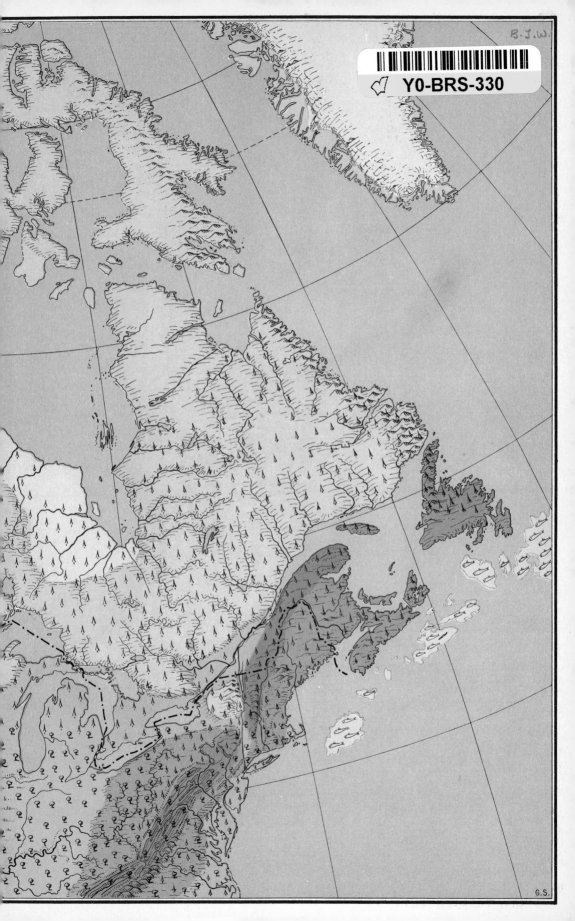

CANADIAN-AMERICAN RELATIONS
1849–1874

THE RELATIONS OF
CANADA AND THE UNITED STATES

———

A SERIES OF STUDIES
PREPARED UNDER THE DIRECTION OF THE
CARNEGIE ENDOWMENT FOR INTERNATIONAL PEACE
DIVISION OF ECONOMICS AND HISTORY

JAMES T. SHOTWELL, *Director*

CANADIAN-AMERICAN RELATIONS
1849-1874

BY

LESTER BURRELL SHIPPEE

UNIVERSITY OF MINNESOTA

NEW HAVEN : YALE UNIVERSITY PRESS
TORONTO : THE RYERSON PRESS   ⟂
LONDON:HUMPHREY MILFORD:OXFORD UNIVERSITY PRESS
FOR THE CARNEGIE ENDOWMENT FOR INTERNATIONAL
PEACE : DIVISION OF ECONOMICS AND HISTORY
1939

EDITOR'S INTRODUCTION

THIS book is the first volume in a group of works contributed by American historians to the historical section of the series of Canadian and American studies issued under the auspices of the Carnegie Endowment for International Peace. As such it ought to be particularly welcomed by a large body of American readers. It, like the other volumes being prepared in this group, has two aims, one general, one specific. The broad general aim is to contribute to a new orientation—and an orientation very much needed—on the part of both writers and readers of American history. In the past it has been almost as difficult to get Americans to think continentally as to get them to think internationally; indeed, in some ways even more difficult. To be sure, Americans are accustomed to hear patriotic speakers refer to the Republic as "continental" and to read of its "continental position." They recall proudly that the first Congress of the nation was called a Continental Congress, and its first army a Continental Army. But their use of the term is in itself a token of their somewhat provincial point of view, for it simply excludes everything outside American borders. In actual fact the United States occupies less than half the continent. A vast deal of history, interrelated with and affecting its own, has been made north of its upper boundary. The aim of this group of books is to help readers to see that the histories of the United States and Canada cannot be fully understood if held within their own frontiers; to help them to understand that the evolution of democracy in North America has been and still is conducted on a truly continental scale; to enable them to realize that the great stage of affairs in which we are concerned stretches uninterrupted from the Rio Grande to the Arctic. This broader orientation will throw much of American as well as Canadian history into a new perspective.

The narrower and more specific aim of Professor Shippee's volume also deserves a word. It deals with events and forces which, when rightly considered, are of surpassing interest to Americans and Canadians alike; for it elucidates one of the greatest decisions in the history of the nineteenth century on the North American continent —a decision of no small moment to the entire world. This was the final decision that Canada and the United States would pursue separate yet friendly ways, each with its individual characteristics, its special position, and its own national destiny.

One of the unique relationships of modern history is that which has developed between the United States and Canada—a relationship full of instruction and hope to mankind at large. It is perhaps not strange that three of the British Provinces in North America should have clung to the Crown in those years, 1775–1783, during which thirteen other Provinces broke away from it. Good historical reasons existed for their continued loyalty. But it is assuredly remarkable that the separation between the two groups—each destined to expand westward to the Pacific—should have endured so long and yet on the whole so amicably, with such increasing acquiescence on both sides in its propriety and healthfulness, and such a growing conviction that it should be perpetuated. It is assuredly remarkable also that the special relationship which Canada holds as intermediary between the United States and Great Britain should have developed so naturally, so steadily, with so little friction, and with large results of usefulness. Dr. Shippee's scholarly and interesting book deals with that crucial period in which Canada attained her majority and undertook those independent responsibilities toward the United States and Great Britain, which she has since maintained and enlarged. Not a shot was fired between Canadians and Americans in these years. Yet the evolution which then took place was full of the tensest drama, which cannot but quicken the pen of any historian who writes upon it.

Among the nations of North America, Canada alone owes allegiance to the Old World. She has maintained that allegiance in spite of the fact that her people are of numerous racial stocks and are curiously divided into two great linguistic groups. She has maintained it in defiance of what would seem the plainest demands of geography. The boundary line between Canada and the United States is in great part one of the most artificial in the world; as André Siegfried has said, its very straightness attests its artificiality. The inhabited portion of Canada is for the most part little more than a long strip glued to this boundary; a strip, moreover, broken in the middle by the great gap of the Laurentian Shield, so that part of Canada is geographically attached to the western half of the United States, part to the eastern half. Canada has maintained her allegiance, again, in spite of cultural and economic demands which pull strongly in another direction. The English-speaking people of Canada, in tastes, training, and thought, are far more like those of Massachusetts or Kansas than of any European land. The strongest of her commercial ties all lead across the border; and that economic importance which would make Canada one of the richest of prizes to any great aggressive Power is primarily an importance to the United States. Yet the boundary line holds; the two peoples stand apart, happy in their political separation; the Canadians occupy a halfway house between the British Commonwealth and the Republic. And men have ceased not merely to question this situation but even to think about it.

This was not true in the year which Dr. Shippee takes for his starting point. It was beginning to be true in the year with which he concludes. The decision of the Canadian and American peoples to accept their separation and to make the most of it was taken, half consciously, half unconsciously, in the crowded decades of which he writes. It was made in part by deliberate choice, and in part by the more or less accidental operation of events. When in 1854 Washington concluded an agreement for commercial reciprocity with all the Canadian Provinces, it seemed possible to many observers that a union between these Provinces and the United States might follow before many years had passed. A great number of Americans desired such a union, and many were ready for active steps to attain it. When the victorious North emerged from the Civil War with powerful armies at her command, with new grievances against Great Britain, and with a fresh expansionist fever burning in her veins, many would have pronounced the union of Canada and the United States altogether probable—some would have said inevitable. Yet the American Congress refused to renew that reciprocity agreement which might have had such large political consequences. American fishermen contrived to irritate Canadian feeling, and Fenian expeditions equipped on American soil to outrage it. The conciliatory genius of Hamilton Fish and the Gladstone Cabinet wiped away, in the greatest arbitration yet known to history, the outstanding differences between the United States and the British Empire. With confederation the new Canadian nation at last emerged, and in its emergence found a multitude of welcoming friends below the border, content to share the continent with a country which would combine some of the best elements in British and American institutions, and to add traits that were all her own.

This is the story which Dr. Shippee has had to tell; it is a story of many and far-reaching implications, and he has told it with a due sense of its greatness.

ALLAN NEVINS

AUTHOR'S PREFACE

THIS story of a quarter of a century of Canadian-American diplomatic relations is a part of the historical portion of the larger comprehensive study of Canadian-American relations in all their ramifications sponsored by the Carnegie Endowment for International Peace.

The year 1849 had a peculiar significance. It marked the culmination of mounting uneasiness in the British North American possessions, and particularly in United Canada, which broke out in a vigorous though limited movement for union of Canada with the United States. In like manner, 1874 was a year in which there began a short respite from almost constant agitation affecting the United States and British North America. Between these two dates came a short-lived reciprocal trade arrangement, the American Civil War and its aftermath of suspicion tinged with no little bitterness on both sides, the culmination of the confederation movement among the British Provinces, and the Treaty of Washington with its attempt to settle *en masse* all the grievances of past years. The everlasting quarrel about the Northeast fisheries rose twice to unseemly bickerings and acrimonious recrimination and twice was laid on the shelf by what at the time seemed a satisfactory solution. Boundary questions, except for the serio-comic San Juan affair, were practically nonexistent; the previous quarter-century had those to struggle with, and the succeeding twenty-five years developed a new one. Annexation, a running concomitant of Canadian-American and British-American affairs from 1775 to at least 1911, aroused feelings of peculiar virulence in the period from 1849 to 1874—a patronizing condescension on one side and a perpetual agitation on the other. There were, in short, very few of these twenty-five years which did not afford somewhat more than ordinary irritability on both sides of the border.

The United States and Canada are probably more intimately bound to each other by cultural and economic ties than any two other countries one can easily recall. Nevertheless, on each side of the frontier there is almost abysmal popular ignorance of and misinformation about the history of their relations or of their present-day interdependence. Canada means far more to the United States than any one of the Latin-American countries, yet contrast the gallons of ink and thousands of pages devoted to the latter with the paucity of contributions on the former. General American histories, once beyond the Revolution, ordinarily forget the northern neighbor except for a passing reference in connection with the War of 1812 and the Maine–New Brunswick boundary dispute. Of late years monographs have begun to appear, and scholarly articles are not as sparse as they once were. Histories of American diplomacy and of foreign policy perforce have to turn an occasional eye northward, but until the appearance of H. L. Keenleyside's *Canada and the United States*, published in 1929, there had been no serious attempt to cover the sweep of Canadian-American relations.

All this means that in reconstructing the story of these twenty-five years most reliance has had to be placed on documents of one kind and another. The Public Archives of Canada at Ottawa and the archives of the Department of State and the Library of Congress at Washington have been most frequently resorted to for materials. The extensive reproductions in the Library of Congress of British Foreign Office and Colonial Office papers in the Public Record Office in London have been of first importance. The Library of Congress already had reproductions of these papers up to March 4, 1869, and has now received copies of Foreign Office papers up to March 4, 1877, which were secured by the Carnegie Endowment for International Peace. Private papers, such as those in the Howe and Macdonald collections at Ottawa, the Pierce, Marcy, Davis, Chandler, and others at Washington, have been useful. Especial mention should be made of the Hamilton Fish Papers so thoroughly used by Dr. Allan Nevins in preparing his biography of that Secretary which Dr. Nevins allowed me to read in proof. Acknowledgment of sources in general is to be found as usual in the footnotes.

May I add that grants from the Carnegie Endowment for International Peace and from the Fluid Research Fund of the Graduate School of the University of Minnesota made possible obtaining materials not locally available. I wish to acknowledge my appreciation of kind assistance from the late Sir Arthur G. Doughty and from Dr. James F. Kenney as well as other members of the staff of the Dominion Archives; from the late Dr. J. F. Jameson, Dr. T. P. Martin and others in the Manuscript Division of the Library of Congress; and from Mrs. Natalia Summers of the Department of State. I particularly wish to state my indebtedness to Dr. James T. Shotwell, General Editor of this Series, and to Dr. Allan Nevins, the Editor of the American historical studies. Professors Chester Martin, J. B. Brebner, and H. A. Innis have read the manuscript and have made many useful suggestions of which I have been glad to avail myself, and my colleague, Professor A. L. Burt, has given me many hints. None of these, however, are to be held responsible for the shortcomings of the volume.

LESTER BURRELL SHIPPEE

Minneapolis,
    December, 1938.

CONTENTS

MAPS

ABBREVIATIONS

CO   Colonial Office Series

D.S.   Department of State, Washington

FO   Foreign Office Series

G   Correspondence between the Governors-General of Canada and the Colonial Office; between Governors-General and the British Ministers at Washington; interprovincial correspondence; correspondence between the Colonial Office and various individual Provincial Lieutenant-Governors

L.C.   Library of Congress, Washington

P.A.C. Public Archives of Canada, Ottawa

P.R.O. Public Record Office, London

(See Appendix I: Manuscript Materials.)

CANADIAN–AMERICAN RELATIONS
1849–1874

CHAPTER I

ANNEXATION

OF all the remedies that have been suggested for the acknowledged and insufferable ills with which our country is afflicted, there remains but one to be considered. It propounds a sweeping and important change in our political and social condition, involving considerations which demand our most serious examination. This remedy consists in a "Friendly and peaceful separation from British connexion, and a union upon equitable terms with the great North American confederacy of sovereign States."[1]

THUS did a group of prominent citizens of Montreal in early October of 1849 approach the public in their "Address to the People of Canada," the famous Manifesto. Alternatives to annexation they rejected as visionary or impracticable: "The revival of protection in the markets of the United Kingdom" was forbidden by the policy adopted by the Empire; "the protection of home manufactures" would fail for want of a market; "a Federal Union of the British American Provinces" offered alleged advantages which were too problematical to be relied upon and would, moreover, not solve the question of markets since there was too great similarity in many of the products of Canada and of the Maritime Provinces, and inadequate demand. "The independence of the British North American colonies as a Federal Republic" demanded a strength which was lacking and threatened expenses beyond the capacity of the colonies; "reciprocal free trade with the United States, as respects the products of the farm, the forest, and the mine" might meet some demands, but would not give the North American continent for a market, stimulate manufactures at home, or allay party violence.

The proposed Union would render Canada a field for American capital, into which it would enter as freely for the prosecution of public works and private enterprise as into any of the present States. It would equalize the value of real estate upon both sides of the boundary . . . , whilst, by giv-

1. *Sessional Papers, 1850* (Great Britain), Cd. 1181, XXXVIII, 11–13.

ing stability to our institutions and introducing prosperity, it would raise our public, corporate, and private credit. . . . It would render our rivers and canals the highway for the immigration to, and exports from, the West, to the incalculable benefit of our country. It would also introduce manufactures into Canada as rapidly as they have been introduced into the Northern States. . . . Nor would the United States merely furnish the capital for our manufactures. They would also supply for them the most extensive market in the world, without the intervention of a Custom-House officer.

Railroads would be built; the value of Canadian agricultural products would be raised to the level of that in the United States; timber sales would boom, shipbuilding would increase and shipping interests prosper; economies in governmental expenses could be effected; and "in place of war and the alarms of war with a neighbour, there would be peace and amity between this country and the United States." A new day would come in political life, for "it would change the ground of political contest between races and parties, allay and obliterate those irritations and conflicts of rancour and recrimination which have hitherto disfigured our social fabric."

Nor would the amicable separation of Canada from Great Britain be fraught with advantages to us alone. The relief to the Parent State from the large expenditure now incurred in the military occupation of the country—the removal of the many causes of collision with the United States, which result from the contiguity of mutual territories so extensive, the benefit of the larger market which the increasing prosperity of Canada would create, are considerations which, in the minds of many of her ablest statesmen, render our incorporation with the United States a desirable consummation.

Not only would Canada and Great Britain benefit by annexation, but for the United States as well there were "many important inducements."

. . . The withdrawal from the borders of so powerful a nation, by whom in time of war the immense and growing commerce of the lakes would be jeopardized,—the ability to dispense with the costly but ineffectual revenue establishment over a frontier of many hundred miles,—the large accession to their income from our customs,—the unrestricted use of the St. Lawrence, the natural highway from the Western States to the ocean,

—are objects for the attainment of which the most substantial equivalents would undoubtedly be conceded.

Back of this Manifesto, signed in a few days by over a thousand financial and political leaders in Montreal,[2] lay a story of economic distress and deep political dissatisfaction. Almost simultaneously the British Parliament had bestowed responsible government upon Canada and had, by a shift from protection to essentially free trade, disturbed an economy which had been geared to a market which gave a preferred position to British colonies.[3]

Politically, the story has its roots deep in the irritations which had burst out finally in the Rebellion of 1837. Lord Durham's epoch-making Report, summing up the situation in the years immediately following the Rebellion, recommended, except as to the Governor and his Secretary, the extension to Upper and Lower Canada of the principle of responsibility of all officers to a united legislature. Governors, unsympathetic with this innovation, prevented an immediate consummation of Durham's recommendation, but when in 1847 the Earl of Elgin and Kincardine was appointed Governor-General by the Whig government, there came an opportunity to realize what had been foreshadowed by the Report. Keeping impartially aloof from the general election of 1848 and not exerting the influence which governors had been accustomed generally to use, Lord Elgin saw the overwhelming defeat of the party which had for years dominated Canadian politics. He asked the leaders of the Reform party to form a government, and thus there came into being the Coalition government of Lafontaine and Baldwin.

This overthrow of the Family Compact, that little group of office-holders, merchants, and professional men so long dominant in the

2. Among them were J. J. C. Abbott, later a premier, John Rose, D. L. Macpherson, John Redpath, Robert Jones, T. Workman, and L. H. Holton. C. D. Allin and G. M. Jones, *Annexation, Preferential Trade, and Reciprocity* (Toronto and London, 1911), pp. 114–115. This work has a wealth of material from newspapers, pamphlets, and the like. For a brief account see O. D. Skelton, *Life and Times of Sir Alexander Tilloch Galt* (Toronto, 1920), chap. vi.

3. See the volume in this Series by D. G. Creighton, *The Commercial Empire of the St. Lawrence, 1760–1850* (Toronto and New Haven, 1937), chaps. xii, xiii; also Gilbert N. Tucker, *The Canadian Commercial Revolution, 1845–1851* (New Haven, 1936), *passim*, especially chap. v.

Council of Upper Canada and not without their counterparts at Montreal and its neighborhood in Lower Canada; this smashing defeat of Tory Loyalists, who, especially after the events of 1837, had considered themselves the special guardians of the imperial interest —the loyalists *par excellence* to whom should be entrusted the reins of government that they might not fall into the hands of erstwhile rebels—left a legacy of bitterness not easily measured. This rancor was the more intense because the election stirred again the embers of racial antagonism; the French had almost unanimously voted for members put forward by the Reform party, and the Tories lost in every French-Canadian constituency. In Lower Canada—since the Act of Union of 1841 united with Upper Canada in a single governmental unit—the British element was in the minority. This minority, however, was dominant in Montreal and represented the commercial as against the prevailing agrarian economy of the rest of Lower Canada outside the Eastern Townships; while it had never been able to dictate the policies of the Province, it had, nevertheless, by maintaining a majority in the Council, been in a position to thwart the Assembly with its preponderance of French. In economic interest Montreal was more in harmony with the British elements of Upper Canada than with the French of Lower Canada. Now, as a result of the election and the complaisance of the Governor-General, they beheld influence and spoils pass not only into the hands of the Reformers but to a considerable extent into the hands of the French.

A Reform government, with a goodly majority at their back, could and did push the Rebellion Losses Bill through Parliament, despite the charge that many who would be compensated as a result of its enactment had stood on the wrong side of loyalty in the late unpleasantness. Vain efforts were made to have Lord Elgin withhold his assent or refer the measure to England; a Tory deputation set out for London on an equally vain quest to find support for their contention that the bill should be disallowed. Popular feeling, mirroring the animosity of Parliamentary discussion and newspaper editorial, vented itself when a mob stoned the Governor-General's carriage, hurled insults at him, and burned the Parliament buildings in Montreal. Ill-feeling would no doubt have been deep-seated in any case, but political vindictiveness was nourished in the prevailing gloom of an economic depression.

As long as remnants of England's seventeenth- and eighteenth-century mercantilism were in evidence, Canada and the other British-American colonies had basked in a preferential position which had produced something like boom times on the eve of the reversal of British policy. Canada's products for export, raw materials almost entirely, found in England a favorable market, since they were protected from foreign competition by prevailing high duties on other than colonial importations. In 1843, at the instance of the Colonial Secretary, Lord Stanley, the Canadian Corn Act was passed; this reduced even farther the duty paid by colonial grain and flour, on condition that Canada impose duties upon American grains but permit the entrance into British ports of flour made in Canadian mills from American wheat on the same terms as that made from Canadian wheat. This act stimulated, especially in Upper Canada, grain-raising and milling and importation of American wheat for milling. Needless to say, Canada rejoiced at this further manifestation, at the same time almost dying gasp, of protectionism in England fighting a losing battle against the forces of liberalism, which demanded more attention to the needs of rising industry with its millions of workers dependent upon outside food supplies. Transportation, too, shared in the transitory prosperity, for Canada's rivers and extensive and partly completed canal system were crowded with craft laden with products of the interior.

Then, in 1846, came the end of the dream. With the end of England's Corn Laws her markets were open to the world, with no preference to colonies or to anyone else. Wheat from the New World which had gone from American fields to Canadian mills and then down the St. Lawrence to the sea now flowed more cheaply through American channels to New York or some other eastern port and thence to England. Prices of foodstuffs were no longer artificially stimulated; Canada had to compete against a system which enjoyed rail transportation and, in many instances, shorter routes. The farmer, the miller, the river or canal boatman all suffered alike and in their train carried down a host of subsidiary enterprises which had been tuned to the primary economic processes of the land.[4]

It is true that with her removal of colonial preference England, to

4. D. L. Burns, "Canada and the Repeal of the Corn Laws," *Cambridge Historical Journal*, II (1926–28), 252–272.

all intents, gave into the hands of her dependencies control over their own fiscal arrangements; they could, in Canada, lower the barrier hitherto raised against American goods, or they could create higher ones. Canada took advantage of this permission to eliminate all differentials, making her tariff schedules uniform when applied to other colonies, to the Mother Country, and to foreign nations. Especially notable was the reduction of duties upon American manufactures. Nevertheless, all the efforts of the Canadians to offset the losses entailed by English free trade were unavailing, while the United States, with Congress and popular opinion engrossed in the Mexican War and its outcome, in the questions of territorial organization which arose from the acquisition of new territories, and in the quadrennial presidential election, would pay no attention to overtures looking toward some sort of reciprocal trade undertaking. No wonder the new Governor-General was appalled at the economic outlook:[5]

The downward progress of events! These are ominous words. But look at the facts. Property in most of the Canadian towns, and more especially in the capital, has fallen fifty per cent. in value within the last three years. Three-fourths of the commercial men are bankrupt, owing to Free-trade; a large proportion of the exportable produce of Canada is obliged to seek a market in the States. It pays a duty of twenty per cent. on the frontier. How long can such a state of things be expected to endure?

"Commercial embarrassments," Lord Elgin continued, were the real difficulty, for, in his opinion, political discontent would evaporate as soon as conditions improved. All that was needed to carry the country through a transition stage was elevation of its economic status to an equality with its neighbor below the line. "If free navigation and reciprocal trade with the Union be not secured for us, the worst, I fear, will come, and that at no distant day." Although Parliament opened British markets to goods from all nations and from its colonies on equal terms, it still retained enough of the old Navigation Laws to restrict to British bottoms the carrying trade between colonies and the homeland. This benefited the British shipowner but bore heavily upon the colonies. Montreal saw its trade slipping away to New York and other American ports, especially since Congress, in 1847, made it

5. *Letters and Journals of James, Eighth Earl of Elgin,* ed. by Theodore Walrond (London, 1872), p. 70.

possible to ship in bond through the United States to a Canadian destination goods landed at an American port. The manifest unfairness of such a situation was borne home to the British Government, particularly when the Governor-General, Boards of Trade in Canada and Canadian public opinion in general harped upon the inequality and demanded a repeal of the antiquated laws. The Liberal ministry, recognizing the justice of the complaints, finally, in 1849, brought in a bill to amend the Navigation Act which, despite vigorous opposition from the Conservatives, was enacted into law, but too late to affect trade during that season.

To make a dismal picture darker there was the immigrant problem. The Irish famine was driving thousands of destitute men and their families to the New World, where the British Provinces, especially Canada, received their share if not more. During the summer and autumn of 1847 it was estimated that close to one hundred thousand refugees were landed at Quebec, whence they were distributed throughout the Province. "The immigration which is now taking place,"[6] wrote Elgin,

is a frightful scourge to the province. Thousands upon thousands of poor wretches are coming here incapable of work, and scattering the seeds of disease and death. Already five or six hundred orphans are accumulated at Montreal, for whose sustenance, until they can be put out to service, provision must be made. . . . Political motives contribute to swell the amount of dissatisfaction produced by this state of things. The Opposition make the want of adequate provision to meet this overwhelming calamity, in the shape of hospitals, &c., a matter of charge against the Provincial Administration. That section of the French who dislike British immigration at all times, find, as might be expected, in the circumstances of this year, a theme for copious declamation. Persons who cherish Republican sympathies ascribe these evils to our dependent condition as colonists.[7]

In such a setting as this, then, appeared the Manifesto, warnings of which had not been lacking in the previous months. Indeed, even

6. *Ibid.*, pp. 42–43. See Gilbert Tucker, "The Famine Immigration to Canada, 1847," *American Historical Review*, XXXVI (Apr., 1931), 533–549.

7. The Governor stated his opinion that the British Government ought to assume the cost of this extra burden thrust upon the provinces; subsequently the colonies were reimbursed from the British Treasury.

before the election of 1848 there had been mutterings about the evil state of the Province as contrasted with the happy condition of the United States. These mutterings had grown louder and multiplied after the defeat of the Tories, and, after the passage of the Rebellion Losses Bill, increased in intensity until there was general expectation that the rumblings would soon produce a reverberating clap of thunder.

The Manifesto served as a crystallizing point for political bitterness and economic discontent. It appealed to the few who believed that there was no way out of the morass except by annexation; it served many English Tories, writhing under a government in which they did not share and which they charged was shot through with republicanism and tinged with disloyalty, as a vent for their spleen; it received whole-hearted approbation from a small group of Americans resident in Canada and from many Irish who welcomed any method of weakening the Empire and flouting England.

Many Tory papers, particularly at Montreal, immediately jumped into the fray with their support of the sentiments of the Manifesto. Public meetings were held in widely scattered places, either to endorse the stand of the Montreal group or to formulate their own. "Letters to the editor" and pamphlets galore spread the doctrine.

The agitation, however, was by no means one-sided. Opposition or "connectionist" meetings, counter-manifestoes, a battery of newspapers as vigorously took up the cudgels against annexation and for continued political connection with England. While a few on this side strove to minimize the significance of the grievances which the annexationists listed, most of them admitted that the situation was bad and something must be done, although to them no condition could be so desperate as to demand the remedy of annexation. Reciprocal free trade or preferential tariff arrangements with the United States seemed not hopeless, and some brought forward the project of a union of the British Provinces in some kind of federated system. If, indeed, reciprocity should prove to be out of the question, federation perhaps appealed most strongly to a large number. The British-American League, loosely organized in the early part of 1849 to bring about some sort of collective action for the amelioration of Canada's ills as well as a united front against threatened French domination, represented at the outset the widest variety of opinion, as shown by the make-up of the first convention which met at Kingston in July.

Although the High Church Tories of Upper Canada formed the backbone of the Convention, yet among the delegates were to be found Annexationists, supporters of independence, advocates of a federal union of the British American colonies, provincial partitionists who demanded a repeal of the Act of Union, Orangemen with pronounced anti-French views, and even a few Radicals who clamoured for popular elective institutions.[8]

Annexationists found themselves in a decided minority at the convention, and during the course of the summer and autumn there was a tendency for them to withdraw into an association of their own, although to the end there remained at least a trace of the annexationist spirit in the ranks of the League. By the time the League met in November for its second convention, however, preponderant sentiment appeared to be for either a federative or a legislative union of the colonies.[9] This was not so much out of favor for union in itself as from a view that some such step was the only thing that would avert annexation. As one of the influential delegates, J. W. Gamble, who at heart was in favor of independence, put it, "A union of this kind would leave the people nothing to desire from annexation, because, in a few years, this country would be in quite as prosperous a state as the other side of the line."[10]

Both among the members of the League and especially in the ranks of Tory annexationists there was a yearning for a return of England to her policy of colonial preference, of protection in general; hence it is quite possible that many who spoke so loudly for annexation did

8. Allin and Jones, *op. cit.,* p. 61.

9. *Minutes of the Proceedings of the Second Convention of Delegates of the British American League* (Toronto, 1849).

10. *Speech of J. W. Gamble delivered at the Convention of Delegates Saturday, November 3, 1849, etc.* (Toronto, 1849), p. 5. The Convention went on record "That it is a matter of regret . . . that the subject of a separation of this Colony from the Mother Country, and of Annexation to the United States of America, has been openly advocated by a portion of the press and inhabitants of this Province; and this Convention unhesitatingly records its entire disapprobation of this course and calls upon all well-wishers of their country to discountenance it by every means in their power."

it with a hope that the British Government, fearful of losing colonies, would repent and turn back to the pre-1846 system. Such hopes could have had very slight foundations, since the Liberal government in England had unmistakably shown their determination not to retrace their steps, and neither by word nor deed held out the slightest comfort or prospect of change.

To a small degree there was an opportunity to judge of the relative strength of annexationists and connectionists, in places where the former had seemed to gain the greatest following, beyond what could be gathered from newspaper editorials and meetings. A few elections had this issue as the predominant one, notably one in Sherbrooke County, in the heart of the English-dominated section of Lower Canada. Here A. T. Galt, one of the signers and circulators of the Manifesto, had resigned his seat in the legislature. J. S. Sanborn, a young lawyer from the States who had been a resident of Canada for a few years, was put forward by the annexationists in the by-election. A loyalist candidate was put up, although there seemed little object in contesting the seat in such a hotbed of annexation sentiment. Following a heated contest, the returns showed that Sanborn had been elected by a narrow margin, much narrower than there had been any reason to expect when it is considered that Galt in this same Riding had been able to pile up a formidable list of signers of the Manifesto barely four months previously.

Whether the Sherbrooke election may be taken as the turning point in the movement of 1849–50 or not, certainly from that time forward annexationists were losing ground. By summer of 1850 the movement was on its last legs, and before the close of the year it was moribund if not dead. Whatever strength the annexationist cause had was principally centered in Montreal and in the Eastern Townships; outside of these areas in Lower Canada it had made no appreciable headway. In Upper Canada, although there economic distress was perhaps as great as at Montreal,[11] annexation had made no headway at all, al-

11. Lord Elgin wrote: "I have lately spent several weeks in the district of Niagara. . . . The inhabitants are for the most part U. E. Loyalists, and differ little in habits or modes of thought and expression from their neighbours [across the boundary]. Wheat is their staple product. . . . Now it is the fact that a bushel of wheat, grown on the Canadian side of the line, has fetched this year in the market, on an average, from 9d. to 1s. less than the same quantity

though scattered proponents might occasionally be found. In Lower Canada adherents were principally from two groups: Tory business-men and politicians, chiefly the former, and radical French under the leadership of L. J. Papineau. Papineau and his Rouge party repre-sented anti-clericalism and radicalism, dissatisfaction with what they considered the temporizing methods of the Lafontaine-Baldwin gov-ernment and of the Reformers generally, admiration for the elective system of the United States, and zeal for union. No stranger bedfellow for Papineau could be found than Sir Allan McNab, leader of the extreme Tory element, yet for the time they found common ground in annexation. Such an unnatural alliance would be unable to stand much buffeting of adverse winds.

Among the French generally in both Upper and Lower Canada the annexation movement made little progress, although this was not for want of effort; French annexationists wooed their fellows vigorously and, through such papers as *L'Avenir*, Papineau's own organ, pre-sented as appealingly as possible the advantages of a change of alle-giance. Opposed to Papineau on principle, the clergy were doubly opposed on this question of annexation: they knew that in the United States their church would not have the privileged position it held in Canada; moreover they were fairly sure that, if the example of French-Canadians who had already gone to the United States was any criterion, their hold over the laity would be far less firm than it was in Canada. Beyond all this Lord Elgin made it a point to show especial attention to the French clergy, who responded by keeping their flock in line. In the Sherbrooke election Sanborn's vote came from the Eng-lish element; he got no support whatever from the French, who voted for his loyalist opponent. As a French-Canadian historian summed it up:

French-Canadians had no sympathy with Americans, with whom their ancestors had often been at grips on the field of battle. Monarchists and conservatives by institutions, habits and education, they detested repub-

and quality of the same article grown on the other. Through their district coun-cil . . . [they] have protested against the Montreal annexation movement. . . . I am confident, however, that the large majority of the persons who have thus protested, firmly believe that their annexation to the United States would add one-fourth to the value of the produce of their farms." *Letters and Jour-nals of Lord Elgin*, p. 104.

lican principles. They knew that under the British flag they would find perfect security for their institutions and privileges, while with annexation their national existence would run great risks.[12]

Much was made by the annexationists of the point that many English statesmen had outspokenly predicted the eventual separation of the colonies; they quoted from leaders who had not hesitated to indicate that, under free trade, the colonies became a burden rather than a source of strength.[13] There was, in truth, considerable ground for the statement in the Manifesto which indicated that England was anxiously waiting the day when the colonies should be ready to go on their own. These statements, however, were not official, although in some cases emanating from important political leaders. Official, however, was the statement in the dispatch sent by Earl Grey, Secretary of State for the Colonies, to Lord Elgin and by him given to the press:[14]

With regard to the Address to the people of Canada in favour of severing the province from the British dominions for the purpose of annexing it to the United States, . . . I have to inform you that Her Majesty approves of your having dismissed from Her service those who have signed a document which is scarcely short of treasonable in its character. Her Majesty confidently relies on the loyalty of the great majority of Her Canadian subjects, and she is, therefore, determined to exert all the authority which belongs to Her, for the purpose of maintaining the connexion of Canada with this country, being persuaded that the permanence of that connexion is highly advantageous to both.

Your Lordship will, therefore, understand that you are commanded by Her Majesty to resist, to the utmost of your power, any attempt which may be made to bring about the separation of Canada from the British dominions, and to mark in the strongest manner Her Majesty's displeasure with all those who may directly or indirectly encourage such a design.

12. Louis P. Turcotte, *Le Canada sous l'union, 1841–1867* (Quebec, 1871–72), II, 124.

13. Cobden's Bradford speech, advising extension of self-government to the colonies and ultimate independence, was utilized by the annexationists. Allin and Jones, *op. cit.,* p. 267.

14. Dated January 9, 1850; *Sessional Papers, 1850* (Great Britain), Cd. 1181, XXXVIII, 23–24. Conveniently found, as to its essential parts, in Allin and Jones, *op. cit.,* pp. 268–269.

Official likewise was Lord John Russell's statement when in the course of a speech delivered in the House of Commons he fully defended the course taken by the Governor-General:[15]

I have, however, seen bitter complaints on this subject; and I have seen that some persons have even gone the length of proposing that, instead of remaining subject to Her Majesty, the province of Canada should be annexed to the United States. To that proposal, of course, the Crown could give nothing but a decided negative; and I trust, although such a suggestion has been made, that, from the characters of several of the gentlemen who are members of the Association, it is not their intention to push their project of joining a neighbouring State to the ultimate result of endeavouring by force of arms to effect a separation from Great Britain; but that, knowing the determined will of the Sovereign of this country, and of Her advisers, not to permit that project to be carried into effect, they will acquiesce in the decision of the Crown.

To many, including Lord Elgin, the forcefulness of this statement was reduced by what Lord John said toward the close of his speech: that he anticipated the time when some of the colonies would have become so strong that they would say they were ready to maintain their independence. That time had not yet come but England must face the possibility.

Lord John's speech on the colonies seems to have been eminently successful at home. It is calculated too, I think, to do good in the colonies; but for one sentence, the introduction of which I deeply deplore—the sting in the tail. Alas for that sting in the tail! I much fear that when the liberal and enlightened sentiments, the enunciation of which by one so high in authority is so well calculated to make the colonists sensible of the advantages which they derive from their connection with Great Britain, shall have passed away from their memories, there will not be wanting those who will remind them that, on this solemn occasion, the Prime Minister of England, amid the plaudits of a full senate, declared that he looked forward to the day when the ties which he was endeavouring to render so easy and mutually advantageous would be severed.[16]

15. Hansard, 3d Ser., CVIII, 551.
16. Elgin to Grey, Mar. 23, 1850; *Letters and Journals of Lord Elgin,* p. 115. "Little Englanders" made considerable of the military expense entailed by the colonies. See C. P. Stacey, *Canada and the British Army, 1846–1871* (London, 1936), especially chaps. iii and iv.

In the face of such official pronouncements the annexationists could no longer maintain, as they had during the height of the agitation, that separation and annexation would be viewed with indifference if not with pleasure by the British Government and people. Many who had reluctantly lent a listening ear to the Manifesto and its supporters because of doubt about their continued welcome in the British family now could exhibit their loyalty and confidently discount an argument which had been used with so much effect.

Other elements came to the support of the loyalists. The relaxation of the Navigation Laws, though tardy, had not been without effect. A good harvest in 1849, better prices for commodities, due in part to the influx of Californian and Australian gold, and a general lightening along the economic horizon, all conspired to lift Canadians from their gloom and turn them from clutching at the straw of annexation as the only hope for rehabilitation.[17] Then, too, efforts had not been lacking on the part of the government to emphasize how strong a motive with many annexationists was political disappointment, and the anti-annexation press, particularly that which supported the Reform government, did not hesitate to play up this aspect of the situation. Even in the weeks when annexationism was most vocal, only a small part of the Canadians supported it; after the British Government spoke in no uncertain terms, and in the face of an improved economic outlook, the movement was doomed.

The Manifesto appeared in Montreal and it was primarily addressed to Canada. Nevertheless, simultaneously a feeble echo was heard in the Maritimes, particularly New Brunswick and Nova Scotia. Here England's shift of economic policy had also brought disturbance, but lumber not grain played the principal rôle. Under colonial preference timber enjoyed special favors in British markets; now, with those markets open to everybody, it could not for the time adjust itself to the competition of Baltic products, although open winter ports and no longer shipping routes rendered Maine competition

---

17. *Punch in Canada* poked fun at the movement. In one issue it printed a "business flourometer":

"Flour, 33s. per barrel—loyalty up.
Flour, 26s. per barrel—cloudy.
Flour, 22s. per barrel—down to annexation."
Quoted in Allin and Jones, *op. cit.*, p. 131.

relatively harmless.[18] As in Canada, so in the Maritime Provinces there had been going on a struggle for responsible government which had its beginnings as far back as that in Canada. While there had been no rebellion the struggle had, nevertheless, been accompanied by much bitterness and hard feeling, and, as in Canada, the transition to a new governmental system left soreness and rankling.

In the Maritime Provinces, moreover, the fisheries question was an ever-present feature whenever anything involving the United States arose.[19] To a limited degree the fisheries affected Lower Canada along the Gulf of St. Lawrence, but it was never the outstanding issue that it was for Nova Scotia and Prince Edward Island. Ever since the Convention of 1818 had defined the privileges to which Americans were entitled there had been intermittent friction, although in 1845 temporary understanding of how the terms of this convention should be interpreted had been reached, and during the next few years the issue was relatively quiescent.

In Nova Scotia owners and operatives of bituminous coal mines looked longingly at possible markets of the United States, especially of New England, where their product could compete with the coal of the Middle States were it not for tariff restrictions, which erected a formidable barrier. The feeling that the Maritime Provinces had in their fisheries something to trade for freedom of American markets, to say nothing of the racial affinity between the people of the two regions, had from time to time brought up the idea of some sort of union which could be urged as mutually beneficial to both sides. As in Canada, so here on the Gulf there was a residuum of sentiment which might be roused under favoring circumstances.

This combination of factors, then, produced in the hard times of 1848 and 1849 reactions similar to those in Canada. The annexationists were loud if not numerous, although proportionately more numerous than in Canada. The reaction set in in much the same fashion and for about the same reasons, so that by the time 1850 was well started the movement had risen to its crest and was rapidly declining,

18. I am indebted to Professor J. B. Brebner for the suggestion of Baltic competition. See W. M. Whitelaw, *The Maritimes and Canada before Confederation* (Toronto, 1934), especially chap. iv.

19. On the general topic see the forthcoming volume in this Series by H. A. Innis, *The Cod Fisheries: The History of an International Economy.*

to become no more than a subterranean rumbling which broke out from time to time in a brief flare-up of feeling.

What, in the midst of this Canadian agitation, was the response of the people of the United States? It would seem no more than natural for a people who in the Revolution had striven to secure the adherence of the "fourteenth colony," some of whom had believed the War of 1812 would secure that colony, and who, along the border, had hailed the Canadian Rebellion of 1837 as a forerunner of union with the United States, to give to the movement every possible encouragement.

Interest there was in the United States, particularly in the common-wealths along the border. Many papers, although not the more in-fluential metropolitan dailies, followed the movement with encour-aging words. French-Canadians in the United States hailed the annexationist agitation with joy.[20] Meetings were held at several dif-ferent centers, where resolutions were drawn up or addresses framed. The legislatures of Vermont and New York expressed their approba-tion of the movement and recommended its encouragement. In the Northwest annexation was joyfully contemplated, for that would mean the opening of Canadian waterways to the States, lower freight rates, and generally improved conditions for the farmers of the area. Commercial bodies in cities like New York and Boston were not averse to the idea; they would welcome additional trade which would flow through them to and from Canada. Yet, in all expressions of approba-tion there was careful refraining from any invocation of the use of force or doing anything that would result in impairing the relations with Great Britain.[21] There was a marked difference in the tone of ex-pression from what there had been during the Maine boundary con-troversy or while the Oregon question was still unsettled; then, many a man in responsible position had delivered himself of sentiments which were, to say the least, provocative, and had not hesitated to pre-

20. See "Adresse des Canadiens de New-York et des environs, à leurs com-patriotes du Canada," published in *L'Avenir* in January, 1850; printed in Allin and Jones, *op. cit.*, pp. 303–308, 385–390.

21. The resolution of the Vermont legislature of 1849 contained this state-ment: *Resolved.*—That the peaceful annexation of Canada to the United States, with the consent of the British Government, and of the people of Canada, and upon just and honorable terms, is an object in the highest degree desirable to the people of the United States.

dict the early flying of the American flag from the North Pole to the Isthmus of Panama.[22]

"Manifest Destiny" had been partially fulfilled by securing Oregon to the forty-ninth parallel; Texas had been admitted to the Union; the Mexican War had just ended, with the United States in possession of New Mexico and California. But Manifest Destiny still fell far short of what its promoters predicted and encouraged, so that this Canadian agitation should have fitted in perfectly with the prevailing temper and have been used to the utmost in forwarding the dreams of those who envisaged a united republic extending over the whole North American continent. On the contrary the Administration was discretion itself, so far as it made any outward manifestation of an interest in what was going on.[23]

This did not mean, however, that it was entirely indifferent to what was occurring. In July, 1849, Secretary of State Clayton notified Israel D. Andrews that he had been appointed Special Agent to visit British North America in order to collect statistics and general information about existing conditions and future prospects relative to commercial and political affairs as they affected the United States.[24] While the inspiration of this mission grew out of the efforts being made by the Canadian Government to secure some sort of reciprocal trade arrangement, Andrews understood his instruction to mean that he was to keep his eyes open to whatever might be going on. From St.

22. Senator Cass's speech, for example, which was delivered at a Fourth of July celebration in 1843. *Niles' Register,* July 29, 1843.

23. In this connection it is not without interest to quote the summing up of the two Canadian historians whose work has been frequently alluded to in these pages: "The conduct of the Government at Washington was strictly proper. No neutral power in time of war could have observed a more scrupulous impartiality. Throughout the course of the annexation movement President Taylor carefully refrained from even an appearance of desiring to meddle in Canadian affairs. Neither by word nor action did he lend the slightest encouragement to the Canadian Annexationists. It would have been easy for him greatly to embarrass the Canadian Government in its efforts to relieve the distress of the province. The question of reciprocal trade was the crux of the Canadian situation, yet he endeavoured to assist the Canadian authorities in securing the passage of a Reciprocity Bill through Congress. The attitude of Congress was equally impartial, even though not as friendly to Canada." Allin and Jones, *op. cit.,* p. 380.

24. The correspondence is in Special Agents, Vol. XVI (D.S.).

John, New Brunswick, at the end of the month, he wrote that there was a great change in attitude from what he had found four months before; now there was much talk about independence and annexation which would not be the case if the colony had not lost its protection in the British market. "The political hacks and the cliques are opposed to annexation or indeed any change if they are paid and can enjoy the patronage and emoluments of office." Annexation was more for the people, and it would take time to give them courage to make themselves felt. Writing again the next day, August 1, he said that he found sentiment divided between confederation, which was advocated by those in power aided by others not normally in politics who had not felt the pressure of the times, and annexation, which was supported by real estate owners who wanted their property's value increased and by all of those who had no faith in the colonial or confederation system. From Montreal, August 29, he sent a letter depicting the past and present dissatisfaction in Canada. "One of the first men here" he reported as saying that there was no salvation for the country except being swallowed by the boa constrictor, the United States, and in case war arose between the United States and England not one Canadian in ten would take up arms for England. It was Andrews' opinion that the annexation movement could be deferred but not defeated.

Andrews remained in Montreal until after the Manifesto appeared. He conferred rather frequently with leaders of the annexation movement and apparently was infected by their enthusiasm, for he reported that agitation was spreading rapidly in Lower Canada and would get beyond the power of England to stop. "They beg of me to conjure you," he wrote Clayton on October 20, "to protract the negotiation [for reciprocity] and finally refuse the terms offered by Great Britain," in order to forward the cause.

These communications from the special agent Secretary Clayton acknowledged but upon them he made no comment. He, as well as anyone, knew the obstacles which lay in the path of any official who came out for annexation of any of the British North American provinces at that time. The success of Manifest Destiny had stopped its own progress. The territory gained by the Mexican War had raised again the slavery controversy, so that from the time the Treaty of Guadalupe Hidalgo was ratified in 1848 until the passage of the Compromise measures of 1850 the question of how these territories should be organized was a paramount political issue. Even if the South succeeded in keeping the new regions open to slavery, it was obvious that the institution would never thrive there, as Webster pointed out in his Seventh of March speech; no real gain in Congress then could be expected from states which might be formed. Therefore, implacable opposition to the annexation of any more territory to the north, where free-soil states could be created, was to be expected from a united-front South.[25]

In Congress no less than in administrative circles the ground of annexation was warily trod. That the South stood ready to withdraw from the Union if at least a portion of its demands were not met was thoroughly believed by many Northern leaders, and these same leaders as fully believed that if secession took place then it meant the irretrievable split of the Union. They were careful then to give no further ground for ill-feeling by advocating annexation of Canada. However, it is improbable that either Congress or the Administration would have taken any other course had there been no controversy between the sections over organization of territories. It was at this same time that Central American affairs had become so complicated in the conflicting claims of the United States and Great Britain that Clayton and Sir Henry Bulwer worked out a compromise in their treaty; the Cuban question was in one of its acute phases. No political faction would make annexation a campaign issue, and any attempt to make it a party question fell flat.

All this did not mean that the ultimate destiny of Canada was a matter of indifference in American public opinion. There was some feeling that Canada in the natural course of events would become a part of the Union; there was no need to rush affairs, particularly if it meant stirring up unnecessary trouble in other quarters. An editorial in the Toledo *Blade* put some border sentiment thus:

25. In a letter dated Montreal, August 29, 1849, Andrews said that the colonists were strong and ardent opponents of slavery, and the position occupied by the United States in respect to that institution "together with the anticipated opposition from the South to annexation is used with great force in the Colonies by all those who oppose annexation, and indeed by many who are strong annexationists—they fear that any movement among the Colonists would be rendered abortive by Southern influence."

The true policy of the Government is that of passiveness. It behoves us to keep a watch upon ourselves in this regard, while tempted so strongly by our Northern neighbours to depart from it. There is no cause for our becoming anxious or excited upon the subject—when the fruit is fully ripe it will fall into our lap without any exertion on our part.[26]

If ultimate annexation could thus complacently be contemplated by those Americans who took the trouble to consider the issue, it is no more than fair to quote as an antidote the judgment of the biographer of one of the signers of the Manifesto, Sir Alexander T. Galt:[27]

The riots in Montreal and the annexation movement which followed were not the outcome of deep conviction, or of any permanent hostility toward the Mother Country. They were really incidents in the painful readjustment of Canada, and especially Lower Canada, to the rapidly changing commercial and political situation at home and in Great Britain. They were the aftermath of the granting of responsible government, a last protest against the change in the constitution of the country and in its relations to the Mother Country. The leaders resented England's acquiescence in the demand for self government, in her abandonment of political control over the colony, especially when that abandonment meant the loss of the outside power which had hitherto made it possible for the minority in the province to have its way against the majority. They resented also the abandonment of the trade preference, which had been an incident of the old colonial system. The Empire had been interpreted to mean racial supremacy and trade profit; and now that both were threatened, the Empire appeared to such interpreters to have no longer any excuse for existence.

26. Quoted in Allin and Jones, *op. cit.*, p. 384.
27. O. D. Skelton, *op. cit.*, pp. 145–146.

CHAPTER II

WORKING FOR RECIPROCITY

"WHETHER these colonies remain separate and disunited as at present, or formed into one confederation, they must have reciprocal free trade with the United States or they will be annexed."[1] This was the opinion of Special Agent Andrews as he looked over the field not only in the Maritime Provinces but also when he reached Montreal. Lord Elgin shared this view when, in November, 1849, he wrote in a most pessimistic vein to Grey:[2]

I have always said that I am prepared to assume the responsibility of keeping Canada quiet, with a much smaller garrison than we have now, and without any tax on the British consumer in the shape of protection of Canadian products, if you put our trade on as good a footing as that of our American neighbours; but if things remain on their present footing in this respect, there is nothing before us but violent agitation, ending in convulsion or annexation. . . . You have a great opportunity before you—obtain reciprocity for us, and I venture to predict that you will be able shortly to point to this hitherto turbulent colony with satisfaction, in illustration of the tendency of self-government and freedom of trade, to beget contentment and material progress. . . .

While a discontented minority were talking separation and annexation, and die-hard Tories proclaimed their discontent if England persisted in her new policy of free trade and refused to return to protection, the Canadian Government was bending its efforts to obtain better trade relations with the United States in order to find there a market which should compensate for what had been lost across the seas. Such a market must afford an outlet for the products of "land, mine and sea," and this outlet could come only through a more liberal policy on

1. Andrews to Clayton, St. John, Aug. 1, 1849; Special Agents, Vol. XVI (D.S.). For Andrews and his activities, see below, Chapter IV. Two studies of the framing and working of the Reciprocity Treaty are Charles C. Tansill, *The Canadian Reciprocity Treaty of 1854* (Baltimore, 1922); and Donald C. Masters, *The Reciprocity Treaty of 1854* (London, New York, and Toronto, 1936). The latter is the more comprehensive and thorough treatment.

2. Nov. 8, 1849; *Letters and Journals of Lord Elgin,* pp. 102–103.

the part of the American Government with respect to import duties. Unquestionably the preponderant majority of Colonials considered some sort of reciprocal arrangement the best solution of their problems, and there were indications that the ranks of the annexationists would be depleted if assurance could be had of relief from economic ills through reduction or elimination of duties at the border. In the States feelings might be mixed, but there were signs that even there this procedure would meet with considerable favor.

Tangible evidence of this sentiment on both sides of the line is found in legislation proposed both in Congress and in the Canadian Parliament in 1848. Grinnell introduced in the House of Representatives a measure providing that when a similar law was enacted by Parliament a list of natural products[3] should be permitted to enter the United States from Canada free of duty. Parliament responded by an act which stated that

Whereas a bill has been introduced into the Congress of the United States of America having for its object the removal of the duties now levied on the articles enumerated in the schedule to this act annexed, being of the growth and production of Canada, whenever and so long as similar articles, being of the growth and production of the United States, shall be admitted into Canada free of duty ; and whereas it is desirable to meet this proposition on the part of the United States by a corresponding action on the part of this province:

Be it therefore enacted, etc., That whenever, under any law of the United States of America, heretofore passed or hereafter to be passed, the articles enumerated . . . shall be admitted free of duty into the said United States of America, then similar articles . . . shall be admitted into this province free of duty, when imported direct from the said United States.

The Canadian proposition became law, contingent only on reciprocal legislation by the United States. The American bill was passed by the House of Representatives but failed to receive attention in the Senate during that session, despite cordial approval of the Treasury

3. The schedule of articles included: grain and breadstuffs of all kinds, vegetables, fruits, seeds, animals, hides, wool, butter, cheese, tallow, horns, salted and fresh meats, ores of all kinds of metals, ashes, timber, staves, wood, and lumber of all kinds. See *House Reports,* No. 4, 32d Cong., 2d Sess., p. 66, where the text of the Canadian act is quoted also.

Department and its assurance that such legislation would not run counter to any existing engagements of the country. On the contrary, it was the opinion of this department that similar reciprocal arrangements on the same terms might be extended to other countries.[4] In the succeeding short session, 1848–49, the Senate did, indeed, give brief consideration to the matter at the instance of Senator John A. Dix of New York, who supported the proposition wholeheartedly. Canada, he said,[5] had shown itself more than willing to meet the United States half way, and people on both sides of the border were anxious for the elimination of commercial restrictions.

. . . The Legislature of Canada has labored for many years, by all means in its power, to get rid of the restrictions by which commerce between them and us has been embarrassed; the most liberal course has been adopted on their part, by abolishing the old system of differential duties, and placing us on a footing with the mother country in relation to the exchange of products. I really hope that this policy on her part may be met by a corresponding spirit on ours. . . .

While a handful of Senators took occasion to express their views on the question it was clear that there was to be no action. It was equally clear that sectionalism, which was tingeing all the issues before that Congress and its successor, likewise appeared in this limited discussion: the Southern Democrats were not going to allow the passage of the bill.[6]

All this, however, was merely a preliminary skirmish, at least so far as British North America was concerned. In September, 1848, delegates from Canada and the three Maritime Provinces had met at Hali-

4. Young, Acting Secretary, to Grinnell, Chairman, House Committee on Commerce, May 1, 1848; *House Ex. Docs.*, No. 64, 31st Cong., 1st Sess., pp. 13–14. Young's list omitted some articles of the Canadian list: vegetables, fruits, seeds, butter, cheese, ashes, and staves.

5. *Congressional Globe*, 30th Cong., 2d Sess., p. 182. Later, January 23, 1849, Dix went into a detailed analysis of the proposition. *Ibid.*, pp. 327–332.

6. J. C. Westcott of Florida (*Cong. Globe*, 31st Cong., 2d Sess., p. 185) virtually accused his Southern colleagues of banding together against it. J. M. Niles of Connecticut, S. A. Douglas of Illinois had a few favorable words; Pearce of Maryland, Hunter of Virginia condemned the bill; and Phelps of Vermont thought that it would be of benefit only to Canada unless manufactures were included in the free list.

fax to discuss the whole situation and, probably so far as Canada was concerned, to find out how far the Maritimes were willing to use their trump card, the fisheries, in effecting a satisfactory arrangement. The British Chargé, John F. T. Crampton, had watched the course of events in Washington during the winter and had kept Lord Elgin as well as the Foreign Office informed about progress or lack of it. Elgin himself had dinned into the ears of Lord Grey, the Colonial Secretary, the imperative necessity of getting reciprocity unless England was willing to face the possibility of loss of the Colonies. With the Thirtieth Congress at an end, with a new political alignment bringing a Whig President and a Whig Congress to Washington, the stage was set for an intensive campaign.

Crampton fired the first gun by addressing to Secretary Clayton, before that gentleman had got acquainted with his office in the Department of State,[7] a communication in which he traced the course of reciprocity to date, pointed out the eminently reasonable stand taken by Canada, suggested that New Brunswick would like to be included in the scheme if it worked out, and asked, in diplomatic terms, whether the new administration was willing to proceed with it, perhaps by treaty.[8] Having received no reply to his inquiry in the course of the next three months, on June 25 Crampton gently reminded Clayton that he had sent such a note and also informed him that the Governor-General of Canada had asked one of his "chief officers," William Hamilton Merritt, to go to Washington to ascertain the disposition of the Government there. He enclosed a long memorandum which Merritt had prepared to show the advantage which would accrue to both parties through reciprocity, as well as copies of the letters which had passed between Grinnell and the Treasury Department, demonstrating that the preceding administration had looked favorably upon the idea.[9]

This time there came a quick response from the Secretary, who

7. Mar. 22, 1849; *House Ex. Docs.*, No. 64, 31st Cong., 1st Sess., pp. 2–5.

8. Sir Edmund Head, Lieutenant-Governor of New Brunswick, had been authorized by the Colonial Office to communicate directly with Her Majesty's Legation in Washington, and Sir Edmund was not slow in taking advantage of this permission. A considerable correspondence went on between Crampton and Head. CO 188:177 (P.R.O.).

9. This correspondence is in *House Reports*, No. 4, 32d Cong., 2d Sess., pp. 53–63.

stated that there were but two ways in which the proposed arrangement could be made: by a law enacted by Congress, or by a treaty or convention. To the first method there could be no constitutional objection, but the President was doubtful of the propriety of handling a matter involving revenue by a treaty, which would leave the House of Representatives out of its consideration. A British Minister, Clayton pointed out, could introduce a measure in Parliament, but all the President could do was to recommend legislation to Congress, and, at its next session, he would bring the subject to the attention of that body. To Merritt, Clayton wrote[10] a few days later that the American Government could do nothing but wait until the British Government was prepared to treat on the subjects of reciprocity, the fisheries, and navigation of the St. Lawrence and the canals; as yet Crampton was instructed to treat only on the subject of the bill introduced in the Canadian Parliament.

Both Merritt and Crampton might well have noted the direction which incidental discussion had taken in Congress. While not specifically connecting these other matters with the question of reciprocity, several Congressmen had brought up the desirability of securing for the United States greater privileges for American fishermen in the waters of British North America, and representatives of the Northwest in particular had let it be known that their principal interest lay in obtaining unhampered outlets for the products of their constituents. The Province of Canada concentrated on reciprocal free trade; Americans, to judge by remarks in Congress, were far less concerned about this than they were about concessions which might possibly be gained in return from both Canada and the Maritime Provinces. Clayton's statement to Merritt was just a notification, or even warning, in a semi-official manner, that all the issues must be tied together.

A week later[11] Clayton informed Israel D. Andrews that the President had appointed him Special Agent to prepare a report, before Congress should meet, on (1) the trade and commerce of each British North American Colony, (2) the tonnage of each, (3) tonnage engaged in the fisheries, (4) the number of men employed in the fisheries, (5) the cost of building vessels in the Colonies, (6) the cost of sailing vessels, (7) the amount of coal exported to the United States, (8) the

10. Clayton to Merritt, June 30, 1849; Special Agents, Vol. XVI (D.S.).
11. July 7, 1849; Special Agents, Vol. XVI (D.S.).

amount of fish exported to the United States, (9) the amount of coal imported from the United States into each Colony, (10) what agricultural products and what manufactures were imported into the Colonies, the salaries of the chief public officials, debts and resources of each Colony, and what would be the benefits of having the St. Lawrence and the canals opened to Americans. Andrews proceeded at once to Nova Scotia and New Brunswick and thence made his way to Canada, where, as has already been noted, he watched the course of events, apparently hobnobbing more with annexationists than with other groups, but, nevertheless, managing to secure a fairly good picture of the situation, although colored too much by his belief that the annexationists were much stronger than they really were and that separation was imminent.

In London, Canadian agitation culminating in the Manifesto, as well as reiterated warnings of Lord Elgin that something had to be done, had stirred the Government to action. Sir Henry Bulwer was appointed Minister, specially charged with securing a reciprocity agreement and with adjusting the complicated Central American situation. Furthermore, the Colonial Office had instructed the Lieutenant-Governors of the Maritime Provinces to get in touch with Lord Elgin and send him any pertinent information relating to their Provinces which he ought to have to guide him in his consultations with Sir Henry.[12] Lieutenant-Governor Harvey wrote from Halifax that so far as Nova Scotia was concerned he believed that the topics discussed at the conference of the previous September would form a satisfactory basis for an arrangement, but "should the American Government be indisposed to establish a reciprocal interchange of staple productions (in favor of which a very strong feeling exists in this Colony) unless the reserved rights of Fishery be also conceded I have respectfully to request that no step may be taken to compromise the interests of Nova Scotia by such concession until an opportunity is afforded to me to consult the Legislature which meets on the 17th of January." In February, Harvey informed Lord Elgin that while as yet the legislature had not formally discussed the questions left undecided at the conference, i.e., "the opening of the Colonial coasting

12. See J. Harvey to Elgin, Dec. 13, 1849; Donald Campbell, Prince Edward Island, Dec. 17; I. Gaspard Le Marchant, Newfoundland, Dec. 31. All in G '44–'58 (P.A.C.).

trade, and the surrender of the exclusive rights of Fishery," he had reason to believe that "respectable Majorities are prepared to sanction both measures should Sir Henry L. Bulwer be thereby enabled to secure for the Empire and its Dependencies a further extension of commercial privileges, and especially the free admission of our Fish, Coal, and other Staples into the American Markets."[13]

Lieutenant-Governor Campbell believed that Prince Edward Island would benefit by the proposed arrangement; he enclosed a copy of an Address to the Queen which prayed that the fisheries of the Island be thrown open to citizens of the United States, at the same time giving it as his opinion that it would have been more prudent for the Islanders to have communicated confidentially with Her Majesty's Government before "offering their fisheries to the Americans without stipulating for any equivalent." Assuming, however, that there would be a reduction in the duties levied by the United States upon imported fish and abolition of American bounties, he saw no reason why the Island might not build up a profitable industry, for there were no better fishing grounds about the Gulf than those off its shores. One point of importance for the Island he did emphasize; it would be of inestimable importance if the Americans would admit to their registry foreign-built vessels when those became the property of American citizens: "I believe that our Island shipbuilders could supply them with vessels at such a price per Ton as would command the market, and not only liquidate all demands that might be incurred for imports, but in my opinion, leave a considerable balance in favor of the Colony."[14]

13. Harvey to Elgin, Feb. 20, 1850; G '44–'58 (P.A.C.). On March 9 Harvey informed the Governor-General that resolutions had passed the House of Assembly and he thought they would be approved in the Legislative Council. "The Fisheries, Your Lordship will perceive, are not named in the Resolutions but the policy or impolicy of their surrender on any terms was freely debated in both Houses. A minority in both Branches are unwilling to cede the exclusive Fishery unless in exchange for a participation in the United States Coasting Trade and the admission of Colonial built ships to the privilege of Registry, in addition to the free admission of the articles named in the Resolutions, and a smaller number, including two of my Executive Council are of opinion that the opening of the Fisheries under any circumstances would be very prejudicial to the Province."

14. Campbell pointed out that figures showed that the trade between the Island and the United Kingdom was the only trade which showed a favorable balance for the Island which was "drained off by the trade with the British

At about the same time Lieutenant-Governor Head sent word that New Brunswick would be unwilling to concede "privileges affecting the fisheries or other rights here reserved to British subjects" unless admission to American markets on "fair terms" was secured for rough and sawed lumber, fish, and "such minerals as grindstone building stone gypsum & perhaps Bitumen."[15]

Writing from Government House at St. Johns, Newfoundland, Lieutenant-Governor Le Marchant was very doubtful whether his colony should be included in the proposed arrangement. The other provinces had agricultural or mining products to sell in the United States, but Newfoundland had nothing but its fish, and it was a question whether opening the inshore fisheries to Americans would not be too great a price to pay for what little advantage would be obtained. The market for fish, he explained, was becoming every year more restricted, the improvidence of the fishermen of Newfoundland undoubtedly contributed to the depressed condition of the industry, and keener competition with the Americans might aggravate that condition. If, however, the other colonies entered into the arrangement to the exclusion of Newfoundland, then the latter would be in a worse state than at present. His personal opinion was that "if the rights of private proprietors be preserved, and foreigners excluded from fishing within the mouths of rivers, and *especially if the bounties granted by the American Government be suspended, (which should be stipulated for)* I cannot but think that the value of property will be enhanced, the resources of the fishery be more extensively and profitably developed, and the prosperity of the great body of the population be materially advanced by the contemplated arrangement. . . ." But, since these were his personal views, he thought it would be politic to

Colonies and the United States. This is certainly very unsatisfactory, and I regret to observe that the disparity between the imports and exports appears to have gone on increasing yearly." Dec. 17, 1849; G '44–'58 (P.A.C.). Lord Grey could not agree with Campbell on this point of unfavorable balance and said that "opinions implied in your Despatch would naturally lead to Attempts to guard the Province against the supposed loss by some Restrictions upon the Freedom of Commerce, which would not be otherwise than disadvantageous to the Colony, and I am anxious that in your communications with the leading Inhabitants you should discourage as far as is within your Power all such Ideas." Jan. 15, 1850; FO 115:106 (P.R.O.).

15. Head to Elgin, Feb. 27, 1850; G '44–'58 (P.A.C.).

"reserve the question as respects Newfoundland, so that this colony may hereafter be included in the arrangement, if upon more mature deliberation it may be considered to our advantage."[16]

While inquiries were being made on both sides during the summer and autumn of 1849, Sir Henry Bulwer finally arrived in the United States to take over the duties of the Legation which had latterly been entrusted to Crampton as Chargé. Relying upon Clayton's assurance that the President would bring the subject to the attention of Congress, no steps were taken until that body convened. In his Annual Message, however, President Taylor made no mention of Canada or of reciprocity. Nevertheless, in both houses the matter was brought forward when McLane of Maryland reported from the House Committee on Commerce a bill similar to the one the previous Congress had considered, and Douglas of Illinois obtained leave to introduce one in the Senate.[17] Douglas' proposition emphasized Clayton's warning to Merritt by coupling with reciprocity the question of navigation. Both measures slumbered in committee for over a month, but on March 15 McLane addressed an inquiry to Secretary Clayton. He said that a bill for reciprocal free admission of certain Canadian and American products had been introduced but had been recommitted with a view to including in it a provision for free navigation of the St. Lawrence and thus assimilating it to a bill pending in the Senate; the committee, he said, was not disposed to add this provision if such navigation could be secured by treaty, and if the Secretary could assure him that free navigation would be tendered citizens of the United States upon satisfactory terms, the committee would feel it more satisfactory to recommend the passage of the bill in its existing shape.

Bulwer, in response to Clayton's inquiry based on McLane's letter,

16. Dec. 31, 1849; G '44–'58 (P.A.C.). Bulwer was instructed by Palmerston, January 25, 1850, to reserve for Newfoundland to this effect. FO 115:106 (P.R.O.).

17. McLane brought in the bill on January 29, 1850; it was read twice and referred to the Committee of the Whole. On March 13 this committee, without having discussed it, was discharged from its consideration and it was referred back to the Committee on Commerce. McLane's bill made some concessions, especially with an eye to the Maritime Provinces, by adding to the free list eggs, stone and marble, masts and spars, and gypsum. Douglas introduced his bill on January 11, when it went to the Committee on Commerce. *Cong. Globe,* 31st Cong., 1st Sess., pp. 238, 512, 324.

replied, on March 27, that his instructions allowed him to say that if Congress enacted a measure corresponding to the Canadian act "Her Majesty's Government will be ready to respond to any application which the United States Government may then address to it on the subject concerning which you have now applied to me, by at once consenting to open the navigation of the river St. Lawrence, and of the Canals thereto adjoining . . . to the shipping and citizens of the United States" subject to the privilege of withdrawing the concession.[18] A copy of this correspondence Clayton sent to McLane with a covering note in which he related briefly what had taken place the previous summer, including the statement that the President had declined to treat upon the subject, since that course would have excluded the House of Representatives from a decision in the matter. In the middle of May all this, together with copies of the correspondence with Crampton on the subject, was sent to the House by the President, whose message stated that he had not considered the markets of Canada equivalent to those of the United States and he had, therefore, directed the Secretary of State to see what else could be obtained.

The receipt of this communication together with the fact that, as McLane announced on May 16, the table was cluttered with petitions

18. This interchange is found in *House Reports*, No. 4, 32d Cong., 2d Sess., pp. 71–72. Before this inquiry reached Bulwer he had inquired of the Foreign Office what attitude he should take if Congress persisted in linking the two subjects; the response of Palmerston, dated March 22 and consequently not received by Bulwer until after his note to Clayton, read: ". . . Her Majesty's Government deem it advisable to procure, if possible, the omission of the clause relating to that subject, but at the same time they are of the opinion that it would be better to accept that clause than risk the Loss of the bill." FO 115 : 106 (P.R.O.).

On May 2, 1850, Buel for the Committee on Foreign Affairs brought in a report (*House Reports*, No. 295, 31st Cong., 1st Sess.) in which the right of navigation of the St. Lawrence was claimed under the Treaty of 1783, and even under that of 1763. The argument was based on one of Adams' in 1823 which claimed for the hinterland the right of navigation when the river had its mouth in the sea on the coast of another country. The strongest argument, however, the committee claimed was commercial necessity.

Reporting this to Lord Palmerston, Bulwer stated that the tone of the report was not unfriendly to Great Britain, although the ground taken was contrary to rights for which this country had always contended. June 17, 1850; FO 5 : 513 (P.R.O.).

for Congress to try to secure the free navigation of the river now that the season was at hand when this privilege would be most valuable, caused McLane to ask to have the bill put on its passage. He explained that it was the same measure which the House of the last Congress had passed and, as free navigation could also be secured, the committee recommended approval. But the House was of a different mind. There was no general discussion of the topic but what there was showed conclusively that there was little chance of legislation, and the session ended with no record vote upon it. In the Senate there was even less consideration. The matter was somewhat complicated with the issue of opening American coastwise trade to British vessels to meet the concessions which England's modified Navigation Act had effected. This, of course, was of special interest to the shipping of the Maritime Provinces, where there was particular desire to have trade between the Atlantic and Pacific coasts of the United States opened to them. Such desires, however, fell upon deaf ears, for there was no inclination to make more liberal provisions for shipping than there was to accord reciprocity.[19]

At the following short session Douglas in the Senate attempted once more to have reciprocity and St. Lawrence navigation taken up, but, although a day was set for its consideration, nothing was done by this body. In the House, William Duer of New York sought to resurrect the last session's bill. In a brief discussion which followed, McLane once more explained the significance of the bill and spoke of the value of Canadian trade. "This enlargement of our northwestern power and trade," he said, "is equivalent to the admission of several new states, in a commercial view, while it relieves us from all political agitation upon the northern frontier; leaving the people on either side free to cultivate a fraternal community of interest and feeling. . . ." Such an expression, eminently reasonable as it was, could hardly be said to be calculated to win over Southern votes for the proposition, and the

19. See *Cong. Globe,* 31st Cong., 1st Sess., p. 464, for Senate, and pp. 1009, 1011, for House reciprocity discussion. The question of coasting trade was linked with certain communications Bulwer had made which also referred to proposed changes in duties on coal and iron. Congressman Samuel Calvin of Pennsylvania considered Bulwer's "interference" as "unprecedented, impertinent, arrogant and highly offensive." He denounced Robert J. Walker as being a traitor in protesting the raising of duties. *Ibid.,* App., pp. 610–612.

net result was the same as that of the last session: no reciprocity legislation was enacted.[20]

From the Legation the British Minister had been anxiously watching Congress' reaction to the proposition, and he kept the Foreign Office in touch with whatever progress there was. Senator Douglas, he wrote Lord Palmerston on February 18, 1850,[21] had brought forward a bill much like that under consideration in the House, except that he had annexed to it a provision for free navigation of the St. Lawrence. "I have had Mr. Douglas spoken to upon the subject," he remarked, "with a view of dissuading him from the addition, and leaving the matter to which it refers for subsequent decision, but he says that without this provision the Bill will be lost in the Senate, and that with it he is sure of success." It was desirable, he thought, that both bills should be alike and asked his superior whether he should try to get Douglas to conform to the House bill or have the latter modified to match the Senate's. Two weeks later[22] he reported his anxiety about the Canadian reciprocity bill. The navigation issue was a complicating factor, although he learned that Senator Dix had seen a copy of a dispatch from the Colonial Office wherein was stated the willingness of Her Majesty's Government to grant the privilege whenever the legislature of Canada desired it. Dix had shown the dispatch to several members of both houses of Congress. Furthermore, Bulwer understood that Merritt, when he was in Washington, had expressed a conviction that the Canadian legislature would put no obstacles in the way of granting the free navigation.[23]

When the bill was brought up in the House in May, Bulwer's hopes rose and he announced, after describing the parliamentary sparring, that the position had become very favorable, and it seemed now to be principally a question for the proponents of the measure as to what was the best method of procedure. The desire of New Brunswick and Nova Scotia to be included in the arrangement had raised new diffi-

20. *Cong. Globe,* 31st Cong., 2d Sess., pp. 750–751.

21. FO 5:511 (P.R.O.).

22. To Palmerston, Mar. 2; FO 5:512 (P.R.O.). While Bulwer mentioned "Mr. Grenell's" bill, he probably meant McLane's.

23. The Foreign Office was a little concerned about how this information had got out. Bulwer traced it to a dispatch written by Lord Grey in 1847 which was published by Parliament. Merivale to Addington, Apr. 2, 1850, FO 115: 106; Bulwer to Palmerston, Apr. 16, 1850, FO 5:512 (P.R.O.).

culties and would probably cost some votes,[24] although there was no doubt about the strong wish of these provinces to share in any reciprocal trade arrangement. To Lord Elgin, who forwarded to Bulwer the wishes of New Brunswick, he wrote at length outlining the whole story of his connection with the affair and emphasizing the complications raised by the Maritime Provinces.[25] He could, however, report in July that the House Committee on Commerce had decided to include in the scheme not only New Brunswick and Nova Scotia but also Prince Edward Island, although the agitation by these colonies had produced an increasingly unfavorable effect upon the public mind. He still did not despair of success, although the death of the President was an impediment and the prevailing sickness in Washington disposed Congress to end its session as soon as possible.[26]

But the session dragged on without affording much comfort to the British Minister or to those who hoped for reciprocity with Canada. In September, toward the end of this protracted session, Bulwer, in a long dispatch,[27] summed up his impressions of the situation. Great excitement over the slavery question and interminable speeches had prevented other business from being adequately considered. The Senate with some difficulty finally got a report from the Committee on Commerce, although this report was not quite so favorable as that of the House committee; specifically it left lumber off the schedule at the instance of Senator Hamlin of Maine, who assured Bulwer that the sole reason for so doing was the existence of large stocks on hand and that, as soon as those should be reduced, lumber could be added. McLane in the House and Douglas and Hamlin in the Senate had made two or three unsuccessful attempts to bring the bill up. The Whigs, with Webster at their head, had taken up the protective tariff; the Whig press denounced the reciprocity measure, and some of the Sena-

24. Bulwer to Palmerston, May 20, 1850; FO 5:512 (P.R.O.). A little later, June 3, he wrote that those favorable to the Canadian bill felt that inclusion of the other two provinces would endanger the whole proposition (FO 5: 513). Bulwer received in the middle of May a petition, numerously signed, from the Chamber of Commerce and inhabitants of St. John asking that New Brunswick be included.

25. Bulwer to Elgin, June 2, 1850, FO 5:513 (P.R.O.); also in G '41–'52 (P.A.C.).

26. Bulwer to Palmerston, July 15, 1850; FO 5:513 (P.R.O.).

27. To Palmerston, Sept. 23, 1850; FO 5:515 (P.R.O.).

tors spoke in a hostile spirit against it. On the other hand, Bulwer felt that he had secured the support of most of the leading Southern Senators, while those from the West were favorable on account of the St. Lawrence, and, if a vote could be got, he thought there might be a majority of a half dozen or so. A few days later Bulwer wrote that the illness of Senator Douglas killed all chances of action in the Senate that session and that the House was so choked with business that it was "utterly impossible" to get the bill up. The only thing to do was to wait until the next session, when the measure would be in the same position as it then stood.

To his own testimony Bulwer added that of T. W. Dimscourt, "a very able gentleman, who has done all that lay in his power to assist me in managing this matter with Congress," and who had been sent by the Canadian Government for the purpose.[28]

Since your return to Washington and the determination of the Southern Senators to support the measure with their votes, with the understanding that they would not be led into any debate on the subject; I could not doubt but that the measure would be carried in its present shape by a fair majority. . . . The reluctance of the Southern Senators to take any part in the debate, and the fact of Senr Douglas being the only person whose constituents had any direct interest in the measure—the advanced stage of the session which will close upon Saturday, the mass of public business to be done, and private bills which everybody has in hand, assures me that all hopes . . . fell with Senr Douglas upon his sick bed.

Once during the session Bulwer had had a little gleam of hope in the matter of American registry for British-built ships, for at one time the committee had voted five to four in its favor.[29] At least, he felt that there was a possibility of securing registry for foreign-built vessels which had been repaired in American ports, but this concession went the way of reciprocity. In like manner, when a complaint came from Nova Scotia and New Brunswick that American Treasury regulation had stiffened so that no longer were Provincial vessels allowed to discharge cargo at ports of delivery, only in ports of entry, no satisfaction was obtained;[30] for when a bill allowing British vessels to unload

28. Dimscourt's letter to Bulwer, dated Sept. 26, was enclosed in Bulwer to Palmerston, Oct. 7; FO 5:515 (P.R.O.).

29. Bulwer to Palmerston, June, 1850; FO 5:513 (P.R.O.).

30. Bulwer to Palmerston, Aug. 18, 1850; FO 5:514 (P.R.O.).

at both types of ports was called up by Grinnell, he attempted to amend it by proposing a general increase in import duties, and no action was taken.

The Thirty-first Congress, then, came to an end with the cause of reciprocity no farther advanced than it had been at the beginning, and this in spite of the fact that Lord Elgin had commissioned Francis Hincks, the Inspector-General of Canada, to go to Washington to put before the proper persons the reasons why mutual concession would be of benefit to both peoples. Hincks gave McLane a long and detailed statement of the value of the commerce between Canada and the United States and pointed out what concessions the former had already made by removing differential duties which had previously favored Great Britain. He concluded his communication with a scarcely veiled threat that if the American Government did not change its attitude it would be necessary for Canada to resort to retaliation by reimposing differential duties and by closing Canadian canals to American users.[31]

When Congress adjourned *sine die* in March, 1851, all that Bulwer could point to in the way of progress was the introduction of a couple of resolutions in the Senate during the closing days calculated to "facilitate some correspondence" between Webster, now Secretary of State, and himself. On the other hand, he was under pressure from Canada, for Lord Elgin informed him in a private letter, dated March 21, 1851, that unless some satisfactory reason could be found to delay proceedings he would be under necessity of acceding to the desire of the Council, which wished to close Canadian canals to American shipping; as to what the "satisfactory reason" must be, Hincks informed him that this would have to be assurance from Secretary Webster that he would enter into negotiations for the purpose of arriving at a convention which would place the intercourse between Canada and the United States on a reciprocal footing.[32] Immediately Bulwer approached Webster, with the result outlined in a communication addressed to Lord Elgin on April 1.

31. *House Reports,* No. 4, 32d Cong., 1st Sess. The letter to McLane, dated Jan. 6, is in Seymour's Report, *House Reports,* No. 4, 32d Cong., 2d Sess., pp. 19–20.

32. Bulwer to Palmerston, Mar. 31, 1851; FO 5:528 (P.R.O.).

I received your letter of the 21st Ultimo, and read it to Mr Webster, and as Mr Webster seemed disposed to entertain the question of a negotiation I sent him a note which I had previously prepared. . . .

.   .   .   .   .

I must now proceed to tell you that having seen Mr Webster twice upon the matter, all I have been able to obtain from him is that when he returns to Washington in the course of a fortnight or thereabouts, he will enter into the matter with me with the disposition to bring it to some satisfactory termination, and that in the meantime it will be submitted to the President.

I have also seen the President who will not commit himself distinctly upon the matter, but stated that he was disposed to consider it with attention; that he had been inclined to think that by an interchange of agricultural or natural products alone, this country would have nothing to gain, since the Canadas and the United States were competitors in the same commodities, but that the great consumption of American manufactures in Canada introduced a new view of the question which had not at first struck him. My idea is that you should now write me an official letter stating the course that you would be prepared to pursue at a particular date if nothing was done here previously to satisfy the just expectations of the Canadians.

I think it would also be well that all the North American Provinces . . . made me a similar communication and that a positive period were *fixed*, beyond which further delay would not be accorded. . . .[33]

Bulwer found Webster reluctant to take any decisive step but finally, reversing somewhat the previous stand of the Administration that nothing could be done without Congress, agreement was reached that they should forthwith treat upon the subject and if they were agreed the President would recommend the view adopted to the favorable consideration of Congress at the earliest opportunity; Webster even went so far as to agree to remain in Washington longer than was his wont in order to settle the affair.[34] This assurance was hardly enough to satisfy the Canadians, who were more and more inclined to retaliation. Lord Elgin informed Bulwer that Hincks was now ready

33. Bulwer to Elgin, Apr. 1, 1851; G '40–'60 (P.A.C.). Bulwer's note to Webster mentioned in the above is printed in *Senate Ex. Docs.*, No. 1, 32d Cong., 1st Sess., pp. 83 ff.

34. Bulwer to Palmerston, June 22, 1851; FO 5:529 (P.R.O.).

to recommend closing the canals; that resolutions were to be proposed in Parliament to place a duty of 20 per cent on American goods and restore differential duties; and that the Imperial Parliament be requested to put duties on goods enumerated in the Canadian reciprocal proposal equal to duties levied by foreign countries on those goods when imported from Great Britain.[35] These threats were not carried into effect during 1851, partly because Bulwer was satisfied that the negotiation was progressing and that the President was prepared to recommend to Congress some general arrangement of commercial intercourse between the Provinces and the United States, and partly, perhaps, because the Canadians had no such real intention. Fillmore, in his Annual Message of 1851, did include this statement:

Your attention is again invited to the question of reciprocal trade between the United States and Canada and other British provinces near our frontier. Overtures for a convention on this subject have been recently received from Her Britannic Majesty's Minister Plenipotentiary, but it seems to be in many respects preferable that the matter should be regulated by reciprocal legislation. Documents are laid before you showing the terms the British government is willing to offer, and the measures which it may adopt, if some arrangement upon this subject shall not be had.[36]

Congress, however, appeared to be in no hurry to deal with the subject of the President's recommendation. The session advanced and no move was taken until, on February 7, 1852, Thomas H. Bayly of Virginia asked unanimous consent to take up a message just received from the President which, he was informed by the Secretary of State, was important and should receive early consideration. The message transmitted a report of Secretary Webster's[37] which called attention to the passage in the President's Annual Message where allusion was made to the prospects of a negotiation. Great Britain, announced Webster, was willing to enter into an arrangement whereby American vessels could participate fully in the fisheries on the shores of the Brit-

35. Enclosure Elgin to Bulwer in Bulwer to Palmerston, July 7, 1851; FO 5:529 (P.R.O.).
36. *House Ex. Docs.,* No. 2, 32d Cong., 1st Sess., p. 8. The enclosures included Hincks's memorandum; the proposal to close the Canadian canals; and resolutions regarding possible increase in duties on American commodities.
37. The report is in *Cong. Globe,* 32d Cong., 2d Sess., pp. 540 ff.

ish Provinces, with the possible exception of Newfoundland for the present, together with the right to use the shores for curing and drying fish, on condition that Canadian fishermen could have the same privileges on American shores and the right to take fish and fish products into American ports free of duty. The British Government, Webster went on, desired to couple with this, as a part of the arrangement, reciprocal free trade in natural products and free navigation of the St. Lawrence, and of the Welland and Rideau canals. Time only was needed to work out a satisfactory agreement; the imminence of the fishing season, however, did not allow delay in adjusting this part of the general plan but the British Government was unwilling to dispose of this part separately. Nevertheless,

the Secretary of State is of opinion that under the circumstances of the case, if Congress should pass an act admitting provincial fish free of duty into the United States, on condition that the fishermen of the United States are admitted to a full participation in the provincial fisheries, the Government of Great Britain would give effect to the measure by the requisite legislation on her part, in the expectation on both sides that the question of reciprocity, and of the use of the St. Lawrence and the canals connected with it, will be taken up hereafter, with a favorable disposition to come to a mutually advantageous agreement on that part of the subject also.

Even if such an act should fail to produce the desired result, which is not apprehended, it would relieve the United States of the responsibility for the consequences.

The report was referred to the Committee on Foreign Relations. Four days later Seymour of New York, for the Committee on Commerce, asked unanimous consent to introduce a bill having to do with the subject of the President's message; it was then, on Seymour's motion, recommitted to the Committee on Commerce. On February 16 it was called up, but postponed until the next day, when Seymour made a speech in its support. Clingman would amend it to open reciprocally the ports of Canada and the United States to the shipping of each, and Washburn of Maine would strike out the specific enumeration of items and provide reciprocal free trade in "all articles of the growth, production or manufacture" of British North America and the United States. Then, as unfinished business referred to the Committee of the Whole, it slumbered on the Speaker's desk, while the British Minister

and the Provincial Governments watched in vain for signs of activity.
The session dragged along into mid-summer with Congress showing no
signs of getting back to reciprocity while it tediously argued land
grants to railroads. In the opinion of the Colonial and of the British
Governments it was time to administer a jolt.[38]

38. In January, when Senator Cass was trying to have taken up a resolution
relative to any power's trying to annex Cuba, John P. Hale of New Hampshire
presented a resolution to add to Cass's to the effect that the United States would
view all attempts of any foreign power to acquire Canada as unfriendly acts
directed against the United States and to be resisted by all means in their
power. This, of course, was a bit of sparring, sectional and political. *Cong.
Globe,* 32d Cong., 2d Sess., p. 226.

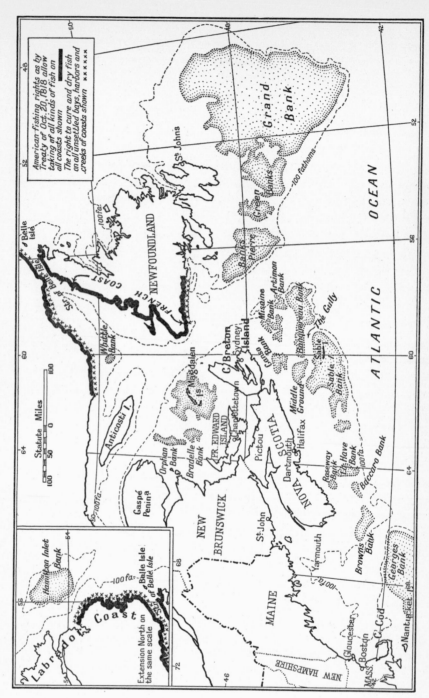

The Fishing Banks from Cape Cod to Labrador

CHAPTER III

STILL AT WORK

An instrument which could be used with great effectiveness to produce a shock lay at hand: pressure through restrictions upon Americans in their fishing activities off British American shores. From the time independence was gained the Northeast fisheries formed a perennial source of actual or potential friction between the United States and British North America, or, officially, between the United States and Great Britain. The War of 1812 was considered by England to have put an end to the "liberties" granted in 1783 and, despite protests of the American Commissioners at Ghent, those liberties were not restored. A new Convention, that of 1818, placed upon a specific and lasting basis much more limited privileges, which included the right of Americans to take and cure fish on restricted parts of the British coasts, while their fishing vessels could put into ports only to obtain shelter, wood, and water. In the cod fishery this limitation was not usually significant, but for mackerel, herring, and certain other varieties of fish, as well as in the matter of obtaining supplies, bait, and the like, the restrictions were onerous. Generally, however, there had been no great disturbance because, on the whole, British authorities had been lenient in interpreting and enforcing the convention. The people of the Maritime Provinces viewed the situation with mixed feelings. Trade brought by American fishermen, so far as it existed more or less on toleration, was welcomed; on the other hand, there was a natural desire to exploit for themselves the rich resources upon their shores and to exclude therefrom Americans, who enjoyed a protected market at home and who, moreover, received bounties when they engaged in the cod fishery.[1]

1. M. H. Perley maintained that, despite efforts of the American Treasury Department, "with the whole system of American fishing bounties, there appears to co-exist an organized system of frauds" while "vast sums of money go annually into the pockets of unscrupulous men, while it is exceedingly doubtful if the actual fishermen are at all benefited thereby." *Report on the Fisheries of the Bay of Fundy;* Laid before the House of Assembly and ordered printed, 15 March, 1851 (Fredericton, 1851), p. 111.

The Maritime Provinces, except possibly Prince Edward Island, were reluctant to admit Americans on an equal footing to the fisheries; they were more interested in preventing interlopers from enjoying what they considered their own treasures.[2] But, if the fisheries were to be surrendered, there must be reciprocal free entry of natural products, including New Brunswick lumber and Nova Scotia coal, as well as American registry for British-built vessels.[3] The legislative assembly of Prince Edward Island, which had in 1849 been ready to admit Americans to the fishery without bargaining, in 1852 by resolution demanded equivalent privileges in terms of reciprocal free trade;[4] Newfoundland and Nova Scotia would not open their fisheries without concessions, and the Island must take the same stand.[5]

The session of the Thirty-second Congress dragged on. There was time to debate interminably land grants to railroads; much discussion of the interpretation of the Clayton-Bulwer Treaty occurred.[6] There appeared to be no time to consider reciprocity, at least so long as protectionist Whigs controlled Congress. It was, then, in the opinion of the British Government time to resort to measures of a more positive nature. On July 5, following an instruction of June 15, 1852, John

2. "The intrusion of American fishing vessels upon the fishing grounds of the Bay of Fundy is loudly complained of everywhere by the Fishermen of the Bay. Measures are required for keeping these vessels without the limits established by the Convention of 1818, either by requesting the services of some of the smaller vessels belonging to the Royal Navy, or else by employing Fishery Cutters at the joint expense of New Brunswick and Nova Scotia." Perley, *op. cit.*, p. 115.

3. T. B. Livingston to Clayton, Mar. 1, 1850; Consular Letters: Halifax, Vol. V (D.S.).

4. *Royal Gazette*, Charlottetown, Feb. 9, 1852.

5. Canada, less vitally interested in fisheries, had navigation of the St. Lawrence and the canals as bait. On February 20, 1852, Elgin transmitted to the Colonial Office a Minute of the Council, based upon a memorandum of Inspector-General Hincks which read in part: "pending the decision of the Congress of the United States during the present Session on the question of Reciprocity, it is expedient that the navigation of the River St. Lawrence and of the Canadian Canals should be conceded to American bottoms"; it was the opinion of the Council that necessary instructions for this should be obtained from the British Government as soon as possible. G 462 (P.A.C.).

6. It is possible that the friction generated by this issue, temporarily straining British-American relations, had a part in preventing consideration of Canadian reciprocity.

F. T. Crampton, who had become Minister not long after Bulwer's
recall, made known to the American Secretary of State that orders
had been issued to afford naval protection to British fisheries to prevent a repetition of the complaints so frequently made against encroachments on British rights by both American and French fishermen. He informed Webster that there would be located off New Brunswick, Nova Scotia, Prince Edward Island, and in the Gulf of St.
Lawrence a force of vessels sufficient to prevent infraction of the
treaty.[7] If this move did not immediately secure the desired results it
at least obtained action.

Webster, now in Massachusetts and probably aware that something of the kind was coming, wrote the British Minister on July 17 to
point out the serious situation that would be produced if this threatened interruption by force of privileges long enjoyed were carried out.
He told Crampton that he wished to see him as soon as he, Crampton,
came north. He had, he wrote, recommended to the President that
they, Crampton and Webster, take up at once the full subject of the
fisheries and Canadian trade as a matter of negotiation. Could not
Crampton, meanwhile, prevail with the Provincial authorities not to
institute hostile proceedings against the fishermen until a longer notice had been given or until they could confer? Crampton, he supposed, would see in the papers the official publication he, Webster, had
made.[8] This "official communication" related the gist of Crampton's
note and told how the recent change in the British Ministry had produced a new policy wherein Sir John Packington, the Colonial Secretary, had determined to "*enforce the observance of the Convention*"
with an armed force; that one American fishing schooner had already
been seized; that the various colonies had each provided one or more
armed vessels to supplement the Royal Naval force. Webster quoted
the provisions of the Convention of 1818 and then pointed out that the
British insisted on interpreting its terms as meaning what was stated

7. *Senate Ex. Docs.*, No. 100, 32d Cong., 1st Sess., pp. 154–155.
8. Webster to Crampton, July 17, 1852; Special Agents, Vol. XVI (D.S.).
Webster's "official communication" dated Washington, July 6, was published
in the Boston *Courier*, July 19. It is printed in *Writings and Speeches of Daniel
Webster* (Boston, 1903), XIV, 555–560. The "communication" was probably
antedated and possibly at least partly prepared before Webster left Washington.

by the Law Officers of the Crown when in a Nova Scotia case in 1841 they rendered an opinion:

That by the terms of the Convention, American citizens were excluded from any right of fishing within three miles from the coast of British America, and that *the prescribed distance of three miles, is to be measured from the headlands or extreme points of land next the sea,* of the coast or of the entrance of bays or indents of the coast, and consequently *that no right exists on the part of American citizens, to enter the bays of Nova Scotia, there to take fish, although the fishing, being within the bay, may be at a greater distance than three miles from the shore of* the bay. . . .

Such a construction, Webster considered, would totally disrupt the "extensive fishing business of New England" and be "attended by constant collisions of the most unpleasant and exciting character, which may end in the destruction of human life, in the involvement of the Government in questions of a very serious nature, threatening the peace of the two countries." Webster affirmed that the American Government did not agree with this construction, but made public the information so that Americans could see how the case stood and "be upon their guard."

President Fillmore, upon receipt of Webster's announcement of the change in policy, suggested[9] that he ought to make public a letter in which he should express regret that any misunderstanding had arisen with respect to the Convention of 1818 and say that it, together with the subject of reciprocal trade, would be the subject of an immediate negotiation. He then went on to outline subjects to be included in the negotiation: fisheries, trade, use of the St. Lawrence and the canals. He preferred the trade question to be settled by legislation, but if that could not be done "it may be well to settle it by Treaty, for a limited time." Crampton, while appreciating how this move of his Government had hastened developments, felt it desirable to inform the governments of the British Provinces and the admiral in command of the squadron about the conciliatory attitude of the American Government and to recommend to them to take precautions to avoid collisions

9. A copy of the letter was given to Crampton. It is found, dated July 20, in FO 5:546 (P.R.O.).

which the United States apprehended.[10] He reported a conversation held with the President, who had frankly discussed the issue with him; Fillmore, said Crampton, maintained that the word "headland" was not used in the convention and that, in his opinion, this interpretation was not warranted. The President concluded his remarks by saying he had been urged to send war vessels to the fishing grounds to protect American interests but he had refrained for fear of the consequences so long as the two Governments were not agreed as to the rights they sought to define, and he repeated the suggestion he had made to Webster about a temporary arrangement whereby each side should refrain from insisting on the rights which it claimed and the other denied. In a private letter to Elgin on the same day[11] Crampton recapitulated what he had written to Malmesbury and again urged maintaining quiet until he and Webster could have an opportunity to confer with a view of adjusting the differences, although he feared that British and American interpretation of the terms of the convention would "give rise to a number of cases in regard to which the British & American Govt will find themselves at issue & keep up a great irritation upon the subject here."

Congress, which had been proceeding in blissful ignorance of, or at least indifference to, feelings north of the line, was waked with a rude shock when Webster published his communication telling of the change of policy by the British Government. On July 23 Senator James K. Mason of Virginia, with fire in his eye, rose to introduce a resolution calling on the President for copies of all correspondence on the subject of the fisheries since the Convention of 1818 and to ask whether the Administration had ordered naval forces to protect American fishermen; he did not know what the President had done, but he should have already ordered the whole navy to defend Americans against British cannon.[12] Under unanimous consent his resolu-

10. Crampton to Malmesbury, July 20; FO 5:546 (P.R.O.). Lord Malmesbury became Secretary of State for Foreign Affairs in the newly organized Coalition government under the Earl of Aberdeen.

11. July 20; G '41–'52 (P.A.C.).

12. Mason, needless to say, was a Democrat who was demonstrating Crampton's opinion that much of the noise came from the opposition which wished to put the President in a hole. The discussion of the resolution, where some resentment was shown because Senators were left in ignorance on the matter

tion was considered immediately and provoked a somewhat extensive debate. Hamlin of Maine said it was rumored that there was an ulterior purpose, that of forcing a reciprocal arrangement; we were not permitted to know, he said, whether there was to be negotiation or legislation under duress, but it was wonderful that either should be attempted in such a manner. Senator Cass was sure that Britain's course was one of the most extraordinary in modern times: for thirty years the treaty had been in force and now, instead of soliciting a friendly negotiation as to its meaning, Britain was drawing a sword to cut the Gordian knot. John Davis of Massachusetts soothed ruffled spirits by assuring them that there was no cause for alarm; he understood that the British Minister and the Secretary of State were already conferring at Boston;[13] Senator Hamlin was correct in stating that the matter was connected with reciprocity, and he would call attention to the fact that Canadian rights on the St. Lawrence were being more strictly enforced, while privileges of the rivers and the canals were either refused or reluctantly conceded. In short, the British North American Colonies wished to take their products into the United States without paying duty and they were willing to barter navigation and the fisheries for it. Several of the Senators made the occasion one on which to make digs, more or less subtle, at the Administration; some of them professed to see imminent danger of war, and others scoffed at the idea. There was, however, no real opposition to the resolution and it was adopted.

Complying with the Senate's request, the President on August 2 stated that a vessel had been sent, and transmitted a selection of documents running from 1823 to 1852.[14] In moving the reference of the message and the documents to the Committee on Foreign Relations, Senator Cass, according to the reporter,[15] "spoke for near an hour,"

until informed by the press, is in *Cong. Globe,* 32d Cong., 1st Sess., pp. 1890–1897.

13. It was not until two days later that Webster and Crampton actually met.

14. *Senate Ex. Docs.,* No. 100, 32d Cong., 1st Sess. The special correspondent of the New York *Herald,* August 2, wrote that the subject of the fisheries had engaged the attention of the President for several days; the clerks in the Department of State had worked late Saturday night and all day Sunday copying the documents, and so great was the interest of the President that he visited the department both nights.

15. *Cong. Globe,* 32d Cong., 1st Sess., p. 2049.

contending that the construction of the treaty by Great Britain was untenable and urging the necessity of protecting American fishermen against Britain's most extraordinary course. Several of the Senators aired their views, without adding much to what had already been said; the documents were ordered printed, and that ended the Senate's consideration of the matter that session.[16] If the British and Colonial Governments had hoped to get immediate action their expectations had been dashed, and recourse must be had to negotiations with the executive department.

It was not only in administrative and congressional circles that the new British policy had produced reverberations. Both American and Provincial newspapers had something to say, but opinion on the subject was not unanimous. The Boston *Daily Bee*[17] said that the valuable fall fishing would be broken up and there would be a heavy loss of property; the United States would resist the new claim set up by Great Britain under the Convention of 1818. The Philadelphia *Enquirer*,[18] on the other hand, stated that this was a correct although strict interpretation; after the leniency so long shown, this new strictness clearly was intended to force some sort of arrangement in reciprocal trade. The Boston *Daily Advertiser*[19] maintained that it was bad policy to encourage or countenance fishermen in prosecuting their calling in prohibited waters; it regretted to see such recommendations as that of the Newburyport *Herald*, which would have the fishermen arm their vessels and sink "every British cruiser which molests them outside

16. In a dispatch to Malmesbury (Aug. 15, 1852; FO 5:546 [P.R.O.]), Crampton commented at length on the debate. Soulé's speech especially aroused his attention for "Mr. Soulé belongs to, and, indeed aspires to lead what is called the 'Young America' or 'Manifest Destiny' Party; that is to say, those who possess extreme democratic doctrines in the usual sense of the word . . . ; and also those who urge it to be the duty, as well as the true Policy of the United States to intervene in the affairs of Foreign Nations in support of Democratic & Republican Principles."

Seward's speech contained some remarks respecting British policy which were "very objectionable," but in general stated the question "in a manner more consistent with justice and common sense than has yet been done by any of the speakers on the subject." This was partly because Seward had applied to Crampton for information and the British Minister accommodated as far as he properly could.

17. July 20, 1852.   18. July 22, 1852.

19. July 21, 1852.

those limits, or if overpowered by superior force, go down with their flags flying." In general, the papers of the communities which were directly interested in fishing assumed a truculent tone, while others either were inclined to think that the fishermen *were* poaching on preserves where they had no business or that the whole difficulty ought to be adjusted by amicable agreement.

The papers of the Maritime Provinces in general approved the course taken by the British Government and said that the Yankees knew they were in the wrong and would, after a little bluster, be willing to make some equitable arrangement in return for the privileges which they had been usurping for so long. The St. John *New Brunswicker*[20] held forth in this manner:

The American government may make a little noise about the rigid enforcement of the fishery treaty, and especially about the correct construction put upon it by the Earl of Derby and his Cabinet, but we feel confident it will not frighten John Bull out of his present position. This movement on the part of England has done more to strengthen those feelings of confidence in her powerful and maternal sway, which exist in the hearts of her colonial subjects than any single act of the Russell Ministry, and we feel quite satisfied that the result will prove highly satisfactory.

Hazard's Gazette[21] was equally positive that nothing but good would come from the episode:

. . . We have no doubt but an attempt will be made by the American Government to obtain a modification of the strict letter of the fishery treaty between Great Britain and the United States; but failing, as we believe they will, in this, they will then offer, as an equivalent, reciprocity in certain articles of domestic growth and produce, for the privilege of fishing within the prescribed limits. . . . Our neighbours had so long trampled upon our privileges, that they imagined they had a perfect right to use our fishing grounds for their own benefit. Did they possess such valuable source of wealth, British subjects would not be permitted to take a single fish. The strictest *surveillance* would be exercised to keep off all intruders. The complaints of the Colonists have been loud and long, but little or no attention was paid to them, until the present Ministry came into power. . . . It has been said, and with great justice, that a Con-

20. July 22, 1852, quoted in Boston *Courier,* July 26; found in Consular Letters: St. John, May 20, 1851 to Sept. 13, 1858 (D.S.).
21. Charlottetown, P.E.I., Aug. 3, 1852.

servative Ministry is best for the Colonies, and experience verifies the truth of the observation.

To satisfy public opinion in the United States, the President, as he had informed the Senate on August 2, sent Commodore M. C. Perry with the steam frigate *Mississippi* to look out for the interests of Americans. He, like Admiral Seymour of the British force, was instructed to do nothing to aggravate the disturbance, and to use his influence to have American fishermen avoid provoking trouble.[22]

The Department of State was far from idle during the short period which remained of Webster's life, and the President himself took more than routine interest in the issues involving British North America. As soon as possible, Crampton had set out for Boston whence he went to Nahant, where he and Webster had a brief interview on July 25. Webster gave him a copy of Fillmore's letter with its suggestion of a temporary arrangement, and the next day at Marshfield they discussed the whole matter with evident frankness. Politics, Crampton informed the Foreign Office, appeared to enter into the controversy:

. . . The excitement which has been created by the Publication [of Webster's "official communication"] has been very great, greater than he himself probably wished or intended, and has given an opportunity to the more violent Members of the Senate who are opposed to the Administration, to make some of [their] many appeals to popular Feeling which, although arising much more from a desire to embarrass their political adversaries, than from real alarm or animosity, is nevertheless calculated to have a prejudicial effect upon the satisfactory settlement of the Ques-

22. Consul Norton of Pictou wrote Webster, July 29, 1852, that a vessel should be sent. There were thousands of American fishermen in the Gulf of St. Lawrence and on the coasts of Newfoundland who were entirely ignorant of the construction of the Convention of 1818 as now stated by the British Government, and they would resist by force any attempt to seize them. Consular Letters: Pictou, Vol. IV (D.S.).

Perry, writing from the Gulf on August 26 (Consular Letters: St. John, May 20, 1851, to Sept. 13, 1858 [D.S.]), said the Provincials seemed "to be anxious to draw tighter the bonds of neighborly friendship which undoubtedly prevails at the present time, and they are exceedingly anxious to come to some more satisfactory arrangement with regard to the fisheries by granting to Americans in consideration of an equitable equivalent, privileges of fishing in common with their own Citizens." Almost any concession, thought Perry, would be small payment for the fisheries.

tion. . . . Those who are opposed to the Settlement of these Questions on purely commercial ground, will also be ready to avail themselves of any feeling which would be likely to retard their definitive arrangement.[23]

The British Minister remained in Massachusetts several days. He heard Webster make a public address in which he referred to the existing controversy in very guarded language. He had a number of conversations with the Secretary, who, while reiterating his hope that nothing might be done to excite the New Englanders further, apparently conceded the correctness of the British interpretation of the convention, although he maintained that in 1818 the Americans conceded more than they ought, and he showed Crampton a letter from the President in which the latter, too, apparently had come to consider that the opinion of the Law Officers was sound.[24] Nevertheless, when Crampton returned to Washington a little later (August 5) he found the President less inclined to the opinion given Webster than he had hoped. Fillmore had apparently been influenced by discussion in the Senate, although he admitted that he had not yet sufficiently examined the documents to be well informed on the subject. Crampton had gone to the interview armed with a statement of authorities on the subject of national jurisdiction over bays, including the opinion of Chancellor Kent, "a very high authority in this country," who maintained the correctness of the British stand and substantiated it by the attitude of the United States regarding such indentations as Delaware and Chesapeake Bays. When the President alluded to the supposed "uninterrupted indulgence which had been for many years practically accorded to American Fishermen in exercise of liberty of fishing in British waters" Crampton could present to him a list of seizures made since 1839 which showed that the British claim had not gone entirely unenforced, even though it had not been applied as rigorously as Crampton tried to make out.[25]

While Webster was still at Marshfield and just after Crampton had left for Washington, Andrews appeared with his nearly completed

23. Crampton to Malmesbury, Confidential, July 26; FO 5:546 (P.R.O.).
24. Crampton to Malmesbury, Confidential, Aug. 2; FO 5:546 (P.R.O.).
25. Crampton to Malmesbury, Confidential, Aug. 9, 1850; FO 5:546 (P.R.O.). Enclosed with this dispatch was the list Crampton presented. It showed that between June, 1839, and the latter part of 1851, twenty-eight fishing craft had been seized; of these three had been restored.

report on the state of things in the British Provinces.[26] This report was to be filed at the Department of State and would, Webster thought, be useful to the President in his conversations with the British Minister. It was obvious that Fillmore had hopes of adjusting the fisheries troubles as well as other Canadian issues before the close of his administration; it would be not only a personal triumph but would redound to the credit of the expiring Whig party, which was so seriously under fire. In this desire Fillmore did not stand alone. The British Government was no less anxious to secure an adjustment.[27] The President believed that a temporary solution, to be in effect during the existing fishing season and while feeling ran so high, could be found by prohibiting both British and American fishermen from carrying on their activities in the disputed waters, while British naval units should be instructed to exercise not only discretion but leniency in enforcing their instructions. Lord Malmesbury, however, shared the opinion of the Colonial Office that it would be impossible to deny British fishermen rights about which no question had ever been raised.[28] Disclaiming any purpose of antagonizing the Government or people of the United States by its course and regretting publication of information relative to the protection of the fisheries "without what appears to Her Majesty's Government sufficient inquiry into the circumstances of the case,"[29] Malmesbury argued that the correspondence of 1845 between Lord Aberdeen and Edward Everett yielded a privilege and did not grant a right to American fishermen when they were allowed to fish within the Bay of Fundy outside the three-mile limit, and that the question of the use of other bays and harbors within the headlands was not left to be decided in the future; in other words Great Britain

26. Back in the summer of 1850 Clayton had notified Fillmore that Andrews had made a preliminary report which he thought would be of much service, "but the existence of such an agency should not be made known to the British Government." Clayton to Fillmore, July 20, 1850, Confidential; Webster to Fillmore, July 30 and 31, 1852; Special Agents, Vol. XVI (D.S.). A brief preliminary sketch of the situation is in Andrews to Webster, July 9, 1851; Consular Letters: Montreal and Quebec, Vol. I (D.S.).

27. Malmesbury to Crampton, Aug. 17, 1852; FO 115:121 (P.R.O.).

28. Malmesbury to Crampton, Aug. 11, 1852; FO 115:121 (P.R.O.). Lawrence to Webster, Aug. 13, 1852; Great Britain: Despatches, Vol. LXIII (D.S.). Abbott Lawrence was Minister to England, 1849–52.

29. Malmesbury to Crampton, Aug. 10, 1852; FO 115:121 (P.R.O.).

had "relaxed" her rights as to this one place but did not admit that they were called into question.

Webster, when he returned to Washington in August, showed evidence of a desire equal to the President's to get the matter settled. Not only had he Andrews' report,[30] but the Treasury Department had given its opinion that there was little reason to fear that British fishermen would seriously interfere with the home market if duties were abolished upon their products. Crampton correctly sized up the situation when he reported that the whole affair had distinct political bearings and was not disconnected with the action of the Baltimore Convention, where Webster's candidacy was so summarily disposed of. The Secretary had to present a front firm enough to reassure his Massachusetts supporters yet not so bold as to endanger the relations between Great Britain and the United States. On the last day of August, on the eve of his departure from Washington, Webster had a long conversation with Crampton in which he made very clear his great desire to adjust the question and sought some kind of assurance that the British Government would give such orders that collision would be unlikely. He pointed out that whether from intention or otherwise there had been great leniency for years in enforcing the British conventional rights, so that a great American interest had grown up.

It was clear that neither side was going to press matters. British and Colonial purpose would have been achieved if negotiations with some promise of success might be instituted, and both in Washington and London there were ample signs that the American Government was in a mood to negotiate, although it preferred that the negotiations take place in the United States rather than in London. Various factors and above all the desire of Webster to wind up the affair before the close of Fillmore's administration, since certain Democrats who expected to win the presidential election intimated to Crampton that they were anxious to settle the whole matter as soon as they were in charge of the Government, made things look very promising.[31] Had

30. The report was printed by resolution of the Senate as *Senate Ex. Docs.,* No. 112, 32d Cong., 1st Sess., also as *House Ex. Docs.,* No. 136, 32d Cong., 1st Sess.

31. Crampton to Malmesbury, Confidential, Sept. 6; Private, Sept. 6; Malmesbury to Crampton, Sept. 9, 1852; FO 5:547 (P.R.O.).

Webster lived, none can say whether his expectations might not have been fulfilled, but his death (on October 24), the interim with no Secretary of State, and the tardy appointment of Everett destroyed all chance of immediate action. Anticipating, however, that in due course Webster would be back in Washington to carry on the negotiation, in September Crampton[32] had an interview with the President at which he formally suggested, in accordance with his instructions, that a negotiation upon all the subjects affecting commercial relations of the two countries should be taken up. Fillmore agreed. He agreed also that to reconcile the Colonies to a surrender of their exclusive fishing rights, whatever they were, would require some concessions on the part of the United States, and reciprocity in trade unquestionably was one most desired. He would consent to an arrangement the execution of which should be left contingent upon appropriate legislation by Congress, and, if that body acted favorably, then a treaty embodying the terms could be signed. Crampton, when asked for a memorandum stating the desires of the Colonies, said he could sum them up at the moment; they were: reciprocity of trade in natural products, including those of the fisheries; coasting trade from the eastern states to California opened to Provincials; and admission of British-built vessels to American registry when purchased by American citizens.[33]

A few days later, when the memorandum was delivered, the President "conversed freely" on its various topics and stated that although some were not free from difficulty, nothing should be overlooked to effect the best arrangement possible. He remarked, however, that rumors of retaliatory legislation on the part of Canada would render success more difficult, especially in getting a reciprocity measure through Congress. Crampton, armed with a memorandum of Inspector-General Hincks as well as with confidential communications from Canada, said that nothing had been done as yet, although there was talk of legislation which would effect not retaliation but a resumption of certain commercial restrictions, the permanent abandonment of which had been found inconsistent with the interests of Canada in the absence of corresponding concessions by the United States. Fillmore admitted the correctness of this view but maintained that the con-

32. Crampton to Malmesbury, Sept. 12, 1852; FO 5:547 (P.R.O.).
33. Crampton to Malmesbury, Sept. 12; FO 5:547 (P.R.O.).

templated acts would be looked upon in the United States as retaliation, especially by those who were opposed to reciprocity.[34]

No actual progress beyond this point had been made before Congress convened in December, 1852, although Everett had attempted
to pick up the threads of the affair and Crampton had kept it alive,
spurred on by new instructions from the Foreign Office.[35] The excitement of the summer had subsided while interested parties on both sides
waited to see what their Governments would do, meantime letting their
feelings be known through communications in the press. Fillmore did
not neglect Canadian issues in his Message. He noted the alarm of the
previous summer and the fear that an enlarged naval force in the
fishing waters was there for the purpose of enforcing the British interpretation of the Convention of 1818, but, happily, satisfactory explanations of the real purpose had been given both in Washington and
London. Nevertheless, he went on,

the unadjusted difference . . . between the two Governments as to the
interpretation of the first article of the convention of 1818 is still a matter of importance. American fishing vessels within nine or ten years have
been excluded from waters to which they had free access for twenty-five
years after the negotiation of the treaty. In 1845 this exclusion was relaxed so far as concerns the Bay of Fundy, but the just and liberal intention of the Home Government, in compliance with which we think the true
construction of the convention, to open all the other outer bays to our
fishermen, was abandoned, in consequence of the opposition of the colonies. Notwithstanding this, the United States have, since the Bay of
Fundy was reopened to our fishermen, in 1845, pursued the most liberal

34. Crampton to Malmesbury, Sept. 26, 1852; FO 5:547 (P.R.O.).

35. In an instruction of September 16, Malmesbury had, on advice of Lord
Derby (September 11, 1852), modified his bald statement of jurisdiction over
bays to one where he called attention to the recognized principle of international
law of jurisdiction over waters "in the immediate vicinity of its own coasts" and
cited the United States' claim to exclusive jurisdiction over such places as Cape
Cod Bay, Long Island Sound, and the like. FO 115:121; 5:543 (P.R.O.).

On December 4, 1852, Everett signed a long instruction addressed to J. R.
Ingersoll, who succeeded Lawrence as Minister in London, in which he took
up point by point the various issues which Malmesbury had raised; he paid
especial attention to what had been said about the "relaxation" in the case of
the Bay of Fundy in 1845 and maintained that Malmesbury's interpretation
was erroneous. Great Britain: Instructions, XVI, 154–174 (D.S.).

course toward the colonial fishing interests. By the revenue law of 1846, the duties on colonial fish entering our ports were very greatly reduced, and by the warehousing act it is allowed to be entered in bond without the payment of duty. In this way colonial fish has acquired the monopoly of the export trade in our market, and is entering to some extent into the home consumption. . . .

These circumstances, and the incidents above alluded to, have led me to think the moment favorable for a reconsideration of the entire subject of the fisheries, on the coasts of the British Provinces, with a view to place them upon a more liberal footing of reciprocal privilege. A willingness to meet us in some arrangement of this kind is understood to exist on the part of Great Britain, with a desire on her part to include in one comprehensive settlement, as well this subject as the commercial intercourse between the United States and the British Provinces. I have thought that whatever arrangements may be made on these two subjects, it is expedient that they should be embraced in separate conventions.[36]

The short period remaining of the Fillmore administration witnessed a valiant attempt to secure both treaty and legislation, but time and political and economic opposition balked all efforts. By the middle of December, Crampton could send the Foreign Office a project of a treaty which had received the approbation of Secretary Everett and President Fillmore: Americans might have inshore fishing privileges on equality with British together with the right to use uninhabited shores for curing and drying of fish, exclusive of the fisheries in estuaries and mouths of rivers; reciprocal free trade in fish and fish products was provided; a long list of natural products should be duty-free; Americans were to enjoy free navigation of the St. Lawrence and its canals; and vessels built in Great Britain or in the British Colonies, when the property of American citizens, could have American registry. The agreement should take effect when appropriate legislation had been enacted by the Imperial Parliament and the British Provincial Assemblies and by the Congress of the United States respectively, and should remain in force for ten years and thereafter "until one year after such assent [should] be withdrawn by one of the Parties to this Treaty."[37]

36. *Cong. Globe,* 32d Cong., 2d Sess., p. 7.
37. Crampton's covering dispatch, dated Dec. 15, 1852, and the draft of the project are in FO 5: 548 (P.R.O.).

While in general the project met with the approval of the British Government, now changed so that Lord John Russell was back in the Foreign Office, there were several details, some of them significant, which in their opinion should be changed. There must be specific statement that Newfoundland was not included in the agreement; since coal was an article of so much importance to Nova Scotia that its omission would not only cause discontent but probably would cause the Provincial Assembly to reject the treaty, Her Majesty's Government must insist on its retention; furthermore furs, pelts, and skins might not be left out; metals as well as ores of metals ought to be included in the free list; since the proposal to admit Colonials to the trade between the Atlantic and Pacific coasts of the United States had been rejected on constitutional grounds, it was no more than fair that there should be some equivalent, and the Minister suggested it would be proper for the United States to open her waters, including bays, harbors, etc., without restriction as to distance from the shore in the same manner in which it was proposed to open the Canadian waters.[38]

When this instruction was received by Crampton the congressional session had scarcely a month to run, too short a time to reply to it and get an answer back before March 4, hence he "thought it expedient to state at once to Mr. Everett with entire frankness the decision of Her Majesty's Government." Everett, on his part, avowed his intention to speak with equal frankness and would lay the points before the President.

I have not yet received [wrote Crampton] any official notification of the decision of the American Cabinet, but from several conversations which I have since had with Mr Everett on the subject, as well as with some other Gentlemen in the confidence of the Government, I have reason to fear that their reply will be unfavorable to the Project in so many essential points as to leave me very little hope that any counterproposition will be made to me to which I could agree without entirely losing sight of the Instructions of Her Majesty's Government, and indeed of the Principles to which Her Majesty's Legation has invariably adhered in the discus-

38. The instruction is dated Jan. 15, 1853; FO 115:128 (P.R.O.). On December 31 Ingersoll, Minister to Great Britain, 1852–53, wrote from London that he had had a brief interview with Lord John and had mentioned the proposed negotiation but he was able to get only noncommittal responses. Ingersoll to Everett, Great Britain: Despatches, Vol. LXIV (D.S.).

sion with the United States' Government of the questions involved in the proposed Treaty.[39]

Further conversations with Everett and with Abbott Lawrence, then in Washington, led him to believe that there was no hope that Congress would approve American registry of British-built ships, and he was equally convinced that New Brunswick would never surrender the fisheries without that concession by the United States. Furthermore, there was strong objection, especially by the representatives from Maine, to free admission of New Brunswick lumber unless there should be admitted into the ports of Great Britain, American lumber at the same rates as the colonial product. Coal, as the President had suspected, would not be allowed on the free list and there was dissatisfaction at leaving Newfoundland out of the proposed arrangement, for both Lawrence and Everett said that there was no guaranty that Newfoundland fish and fish oil would not be smuggled free of duty into American ports under pretense of having originated in one of the other Provinces. Metals, also, were objected to, although for no very clear reason.[40]

Crampton's fears were only too well founded, for, on February 13, he informed the Foreign Office that Fillmore had, on the fifth, sent to Congress a message with a report from the Secretary of State saying that it would be impossible to submit at that session a project of a treaty on account of the variety of details to be adjusted and want of time to refer them to England. In the light of these circumstances the President recommended that Congress enact a law to allow free entry of Canadian fish as soon as the Government should be informed that Great Britain would admit Americans to full participation in the fisheries; if such legislation should be passed and England did not respond, "*which is not apprehended,*" then America's skirts would be clear and the responsibility for any consequences would not rest upon her. "With regard to this opinion of Mr. Everett," wrote Crampton:[41]

I would remark to Your Lordship that it certainly cannot have been formed from the language which I have invariably held to him in regard to this matter. I have stated to him distinctly from the beginning of the

39. To Russell, Feb. 5, 1853; FO 5:563 (P.R.O.).
40. Crampton to Russell, Feb. 5, 1853; FO 5:563 (P.R.O.).
41. Crampton to Russell, Feb. 13, 1853; FO 5:563 (P.R.O.).

Negotiation that my Instructions did not allow me to treat the subjects of the Fisheries and of Reciprocity of Trade separately. I have reminded him that the proposal to make the Cession by the Colonies of their exclusive Rights of Fishing part of a general arrangement of Reciprocal Trade with them first emanated from the United States' Government, having been made to me by Mr. Clayton . . . and that the consent of the Colonies, interested in the Fisheries, to relinquish those exclusive Rights, had been obtained on that understanding. I have moreover read to Mr. Everett, confidentially, a Report of the Executive Council of New Brunswick dated December the 11th 1852, a copy of which was transmitted to me by Sir Edmund Head; . . . as well as other Confidential communications from His Excellency, clearly shewing that that Colony would never willingly give up the Right of Fishing secured to it by the Convention of 1818, on the terms of the Measure now recommended to Congress.

It was on the same day that Crampton reported the death of immediate hope for a treaty that he also transmitted to London a copy of a Report from the Committee on Commerce of the House of Representatives, presented by D. L. Seymour,[42] together with a bill dealing with some of the topics which it had been hoped to include in the proposed treaty. The Seymour Report sketched the course of reciprocity agitation and called attention to the interest manifested in this topic not only in the British North American Colonies but in various parts of the United States, and referred to the resources of British America as depicted in Andrews' Report. The bill, as Crampton summarized it, provided that whenever the Government of Great Britain should agree with the Government of the United States that the people of the United States might enjoy equally with British subjects all fishing privileges on the coasts of Newfoundland, Nova Scotia, New Brunswick, Cape Breton Island, and Prince Edward Island; that whenever all leases for the purpose of enjoying the fisheries, when made by American citizens, should have the same binding effect as when made

42. *House Reports,* No. 4, 32d Cong., 2d Sess. The Committee had not only Andrews' Report (*Senate Ex. Docs.,* No. 112, 32d Cong., 1st Sess.) upon the general situation in British North America, but Lorenzo Sabine's "Report on the Principal Fisheries of the American Seas" had been printed by order of the Senate (*Senate Ex. Docs.,* No. 22, 32d Cong., 2d Sess.), and this contained not only a long and detailed account of the fisheries themselves but a history of the fisheries controversy with a wealth of quotation from British, Colonial, and American official and unofficial sources.

by British subjects; that whenever Great Britain agreed, with the assent of the Governments of Canada and New Brunswick, that Americans should have equal privilege of using the St. Lawrence with its canals and the River St. John; that whenever the Government of New Brunswick should abolish duties on timber, cut within the territory of the United States, floated down the St. John and exported thence; and that whenever the President of the United States should issue his proclamation that these measures had been enacted, then there were to be admitted into the United States free of duty a considerable list of natural products, *not* including coal, provided similar articles should be admitted free of duty into the British Provinces. The bill further stipulated that when Great Britain agreed to admit all kinds of American timber and lumber into the British West Indies at no higher duties than charged on similar articles from the British North American Colonies, then, and during the continuation of the reciprocal trade provided for in the bill, all kinds of Colonial timber and unmanufactured lumber should be admitted free of duty into American ports, provided American timber and lumber were admitted free into Provincial ports and into the ports of Great Britain and Ireland. When a duty should be imposed in British ports on American timber, a similar duty should be imposed upon Colonial timber when imported from the Provinces into the United States.

The bill, thought Crampton, was elaborate and "well worthy of the attention of Her Majesty's Government" but its provisions were not "such as would conform to the Terms of such an Arrangement as, under the Instructions of Her Majesty's Government, I should feel myself justified in agreeing to." Specifically, American registry for British-built vessels was missing; important articles such as coal, pelts and furs, vegetables, poultry, plants, trees and shrubs, and printed books were not included in the list of reciprocally duty-free goods, while unmanufactured tobacco, unrefined sugar, agricultural implements, stone, marble, gypsum, rice, sheep pelts, and lard were to be found therein; the lumber provision was especially worthy of attention; and the inclusion of Newfoundland in the general scheme should be noted. Furthermore, there was nothing reserving to the British Government the suspension of free navigation of the St. Lawrence and the canals, and fishing privileges in estuaries were not reserved. In short, while something could be found as a starting point for a reciprocal arrangement, the specific terms varied widely from what was desired. "Defective as the proposed bill is, I do not despair of its being much amended before its final passage by Congress; and in this view I cannot help regretting that the present Executive of the United States did not deem it expedient to sign and submit to Congress the. Treaty as substantially agreed upon between Mr. Everett and myself," for it would have acted as a guide and plainly indicated what was needed to get the assent of the British Government.[43]

Seymour's bill stimulated a small amount of discussion, in which T. J. D. Fuller of Maine contended that lumber interests of the United States were not sufficiently safeguarded, while his colleague, Amos Tuck of New Hampshire, chided him for attempting to maintain a monopoly for Maine, for trying to shape the legislation of the whole country and abandon his free-trade principles, all for the benefit of not more than five hundred men. "There is no need of protection between two countries lying side by side, in which the labor of one is equally expensive as the labor of the other. There is no need of protecting ourselves against Canada. There is no need of protecting ourselves against any country that lies coterminous to us upon this continent."[44]

Lorenzo Sabine of Massachusetts, remarking that it was impossible to mature a reciprocity arrangement in the remaining days of the session, offered an amendment to provide for the fisheries alone. Charles E. Stuart of Michigan, who took charge of the bill when Seymour was called home, thought there was a chance, especially if the bill were not loaded down with amendments.

I see no other way [he said] for the House to say whether they are willing to compromise something in regard to all of these interests for the sake of securing a great and universal benefit. If we were each to stand by our own peculiar interests in our own neighborhood, we should never be able to adjust any national question. . . . I know that it is insisted that a portion of the country I represent, would, in some degree, be prejudiced on account of the influx of wheat and flour from Canada. That may be true; but as an offset to that we secure the free navigation of the St. Lawrence

43. Crampton to Russell, Feb. 13, 1853; FO 5:563 (P.R.O.).
44. The discussion took place February 22–24, and is reported in the *Cong. Globe,* 32d Cong., 2d Sess., pp. 777, 803, 824. Some of the speeches, including Tuck's, are in *ibid.,* App., pp. 197–199.

and its canals, which, I undertake to say, is an equivalent, and, in the end, will turn out to be more than an equivalent. So I think it is with the interest represented by the gentleman from Maine, and so I think this bill provides sufficiently for the interest of those who now desire that the coasting trade shall be opened to Great Britain.

Stuart hoped for a direct vote, but the nearest that could be obtained was one by which the House declined, 111 to 63, to lay the bill upon the table, after which another matter was taken up and the reciprocity bill slumbered out the few remaining days of the session.

In the Senate, John Davis of Massachusetts attempted to have considered a bill to regulate fishing, and, on March 1, proposed, as an amendment to the Civil and Diplomatic Appropriation Bill, that when the President was satisfied that Provincial waters were open to American fishermen, he should issue a proclamation opening American waters to British Provincials, who should enjoy the markets of the United States for their fish and fish oil on the same terms as citizens of the United States. Mallory of Florida, with an eye to preventing Bahamans from sharing in Florida fisheries and to eliminating the danger of emancipated blacks' getting to Florida where labor was paid more than in the Bahamas, argued that the United States had no constitutional right to control the fisheries within three miles of the shore of a State; he was "unwilling to use any language which may, even by implication, be construed into an admission that the General Government may legislate [for] persons within the jurisdiction of a State, afloat or ashore, contrary to the laws of such State." Others, for various motives, came to the support of Mallory, whose amendment was adopted by a vote of 27 to 18, whereupon Davis said it was of little consequence to pass the general proposition; nevertheless discussion rambled on over a variety of subjects until Davis' amendment was defeated.[45]

45. *Cong. Globe,* 32d Cong., 2d Sess., pp. 953–957.

CHAPTER IV

RECIPROCITY GAINED

SUCH information as leaked out during the winter of 1852–53 and particularly the discussion in Congress over Seymour's bill aroused some attention in the United States, especially in New England, and more in the Provinces. There was no disguising the fact that Canadians and, to some extent, other British North Americans desired some workable arrangement, but it was equally observable that sentiment against surrendering much for what was felt to be slight reciprocal return stiffened as time went on; mere reciprocal free trade in fish was no adequate return for throwing open the inshore waters to the Yankees. Some Americans themselves recognized the justice of this position and were inclined to believe that Congress exhibited too great an indifference not only to the requests of the northern neighbors but to the real interests of American business. Nor was there lack of interest on the part of the British Government, as Ingersoll wrote William L. Marcy, the new Secretary of State, in a dispatch of April 22, 1853.[1] In the House of Lords, he reported, Lord Malmesbury, late Secretary of State for Foreign Affairs, had made an inquiry with respect to the negotiation with the United States on the subject of the fisheries, and the reply of Lord Clarendon, now in the Foreign Office, had indicated that the new government was of like mind with its predecessor in this matter. "I have not discovered anything like expectation of difficulty in this matter," remarked Ingersoll.[2]

1. Great Britain: Despatches, Vol. LXIV (D.S.).
2. To Marcy, Apr. 22, 1853, *ibid*. On April 20, 1853, Sir J. Emerson Tennent for the Committee of the Privy Council for Trade addressed to Lord Wodehouse a long analysis of the draft treaty which Crampton had sent in January, and came to the conclusion that to accept this draft with President Fillmore's amendments would amount to abandoning all claims to concessions. On the other hand, their Lordships would deeply deplore Canada's putting into effect her threats of retaliation which would be harmful to the Colonies as well as inflicting injuries on the United States. They would suggest, in view of the changed situation since the repeal of British navigation laws, that the British Government propose an "entire reconstruction" to the United States to replace the commercial arrangements of 1815 and 1818, and pointed out the

The usual delay in undertaking any business of real importance at the beginning of a new administration, especially where there had been a shift in party control, occurred when President Pierce assumed office, so that several months elapsed before anything was done. In June, Ingersoll informed[3] Marcy that when he had fallen into conversation with the Duke of Newcastle, the Colonial Secretary, a few days before, His Grace had obviously sought to inform the American Minister of the views of Her Majesty's Government and sound him about what the new American Government intended to do. The Duke expressed his regret that Fillmore had attempted to separate the issues, for he thought there was much better chance of coming to an understanding if they were combined. Moreover, orders issued to the Admiralty indicated that there was no wish to press matters with respect to the fisheries; while there was every indication that the patrolling squadron was expected to see that there were no violations of what Great Britain considered her rights under the Convention of 1818, nevertheless nothing was to be done which would give an excuse for trouble; warnings, rather than seizures, were to prevail so long as Americans gave no indication of resorting to force.[4]

By July, with the more hungry office-seekers satisfied and routine problems of a new administration somewhat ironed out, Marcy was ready to take up the whole colonial question. James Buchanan had replaced Ingersoll as Minister near the Court of St. James's, and to him, on July 2, Marcy addressed an instruction[5] of a general nature but mentioning that among the issues with Great Britain was the fisheries question: the British Government, said he, held a construction of the Convention of 1818 by which rights fairly claimed by American interpretation were infringed, sometimes threatening peaceful relations between the two countries; "but that treaty when fairly carried out, imposes restrictions which ought to be remedied." Negotiations on this issue and on reciprocal trade with British North America had

advantages of the United States' following England's example and relaxing tariff restrictions. FO 115:129 (P.R.O.).

3. Ingersoll to Marcy, June 10, 1853; Great Britain:Despatches, Vol. LXIV (D.S.).

4. Seymour to Secretary of the Admiralty, July 6, 1853; FO 115:129 (P.R.O.).

5. Great Britain:Instructions, Vol. XVI (D.S.).

been opened by his predecessor and since that time they had been re-sumed with prospects of an early and favorable conclusion; only a few points of difference remained to be settled, and the President believed they could be adjusted.

After Marcy had talked to Crampton about the force proposed to be sent to the fishing grounds, the British Government was pleased with the frank and friendly tone used by the Secretary of State.[6] Crampton was instructed to state that the British Government would meet it in the same spirit, but, Lord Clarendon insisted, Her Majesty's Government could not consent to waive their interpretation of terms, "Bays, Creeks, or harbours" as used in the convention, an interpreta-tion which was consistent with America's own usage with respect to her own coast.

Two months later[7] Marcy informed Buchanan that he had had many conversations with Crampton and that points of difference had been reduced to three or four. He had submitted to the British Min-ister a draft of a treaty which the President approved, and under-stood that Crampton had forwarded the same to the Foreign Minister, who would probably confer with Buchanan. If a fair opportunity arose he was to exert his influence to induce the British Government to yield in their instructions to Crampton. Meantime, the Department of State not only had various earlier reports but had been instigating inquiries of its own and had been receiving advice, sometimes un-sought. Alvin Bronson, for example, wrote from upper New York on August 27, 1853, that he had had fifty years of experience on the Atlantic and forty-four on the lakes,[8] and it was his opinion that

Reciprocal trade with Canada and the lower provinces *will benefit us more than them,* that they can do without us better than we can do without them, notwithstanding *their* great anxiety & *our* indifference. To refuse reciprocity with them is to be like the other states refusing reciprocity with New England, a fishing & navigating people, & Ohio, a grain growing state.

6. Clarendon to Crampton, July 22, 1853; FO 115:129 (P.R.O.).
7. Marcy to Buchanan, Sept. 2, 1853; Great Britain:Instructions, Vol. XVI (D.S.).
8. Reciprocity Treaty (D.S.). It is to be presumed that these years ran simultaneously.

The Secretary of the Treasury informed Marcy that a 30 per cent duty on Nova Scotia coal had yielded from about $48,000 to $73,000 per annum except in 1848, when it ran over $93,000.[9] Edward Everett, now out of office, wrote from Boston[10] that he had conferred with the late deputy collector of the Port of Boston and with Isaac Rich, a "merchant largely engaged in the fish business"; the former had informed him that the cod-fishing bounty could be removed without injury to the fishing business, while the latter maintained that he was sure that men were on "lay" and not wages and that the bounty was indispensable. Under the circumstances Everett was of the opinion that it was not an opportune time to take the bounty away.

The draft which Crampton forwarded to the Foreign Office on September 5 was accompanied not only by his own extended comments but by a copy of Marcy's note to him, describing in great detail all aspects of the proposed arrangement.[11] Crampton pointed out the differences between this draft and the one he had sent the previous January, stating parenthetically that

Mr. Marcy, in declining some of the proposals of Her Majesty's Government, has repeatedly remarked, that he did so, not generally from any objection which he himself entertained to them, . . . but, on the contrary, from a sincere wish to succeed in carrying into practical effect a measure which would conduce to that object. "Were such a measure," said Mr. Marcy, "framed without reference to the existing state of public opinion and the feelings, or even prejudices, if you will, of the multifarious and sometimes conflicting interests of the different sections of the Union, its production would be worse than useless. Such a measure, it is true, might be in accord with my individual views, with those of the President, and of most, if not all of my colleagues—but it would certainly be defeated and its defeat would add strength to the Protectionist party and tend to delay the very object we sought to attain. . . ."

A partial step in the direction of freer trade now could be followed by further advance as soon as public opinion, which, he thought, was veering in that direction, might permit. It was this that made him think the time inexpedient "for an enlargement of the basis of the

9. Guthrie to Marcy, Aug. 27, 1853; Reciprocity Treaty (D.S.).
10. Everett to Marcy, Sept. 2, 1853; Reciprocity Treaty (D.S.).
11. All three documents are in FO 5:566 (P.R.O.).

negotiation including a revision of the Treaty of 1815" (i.e., the British-American commercial convention). The Administration intended to proceed in the direction of free trade as rapidly as possible, but as for a discussion of the whole question of the revision of the tariff, "he would leave it to me, he said, who had been present in 1846 at part of the debates, which then took place on the Tariff question, to judge where that discussion would lead us."

Crampton then proceeded to point out that the new draft made an exception as to shellfish, and Newfoundland was included in the arrangement; Florida coasts were to be excepted from the reciprocal fishing privileges. Inclusion of the Pacific coast in the mutual concessions was a new point. Marcy left out any reference to an engagement to discontinue fishing bounties. In the list of articles on which duties were not to be charged, coal, printed books, and metals were omitted, while rice, tar, pitch, turpentine, lard, stone and marble were added, in order, as Marcy said, to engage the support of another section of the country. The article providing for free navigation of the St. John was new, as well as the abrogation of all duties on timber floated down that river from American territory and destined for other parts of the United States. "Your Lordship will perceive . . . that the Government of the United States is not disposed to yield in regard to the three principal points on which I was directed to insist— viz: the admission of British vessels to American registry, the abrogation of the duty on Colonial coal, and the discontinuance of the bounty to American fishermen," and, he continued, did not seem inclined to offer any equivalent except the slight one of admitting "Furs, tails, etc.," to which Fillmore had taken objection.

Marcy had comments to make on all of the points of difference between this draft and the earlier one. As to the exception in the case of Florida coasts, he said that he doubted such a privilege would be used much if granted, but it was objectionable to a large portion of the United States where it was feared the privilege would be "perverted occasionally to the purpose of facilitating the escape of Slaves." Shellfish he would omit, for their inclusion might open the question of rights in oyster beds and would be sure to arouse a great amount of opposition. On the subject of the bounty, he maintained that it really gave Americans no appreciable advantage, especially since it was confined to the cod fishery; the amount was not large and was practically offset by the fact that Americans had to pay a duty of about 30 per cent on salt while British fishermen imported theirs free of duty, and there was little expectation that salt would go on the American free list since it was a revenue article. The omission of a reciprocal right of Colonials to use American canals was explained from the fact that it could only extend to canals which the Federal Government, as distinct from the States, owned or controlled and there were none of these. Furthermore, since income was the principal object of those who controlled these canals, he had doubts whether there would ever be an attempt to deprive British subjects of their use. On the question of American registration of foreign-built vessels, Marcy pointed out:

The shipping interest in this country, as it is in yours, is one of very great importance, and our Gov^t look to it, & will watch over it with the deepest concern. The tendency of our legislation has been of late evidently towards a relaxation of restrictions upon foreign commerce, but its progress in that direction must be cautious & conformable to public opinion. Such an innovation in our navigation policy such a material change in regard to the ship building interest as is proposed would not be wise, nor would it be sustained by those, whose approval is required to secure success to the measure. Besides, the competition between British Colonial Shipbuilders & those of the U. S. would not be waged on equal terms. Many of the articles used in the construction of vessels in the U. S. are, under our financial system, revenue articles, & of course are more costly here than in the British Provinces.

The proposal to allow Colonials to engage in the coasting trade between the Atlantic and Pacific coasts was "met by a constitutional objection, which cannot be removed without leaving open to H M's Subjects upon the Atlantic as well as the Pacific coast our entire coasting trade, & it will not, as I understand, in the face of this difficulty, be any further pressed." Omission of "metals of Ores" was due principally to the indefiniteness of the expression; it might apply to all sorts of metals in various stages of manufacture; "under it many invasions of the revenue laws of the respective countries would be sheltered." As to the omission of coal, Marcy was convinced that it could be defended as strongly as the British had defended the omission of unmanufactured tobacco and unrefined sugar; neither had the Americans any

great interest in excluding free coal, nor the Colonials a great interest in its admission,

but it is to be feared that those engaged in the coal business are not yet
prepared to take this view of the subject. The owners of coal quarries
were not long since, & probably are now, very urgent for high duties upon
foreign coals, as an incidental protection to their interests: they were
sturdy opponents to our tariff law of 1846, because it reduced the import on foreign coal, & have since urged an increase of such duty on that
ground.

Nearly two months after Crampton sent the draft treaty to the Foreign Office, Buchanan, in the course of a general discussion with Lord
Clarendon, remarked that he had been informed by Mr. Marcy that a
project had been forwarded and asked if His Lordship had received
it.[12] Clarendon replied that he had, but that the proposition did not
appear to him to be reciprocity. Buchanan said he had no instructions
on the subject but he would be glad to furnish any information at his
command and added that he thought the American Government with
equal justice might say it was not a reciprocity treaty. Clarendon,
Buchanan reported, reiterated his statement but spoke only about
fishing bounties, on which he laid great emphasis, while Buchanan
maintained that a market of twenty-five million people free to Canadian fish would in itself amount to more than the surrender of exclusive Provincial fishing rights, yet the United States were willing to
yield great additional advantages in the reciprocal free trade in a
number of articles.

That something might be coming of the steps thus far taken was
indicated by President Pierce in his Annual Message of December 5,
where he said:[13]

For some years past Great Britain has so construed the first article of
the convention of the 20th of April, 1818, in regard to the fisheries on the
northeastern coast, as to exclude our citizens from some of the fishing
grounds to which they freely resorted for nearly a quarter of a century
subsequent to the date of that treaty. The United States have never

12. Buchanan to Marcy, Nov. 1, 1853; Great Britain: Despatches, Vol.
LXV (D.S.).

13. J. D. Richardson, *A Compilation of the Messages and Papers of the
Presidents, 1789–1897* (Washington, 1900), V, 208.

acquiesced in that construction, but have always claimed for their fishermen all the rights which they had so long enjoyed without molestation. With a view to remove all difficulties on the subject, to extend the rights of our fishermen beyond the limits fixed by the convention of 1818, and to regulate trade between the United States and the British North American Provinces, a negotiation has been opened with a fair prospect of a favorable result. To protect our fishermen . . . I deemed it expedient to station a naval force in that quarter during the fishing season.

In answer to a resolution of the House of Representatives of the third of January, 1854, he submitted papers which explained further what had been done during the previous season.[14] Commodore W. B. Shubrick, in command of the *Princeton, Fulton,* and *Cyane* at Portsmouth, New Hampshire, was to interview Admiral Seymour at Halifax and inform him of the President's interpretation of the treaty; i.e., that Americans were entitled to enter bays more than six miles wide at the entrance. He was to warn all Americans of the importance of observing strictly the rights claimed, to remonstrate "respectfully but firmly" if anyone interfered with those rights, and to take steps best calculated to check any resort to violence except in self-defense. Shubrick reported his interview with Seymour, who concurred in the desire to avoid any cause of offense and said that he was not at liberty to depart from his instructions, which were to carry out the views of his Government in the mildest manner and to make no seizures except in cases of undoubted infraction. Shubrick reported that he was unable to get from Admiral Seymour the exact tenor of the instructions but he surmised that they were to make no seizures unless vessels were fishing within three miles of the shore. When the latter showed the report of the seizure of the *Starlight* by the *Basilisk* and was asked if the seizure was within the three-mile limit, he smiled and said "for flagrant violation—it says nothing about your bays."

After waiting some weeks Buchanan reported that he again asked Clarendon what had been done about Marcy's project. According to his dispatch[15] Clarendon was not hopeful of the success of the scheme: the proposal was too hard a bargain and too unacceptable to Nova

14. *House Ex. Docs.,* No. 21, 33d Cong., 1st Sess.

15. Buchanan to Marcy, Jan. 10, 1854; Great Britain: Despatches, Vol. LXV (D.S.).

Scotia and the other North American Provinces. Buchanan, after endeavoring to show that the bargain was not a hard one, went on to say:

My Lord! the British Statesman, particularly at the present momentous crisis in the affairs of the world, who shall be instrumental in settling all the questions pending between the two Governments, on fair and honorable terms & thus converting Great Britain and the United States into nations kindred in friendship, as they already are in blood, will do more for his country, & indeed for both countries than any Statesman who has arisen in England since the days of Lord Chatham.

Lord Clarendon responded in the same spirit but still maintained that the United States demanded too much. Buchanan suggested that at least some effort should be made to avoid collision on the fishing grounds, which might be done by adopting as a temporary measure a single article providing for American right to fish the disputed waters in return for free entry of Canadian fish and in addition reciprocal free trade in the articles named in Marcy's schedule. This suggestion, which Buchanan told Clarendon he made without instructions, seemed to appeal to the British Minister, who took it down for consideration and appeared to find objection only to the possibility of collision if Americans had the right to dry and cure fish on shore, which Buchanan maintained would be avoided if the right should not be exercised without consent of the owner of the land. "I am persuaded," wrote Buchanan, "that it is the strong opposition of the Colonists, and especially those of Nova Scotia, which has prevented the conclusion of your treaty." The suggestion, Buchanan was convinced, obtained the apparent favor of Lord Clarendon from its clear presentation of a *quid pro quo:*

It could not have been from any other cause; inasmuch as the article would assure to American fishermen all the right specified in the Project; would relieve us from the embarrassing concession to British fishermen of the right to take fish on our coasts, estuaries and rivers, as well as from the question of bounties; and, above all, it would waive the claim to the registration in the United States of vessels built in the British provinces —a claim which ought never to be yielded.

The only objection Buchanan could find with his own idea was that it would not provide for importation of American fish into the Provinces free of duty.

In the light of an instruction sent to Crampton on February 2, it is apparent that Buchanan's uninstructed proposition had no direct effect.[16] Marcy's counterproject was unacceptable with respect to the exception of the Florida coast; the admission to the Pacific coast, on account of the vested rights of the Hudson's Bay Company; the omission of coal, metals, and printed books from the schedule; and refusal of American registry; while the proposition to admit Americans to free navigation of the St. John was quite inadmissible. Under the circumstances Her Majesty's Government saw little advantage in pursuing farther the negotiation; they would, however, prefer that negotiations should be suspended rather than broken off in hope that time might improve the chances of coming to an understanding. Meantime, the situation could be materially improved by mutual legislation on the part of the United States and the Colonies.

As the winter grew shorter, however, and the fishing season of 1854 approached, the possibilities of conflict in the northern waters impressed both Governments. During 1852 and 1853 American fishermen had been restrained from resorting to forceful measures because they understood a negotiation was in progress and there was a good chance of some amicable solution. The good spirit manifested on both sides could not be expected to continue if it were known that the project of a treaty had been dropped.[17] There is little doubt there existed keen desire to get the difficulties adjusted; England, as Buchanan had pointed out to Clarendon, could not wish another international entanglement during the existing European situation; nor did the American Administration yearn to take on additional burdens, with the slavery issue breaking again into the open. The British Government had to take into account the demands of the Provinces, little though those might directly concern the home country, and these demands included some which Marcy knew would never be yielded by the

16. Clarendon to Crampton, Feb. 2, 1854; FO 115:136 (P.R.O.).

17. The anxiety regarding the immediate future is reflected in Norton to Marcy, Feb. 8, 1854, Consular Letters: Pictou, Nova Scotia, Vol. V (D.S.); Buchanan to Marcy, Feb. 24 and Apr. 14, Great Britain: Despatches, Vol. LXV (D.S.); Marcy to Buchanan, Mar. 11, Great Britain: Instructions, Vol. XVI (D.S.); Seymour to Secretary of the Admiralty, Mar. 24, FO 115:136 (P.R.O.).

United States, notably American registry for Colonial-built ships.[18] In the same instruction where Marcy wrote so pessimistically about the probable failure of the treaty and the equally probable clash on the fishing grounds in the coming season, he noted that he had reason to believe Lord Elgin was in England and that Francis Hincks was on his way there. The latter, who had been much consulted in the whole affair, was, he understood, still hopeful of success; he knew as well as anyone the views of the various colonies, and it was barely possible that he might exert a favorable influence on the Home Government. If worst came to worst Marcy would be willing to accept some such temporary arrangement as Buchanan had propounded to Clarendon.

There were, however, other forces at work than those appearing through ordinary diplomatic channels or in legislative deliberations. Two men in especial may be credited with much of the spade work which finally made a treaty of reciprocity possible; one of these was James, Earl of Elgin and Kincardine, Governor-General of Canada, and the other was Israel D. Andrews, long associated with the British Provinces as United States Consul at various points or as Special Agent, and unofficially through his wide acquaintance with and close knowledge of Provincial affairs generally. Andrews has appeared previously in this narrative when he kept successive Secretaries of State informed on public opinion in the Colonies during the days when annexation was widely discussed. He was busy in the Provinces, particularly in the Maritimes, during the winter of 1853–54, feeling the public pulse and exerting an influence to modify opinion which showed itself hostile to any kind of a treaty which the United States seemed likely to approve.[19] That he was busy even before the President sent

18. Marcy to Buchanan, Mar. 11, 1854; Great Britain: Instructions, Vol. XVI (D.S.). The language used in Crampton's communication of the attitude of the British Government on his project conveyed to him the impression that American registry was a *sine qua non*. If that was the case, Marcy wrote, the negotiation "must fail for this cannot be yielded." In a "plain conversation" which Buchanan had with Clarendon on the whole matter and particularly on the fishery aspect, on April 11, the former remarked, "Had General Jackson been President, an immediate collision would have been inevitable." Buchanan to Marcy, Apr. 14, 1854; Great Britain: Despatches, Vol. LXV (D.S.).

19. Information about Andrews' activities is largely derived from the papers in Special Agents, Vol. XVI (D.S.), which is almost entirely given up to this

his Annual Message of 1853 is indicated by a receipt for £78 8s. currency given to Andrews on December 3 by I. P. Keefer, "it being for services and expenses of a journey to Quebec to see the Hon'ble Mr. Ross, the Attorney General of Canada, and Mr. Taché, Commissioner of Public Works, to take certain steps in relation to the Fisheries in the Gulf of St. Lawrence and in Nova Scotia."[20] On December 21 George Coggeswell acknowledged receipt of £41 7s. for traveling to Halifax and back on "government business of a private nature." On March 2, 1854, Marcy wrote Andrews asking an interview as soon as possible in relation to the fishery treaty. There seems to be no written record of this interview, but subsequent communications make its nature fairly clear, for ten days later (March 31) Andrews wrote from St. John that it was a matter of surprise to him and to the Colonials he had seen that nothing had been said there about the negotiations relative to fisheries and trade; up to that morning no information had been sent to the Maritime Provinces, and the first copy of the proposed treaty that any of the officials saw was the one Andrews had received. After waiting some weeks, said Andrews, he returned to Washington to inform Marcy of the "hopeless state of affairs" in the Colonies and to get the Secretary's permission to ask Crampton why the Colonials were being kept in the dark.

The Provinces, said Andrews, were not as they had been earlier. While Britain's change of economic policy had at first produced dismay, things had been changing; no longer would they acquiesce in any treaty on which they were not consulted and which did not greatly benefit them. Furthermore, as he informed Marcy by a letter of March 31, there was an unpleasant feeling resulting from the treatment of emissaries in Washington between 1848 and 1852; "so strong in its

episode. The citations which follow are to this volume, unless otherwise indicated. See also W. D. Overman, "I. D. Andrews and Reciprocity in 1854: An Episode in Dollar Diplomacy," *Canadian Historical Review*, XV, 248–263. D. C. Masters, in "A Further Word on I. D. Andrews and the Reciprocity Treaty of 1854" (*ibid.*, XVII, 159–167), is skeptical about the "Dollar Diplomacy," believing that Andrews was in the affair principally to get out of it what he could for himself. This is also the view of T. H. Le Duc in "I. D. Andrews and the Reciprocity Treaty of 1854" (*ibid.*, XV, 437–438), who notes that Elgin, who was much pestered by Andrews, and Bulwer both thought his activities were due to mercenary motives.

20. Pierce Papers (L.C.). Taché was actually Receiver-General of Canada.

[this feeling's] hold on the public mind that no Colonial Government, since 1852, has ventured to send a delegate to Washington except Newfoundland which had not previously done so, and was recently represented by Mr. Shea (whom you met) to ask for what had been expressly refused or with even worse policy, had been treated with marked indifference and inattention." Neither in Britain nor the United States was there an appreciation of Colonial feeling. Andrews had, after much difficulty, persuaded Crampton to write to the Lieutenant-Governors during the absence of Lord Elgin, and he had already received replies from Head and Sir Gaspard Le Marchant, now Lieutenant-Governor of Nova Scotia, which had been read to Marcy. Another aspect which must not be neglected was the growing prosperity of the Provinces; no longer were they desperate, for England's change of policy had begun to redound to their benefit to such an extent that at the moment they were more or less indifferent to reciprocity with the United States.

Marcy, on April 10, wrote that he was very gloomy over the prospects of the treaty and was not hopeful of improving it "in the way you suggest."[21] "I have always been distrustful," he wrote, "of attempts to change the public opinions of any community by such means as you suggest." He would not have an opportunity to consult the President in time for a letter to reach Andrews and the contingent fund was down to $3,000; the department had asked Congress for $15,000 but the deficiency appropriation bill had not been passed; if he had known that Great Britain would not act except at the caprice of each colony he would never have expected to get anything done. A couple of days later, however, Caleb Cushing, the Assistant Secretary of State, wrote that the business was "arranged" and $5,000 would be placed at Andrews' disposal, and added: "The President is expecting you to produce the results which I heartily trust may be the case." If results were not produced it was not the fault of Andrews; on April 15 he wrote Marcy that he had seen the Governor and Attorney-General of Nova Scotia and was to meet the Council, then would leave for Fredericton and Quebec; he had already communicated with Newfoundland and would address Sir Alexander Bannerman of Prince Edward Island by the next mail. He ascertained (April 20) that Sey-

21. The particular letter to which this is a reply is not in Volume XVI of Special Agents (D.S.), but the suggestion is clear from what Marcy wrote.

mour had been replaced by Admiral Fanshaw, who was said to have instructions of a pacific nature. He also took occasion to tell Sir Gaspard that no American cruisers had been fitted out for service on the fishing grounds and that none would be until after it was found that no treaty could be made.

From Montreal on May 13 Andrews sent a long "private and confidential" dispatch in which he gave a general account of conditions in all the Provinces. Recurring to his visit in Nova Scotia he said that Sir Gaspard had been persuaded to take some responsibility, although he was exasperated at the course taken by the United States and England, as well as by Crampton and the Canadian officials. The struggle in Nova Scotia had been severe but it had been decided finally to send delegates to a conference, although, he added, "I found it necessary to disburse money very liberally; and shall probably require a larger sum than I asked for at the outset." In New Brunswick there was not so much bluster, but feeling ran as deep; "I have therefore taken such measures as the circumstances of the case required in N. B. to moderate the opposition and keep the public mind in a quiet state." Lieutenant-Governor Head was anxious to have a treaty but was unwilling to take any responsibility; however, Andrews wrote, "I was able to reach Fredericton before the N. B. Legislature adjourned, and prevent any discussion of the proposition now under consideration, or any legislative action of an adverse character which would have been exceedingly injurious in the present temper of the public mind." It was in this communication that he stated it had been his duty previously to advise Mr. Buchanan and Mr. Clayton of "the Americanizing influence which the settlement of the North East Boundary Question exercised upon the Colonies." So strong had Webster felt on the present situation, wrote Andrews, that he called it "a fit sequel to the North East Boundary Treaty" and withheld instructions from Lawrence in order that he himself might have the honor of settling the "Great Matter." If a treaty should be made it would be impossible to estimate the amount of American influence which could be exercised over the people of the Provinces. "I am fully justified in stating to you openly and fairly that any expenditure of money within a reasonable amount would be a mere 'bagatelle' in comparison with the immensely valuable privileges to be gained *permanently*, and the power and influence that would be given forever to our Confederacy."

Enough has been said to indicate very clearly what Andrews was doing. Altogether he spent, according to his own account, over fifty thousand dollars, much of which he did not have furnished him but for which he pledged his word. In addition, he spent forty thousand dollars supplied him by the Canadian Government:[22] of this, fifteen thousand went to Moses H. Perley for valuable services of a "general and comprehensive character"; Attorney-General Drummond of Lower Canada was paid five thousand dollars; "Morrison an editor" and Deputy Inspector-General Anderson of Canada each received five thousand. President Pierce later expressed his regret that he was unable to compensate Andrews for all his expenditures[23] and relieve him of the serious burden under which he found himself, for Andrews maintained he was unable to go about his private business or renew his official duties in British America. Once he was thrust in jail for his debt and several times was on bail. Partial relief came through the efforts of a group of Boston merchants, aided somewhat by similar groups in other towns benefited by the treaty, and altogether some twelve to fourteen thousand dollars were raised to free him of his most pressing obligations,[24] but it was not until 1858 that Congress came to his aid by providing in an amendment to the Civil Appropriations

22. Affidavit of Andrews, May 29, 1859; Special Agents, Vol. XVI (D.S.).

23. "I shall always entertain a high appreciation of the valuable services rendered by you in relation to the Fishery question, and other matters during the progress of the negotiations which preceded the Reciprocity Treaty, and, it was a matter of sincere regret that, I could not in the exercise of legal authority and a just discretion embrace in the order of payment, all the items in your account for expenses incurred and money actually paid." Pierce to Andrews, Dec. 12, 1854; Special Agents, Vol. XVI (D.S.).

24. In a folder entitled "Reciprocity and Fishing Treaty between the United States and the British North American Colonies" (Special Agents, Vol. XVI [D.S.]), there is an account of a meeting called by Enoch Train, Samuel Hooper, et al., to obtain subscriptions to defray the expenses of Andrews in securing the Reciprocity Treaty. Rufus Choate, one of those present, said that Andrews was the originator of the treaty; he alone comprehended the importance of the arrangement with all British North America. He had to get favorable action from many local legislatures as well as from Congress, "a body proverbially inert and unmanageable. All this he was the main instrument of effecting, at the abandonment of private interests, and of a wear and tear of body and mind, so exhausting, that, immediately after the result was obtained, he fell into a severe sickness."

Bill for adjusting on the "principle of equity and justice" by the Secretary of State his accounts which were to be paid according to that adjustment.[25]

It is fair to assume that Andrews' activities had something to do with the sending of E. P. Taché, Receiver-General of Canada, and John Ross, Attorney-General of Upper Canada, to Washington early in April to coöperate with Crampton by keeping him informed of "the views and interests of the Canadian Government in relation to the contemplated commercial Treaty with the United States."[26] It is also not unlikely that Andrews may have had some influence with Lord Elgin to the extent at least of adding to his determination, when he went to England for a brief visit in the spring of 1854, to confer with members of the Government in an attempt to work out some sort of a solution no less ardently desired by the British Government than by Lord Elgin himself. Subsequently Andrews commented upon the situation in this manner:

M[r] Hincks had been informed by Sir Emerson Tennant Secretary of the Board of Trade, London, of Lord Clarendon's despatch and of the condition of the negotiations. I stated to M[r] Hincks I thought this Government would resume negotiations upon the basis of M[r] Marcy's *projet* and upon no other, that the question of the Registry of Ships, and the Coasting Trade, would not be entertained, as Lord Clarendon requested, but as a primary condition M[r] Crampton should have more liberal instructions, or that, Lord Elgin, who was at the time in London, should return with ample power to settle the whole question *here*, and I insisted that he, M[r] Hincks, on his arrival in England should call upon Lord Clarendon with Lord Elgin and mature this plan, and I wrote to him by every foreign mail until May, urging him to have the proposed arrangement fully carried out.[27]

25. *Cong. Globe,* 35th Cong., 1st Sess., p. 2572; *United States Statutes at Large,* XI, 327. Andrews' bill for expenses of all sorts, as rendered to the Department of State for the period from May 4, 1850, to August 5, 1854, amounted to $50,911.11. While some of the items specified exactly for what payments had been made, many of them read merely "services and expenses." Accompanying the statement was the assertion that if he had had more time the cost would not have been so great, for the real work was done between December, 1853, and August, 1854.

26. Crampton to Rowan, Apr. 10, 1854; G '51–'58 (P.A.C.).

27. In a statement accompanying a bill rendered to the Department of State, undated, but sometime after June 12, 1858; Special Agents, Vol. XVI (D.S.).

The combination of factors resulted in a detailed instruction to Elgin on May 4, 1854, accompanied by a commission authorizing him to "negotiate & conclude on H M⁸ behalf any Treaty with the United States."²⁸ His Lordship was furnished with copies of the correspondence which had already passed on the subject, including the instruction of February by which the negotiation had been suspended, "but it is possible that the communications which you may have with the President & Mʳ Marcy during your stay in Washington may give you an opportunity of ascertaining whether there is any likelihood at the present time of the negotiation if resumed, being brought to a successful conclusion." Elgin was to find out what, if any, of their demands the Colonies were willing to retract and how far the United States might recede from their contentions; in the "extreme case" of neither's yielding and "more particularly if it originated in the pertinacious adherence of the Provinces to their demands H M's Govᵗ might, however reluctantly, be compelled to look rather to Imperial than to Colonial interests alone, & as in the case of Newfoundland, . . . be driven to consider whether it were right to sacrifice the former for the latter." He was not to appear too anxious to reopen the question lest it should "encourage the Govᵗ of the U. S. still more to enhance their demands." The United States, to that time, had refused to concede four of the five points asked on behalf of the Provinces, and in addition had put forward demands for admission to the fisheries of the northwest coast. "Unless these conflicting pretensions & requirements can be reconciled the conclusion of any agreement between the two Countries is out of the question."

The influence & authority which you so justly possess in the British Provinces may afford you means for inducing the Colonial Govᵗ to modify their extreme demands. On the other hand there are considerations arising out of the existing state of affairs in Europe which may operate with the Gov. of the U. S. & induce it to desire to be well with England at the present time if not from sympathy with the cause for which England & France are now arrayed in arms agˢᵗ Russia, at all events from great material advantages which a commercial nation like the U. S. must derive from the unexampled liberality of the principles in regard to neutrals on which those two powers have announced their intention of acting during the present war.

28. Clarendon to Elgin, Secret, May 4, 1854; FO 115:138 (P.R.O.).

Elgin, however, must not appear at Washington "in the character of an Envoy from H M specially appointed to settle these troublesome questions. The mere suspicion of such a purpose would of itself suffice to render the Gov. of the U. S. still more inaccessible . . . [and] conclude however erroneously, that the British Gov. was prepared to make sacrifices for the sake of averting a discussion with the U. S. while engaged in an arduous warfare with a European Power." If he should ascertain that the Provincial Legislatures were willing to modify their demands, Her Majesty's Government would be prepared "to give effect to such an improved disposition on the part of the local Legislatures"; if, on their part, the United States manifested a corresponding spirit he might at once conclude a treaty on "a basis of mutual concession." Her Majesty's Government, however, would assent to no one-sided settlement. Virtually a free hand was given to bargain, only he must be careful not to yield any contention without a corresponding concession by the United States.[29] He might pursue any course he thought advisable to "discountenance any unreasonable pretensions on the part of the Colonial Gov^t but H M would except in a very extreme case be unwilling that any thing like even moral coercion should be resorted to with that view." While the British Government desired a permanent settlement of fisheries and reciprocity, if that were not possible they would not object to a temporary one.

The position which Y^r L^p occupies in the British Provinces is calculated to give more than ordinary weight to any argument which you may use for the purpose of influencing either the Colonial Legislature or the Gov. of the U. S. The former will see in Y^r L^p an advocate whose able & impartial administration of their general affairs entitles him to the most unreserved confidence & respect; the latter will conclude that your insistence on any specific points is based on considerations which you are well aware cannot be overlooked; & both may hope to obtain by your intervention not only a fair & honourable settlement of the matters in discussion

29. "Y^r L^p will also steadily keep in mind, as a principle never to be lost sight of in negotiating with the U. S. that no concession can safely be made to that Gov. except in return for corresponding concession on its part: that any concession on which it may insist must be purchased by a concession on its side; & that so far from being likely to arrive at a permanent & satisfactory settlement by the adoption of a yielding tone the result in all probability would be the reverse."

between them, but an opportunity of developing the vast natural resources which they possess within their respective boundaries, & of laying the foundation of solid & permanent good will on either side of the border by which their territories are separated from each other.

A few days after this general instruction was given Elgin, Lord Clarendon caused another to be sent after him[30] wherein particular caution was advised about including Newfoundland in any general treaty. The first difficulty grew out of rights which secured "French fishermen from being interrupted in any manner by English competition & it appears that the English Fishermen cannot carry on the cod fishery within the limits specified in the Treaty without interrupting the French Fishermen." The Convention of 1818 gave Americans fishing rights on certain Newfoundland coasts from which English fishermen were practically excluded, at least so far as cod were concerned; it also gave Americans rights in the Strait of Belle Isle and on the coast of Labrador which, "though much coveted by, have never yet been formally conceded to, France." Negotiations had for a long time been going on between England and France over "the precise meaning and effect" of the Franco-British treaty, and

the conclusion of an amicable arrang^t with France [might] be materially impeded, if the result of y^r negotiation with the U. S. should involve a still further concession of rights of fishing on the Coast of Newfoundland from which British Fishermen are now practically excluded & thereby give occasion to remonstrances on the part of France agst the admission of the U. S. to share in a fishery which is now enjoyed without British competition by France.

If, then, any inclusion of Newfoundland in the treaty, apparently desired by both that island and the United States, were contemplated "the rights of France sh^d in terms at least be reserved in any Treaty which Y^r L^p may conclude with the United States." But, further than this, there would not only have to be a stipulation saving the existing rights of France but also those which might be granted as a result of negotiations pending; if the United States could be induced to admit such reservations Her Majesty's Government would not oppose such a proposal, "but as they cannot suppose that the U. S. w^d easily be

30. May 19, 1854; FO 115:138 (P.R.O.).

brought [to] listen to such a proposal, I am not prepared to instruct Y^r L^p to bring it forward."

Another major difficulty which would arise from the inclusion of Newfoundland came from the fact that "it w^d be ruinous for Newfoundland to be included in a Convention founded on this basis [reciprocal freedom from duties] which w^d at once deprive the Island of one third of its limited Revenue." If exceptions should be asked so that in the case of this colony duties might be levied on some of the articles, then other colonies could properly ask for exceptions, and the United States would likewise demand the right to levy duties on certain products from Newfoundland. The only article exported in any quantity was fish, so that would be the only commodity upon which a compensating duty could be levied.

Under these circumstances it is a matter of no small perplexity to determine what course should be pursued. The Legislature of Newfoundland express a desire to be included in the general Convention, & might feel aggrieved if the Island were not brought within its provisions; on the other hand the U. S. profess to entertain the same desire, & might find in the refusal, on whatever grounds, to admit their fishermen to extended privileges on the Coast of Newfoundland, a pretext either for breaking off the negotiation altogether or for insisting with unflinching pertinacity on concessions in other quarters which might not be acceptable to others of the British Provinces.

If, then, "the Legislature of Newfoundland & the U. S. are prepared to make arrangements for the extended admission of American Fishermen to the fisheries on the Coast of Newfoundland the adjustment of the terms on which those arrangements should be effected, can only safely be attempted by a separate Treaty between Great Britain & the U. S. having reference to Newfoundland alone," and Elgin might without further instruction conclude such a treaty if the United States were inclined to enter into such a conditional agreement and Newfoundland was ready to make the necessary revenue sacrifices.

With instructions which left him as nearly a free hand as could easily be conceived, the Earl of Elgin proceeded to the United States, where he faced what appeared to be a very difficult task. His labor, however, was lightened by the desire of the Administration in Washington to secure some sort of an agreement which would prevent what promised to be serious trouble on the fishing grounds; by Canada's great concern about an expanded market in the United States; by the lessened opposition, if not the acquiescence, of the Maritime Provinces brought about in some part by the activities of Israel Andrews; as well as by the political situation in the United States, complicated by a rising tide of sectionalism which involved Southern apprehensions of possible revival of annexationism and extension of free-soil territory. All these circumstances, nevertheless, might not have been sufficient to pull out a reciprocity treaty had there not been added to them the ability of the negotiator to cajole and placate, to win over reluctant support and eventually votes.

Just exactly what took place in Washington cannot be stated with explicitness, for the negotiations were oral for the most part and no considerable body of written documents remains to show the steps by which the agreement was reached. We do, however, have the testimony of Secretary Marcy, written June 5, 1854:[31]

I have been for the last ten days constantly engaged with Ld Elgin on the Fishery & Reciprocity Treaty—We have this morning settled the last points of difference in regard to its provisions—It will be signed this evening & I believe it is in a shape to be acceptable to this country.

Some indication of what had been going on, besides interviews between Marcy and Elgin, is indicated by the biographer of Laurence Oliphant, Elgin's talented, sometimes flippant, rather snobbish, young secretary:[32]

. . . Lord Elgin and his staff approached the representatives of the American nation with all the legitimate wiles of accomplished and astute

31. Draft of a confidential dispatch to Buchanan, in Marcy Papers, Vol. L, No. 44090 (L.C.). Buchanan had been left in the dark about what was going on, for Lord Clarendon, for some reason, did not see fit to impart to him the wide discretion which had been given to Elgin. W. P. M. Kennedy, *Lord Elgin* ("Makers of Canada," Vol. VI [London and Toronto, 1926]), pp. 162–163.

32. Margaret O. W. Oliphant, *Memoir of the Life of Laurence Oliphant and of Alice Oliphant, His Wife* (New York, 1891), I, 109–110. A letter to Oliphant's mother contains this statement: "I have been engaged making arrangements for interviews with Ministers all the morning, and my diplomatic powers are considerably in request, as they are 'cute dodgy fellows, and have always got a sinister motive in the background, which it is sometimes difficult to discover." *Ibid.*, p. 115.

diplomacy. They threw themselves into the society of Washington—which in those days was apparently much more racy and original than it seems to be now, when American statesmen have grown dull, correct, and dignified like other men—with the *abandon* and enjoyment of a group of visitors solely intent on pleasure. Lord Elgin's enemies afterwards described the treaty as "floated through on champagne." "Without altogether admitting this, there can be no doubt," Laurence says, "that in the hands of a skilful diplomatist that liquor is not without its value." The ambassador had been informed that if he could overcome the opposition of the Democrats, which party had a majority in the Senate, he would find no difficulty on the part of the Government. But the young Secretary, keen as was his intelligence, did not see his way at first through the feasting and the gaiety into which his chief plunged. "At last, after several days of uninterrupted festivity, I began to perceive what we were driving at. To make quite sure, I said one day to my chief, 'I find all my most intimate friends are Democratic senators.' 'So do I,' he replied drily."

Something of the round of "pleasure for business" is shown in a letter which contained these words:

At two o'clock our whole party went to a grand luncheon at a senator's. Here we had every sort of refreshing luxury, the day being pipingly hot, and dozens of champagne were polished off. Several senators got screwed, and we made good use of the two hours we had to spare before going to the French ambassador's *matinée dansante* at four. [Here was a repetition of much the same thing.] We then adjourned with a lot of senators to brandy-and-water, champagne, and cigars till twelve, when some of us were quite ready to tumble into bed.

.   .   .   .   .

. . . It is necessary to the success of our mission that we conciliate everybody, and to refuse their invitations would be considered insulting. Lord Elgin pretends to drink immensely, but I watched him, and I don't believe he drank a glass between two and twelve. He is the most thorough *diplomat* possible,—never loses sight for a moment of his object, and while he is chaffing Yankees and slapping them on the back, he is systematically pursuing that object. The consequence is, he is the most popular Englishman that ever visited the United States. If you have got to deal with hogs, what are you to do? As Canning said of a man, 'He goes the whole hog, and he looks the hog he goes,' which is precisely a description of this respectable race.[33]

While he had no Boswell, Marcy no less than Elgin had been quietly using his influence to get support for the general proposition and then for the treaty as it was agreed upon. Nor did he scorn to get others who might have influence to use it where it would be most effective. To some businessmen he wrote, on June 11:[34]

A treaty has been negotiated with G. B. for the Fisheries and reciprocal trade between the U. S. & the British N. A. Provinces. This treaty will soon be laid before the Senate for ratification and the subject must also be acted on by the H. of R. for it cannot go into effect without legislation.

Some opposition to it is apprehended which I think could [be] prevented by correcting erroneous views as to the manner & extent of its operation upon certain interests. I know of no one better calculated to make explanations etc than yourself. *Coal* is on the *free list* and I fear that not only Penn[a] but Maryland & Virginia may oppose the Treaty under an apprehension that the *coal* interest of those states will be seriously injured. I am satisfied that such will not be the effects of the Treaty & that if all the facts in regard to the coal trade & use of the article were clearly explained the Senators and members of Congress from those States would support it.

My object in addressing you is to engage your efforts either by your presence here or otherwise to present the subject in its true light. That being fairly & fully done I really think the Treaty would be acceptable in & out of Congress.

The treaty represented a compromise between the extreme demands of the United States and sum total of the desiderata of the Provinces. On the fisheries issue Americans got most of what they had desired: right to fish the inshore waters of all the colonies on the Atlantic except Newfoundland, but not the privilege of taking salmon, shad, or shellfish, or of taking fish in mouths of rivers; the shores of these areas could be used for drying nets and curing fish so long as private property and British fishing were not interfered with. Similar rights were extended to British subjects along American shores north of the

33. Oliphant, *op. cit.,* I, 118–120.
34. Draft of letter to Roggers and Bronson in Marcy Papers, Vol. L, No. 44114 (L.C.).

thirty-sixth parallel, thus automatically eliminating Florida waters. A commissioner was to be appointed by each side, together with an umpire, and the three were to decide what places were to be reserved from common right of fishing. Americans were to have the use of the St. Lawrence and the Canadian canals between the Great Lakes and the sea, while British subjects had free navigation of Lake Michigan, and the President engaged to urge upon the States concerned the extension of similar privileges to British subjects on American canals. Marcy secured exemption from duty on lumber cut on American soil and floated down the St. John when that lumber was destined for an American port, but he did not get free navigation of that river. One article listed products which were to be mutually admitted free into the Provinces and the United States; in this list appeared coal and lumber, a concession to Elgin's persuasive powers, as well as furs, skins, and tails. On the other hand, the British Provinces would admit tar, pitch, turpentine, and rice which Marcy had urged to draw in Southern votes, as well as unmanufactured tobacco; sugar was not included, nor were printed books. In general, the articles on the free list were natural products of the mine, land, and sea; dyestuffs, in which there was comparatively little trade, fell over the line into the manufactured or semi-manufactured class. Article Six of the treaty provided that it should extend to Newfoundland as far as applicable, but if legislation of the Imperial Parliament, the Assembly of that Island, and the Congress of the United States should not embrace the Colony of Newfoundland then the article would have no effect, but this would not impair the rest of the treaty. The provisions of the treaty would operate for ten years and for so long after that as all parties desired, reserving to each side the right to abrogate on twelve months' notice after expiration of the ten years.

In view of the long struggle, the general indifference exhibited in the United States, as well as the active hostility displayed so frequently, Oliphant was perhaps exaggerating a little but not much when he wrote home, "We are tremendously triumphant; we have signed a stunning treaty."[35] Lord Elgin was less exuberant but none

35. Oliphant, *op. cit.*, I, 130. His description of the final scene would probably not have pleased Americans very much: "It was in the dead of night, in the last five minutes of the 5th of June, and the first five minutes of the 6th . . . that . . . four individuals might have been observed seated, their faces

the less satisfied when he wrote the Foreign Office from Government House in Quebec[36] an account of what he had done. The principal obstacle, he remarked, had been the case of Newfoundland, on which he had received the final instructions of May 19, only two days before it was necessary to leave Washington. The simplest way to handle the situation, according to Elgin's notion, was to leave the Island out of the arrangement altogether and make it the subject of a separate understanding, but Marcy, "who I am bound to say evinced in all his communications with me great candour & fairness," was unwilling to adopt this course, fearing that it might lead to "embarrassing discussions in the Senate." So, too, with the matter of reserving French rights; here Elgin asserted that he was most desirous to avoid anything which would embarrass the Government in its negotiations with France, but at the same time he believed, "and in this opinion M[r] Crampton fully concurred, that so favourable an opportunity for settling important questions which had been long pending . . . might not again present itself & that I ought not to shrink from assuming any responsibility which the faithful discharge of the duty which Y[r] Lordship had imposed upon me, might entail." Marcy could not be induced to include registration of colonial-built vessels; "it is very obvious, however, that if, in consequence of the refusal of this boon, the cost of carriage in colonial vessels is rendered permanently lower than in vessels of the U. S. the evil must soon correct itself." If Great Britain should use the option of closing the canals to American use,

expressive of deep and earnest thought, not unmixed with cunning. . . . Two were young and two aged,—one, indeed, far gone in years, the other prematurely so. He it is whose measured tones alone break the solemn silence of midnight, except when one of the younger auditors . . . interrupts him to interpolate 'and' or scratch out 'the.' They are, in fact, checking him; and the aged man listens while he picks his teeth with a pair of scissors, or clears out the wick of the candle with their points and wipes them on his hair. . . . [The treaty is signed by Elgin] and then it is placed in the hands of the venerable file, whose hand does not shake, though he is very old, and knows he will be bullied to death by half the members of Congress. . . . Why should the old man fear? Has he not survived the changes and chances of more different sorts of lives than any other man? and is he afraid of being done by an English lord? So he gives us his blessing, and we leave the old man and his secretary with our treaty in our pockets." *Ibid.*, pp. 130–132.

36. Elgin to Clarendon, June 12, 1854; FO 115:139 (P.R.O.).

the counter-right of suspending the free list was to apply only to Canada. Elgin stated that, as soon as the United States Senate had ratified the treaty and the necessary legislation had been passed, he would endeavor to obtain similar legislation in Canada and would urge upon the Lieutenant-Governors of the other Provinces to take necessary steps in their jurisdictions. He recommended that the Admiral on the North American Station be instructed with reference to the fisheries so that all possibility of collision might be avoided. He closed his dispatch by stating that it was his "deliberate opinion, founded on a knowledge of the condition of these colonies, derived from long residence in this quarter, that the favourable results of this Treaty, should it come into operation, on their prosperity and progress, will be found very far to exceed what its most sanguine supporters here ventured to anticipate."[37]

On August 4 Crampton could notify the Foreign Office that two days earlier the Senate had ratified the treaty and on the previous day Congress had passed the legislation necessary to put it into effect.[38] While we have no direct information about the discussion in the Senate or how members of that body voted[39] it would appear that the action was almost as perfunctory as that by which the act to carry the treaty into effect was passed by both houses. In the House of Representatives there was neither discussion nor record vote.[40] The next day, when the Senate received the House bill, the only remarks made were by James A. Pearce of Maryland, who said:

It is not my intention to interpose any Parliamentary objection to the passage of the bill, and still less is it my intention to argue against the provisions of the bill. But I am not willing that it shall be passed without making it known publicly that neither the treaty nor the bill consequent

37. Abbott Lawrence, ex-Minister to England, wrote Marcy from Boston, June 17, 1854 (Reciprocity Treaty [D.S.]), that Elgin spoke "in very handsome terms of your ability, patience, and courtesy during this important negotiation." Lawrence himself thought the treaty one of the most important acts of Government since 1815. Marcy to Buchanan, June 12, 1854; Great Britain: Instructions, Vol. XVI (D.S.).

38. Crampton to Clarendon, FO 5:598 (P.R.O.).

39. In subsequent discussions, notably on May 10, 1858, some of the Senators announced that they had *not* voted for the treaty.

40. Aug. 3, 1854; *Cong. Globe*, 33d Cong., 1st Sess., p. 2135.

upon it, meets my approbation. I am utterly opposed to them. I wish that to be known.[41]

The preparatory work had been well done. Some of it was undoubtedly to be found in the persuasive diplomacy of Lord Elgin, but even he would have been powerless had there not been circumstances of a political nature entirely removed from the subject matter of the treaty as such. Perhaps the words of Senator Jacob Collamer of Vermont, spoken on May 10, 1858, in debate upon a bill to abolish fishing bounties, speak some of the underlying factors:[42]

I fancy that when we really come to examine the motives which led to that treaty, we shall not be able to charge them so exclusively upon one quarter as the Senator from Louisiana seems to suggest. I have been strongly impressed with the idea that the treaty was made for the purpose of persuading Canada not to join the United States, lest it might alter the balance of political power between North and South. I think that was really at the bottom of the matter; because if they could have all the advantages of trade with this country, and through it, without contributing anything to the support of our Government, they would not be very likely to be as anxious to join us as they had been for several years before; and they were quieted in that manner. They now derive all the advantages of receiving their importations through this country duty free, without contributing to the support of our Government. Under such an arrangement they will probably be very quiet, and will not undertake to join the North to disturb the political balance of the country. I fancy that, in point of fact, that consideration entered into the treaty more deeply than anything else, though I am not in "the secrets of the prison house. . . ."

41. *Cong. Globe,* 33d Cong., 1st Sess., p. 2212.
42. *Ibid.,* 35th Cong., 1st Sess., p. 2031.

CHAPTER V

THE RECIPROCITY TREATY IN OPERATION

RECIPROCITY, limited to be sure, had been accomplished. Would it work? All depended on the practicability of the terms of the agreement and the spirit in which those terms were interpreted on both sides of the boundary. The two critical points were the fisheries and the adequacy of the trade provisions. Almost immediately peace descended upon the fishing grounds. A few days before Congress acted to put the treaty into effect, Sir Edmund Head reported to Mr. Crampton, on July 29, that the fishing schooner *Ellen* had been seized while within three miles of the coast of New Brunswick, and Crampton, thinking that such an act at that time was much to be regretted, telegraphed Admiral Fanshaw his hope that the vessel might be released even though the treaty was not yet functioning. He had not sent off his dispatch to Lord Clarendon explaining the matter when he received word that his suggestion had been anticipated, and an opportunity taken to demonstrate the determination of British authorities to live up to the spirit of the new accord.[1]

The Government of the United States was anxious to have the Provincial authorities take steps immediately to relieve American fishermen of penalties during the existing season should they desire to avail themselves of the advantages which would accrue when the treaty should be in full effect. A suggestion was transmitted through the usual channels to the Lieutenant-Governors of the Maritime Provinces that it would be well to comply with the request. When Le Marchant of Nova Scotia, the Province most significantly affected, placed this suggestion before his Executive Council, that body displayed a certain reluctance to anticipate the requisite legislative action of the Province. "Your Excellency," they said,[2]

is invited in effect to assume that it [the Legislature] will sanction the Treaty. . . .

1. Head to Crampton, July 29, and Crampton to Clarendon, Aug. 7, 1854; FO 5:598 (P.R.O.).
2. FO 5:599 (P.R.O.). The Minute was dated Sept. 14, 1854.

. . . Your Exc^y is not unacquainted with the *fact* that the People of Nova Scotia generally are deeply impressed with a sense of the magnitude and importance of the privileges which they will be called upon to concede, as well as of their constitutional exclusive right to legislate in relation to them, and that a difference of opinion amongst our leading men exists as to the expediency of granting to the Citizens of the Union, on the conditions of the Treaty, a community of enjoyment of our Fisheries whilst the corresponding concessions are deemed by many to fall very far short of what on grounds of fair Reciprocity, they ought to be; and yet this knowledge of the conflicting sentiments of Nova Scotians & the possible influence upon future Legislation that opinions adverse to the Treaty may exercise Your Excellency virtually is required to ignore.

Less eagerness on the part of the United States to grasp prematurely the concessions of the treaty would have appeared more seemly, opined the Council. Verily the path of a Colonial Secretary was not strewn with roses. It was hard to answer such an eminently sensible argument, and equally difficult to make the Government of the United States, which the British Government desired to placate, understand why a little province like Nova Scotia could thus calmly set itself in opposition to Imperial wish.

But the American Administration was not altogether lacking in a sense of the fitness of things. When Crampton[3] pointed out to Secretary Marcy, who had informed him that there was no possibility of his Government's relaxing its regulations respecting duties on imports before the Provincial legislatures should have passed the requisite acts, that some temporary arrangement might be worked out, the latter responded in a conciliatory manner by stating:

Should British fish, caught after the inshore fisheries were opened, be brought to our markets, and duties paid thereon, it would be reasonable to expect that an application to Congress to refund the duties founded upon such equitable considerations as the case would present, would be successful, or if, such fish thus taken should be put in warehouses, and bonds for the duties thereon given, Congress would, I believe, authorize such bonds to be cancelled and given up, without requiring the fish to be exported.

3. To Clarendon, Oct. 16, 1854, enclosing Marcy to Crampton of Oct. 10; FO 5:599 (P.R.O.).

And this, in fact, was the solution reached, not only with respect to fish but in the matter of other goods.[4] The desire of Americans to have the terms of the Reciprocity Treaty extend to the Pacific coast, and especially to include Vancouver Island within its application, was not considered feasible or possible by the British Government, even though some of the inhabitants of the Island were anxious to be included, for rights already granted to the Hudson's Bay Company seemed to preclude admission of Americans to the fisheries of the coast. The British Government apparently would have been glad to extend to that region the general provisions of the Reciprocity Treaty, but Marcy always brought up the fisheries when the issue was broached and the result was stalemate.[5]

In general, the fisheries provision of the treaty worked satisfactorily to both sides. There was, however, one aspect of the matter which created a small amount of friction. Since the treaty excluded Americans from taking fish in the mouths of rivers it was necessary to determine just where rivers ended and the sea began, and for this purpose, as provided by the treaty, there was set up a commission composed of one appointee by each Government with an umpire agreeable to both. From the beginning Moses H. Perley, the British Commissioner, and G. G. Cushman failed to get along well together. "The U. S. Commissioner," reported Perley, "appears desirous of placing the mouth of each river as far up as possible, in order to give American vessels the right to enter the harbours at their mouths, without question or hindrance, under pretense of fishing."[6] To counteract this,

4. See Jan. 20, 24, Feb. 8, 1855; *Cong. Globe,* 33d Cong., 2d Sess., pp. 338, 376, 622. The act was made applicable to fish and other goods imported from Canada, Prince Edward Island, New Brunswick, Nova Scotia, and Newfoundland.

5. Merivale to Booth, Aug. 10, 1855, FO 115:154; Crampton to Clarendon, Feb. 18, 1856, FO 5:641; see also Simpson to Shepherd, Apr. 11, 1856, FO 115:165 (P.R.O.). George Simpson, Governor of the Hudson's Bay Company, maintained that the extension of the terms of the treaty to the Pacific coast would confer no benefits on the people of the British possessions there and would entail "relinquishing valuable privileges."

6. Perley to Clarendon, Oct. 6, 1855; FO 115:155 (P.R.O.). An account of the work of the Commission is found in J. B. Moore, *History and Digest of International Arbitrations to Which the United States Has Been a Party*

Perley determined to insist on ascertaining the mouth of the Hudson, or the extent of New York harbor, at an early date in order to give the American Commissioner some of his own medicine. Besides what seemed to the British Commissioner the grasping nature of the American, the latter made little appeal to him as an individual.

I regret being obliged to state to Y L that Mr. Cushman is a person of very little education, of vulgar manners and disagreeable habits. He had never seen the sea until we sailed from Halifax, and had never before made a trip in a sailing vessel: of course he suffered much from sea-sickness. He does not even know the names of the fishes caught on these Coasts, and has very crude and imperfect ideas of the modes of conducting the fisheries generally. It w^d almost seem that he had been appointed Commissioner with special reference for his unfitness for the office in every respect.

The annoyance of working with Cushman, however, had to be borne for a time. He was a political appointee and could not be summarily dismissed; "although the inefficiency of Mr Cushman, the United States Commissioner, was acknowledged by Mr Marcy, there were considerations which prevented the United States Government from acceding to Mr Crampton's proposal, that another person should be appointed in his place, as provided by the 1st article of the Treaty."[7] Eventually Cushman was quietly dropped.

All troubles did not cease with a new commissioner, for British and American representatives did not always see eye to eye and it was necessary for the umpire, J. H. Gray, to make final decision in a number of cases. With the awards of that gentleman "certain parties" in the United States expressed dissatisfaction, and the Government "identified itself with the opposition" and requested the selection of another umpire. Her Majesty's Government were considerably embarrassed by this turn of affairs, for they were convinced by the testimony of Perley and others, including Admiral Henry W. Bayfield, that Gray had acted in a spirit of impartiality and fairness. But the formal request of Secretary Lewis Cass, who succeeded Marcy in 1857, that Gray should no longer serve had to be complied with, although simul-

(Washington, 1898), Vol. I, chap. xiii. Following Cushman, Benjamin Wiggin was Commissioner for nine months; he was succeeded by John Hubbard in 1859, and he by E. L. Hamlin in 1861.

7. Quinley to Clarendon, Oct. 13, 1856; FO 5:646 (P.R.O.).

taneously the British Government directed Lord Lyons, then the British Minister, to ask the American Government to replace Richard D. Cutts, the American surveyor, who had been particularly critical of the decisions of Gray. At the same time, to indicate their satisfaction with Gray's work, he was given "a responsible and important office in the Colony of Prince Edward Island by the Duke of Newcastle" which showed him that "H. M.'s Gov^t continue fully to appreciate [his] merits." The work was pushed forward when the newly appointed American Commissioner, Hubbard, working amicably with Perley, "would not permit the slightest interference on the part of Mr. Cutts with the business of the Commissioners," and "behaved in the most honorable and straightforward manner, conceding everything that could be properly asked, & exhibiting an earnest desire to perform his duty fairly & impartially."[8]

After the season of 1855 it was evident that the fisheries provisions of the treaty were working satisfactorily. At its close the Lieutenant-Governor of New Brunswick reported[9] that the British and American fishermen had conducted their operations in "perfect harmony"; while there had been violations of the fishing laws there was no reason to believe that foreign fishermen were peculiarly responsible for illegal practices. Similar testimony was obtained from American consular officers in the other Maritime Provinces. This does not mean, of course, that there never was any friction; that would have been too much to ask. The question early arose as to whether American fishermen were bound by local regulations which applied to British fishermen. In an instruction to Crampton the Foreign Office let it clearly be understood that the treaty did not confer immunity from such restrictions.[10]

In a few minds, notably Perley's, the treaty seemed to contain dan-

8. Russell to Lyons, July 7, 1860; Perley to Russell, Nov. 25, 1860; FO 115:223 (P.R.O.). There is a voluminous correspondence over this matter of determining the limits of American rights, much of which is found in FO 115: 222 and 115:223 (P.R.O.). See also Cass to G. M. Dallas, Nov. 3, 1859; Great Britain: Instructions, XVI (D.S.). Dallas was Minister to England, 1856–61.

9. S. H. Manners Sutton to Grey, Nov. 11, 1855; FO 115:156 (P.R.O.). Sutton became Lieutenant-Governor of New Brunswick when Head replaced Elgin as Governor-General.

10. Oct. 11, 1855, FO 115:155; Sutton to Crampton, June 15, 1855 (Enclosure), FO 5:621 (P.R.O.).

gerous possibilities of reviving or stimulating annexation sentiments, one of the things it was intended to avert. Perley's suspicions, reported to London, in due time reached Lieutenant-Governor Darling of Newfoundland where, particularly, Perley felt there was the greatest menace. Darling did not question Perley's conclusions and believed that there was "no limit to the projects of annexation which are discussed, approved & even pronounced feasible in that country [the United States]," but, he concluded,

no scheme of the kind . . . could, I conceive, be *deemed by reasoning & reflecting men less probable of accomplishment* than that of wresting Newfoundland from Great Britain.

I have good reason to believe, both from occasional opportunities of personal observation, & from information from various sources which I think reliable that any feeling but one of cordiality exists between the native population of this Colony as a Body, & the Citizens of the U States.[11]

Perley agreed with Robert Bunch, back in England on leave from consular service in the United States, who thought he found evidence that

certain Citizens of the United States were actively engaged in an endeavor to excite in the Island of Newfoundland a feeling of hostility towards Great Britain, with the view of procuring at some future period, the annexation of that Colony to the United States. The persons principally concerned in this alleged attempt are a M[r] Field, the President, & a M[r] White, a Director of the Submarine Telegraph Company which has undertaken to connect Newfoundland with the American Continent, & subsequently with Europe.[12]

The American Consul at Halifax[13] reported to the Department of State that the people of all the Maritime Provinces, including New-

11. Darling to Labouchere, June 10, 1856; FO 115:166 (P.R.O.).

12. Bunch to Clarendon, Sept. 25, 1856; FO 115:166 (P.R.O.). In a letter of March 10, 1857, Perley returned to the charge that the officials of the cable company were in some deep, dark plot (FO 115:174). They had, he said, got a foothold in Newfoundland and were busy selecting the most favorable sites under the terms of their concession.

13. Albert Pillsbury to Cass, Mar. 12, 1857; Consular Letters: Halifax, Vol. VIII (D.S.).

foundland, were greatly excited over a rumored proposed fishing treaty between Great Britain and France, and contended that if this treaty were persisted in, they would dissolve their allegiance and put themselves under the protection of the United States. In the course of time it appeared that Governor Darling was better informed of the real situation than either Commissioner Perley or Consul Pillsbury, for, if the former's fears were not allayed, at least he did not continue to lay them before his superiors.

One of the grievances of the fishing Provinces, and a matter frequently mentioned when opening fishing grounds to Americans was under discussion, was the American system whereby those engaged in the cod fishery received a bounty based on tonnage of vessels. This benefaction, the Provincials thought with a certain amount of reason, gave Americans an unfair advantage, and they were of the opinion that if inshore rights were conceded, then bounties should be eliminated. In the United States as well they were questioned, both as to their inherent utility and on the ground that the Provincials had a real cause of complaint. It was not, however, until January, 1857, that an attempt was made to introduce bills in Congress to repeal the act of February 9, 1816,[14] but objection of W. S. Damrell of Massachusetts prevented consideration in the House, and in the Senate C. C. Clay's effort to attain the same end resulted in a similar failure.[15] Local opposition to repeal of bounties was manifested in a set of resolutions framed by the Massachusetts legislature strenuously resisting any such action.[16] Recourse to the argument that the fisheries formed the training place for the personnel of the navy and thus for the defense of the country was always had by someone whenever the question of bounties was raised. Despite the fact that apparently cogent reasons were shown why the argument was invalid, it was always used and with telling effect.

Clay brought the matter up again in the Thirty-fifth Congress,[17]

14. *Cong. Globe,* 34th Cong., 3d Sess., p. 318.

15. *Ibid.,* pp. 217, 378, 661.

16. *Senate Misc. Docs.,* No. 26, and *House Misc. Docs.,* No. 41, 34th Cong., 3d Sess. The legislature of Maine also took this ground. *House Misc. Docs.,* No. 28, 35th Cong., 1st Sess.

17. May 4, 1858; *Cong. Globe,* 35th Cong., 1st Sess., pp. 1930 ff., 2020, 2048–2049, 2070–2075, 2238. *Senate Reports,* No. 10, 35th Cong., 1st Sess.

precipitating a protracted discussion, in the course of which Collamer of Vermont came to the rescue of the American Navy once more. With the Senate this time, however, the navy and the perils which threatened it had less influence, for the bill passed by a majority of thirty to twenty-four.[18] Sectionalism is apparent in the vote, for there were but four Senators from the Northeast who voted in its favor, while opposition to repeal, principally Republican, was found in New England and New York with support from Wisconsin, Michigan, Minnesota, Tennessee, California, and Ohio. The Senate bill did not reach the floor of the House that term, and when an attempt was made to call it up at the succeeding short session it was blocked by Davis of Massachusetts, who objected to a suspension of the rules.[19] At almost every session until the expiration of the Reciprocity Treaty some little attempt was made to secure a repeal of the bounty system, but at none did it get as far as it had in 1858.

If there were questionings and some misgivings in the Maritime Provinces, where, after all, the real price of the Reciprocity Treaty was paid, almost unanimous approbation greeted it in Canada which stood to gain out of all proportion to its sacrifices, for the interest of Lower Canada in the fisheries was as nothing compared with that of the Maritime Provinces. The administration press could and did "point with pride" to the achievements of the Government. "The treaty includes more articles than the American Government were ever before willing to permit to be exchanged, duty free, between the two countries," said the *Daily Leader* of Toronto when it announced that the instrument had actually been signed.[20]

18. *Cong. Globe,* 35th Cong., 1st Sess., p. 2239. The clerk stated that there were twenty-five votes in the negative, but the yeas and nays show only twenty-four.

19. *Ibid.,* 35th Cong., 2d Sess., pp. 7, 363, 1197. Houston of South Carolina was called to order by Washburne of Illinois when he asked if there was "a design to suppress the bill." *Ibid.,* p. 363.

20. June 8, 1854. The *Leader* could not refrain from a little crowing: "Were we inclined to throw back the taunts with which the opposition press has assailed the advocates of Reciprocity, we might, in this hour of triumph, do so with effect. It will be sufficient to direct attention to the unpatriotic efforts of those who ridiculed every step taken by the Government to secure that Reciprocity which unwearied perseverance has at length obtained. . . ."

Never perhaps was the mutual necessity of concluding such a treaty so strongly felt as at the present time. The Americans desired free access to our fisheries and we to their markets with our raw produce. The object of each has been accomplished; the desire of both fulfilled. The commerce of the two countries will be almost infinitely increased. The general effect of the measure, so far as Canada is concerned, will be to increase the value of the productions of the soil. The results of the aggregate labor of the people of Canada will bring a higher remuneration. Labor will yield more and property become more valuable.

When the opposition press continued to point out obstacles still standing in the way of consummation of the pact, especially the possibility of Nova Scotia's obstinately refusing to enact necessary legislation, governmental organs ridiculed the idea that this Province would fly in the face of its own interest and voluntarily cut off a market for its fish. Furthermore, it maintained it must not be forgotten that, after all, there was an Imperial factor involved, and it was a question how far the British Government would go "in maintaining on behalf of the Colonies, at a serious expense to herself, a commercial privilege, so provocative of jealousy, irritation and collision."[21] Events of the past few years had shown that Britain was no longer inclined to let colonial whims divert her from a course in which she had set her foot.

The last appeal to England by New Brunswick and Nova Scotia, even under the protective Administration of Sir John Packington, was positively disallowed as involving deviation from the settled commercial policy of England. . . . It was certainly but natural to expect, that a Government more devoted than Lord Derby's to a liberal commercial policy would not lose the first opportunity of removing so obnoxious a Convention [of 1818]—at whatever expense of Colonial prejudice.

That securing reciprocity was not disconnected with the internal situation in the United States was a fact not overlooked by Canadians, and no illusions about a gratuitous gesture were cherished.[22]

When the announcement was made that the Commercial Treaty had been signed at Washington . . . the leading Protectionist journals of the

21. *Daily Leader,* Toronto, June 14, 1854.
22. *Ibid.,* June 19, 1854.

North, more particularly those which represent the Free Soil interest, gave a distinct intimation of their concurrence in the terms of the Convention. The *Tribune*, for instance, hitherto foremost in its opposition to the establishment of Free Trade between the Colonies and the United States, expressed its readiness to give the new arrangement a trial; and more—as was generally supposed—in banter than in earnest, suggested the probability of the new Commercial Treaty paving the way for annexation. Annexation, as interpreted by the Free Soil party, is an indispensable preliminary towards imposing an effective check on the aggressive policy of the south. It is, in other words, the question which, in diplomatic phraseology, is described as the Balance of Power. . . .

Despite sectionalism and even the recurrence of annexationist talk, Canadians were disposed to believe that on both sides of the boundary there would be enough sensible opinion to recognize that, after all, this was a plain matter of business whereby both parties were likely to profit.

Lord Elgin, upon his return to the Provinces, had immediately recommended to the Canadian legislature the enactment of appropriate legislation and, through the respective Lieutenant-Governors, he suggested the same procedure to the other Colonies. By the time Congress met in December, Canada and New Brunswick had already acted; Nova Scotia was ready shortly after; and Prince Edward Island, after the enactment of a measure which did not, in the opinion of the Secretary of the Treasury, quite meet the terms laid down by Congress in the previous summer, amended its legislation to the satisfaction of both the Treasury and the Department of State.[23] On January 5, 1855, Secretary Marcy addressed a communication to the Chairman of the House Committee on Commerce[24] calling his attention to the reference in the President's Annual Message to the action of Canada and New Brunswick, transmitted letters from the Secretary of the Treasury and the British Minister together with copies of regulations framed by the Treasury Department, and recommended that Congress take action to refund duties which had been paid upon goods included in the free list of the treaty. On January 20 Fuller introduced a bill "to amend an act to carry into effect the Treaty between the

23. The correspondence of Marcy, Guthrie, Crampton, Elgin and the Lieutenant-Governors is found in FO 5:599 and 5:600 (P.R.O.).

24. *House Misc. Docs.*, No. 21, 33d Cong., 2d Sess.

United States and Great Britain, signed the 6th of June, 1854 and approved the 5th of August, 1854."[25] Four days later Seward reported in the Senate a similar measure,[26] called the bill up on February 8, and, after a perfunctory question whether all the Provinces had acceded to the treaty, the measure was passed. On March 1 the House adopted the Senate bill and reciprocity was in full effect.[27] Whatever may have been the doubts of some Congressmen and Senators, they did not appear in the record, and the intention to carry out the terms of the treaty was manifest in the almost casual manner in which the action was taken. The die had been cast and reciprocity was to be tried. Andrews, who had assisted in preparing the ground for the treaty in the Maritime Provinces, wrote Secretary Marcy from Boston in July[28] that "although the Treaty has only been in effect a short time, yet its beneficial effects are already felt and appreciated throughout the Northern Section of America, from Lake Superior to Newfoundland and time alone will prove that its provisions are in unison with the feelings and interests of our fellow citizens."

Canada, too, liked reciprocity thus far. A Report of a Committee of the Legislative Assembly of Canada submitted for the consideration of the Legislature a series of propositions including free trade between the British North American Colonies, on the same basis as it existed in the United States or in the "German confederacy in Europe"; extension of the principle of reciprocity between Canada and the United States to manufactures, shipping, and the coasting trade; removal of all duties from raw materials and all cheap, heavy, and bulky articles imported by way of the St. Lawrence; improvement of the St. Lawrence and reconstruction of its canals and the Champlain

25. *Cong. Globe,* 33d Cong., 2d Sess., p. 338.

26. *Ibid.,* p. 376.

27. On February 10 Crampton wrote Clarendon (FO 5:619 [P.R.O.]) to enclose the bill which "upon consulting with Mr Seward by whom the Bill was reported, the terms of the Bill appeared to us to embrace all the provisions necessary for carrying into execution the intended arrangement, as well with regard to Prince Edwards Island, as with regard to the other colonies."

In his report for the fiscal year ending June 30, 1855, the Secretary of the Treasury announced that duties refunded on importations from the British Provinces up to November 1, 1854, amounted to $555,887.09. *House Ex. Docs.,* No. 10, 34th Cong., 1st and 2d Sess.

28. July 2, 1855; Consular Letters: Montreal and Quebec, Vol. I (D.S.).

canals; abolition of the warehouse system and, instead, extension of credit to the importer. William Hamilton Merritt, long active in the interests of reciprocity, made these recommendations the subject of a discussion which he published in a pamphlet.[29] He admitted that there would be active opposition to such a sweeping innovation not alone on account of its novel and radical ideas but because it would strike at a vested interest, and "we have not yet a sufficient growth of Canadian feeling to advocate any measure with no other motive than promoting the interest of Canada." It was, however, something worthy of consideration and in his opinion rather simply attainable: merely reciprocal legislation forced through by public opinion. Simple as was the plan—just mutual legislation removing all duties—it presupposed a willingness on the part of the United States to tear down an important section of the protectionist wall which was appearing more and more important to a large portion of the North. It proposed abolition of a customs frontier which would result in closer economic relations, and that in turn could not fail to raise again the specter of political association. Canadian national sentiment might be weak, as Merritt asserted, but it was not so feeble as to invite voluntarily the revival of annexationism. Nevertheless, the very fact that a legislative committee could bring in such a report and that it could receive enough attention to provoke discussion is evidence that the sentiment which had brought reciprocity was strong enough to consider the possibilities of its extension.

Outside of Upper Canada there was a belief that relations with the United States were bound to become economically closer. The Legislative Council of New Brunswick and the Council of the Quebec Board of Trade at almost the same time[30] expressed a desire to have some kind of Provincial representative resident in the United States to look after the interests of the Colonies. Separate representation of the

29. *Remarks on the Extension of Reciprocity between Canada and the United States (Now Confined to the Growth and Produce of Each) to Manufacturers, Shipping & Coasting, and Establishing a Commercial System Adapted to the Geographical Position of Canada* (St. Catherines, 1855). The *Remarks* contains a statement of the Committee Report.

30. Sutton to Russell, Apr. 18, 1855; Sir Edmund Head to Russell, Apr. 24, 1855; FO 115:153 (P.R.O.). Lord John Russell was now Secretary of State for Foreign Affairs.

Provinces, however, did not strike a responsive chord in London. Sir Edmund Head, now Governor-General in place of Elgin, was to inform the Quebec Board of Trade[31] that

although H. M.'s Gov[t] do not consider from the information in their possession that it is requisite to create the appointment prayed for, they will direct the British Minister and Consuls in the U. S. to pay special and constant attention to the interests of H. M.'s North American Subjects residing in that country, and that they trust that the instruction they thus propose to give will sufficiently accomplish the object of the gentlemen who have addressed you upon the subject; which will indeed be better attained in this way than by the employment of agents who could not speak with the whole weight of authority of the Imperial crown.

The life of the Reciprocity Treaty falls into two divisions. The first covered the period from the winter of 1854–55, when the treaty was put into operation, down to the spring of 1861, when the American Civil War introduced extraneous elements which in themselves had really nothing to do with reciprocal commercial relations but which inevitably became intertwined with them. The second period is that of the Civil War and beyond, to the abrogation of the arrangement in March of 1866. For the first six years on the whole there was no serious expression of desire to change materially the existing situation, unless to liberalize it.[32] This does not by any means indicate that there were no causes of friction, but in contrast to the general satisfaction, the irritation was slight. Provincial critics called attention to two phases in particular: the tendency of American officials to place a rather narrow interpretation on some of the terms, and to hamper the spirit of

31. Russell to Head, May 23, 1855; FO 115:153 (P.R.O.).

32. Testimony to the relief felt in official circles in England over the temporary settlement of the American-Canadian issues is naïvely given by Buchanan in a dispatch to Marcy on December 7, 1855:

"I need not repeat to you the news, which you will find detailed in the public journals, respecting the present tone of feeling in this country towards the United States. There is one incident, however, of sufficient significance to justify a passing notice as indicating the feelings of the most respectable classes of the population of London in regard to our country. At the reception of the King of Sardinia in Guildhall, on Tuesday last, when the entrance of the American Minister was announced, he was received with spontaneous, loud and reiterated cheers. This was so marked as to attract the attention of every person in that large assembly." Great Britain: Despatches, Vol. LXVIII (D.S.).

the treaty by consular regulations; the other aspect involved the old question of registration of vessels and reciprocal coasting privileges. Americans, especially those who were strongly protectionist in their leanings, believed that Canada was violating the spirit of the treaty by raising duties upon manufactured goods which were not affected by the free-trade article.

Free interchange of raw products, especially of grain, led to a very considerable increase in shipping on the Great Lakes,[33] but Canadians found that there were obstacles to their carrying trade which, they maintained, did not obtain in the case of American shipping. Rae Brothers and Company of Hamilton, early in 1857, spread their grievances at large in the Toronto *Globe*, took the matter up with Inspector-General William Cayley of the Customs Department, and then approached Secretary Marcy direct, making a general case on the basis of specific experiences they had had.[34] They put the questions in this form:

1st If we loaded one or more of our vessels (British bottoms) at Chicago, or any other American Port in our inland waters, for Ogdensburg, & enter said cargoes at a British port *in transitu*, such as St Catherines or Kingston, discharge cargo at such British port & transship afterwards per same vessel, or in a river barge for port of destination, will such act be considered by your Gov^t as a violation of the coasting trade?
2nd Can British, or Canadian Vessels carry grain from one American port to another, on payment of 50 cents a ton tonnage dues at this port of destination, without being liable to seizure or confiscation?
3rd Is the tonnage due payable on Custom House or carpenter's measurements?

33. In a memorandum to the Colonial Secretary, Lytton (Aug. 30, 1858; FO 115:192 [P.R.O.]), Head gave an account of the working of the Reciprocity Treaty; among other things he stated: "H. M.'s Gov^t are already in possession of the reports of Mr Consul Wilkins of Chicago. What do these documents show? They prove that since the year 1854 under the Reciprocity treaty a new line of communication has been opened. It appears that in 1854 the number of British vessels entering Chicago was 5 and clearing from it 6. In 1855 these numbers rose to 77 and 61. In 1856 to 110 and 104, in 1857 to 119 and 101. The imports of lumber in British vessels were in 1850, *nil*, in 1857 about 15,000,000 feet."
34. The correspondence is in FO 115:179 (P.R.O.). The inquiry addressed to Marcy was dated Feb. 20, 1857.

Secretary of the Treasury Guthrie, to whom the inquiry was referred, gave an unequivocal response to the Canadian questions: the Act of 1817 absolutely prohibited foreigners' engaging in coastwise trade. It was the experience of Rae Brothers and others that led Inspector-General Cayley to address a memorandum (June 16) to Sir Edmund Head, then in London, asking him to take the matter up with the Colonial Office to see if something could be done to secure a more liberal attitude on the part of the American Government. Pointing out that such liberalization would not affect the revenue laws of either country, he argued that

. . . These restrictions, it is very generally urged by commercial men, both American & Canadian, might with advantage be relaxed, and it may also with truth be stated that in the interpretation and carrying out of these laws, the Canadian Auth^{ties} are more liberal than the American. By the laws of either country the coasting Trade is closed to foreign vessels. No Canadian vessel can carry freight from one American Port to another; and so with American vessels passing between two Canadian Ports, but, according to Canadian usage, freight may be carried in American vessels between two Canadian Ports if landed and transshipped at some intermediate American Port. Not so as regards Canadian Vessels, according to the principle laid down by Mr Guthrie Secretary of the U. S. Treasury in his letter to Messrs Rae Brothers, inclosed.

The Board of Trade, with whom the Colonial Office took up the proposition, ascertained that the Board of Trade of Toronto had approached the Board in Chicago asking it to coöperate in taking steps with their respective governments to induce them to "grant the free navigation of the Inland waters common to both countries to the Inhabitants of each alike." Conceding that such a course would be of great advantage to both parties, the Board of Trade, nevertheless, had learned that the people of Lower Canada would be averse to opening in this manner the St. Lawrence below Lake St. Francis; consequently they thought that an arrangement should be limited to the "navigation of the Great Lakes and of the waters of the St. Lawrence above Lake St. Francis. With this limitation it appears to their Lordships that a proposal might be made at a favourable opportunity by H. M. Min^{ster} at Washington to the Gov^t of the U. S. for the mutual concession of complete freedom of navigation, including the coasting trade, in the Inland waters between the U. S. & the British North American provinces."[35]

But the American Government was not then susceptible to the arguments which seemed so logical to Canadians and to the British Government. The coasting trade was jealously guarded and any breach in its exclusiveness was not viewed with a hospitable eye. Moreover, from time to time there came indications that the entire reciprocity arrangement was being subjected to a scrutiny which was not always favorable. In the spring of 1858 the whole matter came up in the Senate for a limited discussion when the question of fishing bounties was under consideration. Senator C. C. Clay bluntly put to Hamlin the question of whether or not he favored the treaty, and Hamlin as bluntly said "No."[36] Did not the New England men support it? asked Clay. Some did and some did not, responded Hamlin. Both Hamlin and Fessenden denied that the treaty was made at their instance, as Clay intimated. "I threatened very hard at the Department," said Hamlin,

that if they did not deal a little more justly with us, I would exert my humble influence against it. I was quiet because I found that my opposition would do no good. I find that of the productions of the mines, the forest, and agriculture, there have been imported into the United States $9,502,000 over and above what we have sent to the Provinces—not a very small or inconsiderable item when we reflect that the articles are brought directly into competition with ours. What is true of the whole treaty, is still more particularly and significantly true in relation to the fisheries.

But Judah P. Benjamin of Alabama, a few days later, charged that the eastern and northern States had secured all the benefits of the treaty and now they wanted continued bounties to help them to compete with imported fish.[37] "The whole burden of the reciprocity treaty, then, is to be thrown upon the part of the country which does not catch the fish." Hamlin's statement about trade is typical of many such flat pronouncements, yet an examination of figures annually reported to Congress by the Treasury Department does not bear out his conten-

35. Booth to Merivale, Sept. 25, 1857; FO 115:179 (P.R.O.).
36. May 6, 1858; *Cong. Globe,* 35th Cong., 1st Sess., p. 1996.
37. *Ibid.,* pp. 2030–2031.

tion. The Report[38] covering the fiscal years from July 1, 1851, to June 30, 1856, shows that total exports from the United States to the Provinces had jumped from $13,140,642 in the year 1852–53 to $29,029,349 in 1855–56; of this $22,714,697 represented domestic goods and the rest foreign, the former having more than tripled while the latter had increased very slightly. At the same time Canadian exports to the United States had increased from $17,550,718 to $21,310,421. Reports for subsequent years told much the same story. In other words, while Provincial, especially Canadian, exports to the United States were steadily climbing, those from the United States to the Colonials were also advancing and always keeping ahead.

These recurrent intimations of dissatisfaction on the part of at least some sections of American public opinion could but raise a degree of alarm in the Provinces; there must be some fire where there was all this smoke. Then, too, there continued to be imposed petty restrictions upon Canadian trade which were not so much injurious as annoying, as Sir Edmund Head, in a report on the general economic situation in the Provinces with special reference to the working of reciprocity, pointed out to the Colonial Office.[39] In it Sir Edmund also took note of the navigation issue. Calling attention to a report of a committee of the Canadian Legislative Assembly, in which he did not express complete concurrence, he could say that

the statement . . . with reference to the impediments offered to British vessels by the navigation laws of the U. States is peculiarly important, and I would strongly urge that the adoption of some more liberal system should be pressed on the U. States Gov^t. Even if it were confined to the lakes, the boon would be great and the power of shipping goods from one American port to another, or one British port to another, by British or American vessels respectively, would be nationally beneficial. As a matter of course the admission of British built vessels to an American registry and the opening of the coasting trade on the sea Board would be a great additional advantage.

38. *Senate Ex. Docs.,* No. 3, 34th Cong., 3d Sess., p. 126. See S. A. Saunders, "The Reciprocity Treaty of 1854: A Regional Study," *Canadian Journal of Economics and Political Science,* II, 41–53, for an account of effects in the Maritimes; also Saunders, "The Maritime Provinces and the Reciprocity Treaty," *Dalhousie Review,* XIV, 355–371.

39. Head to Lytton, Aug. 30, 1858; FO 115:192 (P.R.O.).

The Governor-General was prodded by his Executive Council, which was made uneasy by reports from the United States, to take the matter up with Lord Napier, now the British Minister in Washington, and find out how much there was in the rumors. The latter reported[40] that he had made inquiries and found that King had introduced in the Senate a resolution contemplating an end of the agreement as soon as its terms allowed, and in the House some hostile remarks had been made in debate. A proposition to enlarge freedom of commerce was before the American Administration but no reply had been made to the overture. Napier believed that there was no immediate intention on the part of the Government of the United States, or any well defined project, to abrogate the treaty, "the benefits of which are very generally recognized." His Lordship, however, felt constrained to warn the Provincials that

the high scale of duties now established by the Canadian Tariff has produced in some quarters a feeling of dissatisfaction which may eventually result in a serious movement against the stipulations of the Reciprocity Treaty. It is urged that, while, under the Treaty Canada has the advantage of pouring her raw productions into the United States free of charge, the American Trader, whose exports to Canada consist, in considerable part, of manufactured goods, is met on the Canadian frontier by a high Tariff.

Spurred by the communication from Head, Lord Napier took occasion to ask Secretary Cass if there was any design on the part of his Government to terminate the Treaty of 1854. Cass replied that he personally had always been favorable to the treaty, but that there was much difference of opinion along the frontier where each locality judged of its merits by the way it affected local trade and industry; while he could not say what the opinion of the Government might eventually be, for the present the question was not being considered.[41] It cannot be denied that both Napier's hint to Head and Cass's veiled suggestion touched the principal fact which gave Americans an excuse if not a reason for attacking the treaty: Canada, the principal

40. Napier to Head, Feb. 28, 1859; G '59–'63 (P.A.C.). See also Napier to Malmesbury, Feb. 28, 1859; FO 5:711 (P.R.O.). Malmesbury was Secretary of State for Foreign Affairs in the short-lived Derby Ministry, 1858–59.
41. Napier to Malmesbury, Mar. 2, 1859; FO 5:712 (P.R.O.).

offender, had raised duties upon certain types of manufactured goods, and in the United States there were those who considered that this was a violation of the spirit if not the letter of the compact. It had apparently been assumed that the very low rates levied in the Provinces when Elgin got his treaty would remain unchanged and that Americans would continue to enjoy benefits which their proximity afforded. Canadians, on the other hand, were not convinced that the Americans had a real cause of complaint. Head informed the Colonial Secretary[42] that he had conferred privately with Alexander T. Galt, Minister of Finance in Canada, who prepared a memorandum for the consideration of the Executive Council, whereupon that body formulated a report in which they stated:

That no just ground exists for the Gov^t or Congress of the U. States to complain of the action of Canada in the arrangement of her duties on imports, because they are imposed on articles not included in the Treaty, and are equally levied on productions of the Mother Country as on those of the United States; while, in point of fact, similar articles produced in Canada, are, with scarcely an exception subject to higher duties under the American Tariff. That the question of the rate of duties & the articles upon which they may be imposed is however wholly within the control of the Canadian Legislature, & must be governed by considerations of what is necessary for the maintenance of public faith & best for the interests of the Canadian people. That when the American Gov^t are prepared to remove their duties on productions or manufactures common to both Countries, the Gov^t & Legislature of Canada will no doubt be ready to give the proposal their most favorable consideration, so long as they do not thereby impose differential duties in favor of the Foreigner to the prejudice of their own fellow subjects the manufacturers & producers of the Empire.

As can be imagined, the *tu quoque* argument made little impression upon Americans. In the middle of the century, as at almost all other times in the national history of the United States, the framing of tariff measures was looked upon as a purely domestic matter in which no foreigner, irrespective of how adversely he might be affected, could have anything to say. When the argument was turned around and applied against Americans, it merely demonstrated the general un-

42. Head to Lytton, Confidential, June 13, 1859; FO 115:204 (P.R.O.). The report of the committee of the Executive Council was enclosed with the dispatch.

reasonableness if not utter perversity of foreigners as a class. The Canadian maintained that so long as he did not touch directly the articles mentioned in the treaty, no complaint could logically be entertained; the American contended that he had entered upon the reciprocal arrangement upon the basis of *status quo* and any adverse change was a breach of good faith. Moreover, Americans steadfastly refused to consider a modification of their navigation laws, while the Canadians were convinced that mutual registration of vessels and reciprocal throwing open of the coasting trade would not only be witness of good neighborhood but would be economically advantageous to both sides. When Napier was succeeded in Washington by Lord Lyons, that gentleman was instructed that, on the basis of information received from his predecessor, it was not feasible to press for consideration on this point; he was, nevertheless, "to bear this matter in mind in case any favourable opportunity should unexpectedly offer itself for bringing it forward with any chance of success."[43]

The new British Minister was not long in finding out that Napier's estimate of the situation was sound: not only was there no possibility of extending reciprocity, but signs indicated that there might be difficulty in maintaining the treaty through its stated ten years. He had been in Washington only a short time when his attention was called to an article in the *Constitution*, generally recognized as an administration organ, wherein the writer seemed "to anticipate and to be disposed in some sort to justify the abrogation by the U. S. of that [Reciprocity] Treaty." Cass, to whom he pointed out the article, said that neither he nor the President had previously seen it and he was sure that it had been inserted "from inadvertence."[44] Even more uneasiness was roused by the fact that the Honorable Israel T. Hatch, a former Congressman, had been appointed by the President, as Lyons

43. Edmund Hammond (for Russell) to Lyons, Oct. 6, 1859; FO 115:206 (P.R.O.). The instruction enclosed a communication from the Committee of the Privy Council for Trade (Booth to Merivale, Aug. 10, 1859) recommending that H. M.'s Government take up with the United States this matter of registration and of the coasting trade. The Foreign Office warned both the Board of Trade and the Colonial Office (Hammond to Merivale, Sept. 30, 1859) that their information was that it was useless to press either of the issues at the moment.

44. Lyons to Head, Oct. 19, 1859; FO 5:716 (P.R.O.).

understood, to "examine into the effect of the Reciprocity Treaty upon the Revenue and upon the Trade between Canada and the United States."[45] Cass tried to reassure him by saying that Hatch was one of four or five inspectors the Treasury was accustomed to send out to examine into questions of revenue, the conduct of the customs house and marine hospitals, and to audit accounts of customs officials on the Canadian frontier. The inclusion of instructions to look into the matter of Canadian trade was of no particular significance. But when a report came from the British Consul at Detroit that it was understood that Hatch was to recommend "in the strongest possible terms" abrogation of the treaty, he could not fail to be concerned.[46]

Hatch fulfilled the worst of Lyons' suspicions when his report was submitted to Congress and published.[47] That it did not represent a universal opinion Lyons was convinced, for Senator Rice of Minnesota spoke to him about it and said that he, Rice, had spoken to the President on behalf of his constituents and expressed his "strong distrust" in the soundness and impartiality of Hatch's conclusions, and gave the Minister a copy of a resolution of the Minnesota legislature asking the President to negotiate for an extension of reciprocity. He told Lyons that he would have J. W. Taylor of St. Paul report on the same subject, for Taylor was well acquainted in Canada and was familiar with the significance of the trade between the American and British Northwest.[48] The Annual Report of the Secretary of the Treasury[49] demonstrated that what had been true earlier continued

45. Lyons to Head, Oct. 6, 1859; G '59–'63 (P.A.C.).

46. Lyons to Head, Dec. 16, 1859; G '59–'63 (P.A.C.). Donohoe, the Consul at Buffalo, stated that he had seen Hatch and had suggested to him a poll of the Lake cities to find out their views; he was convinced that, with the possible exception of Buffalo, Rochester, and Oswego, all the cities would be in favor of continuing the treaty. Donohoe to Lyons, Buffalo, Dec. 12, 1859, G '59–'63 (P.A.C.); Lyons to Russell, Dec. 20, 1859, FO 5:716 (P.R.O.).

47. Hatch Report, *House Misc. Docs.,* No. 96, 36th Cong., 1st Sess. Taylor's Report, referred to below, is in the same document.

48. Lyons to Russell, Jan. 21, 1860, with enclosure of Rice to Lyons, Private, same date; FO 5:738 (P.R.O.).

49. *Senate Ex. Docs.,* No. 3, 36th Cong., 1st Sess. *Senate Ex. Docs.,* No. 23, 36th Cong., 1st Sess., in a reply to a resolution of March 16, 1860, gave statistics of trade between the United States and British North America from 1851 to 1859 in a more detailed form than the Annual Report.

to obtain; while the depression following the financial crisis of 1857 had reduced the volume of both imports and exports, the fiscal year ending June 30, 1859, showed that the trade had about regained its former dimensions and that the value of exports to the Provinces amounted to $28,154,174 ($6,384,547 reëxported foreign goods, $21,769,627 domestic goods) while imports from the Provinces totaled $17,645,158. The Board of Trade of Chicago passed resolutions[50] to indicate how beneficially the treaty had worked for the Northwest, expressing their conviction that the move for abrogation was instigated by certain railroads which objected to water competition. Israel D. Andrews popped up again in a communication to both houses of Congress[51] to express his deep concern over movements threatening the abrogation of the treaty: trade had more than trebled in four years and would continue to grow; even if Canada had violated the spirit of the treaty by recent tariff legislation, no retaliatory legislation would be justified "which will produce no less evil in this country than Canada" as well as being manifestly unjust to New Brunswick, Nova Scotia, Prince Edward Island, and Newfoundland. Attacks on the treaty might be rampant, but there were champions willing to rise to its defense.

Throughout the summer of 1860 Lyons continued to watch with uneasiness evidences of agitation against the treaty, the more so because in the presidential campaign protection was a real although not the most prominent issue. He took some comfort, when he sent copies of Hatch's and Taylor's Reports to Sir Edmund Head, in noting that the Secretary of the Treasury, in transmitting them to Congress, took occasion to state that the views were those of the writers and that the Department had not given its sanction and approval.[52] In November he reported[53] that fear in Canada increased over defending the treaty against the efforts of the party in the United States bent on its abrogation, the Republican party, which was almost sure to win the election; his own hope was to get some manufactured articles added to the free list so that the present opposition would be enlisted in its support. This, however, was problematical, for he learned that Canadian fi-

50. *House Misc. Docs.*, No. 89, 36th Cong., 1st Sess.
51. *House Misc. Docs.*, No. 92, 36th Cong., 1st Sess.
52. July 10, 1860; G '59–'63 (P.A.C.).
53. Lyons to Russell, Nov. 5, 1860; FO 5:739 (P.R.O.).

nances would not stand the loss of revenue entailed by such a course. Nevertheless, the Canadian Government would do everything to allay suspicion and jealousy on the American side of the border and would endeavor to put duties on manufactured goods at the lowest possible point.

Well might the British North Americans and the British Minister fear the outcome of the election which brought into office a party imbued with old Whig ideas of high protection. Then, when secession took from Congress men who had stood in the way of translating these ideas into legislation, the road was clear for putting into effect policies which had been blocked for years by Southern Representatives and Senators. Nor was the dominant party slow to act, for one of the few significant pieces of legislation passed by that rump Congress was the Morrill Act, with its protective features sticking out at all points. Lyons had watched the course of the bill through both houses, careful, as he reported to the Foreign Office,[54] to keep from suggesting any "doubts or apprehensions" and drawing comfort from the fact that in the general tariff modification in 1857 there had been no question of making any change in trade relations with the Provinces. After the session had ended he sought an interview with Salmon P. Chase, Secretary of the Treasury, to ascertain just what effect the new law would have.[55] Chase told him "he supposed I had heard that alarm was now felt on the subject in Canada. He told me that he had received a communication about it from a gentleman in Canada, and that he had written to allay his correspondent's apprehensions, and had informed him that he might make any use of the letter except an official one." The Secretary did not construe the law as in any way interfering with the execution of the treaty, and when Lyons said that customs officials on the border might attempt to levy duties according to the new schedules, Chase had replied, "They will not be allowed to do so." He recommended that the matter be kept quiet and as little as possible said about it.[56]

For the moment, then, reciprocity was safe, even though any idea of

54. Confidential, Mar. 11, 1861; FO 5:761 (P.R.O.).
55. Lyons to Russell, Mar. 25, 1861; FO 5:761 (P.R.O.).
56. In the course of the discussion of the bill in the Senate Stephen A. Douglas had taken occasion to express his desire for establishing a real Zollverein which would embrace not only Canada and the United States but all of

the extension of its principles into a wider realm was out of the question. After the spring of 1861, however, reciprocity became intermingled with the issues of the Civil War and the attitude of the British everywhere, including the Canadas, toward that struggle, and was no more to be evaluated on its own merits. The experiment could no longer be carried on with reference only to economic factors.

Note. The decade of the Fifties cannot be left without some passing references to the attempt to secure men in the United States for service in the British Army during the Crimean War, and the demand for the recall of Crampton as a result of his activities. Strictly speaking, this whole matter does not enter into the story of Canadian-American relations, for it was looked upon as something between Great Britain and the United States, and there is little indication that popular opinion in the latter country considered the British Provinces as in any way specifically connected with it, at least so far as to affect their mutual relations. Sir Edmund Head, the Governor-General; Sir Gaspard Le Marchant, Lieutenant-Governor of Nova Scotia; and Joseph Howe, the Nova Scotia agent whom Crampton used, were, it is true, residents of British North America, and the first two were responsible officials there. But American indignation was directed against the British Minister and, back of him, the British Government. So far as others were connected with the affair they were looked upon as instruments of the British Government and not as Canadian or other Provincial officials. That the episode was, in popular estimation, linked with the whole range of British-American relations, which necessarily included Canadian relations, cannot be denied, but there can be no ground for believing that generally any responsible person on either side of the frontier thought that the unfortunate event had the slightest bearing on the relations between the United States and the British North American Provinces.

A discussion of the affair is to be found in Richard W. Van Alstyne, "John F. Crampton, Conspirator or Dupe?" *American Historical Review*, XLI, 492–502; H. B. Learned, "William Learned Marcy," in *American Secretaries of State and Their Diplomacy* (New York, 1928), VI, 145–294; and J. Bartlet Brebner, "Joseph Howe and the Crimean War Enlistment Controversy between Great Britain and the United States," *Canadian Historical Review*, XI, 300–327.

North America and the islands of the Caribbean. (Feb. 20, 1861; *Cong. Globe*, 36th Cong., 2d Sess., pp. 1051–1053.) Needless to say Douglas' ideas found little response in a congress bent on taking advantage of the absence of Southern Democrats.

CHAPTER VI

PROBLEMS OF THE CIVIL WAR

THE question of retaining the reciprocal trade agreement affecting British North America was in part a by-product of the whole Civil War situation. That struggle taught Americans, perhaps for the first time in their national existence, certainly for the first time since the Revolution, that the attitude of foreign countries was a vital factor in domestic affairs. What Europe thought and did, and especially what England's attitude was to be, was brought home in a peculiarly significant manner throughout the whole period; and where England was concerned, there British North America figured. It may be said at the outset that in view of intensified feeling in the North, of the disposition to judge of peoples by their attitude toward the two sections, of hypersensitiveness pervading popular ranks and official circles, the surprising thing is that more friction did not develop and more trying situations arise. It speaks volumes that, despite hot words and inflamed tempers, some untoward incident did not explode a mine to precipitate a contest which would have been to the last degree deplorable and disastrous. Half a century of dwelling in peace, if not always in harmony, had done something.

Foremost among potential bases of grievance on the part of the Union was that intangible thing known as public opinion. The North, as a whole, desired to be approved. Just as in earlier years the words of every European who traveled in and then wrote about America were scanned to see whether there was approval or disapproval of American institutions, customs, or manner of life, so during the Civil War the North looked for approbation and winced at every criticism. The average citizen was convinced that his cause was just and he wanted everybody to bolster his opinion by agreeing with him. *Mutatis mutandis*, the same thing may be said of the general run of Southerner, who, however, wanted in addition at least benevolent neutrality if not active assistance.

The first reaction of Canadian and generally of British North American public opinion to secession and the impending struggle was favorable to the North. It seemed to presage an end of slavery, an institution which found scant sympathy north of the boundary over which, during the Fifties after the new Fugitive Slave act went into operation, many a runaway negro had fled, assisted by abolitionists in the United States and, if not exactly welcomed, at least tolerated in Canada. On the whole, moreover, there was deprecation of an attempt to break up the Union. The sentiment expressed by the legislature of Prince Edward Island[1] found an echo generally throughout the Provinces:

The House of Assembly of Prince Edward Island now in session having learned with deep sorrow and regret that actual hostilities have commenced between the northern and southern Sections of the United States of America with whose people we are bound by the ties of common brotherhood—most sincerely expresses its fervent hope that peace with all its attendant blessings may speedily be restored to that country.

Even the truculent and generally Anglophobe New York *Herald*,[2] commenting on the news that 750 British subjects in New York City had volunteered for military service, remarked: "The sympathy which is felt both in England and Canada for this movement is very strong, and may be accepted as an index of the popular feeling throughout the British dominions in favor of the Union and its preservation at all hazards." The Toronto *Globe*[3] stated after news of the first Battle of Bull Run had been received:

We have no doubt that the effect of this battle will be greatly prolonged by the result of this first great event. Looking at the effect of the contest on Canada, we regret such a denouement. Trade languishes and will languish while the war lasts. Every Canadian who desires to see his country prosperous should pray for the speedy success of the Northern arms and the prompt suppression of the slave power.

This first rather generally voiced support of the North soon began to be tempered. When Lincoln, and Congress as well, let it be understood that the North was fighting not to put an end to slavery but to preserve the Union, the ardor of anti-slavery men in the Provinces was damped as effectively as was that of abolitionists of the United States;

1. Apr. 27, 1861; FO 5:764 (P.R.O.).
2. May 12, 1861.
3. July 23, 1861, reprinted in New York *Herald,* July 27.

it was one thing to fight to end an anachronistic institution, quite another to coerce reluctant people into a political association they apparently detested. Nor could Canadians forget the annexation bogey, and it could have been no comfort to them to see one of the most ardent of Northern expansionists heading the Department of State, a man whose blustering foreign policy struck Lord Lyons as one of the most dangerous features of the international situation. "Canada is," he wrote to Head, "as you know, looked upon as our weak point." To Russell he wrote:

In the case of England I am inclined to think that this Government believes that apprehensions for Canada will induce us to avoid a contest. They undoubtedly look upon Canada as our weak point. Mr. Seward, who is no doubt as ignorant of the feeling in the British North American Provinces, as he has proved to be of that of the feeling in the Southern parts of this Country, very probably supposed that there is a strong American feeling in Canada. He publickly advocated, during the Presidential Canvass, the annexation of Canada as a compensation for any loss, which might be occasioned by the disaffection of the South.[4]

But to this persistent fear that the United States might sometime attempt to make good the threats often uttered by irresponsible persons and not entirely absent from the words of those whose positions should have made them more reticent, were added other factors to change the sentiment in the Provinces. Old animosities of 1776 and especially of 1812, when Canada, quite removed from the alleged causes of the war, was made to suffer, were revived, and all the heartburnings of a former day lived over again. Moreover, among Conservatives and some who called themselves Liberals there was profound skepticism about the spirit of democracy which they thought was running wild in the United States; equalitarianism, bad manners, corruption in public life—all those things which British writers and sophisticated Provincials were wont to deprecate in the States and which they almost invariably associated with democracy were cited in

4. Lyons to Russell, Confidential, May 20, 1861; FO 5:764 (P.R.O.). Practically the same words were written to Sir Edmund Head a couple of days later. Lord Newton, *Lord Lyons: A Record of British Diplomacy* (London, 1913), I, 40. If Lyons could have seen that famous memorandum resurrected years after by Nicolay and Hay, he would have been doubly disturbed.

contrast to what they were pleased to call the more urbane institutions of a settled society like England's or Canada's.[5]

Recognition of belligerency of the Confederacy by England in May loosed a flood of adverse criticism in the North, and this tide embraced the British Provinces where, by the late summer of 1861, most of the organs of the Conservative party followed the tone of the London *Times* and other English newspapers. When the capture of the Confederate envoys, James Mason and John Slidell, from the British steamer *Trent* stimulated anew Northern animosity and there was talk of war in which the invasion of Canada figured prominently, newspapers on each side of the line indulged in editorials which were calculated to sting. In all of this James Gordon Bennett's New York *Herald* took a leading part, carrying on its policy of Anglophobia with particular reference to Canada. In one of his milder pronouncements the New York editor thus admonished the northern neighbors:[6]

We perceive that the Canadian press still continues to make unnecessary bluster about the arrest of Mason and Slidell. The fact is that most of the Canadian journals are directly hostile to the government of the United States in this struggle against rebellion, and they make the capture of the rebel envoys a pretext for showering their abuse upon the federal government, and making as much bad blood out of the matter as possible. They resemble a pack of dogs yelping and barking and making all the noise they can at the sight of a stranger, till they are silenced by a word from their master.

Newspapers in the United States in general forebore to pay much attention to Canada, except when some particular incident called forth comment. In Congress, Canadian questions did not receive much attention until toward the end of the struggle. In Canada, too, there was something of a reversal of opinion. While in certain of the large cities, particularly Montreal and Toronto, majority sentiment was for the South throughout the period, the press of the country in general was swinging back in some degree to pro-Northernism.[7] Never-

5. "In those days Conservatives, even Liberal-Conservatives, still retained something of conservatism; they were prone to doubt the wisdom of a wide suffrage and the unchecked play of the elective principle." O. D. Skelton, *Life and Times of Sir Alexander Tilloch Galt,* p. 311.

6. Nov. 25, 1861.   7. Skelton, *Galt,* pp. 320–321.

theless, as late as May, 1863, the American Consul at Quebec was reporting his regret at having to say:[8]

Many painful manifestations are frequently shown of an unkindness towards our government that seems difficult to reconcile with the protestations of attachment made by some, as an evidence of the state of feeling existing here with a portion and I fear a very large portion of the rulers of this Province now assembled in Parliament I beg leave to relate a circumstance which occurred on the P. M. of the 6th inst. A telegram was received here, that the Army of the Potomac under Maj. Gen. Hooker had been defeated; the despatch was published in slip form with the usual sensational headings. . . . One of the slips was taken into the Chamber of the lower branch of Parliament by a member [where it was read and received with applause in which a member of the late ministry joined].

Reporting a debate on the militia bill, on May 21, Consul Ogden described the opposition as distinctly favorable to the Confederacy, while the Government maintained that Canada was governed by its people and not by Downing Street or Lombard Street and asserted that a standing army would be viewed by the United States as a standing menace.

Specific causes of irritation on the Canadian side, more or less persistent, included recruiting of young men for the Northern armies by means open, in many cases, to criticism. Some Canadians left home to volunteer their services to the Union[9] and while this might raise protest it could not make international complications. When the zeal of American officers went so far as to cause the sending of military police into Canada to take back deserters, there was trouble with local authorities and considerable diplomatic stirring.[10] But the real grievance

8. Charles S. Ogden to Seward, May 9, 1863; Consular Letters: Quebec, Vol. I (D.S.).

9. New York *Herald,* May 14, 1861. Lt. Col. Rankin, an officer of the Canadian Provincial Militia, wished to get a leave of absence in order to raise a regiment of Lancers for service in the Army of the United States. Rankin, needless to say, did not have his request granted. Considerable correspondence between Head, Lyons, the Foreign and Colonial Offices was exchanged on the matter in October, 1861. FO 5:772, 115:247 (P.R.O.); G 231 (P.A.C.). Passing references to recruitment of British subjects are found in F. H. Shannon, *The Organization and Administration of the Union Army, 1861–1865* (Cleveland, 1928), II, 71 ff.

10. Head to Lyons, Oct. 1, Billings to McEwen, Oct. 2, 1861; FO 5:772

grew out of efforts to entice into the armies of the North any likely young men who could be induced to come across the border. The practice became especially prevalent in 1863 and 1864, when the Union had been obliged to have recourse to the draft, when bounties bred a class of brokers who made it their business to get substitutes for Americans who had money enough to buy their way out. It was a notorious fact that crimps, official and otherwise, lay in wait for newly arrived immigrants, who frequently found themselves, how they knew not, on the way to battle field or training camp when they had been expecting to reach the farm lands of Illinois or Wisconsin. It was not strange then that the young manhood of Canada and the Maritimes was looked at with a covetous eye. The British Consul at Boston reported several instances where his official assistance was sought to facilitate enlistment of British subjects, although ostensibly the purpose was something else. The most barefaced approach was when he was interviewed by a man who wanted definite information as to what liability he would incur if he tried to raise recruits for the Northern army along the Canadian border.[11]

He was evidently a very shrewd specimen of the Yankees & apparently largely supplied with Funds which he exhibited to me. He made no disguise as to his intentions or purposes, and only wanted to know how far the recruiting law of Canada would touch him and his partners. On my telling him that it was illegal and that he would have to bear the consequences, he said that "he supposed it was no harm to invite men over the boundary line to have a good time at a farm on this side of it, and that there they w^d be free to do as they pleased." He also said "He presumed there was no hindrance to his hiring Canadians for farm service and that they need not come over the line to effect that bargain."

From the general conversation of this amiable gentleman, Consul Lousada got the impression that there was "an organization on some large scale for enlisting British subjects in Canada," and experience had taught him that "those who are foolish enough to be once enticed over the line on any such pretext will find it pretty hard work to get back again, out of the clutches of those recruiting gentry."

(P.R.O.). Backers to Townshend, Oct. 21, Seward to Lyons, Oct. 24, 1861; FO 5:773 (P.R.O.).
    11. F. Lousada to Lyons, Dec. 5, 1863; FO 5:899 (P.R.O.).

The very day Lousada had his interview with the "shrewd Yankee" he received a communication inquiring about the feasibility of getting certificates of citizenship for certain Welshmen whom a quarry master in Vermont wished to employ, alleging that these men would come if they were assured they would not be forced into military service. The skeptical Consul declined to give such certificates on two grounds:[12]

Firstly that altho' there was no law holding aliens to military service in the U. S. yet practically such service was obtained every day by means almost amounting to compulsion and redress was so difficult as to be almost unobtainable.

2^{ndly} I was perfectly aware of the use intended to be made of my certificate and that "Wales" meant the "Canada Borders." The applicant denied this but admitted that such use *might* be made of the document.

A few months later Lousada was called upon by some persons who alleged they wished to hire three hundred laborers in Canada and Nova Scotia to "work at some patent brick works here [Boston]" and wanted a certificate from the Consul to show that it was a bona fide transaction. "I refused to give any such document, and did not disguise from them that it was clear to me this was one of the schemes for recruiting the United States Army and that I should consider myself culpable if . . . I aided in deluding the poor men they were going to employ in their alleged patent brick making."[13]

These schemes to get Canadians into the United States reported by the Consul at Boston were samples of what the Legation at Washington was receiving from other consulates and from private sources of information pretty constantly through the latter part of 1863 and in 1864. At the same time there were coming in numerous complaints from British subjects who sought the aid of their government to get out of military service. "Very little success, however, attends my endeavors to obtain redress for these wrongs," Lyons reported to the Governor-General.[14]

My remonstrances are courteously acknowledged by the Secretary of State, and forwarded by him to the Secretary of War, the Secretary of

12. Memorandum to Lord Lyons, Dec. 5, 1863; G 231 (P.A.C.).
13. Lousada to Lyons, Apr. 5, 1864; G 232 (P.A.C.).
14. Lyons to Monck, Aug. 8, 1864; G 233 (P.A.C.). See also Burnley to

War orders an investigation, or rather calls upon the recruiting officers for a Report. The Recruiting officers commonly report that they never enlist any one except in the most lawful and scrupulous manner that in the particular case referred to them, the allegations of the complaint are utterly false and this enlistment was in all respects lawful and correct. I endeavor to obtain further evidence, but it is very seldom that any can be obtained, except that of the recruit himself and the recruiting officers. From the crimps and agents of course no testimony can be obtained in proof of their own iniquities and the result commonly is that after a controversial correspondence with me of more or less length the United States Government acts upon the report of its own officers and retains the recruit.

Lyons did not pretend that all or perhaps even the greater part of the complaints were well founded: some men enlisted voluntarily, some were not British subjects, some enlisted to get the bounty through collusion with recruiting agents; "but that there is in full activity a system of enticing Her Majesty's subjects to come from Canada to enlist, and even of kidnapping them and carrying them across the frontier, can hardly be doubted."[15]

At the beginning of the war considerable uneasiness was occasioned in Canada by the presence of persons who were presumed to be Union agents, sent more or less secretly for some undisclosed purpose. One of these, Lyons heard, was George Ashmun, who had nominated Lincoln at the Chicago Convention. If secrecy was desired, it was a vain hope, for the New York *Herald* on April 17 came out with a paragraph saying that it was supposed Ashmun was sent to Canada as a confidential agent to explain the political situation in the United States. When the British Minister drew Seward's attention to the statement the latter "betrayed a good deal of confusion." Ashmun turned up in Canada, paid a visit to Sir Edmund Head and, in the presence of Cartier and Vankoughnet, started to tell about the "true

Seward, Sept. 16; Seward to Burnley, Sept. 19; Lyons to Seward, Nov. 16, 1864; *Diplomatic Correspondence, 1864–65,* Part II, pp. 708, 712, 777–778. *Diplomatic Correspondence* was the title given, from 1861 to 1868, to the series afterwards called *Foreign Relations*.

15. John A. Macdonald, the Canadian Premier, had the same opinion: to J. Moody, Mar. 27, 1865; Macdonald Papers: Letterbooks, VIII, 12–14 (P.A.C.).

position" of the United States, whereupon the Governor-General said he had no authority to recognize him or any other agent. Ashmun then denied that he was an accredited agent but said he thought it might do some good to present the real facts, especially as it was understood that Southern agents were in Canada buying arms. Forwarding Head's account of the interview, Lyons wrote: "This sort of proceeding is not inconsistent with Mr. Seward's individual character; but it is difficult to conceive what he can have hoped to effect by it in the present instance." Russell's instruction which crossed this dispatch directed Lyons to say to Seward that the sending of an agent without previous notice had created an "unfavorable impression" on Her Majesty's Government. Later, in June, Seward on his own initiative introduced the matter to say that the object of Ashmun's mission was "to ascertain the feeling in Canada with regard to fitting out Privateers on the St. Lawrence," and as soon as Lyons had spoken to him on the subject Ashmun had been recalled. This little venture into quasi-diplomacy was not repeated.[16]

All kinds of rumors were going about regarding the designs of the United States, or at least of American citizens, upon Canada. One of the wildest was that concocted by one George Manning, who, in a statement prepared to warn Canadian authorities, outlined a dastardly plot:

I was waiting on Friday Evening to consult D^r —— when an earnest discussion in the adjoining room attracted my attention. In the course of the conversation it was proposed to buy several newspapers in Canada East for the purpose of agitating a junction of that Province to the United States. This proceeding was at the instigation of Mr W. Seward who it was said would pay all the expenses out of the United States Secret Service fund. . . . British subjects alone were to be the active operators in Canada, and no American was to appear publicly amongst the annexationists. It was stated that Mr Hamilton Merritt was to be the Territorial Governor, and Mr Woodruffe Secretary of State. Mr Sinclair a stout man with a red face a native of Scotland (by his accent) took a prominent part in the discussion, as did a young man the son of Mr W. Seward. In the

16. Lyons to Head, Confidential, Apr. 19; Lyons to Russell, Apr. 22; Head to Lyons, May 3; Lyons to Russell, May 11, 1861; FO 5:762 (P.R.O.). Russell to Lyons, May 16; FO 115:241 (P.R.O.). Lyons to Russell, June 17, 1861; FO 5:766 (P.R.O.).

course of the conference a letter was read from a person named Moses Perley of Sᵗ Johns New Brunswick, in which he said that the same course as that proposed in Canada could be pursued there; and referred the person to whom he wrote to Mʳ Andrews the former American Consul in British North America.

When the Governor-General got this strange yarn he passed it on to Lord Lyons, at the same time saying he did not believe one word of it, because

in 1856 (I think) this same Mʳ Manning called on me in Toronto and told me privately *a story of exactly the same kind*. The accidental discovery *then* took place in a Hotel at Washington where he was calling, not on a doctor, but on a Lady. Seward was, as now, the Arch-conspirator. Hamilton Merritt, and Perley were both named. What gave probability to the matter then was that Mʳ Manning in his selection of names in Canada, certainly named those who were more or less likely to take part in such a plan. . . .

It is utterly incredible that the same man should have two opportunities of detecting by fortunate accident Mʳ Seward's plots against Canada. In 1856 (if that was the year) this was told me immediately after Seward made his violent Anti-British speech.

Head wished the British Minister to find out what could be learned of this Manning.[17]

The British Provinces were not, of course, directly affected by actual hostilities between the belligerents; the battle fields were far from the international frontier. Operations upon the high seas, however, occasionally caused some perturbation. Naturally most shipping from the Maritimes into the Gulf of Mexico or to the West Indies was suspect, sometimes with cause, and complaints found their way eventually to Washington and to London about the unceremonious treatment dealt out by Federal war vessels.[18] Since some

17. Statement of Mr. Manning, New York, June 1, 1861; FO 5:765 (P.R.O.). Head to Lyons, June 9, 1861; FO 5:766 (P.R.O.). Consul Archibald in New York (to Lyons, June 1, 4; FO 5:765 [P.R.O.]) learned he claimed to be a British subject, one time a lieutenant in the navy; he served with the Neapolitans and claimed to have accompanied Scott to Vera Cruz.

18. Russell to Stuart, Aug. 14, 1862, enclosing a complaint from Murphy & Twining of Halifax, whose brigantine *Annette* had been examined by the offi-

blockade runners were built in Provincial ports and departed thence, it was not surprising that a close watch upon them was maintained wherever possible.[19] More serious, in the eyes of Provincial officials, was the custom of Federal vessels of ignoring municipal regulations in efforts to stop trade with the enemy. Toward the close of the war this was apparently more prevalent than in the earlier days. The Lieutenant-Governor of Nova Scotia asked the British Minister to make representations to the American Government regarding the practice of Federal cruisers' anchoring "in the immediate vicinity of the Port of Halifax with a view apparently to chasing or visiting vessels leaving that port," and to request that they be ordered to anchor "in the appointed place, or [proceed] forthwith to sea without communicating with the shore." When this complaint was brought to the attention of Gideon Welles, Secretary of the Navy, he explained the apparent infraction of regulations by stating that probably the offending vessels had left a home port before information had been received about these rules and promised that word would be got to them as soon as possible.[20]

It was also in the latter part of the war that British subjects in the Provinces were especially affected by an executive order, issued December 17, 1864,[21] stating that no traveler, excepting immigrants entering an American port by sea, might come into the United States without a passport, a "regulation intended to apply especially to persons proposing to come to the United States from the neighboring British Provinces." The recent St. Albans raid[22] had been the immediate reason for the issuance of this order. The regulation itself and the method of its enforcement almost immediately raised a howl of protest in the Provinces and also in some of the States. On a border crisscrossed by highways and railroads, where every day many indi-

cers of the *Rhode Island* in the Gulf of Florida, an example of what the firm alleged was happening frequently. FO 115:293 (P.R.O.).

19. New York *Herald,* Sept. 12, 1863, carried a Toronto item to the effect that it was understood a couple of steamers were building at Quebec to run the Southern blockade.

20. Macdonald to Lyons, Sept. 30; Burnley to Seward, Oct. 1; Seward to Lyons, Oct. 4; Welles to Seward, Oct. 1, 1864; *Diplomatic Correspondence, 1864–65,* Part II, pp. 717, 738–739. FO 5:962 (P.R.O.).

21. Richardson, *Messages and Papers,* VI, 274.

22. For the raids and other demonstrations see Chapter VII.

viduals went to and fro from one country to the other, such a restriction was bound to cause great inconvenience and yet prove ineffective in stopping raids.[23] Premier Macdonald believed that, while it would not do for Canada to apply directly for its rescinding, there was "no reason why individuals or incorporated companies like Railways should not join in their exertions with Americans from the Western Frontier to procure its withdrawal."[24] There was no question that the regulation caused loss to Canada, but it would not do for the Government to go "on its knees to the U. S. Government" to secure its revocation.[25] The Provincial government of New Brunswick, however, was less devious in its policy; through the Lieutenant-Governor direct appeal was made to the Legation in Washington to try to bring about its recall. Chargé Burnley did his best with the Department of State but found Seward "invariably obdurate on this point until there was some show of justice towards this side by the Canadians."[26] When, however, the Canadian Parliament passed an Alien Bill and an Indemnity Bill the order was withdrawn as to that Province, but maintained for the others. Ending of hostilities, of course, brought a removal of the order in its entirety, so the Maritimes did not have to suffer long under its inconveniences.

If the Provinces had their grievances against the United States, the latter's people and Government were doubly sure that no one could doubt where the true causes of irritation lay. Perhaps the deepest sense of being wronged came from allowing Confederates and Confederate sympathizers to remain in Canada and to some extent in the Maritimes. Early in the struggle, but after it became clear that the North was to have no easy time in imposing its will, there appeared many expressions of Northern exasperation. Canada, it was believed, welcomed the expatriated Rebels, who increased in number as time went on. They "thronged" St. Catherine's and "toadied to all the

23. New York *Herald,* Dec. 20, 1864.

24. To Swinyard, Dec. 23, 1864; Macdonald Papers: Letterbooks, VII, 105–106 (P.A.C.).

25. To Swinyard, Jan. 1, 1865; Macdonald Papers: Letterbooks, VII, 174–175. On January 16 the New York *Herald* carried a number of excerpts from Canadian papers complaining about the passport order.

26. Burnley to Russell, Mar. 13, 1865; FO 5: 1016 (P.R.O.).

round and oily men and women at Toronto and Montreal."[27] Vallandigham's hastened departure from Ohio in 1863 and his eventual settling in Niagara Falls and then Windsor, where he carried on his gubernatorial campaign from a foreign land, seemed to be rubbing in what was looked upon as an abuse of asylum.[28] Then, when some of these expatriates, voluntary and otherwise, consorted together and hatched up plans to aid the South, the North was sure that Canada's neutrality laws were either deficient or laxly enforced. It would have been gratifying if the Provinces had refused absolutely to admit Southerners and their friends but the least that should be done, it was felt, was to render them harmless. "Mr Seward," wrote Lyons confidentially to Lord Russell,[29] "has spoken to me more than once during the last few days of the alarm with which the use recently made by the enemies of the United States of the neighbouring British Territory had inspired him. He has said that he should entertain the most serious doubts of the possibility of maintaining cordial relations if the public mind should be excited by a recurrence of such events" as the Johnson's Island affair or the *Chesapeake* episode. "It would . . . be at all events scarcely possible to prevent some demonstration of resentment against the Provinces themselves."

Many of these refugees in the Provinces were accredited agents of the Confederacy; some went there to secure munitions and supplies, others to influence public opinion. All of them talked freely and most of them had no trouble in finding sympathetic hearers even if they did not receive a great deal of tangible aid. It is true that the North also, in the early part of the war, tried to buy arms in Canada and Nova Scotia, but that was a different matter. Private citizens and even State governments attempted to eke out meager supplies of armament at the outbreak of the Rebellion, not from manufacturers, of whom there were few in the Provinces, but from Provincial governments or from local units. When it was found that the Provincial authorities were

27. New York *Herald,* June 1, 1863.

28. J. L. Vallandigham, *Life of Clement L. Vallandigham* (Baltimore, 1872), pp. 317 ff.

29. Dec. 24, 1863; FO 5:900 (P.R.O.). See *Official Records of the Union and Confederate Navies in the War of the Rebellion* (Washington, 1894–1922), 2d ser., III, 174, 1234–1239, 1103–1188 *passim* for activities of Thompson, Holcombe, *et al.*

not permitted under the law to sell or loan such things, there was a degree of resentment exhibited.[30]

Although Northern feeling about the Provinces was based upon a conviction that they, like England, were not in harmony with the Northern point of view and harbored altogether too tender sentiments toward the South, it was a series of actual hostile demonstrations launched upon the Union from Canadian soil that formed the basis of the exasperation[31] and caused most of the alarms which rose and subsided throughout the four years, and led to much agitation about defense on both sides of the line; and the agitation in turn brought about some definite steps in that direction. That some alarm about the safety of British possessions might have been experienced at the very outbreak of the struggle is understandable. Nevertheless, for the greater part of 1861 there was much more talk of increasing Canadian defenses than there was specific augmentation of military personnel and fortification. Rumors filled the air of regiments from India, of transfer of troops from Halifax to Quebec or Montreal, of spending large sums on strengthening the fortifications of Quebec, of organizing volunteer companies of militia on a large scale, of fortifying various points along the St. Lawrence and on the Great Lakes. "Montreal, Logan's Farm, Hochelaga, and the Island of St. Helena are crowded with troops, and it is rumored in Canada that the Great Eastern will return with additional forces for Quebec."[32] It was, however, the *Trent* affair that made all these unverified stories begin to have substance. War spirit in the United States was matched by truculence in England, and Canada would be the battle ground if trouble did come. Thurlow Weed, writing from London,[33] said that England expected and anticipated war and was making "immense preparations."

There is, with but few individual exceptions, but one voice here. All are for war, first on account of the Honor of the Flag, and next because they

30. Some correspondence passed between the British Legation and Canada on this matter. FO 5:763, 765 (P.R.O.).

31. See Chapter VII.

32. New York *Herald,* Aug. 23, 1861. American newspapers, among which the *Herald* was by no means the most reticent, snatched up these rumors and gave them currency.

33. To Zachariah Chandler, Dec. 7, 1861; Chandler Papers (L.C.). The letter appears to be dated 1871, but the context shows it was written in 1861.

think we want to quarrel with them. All that we have said [and] done in sympathizing with Rebellion in Ireland, Canada, &c. and in sending home their militia during the Crimean War, is remembered now.

This war spirit which Weed found in England was reflected in Canada, but there it was mingled with alarm because of the vulnerable situation of that Province.[34] Everybody was talking war and defense. Even Lord Lyons, who preserved throughout his trying mission in Washington an equable and fair-minded attitude, believed the opportunity should be used to do something for Canada.[35] Here and there could be found a calm estimate of the situation, sometimes couched in ironical terms. The Hamilton *Times*, for example, sized up the situation in these words:[36]

Every place must be fortified and that immediately, and where there is no place to fortify one must be made. Chatham wants to know if it is not to have a wall built around the clearing; Caledonia insists on being put in a complete state of defence, lest the Yankees should run up Grand River on skates during the winter, or come down like grasshoppers on rail. Simcoe goes in for as many Armstrong guns as can be spared in all other parts of the Queen's Dominions; Port Dover will not be satisfied with anything short of a belt of forts all along Long Point; while Dundas is about to ask for the erection of heavy batteries at no less than fifty places, the chief of which, however, is to be on Pic-nic Point, to command the pass of Smoky Hollow, Ancaster Heights, and "the Gorge" below! The other fifty batteries are to be so placed that no hostile gunboat dare show her prow in Coot's Paradise, nor attempt to reach the harbor at the "head of navigation." All the works are to be constructed by resident engineers, mounted by cannon of home manufacture, manned by local fire companies, and officered by militia genii "to the manor born." These, however, are only a few of the things demanded by the mania of to-day . . . and if every

34. On December 24, 1861, the New York *Herald* carried four columns of quotations from Provincial papers all sounding the same note. They included the *Globe* and *Leader* of Toronto, the Barrie *Spirit*, Collingwood *Enterprise*, Montreal *Gazette*, London *Free Press*, and Kingston *Whig*. All through December and later, similar excerpts were printed.

35. From a dispatch to Russell, Dec. 27, 1861. Newton, *Lord Lyons*, I, 72. See Stacey, *Canada and the British Army, 1846–1871*, chaps. vi and vii, for a more detailed account of Canada's preparations.

36. Reprinted in New York *Herald*, Dec. 13, 1861.

house in the Province be not immediately fortified, the Palmerston Cabinet had better look out for a vote of want of confidence from Canada.

So far as newspapers were concerned each side egged on the other. In the United States, Canadian talk of defense was interpreted as animosity. The Provincials hoped that war would come, ran comments in the more unrestrained publications; they entertained the "bitterest rancor and enmity" toward the Union; there were even paragraphs in Ministerial papers advocating seizure of Maine so that Portland could be obtained; although the United States would never seek territory at the expense of a neighbor, the probable result of a war would be the annexation of everything right up to Hudson Bay.[37] While no such warlike preparations were made in the Provinces as some people demanded or as the more lurid press of the United States predicted and sometimes asserted, there was, nevertheless, some augmentation of forces from England, and the Provincial governments took steps to put their militia on a better footing. All that was done, however, was not on a scale calculated to occasion much perturbation in the American Union, although the possibility that there might come a day of trouble was never quite out of the minds either of the Provincials or the British Government. Occasional references appeared in the correspondence from time to time and were not wholly absent from the newspapers. In May, 1864, T. L. Gallway, Lieutenant Colonel in the Royal Engineers, prepared in response to a request from Lord Lyons a fairly detailed report on "the probable operations of the forces of the United States in case of war with England."[38] After the St. Albans raid and the ill-considered stand taken by General Dix, aggravated by wild talk which ran through the North, Canada increased her militia in service on the border, quite as much, however, to prevent further untoward happenings as to guard against possible incursions from across the line.

All the agitation about border defense was not confined to the Canadians. The *Trent* episode was a major factor in turning American thoughts to the frontier. Lincoln, in his first Annual Message,[39] speak-

37. New York *Herald,* Feb. 3, 1862. This was the purport of a long communication from its Quebec correspondent.
38. Gallway to Lyons, May 27, 1864; FO 5:954 (P.R.O.).
39. Richardson, *Messages and Papers,* VI, 46.

ing of defense generally, added: "I also in the same connection ask the attention of Congress to our great lakes and rivers. It is believed that some fortifications and depots of arms and munitions, with harbor and navigation improvements, all at well selected points upon these, would be of great importance to the national defense and preservation." For the Select Committee in the House of Representatives, to which this portion of the Message was referred, Arnold, reporting on February 12, 1862, spoke of the good feeling which had prevailed since the War of 1812 and how for nearly half a century the "few and imperfect" fortifications along the border had been allowed to fall into decay.

We had come to regard it as scarcely within the range of possibility that we should go to war with our neighbor over the line. This very neglect of the means of defense recent events have indicated has increased the danger and liability of war; so that it seems that the best security for peace is to be prepared for war. The defense of the great lakes and rivers, therefore, is suggested by the President to the consideration of Congress as a measure likely to promote peaceful relations between the two nations.

The body of the report contained an elaborate scheme embracing (1) a list of places to be fortified or strengthened all along the border; (2) a proposition to establish a national foundry and naval depots on the upper lakes; and (3) enlargement of the Illinois-Michigan Canal for military use and deepening of the channel across the St. Clair Flats.[40] This and other documents received a little attention in Congress, but fading of the immediate danger created by the capture of Mason and Slidell, together with more pressing exigencies of the struggle with the Confederates, drove northern border issues into the background.

A year later, when the *Alabama* was upon the high seas and when other commerce raiders were believed to be building in England and when once more people were contemplating the possibility of war with England, another Committee, that on Naval Affairs,[41] took up the

40. *House Reports,* No. 23, 37th Cong., 2d Sess. Arnold brought in a bill, but beyond reference to the Committee of the Whole nothing was done with it. *Cong. Globe,* 37th Cong., 2d Sess., pp. 1966, 2819.

41. *House Reports,* No. 4, 37th Cong., 3d Sess. When in 1862 an armed vessel, ordered by and built under the direction of a Confederate agent in the Laird

question of how war vessels could most easily be put upon the Great Lakes where, it was assumed by their report, the principal theater of hostilities would be if war came. The committee had no serious apprehension that Great Britain could send into the lakes any considerable force of gunboats, although vessels could be built on the north shore and those already used in commerce could be armed. After deliberate consideration they came to the conclusion that the best method of meeting this possible menace was to follow the same course; namely, build boats at the lake ports, for the proposal to utilize the Illinois-Michigan Canal in the West, and the Erie Canal in the East was not practicable; the locks were too small and their walls too weak to handle gunboats, and the cost of enlargement would be too great. The committee assumed that ample warning would be had of activity in Canadian ports; until then this "watchful waiting" would not bring about any violation of the Rush-Bagot Agreement of 1817.[42]

The question of more adequate canals as a part of American frontier defense was one which occupied a good deal of Congress' time throughout the war but more especially from 1863 to the end. It had an Eastern and a Western phase. In the East the matter was complicated because there were two rival schemes; one was to enlarge the Erie Canal to a size suitable to accommodate gunboats, and the other proposed to duplicate the Welland Canal by constructing one around the American side of Niagara Falls. In the West the principal proposal was that of enlarging the Illinois-Michigan Canal to provide

shipyards on the Mersey, started its career as the cruiser *Alabama,* opinion in the Union was settled that British neutrality laws were insufficient and British attitude was hostile. From this time to the conclusion of the Treaty of Washington in 1871, the *"Alabama* Claims"—and the term included all the claims arising out of the depredations of all the Rebel cruisers—rankled in Northern minds, and, in a sense, came to typify the resentment of Northerners toward Great Britain. While there are several references to the *Alabama* Claims in the pages which follow, their story lies outside the scope of this study except as it impinges occasionally on Canadian-American relations.

42. This same Congress had a set of resolutions from the legislature of Maine demanding immediate steps for the protection of the Northeast frontier. *House Misc. Docs.,* No. 17. The following legislature demanded a military railroad from Bangor to the frontier as well as general protection of the frontier. *House Misc. Docs.,* No. 75, 38th Cong., 1st Sess. A select committee returned a report (*House Reports,* No. 119) backing up the Maine contentions.

direct connection between the Mississippi and Lake Michigan; this was rivaled, but only feebly, by the Fox-Wisconsin route. A combination of the Eastern and Western proposals would, it was alleged, provide an all-American internal waterway from the Mississippi Valley to the Atlantic Ocean. Much was made of the idea on nationalistic grounds; it was a reproach to Americans to have to depend on foreign waterways and it was dangerous because war or something else might close this route. It is to be suspected that something more than notions of national defense influenced the advocates of an all-American waterway, for it is noticeable that the principal support of rival schemes and even of complementary plans came from representatives of those states which would most directly benefit. W. S. Holman of Indiana thought so, to judge by some remarks made on the Report of the Committee on Naval Affairs.[43]

The Thirty-eighth Congress (1863–65) continued the same discussion with the same proponents. This time when the bill for the Illinois-Michigan Ship Canal came to a vote it was passed by the House, 77 to 68,[44] but it died with that Congress in the Senate. When the next Congress met the war was over, and while there were still rumblings of these measures no very serious attention was paid to the Illinois-Michigan scheme. The Niagara proposition continued to be agitated for several years, always with emphasis on nationalistic grounds. Nevertheless, one gathers that even during the war, and certainly after it, there were other factors which operated, chiefly desire for competition between railroads and waterways.

The Civil War could not fail to bring into question the working of the Rush-Bagot Agreement of 1817 respecting limitation of armaments on the Great Lakes.[45] As early as August, 1861, inquiries were

43. Feb. 6, 1863; *Cong. Globe,* 37th Cong., 3d Sess., p. 772. Porter of Indiana (*ibid.,* p. 813), virtually charged the supporters of the Illinois-Michigan and of the Erie Canal enlargement of log-rolling, for while at the last session each was trying to jockey the other out of position, now they seemed to be working in closest harmony.

44. Feb. 2, 1865; *Cong. Globe,* 38th Cong., 2d Sess., pp. 567–570.

45. Back in 1857 and 1858 there had been some correspondence between the American and British Governments over the use of the *Michigan,* a vessel of 582 tons burden armed with one heavy gun. Explanations showing that this vessel was used to aid shipping on the lakes satisfied both the Canadian and

made into alleged violation of the agreement on the part of the American Government but explanations of Secretary Seward that there had been no change from the situation existing before the outbreak of hostilities were accepted as satisfactory, and the matter rested until after the alarms raised by the *Trent* affair. Then, what with the report of the special committee and resolutions of various State legislatures demanding frontier protection, the issue was brought momentarily into question, but again no action resulted.[46] A further agitation resulted from Lincoln's recommendation in his Annual Message of 1862 which elicited the Report of the House Committee on Naval Affairs. Such a discussion drew the attention of the British Minister, who followed the subsequent debate with interest but could report that the bill to carry into effect the recommendations was defeated as it had been at the previous session.[47] The activities of Confederate agents in Canada during 1863 and 1864 produced more rumors of American violation of the spirit of the agreement and eventually the passage by the House of Representatives of a joint resolution in relation to the "treaty of 1817."[48]

Her Majesty's Government noted what had taken place, and Lord Lyons was instructed to inquire whether the Government of the United States intended to put an end to an arrangement which "worked satisfactorily for nearly half a century," for the British Government "would view the abrogation of it with great regret and no little alarm." Seward replied that, in view of recent proceedings upon Lake Erie, it had been found advisable to augment the armed vessels on the lakes to prevent a recurrence of such unfortunate happenings. He wished it to be understood, however, that "any excess which may thus be occasioned . . . over the limit fixed by the arrangement of April, 1817,

British Governments that while technically there was a violation of the agreement, practically there was none, and the Canadian authorities were quite willing its use should be continued. FO 5:671, 5:672, 5:693, 115:176, 115:190 (P.R.O.).

46. *Senate Misc. Docs.,* No. 33, 37th Cong., 2d Sess.; *Cong. Globe,* 37th Cong., 2d Sess., pp. 1966, 2819. Lyons to Russell, Feb. 15, 1862; FO 5:825 (P.R.O.).

47. Lyons to Russell, Jan. 23, Feb. 16, 1863; FO 5:875, 5:877 (P.R.O.).

48. *Cong. Globe,* 38th Cong., 1st Sess., pp. 2909, 3084. No action was taken in the Senate.

will be temporary only; and as it has been made necessary by an emergency, probably not then foreseen, may not be regarded as contrary to the spirit of the stipulation of that instrument."[49] But in October, 1864, Lyons was given a copy of an instruction addressed by Seward to Charles Francis Adams, Minister of the United States in England, by which the latter was directed to give notice to Lord Russell that "in conformity with the Treaty reservation of that right . . . at the expiration of six months after he shall have made this communication, the United States will deem themselves at liberty to increase the Naval Armament upon the Lakes, if, in their judgment, the condition of affairs in that quarter shall then require it."[50] The reasons adduced to support this step included Confederate activities on the lakes and the "insufficiency of the British Neutrality Act."[51]

When Congress met the question arose as to whether the President had any constitutional authority to take such a step without the concurrence of at least the Senate. Some were inclined to consider it an act of executive usurpation, but as a whole both houses agreed to stand behind the action by adopting a joint resolution reading: "That the notice given by the President of the United States to the Government of Great Britain and Ireland to terminate the treaty of 1817 regulating the naval force upon the lakes, is hereby adopted and ratified as if the same had been authorized by Congress."[52]

In Canada the determination of the United States was viewed with regret and some alarm, although the milder papers recognized that there was ground for some action to put a stop to Confederate depredations. The Toronto *Globe*[53] commented upon the satisfactory manner in which the agreement had worked, how it had been the means of great savings and how, under the new situation, "we are left only a

49. The correspondence, running from Aug. 4 to Nov. 3, 1864, is in *Diplomatic Correspondence, 1864–65,* Part II, pp. 668, 716, 718, 729, 739–740.

50. Lyons to Russell, Confidential, Oct. 28, 1864; FO 115:409 (P.R.O.). Adams to Russell, Nov. 23, 1864; *Diplomatic Correspondence, 1865–66,* Part I, pp. 5–8.

51. See Russell's long answer in which he goes in detail into this whole question of neutrality. Russell to Lyons, Nov. 26, 1864; FO 115:405 (P.R.O.), printed in part in *Diplomatic Correspondence, 1865–66,* Part II, pp. 18–20.

52. *Cong. Globe,* 38th Cong., 1st Sess., pp. 44, 292, 311–315, 596.

53. Dec. 13, 1864, reprinted in New York *Herald,* Dec. 16.

choice between a large outlay for naval purposes and the unpleasant alternative of remaining in a state of insecurity."

The parties to whom we owe this altered state of things are those Confederate refugees who have endeavored to make the Northern states the scene of piracy and robbery. Much as we regret the determination of the American government, we can hardly be surprised at it. *We cannot expect Mr. Lincoln and his Ministers to sit quietly by and witness such acts as the plundering of the two steamers on Lake Erie two or three months since without taking some steps to protect the commerce of their people.* Not only did these robberies occur; not only have other outrages of a similar character occurred; not only is there plenty of evidence that the outrages which have taken place are but a small portion of those which have been projected—that, in fact, they are part of a regularly planned system; but there is, moreover, *a systematic effort made in this country to defend the pirates and raiders from the consequences of their crimes.*

So far as the United States was concerned the action was reasonable and satisfactory, but "the appearance of a number of gunboats on our inland seas is a different matter." Their presence would be a standing menace to the cities of Upper Canada and the only solution would be building of a similar fleet for their defense. This was the view pretty generally expressed throughout Canada: if America armed on the lakes, so must Canada, and it was an Imperial as well as Provincial problem.

Things were not as bad as they seemed, however. The Civil War was already drawing to its close when the determination of the American Government was reached. By the next spring it was only a matter of time, and a short time, when the Confederacy should collapse. True to his previous statement that the changed policy was a temporary one due to an emergency, Seward, in March, 1865, instructed Adams to notify Russell that the United States was quite willing to let the agreement remain as "practically in force." The Government had not built and was not building any vessels to put upon the lakes, and they hoped that so long as the United States observed the old understanding the British Government would likewise abstain.[54] This stand quite met the approval of the British Government, for, as Russell informed Sir

54. Seward to Adams, Mar. 8, 1865; Great Britain: Instructions, XX, 89 (D.S.).

Frederick Bruce,[55] British Minister after Lord Lyons, "it would be a great misfortune if the two powers should in time of peace attempt to rival each other in the amount of their Lake armaments and it would not be satisfactory to the feelings of the Canadians that the United States should have a large armament on the Lakes while the British Government should be there wholly unarmed." The only question was whether this instruction of Seward's was to be considered a formal reinstatement of the Rush-Bagot Agreement, since the abrogation had not in so many words been rescinded. It was made clear that this was Seward's intention and Russell accepted the interpretation.

55. Mar. 24, 1865; FO 115:432 (P.R.O.).

CHAPTER VII

CONFEDERATE BORDER ACTIVITIES

It is difficult to find any evidence to show that the governments of Canada and the Maritime Provinces exhibited any reluctance in enforcing their neutrality laws or negligence in putting them into effect; how effective the laws were was another question. It was but natural, nevertheless, that in the United States all hostile demonstrations set in motion by Confederate agents in British possessions should be taken as evidence of Provincial sympathy for the South and enmity toward the Union. Every time, then, that some unfortunate occurrence took place there was a renewed outburst of feeling against Canada. During the early part of the war there were no instances of Confederates' trying to make use of the Colonies for armed expeditions into the Northern States.[1] But as usual there were rumors of such doings. There was a story that Vermont was to be invaded from Canada; when sifted this dissolved into a trip across the border by a couple of Canadian politicians to fight a duel.[2] In those early days of 1861 and 1862 Canada had not become a refuge for soldiers escaped from Northern military prisons or for deserters and draft evaders, and Confederate agents, such few as there were, were merely trying to purchase munitions and supplies, unsuccessfully as a rule.

In 1863 and especially in 1864 the picture began to change. Then the British possessions had begun to receive appreciable numbers of Confederates. Growing desperation of the Southern cause made the Richmond government turn to wild expedients by which Northern attention might be drawn to consider the defense of its own soil and so relieve pressure at the South.[3] Late in 1863 Canadian officials be-

1. Governor Andrew of Massachusetts was considerably alarmed, at the very beginning of hostilities, when he was led to believe that the steamer *Peerless* had been sold to Confederate agents for use against American shipping. Head to Lyons, Apr. 29; Head to Andrew, Apr. 27, 1861; FO 5:763 (P.R.O.).

2. New York *Herald,* May 20. The duel did not come off since it appeared that the seconds had forgotten the ammunition.

3. Some concern was created by reports that the Confederates were attempting to fit out privateers at Vancouver Island. Lyons to Governor of Vancouver

came disturbed about rumors "in relation to projected movements from Canada by Rebel refugees."[4] As related by the Canadian Provost Marshal General, Colonel Hill,

These rumours have generally looked to an occupation for a time of the Northern lakes, the release of Prisoners at Johnson's Island and Chicago, and the seizure of the U. S. Steamer "Michigan"—and have generally been so wild that I have not attached any importance to them. In the last few days disclosures have been made to myself and Col: Smith that I place some reliance on. A Rebel Agent has just arrived at Windsor with certificates of specie deposit in places in the rebel states amounting to over $100,000. These certificates are signed by Mr Meminger, and are drawn in favour of Henry Marvin. This agent also bears a recommendatory letter from Mr Benjamin in favour of Mr H. Marvin. These certificates I am told can be readily negotiated at Windsor and are of a similar character to those negotiated in Europe. . . .

That some project of magnitude is in contemplation I feel very certain, and I have communicated with the U. S. Consul General at Montreal.

After writing this, Hill learned that most of the refugees had left Montreal and everything pointed to an attempt upon Johnson's Island;[5] to that place he dispatched a couple of officers to explain to the authorities what he had heard. Seward, upon receipt of the information from Lord Lyons, informed the latter that Major General Dix had been immediately sent to the frontier, and, at the President's request, Preston King had been designated to go to Canada to confer with Lord Monck, who succeeded Head as Governor-General in 1861. The Secretary expressed his and the President's thanks for the information "conveyed in so just and liberal a spirit."[6]

Island, Apr. 16, 1863; FO 5:882 (P.R.O.). Lyons to Seward, May 21; Seward to Lyons, June 3, 1863; *Diplomatic Correspondence, 1863–64*, pp. 612, 626 (*House Ex. Docs.*, No. 1, 38th Cong., 1st Sess.).

4. Lt. Col. B. H. Hill to Fry, Nov. 9; FO 5:896 (P.R.O.). Lyons to Seward, Nov. 11; Lyons to Russell, Nov. 13, 1863; *Diplomatic Correspondence, 1863–64*, Supplement, p. cxxxvii.

5. This island, near Sandusky, Ohio, provided quarters for a very large number of Confederate prisoners. See below, pp. 139, 143–144.

6. Seward to Lyons, Nov. 12, 1863; FO 5:896 (P.R.O.). Lyons remarked to Monck, when he conveyed the information, that he thought Seward had acted a little precipitately in sending a special agent who could have no official communications with the Governor-General in any case. (Nov. 13, *ibid.*) Both,

The news that Canadian officials had acted so promptly was appreciated by the public as well as the Government of the United States, but Bennett had to qualify his approval by saying that "Canada exposed this rebel plot for the same reason that England stopped the rebel rams. It was her interest to do so. She could not do otherwise with safety."[7]

We thank the Canadians, then, for their friendly warning, and assure them that if, at some future period, they shall desire to drop into our delightful family party of States, and share with us the privileges and blessings of a republican form of government, they will be all the more welcome on account of their present neighborly conduct. . . . Vallandigham and Jewett have lost a magnificent opportunity in this matter. They are both in Canada, and if they are as clever as they profess to be they both knew all about this rebel plot. Had they revealed it to our government they would have been invited to return in triumph and honor. . . .[8]

The plot failed completely. Prompt action of the Canadian officials, orders of the Governor-General that no suspected vessel should pass through the Welland Canal, coöperation between the Premier and General Dix quashed the thing completely. Nevertheless, Seward could not refrain from garnering a little public acclaim by sending an instruction to Minister Adams[9] in which he referred to the "embarrassments of the British government in regard to our affairs [as arising] from the one cause—the error of investing the insurgents with a belligerent character," and then contrasted British action with that of the Canadian authorities who "have not been slow to discover the duties devolved upon them by comity and international law, and they

however, agreed that he should be received "civilly" but that only oral conversations should be held.

7. New York *Herald,* Nov. 14, 1863. The "rams" were two war vessels being built in England. Lord Russell, desiring no more *Alabama* episodes, prevented their leaving, although he had no definite proof they were destined for the Confederacy.

8. While this reflected popular majority opinion in the North about Vallandigham, it grossly maligned this gentleman, who at no time sought to aid the South or to wage war against the Union.

9. Nov. 17, 1863; *Diplomatic Correspondence, 1863–64,* Supplement, p. lxii.

have acted promptly and effectively in fulfilling these obligations. Her Majesty's Government cannot fail, I think, to approve of this course, because it is conservative of their trans-Atlantic empire." It was in accord with Seward's instructions that Adams inquired of Earl Russell whether "seeing what has taken place in Canada and in this Country, Her Majesty's Government could not either by law or Convention alter the terms of the Foreign Enlistment Act so as to make it more effectual."[10] Russell admitted that this was important and should be considered, but while the cases of the *Alexandria* and the rams were pending it was not possible to know what the law really was or whether it needed alteration. No change, however, was made in Canadian law until the session of Parliament in 1865.

Meantime, throughout 1864 rumors, most of which had but little foundation in fact, continued to multiply and to keep both Canadian and American officials on the *qui vive*. In January, 1864, the American Consul-General in Montreal sent word of a gathering of Confederates at Windsor.[11] From Adams came a copy of the *Index*, published by Confederates and Southern sympathizers in London, containing an account of an abortive attempt to free the prisoners of Johnson's Island. According to this paper[12] every effort had been made to avoid raising any question of infraction of Canada's neutrality laws: "Not an article was obtained in Canada. Even medicines and surgical instruments were furnished from New York, and all correspondence with the prisoners was carried on through the personal column of the New York Herald." The aid of British officers and Canadians was refused. "The basis of our operations was to be on Yankee territory, the means for carrying out our object, viz: the release of prisoners, were to be obtained there alone. This principle was adhered to in good faith. . . ." When all preparations were completed, "with the aid of friends in the federal States, the very day before it was to have been executed it reached the ears of the governor general, and the Yankees, being immediately warned by him, it became impossible."

In March came a communication from Colonel L. C. Baker, an

10. Russell to Lyons, Dec. 3, 1863; FO 115:350 (P.R.O.).
11. The correspondence is in *Diplomatic Correspondence, 1864–65,* Part II, pp. 193–194, 484, 505.
12. Sent Feb. 20, dated Feb. 18, 1864. *Ibid.,* p. 195.

agent of the War Department,[13] that the *Montreal*, a small schooner commanded by a former lieutenant in the Confederate Navy, was lying in Rondeau Harbor not far from Chatham, Upper Canada. On board she had a crew of fourteen men, nearly all escaped prisoners of war, two 24-pound guns, and a variety of ammunition. Near Port Stanley was the *Saratoga*, with four 18-pounders and a crew of sixteen men. Both vessels were said not to be dismantled, as was the custom in the winter, but in condition to sail at short notice. The crews, when talked to by a representative of Baker's, did not hesitate to avow their intention of preying upon American shipping as soon as navigation should be opened. Lyons, when notified of these allegations, transmitted information to Monck, who immediately gave orders that the vessels, if actually as represented, should be prevented from pursuing their objectives. Colonel Moses Wily investigated and found that the only vessel in Rondeau Harbor answering at all to the description was the *Cataraque*, recently purchased by a Captain Whitby, an Englishman who had never been in the service of the Confederacy; on this vessel were the captain, his wife, and one man, and its arms consisted of a rusty old four-pounder used for salutes and a double-barreled fowling piece. No vessel at all could be found in the vicinity of Port Stanley. These findings were corroborated by the Federal General Terry from Johnson's Island.[14]

A little earlier, in December, a few Confederates had seized the *Chesapeake* on its regular trip from New York to Portland.[15] This exploit was more or less a volunteer affair with considerable question as to whether any authority had been given to the participants by the Confederate government, for the conduct of the captors was anything but regular. They made their way to Halifax, stopping at several points to sell parts of the cargo, and then abandoned the vessel which

13. Baker to Stanton, Mar. 8, 1864; *ibid.*, pp. 549–550.

14. Wily to Macdonald, Confidential, Mar. 29; *ibid.*, pp. 585–586. Wily said that he searched all the creeks in the vicinity. He could find no record of the registry of any *Saratoga* on the upper lakes.

15. Nicolay and Hay, *Abraham Lincoln* (New York, 1890), VIII, 14. Holcombe to Benjamin, Apr. 1, Apr. 26, 1864; *Official Records of the Union and Confederate Navies in the War of the Rebellion* (Washington, 1894–1922), 2d ser., III, 1072–1075, 1103, 1154. Seward to Lyons, Mar. 21, 1864; *Diplomatic Correspondence, 1864–65*, Part II, pp. 562–563.

was taken in charge by Provincial authorities, turned over to the owners, furnished with coal through the courtesy of the Cunard Company, and sent back to New York. The captors were arrested in New Brunswick, released on *habeas corpus*, and then sought under new warrants. No great zeal in pursuit was displayed, however, for, as the Confederate Agent, James P. Holcombe, reported to J. P. Benjamin, Secretary of State of the Confederacy, their arrest would cause quite as much embarrassment to the British as to the Confederate government in trying to solve their legal status; furthermore, public opinion in the Provinces would not permit their being treated as pirates. The facts appeared to be that two Confederate citizens, Braine and Parr, escaped military prisoners, started to execute a scheme planned by Vernon G. Locke, a British subject who, masquerading under the name of Parker, had commanded the privateer *Retribution*. The plan had been to go to a British port for fuel and then take the *Chesapeake* to some Confederate port, but Braine upset everything by his inexplicable conduct.[16]

In June, 1864, the Department of State was informed that "unusual numbers of persons hostile to the United States" were passing through St. John, New Brunswick, on their way to Canada, and Secretary Seward asked Lyons to bring this to the attention of Lord Monck that he might ascertain what were the facts of the matter. After inquiries had gone the customary rounds, Seward was notified that the Lieutenant-Governor of the Province could find no evidence either of a projected raid or of the presence of "unusual numbers" of "persons hostile to the United States."[17] It is possible that the story grew out of the activities of Holcombe, who had been especially charged with the task of repatriating a number of escaped war prisoners who had sought refuge in the Provinces. Supplied with a considerable fund, he planned to herd these refugees to Halifax and thence send them to Bermuda, where they might hope to reach a Southern port on a blockade runner. These men, to be sure, would be traveling east and not west, but this fact might easily have escaped

16. Holcombe to Benjamin, Apr. 26, 1864; *Official Records . . . Navies,* 2d ser., III, 1103. Benjamin to Holcombe, Apr. 20, 1864; *ibid.,* pp. 1095–1097.

17. *Diplomatic Correspondence, 1864–65,* Part II, pp. 623, 637, 657–658, 660.

the attention of some informant who was keyed to see a "reb" and a prospective raider on every corner.[18]

All through the summer and into the autumn rumors of projected raids plagued army officers whose duties brought the border within their jurisdiction. Most of the stories proved to be either baseless or much exaggerated. Nevertheless, credence would be given to the next yarn and telegrams would fly between city and state authorities on the one side and military commanders and the War Department on the other, with the Department of State raising its voice when the clamor became too pronounced.[19] There was, however, some ground for a moderate amount of alarm. In Canada three special agents, Holcombe, C. C. Clay, and Jacob Thompson, were charged with lighting backfires against the Union. Their arrival in the Province was timed to coincide with the American presidential campaign of 1864, for it was believed that in the Northwest, especially in Ohio, Indiana, and Illinois, there was a large body of persons tired of the war who would coöperate with the South in an effort to bring it to an end. The Knights of the Golden Circle had become the Order of American Knights and then, in 1864, the Sons of Liberty.[20] The "Sons" north of the Ohio, optimistically estimated in the South to be at least half a million, were expected to work with their brothers in Kentucky and Missouri to bring about a political overturn in the North which would work to the advantage of the Confederacy. The agents in Canada did

18. *Official Records . . . Navies,* 2d ser., III, 1035–1036, 1103–1105, 1120, 1187–1188, 1239–1240. Holcombe to Monck, May 9, 1864; FO 5:950 (P.R.O.). The New York *Herald* was skeptical of the good faith of the Provincial authorities, for, it said (July 24, 1864), they were incensed at the zeal of Consul Howard, who had turned in the alarm. "He is a worthy, upright and reliable gentleman, which is more than can be said of any of the Bluenoses among whom he lives."

19. In *The War of the Rebellion: Official Records of the Union and Confederate Armies* (Washington, 1880–1901), 1st ser., Vols. XXXIX, XLIII, XLV, XLVI; 2d ser., Vols. II, VII; 3d ser., Vols. I, III, IV; and 4th ser., Vol. III, are to be found scattered communications, usually telegrams, illustrating this point. *Diplomatic Correspondence, 1864–65,* Part II, pp. 674–678.

20. See discussion of the orders and their activities together with the aspirations of the Confederacy about them in J. F. Rhodes, *History of the United States from the Compromise of 1850 to the McKinley-Bryan Campaign of 1896* (New York, 1920), V, 317 ff.

not expect to enlist any direct foreign aid; they betook themselves north of the border because from here they could get in touch with disgruntled elements in the Union and strive to bring about what they supposed was the common end. Holcombe, who stayed at Niagara Falls most of the time he was in Canada, reported seeing and talking to Leigh Richmond and Benjamin Wood of New York, Buckalew, Black, and Van Dyke of Pennsylvania, McLean of the Cincinnati *Enquirer*, and Weller of California; Thompson saw and talked with Vallandigham, and they received messages from Voorhees and Pendleton of Ohio.[21] Strictly speaking, their activities did not involve Canadian-American relations unless their zeal led them to violate Canadian law, and this they apparently sought usually to avoid. To the average Northern eye, however, Canada was involved because these agitators were operating from Canadian soil, and the rank and file of Unionists drew no distinction between an exile in a foreign land doing what he legally could to forward the cause of his country, and Canadian aid to and participation in Confederate machinations. So far as popular opinion was concerned this was only hair-splitting: Canada was helping the Rebel cause.

The principal specific objective of these Confederate agents which might affect the relations between Canada and the United States centered about a scheme to obtain possession of the *Michigan*, the only American armed public vessel on the upper lakes, and to free military prisoners held at various points close to the border. The large concentration of prisoners of war at Johnson's Island, and another at Camp Douglas near Chicago, were especially kept in mind. C. H. Cole, a refugee Confederate officer in Canada, was sent by Thompson to see what could be done about the *Michigan*.[22] At first he tried to bribe her officers and "buy" the vessel; failing in this he received permission from his superiors to try to take her, because it was felt that the *Michigan* was the only real obstacle in the way of a successful attempt to free the prisoners. Cole's plans were suspected by Union officials, and he was arrested without having been able to get word to a subordinate,

21. Holcombe to Benjamin, Nov. 16, 1864; *Official Records . . . Navies,* 2d ser., III, 1234–1239.

22. Thompson to Benjamin, Dec. 3, 1864; *Official Records . . . Armies,* 1st ser., XLIII, Part II, 930–936. This communication, not received at Richmond until Feb. 13, 1865, recounted the general activities of the agents.

Burleigh (or Burley), who, on September 18, with a small body of men had seized a little steamer, the *Philo Parsons*, when on her run to Sandusky. The *Parsons* was halted at Bass Bay to take on wood; while there another little lake steamer, the *Island Queen*, came alongside, was boarded, the passengers and crew driven off, the vessel towed out of the harbor, scuttled, and set adrift. Everything seemed propitious for continuing the enterprise, but, as the *Parsons* neared Sandusky, Burleigh's men refused to make an attempt on the *Michigan*, so the vessel put into Sandwich, Upper Canada, where, after being partly plundered, it was abandoned and the captors scattered. This failure marked the end of serious efforts to free the Johnson's Island prisoners, although rumors of further attempts continued to circulate.[23] No Canadians were allowed to participate in these enterprises, although it appeared that volunteers could have been found had they been wanted; nor was there any complaint that Canadian authorities had failed to take all proper steps to forestall any illegal activities.[24] All attempts by Confederate agents to effect release of prisoners were abandoned after the Johnson's Island fiasco, except that Captain Hines still believed he could do something about Camp Douglas, but here, as Thompson reported, "treachery defeated him."[25]

Previous efforts made by Confederate agents in the British Prov-

23. In addition to Thompson's account, see communications between the War Department and officers in Ohio, *ibid.*, pp. 426–428; Seward to Adams, Oct. 24, 1864, Great Britain: Instructions, XIX, 491–503 (D.S.). Newspapers, of course, carried extensive accounts; e.g., New York *Herald*, Sept. 24, 1864. Detailed account in Adams to Russell, Nov. 23, 1864; *Diplomatic Correspondence, 1865–66,* Part I, pp. 5–8.

24. A detective under orders from the Provost Marshal at Buffalo reported that the Confederate officers were "educated, reticent and shrewd" men who held secret meetings where no Canadians were allowed to be present. A. M. Harper to Brig. Gen. T. A. Rowley, Sept. 26, 1864, *Official Records . . . Armies,* 1st ser., XLIII, Part I, 929–931; Donahoe to Burnley, Sept. 26, 1864, G 233 (P.A.C.). It was reported that most of the men engaged in this scheme managed to reach Bermuda. Hill to Dix, Oct. 17, 1864, *Official Records . . . Armies,* 1st ser., XLIII, Part II, 401–402. Colonel Sweet reported (*ibid.,* XLV, Part I, 1076–1077) that he could prove that Thompson had engineered the raids.

25. Thompson to Benjamin, Dec. 3, 1864, already cited; Sweet to Cook, Nov. 6, 7, 1864; *Official Records . . . Armies,* 1st ser., XLV, Part I, 1081–1082.

inces faded into the background when news came on October 21, 1864, that the little village of St. Albans, Vermont, had been raided from across the border. Public opinion flamed to heights greater than at any time since the *Trent* affair; all the accumulated irritation growing out of three and a half years of hostilities now flared out in a burst of resentment that threatened to break every restraining bond. Added to everything else was a feeling of irresistible power arising from a consciousness of military superiority in Grant's steady pounding away toward Richmond, Sherman's devastating march in the interior of the Confederacy, and the gradual encirclement of the South by a tightening blockade which by now left only a port or two still in the hands of Confederate forces. The war was not over but there was little doubt about the outcome. It was time, so people in the North thought, to show the British in Europe and in America that they would stand for no nonsense. The story of the raid itself is very simple. Some twenty-five men under the command of Lieutenant Bennett H. Young attacked St. Albans on October 19, 1864, setting fires, robbing the banks of some $200,000, wounding two inhabitants, one mortally, and then fled back to Canadian territory a few miles away. Young acted directly under authority of the Confederate War Department with the approbation of C. C. Clay, who had advanced a small sum of money. Although the party was not in uniform and bore no Confederate flag, its members proclaimed, when back in Canada, that they had acted under military authority in committing an act of reprisal for the depredations of Sheridan in the Shenandoah Valley.[26] The raiders were pursued, even across the border, by citizens of St. Albans, who together with Canadian authorities arrested thirteen of them including Young.

The first and persisting reaction both in Canada and the North was one of horror and reprobation. The Montreal *Herald* voiced the sentiments of most Canadians when it said:[27]

That these men will meet with any wide sympathy here is what we do not believe. . . . Such an offense, cowardly and larcenous in its own nature, but also in respect to the people among whom its perpetrators have enjoyed an asylum, treacherous and ungrateful, will . . . excite among

26. For a succinct account see Rhodes, *op. cit.*, V, 333 ff.
27. Oct. 21. Excerpt in New York *Herald*, Oct. 23.

Canadians nothing but abhorrence. That sentiment, moreover, cannot but be increased when we know that these malefactors were cruel enough and wanton enough in their cruelty to shoot officers who, in endeavoring to arrest them, were only doing their duty—a duty which truly brave men always respect in others.

The *Herald*, however, maintained that such enterprises had a foundation in *"the encouragement which has been afforded by certain newspapers in this country to the earliest endeavors to commit atrocities of the same description,"* and charged the government with being less alert in forestalling such happenings than its predecessor of the year before. The Lake Erie venture, followed so closely by the St. Albans raid, could only provoke retaliation and perhaps cause the two countries *"to drift into a state of hostilities along the border* before we know in what direction we are going." Similar sentiments appeared in papers of all political stripes. Said the Toronto *Globe*, "Has Mr. Jefferson Davis power to make what seems to our common sense an act of robbery simply an act of war?"

Supposing the raiders had got to St. Albans directly from the Southern States, and had appeared in Canada for the first time after the robbery, their position might then have been that of refugees, whom we could not give up. But should it be proved that the raiders went from Canada into Vermont, as is altogether probable, then the case against them would be a very strong one. . . . Such a thing ought either to be an offence against our laws, or such an offence against American law as would come under the operations of the extradition treaty.[28]

Here was the crux of the matter. Was the offense covered by the extradition treaty, or was it analogous to the famous McLeod affair of 1840, where individual responsibility was lost in official authorization? The Administration in Washington immediately concluded that it came in the former category, for, on October 29, Secretary Seward made formal requisition upon the British Government to issue a warrant for delivery of the thirteen men to persons designated by the Governor of Vermont, men "charged with the crimes of murder, assault with intent to commit murder, and robbery, within the jurisdiction of

28. Oct. 26. Excerpt in New York *Herald,* Oct. 29.

the United States, . . . now held in jail at St. John, in Canada East."[29] To the Confederate agents, on the other hand, there was no question of individual responsibility. Young had, after his capture, shown his authority from the Confederate Secretary of War Seddon to do all the damage he could in way of retaliation; it was the duty of the Confederate government to come forward and avow the official nature of the act and so prevent giving up the men to the Federal Government.[30] No obstacle was raised by the Canadian Government, for, upon receipt of Seward's requisition, Lord Monck caused the British Legation in Washington to be informed that as soon as he should "have been advised that the proofs required by the treaty of extradition have been made in the case of these men, the necessary warrants will be issued for their delivery to the authorities of the United States."[31] Canadian legal processes, however, did not move fast enough for the Department of State. On November 21 Seward addressed a new communication to the British Legation, and two days later sent a long instruction to Adams in which he reviewed the complaints of the United States against what was alleged to be remissness on the part of the Canadian Government. Failure of British Neutrality Acts was charged with being the basis of all this trouble; furthermore, asylum afforded in Canada to such individuals as a "notorious person named Jacob Thompson" made possible these outrages.[32]

Neither the Canadian nor the British Government enjoyed the prospect opened by these unfortunate occurrences. In December the Colonial Office, noting that the attention of Her Majesty's Government had been drawn to what appeared violations of British neutrality, informed Monck:[33]

29. Seward to Lyons; *Diplomatic Correspondence, 1864–65,* Part II, p. 756. Three days later a similar request was made for the extradition of William H. Hutchinson, who was held in jail in Montreal. *Ibid.,* p. 757.

30. [Unsigned] to Benjamin, Nov. 1, 1864; *Official Records . . . Armies,* 1st ser., XLIII, Part II, 914–916.

31. Oct. 31, 1864, *Diplomatic Correspondence, 1864–65,* Part II, p. 762.

32. Adams to Russell, Nov. 23; *Diplomatic Correspondence, 1865–66,* Part I, pp. 5–8. It was in this instruction that Seward directed Adams to give the six months' notice respecting abrogation of the Rush-Bagot Agreement. Intercepted correspondence of the Confederate agents sent to Adams on December 6 showed that C. C. Clay was party to the St. Albans affair. *Ibid.,* pp. 13–14.

33. Cardwell to Monck, Dec. 3, 1864; FO 115:405 (P.R.O.).

These violations of neutrality are a great offense against the British Crown, and H. M.'s Gov^t are of the opinion that the Gov^t of the U. S. have a clear right to expect that the Canadian law shall be found in practice generally sufficient, not merely for the punishment, but also for the suppression and prevention of these border raids.

Seward had reminded Earl Russell of the Congressional Act of 1838 to prevent hostile attempts prepared in the United States against Her Majesty's Dominions, and, while the circumstances were not the same and precisely the same legislation was not apparently called for, nevertheless Monck was advised by the Colonial Office to consult his Government and find out from his Law Officers whether existing acts were sufficient to meet emergencies. If they were not it would be advisable to apply to the legislature for increased powers, which might well be limited to a definite term as had been the Act of Congress. The force of this advice was borne home when, in the middle of December, the magistrate before whom the case of the raiders had been brought, gave as his opinion that the prisoners could not be held and ordered their release.

. . . Grounds for the liberation of the prisoners were based upon the fact that the provincial Canadian Act to carry into effect the Ashburton Treaty had not rec^d the special Royal sanction requisite, That in consequence the Imperial Act must rule & that act required that the warrant under which the prisoners were arrested should be signed by the Govr Gen: that failing that the court possessed no jurisdiction & the order was accordingly issued to liberate the Prisoners.[34]

This decision aroused almost if not quite as much consternation in Canada as in the United States. Said Premier Macdonald in a private letter:[35]

The unhappy and mistaken decision of Coursol at Montreal has had a most unfortunate tendency, from the fact of his being called Judge Coursol, his decision is considered a judicial one in the U. S. He was merely acting in his capacity as Police Magistrate, and altogether mistook his duty, when he presumed to judge as to his right to discharge those prisoners. It was his duty to assume that he had the authority,

34. Burnley to Russell, Dec. 15, 1864; FO 115:409 (P.R.O.).
35. To Thos. Swinyard, Dec. 19, 1864; Macdonald Papers: Letterbooks, VII, 70–71 (P.A.C.).

under the Statute, and the question of jurisdiction should only have been brought up to be solemnly decided by Superior Courts. A new process has been issued, however, and it is hoped that these men, or the majority of them, will be *re*arrested, and the discredit thrown upon the administration of justice in Canada, removed.

The fact that money, some ninety thousand dollars, found in possession of the raiders, was ordered returned to them added insult to injury.[36]

Advices from various parts of Canada showed that Coursol's decision was highly unpopular.[37] From Montreal came word that the conduct of the magistrate and of Chief of Police Lamothe were denounced, the latter being charged with complicity in the affair and his early dismissal foretold; in Toronto a "profound sensation" was caused, and the best legal authorities condemned the decision as contrary to law; and in Quebec the release was called ridiculous and there was a demand that Coursol should be severely dealt with. Parliament, it was anticipated, would be summoned to convene in January instead of a month later so that adequate laws could be passed. If condemnation in Canada was severe, imagination can picture what was the reaction in the United States. Very temperately for a Bennett publication the *Herald* remarked:[38]

We publish in another column the decision of the Canadian Judge in the case of the St. Albans raiders, whereby it will be seen that he has discharged those miscreants on the plea of want of jurisdiction. At the same time we have received intelligence of the discharge at Toronto of the pirates of Lake Erie. The latter, however, is not an event of so much importance as the discharge of the highwaymen, murderers and robbers of the St. Albans raid, and we have no doubt that the decision in that case will strike with as much astonishment the British and Canadian governments as it will our own government and people.

The New York *Evening Post*, not ordinarily chauvinistic, bitterly stated:[39]

36. Seward to Adams, Dec. 19, 1864; *Diplomatic Correspondence, 1865–66,* Part I, pp. 49–51.

37. New York *Herald,* Dec. 16, 1864.

38. Dec. 14, 1864.   39. Dec. 14, 1864.

It would seem to be idle, after the farce acted at Montreal, for our government or people to expect justice from the local tribunals of Canada. The mode in which they have conducted the case shows that either sympathy or venality is likely to control their decisions in all subsequent proceedings, as it has in the present case. Even the wretched pretext of a "Commission from Richmond" will no longer be needed to shield these robbers and murderers from legal responsibility. Two courses, therefore, are alone left us to pursue: first, to demand from the imperial government such a police of the Canadian frontier as will secure our villages and towns from the descents of rascals who take the name of rebel; or, secondly, in the event that this is not promised, to take the mode and measure of redress into our own hands.

By now Congress was in session. In his Fourth Annual Message President Lincoln[40] referred to the "insecurity of life and property in the region adjacent to the Canadian border," stated that he had given notice for the termination of the Agreement of 1817, and raised the question as to whether rights of transit established by the Treaty of 1854 should be continued.

I desire, however, to be understood while making this statement that the colonial authorities of Canada are not deemed to be intentionally unjust or unfriendly toward the United States, but, on the contrary, there is every reason to expect that, with the approval of the Imperial Government, they will take the necessary measures to prevent new incursions across the border.

It did not need the President's words to arouse Congress to a consideration of the frontier happenings. In various ways the subject came up and was debated hotly, part of the occasion being afforded by Chandler's reading to the Senate[41] a news item about the discharge of the prisoners, telling how the border was seething and how it was swarming with armed men while Canadian authorities were apparently bent on protecting the raiders; Vermont might submit to such outrages but the Northwest would not. Then the Senator presented a resolution, prefaced by a characteristic preamble, desiring the Committee on Military Affairs to "be directed to inquire into the expedi-

40. Richardson, *Messages and Papers*, VI, 246.
41. Dec. 16, 1864; *Cong. Globe*, 38th Cong., 2d Sess., pp. 33–34. *Senate Misc. Docs.*, No. 5, 38th Cong., 2d Sess.

ency of immediately enlisting an Army Corps to watch and defend our territory on the lakes and Canadian line from all hostile demonstrations."

Commenting on the discussion of this and other examples of the excitement in Congress, Chargé Burnley informed Earl Russell that the whole debate was worthy His Lordship's "attentive perusal":[42]

Mr Sumner, Mr Johnson & Mr Hale took a very fair view of the case the first alluding to the St Albans Raiders stating that in his opinion "the whole proceeding was a trap in which to catch the Gov[t] of our country." "It was hoped that in this way the rebellion would gain powerful British intervention which would help restore its failing fortunes."

This is a feeling pretty generally felt & understood among the more sober of the Americans & therefore General Dixs order without being positively blamed was considered too farreaching in its tendencies to warrant its standing as it was unfairly promulgated, considering the efforts made by the Canadian Administration to remedy the precipitate action of the Judge.

Burnley did not believe, from the general tenor of the discussion, that there was any possibility of preventing Congress from ordering the abrogation of the Reciprocity Treaty. The less "sober" among the Americans, whether they were in Congress or out, made no attempt to conceal their feelings or to restrain their condemnation of Canada and their desire to strike back, at least through trade.

It did not need these warnings from the United States to awaken the Government of Canada to the necessity of taking action at once. The Governor-General called out militia to be stationed at strategic points to prevent further excursions into the United States. Gilbert McMicken was appointed Stipendiary Magistrate "with full powers to organize a Detective and Preventive Police Force, for the purpose of watching and patrolling the whole Frontier from Toronto to Sarnia," and was particularly instructed to "put himself in common with the American Authorities at Buffalo and Detroit." He was, said Macdonald,[43] "a shrewd, cool and determined man, who won't easily lose his head, and who will fearlessly perform his duty." Parliament was called to meet in session on January 19.

42. Dec. 23, 1864; FO 115:409 (P.R.O.).
43. Macdonald to Swinyard, Dec. 19, 1864; Macdonald Papers: Letterbooks, VII, 70–71.

Impetus to Canadian activity had been provided by Major General Dix, the commanding officer for the Northeast department, who, as soon as he had heard of the St. Albans raid, telegraphed the commanding officer at Burlington, Vermont: "Send all the efficient force you have to St. Albans, and try to find the marauders who came from Canada this morning. Put a discreet officer in command; and, in case they are not found on our side of the line, pursue them into Canada, if necessary, and destroy them." It did not take long for this order to be noticed by Canadian authorities, for, on October 26, Lord Monck brought it to the attention of the British Legation.[44]

While no one would be inclined to scan too narrowly the conduct pursued by the citizens of St. Albans, while smarting under the effect of the outrage to which they have been lately unfortunately subjected, it is obvious that an order such as . . . [General Dix's], if issued by a responsible officer of the United States, would be liable to a different construction, and might, unless remonstrated against, be drawn into a precedent in the future.

Burnley was to assure the Secretary that British authorities had the "most earnest desire" to coöperate with the Americans in keeping peace on the border. Less inclined to bluster than he had been three years earlier, Seward, nevertheless, in answering Burnley's note turned the subject by saying that while his Government had been considering Lord Monck's inquiry about Dix's order, their requisitions for the return of the offenders had remained unanswered, and there were rumors that further raids were being projected.[45] Fortunately there was no occasion for any officer to follow literally Dix's order, and before anything new turned up the President, on the advice of General Grant, had disapproved the part of the order which directed an invasion of Canadian territory.

Dix's order was, of course, popular in the United States, just as it was highly unpopular in Canada, although even here was found occasional expression of the opinion that in some cases such action might

44. The correspondence is in *Diplomatic Correspondence, 1864–65,* Part II, pp. 754–755, 759–760, 782–783, 812; Part III, p. 16. See also *Official Records . . . Armies,* 1st ser., III, Part II, 799–800.

45. Monck rather resented the imputation that his Government had been unnecessarily delaying matters. Monck to Burnley, Nov. 12, 1864; *Diplomatic Correspondence, 1864–65,* Part II, p. 783.

be justified even though not expedient. Dix ought to have remembered, ran the comments, that the real purpose of the raids was to embroil the United States with Great Britain, to create that bad feeling which Southerners had been striving for all along.[46] The Montreal *Gazette*[47] believed that the Federal authorities had no excuse to cross the border in the way Dix proposed unless Canada showed unwillingness to respect the first principle of international law; furthermore, the United States should not complain of carelessness on the frontier since it had been of aid to kidnapers in getting recruits for the Union armies. The New York *Herald*[48] traced the rescinding of the order to the Secretary of State, who had "opposed the manly policy with which the General commanding this Department has sought to secure our border towns from outrage and pillage." Perhaps, however, the rescinding was not wholly to be regretted,[49] for Dix himself, while bowing to the decision of his superiors, felt no compunctions about his course as he clearly indicated at a banquet where, in a flowery speech, he maintained the correctness of his course.[50]

The question which the Secretary of State pressed and with which the Provincial authorities struggled was the very practical though legally entangled one of whether the raiders were to be rearrested and extradited to the United States.[51] After their discharge by Magistrate Coursol most of these gentlemen had betaken themselves to New Brunswick, where shortly they were again under arrest. The judge allowed them thirty days to procure evidence from Richmond[52] and

46. Toronto *Leader,* Dec. 15. In New York *Herald,* Dec. 18.

47. Dec. 15. In *Herald* of Dec. 18. Macdonald thought the order of General Dix "most unfortunate and uncalled for. It did not affect us in any manner as Canadians but it was a direct insult to the Sovereignty of England." To Swinyard, Dec. 19, 1864; Macdonald Papers: Letterbooks, VII, 70–71 (P.A.C.).

48. Dec. 18.

49. Dec. 21. The *Herald* thought the change might have come from political rivalry between Seward and Dix.

50. New York *Herald,* Jan. 1, 1865.

51. The newspapers followed the course of events with information as well as misinformation, while a lively correspondence went on between Washington, London, and the Provinces. The pertinent portions are in *Diplomatic Correspondence, 1865–66,* Part II, pp. 32–93, *passim,* with an occasional unprinted dispatch or instruction in FO 115:405 (P.R.O.).

52. New York *Herald,* Jan. 10, 1865.

the case finally came up on February 10, 1865, when another stay was requested and refused. Messengers sent to Richmond almost to a man met with bad luck; one was arrested and hanged as a spy in Ohio; one, captured in Wilmington, escaped and returned to Canada; while another reached Washington only to have his request for a pass to see him through the lines to Richmond refused even though the British Chargé intervened in his behalf.[53] Toward the end of March, Judge Smith discharged the raiders on the ground that they were exercising belligerent rights, a decision which might have been expected, since, as the Law Officers of the Crown ruled, if they were Confederate officers and enlisted men under the orders of C. C. Clay, there was no case against them.[54] Immediately after their discharge, however, they were arrested once more on a charge of assault to commit murder in the Queen's dominions. The principal actor in the *Philo Parsons* affair, Burleigh, did not escape extradition. In spite of the fact that the original document signed by Jefferson Davis authorized him to make reprisals upon persons and property of the United States, the Chief Justice of the Queen's Bench, sitting with three other judges at Toronto, decided that his offense was extraditable, and on February 3, 1865, he was turned over to a Provost Marshal at Suspension Bridge.[55]

Before the raiders' cases were decided the Canadian Parliament had met, and the Governor-General in his Address referred directly to the "outrages . . . committed on the commerce and territory of the United States of America by persons who, after the perpetration of these acts have sought refuge on Canadian soil." He told what had been done to prevent similar occurrences and asked the legislature for stronger powers to deal "with persons who, while availing themselves of the right of asylum which has always been allowed on British soil to political refugees from all foreign countries, may be unmindful of the implied obligations which, by their residence among us, they contract to obey our laws and to respect the declared policy of our sovereign."[56]

53. New York *Herald,* Feb. 10, 1865.

54. *Ibid.,* Mar. 30, 1865. Russell to Bruce, Apr. 1, 1865; FO 115:433 (P.R.O.).

55. New York *Herald,* Jan. 12, Feb. 4, 1865. Rhodes, *op. cit.,* V, 335.

56. Canada *Gazette,* Jan. 19, 1865. In *Diplomatic Correspondence, 1865–66,* Part II, p. 56.

The debate on the Address showed that a majority of the House was determined to stop abuses; a special committee was appointed to look into the action of Coursol, and Finance Minister Galt in his estimates included an item to make good the money which had been restored to the raiders on their release.[57] On the crucial divisions the Government showed a good majority, and the important measures of amending the Neutrality Act and passing an Alien Act, to curb the activities of political refugees, were enacted without difficulty.

The events of September and October, 1864, marked the high point in attempted excursions across the border. Barren as they were in the production of anything except exasperation, they came closer to accomplishing something than any attempts which were planned before or after. Alarms there were in plenty during the next five months, but most of them were merely alarms. Vigilance on the part of Provincial authorities both before and after the amended Neutrality Act, and watchfulness on the part of Federal officials, together with the cooperation between the two, nipped in the bud every effort instigated by Clay, Thompson, and their associates. Early in April, when practically all danger of further expeditions was past, Seward,[58] calling attention to the fact that "evil-disposed persons have crossed the borders of the United States, or entered their ports by sea from countries where they were tolerated" to commit felonies within the United States, announced, on the authority of the President, a reward of five hundred dollars for the arrest of any person convicted subsequently of aiding and abetting such offenders.

The detailing of all the false alarms would be a wearisome task for both writer and reader, but a sample or two will illustrate what was taking place. On November 25, 1864, the War Department asked Seward to bring to Lord Lyons' attention "reliable information" which Dix had received that about forty rebels at Marysburg, Prince Edward County, Canada, were drilling regularly, seemed to have plenty of money, and were reported to have belonged to Morgan's corps. Immediately Canadian machinery was set in motion. London

57. New York *Herald,* Jan. 25.

58. The notice, dated April 4, 1865, is in *Diplomatic Correspondence, 1865–66,* Part I, p. 304.

was informed of the rumor and Lord Russell assured Adams[59] that the Governor-General had been instructed to take every precaution that no violation of neutrality should take place; "if it should appear that the persons concerned in such inroads are for any reason not subject to extradition, they & others must in some way be effectually prevented from committing . . . offences [similar to that at St. Albans] against a neighboring state." Eventually the office of the Attorney-General for Upper Canada received from an officer sent to Marysburg the intelligence that "no traces of any such organization" could be discovered; he was confident "that the county of Prince Edward is free from any such illegal combination."[60] Late in December there was a story that two or three hundred men at Halifax were plotting "predatory attacks on the commercial shipping of the citizens of the United States." By direction of Lord Monck the Lieutenant-Governor of Nova Scotia was instructed both to ascertain the facts and to cooperate with the American Consul. The Lieutenant-Governor reported[61] that he had "instituted searching inquiries with a view to ascertaining whether any such organization had really been set on foot," but "he had not been able to discover any adequate reason for the suspicions entertained by the United States consul." And thus it continued: rumor after rumor with but little to back them up.

One of the stories, however, did have some foundation in truth. Thompson reported to Secretary Benjamin[62] that Dr. James T. Bates of Kentucky had, with Thompson's aid, bought the little steamer *Georgiana*. Then, wrote Thompson, the wildest rumors began to go about; the *Georgiana* was investigated more than once and nothing out of the ordinary was found, although suspicion was still rife. "The bane and curse of carrying out anything in this country," said Thompson, "is the surveillance under which we act. Detectives, or those ready to give information, stand at every street corner. Two or three cannot interchange ideas without a reporter." If the *Georgiana* was purchased for some sinister purpose, as she probable was, there

59. Dec. 16, 1864; *Diplomatic Correspondence, 1865–66*, Part I, p. 61.
60. *Ibid.*, p. 33. Most of the correspondence is in *ibid.*, *passim*, and Part II, pp. 812–813.
61. Russell to Adams, Mar. 11, 1865; *ibid.*, Part I, p. 248.
62. Dec. 3, 1864; *Official Records . . . Armies*, 1st ser., XLIII, Part II, 934.

was no opportunity for action except by investigators representing both Canada and the United States.[63]

As a part of the program to put a stop to Confederate activities in Canada the Governor-General issued in December, 1864, a proclamation[64] forbidding exportation of "warlike stores or munitions of war." This gave rise to another crop of wild stories but none more amusing than the particular incident which immediately provoked the proclamation. It seems that there was a certain Vermonter living in Guelph, Upper Canada, who told of a neighbor's having had in his yard for a year or more a 14-pounder; suddenly this gun disappeared and the Vermonter was sure that it had been packed to be sent to some Southerners. To make the story more convincing he had heard that a foundry at Guelph had been casting shot and shell of a caliber that would probably fit the gun; since these manufacturers were strong Southern sympathizers the inference was clear. The details of the story were pretty vague, but that did not prevent all possible machinery being set in motion to trace that gun. A heavy box marked "potatoes" but suspected of containing the gun, after various false clues had been followed up, was thought to have been shipped to a port in Michigan, and then lost sight of,[65] although Seward had been warned of the whole affair. While no complaint was made of lack of zeal on the part of Canadian authorities, this was one of the examples which demonstrated the difficulty of dealing with affairs affecting Canada or any of the British Provinces and the United States. "The consul at Halifax," Seward stated to Burnley,[66] "addresses the department, I address you, and you, under the leave of your home government, communicate with the governor of Nova Scotia at Halifax," and added that he would in compliance with Burnley's "expressed wish," instruct the Consul to make known directly to the Governor-General "whatever he may learn that shall be important to be known by him in preventing hostile proceedings in the province of Nova Scotia against

63. *Ibid.*, 1st ser., XXXIX, Part III, 656–657, 694; XLIII, Part II, 552, 603. *Diplomatic Correspondence, 1865–66,* Part II, pp. 771–778.

64. Hammond to Rogers, Dec. 9, 1864, with enclosures including a Report of the Executive Council; FO 115:405 (P.R.O.).

65. The correspondence is in FO 115:405 (P.R.O.).

66. Mar. 14, 1865; *Diplomatic Correspondence, 1865–66,* Part II, pp. 95–96.

the United States." It was unfortunate that this simple procedure could not have been devised earlier to the benefit of both countries.

Exasperating as were the few raids which really took place, the surprising fact is that there were not more of them, more destructive to lives and property of the people of the North. Surprising but gratifying, but, even so, the events of the latter part of 1864 aroused such resentment in the Union that the rising tide of indignation desiring to vent itself in abrogation of the Reciprocity Treaty could no longer be held back.

CHAPTER VIII

THE CIVIL WAR AND THE END OF RECIPROCITY

WHETHER reciprocity uncomplicated by issues raised by the war between the States would have passed through its stipulated ten years with no more grumbling than had been heard down to 1861, and then, with modifications to meet some of the plaints of the discontented, have been renewed for another period of years, is one of those things which belong to the realm of prophecy and not of history. One cannot help guessing, however, that the chances for its continuation were relatively good, and that, on the whole, the malcontents were far less numerous than those who believed there was more good than evil in the arrangement. But such a peaceful development was not to be. The war, with its demands for money, made men look askance at goods coming over the border without paying duty; fishermen coveted inshore privileges but resented invasion of their market by free Canadian fish; anger in the North over the attitude of the British, whether American or European, toward secession and the following struggle added to the ranks of those who were critical of the Elgin Treaty and exaggerated the deficiencies of the pact.

After the adjournment of Congress in March, 1861, and the inauguration of the new administration, political leaders were too occupied with immediate problems to pay much attention to a relatively minor matter like Provincial trade and the treaty regulating it; a Republican administration not only had to oust Democratic officeholders and fill positions with "loyal" men, but some decision had to be reached on secession. The period of quiescence continued throughout spring and summer and on until Congress was in regular session in the winter of 1861–62,[1] although rumblings found vent in newspapers, especially in connection with the persistent campaign for annexation which was being carried on under the instigation of James Gordon

1. On August 2, 1861, Lyons wrote Sir Edmund Head (Newton, *Lord Lyons*, I, 50): "We have nearly got through another Tariff Bill without a serious attack upon the Reciprocity Treaty, thanks more to the haste, I am afraid, than the good will of the Legislators."

Bennett and his New York *Herald*.[2] It was the opinion of Lord Lyons, an opinion shared by the home government and those of the Provinces, that the best policy was to lie low and watch developments.[3]

When Congress met in the winter the subject of reciprocity was raised and resulted in a voluminous, penetrating, and fairly well balanced report from the House Committee on Commerce presented by its chairman, Elijah Ward, on February 5, 1862.[4] The immediate incentive to the committee's activity had been resolutions passed by the New York legislature calling attention to a statement in President Buchanan's message to the Thirty-sixth Congress which stressed the inequities of the situation where Canada levied such high duties upon imports of manufactured goods and discriminated against citizens of the United States in administering tolls on Canadian canals; a policy of retaliation, the legislature believed, would injure the people of Upper Canada who had "never failed in their efforts to secure a permanent and just policy for their own country and ourselves." New York senators and representatives were, therefore, called upon to take such steps "by commissioners or other means" as would protect the United States and provide a system reciprocally beneficial originally "intended and expressed" by the treaty.

After a historical survey of conditions which resulted in the Treaty of 1854, the committee examined its operation and concluded that Canada, influenced by the commercial classes of Lower Canada, had entered upon a policy which did distinctly discriminate against Americans for the benefit of Montreal and Quebec and for certain railroads. The report recognized the close economic relationship between

2. See Chapter IX.

3. Lyons to Russell, July 15, 1861; FO 5:767 (P.R.O.). Lyons spoke of an article in the *National Republican,* "considered in some sense the Organ of the Present Government, although they repudiate all responsibility for the Articles which appear in it," wherein it was suggested that the United States put an end to the treaty as soon as the ten years should have expired, a suggestion "not so objectionable as the violent proposals which have been not infrequently made to terminate the Treaty at once by a direct breach of faith." At about the same time, July 13, Andrews wrote Seward (Special Agents, Vol. XVII [D.S.]) that he had heard rumors of abrogation of the treaty and hoped that nothing would be done hastily to prejudice the real interests of both countries.

4. *House Reports,* No. 22, 37th Cong., 2d Sess. This Report contains the resolutions of the New York legislature.

the two regions and the large interchange of commodities which took place. The Canadians, too, recognized these facts, for the report of a Canadian Parliamentary Committee in 1858 advocated removal of all duties between the Provinces, and advised that "*the principle of reciprocity with the United States may be extended to manufactures, the registration of Canadian and United States built vessels, and to the shipping and coasting trade, in the same manner as to the productions of the soil.*"[5] But, the Ward Report went on, Canada had not lived up to its professions; under an enactment of 1860, vessels, having paid toll at the Welland Canal, received a rebate if they entered the St. Lawrence or any Canadian port, a procedure which created "a discrimination of ninety per cent against vessels going to American ports, besides a free passage through the canals of The Galops, Point Iroquois, Rapid Flat, Favian's Point, Cornwall, Beauharnois, and Lachine—a discrimination against the forwarders and millers of Rochester, Oswego, and Ogdensburg, the carrying systems of New York, and the shippers and merchants of that port."[6] Canada had maintained that it was necessary to increase duties upon manufactured products in order to raise necessary revenue; nevertheless, by a proclamation of November 30, 1860, the harbor of Gaspé Basin had been constituted a free port embracing the Magdalen Islands, Anticosti Island, and the eastern limits of the province on the coast of Labrador. The free port of Sault Ste Marie in like manner opened a shore line of not less than four hundred miles, whence goods, paying no duty, could be smuggled into the United States. Moreover, a very large proportion of the revenue raised in Canada went to service the debt created by building railroads and canals "to compete with American interests, and in fruitless but persistent efforts to divert the trade of western States from the natural channels it had already formed," and the committee quoted Minister of Finance Galt to show that it was the avowed purpose of the Canadian Government to effect such discrimination.[7]

It is, of course, a little hard to understand why the Canadian Government should not adopt means to promote the welfare of its own citizens, but to the committee of the House of Representatives this apparently was an indication of some malign intent. On the other

5. *Ibid.*, p. 8.　　　　　　　　6. *Ibid.*, p. 12.
7. *Ibid.*, p. 14.

hand, it appeared that these efforts to build up Montreal and Quebec at the expense of American towns on the Atlantic seaboard were by no means satisfactory to all of Upper Canada which, through Boards of Trade in various towns, protested that the

proposed policy of the inspector general practically shuts the door to the admission into Canada of the leading articles of commerce hitherto purchased in the great markets of the United States, and *forcing Upper Canada to import via the St. Lawrence, or pay an enormous increase of duty.*[8]

Along the northern border of the United States there was no question about the advantages of a "true" reciprocity with the British Provinces; Milwaukee, Chicago, Detroit, Cleveland, Ogdensburg, and other cities had expressed themselves through their Boards of Trade in favor of casting "the sentiment of the frontier into a useful and permanent form, by the removal of restrictive laws, and by opening such channels of trade as, beginning at the frontier, will enrich the interior of their various States, concentrating wealth and commerce at our seaports, increasing our shipping, and adding materially to our national resources."[9] Agreeing with this view, the committee recommended that "three commissioners be appointed by the President of the United States to confer with persons duly authorized by Great Britain . . . with a view to enlarging the basis of the former treaty, and for the removal of existing difficulties."[10] While the recommendations of the committee appeared on their face open-minded and liberal, it is observable that no mention was made of two points which the Colonials always stressed: mutual registration of vessels and the coasting trade.

Lord Lyons had been paying close attention to what had been taking place in Congress and to the mutterings of the press. He had

8. *Ibid.*, pp. 20–21.   9. *Ibid.*, p. 22.

10. *Ibid.*, p. 32. The committee might have added St. Paul to its list of frontier towns, for, on January 17, 1862, J. W. Taylor presented to the Chamber of Commerce a memorial which was unanimously adopted: this urged the maintenance of national good faith, for all parties up to that time *had* observed in good faith the terms of the treaty; it urged upon Congress taking up in due time the question of continuance of the treaty with enlargement of its provisions "to the proportions of a Zoll-Verein or Customs Union." *Senate Misc. Docs.*, No. 26, 37th Cong., 2d Sess.

spoken[11] to Secretary Seward on February 1, 1862, of an instruction directing him to request the President to interpose his veto should there be any action taken to abrogate the treaty. Seward had assured him that there was no intention on the part of the Administration to take any step violating the terms of the existing arrangement. Lyons did, however, see the President on February 12,[12] and repeated the substance of what he had said to Seward.[13] "The President answered that until he had been informed by Mr Seward that anxiety was felt on the subject by Her Majesty's Government, he had not been aware that an idea of disturbing the Treaty existed in any quarter. I might, he added, rely upon his determination to maintain the good faith of the Nation. 'In this and in all matters' he said in conclusion 'we desire to be good friends with you if we can.' " The Ward Report, while it charged that the Canadian Government "of set purpose" had acted contrary to the spirit of the Treaty, did not, Lyons noted,[14] "recommend any of the violent retaliatory measures which have been sometimes advocated in this country; on the contrary they rather suggest negotiations for extending the system of Free Trade between Canada and the United States, and even for establishing a complete customs-union between the two countries, on the principle of the German Zollverein." An addition to the list of undutiable articles might, in Lyons' opinion, serve to enlist additional support, especially if some manufactures were included, but in view of Canadian finances it appeared that this was out of the question and the best thing to do was to "avoid as far as possible all agitation on the subject of the Treaty."[15]

Congress at this session (1861–62) took no action upon the Ward Report nor upon any of the petitions and memorials submitted for or against abrogating the treaty.[16] Nor did it in the concluding short session turn its attention to the matter. The winter of 1863–64, how-

11. Lyons to Russell (draft), Feb. 7, 1862; FO 115:298 (P.R.O.).
12. Lyons to Russell, Feb. 14, 1862; FO 5:825 (P.R.O.).
13. Lyons to Russell (draft), Feb. 14, 1862; FO 115:298 (P.R.O.).
14. Lyons to Russell, Feb. 25, 1862; FO 5:825 (P.R.O.).
15. A resolution of the Maine legislature, dated Mar. 19, 1862 (*Senate Misc. Docs.*, No. 74, 37th Cong., 2d Sess.), called for abrogation as soon as possible and lent point to Lyons' remarks.
16. A joint resolution (*Cong. Globe,* 37th Cong., 2d Sess., p. 1847) was introduced in May authorizing the appointment of commissioners to negotiate a new treaty based "on the true principles" of reciprocity and authorizing the

ever, found a different state of affairs; the new Congress was apparently bent on eliminating the treaty as soon as its terms would allow, even if, as some desired, they did not go to the point of actually violating its provisions by an earlier abrogation. Hardly was the House organized before J. S. Morrill gave notice that he would introduce a joint resolution for abrogation, and a week later it passed its first and second readings and was referred to the Committee on Commerce.[17] No serious effort to bring it up was made until May, and then the fireworks began.

In the interim, diplomacy complicated with new difficulties was struggling with the issue. In December, 1863, E. M. Archibald, the British Consul at New York, complained to Lord Lyons[18] that new and embarrassing restrictions had been imposed upon shipments of general merchandise from that port to British North American ports. In the case of one vessel, laden with flour, pork, butter, and other provisions, the shippers had to give security, "in double the amount of the invoice," that the cargo would be landed at Harbor Grace and that no part should be directly or indirectly transshipped for the port of any insurrectionary State "or in any manner used for the aid and comfort of the insurgents. . . . The peculiar and oppressive nature of this bond is the requiring one of the sureties to be possessed of *real estate* of double the value of the invoice." The other cases were of a similar nature. Since Newfoundland was supplied in great measure from the United States, these almost prohibitory restrictions might easily cut off all legitimate trade. Archibald pointed out to the Collector of the Port of New York[19] that the people of Newfoundland were not interested in American political questions and had no trade, direct or indirect, with the insurgent States of the Union; nor had they any trade

President to give notice terminating the existing "unsatisfactory" treaty. No action upon it was taken.

17. *Cong. Globe,* 38th Cong., 1st Sess., pp. 9, 19. On February 25 Rufus P. Spaulding of Ohio brought the matter up and voiced the usual complaints, while the next day De Witt C. Littlejohn of New York protested abrogation, which would arbitrarily interrupt trade and commerce. *Ibid.,* pp. 2481–2482, 2505. Lyons reported he notified Seward that notice could not be given till the end of the ten years. Lyons to Russell, Jan. 12; FO 115:406 (P.R.O.).

18. Dec. 31, 1863; *Diplomatic Correspondence, 1864–65,* Part II, pp. 469–470.

19. Dec. 31; *ibid.,* p. 471.

with Bermuda or Nassau. Lord Lyons took the matter up with Seward[20] and again, in the middle of February, found himself "called upon to remonstrate against restrictions placed upon trade between New York and places within the Queen's jurisdiction." To this Seward replied that it appeared from a report of the Treasury Department that there was reason to believe that shipments from New York ostensibly for Newfoundland were really for Nassau and Bermuda, so that "bonds were, in one or two instances only, some months ago, required on cargoes for Newfoundland. That requirement has, however, now been discontinued."[21] But Seward was evidently misinformed, for renewed complaints came from Archibald that even more onerous restrictions were being imposed.

What so far had been only the result of executive order threatened to become fixed permanently as law when Lyons learned that Wade had introduced in the Senate a bill to repeal so much of the acts of March 3, 1845, and August 6, 1846, as authorized transportation of goods imported from foreign countries through the United States to Canada, or from Canada through the United States for export to foreign countries. "I went," wrote Lyons, "immediately to Mr Seward and begged him to give his attention to this matter and to consider whether the enactment of the proposed Bill would not have a most unfavourable effect not only on the commercial relations between Canada and the United States, but on the political relations between the United States and the Empire at large." Seward promised to look into the matter and asked Lyons in the meantime not to "make any stir about it." A little later he received from Seward confidentially a copy of a dispatch from J. R. Giddings, the American Consul at Montreal, "reporting that supplies were sent to the Southern States from Canada, which passed through the United States in bond, and were shipped at New York." Seward also confidentially informed Lyons that Wade's bill had been introduced on account of irritation over Giddings' arrest, which was "exercising a very unfortunate influence, with regard to the motion for abrogating the Reciprocity Treaty, and on all matters relating to Canada." He had, so he told Lyons, succeeded in arresting Wade's bill, "which was more dangerous than the

20. Jan. 6, 1864; *ibid.*, p. 469.
21. The correspondence is in *ibid.*, pp. 520 ff.

motion respecting the Treaty, because if it had passed it would have taken effect immediately."[22]

Such satisfaction as might have been drawn from this assurance was short-lived. In a little over a month Lyons had sadly to report that bonds were still being demanded, despite his efforts to have them eliminated. "Every effort," he wrote the Colonial Office,[23] "has been made by Her Majesty's Government, and by me acting under their orders, to induce the United States Authorities to refrain from imposing these and similar restrictions on the trade with British Possessions; but I regret to say that little or no success has hitherto attended these efforts." The Secretary of State did admit in reference to one of the complaints that "the Collector was believed to have exceeded the requirements of the Act of Congress" and had been notified to that effect, but the Secretary "still however maintains that the Collector must be left to exact Bonds according to his own discretion."

There was brought to Seward's attention in January, 1864, the fact that a large shipper of cattle in Canada had suddenly found he could no longer import live hogs over the Suspension Bridge at Niagara and had laid a complaint before the proper authorities of his country. In due course this had gone before the Canadian Executive Council, which, in a committee report, asserted that the finding of the Finance Minister be approved when he stated that there must have been some misapprehension on the part of the American customs officials of their orders since "they have not been construed as prohibiting the exportation of live hogs to Canada at any other point." Up to the time of this action there had been continuous and large shipments of live stock into Canada, and no one suspected that certain orders of the War and

22. Lyons to Russell, Feb. 23, 1864; FO 5:945 (P.R.O.). Seward's and Giddings' letters were enclosed. In an unofficial dispatch to Seward, February 19, Lyons said he had no recollection of any such shipment as Giddings mentioned nor of giving any general advice which would have served as official approval of the alleged transaction. *Ibid.*

W. D. Overman, in "Some Letters of Joshua R. Giddings on Reciprocity," *Canadian Historical Review*, XVI, 289–296, indicates Giddings' bitterness, especially over his arrest for alleged complicity in the kidnaping from Montreal of a British subject who had been employed in New York. Giddings was released and the complaint dropped, but he was convinced that he was the object of Southern machinations.

23. Lyons to Gordon, Mar. 28, 1864; CO 188:177 (P.R.O.).

Treasury Departments relative to the shipment of arms and munitions could apply to such commodities. The Finance Minister was of the opinion that the prohibitory order did not transcend the rights of the United States, nor could it be looked upon as an "interference with the reciprocity treaty, such order having no bearing upon our exports to the United States." The case, then, appeared without remedy "except by special representation of the government at Washington, founded upon the fact, which is so abundantly established by official returns, that long after the promulgation of the orders in question in the United States, and before . . . [they] were generally known to the trade in Canada, importations of live stock continued to be made as usual . . . justifying the impression that the prohibition was not considered by the customs authorities of the United States as extending to the exportation of live stock." Seward's reference to the order of the Treasury Department placing the prohibition upon grounds of possible shortage of meat in the United States was mildly scoffed at by Lord Lyons, who said that, since there was no prohibition upon the shipment of meat to the Provinces, nothing was achieved by the order.[24]

Anthracite coal, too, was placed on the prohibited list. While this, wrote Lyons,[25] presented "no such anomaly as that just adverted to it is productive of far greater inconvenience to the people of Canada than the other regulation."

There are scattered through the western part of the province numerous iron foundries and other factories which have heretofore been wholly supplied with fuel from the United States, consisting mainly of anthracite coal. . . .

The prohibition is believed to have been solely designed to prevent American coal from passing into the hands of the enemies of the United States, or being used for purposes hostile to the United States, neither of which consequences would be likely to flow from the exportation of coal to Canada, at points so remote from the sea as to preclude the probability, if not the possibility, of any intercourse with the enemies of the United States.

24. The documents are in *Diplomatic Correspondence, 1864–65,* Part II, pp. 485 ff.; G 232 (P.A.C.).

25. Lyons to Seward, Mar. 15, 1864; *Diplomatic Correspondence, 1864–65,* Part II, p. 559.

Reasonable as the statement appeared to be, it elicited no favorable response from the Department of State. The measure, said Seward,[26] had "been adopted after due deliberation and has been dictated by public exigencies growing out of the present civil war."

With reference to this article, however, another element has measurably, at least, influenced the policy of this Government, namely, the notorious fact that fuel of that character is, for obvious reasons, preferred by blockade runners, who before the restriction went into effect, were in the habit of supplying themselves with this article at those ports in Her Majesty's possessions near us which, ever since the spring of 1860 [sic] they have made the basis of their operations.

"Your Lordship," remarked Lyons in sending this note to the Foreign Office,[27] "will observe that Mr Seward, while holding out no hope of any relaxation of the prohibition, takes little notice of the arguments tending to show that the exportation of cattle and coal to Canada might be permitted without interfering with the general objects with a view to which the prohibition is enforced." The regulation, he thought, was in part applied because the Government of the United States wished to make no exception to a general rule: he believed that the French authorities had applied for a small amount of coal for their squadron in the Gulf of Mexico, and there was "certainly no desire in the United States to facilitate in any way the operations of the French Forces on this side of the Atlantic, and this may be one reason why it is thought desirable to enforce rigorously in all cases the prohibition to export live stock and coal."

But apart from all these inconveniences caused by real or supposed war necessities of the United States, the chief issue was what was going to happen to the Reciprocity Treaty. The anxiety of the British Minister, so frequently communicated to Secretary Seward, was real and persistent. The latter avowed, not only to Lyons, but also to Adams[28] in London the desire of the American Government to let matters remain as they were and not to stir up more trouble by taking precipitate action looking toward abrogation. Nothing, he said, could be more foreign to the purpose or desire of the Administration

26. Seward to Lyons, Mar. 18, 1864; *ibid.*, p. 561.
27. Lyons to Russell, Mar. 28, 1864; FO 5:946 (P.R.O.).
28. Feb. 8, 1864; Great Britain:Instructions, Vol. XIX (D.S.).

than to view rising difficulties about the treaty as anything but mere demonstrations. Nevertheless, he was forced to admit that there was actual discontent with the reciprocity arrangement: there was a valid argument to be drawn from the loss of revenue; there was a feeling of dissatisfaction produced by the coöperation of British subjects and more especially by those in the nearby colonies with the "slave insurrection," which had brought on a legislative agitation of the questions which the President would gladly have postponed to a more convenient day. Opposition to the treaty seemed to be gaining strength. He authorized Adams to discuss the subject with Lord Russell, and the result of their conversations was reported by Adams on February 26.[29] His Lordship said he had received information from Washington on the matter; he understood the position of the American Government and their disinclination to "disturb the treaty. He could say no more than that he regretted such a consequence, as at the present time he saw no present way of avoiding it."

In British North America it was obvious that so much hostile discussion could not fail to produce growing uneasiness. In the House of Assembly of Newfoundland, for example,[30] several returns on the working of the treaty had been laid on the table and the subject had been discussed for three days on a motion to the effect that the treaty had operated to the benefit of the Colony and should be continued. An amendment, proposed by the Attorney-General, stated that the treaty had not produced *all* the benefits expected and it was to the advantage of the Colony to wait the opening of further negotiations in the expectation of obtaining further concessions such as abolition of fishing bounties. The amendment was carried by a vote of fourteen to ten. In common with New Brunswick and other colonies, Newfoundland felt justified in demanding compensation for closing the Southern market by the blockade, although no formal statement to this effect was adopted. In Canada a Report of a Committee of the Executive Council, adopted on February 19,[31] called attention to agitation in Con-

29. Adams to Seward; *Diplomatic Correspondence, 1864–65,* Part II, pp. 244–245.

30. Convers O. Leach to Seward, Mar. 9, 1864; Consular Letters: St. Johns, Newfoundland, Vol. IV (D.S.).

31. Enclosed by Russell in an instruction to Lyons, Mar. 22, 1864, together with a covering letter from the Colonial Office. FO 115: 402 (P.R.O.).

gress which had as an "avowed object the abrogation of the Treaty at the earliest moment consistent with the stipulations of the instrument itself." The Committee maintained that it was impossible to express in figures the "extent to which the facilities of commercial intercourse created by the Reciprocity Treaty have contributed to the wealth and prosperity of this Province," and it would be difficult to exaggerate the importance Canadians attached to a continuation of the arrangement. Not alone was there an economic consideration; it had a political significance:

Under the beneficent operation of the system of self government which the later policy of the mother country has accorded to Canada in common with the other colonies possessing Representative institutions combined with the advantage secured by the Reciprocity Treaty of an unrestricted commerce with our nearest neighbours in the natural productions of the two Countries all agitation for organic changes has ceased—all dissatisfaction with the existing political relations of the Province has wholly disappeared.

Mere commercial convenience, the committee hastened to state, was not the basis of their loyalty to the Crown, a loyalty which would not be in the slightest diminished by withdrawal of such privileges by an unfriendly foreign power; nevertheless, commercial prosperity and political contentment were closely associated.

The Committee Report was by no means the first indication that the Canadian Government viewed with apprehension increasing tension over the treaty. In the summer of 1863 the question of finding out just how the land lay had resulted in the suggestion of sending a special representative to Washington to confer with Lord Lyons and to sound out the possibilities of the future. No immediate action was taken, but, when Congress met and the issue was uppermost again, the Premier, John Sandfield Macdonald, approached George Brown, editor and proprietor of the powerful Toronto *Globe*, leader of the "Clear Grit" faction and foremost Liberal, on the subject.[32] The Government, he said, had not failed to notice the agitation in the United States.

32. Macdonald to Brown, Jan. 7, 1864. Alexander Mackenzie, *The Life and Speeches of the Hon. George Brown* (Toronto, 1882), p. 83. "Clear Grit" was the radical faction of the Liberal party; Brown went over to it in 1850.

. . . If we have abstained thus far from indicating by any public announcement the policy to be adopted, or from taking steps either by representing the anxiety we feel to the home government, or to the British Minister in Washington, with a view to imperial action, it is because we were waiting the result of events we could not control. The aspect in which the matter now presents itself admonishes us to prepare for the fight. We have considered that the first movement to be made is to select a competent individual who could be entrusted to deal with the subject at Washington, and who by his position could approach all parties at that capital.

Brown, in the opinion of the Government, was that person and his co-operation was bespoken "in any way you may feel disposed to lend it toward maintaining the treaty as it is; or, if that should be found impracticable, to promote the best terms that can be secured in any new arrangement that may be agreed upon as the basis of a fresh treaty." Macdonald added in a postscript that "during an interview I had with Mr. Seward in New York, he strongly recommended this course to be taken early—namely, having a quasi-political agent to remain at Washington for some months, with whom he and Lord Lyons could confer informally from time to time on matters concerning Canada." Brown was heartily in accord with the idea, but thought Luther M. Holton and not he was the man to send,[33] and made many suggestions for arousing to action sympathetic support in the United States.

The British Minister was positive that the Canadians were making a mistake by pressing the matter at that time.[34] The more they agitated the surer would the people of the United States be that Canada was gaining and the United States losing by the arrangement. But Seward, who had previously been of the opinion that any move by the Canadians would result badly, Lyons found, had changed his mind. "He now thinks that discussion on the subject cannot be avoided, and a good effect would be produced by visits to Washington of influential Canadians coming 'on their own hook' and talking in a friendly manner to Senators and Deputies,"[35] although he did not have any great hope of staving off action by Congress. Finally, the Honorable John Young, a leading businessman of Montreal, was charged with the mis-

33. *Ibid.*, p. 84.
34. Lyons to Monck, Jan. 28, 1864. Newton, *op. cit.*, I, 123–124.
35. Lyons to Russell, Feb. 9, 1864; *ibid.*, pp. 125–126.

sion and sent in a confidential capacity by Lord Monck to Washington. On the basis of his report the Governor-General[36] believed that the Government of the United States, "though friendly to the maintenance of the Treaty, will not be able to defeat in the Legislature the motion calling upon the President to give the year's notice for its abrogation." Even if there were no danger of abrogation, Canadian trade would be disadvantageously affected unless some new arrangement should be made for a "*fixed*" period, since "operations of trade will soon accommodate themselves to conditions however hostile if they are fixed, but they are paralyzed by those that are precarious or uncertain." But Lord Lyons had not changed his opinion that the best course to follow was that of "watchful waiting."[37] Perhaps the feeling in Canada was so strong that something in the way of negotiation would have to be undertaken, but conditions were not propitious. The Canadians wanted a treaty and one about the same as the existing one; in the United States, however, a considerable party desired no treaty for revenue reasons, others wanted one with manufactured articles included, while, he went on, "a number, and I am afraid not a small number, of influential men are actuated by a feeling of irritation against England, and particularly against the neighbouring British Provinces."

There are moreover not a few who look to the annexation of Canada to the U. S. who desire to cause the separation to be felt by the Canadians as an inconvenience, and who possibly even hope that the Canadians may be brought to regard restrictions on commercial intercourse as greater evils than the conscription and the heavy Taxation to which a union with this country would render them liable.

Besides all this Americans "do not believe that we shall ever really exclude them from the Fisheries or from the Navigation of the St Lawrence. A threat to do so from the mouth of the British Negotiator would have very little effect, unless strong measures were to convince the opposite Party that there was a firm determination to execute it."

That the British Minister, basing his views upon an observation of things American from close at hand, was better informed than Cana-

36. Monck to Newcastle, Confidential, Mar. 15, 1864; FO 115:403 (P.R.O.).

37. Lyons to Russell (draft), Mar. 28, 1864; FO 115:406 (P.R.O.).

dians, whose views were colored by wishful thinking, was amply demonstrated by what soon took place in Congress. Furthermore, both the Foreign Office and the Colonial Office were agreed that "at the present moment the attitude of observation is that which is most prudent to preserve, in the hope that the Resolution may not be passed by both Houses."[38] A change in the Canadian Government, too, had a deterring effect, for the Governor-General had not yet had time to consult with his new advisers to ascertain "whether in the hope of obtaining a satisfactory treaty with U. S. as well as upon other grounds they may not be disposed to entertain the question of a general reduction of the customs duties of Canada."

In the House of Representatives the voluminous Report of the Committee on Commerce had remained practically unnoticed until, on the first of April, 1864, Chairman Ward obtained the floor to report back a resolution based upon it and to enter a motion to have a substitute, prepared by the committee, considered by the House within a month.[39] The substitute, after rehearsing in a long preamble the reasons for taking up the matter, stated that

The President of the United States be, and he is hereby, authorized and required to give notice to the Government of the United Kingdom of Great Britain and Ireland that it is the wish and intention of the Government of the United States of America to terminate the said treaty at the end of twelve months from the expiration of ten years from the time when the said treaty went into operation as aforesaid;[40] such notice to be given at the expiration of the said term of years, to the end that the said treaty may be abrogated as soon as it can be done under the provision thereof, unless a new convention shall before that time be concluded between the two Governments by which the provision shall be abrogated or so modified as to be mutually satisfactory to both Governments. And that the President of the United States shall be, and he is hereby, authorized to appoint three commissioners, by and with the advice and consent of the Senate, for the revision of the said treaty, and to confer with other commissioners duly authorized therefor, whenever it shall appear to be the wish of the Government of Great Britain to negotiate a new treaty based upon the true principles of reciprocity, and for the removal of existing difficulties.

38. Elliot to Hammond, May 7, 1864; Layard to Rogers, May 9, 1864; FO 115:403 (P.R.O.).

39. *Cong. Globe,* 38th Cong., 1st Sess., p. 1387.

40. This date was fixed by the preamble as March 16, 1855.

It was not until May 17 that the Speaker announced that the resolution was entitled to the floor.[41] The next day Ward presented the subject and recapitulated the arguments of the report, pointing out the similarity of institutions in the British Provinces to those of the United States, the desirability of removing objectionable features of the existing treaty and cementing commercial relations of the two countries in a firm and lasting manner. "I am less desirous," said he, "of a union of the Governments than for a union of the people. I do not wish to admit into our family of States any who are not imbued with the spirit of our institutions and do not appreciate as we do the benefits resulting from them, or the principles on which they are established." Much was made of Canada's increase in import duties which had caused, according to Ward, a drop in exportation of manufactures into that Province from the United States to the extent of some three millions of dollars in value between 1859 and 1863; the natural route for goods to flow into Canada was through New York and Boston, but the Canadian tariff diverted this trade to other channels. In the matter of grain and flour it was not so much a question of consumption on both sides of the frontier as one of commerce and transportation: if the whole grain crop of the United States were sold to Canada and went down the St. Lawrence to Europe it would not raise the price in the Province, but American railroads and canals would suffer. There was danger that all the colonies would go on a free-trade basis, whereupon it would be impossible to enforce American tariff regulations upon the northern frontier; unlimited smuggling would break down the American system. In general, Ward trusted that

there are few who deem it the part of wisdom or sound policy, or consistent with due regard to the character of the nation represented by us here, to attach any weight to whatever ebullitions or temporary ill-will may have arisen from individuals in the provinces or Great Britain. These manifestations, having their sources in ignorance or unworthy motives, may safely be left to the class of minds in which they originated.

The debate went on at intervals until May 26. Justin S. Morrill of Vermont moved an amendment[42] to authorize the President flatly to abrogate the treaty with no reference to further negotiations or to a

41. *Cong. Globe,* 38th Cong., 1st Sess., pp. 2298, 2333 ff.
42. May 19; *ibid.,* p. 2364.

new treaty. His colleague, Frederick A. Pike,[43] was equally sure the country demanded abrogation and he would put the date as early as possible, arguing that the ten years were up on September 11, 1864. As to the fisheries he maintained that all the people of his State wanted was the abolition of free entry of Canadian products: the fishing interest, he asserted, had no hand in bringing the treaty about; it was the Canadian Government and Canadian money circulating freely in Washington, "lubricating official channels. . . . As to the provinces, they are as nearly incorrigible as people can be."

But all arguments were not along this line. Isaac N. Arnold of Illinois[44] said the West needed the treaty, for its abrogation would shut off the St. Lawrence, and any representative of Minnesota, Iowa, Wisconsin, Missouri, Michigan, Ohio, Illinois, or Indiana would know that those States had been taxed for years by transportation charges through the United States. Answering a question of Morrill's, he maintained that not only were American routes insufficient but that Canadians used American waterways and railroads less than Americans used Canadian. He would remedy the evils of the treaty but not abrogate it, and to that end proffered an amendment[45] authorizing the appointment of commissioners to effect changes if possible but otherwise to abrogate. In general, the voice of the West echoed Arnold's words: they admitted changes might be necessary but they wanted reciprocity. Another note, not a new one, was injected by John V. L. Pruyn of New York when he said:[46]

I take the ground that we are willing to see reciprocally broad relations between Canada and this country. We have no desire to check the growth of Canada, but on the contrary we wish to see her developed, for in time she is to be annexed to us and form a part of this country, and I look upon her growth and prosperity with the highest satisfaction. It may not be in five or ten years that this will be brought about, but the logic of events will bring these provinces to us in time.

Portus Baxter of Vermont[47] told how, when Great Britain turned to free trade, the Canadians sent delegations to Washington to press for reciprocity, how the question of annexation was raised by the present

43. *Ibid.*, pp. 2364–2368.
45. May 24; *ibid.*, p. 2455.
47. May 26; *ibid.*, p. 2502.

44. May 19; *ibid.*, pp. 2368–2369.
46. May 25; *ibid.*, pp. 2482–2484.

head of the Canadian Government, and how the Southerners conceded the treaty to head off annexation. If Congress should provide for the commission recommended by the committee he would wish to amend the bill to read "a commission to arrange terms for continuing, in a dignified position, the wet-nurse of the sick British colonies."

Finally, after hours of discussion, the issue came to a vote on May 26. Both Morrill's and Arnold's amendments were defeated. Then Thaddeus Stevens of Pennsylvania moved to lay the original resolution on the table, thinking it better to let the treaty run another year; this was lost, 76 to 73. He then proposed postponing it until December and this was carried, 77 to 72. In the Senate, Lot M. Morrill of Maine sought leave to introduce a resolution requiring the President to give notice,[48] but the matter went no further that session. A breathing space was afforded friends of the treaty in the United States, and the Provinces gained a little hope that abrogation might be staved off.

With abrogation temporarily laid aside the British Minister could feel that the burdens placed upon him by Colonial interests were somewhat lightened, but by no means removed. Bonding and restrictions upon exports to Canada still occupied his attention, and he continued to urge upon Seward the unreasonableness of some of the war-time measures. Only partial relief could he obtain for those who shipped goods by sea to the Maritime Provinces, and particularly to Newfoundland. In the words of the Collector of the Port of New York,[49] the complaint was unfounded with respect to Prince Edward Island, for no bonds had ever been required on goods sent to that Colony and only in a limited way in the case of Nova Scotia and New Brunswick.

This exaction is made for the reason that an illegal traffic has been carried on, and still is to some extent, between the principal ports in those provinces and the British West Indies, and ports and places under the control of persons in rebellion against the authority of the United States; and it is believed that such illegal trade would be carried on to a large amount, were it not that such bonds are exacted on shipments of such articles from this port.

48. Jan. 8, 1864; *Cong. Globe*, 38th Cong., 1st Sess., p. 134.
49. Clinch to Chase, May 25, 1864; *Diplomatic Correspondence, 1864–65*, Part II, p. 632.

To Lord Russell[50] the arguments of the American Secretary of State were feeble, to say the least, and he caustically instructed Lyons to

. . . remark to Mr Seward that if the blockade of the Southern Coasts cannot be rendered efficient by the naval power of the United States without recourse to those irregular and unprecedented methods of harassing and intercepting within the United States the ordinary trade of Neutral Powers, those Powers might well be justified on their part in treating this as a virtual admission that the blockade is not adequately or legally maintained and in declining under such circumstances any longer to recognize its legality.

Such a statement was very interesting coming from the man who had blandly asserted in Parliament more than once, in response to angry protests, that the British Government regarded the blockade as effective. Protests produced better results regarding export of coal to Canada, for a hint from Seward to Lyons[51] led to the issuance of a proclamation by the Governor-General of Canada, authorizing the prohibition, from time to time, in addition to arms, munitions, and military or naval stores already provided for, of *"exportation from our province of Canada of anthracite coal* in any manner or way whatever." This statement produced a Treasury Order of August 17 rescinding the previous one to the extent of allowing unrestricted exportation of anthracite coal to Canada, except by sea.[52]

If, however, the colonials had derived comfort from the postponement of abrogation of the treaty and from relaxation of restrictions in some minor ways, the late autumn showed that this was but a momentary lull before the storm. The raid on St. Albans, the *Chesapeake* affair, and the resulting increase in exasperation in many parts of the United States directed anew the attention of Congress to Canada's vulnerable spot. "In the presence of such facts," an editorial in the

50. Russell to Lyons, July 16, 1864; FO 115:404 (P.R.O.). Lyons to Seward, Aug. 4, 1864; *Diplomatic Correspondence, 1864–65,* Part II, pp. 667–668.

51. Lyons to Monck, July 11, 1864; G 233 (P.A.C.). Lyons to Seward, Aug. 3, 1864; *Diplomatic Correspondence, 1864–65,* Part II, pp. 682–683. Lyons to Russell, Aug. 5, 1864; FO 5:957 (P.R.O.).

52. *Diplomatic Correspondence, 1864–65,* Part II, p. 688. Lyons expressed the thanks of the Governor-General in a note to Seward, Aug. 3. *Ibid.,* p. 682.

New York *Herald* stated,[53] "we repeat that it becomes one of the first duties of the new Congress to manifest its resentment at the unfriendly and dishonest treatment by doing away with the treaty under which Canada derives such substantial commercial advantages from us." And Congress took it as one of its first duties. The House proceeded immediately to pass the joint resolution to terminate the Reciprocity Treaty on March 16, 1866; the Senate received it on December 14, when after a brief discussion the Committee on Foreign Relations took it and reported it back on December 19 with a substitute.[54] From the first there was little doubt that the Senate would adopt the resolution in some form. Much attention in the debate was paid to border raids and the supposed threat of similar occurrences, and it was clearly apparent that resentment played a great part in the motives actuating Senators. J. R. Doolittle of Wisconsin hoped that Canada would stop the raids, for if they were not halted it meant war, which he hoped could be averted; but if it must, let it come: "We will end the question whenever it does come by perfect free trade between Canada and the United States, and by putting an end to the jurisdiction of Great Britain in any of those provinces in North America."[55] This was the spirit if not the words of most of those who spoke for abrogation. Not many agreed with J. W. Grimes either in prophesying the ruin of Canada or in wishing it.[56] But there were fewer who would stand with John Hale of New Hampshire, who came out flatly against any hasty action; the time to show resentment, he said, had been in the Mason and Slidell affair, not now, when nothing should be done, even in debate, to excite feelings. "I have totally disagreed with those who would repeal this reciprocity treaty. I think it is a great measure of good, not only to the comfort but to the military ability and to the naval force of this country."[57] A few rallied to Hale's side—Alexander Ramsey

---

53. Nov. 9, 1864.

54. *Cong. Globe,* 38th Cong., 2d Sess., pp. 34, 35, 71. The Senate Committee substitute was much more succinct than the original resolution; *"Resolved, etc., That* notice be given of the termination of the reciprocity treaty, according to the provision therein contained for the termination of the same; and the President of the United States is hereby charged with the communication of such notice to the Government of the United Kingdom of Great Britain and Ireland." *Ibid.,* p. 96.

55. *Ibid.,* p. 57.   56. *Ibid.,* p. 60.   57. *Ibid.,* p. 60.

of Minnesota, Reverdy Johnson of Maryland, T. O. Howe of Wisconsin—but they pleaded in vain against a hostile majority which wished to strike a blow that would hurt. Charles Sumner, the pontifical chairman of the Committee on Foreign Relations, loftily maintained that the only value to the United States was found in the fisheries provision; commerce had increased, but who could tell whether it was from the treaty or on account of the increase of population in the Provinces; navigation of the river and the canals was a negligible matter, and the United States was suffering from loss of revenue due to the free list. Except for making known to their constituents their individual stand, and except for the inevitable necessity of senatorial debate, there might as well have been a vote on the day the committee returned its report, for minds were made up and anything said in debate was merely words for the *Congressional Globe*. The Congress of the United States was determined to end reciprocity. Motives were found in a mixture of belief in alleged inequities of the treaty and firm conviction that, as a whole, the Provinces, especially United Canada, had been unsympathetic to the North in word and deed.

CHAPTER IX

INDEPENDENCE, CONFEDERATION, OR ANNEXATION?

ANNEXATIONIST agitation in the United States, which had been so pronounced in the late Forties and early Fifties and which had met with a little response in British North America, had died down under reciprocity, although seeds of the movement were always present, waiting a favorable moment to sprout. That period came with the American Civil War and its aftermath. For nearly a decade there were in the United States vociferous advocates of absorbing part or all of the British continental Provinces, and, at times, these agitators found no inconsiderable support in various parts of the country and aroused more than a little concern north of the border. In British North America, on the other hand, this was the time when a movement for changing the status of the individual Colonies in their relations with each other and with Great Britain assumed formidable proportions and eventually produced the Dominion of Canada in 1867. The path to confederation was by no means smooth. Large sections of the Colonial populace were content to let things remain as they were; they believed that both economic advantage and political security were bound up with a maintenance of existing relations with the Empire, that the interests of the different Colonies were so diverse that any sort of a union would entail too many sacrifices and lead to dangers the extent of which no one could foretell. At the other extreme was an active group convinced that the time was approaching when the Colonies would be ready to break the Imperial tie and assume the position of an independent nation. Between these two extremes were those who felt that while independence was neither safe nor practicable, a mere antechamber to annexation, continuation of the existing situation was almost equally hazardous. Standing alone, even though a part of the Empire, each Province was too small to be an effective unit either in maintaining a position of economic stability or of withstanding pressure from the powerful nation to the south. When to this was added more than a suspicion that many leading men in Britain were beginning to doubt the desirability of retaining colonies, and especially the

North American Colonies, those who opposed merging their fortunes with those of the United States felt that there must be found some solution which would relieve Great Britain of at least a part of the expense which those colonies entailed, while at the same time encouraging those at home who were not "Little Englanders."[1]

But there were other motives besides those based on lofty concepts of nationality, imperial welfare, and the like. As the Lieutenant-Governor of New Brunswick wrote Lord Lytton in 1858,[2] after he learned that the Executive Council of Canada had advised the Governor in Chief to recommend to the Secretary of State for Colonies the appointment of a commission to look into the matter, he was surprised that such a proposal should have been made without consulting the other Colonies. Federation, he opined, would be of advantage to the Canadas: it would solve the problem of selecting a seat of government; it would possibly find a solution of the perpetual conflict between Upper and Lower Canada, since it would involve the "severance of the bond" uniting the parts and substitute a "more elastic tie of Federal or Federative character." But a union government would find the Canadas in a preponderant position; New Brunswick, Nova Scotia, and Prince Edward Island would have minority representation and their interests would be subordinated. Either the local governments would retain their existing authority, in which case the central government, with nothing else to do, would soon claim authority on subjects

1. Later, in an instruction from Granville to Sir John Young, the Governor-General (March 28, 1869), to be laid before the Canadian Cabinet, it was bluntly asserted that the Imperial military force in Canada would probably be reduced to 2,000 in Nova Scotia, where Halifax would be considered the Imperial station, while about 4,000 would be left for a time in the rest of the Dominion. Canada must look to the withdrawal of all except a few officers left for training local recruits, although the British Government would introduce a bill to carry out a previous agreement regarding fortifications. Moreover, there was no reason to maintain on the Great Lakes a naval force larger than that contemplated in the Agreement of 1817. FO 115:486 (P.R.O.). See Chester Martin, "British Policy in Canadian Confederation," *Can. Hist. Rev.*, XIII, 3–19, and "The United States and Canadian Nationality," *ibid.*, XXIII, 1–11; C. P. Stacey, *Canada and the British Army, 1846–1871*, chap. ii; and, particularly, R. G. Trotter, *Canadian Federation: Its Origins and Achievement: A Study in Nation Building* (Toronto and London, 1924), chap. iii and *passim*.

2. Sutton to Lytton, Oct. 2, 1858, Question of Federation of British Provinces in America; CO 188 (P.R.O.).

not purely colonial and lead to collision with the Imperial Government and Parliament; or, if local governments were shorn of their powers, the inhabitants of the Maritime Provinces would soon become dissatisfied with a system which made them Provinces of Canada rather than of the British Empire, "and in the attempt to gain what they had lost, they might, and, as I think, probably would look, not, indeed, to the Government at Washington for assistance, but to the Northern States of the Union." Federal union would be followed by a demand for election of local governors, then of a governor-general, and finally there would be practical if not nominal severance from the Crown. A legislative union of the Maritime Provinces, thought the Lieutenant-Governor, would bring "incalculable benefits" to all three, but no basis existed for tying the Canadas with the Maritime Provinces in any kind of a political union.[3]

But the Civil War, with its continued and sometimes menacing concomitant of annexation, tended to modify opposition to confederation. If a small number of malcontents saw incorporation in the United States as the solution of political and economic ills, by far the greater number feared such a fate: they did not want to cease to be British subjects; they objected to paying the taxes necessitated by the long-drawn-out struggle between the sections; they abhorred American protectionism; they believed that their own system of government was vastly superior to that of the Union; and they prided themselves on a freedom from political knavery which they reprobated in their southern neighbor. In short, they did not wish to become Americans both from practical and sentimental reasons. And yet if England was growing cold and was willing to let her North American Colonies stand on their own feet, if England was tired of footing bills for military and naval protection, tired of being embroiled in nagging disputes engendered by Canadian-American proximity, what was there to do but try to work out some arrangement whereby not a group of sparsely populated isolated Provinces but a consolidated organization, able to make at least the first moves in self-defense, faced a powerful nation? As the tides of fortune in the Civil War rose and fell, and with them talk of

3. For a discussion of the reception of the Canadian proposal and Sutton's dispatch in England, see W. M. Whitelaw, *The Maritimes and Canada before Confederation,* chap. vi.

annexation, even the most reluctant were forced to believe that something had to be done.

Foremost in its pertinacious advocacy of absorbing British North America into the Union was James Gordon Bennett's New York *Herald*. In season and out, upon every conceivable occasion this paper was foretelling, urging, or demanding annexation. When secession became a fact in South Carolina, and the rest of the lower South was rapidly moving in the same direction, the *Herald* was of the opinion that the best thing to do was to let the dissatisfied states go; the South had legitimate grievances which the North refused to acknowledge or redress, but

Each section can find in its expansion in other directions some compensation for the sense of diminished national importance which the dissolution of the existing confederacy must bring home to all. The Cotton States will, in Mexico and the tropical countries bordering the Gulf, find the area which they deem necessary to provide for the rapid increase of their slave population. The Northern confederacy will seek a counterpoise to these acquisitions of its powerful neighbor by absorbing Canada. The English have, therefore, reason to view with alarm the alternative to which republican obstinacy is driving the South. As sure as ever it is consummated, Canada will be lost to the British crown.[4]

Day after day the "renegade Scot" harped upon this note. He cited[5] with approbation Seward's words spoken in St. Paul in September, 1860, when he was campaigning for the Republican ticket:

"I can stand here and look far off into the Northwest and see the Russian, as he busily occupies himself in establishing seaports and towns, and fortifications, as outposts of the empire of St. Petersburg, and I can say, 'Go in; build up your outposts to the Arctic Ocean; they will yet become the outposts of my own country, to extend the civilization of the United States in the Northwest.' So I look upon Prince Rupert's Land and

4. New York *Herald,* Jan. 24, 1861. In the same issue another editorial said: "There is now gaining strength in Canada, and indeed throughout the whole of British North America, a strong revolutionary feeling in favor of a confederation of all the colonies; and should there really be an irrevocable split in the United States, there will be no slight probability of one or more of these forsaking the protection of England and joining the Northern confederacy."

5. Jan. 25, 1861.

Canada, and see how an ingenious people, and a capable, enlightened government are occupied with bridging rivers and making railroads and telegraphs to develope, organize, create and preserve the great British provinces of the North, by the Great Lakes, the St. Lawrence and around the shores of Hudson's Bay, and I am able to say, 'It is very well; you are building excellent States to be hereafter admitted into the American Union.' "

Just as Slidell, Davis, Rhett, Mason, and others had been "toiling for years to build up a Southern confederacy," so "Seward, Wade, Lincoln, Hale and Sumner have been mapping out an immense empire this side of the Potomac, to embrace every acre of territory as far as the Arctic Ocean."

As long as the outcome of secession hung in the balance, up to the time when it was obvious that there was to be no peaceful withdrawal of the South, Bennett sounded this note: let the North absorb the British Provinces to compensate for the loss of the secessionists; the Provinces would gain and so would Great Britain.[6] The extradition case of the Negro, Anderson, in which it was asserted that Canadian self-government was flouted by an appeal to the English Court of the Queen's Bench, was played up to demonstrate that Colonials really did not have the management of their own affairs. "If the case of this negro is permitted to go upon the books as a precedent, the Canadian Judges have really no more power than a county magistrate."[7] When other states followed the example of South Carolina and formally withdrew from the Union, the *Herald* maintained that there should not be a moment's delay in repairing the loss: "Let Mr. Seward, in the 'rump' congress, immediately propose the admission of Canada into the Union of the Northern States, subject to the vote of the Canadian people, which there can be no doubt will be in favor of annexation. . . ."[8] When a Canadian, resident in New York, in a letter to the editor inquired what Canada could gain by annexation and scoffed at the reputed "perturbations" in the Provinces, he was editorially rebuked as ignorant both of the "perturbations" and of the "nature of our confederacy."[9] In short, every scrap of news which remotely bore upon the issue the *Herald* seized upon to drive home the desirability

6. Jan. 26, 1861.   7. Jan. 31, Feb. 4, 1861.
8. Feb. 4, 1861.   9. Feb. 9, 1861.

of annexation, as, for example, when McDougall, "one of the leaders of the opposition from Upper Canada," was reputed to have said that if the evils resulting from the union with Lower Canada were not soon remedied "an alliance between Upper Canada and the Northern States was likely to be formed."[10]

But the South showed that it was not bluffing; the North was insistent that secession had not occurred; and the Provinces showed no disposition to link their fate with the Union. A dialectic struggle became an armed encounter. Then the tone of the annexationist press in the United States, led by the *Herald* in the East, and, more or less, by the Chicago *Tribune* in the West, began to change. No longer was the matter to be left to sweet persuasion, but forcible means should be taken to effect annexation. The *Herald* came forth with the suggestions that North and South should bury the hatchet in a three-year truce, during which they should combine their armies to liberate Santo Domingo and perhaps Cuba from the Spanish, annex Mexico, and then conquer all the West Indies and drive the British from the North American continent.[11] When this proposal fell on stony ground still another note was struck, a note undoubtedly sounding in sympathetic vibration to current rancor against British attitude toward the struggle in the United States. "Let them [the British people] remember, however, that when the termination of our civil conflicts shall have arrived, it may be the turn of our foreign enemies to suffer the consequences of the mischiefs they are attempting to do us. Four hundred thousand thoroughly disciplined troops will ask no better occupation than to destroy the last vestiges of British rule on the American continent, and annex Canada to the United States."[12] And this was the theme of the annexationists during the remainder of the Civil War although, as the struggle intensified, less and less attention was paid to annexation or to much else besides the task immediately at hand. When in the summer of 1862 rumors of European intervention were rife, England and France were warned of the danger of interfering with the domestic concerns of the United States: "We will soon have an army of three-quarters of a million of men disengaged after the suppression of the rebellion, and a fleet of iron-clad vessels which will

10. Apr. 19, 1861.   11. June 27, 28, 1861.
12. Sept. 26, 1861.

sweep the combined navies of France, England and Spain from the face of the ocean; nor will we ever lay down our arms till we wipe out every vestige of foreign sway in the New World."[13] Canadians had their attention called to the coolness displayed by England, as represented by speeches in Parliament and editorials in leading newspapers, while their puny efforts looking toward self-defense were jeered at as insignificant: "How utterly contemptible is the military power of England and her provinces as compared with ours."[14]

While the fulminations of the New York *Herald* cannot be taken as a fair sample of news comment or as representing the opinions of the mass of thinking people of the United States, they do have to be considered as a constant irritant to the susceptibilities of Canadians and other Provincials. Harping upon this string of annexation could but combine with the growing demand for abrogation of reciprocity and a general tone of hostility to all things British, whether in the Old World or the New, to create a feeling of suspicion and distrust north of the border and to promote the idea of confederation as one way out.

By the summer of 1864 confederation definitely was a factor to be reckoned with. This concept, or something like it, had been advocated almost as soon as Britain's revolting Colonies had made good their claim for independence as the United States of America; it had received support ever after that time from a small though influential minority. Now the American Civil War proved to be the activating force, although it must not be supposed that repercussions of this struggle were fundamental causes underlying a movement sponsored at various times by such men as Chief Justice William Smith, Lord Dorchester, Lord Durham, A. A. Dorion, Alexander T. Galt, and others perhaps equally prominent. Ever since the Act of Union, Upper and Lower Canada had been in uneasy political association, constantly bickering over unequal incidence of taxation, the position of French-Canadians, religious differences between French Lower Canada and British Upper Canada, the question of separate schools,

13. June 25, 1862.

14. Oct. 10, 1864. All through 1861 every week and frequently every day saw issues with extended comments on annexation. They became far less frequent as the war settled down into a protracted struggle, so that it was only occasionally any attention was paid to the subject from rather early in 1862 to the end of the war.

the problem of what was to be done with the domain still under the control of the Hudson's Bay Company, and a host of other puzzling issues. Governments had been harassed by embarrassing opposition and were increasingly short-lived. Capital was needed for internal improvements, especially railroads which would link the far-flung provinces; common currency, banking systems, and other concomitants of modern economic society were insistently demanded. None of these issues would be met except under a fundamental reorganization which brought the Provinces together in some sort of a union. Recommendations made in 1858 by the Canadian group who had been so severely reprimanded in the Maritime Provinces had aroused no enthusiasm either in British North America or in England, but now, with the reiterated threat of annexation from the United States, the time was ripe for action.

The movement started under leadership of such men as Charles Tupper, S. L. Tilley, and W. H. Pope, and contemplated a legislative union of the Maritimes. A conference at Charlottetown in September, 1864, exposed the futility of forming so small a union and welcomed delegates from Canada. Collectively the delegations, urged on by railroad and other practical interests, provided for another conference to meet at Quebec later in the year, and from this came the plan which was the basis of confederation three years later. John A. Macdonald, slow to be convinced of the necessity of federation, Tupper, Tilley, Pope, A. T. Galt, E. P. Taché, George Brown, Thomas D'Arcy McGee, William McDougall were leaders who dominated the conference —really a constitutional convention—which elaborated the plan. After the project was launched there remained the task of convincing the people of British America of both its necessity and feasibility, and of securing the acquiescence of the British Government, the latter now much more easily convinced on account of the same thing which pushed forward the movement in the Provinces—the influence of the American Civil War.[15]

15. See Trotter, *op. cit.*, chaps. vii, viii, ix. Lord Monck, then in London, wrote Macdonald on October 26, 1865: ". . . I am much surprised to find how extensively but noiselessly the opinion that the colonies should be allowed to shape their own destinies without interference on the part of the Mother Country is working its way in the public mind. It is in our Colonial Policy, the counterpart of 'non-interference' in our foreign policy & derives its vitality

In the United States this rapid development was viewed with mixed opinion. Those who had been most vocal among the annexationists either ridiculed or reprehended the move. A shortsighted policy was the dictum of Bennett;[16] the Provinces were tied by economic bonds to the United States and would gravitate to them as soon as left to their own devices. There were no real bonds between the upper and the lower colonies and any kind of a union would be an unnatural one. If, however, they were bound to go on, let them confederate and then join the "great republican family" to the south. All suggestions that there was opposition to confederation in the Provinces were seized upon and played up for considerably more than they were worth, although it cannot be denied that opposition there was, loud and insistent.[17] As the work of the conference was made public and the details of organization divulged, some Americans were flattered to note that "while the British people pretend to despise our form of government and to regard it as a failure, . . . they have themselves consummated almost a similar one in their own colonies," although further study seemed to show that, after all, with an appointive governor-general and upper house of the legislature, the change from the existing situation did not amount to much.[18]

As the Civil War drew to a close and finally culminated in the entire collapse of the Confederacy, the tone of American comment about Canada began slowly to moderate. There was no inclination to con-

from precisely the same set of feelings and notions." Macdonald Papers: Governor General Correspondence, I, 101–102 (P.A.C.).

16. New York *Herald,* Nov. 6, 1864.

17. A statement from *Le Pays,* "an influential Canadian journal believed to be the organ of a large party," containing an account of a discussion of the question: "Would not annexation be preferable to Lower Canada in every respect to a legislative union disguised under the name of a Confederation of the British Provinces, such as adopted at the Quebec Conference?" was cited with complacency by the New York *Herald,* January 8, 1865. The unanimous vote of L'Institut Canadien, before which the debate took place, was noted with approbation.

18. New York *Herald,* Oct. 22, 24, 1864. Macdonald, however, thought differently. "We have avoided the weak points of the United States Constitution; we have avoided exciting local prejudices against the scheme by protecting local interests, and, at the same time, have raised a strong Central Government." Macdonald to Cameron, Dec. 19, 1864; Macdonald Papers: Letterbooks, VII, 74–75 (P.A.C.).

tinue reciprocity, as has already been pointed out; nor did exasperation over raids die out immediately, linked as it was with the general
feeling that Great Britain and her North American Colonies had
shown not only a lack of sympathy with the North but had gone out of
the way to demonstrate that coldness. With the exception of an occasional oratorical outburst from some politician or a resurgence of
annexationist talk when the Fenians[19] were most active, or just to fill
in space in newspapers when other news was scanty, there was little of
that demand for immediate revenge by invasion of Canada or employing forces no longer needed on the battle fields of Virginia to overrun
the British North American Provinces. Reconstruction of the Southern States, economic developments in the North and particularly in
the West, in short the readjustments necessarily following a long-
drawn-out struggle, relegated annexationist ideas to a place of relative unimportance. Enough, however, remained to keep the Provincials in a state of nerves and to serve as an argument why confederation
should be pushed to completion at the earliest possible moment.

Among the stronger factors conspiring to promote confederation
was the growing suspicion that England did not much care whether
Canada and the other Provinces remained a part of the Empire, and
particularly that not much more money would be spent to defend them
against threatened attack. John Bright made no bones about where
he stood: the Colonies and England both would be better off if they
parted company. Some of Gladstone's remarks were interpreted to
mean that he too was a "Little Englander." Misrepresentation of
Canadian sentiment, it was alleged, was responsible in part for this
coolness, and Lord Monck was by some held blameworthy for not putting in a truer light the essential loyalty of the Colonials.[20]

When Robert J. Walker, ex-Senator from Mississippi, ex-Gover-
nor of Kansas Territory, and long in political life, but a Unionist in

19. See Chapter X.
20. The Montreal *Gazette* (March 26, 1865), an organ of the Conservative
party then in opposition, charged Lord Monck with "idleness, inanity and
diluted voluptuousness," and maintained that he, under the influence of his
private secretary, had failed to impress upon the home government the essential
loyalty of Canadians. Monck's undeserved unpopularity has begun latterly to
be reappraised and his real constructive work for Canada in a trying time, as
well as his efforts in behalf of confederation, appreciated. See C. P. Stacey,
"Lord Monck and the Canadian Nation," *Dalhousie Review*, XIV, 179–191.

the Civil War, visited Canada in March, 1865, rumors began to circulate that he was there to sound out opinion regarding annexation.
The Montreal *Gazette* openly charged that this was the case, and even
the British Chargé in Washington felt obliged to write home about
the visit.[21] So much stir was made over this episode that Walker felt
constrained to make a categorical denial of the *Gazette*'s charges;[22]
he did not visit as a "Federal Commissioner" and he did not know the
opinions of the Administration regarding annexation; he was not
acquainted with Lord Monck, his secretary, or any member of the
Canadian Cabinet, nor did he visit Quebec, where the Canadian Parliament was assembled. Of course, he knew that Canadians and Americans enjoyed a joint heritage and he did not doubt the two countries
would have a common destiny, but he did not propose to embarrass the
Government by a discussion of the question "at this critical period."
The *Gazette*, he said, wished "to embroil the United States with England on this question, in aid of the Southern rebellion. The *Gazette* is
a violent tory paper, and of course utterly hostile to the North, and
favorable to the Southern rebellion."

As the year 1865 stretched out and merged into 1866, annexation
was far less prominently featured in American public discussion than
it had been for some time. Only casual attention was paid to steps
which were being taken to forward confederation—the visit of
Georges-Etienne Cartier, J. A. Macdonald, George Brown, and Alexander T. Galt to London, the interviews with the Colonial Secretary
to work out a basis for the transition,[23] or even such evidences as appeared of opposition to confederation in Canada. A leading article of

21. Burnley to Russell, Mar. 27, 1865; FO 5:1017 (P.R.O.). Burnley mentioned the *Gazette* article which charged that while Walker's ostensible purpose was to confer "with Confederate Gentlemen on the subject of peace," the
"real mission was to ascertain the temper and disposition of the Canadian
people respecting union with the States and see what could be done to impede
or defeat confederation. . . ." Quoted in New York *Herald,* Mar. 25, 1865.

22. The letter is in the New York *Herald,* March 29, 1865. On April 18 there
appeared in that paper a statement of George N. Sanders saying that Walker
was in Canada at his request to talk over peace plans. Sanders was a Confederate agent, one of four offered a safe conduct by Lincoln in the summer of 1864
to go to Washington to talk over peace plans. They did not go.

23. Reports of these commissioners detailing at length progress of the negotiations are found in Macdonald Papers: Visits to England, Vol. I (P.A.C.).

the London *Times* of December 5, 1865, was thought of sufficient interest to be forwarded to Congress with papers prepared by the Secretary of State and subsequently printed in a Congressional document.[24] Britain, it was stated, would not object if Canadians wished to join the United States, but if such expansion were to be accomplished by fraud, force, or intimidation, that was different. "In that case, not only is there actual wrong done upon our own loyal fellow subjects, and others entitled to our sympathy, but there is also established a prescription, a policy, and a temper ruinous to the future peace and even progress of the world." It was, then, from no jealousy that Englishmen dreaded the "indefinite enlargement" of the United States "by the means too often employed," nor would they "object to any amount of aggregation in America" similar to that going on in Italy and Germany, "only, as a great State we cannot bear to be ousted, outwitted, and coerced, and to see our own people suffer for their loyalty." The "Thunderer," then, virtually gave its permission to the United States to use its powers of suasion upon the Colonies but warned against employment of other means of extending the Union at British expense.

But muttering of forceful means continued from time to time to crop up. In January, 1866, the Toronto *Globe* noted[25] that the Western fire-eater, the Chicago *Tribune*, was lamenting the loss of the opportunity to take Canada in the last war with Great Britain and threatening that when, if ever, that opportunity did return Great Britain's "American colonies will be snatched up by this Republic as quickly as a hawk would gobble a quail." Then there would be a satisfactory northern boundary, along the Arctic Ocean, and the southern one would be movable, eventually to be some day in the vicinity of the Panama railroad. "Cock-a-doodle-doo!" remarked the *Globe*'s editorial:

We don't object to our neighbours giving wing to their fertile imaginations, and seeing, through the distant vista of the future, the natural boundaries to their "great country" which "manifest destiny" seems to fix, provided such contemplation gives them pleasure. It is very silly, but harmless; still, outsiders would think quite as highly of them if they would leave such braggadocio alone, and make better use of their present

24. *Diplomatic Correspondence, 1866–67,* Part I, pp. 27–28.
25. Jan. 17, 1866.

possessions. The South, Utah, and the war debt, require all the attention that the people of the United States can give at present.

Too busily occupied by its quarrel with the President over Reconstruction, Congress, having in the previous session taken its stand for abrogation of reciprocity, paid little attention to Canada in 1865–66. The fishery question slumbered under the license system, and attempts to renew the old or make a new modified trade agreement met with almost contemptuous indifference.[26] It is true that General Nathaniel P. Banks introduced in the House a bill[27] directing the President of the United States "whenever notice shall be deposited in the Department of State that the Government of Great Britain and the Provinces of New Brunswick, Nova Scotia, Prince Edward's Island, Newfoundland, Canada, British Columbia and Vancouver's Island have accepted the proposition . . . made by the United States, to publish by proclamation that, from the date thereof, the States of Nova Scotia, New Brunswick, Canada East and Canada West, and the Territories of Selkirk, Saskatchewan and Columbia . . . are constituted and admitted as States and Territories of the United States." The bill provided that all public property should be transferred to the United States, which would assume the debts of the Provinces to the amount of $85,700,000 and make a grant annually of $1,646,000 to compensate for loss of import and export taxes; the opening of a waterway for steamers from Lake Superior to the Atlantic was contemplated. Even though the measure was scarcely noticed in Congress it did get a little attention outside. The Chicago *Republican*[28] later on brought it up and opined that "however chimerical this scheme may have appeared a few months ago, it bids fair to become a practical one

26. See Chapters XII and XIII.

27. July 2, 1866; *Cong. Globe,* 39th Cong., 1st Sess., p. 3548. Banks's bill was a copy of one prepared by James W. Taylor, Special Agent of the Treasury Department in the Northwest, and incorporated in his report transmitted to Congress June 12, 1866 (*House Ex. Docs.,* No. 128, 39th Cong., 1st Sess.). See T. C. Blegen, "A Plan of Union of British North America and the United States, 1866," *Mississippi Valley Historical Review,* IV, 470–483. The Taylor Papers (MSS.), in the Minnesota Historical Society, give evidence of his interest in the Red River region, for the acquisition of which the bill was actually framed.

28. Quoted in the Montreal *Gazette,* Dec. 11, 1866.

much sooner than anticipated." Intimations from Canada pointed to a "decided, vigorous and systematic movement in favor of annexation"; a meeting at Kingston recently had condemned the Government's course with respect to the Fenian invasion and adopted resolutions "advising the Canadian people to accept the terms of annexation proposed in Gen. Banks' bill," and indications that other meetings would be held were not lacking. Reasons for this change of front the *Republican* ascribed to the disastrous results of reciprocity abrogation; fear of Fenian invasions; "estrangement from the English Government, in consequence of its inability to furnish protection of the country in case of foreign or domestic war"; the breakdown of the confederation "scheme"; and disgust with the Canadian Government, which was trying to force confederation upon an unwilling people.[29]

There were, of course, as there had been at almost any time, intimations of local and usually sporadic dissatisfaction in various parts of British North America. Yet it appears that the discontent was fairly well localized. In Montreal and its vicinity there was a faction of the Rouges dissatisfied alike with existing arrangements and with prospective confederation.[30] In Nova Scotia an indeterminate number openly deprecated a close association with Canada; Joseph Howe, although he never would admit that his advocacy of independence was in any way connected with annexation, had lent prestige to the movement, and when he became more or less reconciled to confederation left behind a disgruntled minority that persisted in believing that Nova Scotia had been sold out. In New Brunswick opinion at the outset had to some degree paralleled that of Nova Scotia, but intensive work in 1866 had swung the electorate into line for confederation.[31] Here and there in Upper Canada a voice was raised for annexation, but it was a feeble note which found few echoes. Professor Goldwin Smith was outspoken in his belief that Canada would do better separated from England and he contemplated annexation with equanimity.[32]

29. The *Gazette* carried an article of similar trend from the Washington *Intelligencer*.

30. Montreal *Gazette*, Feb. 10, Apr. 10, 1866, *et al*. *Le Pays* and *Le Canadien* were organs of this attitude.

31. In the opinion of the Detroit *Free Press*, June 16, 1866, the result of the New Brunswick elections was very heartening to advocates of confederation in the Provinces.

32. In printing Smith's letter the Montreal *Gazette*, January 19, 1867,

After a period of relative quiescence annexationism flared up again, blown by Radical Republicans of the stamp of Zachariah Chandler, Banks, Charles Sumner, Edwin M. Stanton, Benjamin F. Butler, and Henry Winter Davis.[33] They either openly applauded Fenian attempts or covertly encouraged them; they were hostile to reciprocity and had urged its abrogation as a means of forcing annexation; they did not hesitate to express their undying hostility toward England and their confidence that it was only a matter of time when the British flag would be removed from the Western Hemisphere. It was to this group, and to the newspapers like the New York *Herald* and the Chicago *Tribune*, that Sir Frederick Bruce referred, not long after he took charge of the Legation in Washington, when he wrote:[34]

Looking at the hostile state of feeling towards England which has always existed, and has been much increased by the late civil war, I think our policy in this question ought to be based on the assumption that the United States will be, at all events a rival, and possibly an enemy. It is of importance that British North America should be encouraged in every way to maintain her connection with the Mother country, or to become if she separates, an independent Power. The possession of the maritime Provinces would add immensely to the naval power of the United States, while on the other hand, as long as they and Canada are independent, they will from jealousy of their arrogant neighbour remain well affected to Great Britain and constitute a balance of the power of the United States, which other Powers in Europe may well have an interest in maintaining. . . .

Nothing will be more likely to deter this Country [the United States] from war, and to bring about a better treatment of North American interests, than the avowed determination of Great Britain to support by all the force at her command her Colonies as long as they are loyal and to resent injustice towards them as an injustice to herself. There is little sympathy felt towards the United States in Canada, as I am informed,

apologized for "polluting" its columns with it, and proceeded to tear to pieces its statements, and then returned to the attack a few days later (January 22).

33. See Joe Patterson Smith, *The Republican Expansionists of the Early Reconstruction Era* (private edition, distributed by the University of Chicago Press, 1933).

34. To Stanley, Confidential, Sept. 17, 1866; FO 5:1067 (P.R.O.). Edward Henry Stanley was Foreign Secretary in the Cabinet of his father, the Earl of Derby, 1866 to 1868.

and the course pursued by leading men here in the Fenian question has done much to destroy whatever feeling may have existed. Advantage ought to be taken of this alienation by military and financial aid given in a free and friendly spirit to foster this fortunate turn of public sentiment, and to show the Provinces, that their good will is valued, and that their material interests will not suffer in consequence.

In Congress in the winter of 1866–67 there arose a few reverberations from this Radical group. Senator Chandler, when a bill was introduced relative to the sale of ships to belligerents,[35] took occasion to remind the Senate that he had, in December, 1864, brought in a resolution recommending that the Committee on Military Affairs be directed to "inquire into the expediency of immediately enlisting an Army corps to watch and defend our territory bordering on the lakes and Canadian line, from all hostile demonstrations." He had done this in good faith, he said; his intention was that watch should be kept from Montreal and Quebec. Those towns could have been held as hostages for the good behavior of Canada and Great Britain, preventing raids into the United States. The committee had never reported upon the resolution, but Chandler's reminder at this time had double significance when one considers that confederation was well on its way toward accomplishment and recalls, too, that this progress had not passed unnoticed in Congress. Only a month before, Henry J. Raymond of New York had tried to introduce a resolution[36] requesting the President to inform the House "whether any remonstrance has been made by this Government against the proposed consolidation of all the British North American Provinces into a single confederation under the imperial rule of an English prince, or whether the consent of the Government has been given in any way, directly or indirectly, to the consummation of this project." Even if Raymond's rather arrogant proposition did not stir up any discussion in Congress or any extended notice in the country, it did not pass without comment by the Canadians.

We remember, of course [said the Montreal *Gazette*], that certain politicians in Canada have always made it one of their chief objections to

35. Mar. 25, 1867; *Cong. Globe*, 40th Cong., 1st Sess., p. 328.

36. Feb. 27, 28, 1867; *ibid.,* 39th Cong., 2d Sess., pp. 1617, 1646. The resolution went to the Committee on Foreign Affairs, but without leave to report at any time as Raymond had desired.

Confederation that it would probably give offence to our American neighbours; but we certainly never expected that the envious opposition which it might create amongst the latter would ever find expression in formal resolution laid before Congress, or that it would have for its mouthpiece so respectable a politician as Mr. Raymond. . . . Governor Chamberlain of Maine is evidently not the only American who believes in the divine right of the great Yankee nation to meddle in the affairs of every other community and to propagate democracy as Islamism was propagated by the followers of Mahomet.[37]

Returning to the attack a week later[38] the *Gazette* held forth in another long editorial where it stated:

One scarcely knows which is the most deserving of ridicule, the fears of the Congressmen at the danger to the United States to accrue from the consolidation of these Provinces, or the ignorance of the Committee of the Maine Legislature, which, as a peroration to a pretentious disquisition on British colonial history, speaks of union as about to be forced upon the people of the Provinces against their will. The alarm of these poor timorous legislators at Washington, and the philanthropic care for our interests of the lawgivers of Maine, would be very funny if we did not know that they were meant to work mischief. . . .

Not only did these persons ignore facts and falsely state the issue, but they neglected the wholesome advice of the good old Saxon "Mind your own business."

Even Sir Frederick felt called upon to notice Raymond's resolution[39] and sent a copy to the Foreign Office, saying that the designation "the Kingdom of Canada" had caused "much remark of an unfriendly character in the United States and [had] aroused their susceptibili-

37. Mar. 7, 1867.   38. Mar. 13, 1867.
    39. Bruce to Stanley, Mar. 2, 1867; FO 5:1106 (P.R.O.). On August 7, 1869, Macdonald wrote E. L. Montingambert (Macdonald Papers: Letterbooks, XIII, 59 [P.A.C.]): "When in England on Confederation matters the Delegates or a Majority of them were in favor of styling the new Confederation a *Kingdom* but I believe H. M. Government were afraid that it might wound the susceptibilities of the United States, so we compromised on the word *Dominion*. That name had been suggested by you to myself and I believe to others of the Delegation. I am not quite sure either whether the same idea did not suggest itself to Lord Carnarvon without previous consultation with us." See Joseph Pope, *Memoirs of the Right Honourable Sir John Alexander Macdonald, G.C.B.* (London, 1894), I, 312–313.

ties." The Confederation itself, he said, was looked on with mixed feelings in the United States: "*with favour*, by those who do not wish the extension of the States, but who would gladly see the Provinces break their connexion with Great Britain, to which result they think Confederation tends; *with disfavour*, by the ambitious part of the population who desire peaceful or forcible annexation, and who are averse to Confederation because they think it will create the germ of a powerful nationality in sympathy with, if not directly incorporated with, the Old World." Union, thought Sir Frederick, was the important thing at the moment; whatever might be the ulterior views of Her Majesty's Government it would be well to divulge as little of them as possible so that opposition to the scheme in the United States might have little to build upon. By return mail the British Minister was informed[40] that he might refute the rumor that there was to be a formal Kingdom of Canada under the rule of Prince Arthur: the Colonial Secretary had notified the Governor-General that "if this statement obtain currency in Canada I think it desirable that you sh^d be enabled to state that it is entirely without foundation."

But there was to be still another exhibition of failing to mind one's own business. In the special session of Congress which followed immediately upon the adjournment *sine die* of the Thirty-ninth, Banks, from the Committee on Foreign Affairs, brought in a joint resolution which declared[41] that the people of the United States could view only with extreme solicitude the proposal to organize a confederation founded on the monarchical principle without consulting the people of the Provinces, for it would be in direct contradiction to the frequently declared principles of the United States, dangerous to its interests, and tending to increase and perpetuate embarrassments already existing. With no record vote and with but perfunctory comment the resolution was passed, although Chandler said that while he agreed with the principle, he thought the resolution illogical: Canada already had a monarchical form of government, and if the American Government were to make an issue let it insist upon the independence of Canada and "take up arms with Canada on that issue."

All comment in the United States, however, was not so chauvinistic as that of Banks, Chandler, Sumner and Company. To many, con-

40. Hammond to Bruce, Mar. 23, 1867; FO 115:462 (P.R.O.).
41. *Cong. Globe,* 40th Cong., 1st Sess., p. 392.

federation seemed the natural development which might be expected and should be the cause neither of disturbance nor jealousy; perhaps to most of these it seemed a step toward independence but did not necessarily involve annexation. Indeed, it might be anticipated that the new Confederation would become a "populous, rich and powerful independent nation" that would be one of the "most reliable and useful allies" of the United States, and "so long as we continue to bear the burden of our national debt, we cannot foresee the time when annexation to the United States will be more desirable for the new power thus created, than independence."[42] But the New York *Tribune*, commenting on Lord Russell's speech on the Guarantee Bill,[43] observed: "When the experiment of the 'dominion' shall have failed, as fail it must, a process of peaceful absorption will give Canada her proper place in the great North American Republic."

In spite of all comments, adverse and otherwise, the course of colonial amalgamation into a confederation went on with little obstruction, and Parliament in 1867 incorporated into the British North America Act the essential features of the plan worked out at Quebec and further elaborated and refined in London. A royal proclamation fixed July 1, 1867, as the day for inaugurating the Dominion of Canada. Hailed in most of Canada, lukewarmly accepted in New Brunswick, and reluctantly acceded to by Nova Scotia,[44] the new nation—in everything except name—was launched, even though Prince Edward Island and Newfoundland preferred to remain on the outside.

42. New York *Times,* quoted in Montreal *Gazette,* Apr. 17, 1867.

43. Quoted in Montreal *Gazette,* May 18, 1867.

44. For the Maritimes and the Dominion see James Hannay, *The Life and Times of Sir Leonard Tilley, Being a Political History of New Brunswick for the Past Seventy Years* (St. John, 1897), pp. 258–259, 289 and *passim;* Whitelaw, *The Maritimes and Canada before Confederation,* chap. xii, *passim;* Montreal *Gazette,* Apr. 17, 1867.

In the new Dominion, United Canada was split into the two provinces of Ontario and Quebec; in 1870 Manitoba was brought in, while British Columbia came in in 1871 and Prince Edward Island in 1873.

In recognition of their services in bringing about confederation and for other services to the Empire, in 1867 John A. Macdonald was made a Knight Commander of the Bath, and Tupper and Cartier were created Commanders of the Bath. Subsequently, Tupper was knighted in 1879 and made a baronet in 1888. Galt refused an honor in 1867 but accepted a knighthood in 1869. Francis Hincks was knighted in 1869.

It was on these island Provinces that considerable American attention was bestowed for the purpose of preventing their yielding to pressure to unite with the other British North American Provinces. General Benjamin F. Butler took it upon himself to go in person to Prince Edward Island to exercise his powers of persuasion upon the people there. His visit was viewed with considerable anxiety in Canada,[45] although it was wisely decided not to intervene but to leave the situation to local authorities and to the Imperial Government. The wisdom of the course was amply demonstrated in the outcome, for Prince Edward Island later decided to cast its lot with the rest of the Confederation. Newfoundland, however, remained obdurate. Belief that its interests would be better served if it retained its separate status, together with considerable sentiment in favor of a closer relation to the United States, all tinged by a spirit of independence which objected to surrendering any of its functions to a central government in North America, combined to keep this large area with a small population standing alone.[46]

Meantime, American attention had been drawn toward western British possessions. The purchase of Alaska in 1867 had more than a little to do with this, for it was but natural that thoughts should turn toward the area which lay between the forty-ninth parallel and the southern boundary of former Russian-America. Seward, expansionist as he was and flushed by his diplomatic "triumph," could hardly fail to note that between Washington Territory and Alaska lay the Province of British Columbia, and north of Minnesota and the Dakota Territory stretched the vast area over which the Hudson's Bay Company still held sway. It is no more surprising that others should cast a contemplative eye in that direction, as did the editorial writer of the New York *Herald*[47] who remarked:

The information we receive from the Pacific side of the Continent shows that there is a considerable movement, both in British Columbia and Cali-

45. Monck to Macdonald, Sept. 1, 1868; Macdonald Papers: Governor General Correspondence, II, 317–318 (P.A.C.).

46. For a discussion of the "particularism" of the Maritimes, and especially of Newfoundland, see Whitelaw, *op. cit.,* especially chaps. ii–iv.

47. Quoted in the *Gazette,* Montreal, June 18, 1867. See H. L. Keenleyside, "British Columbia—Annexation or Confederation?" Canadian Historical Association *Report,* 1928, pp. 34–40.

fornia and Oregon, to annex to the United States the territory of Great Britain in that part of America. The press and people of Victoria are outspoken in favour of annexation. It is said, also, that Mr. Seward has his eye on British Columbia, and that he wishes to make a settlement with England for the Alabama Claims by the annexation of that territory. . . . The people of this country will certainly find it inconvenient to have different portions of our republican empire separated by foreign territory.

Seward himself lent point to such dreams when, in a speech at Boston, he said: "I know that Nature designs that this whole continent, not merely these thirty-six states, shall be, sooner or later, within the magic circle of the American Union," and found his sentiments roundly applauded by his audience.[48] Other papers joined in the chorus which swelled to a volume sufficiently loud to attract the attention of the British Minister in Washington. "I enclose an article from the 'N. York Times,' " he wrote, "on the conditions and prospects of British Columbia."[49]

I have no means of knowing how far the representations . . . are true. . . . The article describes accurately enough the desire of a large part of the population of the U. S. to obtain possession of Columbia so as to remain without a rival on the Coast of the Pacific.

There is moreover a considerable section of the Western population looking forward to the acquisition of the territory which includes the Saskatchewan River and the Red River settlement—and I foresee that if it is not shortly occupied with settlers who can turn its natural resources to account, it will be over-run by squatters pushing up from Montana with whom the Hudsons Bay Company and the Canadian authorities will find it difficult to deal.

The N. Y. Times is supposed on these general questions to reflect in some measure Mr Seward's opinions which are known to be strongly in favour of territorial extension for the sake of popularity. Indeed I was present at a conversation lately in which Mr Seward urged an American capitalist to form a company for the purpose of buying up the rights of the Hudsons Bay Company, and of thus obtaining the command of what he considers would be the best line for a northern communication between the Atlantic and Pacific Oceans. It is certain that he does not con-

48. Montreal *Gazette,* June 27, 1867.
49. Bruce to Stanley, Aug. 30, 1867; FO 115:466 (P.R.O.).

template in such a contingency that the line between the Lakes and Vancouver's Island will remain in any hands but those of the U. States.[50]

In the winter Senator Alexander Ramsey of Minnesota put in specific form aspirations for the acquisition of the British Northwest when he introduced a set of resolutions touching on reciprocal trade, navigation, common system of patents, copyrights, and the like, and then proposed the purchase by the United States of the rights of the Bay Company including all claims to territory in North America clear through to the Pacific Coast; the northwest territory should be divided and organized into not fewer than three territories "with all the rights and privileges of the citizens and government of Montana so far as the same can be made applicable."[51] Speaking to these resolutions Ramsey called attention to the fact that these northwest Colonies had applied for admission into the Dominion although the people of the Selkirk settlement and those of British Columbia would prefer to enter the American Union; he believed it was the duty of the Government of the United States to put in its bid in opposition to that of the Confederation. Grimes of Iowa interposed an objection on the ground that he was opposed to anything "looking to another reciprocity treaty," to which he was "utterly opposed."[52] Nothing specific came of the Ramsey proposition, but during the session there came up occasional reference when a die-hard annexationist burst out. Rufus P. Spaulding of Ohio was one of these. When the bill for the payment of Alaska was under consideration he delivered himself of this all-embracing declaration:[53]

50. The *Nor'wester,* published at Fort Garry, in its issue of July 27, 1867, commented on the impossibility of the Hudson's Bay Company's continuing long in its control of the Red River region, and quoted with approval Roebuck's statement that "as sure as there is a sun in Heaven, the United States will thrust themselves between us and the Pacific Ocean if some steps are not taken to prevent it." On the whole subject of Manitoba see G. F. G. Stanley, *The Birth of Western Canada* (London, New York, and Toronto, 1936).

51. Dec. 9, 1867, *Cong. Globe,* 40th Cong., 2d Sess., p. 79. *Senate Misc. Docs.,* No. 4, 40th Cong., 2d Sess.

52. On January 31, 1868, Ramsey modified his resolutions to change somewhat the reciprocal trade provisions. *Senate Misc. Docs.,* No. 22, 40th Cong., 2d Sess.

53. July 7, 1868; *Cong. Globe,* 40th Cong., 2d Sess., p. 3810.

. . . My colleague said that we were embarking upon a new political enterprise, that we were endeavoring to acquire territory where there is no contiguity of territory with our own possessions, that we were acquiring foreign possessions. Sir, as an American citizen, and a republican at that, I deny that any territory upon this western hemisphere is to be deemed foreign to the Government of the United States when it seeks to extend its limits. I believe that if anything under the heavens be fated, it is that the American flag shall wave over every foot of this American Continent in course of time.

When J. S. Pike interrupted to say "including South America," Spaulding agreed to that and added that if they had not foolishly allowed Great Britain to interpose 49° instead of 54° 40', contiguity with Alaska would exist. Green B. Raum of Illinois said[54] that if the United States had a traditional policy, it was that of acquiring territory, and he believed that in the lifetime of the pages then running about the chamber "the American flag will wave in triumph over the undivided territory of North America."

Since dissatisfaction with confederation still obtained in parts of the new Dominion,[55] undoubtedly American annexationists were encouraged to continue their assaults. But internal issues made the year 1868 relatively free from any widespread or general agitation of the matter. Even in Canada fears began to subside, at least temporarily. The Dominion Government had been sustained by their Parliament, which was prorogued in May, on every major point except one, and the Government was committed to confederation.[56] Despite all this

54. *Cong. Globe,* 40th Cong., 2d Sess., p. 3813.

55. Macdonald wrote the Archbishop of Halifax (Feb. 4, 1868; Macdonald Papers: Letterbooks, XI, 455–456 [P.A.C.]), that the "repeal fever" seemed to be at its height and he hoped it would soon abate.

56. Macdonald wrote Tupper, May 25, 1868 (Macdonald Papers: Letterbooks, XI, 960 [P.A.C.]), that the reduction of the salary of Lord Monck, even though he was about to leave his post, was due to the Governor-General's unpopularity rather than to his stand on confederation. "Some of his unpopularity is attributable to his being supposed to lean towards the anti-Colonial party in England, and some imprudent expressions of his when he first came to Canada strengthened that opinion. Godley, his private secretary, who is supposed to speak his opinions was an out and out follower of Bright and Goldwin Smith and did not hesitate to state his opinion that the sooner England got rid of her Colonies the better."

President Johnson, in his last Annual Message, returned to the subject. After speaking of the annexation of Alaska and of the Danish treaty, he said:[57] "Comprehensive national policy would seem to sanction the acquisition and incorporation into our Federal Union of the several adjacent continental and insular communities as speedily as it can be done peaceably, lawfully, and without violation of national justice, faith or honor." But no response came from Congress other than the introduction by Representative Pruyn of a proposed amendment which, according to Minister Edward Thornton, had a tendency "to encourage the inhabitants of any other North American countries, of course including Canada, to ask to be annexed to the United States."[58] The Johnson administration was, as a practical political instrument, dead, and everybody was waiting the inauguration of General Grant, including Canadians, who hoped that the new administration would take a firm stand on the Fenians and discourage annexationist agitation but feared that this might not be the case.

As a political factor Grant was an unknown element except for the fact that he had the support of and apparently sympathized with the Radical faction of the Republicans. His Inaugural Address did not throw much light upon the course he proposed to pursue, for the paragraph dealing with foreign affairs was general, vague, and apparently harmless, although Thornton was moved to write:[59] "I look upon the paragraph with regard to foreign policy as menacing towards England, and so it is considered by persons who are well acquainted with the character of the President and his feelings with regard to the questions pending between the two countries." Moreover, the appointment of Elihu Washburne as Secretary of State was not reassuring, since, according to Thornton, that gentleman had "the reputation of not being well disposed toward England." Washburne, however, retained his office for so short a time that he had no opportunity to display his reputed animosity; and his successor, Hamilton Fish, had not been in public office since his pre-Civil War service in the United States

57. *Cong. Globe,* 40th Cong., 3d Sess., App., p. 5.

58. Thornton to Clarendon, Feb. 2, 1869; FO 5:1158 (P.R.O.). In 1868 Edward Thornton became Minister to the United States; Sir Frederick Bruce died in 1867.

59. Thornton to Clarendon, Mar. 8, 1869; FO 5:1158 (P.R.O.).

Senate and had not put himself on record in the matter of American controversies with England and Canada.

While neither the British Cabinet nor Thornton were admitted to the intimacies of official circles in the United States, it required no divination to imagine that there must be some talk of annexation, especially since the Radicals were now in the saddle. Sumner's famous speech, in which he advanced his preposterous claims while delivering the adverse report of the Committee on Foreign Relations on the Johnson-Clarendon Convention,[60] was proof enough of this; while Chandler's resolution, introduced on April 19, 1869, stated that "in the judgment of the Senate the true solution of all the controversies between Great Britain and the United States will be found in a surrender of all British possessions in North America to the people of the United States; and that the President be, and he hereby is, requested to open negotiations as soon as practicable for a settlement of all matters in dispute upon that basis."[61] Echoing Sumner, he placed upon Great Britain responsibility for one-half the cost of the war and declared: "I put on file a mortgage upon the British North American provinces for the whole amount, and that mortgage is recorded and the security is good."

Had members of the Administration confided in the British Minister he probably would not have been surprised but he surely would not have been reassured. Grant, in the bosom of his official family, made no secret of his desire to see the United States annex Canada; he spoke of his wishes to others with whom he felt on terms of intimacy.

60. Reverdy Johnson, who replaced Charles Francis Adams as Minister to England in 1868, negotiated a Claims Convention which lumped the *Alabama* claims with all others preferred by both sides and made no reference to the American contention that they required special consideration as well as some apology. Sumner, as Chairman of the Senate Committee on Foreign Relations, was the only one who spoke in the Senate when he reported that the committee recommended rejection of the convention; he maintained that England, by her "unneutral" acts, was responsible for half the cost of the Civil War and that she should be made to pay more than the cost of the actual damage done by the Rebel cruisers, hinting that perhaps the obligation might be met by turning over British North American possessions to the United States.

61. *Cong. Globe,* 41st Cong., Spec. Sess., Sen., pp. 727–728. See J. P. Smith, "American Republican Leadership and the Movement for Annexation of Canada in the Eighteen-Sixties," Canadian Historical Association *Report,* 1935, pp. 67–75, especially for Sumner.

To John C. Hamilton he stated that one of his chief aims was to acquire Canada.[62] To Fish, in November when the Annual Message was under consideration, Grant expressed the thought that it might be better to let the *Alabama* Claims ride along in the expectation that eventually England would be brought to liquidate them by cession of the Dominion. In a Cabinet meeting he advanced the same idea and found that it met with considerable approval, although Fish, while not averse to the notion of annexation, was convinced that England would never yield to pressure from the United States.

I do not think [he said at this meeting] that it will influence the question of Canada. Great Britain is quite willing to part with Canada when the latter requests it, but will not cede it, in any negotiations, as a satisfaction for any claim, nor until Canada herself unequivocally expresses her wish for separation. I mention that ten years ago in England, Lord Carlisle told me that his government would be glad to part with Canada, which was an expense and a source of weakness to her. Hoar interposes, saying that Mr. Thornton had told him the same thing. President: "If that be so I would be willing to settle at once." And such seemed to be the impression of every member of the Cabinet, so far as I could judge from nods of assent, or slight expressions of concurrence.[63]

This conviction, if conviction it was, did not deter the Secretary from bringing up the matter with Thornton when the latter one day in the course of a general conversation spoke of the rumored possibility of another Fenian invasion that winter (1869–70). "Well," said Fish, "why not withdraw entirely from Canada and remove the pretext for these Fenian threats? At the same time we can settle the *Alabama* Claims immediately."

"Oh," rejoined Thornton, "you know that we cannot withdraw. The Canadians find great fault with me for saying as openly as I do that we

62. The references to most of the citations involving Grant and Fish are in Allan Nevins, *Hamilton Fish: The Inner History of the Grant Administration* (New York, 1936).

63. From Fish's Diary in *ibid.*, p. 230. Earlier in the year, April 2, 1869, Fish wrote John C. Hamilton that the indirect claims might be met by a territorial concession, "but *to suggest this to Great Britain is to assure its refusal.*" *Ibid.*, p. 160. Letters received by Fish from such men as Carl Schurz, John Jay, Motley, and others showed that the idea of exchanging the claims for Canada was widely prevalent.

are ready to let them go whenever they wish, and declare they do not desire it." He added that when his secretary of legation was recently in Montreal, he had inquired into the popular feeling, and learned that scarcely anybody favored annexation.

"If so, this information comes from very different sources than ours," said Fish. "My information is that with the exception of the government officials, bankers, and some few wealthy families, there is a heavy preponderance of sentiment in favor of separation from Great Britain. . . ."[64]

Fish continued to play with the idea and on more than one occasion mentioned it in conversation with the British Minister. Thus, for example, when Thornton spoke to him about a petition from the inhabitants of Vancouver Island, he was told that the "removal of the British flag" from the North American continent "would render easy the settlement of all other questions between the two governments."[65]

Except on the sparsely settled Pacific Coast and in the hearts of the confirmed annexationists in Congress, British Columbia did not figure largely, but with the Red River Colony, the nucleus of the Province of Manitoba, the case was different. This area, separated from Dakota Territory only by an imaginary line, alike in topography, soil conditions, and climate, looked to St. Paul for its economic outlet. Quite naturally the people of Minnesota thought that it was a perversion of nature to have this region connected politically with the Dominion, and Ramsey's resolutions merely voiced the sentiment of most of his constituents. On the other hand, Canadians generally were not inclined lightly to allow a wedge to be interposed between Old Canada and the British possessions on the Pacific Coast. With the formation of the Dominion, negotiations were initiated for quieting the claims of the Hudson's Bay Company and incorporating the Red River settlements in the new Confederation. The affair progressed rapidly. By late summer in 1869 preliminaries had been completed, and the Province of Manitoba was ripe, so Dominion authorities thought, to be taken over.

64. Nevins, *op. cit.,* p. 300.

65. Fish Diary, Jan. 6, 1870; *ibid.,* p. 386. How much was "banter," as Nevins called it, and how much had a basis in real desire on the part of Fish it is impossible to tell. Macdonald called Fish's suggestion of a plebiscite on annexation, "blackguard business." Letter to Rose, Jan. 26, 1870, quoted in M. H. Long, "Sir John Rose and the Informal Beginnings of the Canadian High Commissionership," *Can. Hist. Rev.,* XII, 23–43.

Accordingly William McDougall, as Governor, set out by way of St. Paul for his post. But on the frontier the population, Indians and French-Canadian half-breeds with only a sprinkling of English-speaking whites, were reluctant to lose the guidance and protection of the Company. Badly informed as to plans, they believed they were to be subordinated to "foreign" masters, to lose their privileges, including title to land they had long occupied, and generally to be reduced to an inferior position. Under the leadership of Louis Riel these malcontents organized a kind of government and proposed to stand for their rights, which they felt could be protected in the long run only by securing provincial status.[66]

It was into such a situation that Governor McDougall advanced with his little official family, only to be halted at the boundary, where he demonstrated his ineptitude by issuing blustering proclamations which only served to increase the fears and the determination of the half-breeds. In spite of good advice from his superiors, McDougall pretty successfully confirmed the worst suspicions of the people over whom he was supposed to exercise authority.[67] At best it was a sorry mess. McDougall was convinced that back of Riel were annexationists of the United States egging him on; the postmaster at Pembina, he was sure, was in the plot and using his official position to aid the rebels.[68] Almost frantic appeals for military support were sent back to the Premier and the picture was painted in darkest colors. Fortunately, the Dominion authorities kept their heads, believing with good ground that the trouble was not deep-seated and that with tact it could

66. For the Riel rebellion see Graeme M. Adam, *The Canadian North-West: Its History and Its Troubles from the Early Days of the Fur Trade to the Era of the Railway and Settler, etc.* (Toronto, 1885); Charles A. Boulton, *Reminiscences of the North-West Rebellion, etc.* (Toronto, 1886); and especially G. F. G. Stanley, *The Birth of Western Canada*, pp. 3–176. McDougall's misfortunes were threshed out in Parliament in the spring of 1870. *Dominion Parliamentary Debates, 1870,* 3d Sess., *passim.*

67. Macdonald's government had many anxious moments as the news of the revolt trickled back, and his Letterbooks (P.A.C.), especially Vol. XIII, are filled with copies of communications which demonstrate the realization that McDougall was handling the affair in an unfortunate manner. The illness of McTavish, Governor of the Company, had much to do with the development.

68. Macdonald to McDougall, Nov. 27, 1869; Macdonald Papers: Letterbooks, XIII, 614 (P.A.C.).

be handled. They scoffed at McDougall's fears of a formidable demonstration from St. Paul, especially in the dead of winter.[69] Nevertheless, something had to be done to assert Dominion authority and, at the same time, quiet the fears of the half-breeds. A tactful use of the olive branch and a demonstration of force accomplished the purpose. A commission was appointed to investigate the whole affair, while a small but sufficiently overawing armed expedition showed that no nonsense would be tolerated. This combination, together with the promise of a fair hearing of complaints, led to a compromise which assuaged the apprehensions of the half-breeds and paved the way to inauguration of a provincial government and, soon afterwards, admission into the Dominion with representation in both houses of Parliament.[70]

Needless to say, this episode stirred up comment in the United States and gave a new fillip to annexation talk. Senator Chandler brought in a resolution[71] requesting the President to appoint two com-

69. As Macdonald wrote Judge Gowan (Jan. 13, 1870; Macdonald Papers: Letterbooks, XIII, 886–887 [P.A.C.]), "The Yankees would like to have a finger in the pie I dare say, and so would the Fenians; but the march of *400 miles* from St. Cloud to Fort Garry and the carriage of provisions for such a force is quite sufficient protection from that quarter."

70. The refusal to allow a supply steamer to pass through the American locks at Sault Ste Marie occasioned a long correspondence between the American and British Governments and raised the issue in Congress. Thornton to Clarendon, May 2, 1870, FO 5:1193 (P.R.O.); Thornton to Clarendon, May 15, 1870, FO 5:1193 (P.R.O.); *Senate Ex. Docs.*, No. 88, 41st Cong., 2d Sess.

71. Apr. 19, 22, 1870; *Cong. Globe*, 41st Cong., 2d Sess., pp. 2887–2890. In December the Senate had called for correspondence (*Senate Ex. Docs.*, No. 33). Probably Chandler needed no outside encouragement in his annexationist propensities, but such letters as that written to him by J. W. Carman of Belleville, Ontario, January 1, 1870, certainly had no deterrent effect: "You may or may not be aware that in Canada there is a strong and growing American party—composed of gentlemen 'to the Manor born,' and of every nationality, whose ultimate object is to carry the province or Dominion into the American Union. Of that party I have for many years been a leader, and have as *editor* and publisher been in a position to take a prominent part. During the war I published the only Daily paper in Central Canada—the *British American*, at Kingston, that stood manfully for the Federal cause and I found to my cost that the sentiment of the country was too strong for me. Canada was strongly Secession and the Daily finally had to be suspended. . . ." (Chandler Papers [L.C.]).

missioners to open negotiations with people at Winnipeg with a view to annexation to the United States. He accompanied it with his usual tirade, "a speech of the intemperate character against England for which he is notorious and which brought a smile of recognition to the faces of most of his colleagues," as Thornton reported to Lord Clarendon.[72] Whether it was because of the imminence of extending the Dominion by the inclusion of British Columbia[73] and Manitoba and putting the rest of British North America under the control of Canada; or of a localized agitation for annexation in Nova Scotia;[74] or of a new burst of independence agitation fomented by prominent men like Luther M. Holton, Lucius S. Huntington, Galt, A. A. Dorion, and others, not only in public addresses and communications to newspapers, but even in Parliament;[75] or because of a combination of all these factors; or, on the other hand, whether it was due to a peculiarly virulent chauvinism following the quieting of Reconstruction issues— the fact remains that annexationism was more rampant in the United States during most of 1870 than it had been since the late Forties and early Fifties or has been since the Treaty of Washington. Thornton, transmitting a copy of a memorial "said to have been signed" by a

72. Apr. 25, 1870; FO 5:1192 (P.R.O.).

73. On January 10, 1870, Henry W. Cobbett, delegate from Oregon Territory, introduced a sweeping preamble leading to a resolution proposing to include in any treaty settling the difference between England and the United States a transfer of British Columbia to the latter. It produced little discussion before it was referred to the Committee on Foreign Affairs, but Howard did say that it might be taken as a "very small part" of the payment of American claims. *Cong. Globe,* 41st Cong., 2d Sess., p. 324.

74. The Yarmouth *Herald* was most pertinacious in its advocacy of annexation and opposition to continuance in the Confederation. Transmitting copies of R. J. Walker's letter to the Nova Scotia League of Halifax, Thornton informed Clarendon (Apr. 26, 1869; FO 5:1160 [P.R.O.]): "It points out in glowing and seductive colours the advantages that would accrue to both countries, but particularly to Nova Scotia and even Canada, from their annexation to the United States; but the writer carefully keeps out of sight the additional burthens that would be imposed upon Nova Scotians and Canadians by the enormous taxation and high tariff which rule in this country."

75. *Dominion Parliamentary Debates, 1870,* 3d Sess., *passim.* Charges and countercharges came up in debates on the tariff, fisheries, the conduct of the Manitoba affair, trade relations with the United States, and almost every other topic of discussion.

number of residents of Victoria asking the United States to endeavor
to induce Her Majesty's Government to transfer the colony to the
United States, was moved to comment on the general situation as he
saw it.[76]

This circumstance, the existing disturbance in the Hudson's Bay settlement, and the asserted disaffection in Nova Scotia, are much commented
on by the newspapers of this country, and are looked upon as a beginning
of a separation of the British Provinces from the Mother Country and of
their early annexation to the United States. This view of the matter is
put in connexion with the settlement of the differences with us arising out
of the "Alabama" affair, and the Senators are evidently indulging in the
[i]llusive hope that England has it in her power, and might not be unwilling, to come to an amicable settlement of those differences on the
basis of the cession of our territory on this continent to the United States.

The agitation broke out in various ways in Congress. Pomeroy
made a memorial signed by persons who were not citizens of the United
States an excuse to offer a resolution couched in familiar terms authorizing the President to open negotiations for peaceful transfer of
Canada to the United States.[77] Lawrence of Ohio, speaking on commercial intercourse,[78] believed that "if we resume the trade [as under
Reciprocity Treaty] on a few articles reciprocal interests will hasten
annexation, which will be delayed if Canada finds commercial alliances elsewhere." T. W. Ferry of Michigan, however, opposed reducing the duty upon lumber, for free trade in lumber would put off the
day of annexation: "Compel Canadians to pay a duty on their expor-
tations to our markets, and you will meet them with their own weapons
and force them to seek an earlier union with us, that is sooner or later
inevitable." Moreover, let Americans exploit their own timber at high,
protected prices and when the supply shrank annex Canada and use
hers so that the enhanced price would "inure to the benefit of our own
citizens, who shall then be the occupants and owners of soil now foreign to our borders."[79] L. P. Poland of Vermont introduced a joint
resolution requesting negotiations with Great Britain and the local

76. Thornton to Clarendon, Jan. 3, 1870; FO 5:1191 (P.R.O.). See above,
pp. 199–200.
77. May 19, 1870; *Cong. Globe,* 41st Cong., 2d Sess., p. 3606.
78. May 23, 1870; *ibid.,* App., p. 367.
79. May 24, 1870; *ibid.,* App., pp. 370–375.

governments of British North America with a view to admitting the latter into the American Union.[80] And annexation cropped up in all sorts of discussions, in season and out. State legislatures adopted resolutions in favor of annexation, among them the General Court of Massachusetts, where in the lower branch Charles L. Woodbury, as reported in the Boston *Advertiser*,[81] made "an eloquent speech" supporting the resolution.

He reviewed the arguments in favor of the scheme, and maintained that such a union would do away with the necessity of frontier garrisons; that it would save the expense of the cordon of custom houses, and that it would give New England a market for its manufactures. He said that there are three trunk lines to this city from the west, all of which pass through Canada, and Boston is the commercial outlet for two of these. . . .

"The wishes and interests of the people of the Dominion," remarked the *Gazette*, "don't seem to have entered, at all, into the calculation of the Massachusetts Legislators. New England manufactures were all that was thought of. It seemed to be taken for granted that the people of the Dominion could be bartered like so many sheep, if Great Britain and the United States should agree to it."

Illustrations might be multiplied, but the net result would be the same: in the United States there was a somewhat widely held conviction that the inevitable destiny of the British North American Provinces, whether in the Dominion or out, was eventual union with the United States. Belligerent aggressiveness such as had pervaded expression of this conviction during and immediately after the Civil War no longer was prevalent; in its place was a complacency which to Canadians was quite as irritating though not so alarming. In Canada, confederation had produced something of a sense of security, although too rapid a withdrawal of Imperial protection was deprecated. Confederation, while probably satisfactory to the great majority of people, especially in Ontario and Quebec, nevertheless left some cold; at one extreme was a group of advocates of independence, at the other a very small number who would welcome annexation. Confederation in itself, however, did not solve immediate problems of international rela-

80. *Ibid.,* p. 4601. Thornton to Clarendon, June 21, 1870; FO 5:1193 (P.R.O.).
81. Quoted in Montreal *Gazette,* June 14, 1870.

tions, even though it placed the Dominion in a more strategic position with respect to them. As the winter of 1870–71 drew near and all the old and new issues pressed for settlement, this pulling and hauling between confederation, independence, and annexation had more than a little part to play in setting the stage for a general clean-up.

CHAPTER X

THE FENIANS

At the close of the American Civil War there was a confused mixture of issues which complicated relations between the United States and the British North American Provinces. Some of the problems were of long duration, like the Northeast fisheries question; some were new and in some degree an outgrowth of the struggle between the North and the South. Among the newer issues one of the most irritating was that created by the Fenian movement in the United States. Fenianism grew out of the ever-present Irish problem of the British Empire. A new uprising in Ireland against England had led to stern repressions, and Irish-Americans and Irish sympathizers in the United States sought to embarrass if not to cripple Britain by instituting a movement which would somehow or other remove Canada and the other British North American Provinces from the Empire. At no time do the ends to be attained appear to have been well defined; sometimes they seemed to embrace the establishment of a new republic on the North American continent; sometimes they appeared to be merely a variant of the annexationist movement; and always they sought to annoy England. Whatever the objectives might be, Fenianism gave the Provincial governments many an anxious moment, increased notably their expense for defense, kept the people in the Provinces in a state of agitation and panicky fear, and gave rise to a feeling that the Government of the United States was negligent and callous, demonstrating an animosity toward British North America which, if deserved at all, should have been directed against England.

The first serious attention to this open movement in the United States was aroused in British official circles when the Consul-General at New York, E. M. Archibald, sent, on October 27, 1864, a secret communication[1] to Chargé J. Hume Burnley, in which he enclosed an anonymous letter from a British subject living in Albany together with a copy of by-laws and rules of the Order of the Fenian Brother-

1. FO 5:962 (P.R.O.). See on the general topic C. P. Stacey, "Fenianism and the Rise of National Feeling in Canada at the Time of Confederation," *Can. Hist. Rev.*, XII, 238–261.

hood. Already the Order had established a newspaper, the *Spirit*, and there appeared to be a number of local organizations scattered throughout the larger cities of the North. Its design "to bring about a revolution and to establish a democratic Republic in Ireland," wrote Archibald, "is avowed with the utmost boldness." At that time, so far as Archibald's information went, this appeared to be the principal, if not the only, design of the order; he believed that it would pay to hire a man to keep an eye on the activities of John O'Mahony, the chief executive officer of the Order, and his associates.

Throughout the autumn and winter of 1864 information was quietly gathered until it was clear that the movement was assuming rather formidable proportions, and that, moreover, little attempt was made to keep secret what was going on. So notorious did Fenian agitation become, what with frequent meetings which were freely reported in the papers, that Burnley, on March 14, 1865, in accordance with his instructions, called it to the attention of the Government of the United States.[2] There was no doubt, he said, that "an extensive conspiracy on the part of the so-called Fenian Brotherhood is being openly carried on in the United States, having for its object to promote rebellion in Ireland, and to forward from the United States assistance to the rebels in money, men and arms." So public were the activities and so open the threats that the Government of the United States must have taken note, and "Her Majesty's government might reasonably have expected that while the government of the United States so loudly protest against the proceedings of the confederate agents in this country, [they] . . . should at least have shown their disapprobation of such hostile declarations against the peace and security of the Queen's dominions." Instead, however, an officer of the Army of the Potomac, Colonel J. H. Gleason, had been given leave from his military duties to attend a Fenian meeting in Chicago, and Attorney-General Lynch of Louisiana had taken an active part in a Fenian meeting in New Orleans. Burnley admitted that it might be difficult, under the Constitution of the United States, to prevent or interfere with the meetings, but at least the Government of the United States might disapprove attendance of civil and military officers at them.

2. Burnley to Seward; *Diplomatic Correspondence, 1865,* Part II, pp. 96–97.

Burnley's note gave Seward an opportunity to express prevailing American resentment[3] and at the same time rather smugly to take occasion to demonstrate that the Government did not particularly care whether Great Britain was discommoded or not. So long as a popular assembly did not break the peace or violate municipal or international law it could not be interfered with. The occasion was too good to resist the temptation to advert to Burnley's reference to American representations about Confederate agents.

I must be excused for leaving unnoticed the allusions which your note contains in regard to an assumed hostility of this government towards Great Britain, and I pass over in the same manner the allusion which you have made to the many well-founded complaints which this government has heretofore presented of aggressions committed by British subjects against the peace and sovereignty of the United States. This government could not consent to weaken those complaints by entering, though even more directly invited, into an argument of recrimination.[4]

By the spring of 1865 the immediate Fenian objective appeared to be an invasion of Canada as a means of bringing pressure to bear upon England in order to relieve Ireland, and Canadian authorities were beginning to be alert to the possibilities. Occasional border encounters between individuals emphasized the possibilities, but even yet there was no serious alarm over the situation. As Premier J. A. Macdonald,[5] commenting on the arrest of one exuberant Irishman, stated:

As I think the Fenians are thoroughly disheartened, and as the arrest of men in this Country for acts performed in the U. S., such as joining the Fenian organization there would have a tendency to diminish the friendly relations existing at present on both sides of the line, it is, I think, in the highest degree inadvisable to stretch the law at all. As for those men taken with arms in their hands at Fort Erie, and who aided in shooting down our Volunteers, and for those men who like Murphy were actually on their way to attack New Brunswick we ought properly to adopt a different course.

3. Seward to Burnley, Mar. 20, 1865; *ibid.*, pp. 103–104.
4. Seward's insinuations that this might be a game of tit for tat were echoed in the public press. New York *Herald,* Apr. 20, May 2, 1865.
5. To W. C. Allen, July 2, 1865; Macdonald Papers: Letterbooks, XI, 384–385 (P.A.C.).

As summer stretched on, however, increasing activity, or at least vociferousness, of Fenians caused increased alarm across the border[6] and uneasiness in the British Legation in Washington, although in the latter place the principal concern was over the possibility of sending men and money to Ireland.[7] Nevertheless, Canada was not left out of consideration entirely, for, as Archibald reported to the Governor-General, "I incline to believe that a number of outlaws, men who have been in the U. S. military service, who are probably Fenians, will organize a raid or raids for the purpose of plundering Banks and committing outrages in Canadian towns near the frontier." Rumors of expeditions planned or started continued to flow into the Legation, although it was hard to trace them down and when traced they were found to be much exaggerated. Suspicions that the leaders of the movement were using the organization to raise money which might or might not be devoted to freeing Ireland were rife, and it was believed that appeals were made to the ignorant to get them to subscribe to the cause, dupes who thought that "some great good is to happen to their Country."[8] As autumn came on, the rumors of possible attacks grew more frequent, but when Bruce talked the matter over with Seward the latter "remarked that he thought the Fenian affair was much exaggerated, and that nothing would serve so much to give it importance as that it become the subject of official correspondence."[9] Bruce was disposed to agree with the Secretary of State, but for other reasons.

. . . If Mr Seward were called upon to make any formal declaration on the question, it is very likely that he would accompany it with some expressions of sympathy with the national aspirations which underlie the movement rather than lose for his party the support of the Irish vote at

6. "I hope you have employed Armstrong, and I now, in consequence of this Fenian business authorize you to employ five or six good men more—they should watch the whole Frontier in your beat.

"The Fenian action in Ireland is serious, and the Imperial Government seem fully alive to it. *We* must not be caught napping." Macdonald to McMicken, Sept. 22, 1865; Macdonald Papers: Letterbooks, VIII, 259–260 (P.A.C.).

7. Archibald to Monck, Sept. 16, 1865; G 236 (P.A.C.).

8. J. E. Wilkins to Bruce, St. Louis, Oct. 5, 1865; FO 5:1020 (P.R.O.).

9. Bruce to Russell (draft), Confidential, Oct. 31, 1865; FO 115:438 (P.R.O.).

this critical moment. That such would be the case I infer from his anxiety to repudiate the charge made against him by the Democratic papers on the strength of a statement in the "Times" that he had supplied information about the Fenians to H. M. Gov^t. Now a declaration of such a nature w^d be represented by the Fenian agitation as favourable to them, & by the attention it w^d excite, the Gov^t would be more embarrassed in taking measures to preserve quiet on the frontier, should any measures for that purpose become necessary.

But, said Bruce, there were larger considerations that inclined him to fall in with Seward's ideas: he was more pacific in his views than any other person who would be likely to be put in his place. Moreover, if Southerners were readmitted to Congress it was probable that there would be a coalition of the South and West to restrain the "War-party of the North," for the Southerners could hardly be expected to take a violent attitude toward England, and the West wanted quiet along the border "to develope the resources at her command." Hence, unless otherwise instructed, Bruce proposed to confine himself to private and friendly communication of such specific information as he might obtain. "Mr Seward will readily undertake, & more easily defend, measures of precaution when he can state that the Gov^t has taken them, ex proprio motu, & for the vindication of international obligation, and not at the request of H. M. Gov^t."

Such were the indications of pending incursions by Fenians into Canada, however, that the British Government, speaking through Lord Clarendon who replaced Russell in the Foreign Office, while approving the course Bruce had hitherto pursued, believed the time had come to press things a little harder, and instructed him to this effect on November 16, 1865.[10] The movement had gone to the point where "the Fenian Agitators in the United States have recently set up within the United States, a so-called Executive Government with all the Paraphernalia of Ministers appointed to several Departments, and have established, or are about to establish, in one of the cities of the American Union the seat of such Government." This must be surely looked upon by the American Administration as unprecedented "in the history of the world." As yet, however, in view of what Bruce had written, "Her Majesty's Government will not, at all events for the

10. FO 115:434 (P.R.O.).

present, require you to make an official representation to the United States Government on these matters."

But in the Provinces some more tangible demonstration of the intention of the United States Government to end the continued agitation and threatened disturbance was much desired. As the Lieutenant-Governor of New Brunswick wrote the Colonial Office:[11]

You will observe that Sir F. Bruce while expressing his own opinion of the vigilance of the U. S. authorities has not procured an authoritative announcement from the President of his determination to perform his international obligations and to prevent the territory of the U. S. being made the base for hostile operations directed against this Province although therefore I am bound to believe that the U. S. Gov^t will not fail in their duty in this respect, H. M. Minister gives me no indication of their real disposition, and on this most material point I am left entirely in the dark.

Michel's concern could not have been materially reduced when he received, a few days after writing the above, a communication from the consulate in New York[12] which told of difficulties the Fenians had in raising funds and how the leaders were putting on a bold front by taking an expensive house in that city; how much misery the leader John O'Mahony was causing by raising false hopes and at the same time bleeding credulous Irishmen. O'Mahony, according to an unnamed banker who talked with Archibald, alleged that the Fenians had abandoned the project for raising an insurrection in Ireland and were concentrating on the Canadian venture. When the banker asked O'Mahony how he expected to accomplish anything unless there was a state of war between Great Britain and the United States, the latter had replied that "there was more in the matter than was generally supposed; and hinted that prominent parties in the U. S. Government were encouraging the movement." Another informant of Archibald's, "a respectable person, in appearance," told him that he had been employed as an engineer "in preparations which they were about to make for a raid into Canada on the 25th of October last"; this engineer became dissatisfied and gave information about the scheme, whereupon it

11. Sir John Michel to Under-Secretary Cardwell, Confidential, Nov. 24, 1865; FO 115:273 (P.R.O.).

12. Archibald to Michel, Nov. 27, 1865; G 236 (P.A.C.).

was abandoned; but now, he said, they were contemplating a raid or invasion as soon as the ice on the St. Lawrence was solid enough. On the whole, Archibald stated, he was inclined to believe that the worst of the Fenian movement was past.[13]

Archibald's view was shared by Premier Macdonald,[14] who on December 14, 1865, wrote that from the existing aspect of affairs in New York it appeared that the Fenian conspiracy was broken up and that the design for an invasion of Canada was abandoned; the American Administration would, no doubt, put down at once any attempt at invasion and speedily apprehend all of those connected with the affair. The Canadian Government was being kept well posted on developments. From Detroit[15] came an account of the debates of a Fenian Congress where the Reverend Mr. Carley spoke at length and insisted that "the Irish in America had no right to invade Canada, unless to aid them in establishing a free republic, or in effecting an annexation to America. He thought the Canadians were fully capable of taking care of themselves, without having the Fenians interfere and invade them against their will. This view was approved by the majority of the delegates." A meeting in Cincinnati, however, put a different view on the matter. As the Montreal *Gazette*[16] saw it:

. . . These provinces are clearly indicated as the object of attack by 50,000 men under Major-General SWEENEY of the United States army, who, by way we suppose of showing the value of professions of United States neutrality, appeared in U. S. army uniform, which he probably would not have done had he apprehended any check from his superior officers, or the United States Government, by whom he was reinstated at the request of the Fenians, after being dismissed by Gen. GRANT.

13. From London, Adams sent (Dec. 1, 1865; *Diplomatic Correspondence, 1865,* Part II, pp. 25–26) a clipping from the *Cosmopolitan* (Dec. 2), which showed an alarmist attitude; it doubted whether President Johnson and Russell could much longer keep the peace, for they had allowed "Fenianism to live too long, to grow too large, and to go too far." The Fenians would invade Canada, unite with dissatisfied elements there, set up a provisional government, issue letters of marque against England and "the cost and the consequences who can calculate?"

14. To Crawford; Macdonald Papers: Letterbooks, IX, 34–35 (P.A.C.).

15. Detroit *Free Press,* Jan. 9, 1866.

16. Feb. 12, 1866.

Look, said the *Gazette*, at the howl that went up after the St. Albans raid and contrast it with the supine attitude of the Administration in Washington in face of these recent threats. "In fact this Fenian demonstration is probably winked at by the U. S. Government, in the hope that it may produce a terrorism in these colonies, which may favour their annexation projects; but in this they again commit an error, which will put further off the desired object." One of the sad features of the case was that there were men in Cincinnati, not Fenians or Fenian sympathizers, who "believe them to be quite in earnest." A recent "active movement in arms in New York with the full connivance of the Federal authorities" lent point to the Cincinnati episode. "There may be mischief done, and the blood of many dupes and innocent men spilt; there may also be property destroyed; and both for the blood and the destruction, the United States will be the party." Only a short time later[17] the same paper commented on how, although Great Britain, in common with France, recognized the belligerency of the Confederacy, neither England nor Canada had ever had official intercourse with Confederate agents, but now, according to a "recent American paper,"

A Fenian Delegation, consisting of Mayor Wallach of Washington, B. Doran Killian, George Francis Train, Congressmen Rogers and Hogan, and others, had an interview with the President last evening. The President appointed Wednesday for a special interview, so that papers concerning the recent alleged outrage on American citizens in Ireland can be perused, and a reply prepared.[18]

17. Montreal *Gazette,* Mar. 1, 1865.

18. According to an editorial in the Detroit *Free Press,* April 9, 1866, warlike preparations by Canada were uncalled for. Was there some ulterior motive in all the talk about it? Did the authorities hope to promote the confederation scheme and extinguish the last thought of annexation? "Late attempts to *potterize* them into a union with us have made the Provincials peculiarly sensitive. Their common sense tells them that the continued danger of collision with the States and the crippled state of their commerce, are but a poor compensation for the honor of being regarded as bastard Britons by those who dwell within the shadow of St. Paul's. But with characteristic Anglo-Saxon stubbornness, they will not be driven into dissolving their connection with the old country, and even the prospect of permanent peace and the full development of all their great natural resources will hardly bring them to join Uncle Sam's family."

In the Provinces, as well as in the United States, there was much speculation as to how much support Fenianism found there. In particular was there question about the extent to which French Canadians welcomed the agitation. There was more than a little suspicion that the Rouge faction in Lower Canada, long discontented with existing conditions, harbored designs looking toward coöperation with the Fenians.[19] Mr. Mederic Lanctot, through his paper the *Irish Canadian* of Toronto, was, according to his opponents, doing all that he could to make Canadians believe that Irish Catholics of that Province were "prepared to receive the Fenians with open arms." Toronto, Lanctot maintained,[20] was "evidently in the power of the Fenian element; the Government dares not put a stop to seditious speeches and the display of disloyal banners; it allows a journal to be published which openly declares itself to be Fenian and proves it day by day." If the Government did not dare, with 15,000 men under arms, arrest three or four leaders, "how many hundreds of thousands of men more will be needed to induce the Government to give orders to beat back a Fenian invasion?" That there was discontent in certain groups and that there was strong opposition to confederation cannot be doubted, yet it is apparent that this element which might have been tempted to toy with the idea of coöperating with the Fenians in the United States was, after all, pitifully small.

Throughout the late winter and early spring of 1866 Provincial opinion swung between the beliefs that invasion was imminent and that Fenianism was petering out. The former view, however, began to gain sway. On April 7 a Report of the Canadian Executive Council[21] pointed out that the British Government had come to the conclusion that the Fenians were finally convinced "of the futility of a direct

19. In an editorial in the Montreal *Gazette* of March 14, 1866, there was an analysis which resulted in the conclusion that the two recognized official organs of the Rouges, *Le Pays* and *L'Ordre,* as well as *L'Union nationale,* which had Rouge affiliations, really were sympathetic with Fenianism, although pretending to detest it; that their agitation looked to independence, which could mean only annexation. See Isabel Skelton, *The Life of Thomas D'Arcy McGhee* (Gardenvale, Can., 1925), pp. 440–465, *passim,* for the attitude of a leading Canadian Irishman.

20. Montreal *Gazette,* Mar. 23, 1866.

21. FO 115:450 (P.R.O.).

attack on Ireland and almost the whole energies of this formidable organization seem now to be directed against the British Provinces, and more especially against Canada." Hence, on March 7, it was decided to call out an additional force of 10,000 men, and later still more, so that, by the time of the report, there were 11,000 under arms and another 15,000 could be mustered into service within twenty-four hours. "H. M. Govt.," went on the report, "are no doubt well informed as to the numbers & state of preparation of the Fenian conspiracy but even making every allowance for exaggeration it cannot be concealed that the organization is probably the most formidable in numbers in the warlike training of men & officers & in the possession of improved fire arms that was ever permitted to exist within a State professing to be on amicable terms with the country against w^h such preparations were being openly made." But it was not only the actual strength of numbers which made the conspiracy dangerous, it was the significance of

the tacit support & encouragement w^h it received from large sections of the citizens of the U. S. & from the fact that the termination of the civil war in that country has left an enormous mass of men comparatively unemployed who w^d be apt if a temporary lodgment were made on British soil by the Fenians to rush in thousands into Canada for the purpose of plunder or conquest. Under these circumstances the Committee cannot but regard the position of Canada as one of *quasi* war w^h may at any moment become one of active hostilities. . . .

It had become an Imperial as well as a Canadian problem. A menacing feature of the situation was the presence of seven "Vessels of war called Revenue Cutters on the Lakes of great speed & power & carrying very heavy ordnance"; if these were seized by the Fenians "the whole of the Canadian Commerce on the Lakes would be annihilated and the Lake Towns would be at their mercy." Therefore the committee urged that adequate vessels should be constructed and that long-range guns should be placed "for the defence of Kingston, Toronto, Hamilton and other Lake Towns." The defense of Canada was defense of the Empire, hence Canadians believed that they should not "be left with the support of H. M.'s Land Forces now in Canada to sustain the attack of the enemies of the Empire, and to bear the burden incident to a defence which ought to be made complete in all its parts to ensure success."[22]

From Washington, Bruce reported[23] an interview with the Bond Agent of the Fenian Brotherhood in Washington showing the poor results of attempts either to sell the "bonds" or to make collections. Bruce also reported another interview which a correspondent of the London *Times* had with President Johnson, when, at the instance of the Minister, who had known the interview was to take place, opportunity was taken to bring out the state of public feeling in England on the matter.

The President at first seemed rather indisposed to talk on the subject. But he gradually entered upon it, in the same strain in which he spoke to me in a previous occasion. He reprobated this imperium in imperio thus created, & seemed quite alive to the impropriety and inconvenience of these proceedings. He said that the subject had been frequently discussed by the Cabinet, and that the Gov^t were determined & fully prepared to put down any overt act or enterprise by land or sea. That the state of the law did not allow more to be done; But he frankly admitted that the Gov^t surrounded by difficulties in its internal policy, & anxious to obtain support from any quarter against the violent party of the North, were desirous of avoiding if possible any collision with the popular sentiment of the Irish masses.

This, Bruce thought, was the real opinion of the Government, for it coincided with what Seward had told him.

Bruce's diagnosis would have received confirmation had he been able to see a "confidential" instruction to Adams written in reply to

22. Just after this report was signed Macdonald wrote to Peter Mitchell of Fredericton (Apr. 10, 1866; Macdonald Papers: Letterbooks, IX, 159 [P.A.C.]): "At the moment I am writing this letter you are, I fancy, in great excitement about the Fenians. I really would not be surprised if these Rascals gave you some trouble. . . . They have found that we are too strong for them and therefore they will make a dash at you. But it will end in a fiasco I have no doubt and they will be thoroughly drubbed for their pains if they make the attack. Meanwhile, however, it is an anxious time for you."

23. Bruce to Clarendon (draft), Confidential, Apr. 17, 1866; FO 115:453 (P.R.O.). A week before he had asked whether there was any chance of prosecuting the Fenians under the common law for getting arms to attack a friendly power. He was told such action would not lie either in a State or Federal Court.

the latter's dispatch of February 22, 1866,[24] wherein the American Minister was informed "confidentially" of the sentiments then entertained by the President.

. . . The Fenian excitement as it exists in the United States seems to have merely a political or partisan character. . . . The persons who are engaged in that agitation are, as a general fact, native Irishmen, many of whom, however, have, while others have not, availed themselves of our laws of naturalization. In moving, controlling and directing the Fenian agitation, it is manifest that they are influenced altogether by feelings, sentiments, and views which they cherish as Irishmen, notwithstanding their change of domicile, or place of residence or citizenship. In a few words the Fenian agitation is a British and not an American movement. . . .

After this delicate touch by which the Secretary removed the whole matter from the jurisdiction of the United States and laid the burden upon England, he went on to say that there had been no violation of law brought to the attention of the Government by its own agents, "who are believed to be vigilant," or by complaints from the British Legation, whose "agents of observation" had been placed under no restraint. So long as "neither the character of the agitation, nor the condition of our international relations, is such as to render it wise for this government to denounce the proceedings of the agitators, so long as they confine themselves within those limits of moral agitation which are recognized as legitimate, equally by the laws of the United States and by those of Great Britain" there was nothing the Administration could do. It was "not unreasonable to suppose" that any unlawful undertakings calculated to disturb the peace of Ireland or the British Provinces would "prove not only abortive, but even absurd, unless it should be found that the movement had some connection with an uprising of the country to be invaded." Having thus composed an instruction which could neither wound the Irish in the United States nor present a handle by which it could be charged that the United States did not intend to meet its international obligations, but, at the same time, slyly indicting England, Seward proceeded to include it among documents transmitted to Congress and thus let it become public.

Like the Secretary of State, a great many people of the United

24. *Diplomatic Correspondence, 1866*, Part II, p. 74. Seward's instruction was dated March 10. *Ibid.*, pp. 77–79.

States believed that if, after all the talk, there should come an attempted invasion of Canada or other Province it would be a puny affair, *opéra bouffe*, nothing for the Canadians to get excited about. As the Milwaukee *Sentinel* saw it:[25]

Seriously, it seems strange that any intelligent man on either side of the lakes or of the ocean should believe that there is any expectation or intention on the part of the Fenian leaders to conquer either Canada or Ireland. Just think for a moment of the effort it would require to capture Montreal or Quebec. It would be no holiday affair for the United States, with all our vast armament and resources. What then can an unorganized band of a few thousand, without arms, without a navy, and without resources of any kind at all adequate to such an enterprise, accomplish?
. . . That the United States should suffer an army and navy to be actually organized and fitted out on our own borders for a demonstration against a neighbouring province upon any such scale which need excite alarm, is not supposable, and the frightful demon which England now sees at work in the United States, is but the creation of a guilty conscience in the fresh recollection of her own bad faith towards us. Well, she deserves to be frightened a little, and as long as it is her own devil that is teasing her and not ours, we may be excused if we look on and indulge our devil in a good broad grin.

Such a comment, of course, missed the entire point. It was true that nobody in the Provinces or in the United States expected that the Fenians by themselves could do more than keep the frontier uneasy, but this did not take into consideration the forces which an invasion of any strength might unloose, nor of the wear of constant threats on nerves and resources; it did not count the extra expense to which the Provincial governments, especially that of Canada, were being put, nor the depth of exasperation which was being entertained. It did not take account of the effect of piling this menace, slight as it might be intrinsically, upon the other issues which disturbed relations between the United States and the British Provinces. In addition to all this was the feeling held by many that England ought somehow to clean up the Irish mess and the conviction that Irish-Americans who returned home to engage in insurrection should not be treated the same as other Irishmen. Americans believed that a naturalized citizen was entitled to special consideration when in his homeland, while the British main-

25. Quoted in Montreal *Gazette,* Apr. 19, 1866.

tained that any denizen was subject to the laws of the land while he was there.[26]

Through April and May the situation continued much as it had been, while the Canadian Government and people wavered between hope that nothing would come of the alarms and fear that a raid might take place. The Government of the United States likewise continued to maintain the stand that there was much smoke and but little fire, trusting that things could be nursed along without an outbreak at least until after the elections. Then, on the night of May 31, the storm broke. What actually took place is succinctly outlined in a dispatch sent by Bruce to the Foreign Office on June 4.[27]

The Sweeney & Roberts faction always disapproved of Killian's movement on N. Brunswick[28] & have held out the seizure of Canada as the first step towards the establishment of an Irish Republick. The ease with which Killian's attempt was baffled, and the impression that Roberts had not been successful in collecting funds encouraged the Gov^t of the U. S. in the belief that nothing of a serious character could be effected on the Canadian frontier; and that the precaution taken would be found sufficient to prevent any armed aggression.

On the 31st of May however about 1500 men, who had arrived as passengers of different railways at Buffalo seized some boats in the middle of the night & crossed over to the Canadian side at a village called Fort Erie. The next day they marched down the river in the direction of Ridg-

26. There is considerable correspondence on this point, some of which is published in *Diplomatic Correspondence, 1866,* Part I, in which appears the feeling that a little pressure through Canadian issues might oblige the British Government to take a more complaisant attitude toward American demands growing out of the Civil War.

27. FO 115:453 (P.R.O.).

28. A small group of Fenians under Doran Killian had gathered in Eastport, Maine, close to the New Brunswick border. Murray, the British Consul at Portland, Maine, had been watching the situation, as had Vice-Consul Ker at Eastport (Murray to Bruce, Mar. 19; FO 5:1063 [P.R.O.]). The latter reported: "Our New Brunswick friends are in an intense state of excitement on account of Fenianism, it is said there are some of the so-called Brotherhood here but I am doubtful if such is the case." Murray was reassured by strength of the American military force and by the statement of Washburn, Collector of the Port of Portland, who told him that "as far as he was concerned he w^d use his best endeavors to prevent any breach of the neutrality Laws at this Port. . . ."

way where they were met by the Canadian forces and driven back or dispersed. . . .

Bruce could also report that in the meantime the American Government had acted with commendable promptitude. The *Michigan* and chartered tugs prevented any more Fenians from crossing. By the night of June 2 all the rest of the uncaptured Fenians left Canada and were taken into custody by United States authorities.

The arms which had been lodged at Buffalo, Potsdam, St. Albans, together with ammunition at N. York have been seized—the garrisons at Buffalo, & Rouse's Point have been increased, & other revenue cruisers have been ordered down from their station on the Lake. General Meade has left for the Northern frontier to take the command of the district. The regular forces of the U. S. in the North are however inconsiderable and are inadequate to prevent a movement if the Fenians attempt it in force.

But Bruce had no doubt that vigorous efforts would be made by the Administration to put a stop to all further movements and to "assert the authority of the United States along the frontier, where at this time it may be said practically to be in abeyance." One cause of embarrassment for the Americans was the number of prisoners, some seven hundred, for "the Gov^t has neither guards to look after them, nor prisons in which to confine them, and if they were to land them [they were being detained on the *Michigan*], it is more than probable they would be received by their associates." T. W. Sweeney, W. R. Roberts, and other prominent leaders had disappeared, but Bruce said he had strongly urged their arrest since no movement would be more likely to discourage the Fenians from making further attempts, for rumors had reached him that a new effort was to be made in the direction of Prescott and that Sweeney was in command.

No further raid was tried at this season nor again until four years later. On June 11 Seward, in a note to Bruce,[29] stated that advices received from the border indicated that the "so-called Fenian expedition is now entirely at an end." Coupled with this gratifying information, however, was a complaint, the political implications of which are obvious. General Meade, said Seward, reported that some British or

29. *Diplomatic Correspondence, 1867,* Part I, pp. 237–238.

Canadian troops had crossed the line under a leader named Spear after the raid was over and had taken some prisoners back to Canada and that Canadian agents had threatened these prisoners with immediate execution without legal trial. The reports, remarked Seward, were no doubt exaggerated but the President had directed him to represent that the American Government would regard such an occurrence with serious concern, and requested the British Minister to look into the matter. In a reply[30] dated the same day Bruce stated that he had no information of any such violation of American soil but would institute inquiries in the proper quarters. As to the threats of summary punishment of captured Fenians, "it is not to be denied, nor is it unnatural, that much indignation should be felt against them. But it is a satisfactory circumstance, and creditable to the humanity of those engaged, that the men who formed part of the expedition which crossed at Fort Erie and were taken in the act of attacking the Canadians who turned out to defend their homes, were not summarily disposed of, but were reserved to be dealt with after due investigation." He was confident, wrote the Minister, that there would be every disposition to confine punishment to the offenders "within the limits of what may be required to insure safety for the future" and which would be confirmed "by the decision of a sound and enlightened Public opinion."

That there might be some difficulty in restraining the natural inclination of Canadians to visit condign punishment on the captives, Bruce did not admit to the American Secretary, but, in writing to the Foreign Office,[31] he voiced this fear, yet expressed his hope that the dupes of the Fenian leaders might be dealt with leniently, since nothing would more enlist public opinion in the United States against the Brotherhood and in favor of the Provincials. He did, however, hope that the leaders would be treated severely by the United States for violating its neutrality laws. Sober Canadians, when the first rush of anger had passed, were less inclined to wreak vengeance on the poor fools who had made the mad attempt from Buffalo and more disposed to place the blame squarely where it belonged: on the Government of the United States. If politics had not been played, if there had been

30. *Diplomatic Correspondence, 1867*, Part I, p. 238.
31. Bruce to Clarendon, Confidential, June 11, 1866; FO 5:1065 (P.R.O.).

more attention to international obligations and less concern about how the Irish would vote in the fall, loss of life, loss of property, and loss of respect of the northern neighbor would have been avoided. This was recognized in the United States by those who stopped to think. The New York *Tribune*, certainly no Anglophile sheet, in a leading article maintained:[32]

We do not suppose Messrs. Roberts and Sweeney are any more enemies to-day than they were a month ago, nor that the Government is in possession of any information which had not, in substance, been communicated to it before a blow was struck. *If the Fenians are guilty now, they were guilty then;* and we are at a loss to know why the interposition of our Government should not have occurred before this enterprise had culminated, and before that outbreak of hostilities which a word from President Johnson to those who consulted him might have prevented. *There certainly was no Fenian leader so mad as to suppose that he could conquer Canada plus the United States, nor any leader who would have put his own reputation and the lives of his followers at risk, if he had not believed that this Government would confine its opposition within the rigorous limits of the law.* That Messrs. Sweeney and Roberts are under arrest to-day is only an evidence that they placed too much reliance on what *they were led to suppose would be the policy of the Government.*

A reporter of the New York *World*,[33] who was covering the Fenians at Malone, wrote that

after their arrest Murphy and Heffernan, the Fenian leaders there, waited upon Gen. Meade, and bitterly "complained" of the "perfidy" of the United States Government, asserting that it had allowed them to purchase their arms directly from the United States Arsenals; that it had not objected to their organizing and parading as an armed organization. Mr. Murphy stated that "the United States Government, through Mr. Seward, had encouraged them to make war upon England"; and complained that in spite of this encouragement, and "when they attempted to strike a blow they were crushed by the capture of their arms."

Practically open connivance, such as is implied in this statement, was hardly to be substantiated, but the "hands off" policy of the Govern-

32. Quoted in an editorial in the Montreal *Gazette,* June 13, 1866.
33. Quoted in *ibid.*

ment really amounted to tacit encouragement of the Fenian movement. Not even the valiant fight Johnson was making against the Radicals in Congress over Reconstruction policies and his reluctance to array against him a faction which played with the Irish vote could palliate playing fast and loose with an international situation charged with dynamite.

In Congress, where practically no attention had been paid to the activities of Fenians down to the time of the actual raid, that event and its suppression called forth a few expressions which showed that some had not been displeased with what had taken place and would not be averse to allowing further disturbances. S. E. Ancona, a representative from Pennsylvania, submitted in the House on June 11, 1866, a joint resolution with a preamble which recited the sympathy of Americans with all peoples struggling for independence and nationality, recalled England's alleged "willful neglect to enforce" her neutrality laws, and maintained that the laws of the United States discriminated "most harshly against those who have been and are now our friends" and favored "those who have been faithless, not only to the general principles of comity which should exist between friendly States, but also to the written law of their own nation." The resolution called on the Committee on Foreign Affairs to report a bill repealing the Neutrality Act of 1818 "under the terms of which the President's Proclamation against the Fenians was issued."[34] An attempt to have the resolution laid upon the table was lost by a vote of 112 to 5. Then Robert C. Schenck of Ohio offered a substitute, reading:

Resolved, that the President of the United States, in the opinion of this House, should reconsider the policy which has been adopted by him as between Great Britain and the portion of the Irish people, who, under the name of Fenians, are struggling for their independent nationality; and that he be requested to adopt as nearly as practicable that exact course of procedure which was pursued by the Government of Great Britain on the occasion of the late civil war in this country between the United States and rebels in revolt, recognizing both parties as lawful belligerents, and observing between them a strict neutrality.

Ancona then rephrased his resolution into more flowery terms than before, winding up with

34. *Cong. Globe,* 39th Cong., 1st Sess., p. 3085.

While this Government refuses to aid freedom upon this continent, in Chile and Mexico, from foreign intervention, to which it stands pledged by solemn instructions of our policy and people, it is ignominious and disgraceful to put forth its power with zeal and alacrity to aid an oppressor to an extent not imperatively required by the observed laws of nations.

After an attempt to lay the motion on the table, it was referred to the Committee on Foreign Affairs where it was allowed to rest in peace. Later, on R. P. Spaulding's motion, a resolution was adopted calling upon the President to cause prosecution of Fenians to be discontinued if compatible with the public interest,[35] and Columbus Delano of Ohio secured the adoption of a resolution authorizing Fenians, who had been "illegally" dispersed by the Mayor of Washington, to occupy a building recently erected for the orphans of soldiers and sailors.[36] Having thus blown off steam and made a gesture to placate the Irish vote, the House was content to let the matter drop.[37]

The Administration paid no attention to this ebullition in Congress but continued to pursue the policy it had tardily adopted. It did, however, seek in various instances the release by the Canadian Government of individuals who had been captured as raiders and who maintained that they were innocent bystanders.[38] Most of the requests were complied with when it was ascertained that the prisoners were American citizens. The action of the United States met with cordial appreciation in both England[39] and Canada, although neither the Cana-

35. July 23, 1866; *ibid.*, p. 4048. *House Ex. Docs.*, No. 154, 39th Cong., 1st Sess.

36. July 27, 1866; *ibid.*, p. 4274. In both the House and Senate (*ibid.*, pp. 457, 749, 1633) bills for the defense of the frontier of New England were introduced and referred to appropriate committees, but no discussion or action upon them took place.

37. An editorial in the Detroit *Free Press*, July 7, 1866, stated that one group of Fenian leaders was trying to sell out the Irish vote to the Radicals because this wing of the Republican party promised to repeal the neutrality laws of the United States.

38. There is considerable correspondence over this question in *Diplomatic Correspondence, 1867*, Part I, pp. 239 ff., obviously printed to show the zeal of the Government and to demonstrate that it had no anti-Irish bias. The Governor-General ordered more gunboats for the Lakes without waiting instructions. Monck to Carnarvon, Aug. 16, 1866; G 466 (P.A.C.).

39. Adams reported to Seward, June 21, 1866 (Great Britain: Despatches,

dian Government nor people agreed with the American Government that all danger of further expeditions was over, for throughout the summer preparations for defense continued to be pushed with vigor.[40] It is possible, of course, that some part of this activity was motivated by a desire to impress those who were opposed to confederation with the idea that only by some sort of union could the Provinces hope to maintain themselves from annexation to the United States or defend their borders from hostile demonstrations. There is, however, no reason to believe that this was a dominant motive, for the feverish activity had all the earmarks of being stimulated by genuine alarm. The very fact that Fenians had been allowed to pursue so openly their preparations for an invasion, prior to the actual incursion, might well make the Provincials skeptical about the future.

Bruce, in Washington, also was doubtful whether nothing more was to be feared. In August he reported[41] he had received information leading him to think there might be a renewal of attempts, "prompted no doubt by the sympathy & encouragement extended to them by the H. of Representatives and some leading politicians of the extreme Republican party." In his opinion the Government of Great Britain should not assume that "this mischievous agitation is at an end." While no specific action had been taken by Congress, now adjourned,

the same Congress will sit from December to March, and it is impossible to say whether they will or not on their re-assembling carry out this program [of trying to repeal the neutrality laws], which promises to gain the Irish vote, and to satisfy animosity against England. And when it is recollected, that the object to be achieved by what is called statesmanship in this country is the triumph of the party to which the successful poli-

Vol. XCII [D.S.]), how favorable was the effect upon English public opinion of the course of the United States Government; he had received, he said, in social circles the most marked and pointed expressions of it from leading persons in both parties. Formal thanks of the British Government were expressed in a note to Seward, July 13. *Diplomatic Correspondence, 1867,* Part I, p. 245.

40. Throughout June, July, and August, Macdonald's correspondence (Macdonald Papers: Governor General Correspondence, Vol. I, *passim* [P.A.C.]) was filled with letters having to do with defense, troops from England, location of volunteers, furnishing of arms, and the like.

41. Bruce to Stanley (draft), Confidential, Aug. 2, 1866; FO 115:454 (P.R.O.).

tician belongs, and that questions, especially foreign ones, are made subservient to that end, that the feeling against England is deep-seated & generally entertained, and Ireland is looked upon as a second Poland, I feel much uncertainty as to the course the President may adopt, if he is placed in the dilemma of sacrificing the Irish vote, or of allowing the Fenians to take their chance. I think he is honest, & Mr Seward pacifist—but his honesty may be put to too severe a trial, & Mr Seward's continuance in office becomes every day more problematical, particularly if no progress is made towards an amicable settlement of the questions & dispute between G^r Britain [and the United States].

Both the British Legation and the Canadian Government kept agents in the field to gain information of possible hostile demonstrations[42] and discovered enough to keep them on the alert. In part, this show of vigilance was necessitated by a state of mind bordering on panic which possessed the people living near the boundary line, for they were convinced that other raids were imminent.[43] Nor was the opposition party in Canada loath to take advantage of the situation to attack the Government on the ground that it was too lax in measures of defense,[44] and to charge them with playing fast and loose with the existence of British America. Local officials were prone to make arrests on mere suspicion, and the Government had to check their zeal. Macdonald, writing to a St. Catherine's man who had advised allowing the arrest of persons suspected of being Fenians, pointed out that "the consequence of allowing illiterate Magistrates to arrest every man whom they choose to suspect (and that would be, in the rural districts, every Roman Catholic) would be to drive all that class out of the Country, to ruin many a respectable family by forcing them to sacrifice their property; and to swell the ranks of the Fenian Organization

42. Bruce to Stanley, Secret, Aug. 7, 1866; FO 5:1066 (P.R.O.). Macdonald's Letterbooks throughout 1866 and even after reveal the extent to which this watch was kept.

43. Macdonald to Sir John Michel, Sept. 17, 1866; Macdonald Papers: Letterbooks, X, 140–141, et al. (P.A.C.). "It is really astonishing to witness the panic of the people on the Frontier." To Morrison, Sept. 29; ibid., p. 185.

44. Montreal Gazette, Sept. 11, 1866. "The Globe's idea about calling out all the Volunteers is all nonsense, and no one knows better than Brown that it is so, but he desires to create a fuss and cause discontent." Macdonald to McMicken, Aug. 25; Macdonald Papers: Letterbooks, X, 60 (P.A.C.).

in the United States by every man who has been obliged to leave the Province."[45]

When the trials of the Fenians came on there was loud demand for their severe punishment, despite efforts of the Colonial Office to secure lenient treatment for the effect that would have in the United States, and in spite of representations of the Government of the United States on behalf of those who were American citizens. Even the Montreal *Gazette*, a paper which supported the Government and which had been relatively moderate in its views of the whole affair, maintained[46] that

. . . these men were mere land-pirates coming among us (who have never done them wrong) to rob and subjugate us, or, if we refused to do their behests, to murder us. The laws of civilized warfare do not and cannot apply to them. . . . We only ask for justice. And but one thing can prevent the appeal for mercy being listened to. We must deter from future raids. . . .

If the danger were over the situation would be different, but "when the Fenian leader, President Roberts, [threatens] us in the most stupid rhodomontade if we hang these men,"[47] and prosecutions of Fenians in the United States courts have been abandoned, then mercy would be out of the question. Demands for quick and severe punishment in Canada, however, did not deter the Department of State from appealing to the British Government to interpose on behalf of the condemned men.[48] The court records reporting the trials of the men were sent in transcript to the Department of State at its request, as a favor and not as a right, and, while in most cases it was considered that the proper forms of law had been observed and the accused given the usual benefits, in a few instances question was raised as to whether actual participation in the raids had occurred. Eventually the death sentences were commuted to long-term imprisonment, and, in the

45. To Roland Macdonald, Sept. 29, 1866; Macdonald Papers: Letterbooks, X, 188–189 (P.A.C.).

46. Nov. 5, 1866.

47. Two of the prisoners, R. B. Lynch and J. McMahon, had been tried and condemned to death.

48. The pertinent correspondence is in *Diplomatic Correspondence, 1867,* Part I, pp. 262–265 and *passim.*

course of time, most of the prisoners were released before the expiration of their terms.

During the remainder of 1866 and throughout 1867 the story continued much the same: the Canadians were on the alert in anticipation of further attempts, while the Government of the United States, believing that no more raids were to be expected, nevertheless kept a sharper eye upon the doings of scattered and disrupted groups of Fenians. But toward the end of 1867 and on into 1868 alarm began to be heightened. Revived activity under new leadership gave Fenianism a renewed lease of life, and rumors began to fly thick and fast. Late in December, 1867, the British Consul in Chicago reported to the Legation[49] that a Montreal Irishman who had been living in Chicago stated that "there exists in the large cities of the West a large number of Fenians whose aims are being directed to a raid upon Canada so soon as the ice will permit a large body of men to cross the river St Lawrence" in order to release the Fenian prisoners at Kingston. In February, Macdonald, basing his statement on information from the British Consul in New York, expressed his apprehension to a correspondent:[50]

. . . The United States are now convulsed with the presidential election contest, and the excitement will continue until next December. Both Republicans & Democrats will fish for the Irish vote and therefore will wink as much as possible at any action of the Fenian body. It is only, in my opinion, the want of money that will prevent a serious [in]road. . . . There is a great & increasing want of employment of the labouring classes & great consequent destitution and I fear that the hope of plunder will induce many of these people to cross our Border, so we must always be ready.

Support for Macdonald's fears seemed to be supplied from information that reached the Foreign Office by a roundabout way from Chicago[51] indicating that Fenian factions were likely to compose their differences under the leadership of John O'Neill; that "Andy John-

49. Wilkins to Ford, Dec. 21, 1867; G 238 (P.A.C.).
50. To Ermatinger, Feb. 4, 1868; Macdonald Papers: Letterbooks, XI, 482 (P.A.C.).
51. Hammond to Minister Edward Thornton, Secret, Mar. 7, 1868; FO 115:472 (P.R.O.).

son's administration [would] not impede their progress a great deal" in trying to raise an army to invade Canada in the spring. Canada's detective forces were spurred to greater watchfulness and frontier defense was strengthened. Hope, however, was pinned on the existence of internal Fenian squabbles which might prevent consummation of O'Neill's plans, which, according to reports received by the British Legation,[52] proposed a simultaneous invasion of Canada at three points, "one from the Chicago district, via Detroit, another via & from Cleveland, Buffalo, Toledo &c, and a 3ᵈ, New York, Massachusetts &c. This movement must be defeated by the British Govᵗ for the Govᵗ of the U. S. will not & cannot do it."

When all these indications of new Fenian movements were brought to the attention of Seward, he, as usual, maintained that the danger was exaggerated, and, furthermore:

Whatever danger there may be of a disturbance of the peace of the frontier at the present time, that danger is altogether due to the omission by the British Government to seasonably remove, either by legislation or by negotiation, the indefensible features of British policy on the subject of the rights of naturalized citizens of the United States. . . .

In asking your attention to the subject once more, I do so with a view to averting from this government undue responsibility in the event of new frontier collisions, especially liable to occur in a season of high political excitement in both countries.[53]

52. Abstract of information contained in two letters, Chicago, Apr. 23, 25, 1868, names not given; FO 115:473 (P.R.O.). McMicken, one of Macdonald's detectives (Mar. 26, 1868; Macdonald Papers: Governor General Correspondence, II, 213 [P.A.C.]), stated that it was improbable the factions would unite, for "Politicians would make it their aim to foster this division."

53. Seward to Thornton, May 28, 1868; *Diplomatic Correspondence, 1868,* Part I, p. 430. In a letter to Tupper in Nova Scotia, Macdonald said: "We are threatened with another Fenian invasion, and I am satisfied that we will have another raid before the 1ˢᵗ July unless the American Government acts vigorously. The Fenians rely much upon the Presidential Contest which is now beginning to rise to fever heat. As a body they have declared that they will vote with the party that gives them the most support. The Republicans wont trust them, however, I believe; and I have little doubt that the Irish vote will as usual be cast in the main for the Democratic candidate." Macdonald Papers: Letterbooks, XI, 790–791 (P.A.C.).

Seward lived up to his earlier reputation of being a politician of parts, for the publication of this note was calculated to please the American people by its twisting of the lion's tail; it surely did not hold out much hope that undue activity could be expected from the Government of the United States. Nevertheless, the bark was worse than the bite, for the Administration apparently did not intend to be caught napping as it had been two years before.[54]

Despite alarms and excitement, the summer passed with no actual attempt to duplicate the raid of 1866. By the time the elections were over and it was known that Grant would become president, in the United States, at least, little remained of the expectation that a raid would come. This was the opinion expressed to Minister Edward Thornton by Seward, as the former reported to Sir John Young, the Governor-General.[55] Some months before, at Thornton's request, Seward had asked the Secretary of War to make a secret inquiry along the border. Brigadier General John Pope was appointed to the duty, and, Thornton wrote, "Mr Seward has informed me this morning confidentially that the Secretary of War has transmitted to him a lengthened [sic] and detailed report of the enquiries, all of which, as he assures me, lead to the belief that there does not exist the slightest intention, for the present at least, on the part of the Fenians to enter upon a hostile expedition against Canada." Young was not so confident and persuaded the British Minister to urge Seward not to relax entirely the Government's "vigilance with respect to the proceedings of the Fenians."[56] Thornton was inclined to agree with Seward that the danger of a raid was remote and also concurred in the latter's opinion that "although strictly speaking the United States Authorities might have a right to forbid such an armed procession [as had taken place in Philadelphia], it might be unwise to do so, because such a step might excite the Irish to resistance and irritate them, and might increase the number of their friends among the Americans, who, I really believe, are daily diminishing in numbers." With this assurance the Governor-General was satisfied that the United States would take all necessary

54. Macdonald to Tupper, June 13, 1868; Macdonald Papers: Letterbooks, XI, 873 (P.A.C.).

55. Thornton to Young, Confidential, Dec. 4, 1868; G 573A (P.A.C.).

56. Thornton to Young, Confidential, Dec. 22, 1868; G 573A (P.A.C.).

precautions to prevent a disturbance.[57] Premier Macdonald, too, was reassured, particularly after the Grant administration came into office, for, as John Rose, Dominion Minister of Finance, wrote him, "Mr. Fish is taking the most effectual measures about Fenianism: . . . & I really think that so long as he is there we have nothing to fear;—if vigilance and good faith can prevent it."[58]

For a time there was a lull in concern about Fenianism, except as to the responsibility of the United States for pecuniary compensation for damages and for the expense of Canadian preparations for defense. A little excitement came up in the summer of 1869, when there was some stir in New York among the Brotherhood there, but again difficulty in raising money stood in the way of any effectual move.[59] Fenianism became somewhat entangled with the Cuban insurrection, since there was some thought of directing its energies to filibustering expeditions in aid of the insurgents possibly setting forth from St. John,[60] but this came to nothing. One of the Fenian prisoners, John McMahon, still held in jail, was the subject of continued correspondence until he, too, was finally released.[61] The Canadian Government, however, did not relax its vigilance, for persistent rumors still were running about that an attack was planned, now at this point and now that.[62] In October, Sir John Young could report that there had been rumors of attacks all summer but that they had blown over; now, however, there were new and more disquieting ones. Several hundred men were at Ogdensburg and another force at Detroit, while at various

57. Young to Thornton, Dec. 29, 1868; Despatches to Minister at Washington, XI, 166 (P.A.C.).

58. Rose to Macdonald, written at Montreal on "Tuesday, 1869" after Rose's return from Washington, where he had been from July 8 to 11, sounding the situation as to reciprocity (Macdonald Papers: Rose, '64–'74 [P.A.C.]).

59. Young to Granville (the Colonial Secretary at the time), Confidential, July 16, 1869; Macdonald Papers: Governor General Correspondence, pp. 127–128 (P.A.C.). See also July 23 and July 30, 1869; ibid., pp. 129–130.

60. Macdonald to Sir John Young, July 17, 1869; Macdonald Papers: Letterbooks, XII, 1022–1024 (P.A.C.).

61. Report of the Department of Justice, Ottawa, July 15, 1869; FO 115: 488 (P.R.O.).

62. A. F. Lidell of the Home Office to Foreign Office, Aug. 3, enclosed in Otway to Thornton, Aug. 6, 1869; FO 115:487 (P.R.O.). Fish to Thornton, Aug. 28, 1869; Davis Papers, Vol. IV (L.C.).

places on the frontier the Fenians had thousands of rifles waiting to
be used. He did not fear the conquest of Canada but there might be "a
great deal of bloodshed and marauding and ill feeling caused thereafter."[63]

Mr. Fish, in spite of his doubt whether an expedition would take
place, promised Thornton[64] "to do all that was in his power to prevent
any hostile expedition against Canada from being organized in the
United States, and he promised me to telegraph at once to the Mar-
shals of the United States . . . and to instruct them to use the greatest vigilance with regard to the persons" involved, "and to break up
any attempt at an expedition against Canada."[65] O'Neill was reported
to be leaving New York for Buffalo. A western movement was to be
attempted as a diversion, but the main attack would be along the eastern shores of Lake Champlain, "to take a few lives, plunder some villages & keep the game alive."[66] But again nothing was done. O'Neill
did not leave New York and no invasion occurred. And so things went
on during the rest of the year and into 1870. Then, when in May,
1870, a miserable little band made the long-threatened raid into
Canada from near Franklin, Vermont, it was easily overwhelmed and
driven back. O'Neill and other leaders were arrested in the United
States, tried for and convicted of violation of the laws of the country
and put in prison.

63. Young to Granville, Oct. 14, 1869; Macdonald Papers: Governor General Correspondence, pp. 142–144 (P.A.C.). John Lothrop Motley, who followed Reverdy Johnson as Minister to England, was told by Clarendon: "I beg
also to remind you that the crimes of these men cannot be regarded with reference only to the past; but that the very same conspiracy of which they were
among the most active and mischievous offenders and Agents, is not only busy
at home collecting arms and funds, but is at the moment threatening a hostile
expedition into H. M.'s Canadian Dominion." Oct. 15, 1869; FO 115:488
(P.R.O.).

64. Thornton to Young, Oct. 19, 1869; G '69–'71 (P.A.C.).

65. Macdonald's Letterbooks have numerous references to the possibilities
of raids and the precautions that were being taken to forestall them.

66. Young to Granville, Oct. 25, 1869; Macdonald Papers: Governor General Correspondence, pp. 144–147 (P.A.C.).

CHAPTER XI

THE SAN JUAN WATER BOUNDARY

ALTHOUGH not hoary with age like the fisheries problem, the question of the water boundary provided for in the Oregon Treaty of 1846, with the consequent dispute as to whether San Juan Island and its surrounding islets lay in British or American territory, antedated the Civil War. It was, of course, at that time and down to 1867 not properly a Canadian issue at all, but after confederation and the prospective inclusion of British Columbia in the Dominion, it became not only a matter of concern to Great Britain and the United States but also one of the points at issue between the United States and Canada.

When the long-drawn-out controversy over the Oregon country was finally settled by the Treaty of 1846, the line of demarcation between the possessions of the United States and those of Great Britain was, according to the treaty, to run along the forty-ninth parallel "to the middle of the channel which separates the continent from Vancouver's Island; and thence southerly through the middle of said channel and of Fuca's Straits to the Pacific Ocean." Right of navigation in the channel and in the straits south of forty-nine was to be free and open to both parties. Sparsity of population and dominance of the Hudson's Bay Company in the region prevented any real concern over the location of the actual line for several years; but when, in 1853, the inhabitants of the area north of the Columbia River and especially along the shores of Puget Sound had increased so that Congress set apart the Territory of Washington from that of Oregon, it was soon to become more than an academic question. In 1854, at the first meeting of the legislature of the new Territory, the County of Whatcom was incorporated, and San Juan with its adjacent islets was included within it. Then the matter of jurisdiction came to the surface. Up to that time British authorities entertained no doubt that the island was a part of their domain and had acted accordingly, although there were few people outside the servants of the Hudson's Bay Company who disputed the area with the Indians. Now a few American squatters straggled over to San Juan and they looked to the territorial government of Washington for protection, while the Britishers continued to maintain that they were under the authority of the Queen. Assessment of taxes upon British property, mostly Company property, and the seizure of some sheep to satisfy the assessment, brought the issue to a showdown, which led to an agreement between Secretary Marcy and Crampton in 1855 for temporary joint occupation. An exchange of letters between Governor James Douglas of British Columbia and Governor Isaac I. Stevens of Washington Territory put the arrangement into operation.[1]

In his Annual Message of 1855 President Pierce adverted to the necessity of taking steps properly to determine and mark the boundary, and Secretary Marcy, in February, 1856, called this passage to the attention of the appropriate committee of the Senate, after Crampton had made the subject a matter of communication. In due time Congress authorized the appointment of a commissioner to work with some person representing Great Britain, and appropriated money for the job. The Commissioners proceeded to their task and agreed upon all points except as to which channel about San Juan was the one intended to be specified by the treaty. The American Commissioner, Archibald Campbell, took the ground that it was Haro Canal, lying to the west of San Juan, because that was widest and deepest, while Captain Prevost, representing England, was equally sure that Rosario Strait, on the east side of the island group, was the one intended. Both Commissioners turned in their reports and thus left the issue to the negotiation of the two Governments.[2] In view of the small intrinsic interest involved and of the sparse population in the disputed area, it is improbable that the Foreign Office and the Department of State would have been moved from their slow handling of the question had it not been for a local disturbance which, for a time, made it a matter of rather grave concern to both sides. Some indication of possible trouble had been given by John Nugent, Special Agent, who had been sent to the Northwest in 1858 to inquire into complaints about the treatment of American citizens temporarily or more perma-

1. See *Senate Reports,* No. 251, 34th Cong., 1st Sess., and *Senate Ex. Docs.,* No. 2, Part II, 36th Cong., 1st Sess., pp. 39 ff.

2. J. B. Moore, *History and Digest* . . . , I, 218–222. In the course of their discussions Captain J. C. Prevost suggested, without committing his Government, a compromise line (see map) which Commissioner Campbell refused to consider.

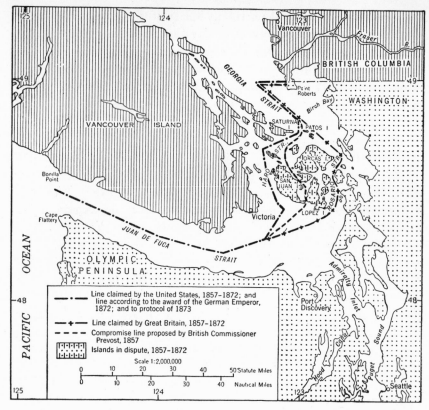

San Juan Islands and the Disputed Boundary

Reproduced with permission from Diplomatic History of the United States
by S. F. Bemis, published by Henry Holt & Co.

nently resident in British Columbia. Toward the end of his report,[3] which dealt almost entirely with the immediate subject of his investigation, he called attention to the disputed water boundary. The "intendment" of the article in the treaty was, in his opinion, merely to see that all of Vancouver Island was recognized as British and that the islands of the Sound belonged to the continent; nevertheless, he concluded, he felt it his duty "to call attention to the design apparently entertained by Great Britain, on the shallowest possible pretext, to deprive the people of the United States of possessions clearly theirs, and

3. *House Ex. Docs.*, No. 3, 35th Cong., 2d Sess.

the importance of which to them, as well as to the government of the
United States, can scarcely be overestimated." This great importance, which he did not specify, can be surmised to be the supposed
value of San Juan as a site for fortifications, since this was more or
less emphasized in later correspondence between the two Governments.

It was in the spring of 1859 that San Juan became the subject of
real discussion as a result of local difficulties. On May 12, 1859, Lord
Lyons stated to Secretary Cass[4] that Her Majesty's Government was
informed that recently American citizens had established "themselves
on the Island of San Juan, in the Gulf of Georgia" and that he had
been instructed immediately to call the attention of the Government
of the United States to the fact. Commissioners, who had been appointed to locate the boundary, he said, had not been able to agree
about the status of this island and so the matter was left to the two
Governments to "enter into direct communication with each other for
the settlement of a question which very closely affects the good understanding between them." His Government hoped, said Lyons, that no
local collision might arise in the meantime "to imbitter a discussion
which might otherwise be conducted with cordiality and good will,"
and that "citizens of the United States will be restrained, as far as the
institutions of this government admit of their being so, from attempts
to settle by unauthorized acts of violence a question" which could
probably be adjusted without difficulty by the Governments.

Back of this natural desire to have the disputed point settled was
information that friction on the island had been increasing.[5] According to the story of the Americans involved, not only was there danger
to the little group from Indians,[6] but on August 2, 1859, the "governor and commander-in-chief in and over the colony of Vancouver's
Island and its dependencies" issued a proclamation to this effect:

The sovereignty of the island of San Juan, and of the whole of the Haro
archipelago, has always been undeviatingly claimed to be in the crown of
Great Britain. Therefore, I, James Douglas, do hereby, formally and

4. *Senate Ex. Docs.,* No. 29, 40th Cong., 2d Sess., p. 218.
5. The correspondence is printed at great length in the Report of the Secretary of War, 1859. *Senate Ex. Docs.,* No. 2, Part II, 36th Cong., 1st Sess.
6. Communication signed by twenty-two persons addressed to Brig. Gen.
Harney, Commander-in-Chief of the Pacific Division of the United States
Army, July 11, 1859; *ibid.,* pp. 44–45.

solemnly, protest against the occupation of the said island, or any part of the said archipelago, by any person whatsoever, for or on behalf of any other power, hereby protesting and declaring that the sovereignty thereof by right now is, and always hath been, in her Majesty Queen Victoria and her predecessors, Kings of Great Britain.[7]

This "protest" did not refer to individual American citizens who had squatted on the island but to the fact that Captain George E. Pickett, on orders from Brigadier General W. S. Harney, had taken a company of soldiers to the island "to protect it as a part of the territory of the United States." Captain Geoffrey Phipps Hornby, commanding officer of the British forces at Vancouver, thereupon, to use his own words,[8] presented "the governor's protest against any such occupation or claim. I represented to you that the fact of occupying a disputed island by a military force necessitated a similar action on our part; that again involved the imminent risk of a collision between the forces, there being a magistrate of each nation now acting on the island, either of whom might call on those of their country for aid." To prevent such a collision Captain Hornby suggested that the joint military occupation might continue until the respective Governments could be heard from, and during the time "the commanding officers of the forces should control and adjudicate between their respective countrymen, the magistrates being withdrawn on both sides, or the action of their courts suspended for the time being. . . ." Pickett, however, stated that as he was under orders he could not allow any joint military occupation until he was directed to do so by General Harney; he did not believe any disturbance would arise and thought that "no discredit can reflect upon either of us, or our respective flags, by remaining in our present positions until we have an opportunity of hearing from those higher in authority."[9]

General Harney seems to have been very much upset over the whole affair and saw in it an attempt on the part of the local British authorities to take the island and hold it. He was the more convinced of this when he learned through Pickett that there were three British war vessels in Vancouver waters and heard of an astounding threat to an American citizen on the island. He started posthaste for Puget

7. *Senate Ex. Docs.*, No. 2, Part II, 36th Cong., 1st Sess., p. 53.
8. Hornby to Pickett, Aug. 3, 1859; *ibid.*, pp. 51–52.
9. Pickett to Hornby, Aug. 3; *ibid.*, pp. 52–53.

Sound and, arriving there, reported to the War Department the horrible state of affairs he encountered.[10]

A week or ten days before my arrival on that island one of the Americans shot a pig belonging to the Hudson's Bay Company, after having been greatly provoked by the person in charge, to whom he had applied to have the pig secured, as it damaged his fields. This request was treated with contempt, and the pig was shot, the American offering twice the value of the animal, which was refused. The next day the British ship-of-war "Satellie," with Mr. [Alexander D.] Dallas on board, who is the chief factor of the Hudson's Bay Company, and a son-in-law of Governor Douglas, visited the island and threatened to take the American to Victoria, by force, for trial. The American resisted, seized his rifle, and in return told Mr. Dallas he might take him, but he would kill him first. I was also informed that the Hudson's Bay Company had threatened at different times to send the northern Indians down upon them and drive them from the island. This statement has since been confirmed to me by some of the most reliable citizens of the Sound. . . .

Already, before sending his account to the War Department, the doughty General had addressed from Fort Vancouver a communication to Governor Douglas, asserting his intention to protect American citizens on the island "from the insults and indignities which the British authorities of Vancouver's Island and the establishment of the Hudson's Bay Company recently offered them." He had, he said, reported the outrage to his Government, which would doubtless seek proper redress; meantime he would not permit a repetition of the insult. Without waiting for a response from Washington he requested the "Senior Officer of the United States Navy Commanding Squadron on the Pacific Coast" to send "such force as you can render available to assist in the protection of American interests in that quarter, and to enable us to meet successfully any issue that may be attempted to be made out of the present impending difficulties."[11] As a more immediate means of defense he ordered several more companies from their quarters at various places in the Northwest to proceed at once to San Juan to back up Pickett's little force. Furthermore, when Governor Douglas, on learning of the sending of a company of American

10. Harney to Col. S. Cooper, Adjutant General, Aug. 7, 1859; *ibid.*, pp. 45–47.

11. *Ibid.*, pp. 53–55, for the two communications.

soldiers to San Juan, had "appointed a justice of the peace and other civil authorities at Victoria, and sent them over in the British ship-of-war 'Plumper' to execute British laws in the island," Harney sustained Pickett in refusing to allow them to land.[12]

By the middle of August the disturbance had come to the point where two not inconsiderable forces faced each other on this little plot of ground and its surrounding waters.[13] Colonel Silas Casey had arrived with five companies "and was busy placing in position eight thirty-two pounders, taken from the steamer 'Massachusetts' " at Harney's orders, and, within three days, four more companies had joined him. The British force comprised "five vessels of war, one hundred and sixty-seven guns, two thousand one hundred and forty men, some six hundred of which are marines and engineer troops."[14] A nice little powder mine.

All this was a savory dish to place before the authorities in Washington and in London, little improved by the fact that General Harney in his subsequent communications with Governor Douglas exhibited a somewhat less truculent attitude and was willing to await instructions before pushing the matter further. In Washington the news from the Pacific Northwest was unexpected and entirely unwelcome. Newspapers carried the story of what had taken place before authentic official information was received, and it was on the basis of these news accounts that, on September 3, 1859, Lord Lyons addressed a note to Secretary Cass calling attention to his communication of the previous May when he had, on instructions from London, urged the desirability of settling the boundary dispute before local clashes complicated the situation. Having received no reply to that note the British Minister told Cass he was "the more earnest in requesting you to

12. Harney to Cooper, Aug. 8, 1859; *ibid.*, p. 56.
13. Harney to General-in-Chief, Aug. 18, 1859; *ibid.*, pp. 59–60.
14. Colonel Casey, who was not far behind his superior officer in determination to let no Briton put anything over an American, did, however, make an amicable gesture when he, on his own initiative shortly after his arrival, sought an interview with Admiral Baynes, to propose that if no British orders were given to prevent Pickett's carrying out his orders, then he would recommend the withdrawal of the American reinforcements. Some stiffness on the part of Baynes stopped the overture, and Harney directed that in the future all official communications be referred direct to headquarters. Casey to Pleasonton, Aug. 12; *ibid.*, pp. 61–63.

enable me to send, as speedily as possible, satisfactory information to Her Majesty's government on the subject."[15] Several conversations took place between Cass and Lyons in which the Secretary of State, while careful not to make any retreat that might jeopardize the future standing of the United States in the disputed area, nevertheless "assured [Lord Lyons] of the regret of the President at the recent difficulties at San Juan, and his confident hope that, by the moderation and friendly feelings of the two governments, it will be attended with no serious consequences."[16] He did not state that the American forces would be forthwith removed, but, to get a true picture of the situation and at the same time to have a person of undoubted authority on the spot to help straighten out the imbroglio, General Winfield S. Scott, Commander-in-Chief of the Army, was dispatched immediately to the Northwest. Positive instructions could not be given this emissary because too little was known in Washington about the actual situation despite the somewhat hectic accounts General Harney was sending in; the main object was to preserve the peace and prevent collisions.

. . . Following out the spirit of Mr. Marcy's instructions to Governor Stevens, it would be desirable to provide, during [the period until the water boundary was settled] for a joint occupation of the island, under such guards as will secure its tranquillity without interfering with our rights.

If, unfortunately, a collision had taken place before Scott's arrival, then he should "not suffer the national honor to be tarnished. If we must be forced into a war by the violence of the British authorities, which is not anticipated, we shall abide the issue as best we may without apprehension as to the result."[17]

15. *Senate Ex. Docs.*, No. 29, 40th Cong., 2d Sess., pp. 224–225. On September 21, 1859, Lord John Russell wrote Lyons that the affair was "very annoying." It was the nature of Americans to "push themselves where they have no right to go," and "the nature of the U. S. Government not to venture to disavow acts they cannot have the face to approve." Perhaps the best thing to do would be to seize an island "to which we have as little right as the Americans to San Juan." Newton, *Lord Lyons,* II, 19.

16. Cass to Minister Dallas, in London, Sept. 22, 1859; *Senate Ex. Docs.*, No. 29, 40th Cong., 2d Sess., pp. 227–228.

17. W. R. Drinkard, Acting Secretary of War, to Scott, Sept. 16, 1859; *Senate Ex. Docs.*, No. 2, Part II, 36th Cong., 1st Sess., pp. 57–59.

Meantime General Harney had been directed by the Secretary of War to act with caution, at the same time not to allow anything to occur which would affect American claims. Fortunately matters remained *in statu quo* until General Scott arrived at Port Townsend soon after the middle of October. He immediately got in touch with Governor Douglas, to whom he proposed a "temporary adjustment of any present difficulty."[18]

Without prejudice to the claim of either nation to the sovereignty of the entire island of San Juan, . . . it is proposed that each shall occupy a separate portion of the same by a detachment of infantry, riflemen, or marines, not exceeding one hundred men, with their respective arms only, for the equal protection of their respective countrymen in their persons and property, and to repel any descent on the part of hostile Indians.

Any modification of this plan would, said Scott, be "respectfully considered." Douglas, in an equally conciliatory mood, responded that at first glance he was satisfied there was no obstacle to an "amicable and satisfactory adjustment . . . either upon the plan suggested by General Scott, or some other that may be mutually agreed to after advisement."[19] Upon second thought, however, the Governor hesitated to commit Her Majesty's Government and proposed[20] that "there should be a joint civil occupation, composed of the present resident stipendiary magistrates, with such assistants as may be necessary, and that the military and naval forces, on both sides, be wholly withdrawn." If military protection should be needed, which he doubted, for more trouble came from internal quarrels than from the Indians, then he saw no objection to landing of such force as might be mutually agreed upon. Scott demurred, because any military located on the island would be subject to the civil authorities and that might cause trouble. Douglas stuck to his guns: he could not alter arrangements made by treaty; he was willing to effect a mutual withdrawal of armed forces, and, as soon as he had received instructions from his Government, would coöperate "in arranging a plan for the temporary maintenance of order and protection of life and property upon the island." Mean-

18. Scott to Douglas, Oct. 25, 1859; *Senate Ex. Docs.*, No. 10, 36th Cong., 1st Sess., p. 60.
19. Memorandum of Lt. Col. G. W. Cray, U.S.A., Oct. 26, 1859; *ibid.*, p. 61.
20. Douglas to Scott, Oct. 29; *ibid.*, pp. 61–63.

time, he assured Scott, "we will not disturb the *status* of San Juan by taking possession of the island, or by assuming any jurisdiction there to the prejudice of the position in which the question was placed by Mr. Secretary Marcy and Her Majesty's representative in the year 1855." Hereupon Scott agreed to withdraw immediately all the American forces except Pickett's small detachment "for the protection of the American settlers (such protection being petitioned for by them) against neighboring and northern Indians." With this Douglas was satisfied; he would communicate the scheme to his Government who would "no doubt accept it as a proof of the desire of the United States to restore the former status of the disputed territory."[21]

Locally, then, the tempest in a teapot was calmed. A working arrangement was effected which produced relative satisfaction while the two Governments wrangled over the question of title. This discussion was entered upon in good earnest in the autumn and winter of 1859, largely confined, however, during a considerable portion of the time to American dissatisfaction with an expression in Lord John Russell's instruction of August 24, where he said "that no settlement of the question will be accepted by Her Majesty's Government which does not provide for the island of San Juan being reserved to the British Crown."[22] This, according to Secretary Cass's interpretation, could only mean that whether Haro Canal, Rosario Strait, or Douglas Channel, which Russell subsequently suggested as a compromise line, were selected, there was no question about the island; it must be British. An explanation in an instruction of November 29 did not remove Cass's objection, and it was not until April 23, 1860, that he was able to say to Minister Dallas that a copy of a note of Lord John's dated March 28 entirely removed the obstacle. A slight but momentary rift in the tenor of peaceful arguing about whether the line followed Haro or Rosario came when Lord Lyons, on June 6, 1860, called the attention of the Department of State to an order issued not long

21. The correspondence between Douglas and Scott is in *ibid.*, pp. 63–68. Douglas' final agreement was dated November 7, 1859.

22. Russell to Lyons; *Senate Ex. Docs.*, No. 29, 40th Cong., 2d Sess., pp. 218–224. The pertinent parts of the correspondence are printed in this document, where are found many of the citations which immediately follow.

Lord John Russell's compromise line approximated that which Captain Prevost had previously suggested. (See map.)

before by General Harney, who directed "the officer in command of the United States detachment to acknowledge and respect the civil jurisdiction of Washington Territory over the island of San Juan, and he goes on to say 'that he is satisfied that any attempt of the British commander to ignore this right of the Territory will be followed by deplorable results which it will be out of his power to control.' "[23] The General, it appears, was a glutton for *faux pas*. Any alarm that the British Minister may have felt was allayed when, two days later, Cass replied that "the orders of General Harney, . . . which appear to be in violation of the arrangement of General Scott, have been read . . . by the President both with surprise and regret." It was hoped, said Cass, that the orders would be found not to "bear the construction which seems naturally to belong to them" and that they would in any case lead to no collision. The episode caused the British Government to seek some more definite statement about the temporary arrangement, pending the final solution, but, according to the American Government, the existing situation was not susceptible of serious difficulty and would suffice for the time.

Settling the water boundary raised the question of the reserved rights of the Hudson's Bay Company in the region which remained under American jurisdiction by the Treaty of 1846. President Buchanan suggested that the United States would be willing to quiet those liens by a money payment, and the Company, when consulted by the British Government, agreed to give up whatever privileges it had retained in the territory of the United States for a payment of half a million dollars.[24] Coupled with this offer was a proposal to submit the question of the water boundary to arbitration, preferably to the head of some sovereign state like the Netherlands, Switzerland, or Sweden and Norway, who should be allowed either to determine which of the two waterways was indicated by the treaty or, if he could not do that, establish a compromise line. Both Governments should bind themselves to accept the award, whatever it might be. Apparently no repetition of the experience had with the Northeast boundary and the award of the King of the Netherlands was desired. This communication remained unanswered, for secession had come and the Government of the United

23. Lyons to Cass; *ibid.*, pp. 256–257. Cass's reply follows, pp. 258–259.
24. Lyons to Cass, Dec. 10, 1860; *ibid.*, pp. 264–265.

States was far too much occupied to take time for such an issue as the sovereignty over a few square miles on the Pacific Coast.

During this period, in 1859 and 1860, Congress was surprisingly quiet about San Juan. It too was occupied with the problems of sectionalism. The only thing of any significance was a report[25] prepared by Henry R. Crosbie and transmitted to the House in answer to a resolution of April 6, 1860. This advocated extension of the laws of the United States forthwith over the disputed area, laying the blame for the events of 1859 upon Governor Douglas, whose "indiscreet action" had caused all the trouble. Little attention was paid to the report, and the matter, so far as Congress was concerned, was to lie over until the Civil War was ended and San Juan was added to the list of questions involving Canada.

Joint military occupation worked successfully for the next six years. The absence of civil government apparently caused no difficulties for the insignificant number of inhabitants until, in 1866, local troubles again began to make their appearance. According to Jared C. Brown,[26] Deputy United States Marshal at Port Townsend, the American Commandant, Captain Gray, had "exercised arbitrary power over the citizens," and his arrest was ordered by the United States District Court for the Third Judicial District of Washington Territory. Gray refused to be arrested, and when a sheriff with a posse was sent after him he met them with force. When the court adjourned Gray was still defiant, and, according to Brown, there was likely to be trouble "unless the Department of State settle the question as to the authority of either the military or civil power over the island." The citizens, he maintained, intended to enforce civil law and Judge Darwin was backing them. Brigadier General O. E. Babcock, sent to investigate the situation,[27] found that the difficulty arose from a man who "owning land lying between the landing and the military post, becoming displeased with the military authority, built a fence across the road leading from the post to the landing" and would not remove it when asked to by Captain Gray, whereupon Gray "ejected him from the island." No immediate trouble was anticipated. Babcock thought

25. *House Ex. Docs.,* No. 77, 36th Cong., 1st Sess.

26. Brown to Seward, Sept. 20, 1866; *Senate Ex. Docs.,* No. 29, 40th Cong., 2d Sess., p. 266.

27. Babcock to Rawlins, Dec. 6, 1866; *ibid.,* pp. 267–268.

that until title to the island was settled the military should be upheld, for if "the military is withdrawn our title to the island is given up." No trouble apparently did ensue and things jogged along as usual.

In the winter, in answer to a resolution from the House of Representatives asking for information on San Juan, the President replied that "it was not deemed advisable, at this juncture, to comply with the request contained in the Resolution."[28] Nearly a year later Major General H. W. Halleck, commanding the Military Division of the Pacific, called the special attention of the War Department, and through it of the Department of State, to conditions on the island.[29] The civil authorities of Washington Territory repudiated Scott's agreement and were bent on exercising the right to collect taxes, execute judicial processes, etc., on the island; "moreover, the United States officers of customs claimed the right to enforce our revenue laws on the same island." Brevet Major Graves had been arrested and put under bonds for resisting civil jurisdiction and Captain Gray had been fined five thousand dollars. "In other words we have this anomalous condition of affairs on that frontier: the military officers of the United States are required to prevent the exercise of civil jurisdiction on the disputed islands, while the civil officers of the same government insist upon its execution, and proceed to punish the former for the very acts which are required of them by the War Department." An impossible situation had developed.

At this point the Senate took a hand. By a resolution of December 18, 1867, it called upon President Johnson for information relating to the occupation of the island, and that gentleman, on February 20, 1868, transmitted a report of the Secretary of State[30] rehearsing the story from the beginning with a multiplicity of documents covering the whole affair. The President noted that in December, 1860, the British Government had suggested arbitration, but he said that the question was not pursued during the war. Then the legislature of Washington Territory raised its voice[31] and called upon the Federal Government to settle the question raised by armed forces which had

28. Dec. 21, 1866; *House Ex. Docs.*, No. 24, 39th Cong., 2d Sess.
29. Halleck to Adjutant General (extract), Nov. 18, 1867, *Senate Ex. Docs.*, No. 29, 40th Cong., 2d Sess., pp. 269–270.
30. *Senate Ex. Docs.*, No. 29, 40th Cong., 2d Sess.
31. *House Misc. Docs.*, No. 79, 40th Cong., 2d Sess.

"defied and disregarded" the processes of the courts of Washington Territory. In the face of this situation the Government was forced to take action, and Seward mentioned the matter to Thornton, who received permission to go ahead on the basis laid down in 1860.[32] The negotiations, however, were not pursued in Washington but transferred to London, where Reverdy Johnson had replaced Minister C. F. Adams. Johnson found the British Government willing to proceed with the matter and he was given instructions[33] to open the discussions providing he was convinced that a treaty, then under negotiation, relative to recognition of naturalization could be arranged; neither an arrangement for San Juan nor on the *Alabama* Claims should be completed before the naturalization issue was satisfactorily settled. Johnson was sanguine after an interview with Lord Stanley[34] and expected in a week or two to have a protocol ready. His expectations were met, for on October 17 he and Stanley initialed a protocol[35] providing for the submission of the issue to a friendly sovereign whose award, whether for one or the other channel or a compromise line, was to be accepted by both parties, although "it is understood that this agreement shall not go into operation . . . until the question of naturalization now pending between the two governments shall have been satisfactorily settled by treaty, or by law of Parliament, or by both, unless the two parties shall in the mean time otherwise agree." The protocol was acceptable in Washington, except that the United States would insist that the arbiter should be the President of Switzerland.[36] Stanley did not object, so an additional protocol specifying the "President of the federal council of the Swiss Confederation" was signed on November 10, 1868. When, however, Johnson inquired whether or not the protocol might be changed to a convention, Seward called a halt; "Let San Juan rest," he telegraphed, for the Claims Convention unless amended was useless.[37]

If arbitration was acceptable to the Administration, it decidedly

32. Stanley to Thornton, Mar. 14, 1868; FO 115:472 (P.R.O.).

33. Seward to Johnson, Sept. 23, 1868; Great Britain: Instructions, Vol. XXI (D.S.).

34. Johnson to Seward, Sept. 25, 1868; *Diplomatic Correspondence, 1868,* Part I, p. 356.

35. *Ibid.,* pp. 362–363.   36. *Ibid.,* pp. 366–369.

37. *Ibid.,* p. 377.

was not in the Northwest. Governor Marshall F. Moore and other officers of Washington Territory on December 17, 1868, signed a memorial[38] protesting against any recognition whatever of the British; they had heard that arbitration had been proposed and they were all against it. Those who negotiated the treaty in 1846 "acted with the full understanding that the Canal de Haro was the boundary. Having already conceded from the line of 54° 40′ to that of 49, for the sake of peace, neither the honor nor the interests of the United States will admit of further surrender of right." From the Canadian side as well came skepticism about arbitration. Cartier and McDougall sent to Lord Granville, the Colonial Secretary, a communication dated December 30, 1868,[39] in which they spoke of the probable imminent inclusion in the Dominion of the British Northwest. They had noted in the President's Annual Message reference to questions pending between Great Britain and the United States and one of these was sovereignty over the island of San Juan. It was, in the opinion of these two Canadian Cabinet officers, of vital importance then to British Columbia and prospectively to the Dominion that "an island commanding the passage by sea of the principal cities, ports and harbours of Her Majesty's possessions on the Pacific Coast should not be surrendered to a Foreign Power." Experience of the past demonstrated that when there was a boundary to be settled there was "the disposition on the one side to concede & on the other to encroach," and there was no rea-

38. *Senate Misc. Docs.*, No. 27, 40th Cong., 3d Sess. Thornton sent copies of the resolution to the Foreign Office, January 25, 1869. A little later, enclosing copies of a petition of citizens of Washington Territory on the subject he commented: "Y. L. will observe that the statements upon which the memorialists form their objection, are for the most part devoid of truth." Feb. 2, 1869; FO 115:490 (P.R.O.).

Benjamin Moran, long-time Secretary of Legation in London, stated in his Journal, May 6, 1869 (Vol. XXII [L.C.]), that Robert McLane called. "He says that his father clearly agreed with Ld. Aberdeen that the Canal de Haro was to be the channel through wh. the boundary of the N. W. Territory was to run and that he would have had it named in the treaty had it been negotiated in London instead of in Washington. But Mr. Buchanan changed the place of negotiations and hence the blunder in the Convention. Our people had surveyed the Canal in advance and found it *was the channel* that separate[s] the Continent from Van Couver's Island, and hence is the one meant altho' not named in the treaty."

39. FO 115:485 (P.R.O.).

son to believe that things would be different this time. If San Juan should be given up, future generations of loyal subjects would have occasion to regret "as bitterly & as unavailingly as the people of New Brunswick, Quebec & all Canada now regret the unfortunate concession of the 'Ashburton Treaty.' "

. . . We cannot help feeling, when we look at the map of Canada, & observe, that on our Eastern frontier the state of Maine by a recent treaty has been thrust, like a wedge, between the provinces of New Brunswick & Quebec, interrupting direct Communication & covering some 800,000 of acres, previously regarded as British territory, & occupied by thousands of British subjects; & that in the West, through ignorance of the natural features of the country in 1773 [*sic*], & under a spirit of concession in 1818, a vast territory was surrendered . . . ; we say we cannot help feeling when we recall these unhappy & as we now find, *costly* blunders of the past, that we are only discharging a solemn duty when we add our earnest warning to the arguments Y. L^P—, as Secretary of State for the Colonies, will use to prevent a similar, & in some respects, a worse blunder, in reference to our position on the Pacific Coast.[40]

Economic factors as well as political ones were not lacking on the American side, as witnessed by two letters sent to Senator George F. Edmunds and by him presented to the Senate.[41] One, written by George Gibbs, stated that it was well known at the time the treaty was concluded that San Juan belonged to the United States; the end of Vancouver Island was the only fortifiable place north of San Francisco and yet it was known that Britain would have yielded all that island rather than fight and they were bluffing then as now; tying the naturalization treaty with the San Juan matter meant that there would be no satisfactory solution of the former until the United States gave up the latter. In the second letter, G. Clinton Gardner asserted that the British probably meant to build a Pacific railway and wanted to occupy the ground first; if the country had been better known in 1846 the United States would have insisted on all of Oregon instead

40. Whatever arguments Granville may have used, he was met with the statement that an arbitration agreement had been entered into with the American Minister. Hammond to Colonial Office, Jan. 15, 1869; FO 115:485 (P.R.O.).

41. Sent by J. Gregory Smith, President of the Northern Pacific Railroad, February 20, 1869. *Senate Misc. Docs.*, No. 14, 41st Cong., 1st Sess.

of surrendering half of it. A board of Army engineers quoted and approved[42] a report of General J. G. Totten's of 1859 where he said that the British had established a naval base at Esquimalt on Vancouver Island, hence San Juan was necessary to them neither for offense nor defense; to offset the advantage already possessed by the British the United States should have a fortified anchorage on or near San Juan Island for, while it would be of use there, it would not on Rosario Strait, forty or fifty miles away.

Although the Claims Convention had been amended to the satisfaction of the Administration and was before the Senate, and the San Juan protocol, turned into a convention on January 14, 1869, embodied a solution acceptable to both Governments, there continued to be delay. A new administration came into office, with Fish in the State Department. To him Thornton mentioned the arbitration proposal and said he hoped the matter would soon be settled; while joint occupation had been amicably carried on for a number of years, at best it was a delicate business. Fish, "who is extremely careful and reserved upon matters of business, possibly because he is not yet well acquainted with the affairs of his Department," merely expressed a hope that the question would be settled.[43] Not much more encouragement did Thornton find for speedy settlement when he understood[44] that there was much opposition from Pacific Coast Senators who were opposed to arbitration, and Senator J. M. Howard of Michigan, who, the Minister was told, "made a violent and intemperate speech against England on the occasion."

It would seem that this gentleman, and Mr. Chandler, his colleague, whose violent speech of yesterday is enclosed in my Despatch, living so near and looking into Canada, cannot contain their covetousness and think that by exciting violence betw: the two countries, they will attain their object of adding that possession to the territory of the U. S.

On the other hand, "Mr. Sumner asserts, perhaps as a counterpoise to the part he has taken with regard to the Claims Convention, that he is doing his utmost to obtain the sanction of the San Juan Convention; but whether Mr. Sumner is sincere in these professions, I would not

42. *Senate Ex. Docs.*, No. 8, 41st Cong., 1st Sess.
43. Thornton to Clarendon, Mar. 29, 1869; FO 115:490 (P.R.O.).
44. Thornton to Clarendon, Apr. 20, 1869; *ibid.*

venture to decide, altho' it is quite possible he may be so if he believes it will be rejected, even if he should vote in its favour." This did not seem to accord exactly with Motley's statement to Clarendon[45] when he told him in June that the recent session of the Senate had not afforded time to take up the matter, although no objection had been raised to it. Nor, for that matter, had Great Britain done anything about the naturalization treaty, even though it was Motley's opinion that the next sitting of Parliament would bring legislation clearing the way for it.[46]

Throughout the summer of 1869, then, the matter remained in abeyance, although some progress was made toward quieting rights of the Hudson's Bay Company and those of its subsidiary, the Puget Sound Agricultural Company.[47] Moreover, maps, embodying the results of the surveys of the commissioners for the boundary under the Treaty of 1846, were prepared and approved by the two Governments, leaving, of course, the disputed portion for such final adjustment as might be made. Autumn came, and then winter, with the assembling of Congress. Then, on the evening of December 24, Thornton received from the Foreign Office a cable with these words: "Remind Mr Fish that the ratifications of the San Juan should be exchanged by the 13th of January."[48] To this the British Minister immediately cabled back that the Senate had adjourned to January 10 and the Secretary of State told him that nothing could be done until after the holiday recess.

Fish, indeed, seems to have been quite taken aback when reminded that the time for exchange of ratifications was so short; he had entirely forgotten the fact, he explained to Thornton. So, too, had Mr. Sumner, chairman of the Senate Committee on Foreign Relations, who said no allusion had been made to it in the committee and he did not know "what their feelings might be as to its sanction." Thornton made no suggestion about agreeing upon an extension of time for

45. Clarendon to Thornton, June 10, 1869; FO 115:487 (P.R.O.).

46. Motley to Fish, June 12, 1869; Index to Despatches, pp. 149–150 (D.S.).

47. Thornton to Clarendon, Sept. 13, 1869; FO 115:491 (P.R.O.). See F. E. Ross, "The Retreat of the Hudson's Bay Company in the Pacific Northwest," Can. Hist. Rev., XVIII, 261–280.

48. Thornton to Clarendon; FO 115:492 (P.R.O.).

ratification "nor did M^r: Fish himself make the slightest advance in that direction."[49] On January 8, 1870, Fish "of his own accord" brought up the matter, saying he regretted that the date for ratification had been overlooked; he asked whether Thornton could suggest a solution. The latter replied "as coldly as possible that I knew of none; that H. M. Gov^t: had done what they could to bring about a settlement of the question to which the Convention related, but that as this was now in the hands of the Senate, it must be left entirely to them."[50] As he had previously indicated in a telegram, the British Minister was not in favor of making the first move to solve the problem

because, whether intentionally or otherwise, the blame of a failure to take the Convention into consideration lay entirely with the Gov^t: and Senate of the U. S. and therefore any proposal to remedy their neglect should come from themselves; and further because I understand that great opposition will be made to the Convention, and that it is not improbable that, if brought up for discussion, it will be rejected.

There was, added Thornton, apparently a determination on the part of the American Government not to settle any of the issues singly but

to wait till a simultaneous understanding upon all of them can be arrived at, and that further there is a growing disposition on the part of the politicians of the U. S., to connect this final settlement, if possible, with the separation at least of all our possessions on this continent from the mother country, which they have for years longed for, and which they pretend to believe is now to be consummated within a brief period.

When Congress assembled after the holidays Thornton was more than ever convinced that there was no disposition to adjust the boundary issue; Henry W. Corbett, a Senator from Oregon, had introduced a resolution asking the Secretary of State to inquire into the expediency "of including the transfer of British Columbia to the U. S. in any treaty for the adjustment of all pending differences between the two countries," and Howard of Michigan had made another rabid speech in which he estimated the *Alabama* Claims at two hundred millions and "thought there would be no objection to receive British Columbia

49. Thornton to Clarendon, Dec. 27, 1869; FO 115:492 (P.R.O.).
50. Thornton to Clarendon, Confidential, Jan. 10, 1870; FO 115:506 (P.R.O.).

as part payment of that sum."[51] In light of these indications the British Government was not going to do anything to present the appearance of anxiety to hasten matters or to ease the American Administration out of a slightly embarrassing position. That Fish did find the situation the cause of some chagrin was evident to Thornton, who reported a conversation[52] with him in which he took some pains to explain why it came about that the convention had not been taken up in the Senate—how busy it had been up to Christmas considering presidential appointments, and how little time there was after recess to deal with so important a matter as this boundary convention. Moreover, said Fish, England had not taken any steps in the matter of naturalization, which, according to Johnson's protocol, was to be got out of the way before other things were dealt with. Parliament, he said, had been in session nearly six months and had done nothing, so that if there was any grievance it lay with the United States rather than England, as Lord Clarendon had intimated to Motley.[53] It is apparent that in the time between Thornton's reminder and the date set for the exchange of ratifications Fish not only had been taking thought but had been going over the correspondence. He had rationalized himself out of the embarrassment and had come to the conclusion that the United States might claim cause for a grievance. Further evidence of this is in the long and detailed instruction sent to Motley on February 15, which contained in much greater elaboration the line of argument Fish had used with Thornton.[54] The fact, too, that this instruction was so soon transmitted to the Senate and by that body printed would make it seem that Fish wished to get his explanation before the public before anything was likely to be done on the British side. It is also probable that the Administration, which wished to command and keep

51. Thornton to Clarendon, Jan. 11, 1870; FO 115:506 (P.R.O.).

52. Thornton to Clarendon, Feb. 12, 1870; FO 115:506 (P.R.O.).

53. "M^r: Fish expressed likewise his regret that on the 12th Ult^o: two days before the term had expired, Y. L. should have stated to M^r: Motley, as reported by him, that H. M. Gov^t: would consider it a discourtesy if the Senate should not take the Convention into consideration before the 14th Ult^o: and that you should have made use of this expression before it could have been known in England whether any action had been taken by the Senate, or not, upon the Convention."

54. Fish to Motley, Feb. 15, 1870; *Senate Ex. Docs.*, No. 114, 41st Cong., 2d Sess., pp. 10–13.

the support of the Radical group of Republicans, was disinclined to push the boundary convention in the face of the annexationist spirit which animated a considerable portion of that group. This instruction would not only show that the United States was not abashed by an expression of British displeasure but would leave the door open to proceed in whatever direction circumstances seemed to dictate.[55]

It was clear that, in consideration of the delay with the boundary convention and the general trend of discussion in the United States over all the issues which involved Canada as well as over the *Alabama* Claims and all that those implied, there was no intention of dealing with one topic alone, and San Juan was to remain to be thrown into the pot with the rest of the problems.[56] At any rate, it is true that this issue did not come up for further consideration during 1870. One aspect of the San Juan matter did, however, receive some attention. The year 1870 was a census year. Should the inhabitants of the San Juan group be included in the enumeration? In July, Thornton addressed a note to Fish suggesting to him "that it would seem unnecessary to take the census of San Juan."[57] Through Assistant Secretary of State J. C. Bancroft Davis, the Minister was informed that it was decided not to make such an enumeration; nevertheless, later in the year it was learned from the Governor of British Columbia that actually the census *was* taken, but Thornton was inclined to believe that "when Mr Fish made the above mentioned communication, neither he nor the Secretary of the Interior was aware of the previous action of the United States officials."[58] Later Fish assured Thornton that this

55. In transmitting copies of a resolution calling upon the Secretary of War to communicate information about the military importance of San Juan, and other documents on the subject, Thornton remarked: "The opposition which is being raised to this Convention and to that for the settlement of claims pending between the two countries, seems to indicate that the people of the United States are indisposed to submit any of these questions to arbitration, possibly owing to an apprehension that the decision of an impartial umpire might not be favourable to their pretensions." Thornton to Clarendon, Mar. 16, 1870; FO 115:490 (P.R.O.).

56. See pp. 361, 364–366 *passim,* 369, 373, 400.

57. Thornton to Principal Secretary of State for Foreign Affairs, July 11, 1870; FO 115:508 (P.R.O.). Thornton to Fish, July 8, 1870; Great Britain: Notes to Department, Vol. XC (D.S.).

58. Thornton to Granville, Oct. 3, 1870; FO 115:508 (P.R.O.).

had been done by inadvertence and, after considerable discussion, it was decided to append a note in the printed schedules indicating that no clear title to San Juan at the moment rested in the United States, although the exact wording of the note was in itself reached with some difficulty.

CHAPTER XII

THE FISHERIES

UNLIKE some of the other post-war difficulties the fisheries issue did not, immediately after the abrogation of the Reciprocity Treaty, assume a menacing or even a critical aspect, although the intensity of the controversy, after a few years, more than made up for the quiescence of the middle Sixties. Neither Canada nor the United States desired to raise a question surrounded with difficulties, even though in the Maritime Provinces there was a disposition to press the matter at once.[1] The British Government certainly did not wish to have the issue raised not only on account of its potentially irritating effect upon the general situation but because, if the Colonials insisted upon complete exclusion of Americans from everything not secured under the Convention of 1818, the cost of preserving colonial rights would fall upon the Imperial Government.[2] Public opinion on both sides of the boundary was mixed. In the United States, while the reciprocity abrogation resolution afforded some satisfaction to a large number of people, there were many, especially in the West, who believed that as a permanent policy the idea embodied in that resolution was not one to be maintained. Some hope had been raised by the negotiations which went on in Washington in the winter of 1865–66. When those broke down, there still remained a notion that Congress might do something before its adjournment,[3] it being understood that reciprocal trading privi-

1. Lord Monck, writing to Macdonald in January, 1866, remarked that Nova Scotia did not wish to come into any common arrangement. "My own opinion," said Monck, "is that we should leave the question in the hands of the Imperial authorities who have been instructed from home to protect the fisheries." Macdonald Papers: Governor General Correspondence, I, 123–125 (P.A.C.). For the whole topic see the forthcoming volume in this Series by H. A. Innis.

2. Cardwell to Monck, Confidential, Mar. 3, 1866; FO 115:449 (P.R.O.). The Colonial Secretary's final admonition to the Governor-General was, "I need not impress upon you the great importance both to the British possessions in North America, and to this country, of avoiding any measure which might produce any feeling of irritation between ourselves and the United States."

3. See editorial from New York *Times*, quoted approvingly by the Detroit

leges and freedom of the fisheries were inextricably interwoven. This attitude was met more than half way by the Canadian Government, which, although their efforts at an adjustment had been disappointed, were far from desiring to render a solution more difficult.

The overture made by the Canadian Government was the license system. According to this any American fisherman could, on the payment of a fee of fifty cents per measured ton of his vessel, continue to have the privileges he had enjoyed under the Reciprocity Treaty: he could fish the inshore waters, land to buy bait, ice, supplies, and whatever he needed, recruit members for his crew, ship fish in bond from a Canadian port; in short he stood on exactly the same footing as a Canadian fisherman except in the mouths of rivers. The fee was nominal, intended only to show that there was a privilege which had to be purchased and not a right to be demanded. Canada, to be sure, was less directly interested in the fisheries than the Maritime Provinces, so that this fee system really involved no particular sacrifice. In Nova Scotia, where fishing was of paramount concern, the system made no appeal. In a discussion in the House of Assembly early in March[4] it was pointed out that after reciprocity went into effect Nova Scotian investment in the fisheries had grown from practically nothing to an impressive amount, and now, if the United States were disposed to yield nothing in trading privileges, the Province should insist upon strict compliance with the terms of the old convention, even to the British interpretation of the headland question. Before the fishing season actually opened, however, the Maritime Provinces were swung into line and each issued licenses recognized by the others. It appears that for the most part Americans took out such licenses and that during the season there was little friction.[5]

The American Administration seemed to be equally anxious that there should be no conflict, as Seward indicated in an instruction to

Free Press, March 6, 1866, deprecating the misunderstandings which would follow the lapse of the treaty. See Chapter XIII for attempts at reciprocity.

4. Montreal *Gazette,* Mar. 17, 1866. Lt.-Gov. Sir F. Williams wrote Macdonald that his Ministers were strongly opposed to issuing licenses to Americans. Apr. 2, 1866; Macdonald Papers: Governor General Correspondence, I, 131 (P.A.C.).

5. It took a little pressure from London to line up the Maritime Provinces. Cardwell to Lieutenant-Governor of Nova Scotia, May 26, 1866; FO 115:450 (P.R.O.).

Minister Adams when he forwarded to him the protocol of a proposition to create a commission to agree upon the limits of common fishing rights in both countries, establish regulations necessary to "secure to the fishermen of the United States the privilege of entering bays and harbors," to seek shelter, repair damage, get wood and water, and to fix penalties for abuses of the privileges.[6] But Congress, as usual, was more truculent. On April 10 a House resolution called upon the President to furnish information about what was being done to protect the rights and interests of Americans on the fishing grounds. Three days later the President informed the House that the Secretary of the Navy had taken preparatory measures to send an adequate force for this purpose, although he believed there was no ground for thinking there would be any collision.[7] The resolution on its introduction had provoked some discussion in which the headland question figured rather prominently; Henry J. Raymond of New York, when reporting the original resolution, somewhat modified by the Committee on Foreign Affairs, had confidently asserted that Americans would never admit the validity of the British contention, and that if England sent a force to maintain it, the United States must be equally prepared to support American fishermen in their interpretation.

Seward's protocol at first struck the British officials very favorably.[8] Both Clarendon and Cardwell thought the idea had merit, but there were some points which needed clarification.[9] When Adams tried to hurry the Foreign Office[10] he learned that the British Government had decided to empower Sir Frederick Bruce "to proceed in conjunction with [Seward], after consultation with the respective provincial authorities," for "the latter had now substantially reached such a position of independence as to make it unadvisable for the government here to attempt to act without regard to them." In Sir Frederick's in-

6. Seward to Adams, Apr. 10, 1866; *Diplomatic Correspondence, 1866,* Part I, pp. 98, 101.

7. *House Ex. Docs.,* No. 88, 39th Cong., 1st Sess. *Cong. Globe,* 39th Cong., 1st Sess., pp. 1720, 1867 ff.

8. Adams to Seward, May 3, 1866; *Diplomatic Correspondence, 1866,* Part I, p. 118.

9. Hammond to Bruce, Private and Confidential, May 5, 1866; FO 5:1060 (P.R.O.).

10. Adams to Seward, May 10, 1866; *Diplomatic Correspondence, 1866,* Part I, pp. 119–120.

struction[11] it was pointed out that it was assumed that the proposed commission would inquire into and define the "questions relating to rights of exclusive Fishery possessed by Great Britain within the Bays and between Headlands which have in former times been a fruitful source of discussion between the two Governments." Her Majesty's Government authorized Sir Frederick to proceed with the negotiation but to take care before he signed the protocol that there was a distinct understanding of the duties of the commission. The Government would not engage to maintain the existing arrangement regarding fisheries during the sitting of the commission, although they "have cordially approved and have recommended to the Governments of the other British Provinces, a proposal made by the Authorities of Canada that American Fishermen should for the present season be allowed to enjoy under special licenses the benefits conferred by the Reciprocity Treaty." They could not agree to maintain this system indefinitely, although they were "perfectly prepared to concert with the United States for substituting for it a more permanent arrangement which, either solely applicable to Fisheries or more generally comprising the common interests of Her Majesty's subjects and those of the citizens of the United States, [should] hold out a promise of mutual interest to both parties and the strongest assurance of peace and good will between the two Governments."

Naturally enough the Provincials, especially in the Maritimes, thought that if they adopted the licensing system with a purely nominal fee some sort of reciprocal gesture could be expected from the Government of the United States. Could not fish be admitted without duty as it had been under the treaty? Spurred both from London and Halifax, Bruce approached Seward, and, on his recommendation, Justin S. Morrill of the House Committee on Ways and Means, to see if the new tariff bill under discussion might not abolish or at least reduce the duty on fish. Morrill, however, held out little expectation of much relaxation, and Seward told the British Minister that the best policy for the Provinces to pursue for the present was one of conciliation, and trust that before long there would be a disposition to deal with the matter in a liberal manner; there was no use in going ahead on the assumption that the people of the United States could be coerced into conces-

11. Clarendon to Bruce, May 11, 1866; FO 115:405 (P.R.O.).

sions.[12] But Canadians and other Provincials felt that a policy of conciliation on one side and indifference on the other was not likely to bring a permanent arrangement about the fisheries. As the Canadian Minister of Finance put it, when Bruce informed Lord Monck of the attitude of officials in Washington, Canada would not be disposed to enter into any arrangement with the United States which merely contemplated offsetting the license system by concessions on duties on fish.[13] This stand effectively put a stop to any progress with Seward's proposition.

Meantime, the far more important subject of confederation was entering upon a new and, as it proved, final stage. After July 1, 1867, it was not a matter of separate colonial but collective action of the Dominion, then comprising Ontario, Quebec, New Brunswick, and Nova Scotia, and individual action by Newfoundland and Prince Edward Island. There was, nevertheless, a complication when Nova Scotia, Prince Edward Island, and New Brunswick, acting before Confederation went into effect, proceeded to raise the license fee to one dollar, while Canada retained the fifty-cent fee. The Duke of Buckingham, the new Secretary in the Colonial Office, was angered but could do nothing.[14] Canada, however, fell in line and raised its fee to one dollar,[15] so that there was uniformity throughout the Dominion and the still separated Provinces. The season of 1867 passed with no serious difficulties, although there was occasional complaint that Americans failed to secure their licenses, preferring to take a chance at not getting caught when they indulged surreptitiously in privileges they were supposed to buy. In part, freedom from friction arose from the practice of the officers of the Royal Navy in giving three warnings before making seizures,[16] and it was a stupid skipper who allowed himself to be caught twice and warned and then ran the risk of being apprehended for a third infringement of regulations. Indeed, this sys-

---

12. Bruce to Clarendon, June 5, June 8, 1866; FO 5:1065 (P.R.O.).

13. June 16, 1866; G 237 (P.A.C.).

14. Monck to Macdonald, July 20, 1867; Macdonald Papers: Governor General Correspondence, II, 62 (P.A.C.).

15. P. Mitchell, Minister of Marine and Fisheries, to Macdonald, Aug. 3, Aug. 8, 1867; Macdonald Papers: Governor General Correspondence, II, 65–66 (P.A.C.). Most of the fishermen had already taken the fifty-cent license.

16. Monck to Buckingham, Mar. 11, 1868; FO 115:472 (P.R.O.).

tem, together with the instruction not to make seizures when there was any doubt in the case, practically rendered the license system completely illusory. This view was shared by the officers themselves, who maintained that it was impossible to prevent poaching when so much leeway was given interlopers. Complaints multiplied, so that as the season of 1868 approached it was proposed not only to do away with so many warnings[17] but also to raise the fee still higher, to two dollars. The Colonial Office was inclined to agree with the Governor-General and his Government, both as to the fee and the warnings,[18] but hesitated to take a step which probably would stir up trouble. The delay irritated the Dominion Government[19] who believed their interests were being sidetracked for Imperial concerns. However, the Home Government finally yielded and approved both the two-dollar license fee and one warning to offenders.

The situation was not becoming any more satisfactory. Throughout the season of 1869 it was complained that the majority of American fishermen refused to take licenses and, at the same time, persisted in doing those things to which fees were presumed to entitle them. Other issues were likewise irritating: the Johnson-Clarendon Claims Convention was rejected to the tune of Sumner's inflammatory speech;

17. "I think whatever the amount of the license fee may be the practice on the part of the officers of the Royal Navy to give three warnings before proceeding to enforce the right to exclude foreigners from the fisheries should be abandoned as tending to render all regulations completely illusory." Monck to Buckingham, Confidential, Mar. 11, 1868; G [unnumbered], pp. 44–45 (P.A.C.).

18. Adderley to Hammond, Apr. 1, 1868; FO 115:472 (P.R.O.). Elliott to Egerton, Apr. 13; FO 115:473 (P.R.O.).

19. Macdonald to W. H. Boswell, Apr. 11, 1868: "You say that Mr. Wells [?] is of opinion that we ought not to increase the Fishing Licenses on American vessels fishing in Canadian waters. The Licenses hitherto granted were of a rate which was merely nominal, and really no protection to the Canadian Fisheries, nor of any value except as an assertion of right.

"The American Government have lately prohibited the repacking of Canadian fish at Boston, so as to fit for the West Indian market. We are therefore cut out of that trade." Macdonald Papers: Letterbooks, XI, 646–647 (P.A.C.). To Tupper, then in London, he wrote, Apr. 30, 1868, "It is a great disappointment to us that the license has not been agreed to at $2.00 per ton by the Home Govt.—there is no justification for any hesitation or refusal in the matter." *Ibid.*, p. 896.

the naturalization question was hanging fire; Fenian claims were un-adjusted; the San Juan boundary was still unsettled; in fact not one of the issues pending at the close of the Civil War and with the abroga-tion of reciprocity had made any appreciable progress. It was at this juncture that John Rose, the Canadian Minister of Finance, went on his first semi-official mission to Washington, primarily to find out whether the American Government was yet in a mood to talk renewed reciprocity.[20] Rose reached Washington and saw Thornton, who took him to call upon the Secretary of State. Fish, as Rose reported to Mac-donald, was "guarded and reserved," although he expressed himself "sincerely anxious to bring about more liberal commercial relations." He said that any action by the Executive would be resented by the Congress and intimated that the initial move must be made by that body. Thereupon Rose stated that questions of navigation of the St. Lawrence and of the fisheries must be dealt with by treaty and that *provisional* arrangements, subject to the approval of Congress, could be made on tariff issues. Fish, said Rose, seemed to fear the loss of revenue, especially if the duty on fish were removed, but Rose pointed out what a small amount this was.

. . . I told him we could not continue the *considerate* policy we had pur-sued ever since the Treaty was repealed much longer—that public opinion would not sustain any Govt. in continuing to overlook the immediate in-terest of their own people; that we had been more than friendly in our efforts to prevent illicit trade springing up on the Frontier—that we had almost winked at the Fishermen exercising their vocation without pay-ment of license dues—that we rarely inquired into the nationality of ves-sels going through the canals—that we had resisted the imposition of duties on their products such as coal—salt—hops—Flour ec—& that unless there [was very?] practical evidence now of a desire to liberalize our trade relations,—they must be prepared for a very different policy at the hands of *any* Govert in Canada.

Canadians, said Rose, were not so dependent on American trade as they had been earlier, and if the United States refused to adopt a more

20. Nevins (*Hamilton Fish*, pp. 212–214) quotes from Fish's Diary the latter's account of the visit, which harmonizes with Rose's own statement in Rose to Macdonald, July 8, 1869; Macdonald Papers: Rose, '64–'74 (P.A.C.). See also Thornton's Memorandum, July 8, 1869; FO 115:491 (P.R.O.).

acceptable policy other foreign lines would be pushed, probably to the detriment of American trade. Thornton thought Rose made some impression on the Secretary of State but Rose was not so sanguine, and, as things turned out, Rose was more nearly correct. It is evident that Fish was sincerely desirous of bettering relations with Canada and had no strong aversion to reciprocal trade arrangements, but, short time as he had been in office, he realized that it was impossible to impress his views upon Congress and believed that, after all, there were more important issues for which strength should be saved when it came to a struggle.

President Grant's first Annual Message had room for a comment on the ill-fated Johnson-Clarendon Claims Convention, could include a disparaging remark about Canadian-American reciprocity, and could call attention to the award of the commission on the Hudson's Bay Company claims and to the findings of the boundary survey commission; but there was no mention of fisheries, no conciliatory gesture. This could have given little satisfaction either in the Dominion or in England. In both places there was a growing feeling that conciliation had been pressed to a point beyond which national honor would not let it go; more significant from a political point of view was the increasing murmur of discontent north of the boundary. A system of licenses, a gesture calculated to invite mutual concessions, had not worked.[21] Instead of bringing about a better relationship, the system had broken down; annexationists led by Bennett and his New York *Herald*, Senator Zach Chandler, and Congressman Ben Butler were making incendiary comments and urging the United States to gobble up the British possessions in North America. Conciliation, according to Canadian sentiment, had had its day. The British Government, which had welcomed admission of Americans through licensing, were now also convinced that the system would not work and were willing to coöperate with the Dominion in trying something else.[22]

21. Thornton wrote Sir John Young, October 20, 1869, that an article in the New York *Tribune* said that Gloucester fishermen were preparing to resist by force the pretensions of the British Government in excluding them from their customary fishing grounds "where they think they have a right to fish." Despatches from the British Minister at Washington, XV, 118 (P.A.C.).

22. Clarendon to Thornton, Dec. 24, 1869; FO 115:489 (P.R.O.).

The intent of the Canadian Government was stated by Macdonald in a letter to Rose[23] on January 21, 1870.

. . . We are going to put an end to all fishing licenses, as the system has proved abortive. The American Fishermen will not take out the licenses & Her Majesty's Navy will take no steps to catch them or drive them off the Grounds. We shall therefore, fit out six cruisers, which will be employed like "La Canadienne" as a Marine Police, and act under our Statute of 1868—31 Vic. Cap 61.

The principal use of Ships of War being on the Station would be the moral support they would give to our Cruisers. In the absence of such ships, American fishermen might combine & resist our Fishery Officers. But if it were known that there were Ships of War in the background, we would have no trouble. All that you can do to press as strongly as possible on Mr. Childers, that the stronger the force, the less likelihood there will be of resistance by the Fishermen, and complications & quarrels with the Americans.[24]

A more detailed explanation of the causes for the change in policy was sent to Rose to present to the British Government in March.[25]

Naturally, the subject of the fisheries and the policy adopted by the Government engaged the attention of the Dominion Parliament when it met in February, 1870; it was referred to in the Address from the Throne and, some three weeks later[26] became the subject of a short discussion, when Thomas Coffin, member from Shelburne, Nova Scotia, moved an address for correspondence about the depredations committed by American fishermen in Canadian waters. The general sentiment was that Canada had been long-suffering and that it was time to take more drastic measures. Aside from some little complaint that the Government had not been active enough in protecting Dominion fishermen against the encroachments of outsiders, there was

23. Macdonald Papers: Letterbooks, XIII, 933–934 (P.A.C.).

24. Rose, now in England, replied that he had a note from Hugh C. E. Childers, First Lord of the Admiralty, which he thought would be satisfactory. "There is a great deal of uneasiness about the *policy* of withdrawing the Licenses wholly, but no disposition to interfere with what Canada thinks best for her interest." Feb. 24, 1870; Macdonald Papers: Rose, '64–'74 (P.A.C.).

25. Macdonald to Rose, Mar. 11, 1870; Macdonald Papers: Letterbooks, XIV, 41 ff. (P.A.C.).

26. *Dom. Parl. Debates, 1870,* 3d Sess., I, 326 ff.

general unanimity of opinion that the time had come for action; no partisan division was noticeable, although A. A. Dorion, of the Opposition, did take occasion gently to twit the Government about pursuing a course which he alleged had not been sanctioned by Imperial authorities.

As might have been and probably was expected, the announcement of this new policy immediately produced a reaction in the United States. During the two previous sessions of Congress the fisheries had scarcely caused a ripple,[27] but now oratory was let loose and resolutions began to pour in. Thornton was considerably disturbed both by the excitement aroused in the United States and by the action which occasioned it, which, he feared, would

excite a good deal of bad feeling amongst the marine population of the New England States and it will require great discretion and prudence, on the part of the Canadian cruisers to prevent collisions with American fishermen which may have very disagreeable consequences, especially as it is not to be supposed that the officers commanding the vessels have as yet so much experience in a service of that nature as H. M. Naval Officers.[28]

Perhaps Thornton was the more concerned since he had been assiduously working upon Secretary Fish to get that gentleman to undertake something which would lead to renewal of reciprocal trade relations.[29] While Fish was willing to talk about the fisheries, he shied off from anything more inclusive. Recounting how he had communicated a proposition which Sir John Young had transmitted on behalf of the Canadian Government, Thornton said Fish had answered by saying that

the Canadian Government seemed to desire a negotiation upon a larger scale than he had contemplated, but this he feared was impossible as long

27. Butler had introduced a resolution of truculent inquiry in June, 1868 (*Cong. Globe,* 40th Cong., 2d Sess., p. 3462). One or two communications from the Administration had supplied some information, but fisheries *per se* could make no headway as an argumentative subject.

28. Thornton to Clarendon, Mar. 14, 1870; FO 115:506 (P.R.O.).

29. The Fish Diary contains a number of entries giving the gist of conversations with Thornton. Nevins' *Hamilton Fish* contains a number of these statements. Thornton's correspondence with the Foreign Office likewise discloses the same facts. See Chapter XIII.

as the majority of Congress were animated by their present feelings upon the subject. He had hoped indeed to make a small beginning of more liberal relations by combining in favour of them antagonistic interests in this country. But he thought it would be out of the power of the supporters of the scheme to carry any measure of the nature suggested, unless the freedom of the fisheries for American citizens were one of the concessions; indeed this was the principal point, and without it, it would be useless even to begin any negotiation.[30]

Fish was inclined to minimize the importance of the right to navigate the St. Lawrence and the canals, but the fisheries were *sine qua non*.

When Thornton received from Canada *official* information respecting the changed policy about licenses he was able to transmit to the Department of State a copy of a memorandum prepared by Premier Macdonald, together with the Act of 1868 which defined the Canadian position and made it clear that the Dominion was in earnest this time. In an accompanying note Thornton reiterated the expression used by the Governor-General: "That the system of granting license to foreign vessels, under the act 31 Vic., cap. 61, be discontinued and that henceforth all foreign fishermen be prevented from fishing in the waters of Canada." These last words, "in the waters of Canada," seemed to Fish to curtail the rights granted under the Convention of 1818, since, subsequent to that instrument, the boundaries of Canada had been changed and certain parts of the Labrador Coast, open to Americans, had been added to Canada. Thornton assured Fish that while he would refer the matter to Sir John Young, he was convinced that there was not the slightest intention of abridging any rights which accrued under the convention.[31] Assurances from London[32] allayed Fish's apprehensions on the point. The Treasury Department, after receipt of official notice, issued a "Circular relating to Canadian In-Shore Fisheries,"[33] wherein American fishermen were warned that licenses were no longer to be issued and that "all fishermen of the United States are prohibited from the use of such in-shore fisheries, except so far as stipulated in the first article of the treaty of October

30. Thornton to Clarendon, Mar. 21, 1870; FO 115:506 (P.R.O.).
31. The correspondence, including a copy of the Fisheries Act of 1868, is printed in *Foreign Relations, 1870*, pp. 407–411.
32. Fish to Thornton, May 31, 1870; *ibid.*, pp. 417–418.
33. *Ibid.*, pp. 411–413.

20, 1818." Authority vested in Canadian officials to prevent infractions of the law was cited, as well as the penalties attached to such infractions; a saving clause touching upon the point raised by Fish was inserted: "It is understood that, by a change of the boundaries between Canada and Labrador, the Canadian territory now includes Mount Joly and a portion of the shore to the east thereof, which in the treaty of 1818 was described as the southern shore of Labrador."[34]

At first it appeared that orders to enforcing officials contemplated prohibiting Americans from fishing "within three miles of the entrance of any bay, harbour or creek which is less than ten geographical miles in width." If this were the intent, thought the British Minister,[35] it was most likely to cause disputes; and he was relieved to learn that Americans were "to be allowed fish every where, even within headlands, provided they do not encroach upon the three miles from the shore, except upon the Coasts where they are allowed to do so by the Treaty of October 20, 1818."[36] Furthermore, the British naval officers were instructed to coöperate "frankly and cordially" with officials of the United States in order "to prevent any possible misunderstanding or chance of collision between American and English fishermen."[37] Even

34. A Report of the Minister of Marine and Fisheries approved in a Report of a Committee of the Canadian Privy Council, dated May 10, 1870, in answer to Thornton's inquiry, contained this statement: "Mr. Thornton was . . . quite right in assuring Mr. Fish, in general terms, that there could be no intention to abridge any rights to which citizens of the United States are entitled by treaty." *Ibid.*, pp. 413–414. In spite of this, considerable correspondence between Thornton and Fish, and between the latter and the Governor-General, took place before the Secretary was completely satisfied that no abridgment of American rights was contemplated. This is printed in *ibid.*, pp. 417 ff. For an elucidation of the Canada-Labrador boundary, see Lawrence J. Burpee, *An Historical Atlas of Canada* (Toronto, 1927), p. 20 of Notes.

35. Thornton to Clarendon, Confidential, May 9, 1870; FO 115:507 (P.R.O.).

36. At first there was some confusion because orders were contradictory, the earlier evidently contemplating seizures in bays. Clarendon informed Thornton that "Lord Granville informs me that the public instructions of the Canadian Gov^t to their cruisers are founded upon former orders, but they have privately ordered their officers not to seize fishing vessels except in the case of their being within three miles of shore." Clarendon to Thornton, May 23, 1870; FO 115:507 (P.R.O.).

37. Wellesley to H. M. S. Royal Alfred, Apr. 27, 1870, enclosed in Thornton to Fish, June 3; Great Britain: Notes to Department, Vol. LXXXIX (D.S.).

such precautions and the limited field of action admitted to enforcing authorities were not entirely satisfactory to the American Administration, which, according to Secretary of the Treasury Boutwell's Circular, interpreted them to mean that whatever leniency might be exercised, nevertheless no abandonment of jurisdiction over bays and harbors was intended. This was, indeed, just what the British meant, as was shown, after a considerable correspondence, in a communication to Sir John Young from the British Minister,[38] who said he would tell Mr. Fish

that the instructions respecting the limits within which the prohibition of fishing is to be enforced against United States fishermen are not to be considered as constituting an arrangement between the Governments of Great Britain and the United States by which Canadian rights are waived, or United States fishermen invested with any privilege; but only as a temporary direction given by the British and Canadian Governments to their own officers in hopes that the question may soon be settled, and in order to prevent any controversy arising on a subordinate point.

Having eventually clarified the situation, then, it remained to see what would happen. That Yankee skippers would mildly submit to be deprived of privileges which they had enjoyed for nearly fifteen years —privileges, to be sure, purchased by their Government or by themselves and now no longer for sale—was not to be anticipated. Some lessons would have to be taught in order to emphasize the fact that conditions were changed and would remain changed until the Government of the United States saw fit to strike a bargain. The first serious lesson came in turning back from the Strait of Canso vessels which then had to take the long way around Cape Breton Island to reach the Gulf of St. Lawrence. Rumor had it that these fishing craft had been seized but later information showed that most were turned away or, at worst, detained for a time. The rumor, however, was enough, according to Thornton, to bring Ben Butler of Massachusetts to his feet in the House of Representatives with resolutions calling upon the President to inform that body "under what pretence of right and under whose orders American Fishing vessels [were] arrested and detained in their voyages in the straits of Canso on their way to the fishing grounds by

38. Thornton to Young, July 20, 1870; G '69–'71 (P.A.C.). Thornton to Fish, July 21; Great Britain: Notes to Department, Vol. XC (D.S.).

armed vessels flying the British flag."[39] "I cannot but regret," said Thornton in reporting the occurrence, "the bad taste, not uncommon in this country, with which Members of Congress allow themselves to propose such resolutions . . . without first asking that enquiries may be instituted thro' the regular channel of the Gov^ts: against whose officers complaints are brought forward." A little later, when forwarding a copy of the resolutions, together with documents received from Canada which made it appear that Butler had no foundation for his statements, Thornton remarked: "It is however well known that Genl: Butler is sufficiently unscrupulous in his assertions in the House, and is probably more so just now because he hopes by that means to gain votes for his re-election for which he will be a candidate in October next."[40]

On the whole, there were surprisingly few serious complaints against the enforcement of Canada's new policy, although complaints galore and bitter were levied against the policy itself. It was the Government of Prince Edward Island, not yet a member of the Dominion but co-operating in administering the new policy, that succeeded in giving the screw a final twist. According to William A. Dart, Consul-General at Montreal,[41] dealers in fish on the Island, Americans, complained that they daily expected the commanders of Her Majesty's vessels to forbid "American fishermen the privilege, heretofore long enjoyed by American vessels of entering its ports to dry fish, purchase supplies, and to reship their fish for ports in the United States." The fishing interest of the island, said Dart, was nearly all in American hands, but "the islanders are quite largely interested in furnishing shippers with supplies of barrels, salt, provisions, &c., who will be nearly ruined by a strict enforcement of the treaty of October 20, 1818." Already "Her Majesty's steamers Valorous and Plover have closed up all trade privileges of landing mackerel in the ports of this island; ordered off a

39. As reported by Thornton to Principal Secretary of State for F. A., July 4, 1870; FO 115:508 (P.R.O.).

40. Thornton to Principal Secretary of State for F. A., July 11, 1870; FO 115:508 (P.R.O.). Fish made inquiry about the alleged seizures, enumerating the vessels involved (July 22, 1870; Great Britain: Notes to, XV, 120–123 [D.S.]), which led to a considerable correspondence revealing the fact that in most cases Americans were violating the regulations and knew they were.

41. Dart to Davis, Aug. 25, 1870; For. Rel., 1870, pp. 422–423.

Gloucester schooner this morning; would not allow her to take bait or supplies,"[42] wrote J. C. Hall from Charlottetown, and insisted that if this interpretation of the orders was persisted in it would completely ruin the fishermen engaged in the trade. He said, "That the . . . commercial relations, including the landing of mackerel, that have existed here for the last six years, should be terminated at once, is to say the least of it, unfriendly to the last degree, and should receive the immediate attention of our Government. The remedy is plain; close up the shipment of goods in bond through the States to Canada."

Feelings were mixed when it came to enforcing literally the terms of the old convention. If Americans were to enjoy privileges respecting the fisheries in British American waters and ports, the Provincials wanted to make them pay in some tangible way; to make them pay they felt they had to bring pressure to bear, but when coercive measures became a boomerang it was possible that the scheme was not working as expected. The Lieutenant-Governor of Prince Edward Island, Robert P. Haythorne, told the American Consul[43] that privately he regretted the course he was obliged to take officially, but as governor of so small a colony he had little power and could not stand against the policy enforced by the Admiralty. Then from Halifax it was reported that Canadian and Imperial authorities were about to prohibit transshipment in bond of American-caught fish from Canadian and other Provincial ports,[44] and the Consul, like his confrere at Charlottetown, recommended "discontinuing or suspending the operation of the bonding system, so far as it relates to shipments between and to and from the British North American Provinces." From Pictou came a similar story. The American Consul reported[45] that strict and literal construction of the Convention of 1818 was forcing most of the American fishing vessels to return to their home ports. "The action of the Dominion government in this respect being calculated to annoy

42. Hall to Dart, Aug. 19, 1870; *For. Rel., 1870*, p. 423. A "Japanese policy," Hall called it.

43. E. Parker Scammon to Fish, Aug. 24, 1870; Consular Letters: Charlottetown, Vol. II (D.S.). Scammon, on August 19, had reported that it was all a scheme to force Prince Edward Island and Newfoundland into the Confederation. *Ibid.*

44. Jackson to Fish, Aug. 25, 1870; *For. Rel., 1870*, pp. 423–424.

45. Malmros to Davis, Aug. 28, 1870; *ibid.*, p. 424.

and harass our fishermen without benefitting, if not seriously injuring, the interests of the people of the maritime provinces, seems to confirm the declaration often made by members of the confederate party . . . that their government intends to retaliate for an alleged illiberal commercial policy on the part of our Government; in other words, that they mean to coerce the United States into a reduction of duties on Dominion goods."

News that Canada was not only excluding Americans from the inshore waters but also denying them privileges they had for many years enjoyed, though not under the Convention of 1818, quickly spread in the fishing communities of New England and produced as quick a response. According to the *Cape Ann Advertiser*, August 26, 1870, the recent acts of restriction on the fishing fleet were absolutely insulting to the flag; there was only one thing to do and that was to maintain strict non-intercourse with the Provinces. The recent events at Prince Edward Island forbidding all mercantile transactions, if approved by Great Britain, showed "that malice and revenge are the inspiration of these acts, and nothing but reciprocity of non-intercourse, shutting out the products of the Provinces from our markets, will bring them to their senses." Davis, in charge of the department at Washington while Fish was at his country home in Garrison, New York, noted in his Diary[46] the receipt of the news and sent for Thornton, who claimed that the treaty gave authority for the restrictions, a point which Davis could not concede. Thornton doubted whether anything could be done about it at Ottawa and said that he supposed the United States would be willing to have the matter tested in the courts. This, said Davis, was something for Fish to decide; he was not inclined to be unreasonable, but the United States could not leave the construction of treaties to the courts. Then, said Thornton, it would better be left to arbitration. Still better, retorted Davis, to drop the claims. The Secretary, when he had word from Davis of the affair, wrote back:[47]

. . . This appears to be a much more serious matter & one requiring prompt & strong remonstrance. I have not the means at hand of reference to the Statute of 1843 (referred to) or other Statutes, but *unless* it has heretofore been admitted, or acknowledged that the Treaty of 1818 ex-

46. Aug. 28, 1870 (L.C.).
47. Sept. 3, 1870; Davis Papers, Vol. VII (L.C.).

cluded American fishing vessels from the ports of British N. A. for any other purpose than that of shelter repairs & obtaining wood & water, we cannot admit the present action, & should make an energetic remonstrance & a reclamation. The object of the Treaty of 1818 was to settle the differences arising out of the claims of the Americans to take & cure fish. It was not intended to limit the commercial rights of American vessels to enter the regular open ports of British America.

Consul Jackson, at Halifax, bombarded by complaints from Americans who were hit hard by the new regulations, tried to obtain from Vice-Admiral Wellesley information as to why these unprecedented restrictions were imposed and drew only a rather stiff reply that the treaty authorized recourse to Provincial ports by American fishing craft only for wood, water, shelter, and repair. "It will be seen by the vice-admiral's communication," said Jackson,

that for the first time since the treaty of peace in 1815 have the imperial authorities prohibited ice, bait, or other supplies from being furnished in the colonial ports to American fishermen engaged in the deep-sea or ocean fisheries. And this prohibition, so extraordinary and unprecedented, was neither announced nor enforced, either by the imperial or Dominion authorities, until after the commencement of the fishing season, when our vessels were on their voyage to the fishing grounds.[48]

Thornton, striving as he was to come to some sort of an arrangement with the American Government on a wide range of disputed topics, was more than a little disturbed by the stiff-necked attitude taken by the Dominion authorities. On a visit to Sir John Young at Quebec he met several members of the Canadian Cabinet. Dr. Charles Tupper tried to convince him that the course pursued was the only logical and probably the only effective one that could be taken, while Sir Francis Hincks asserted that the Cabinet was a "unit" on the question.[49] The arguments, however, did not convince him of the soundness of the position. "Your Excellency," wrote Thornton when he returned to Washington,[50] "may . . . remember that although I declined to

48. Jackson to Fish, Sept. 5, 1870. The correspondence is in *For. Rel., 1870*, pp. 424 ff.

49. Young to Kimberley, Sept. 3, 1870; G [unnumbered], pp. 267–269 (P.A.C.). Lord Kimberley took over the Colonial Office when Granville became Foreign Secretary in 1870.

50. Thornton to Young, Confidential, Sept. 12, 1870; G '69–'71 (P.A.C.).

discuss the interpretation of the wording of the Treaty, I said that even if it really gave us a full right to prevent American Fishing vessels from trading in Canadian ports, I thought it somewhat unfriendly and unneighbourly, and that it might embitter the relations between the two countries which in the interest both of Canada and Great Britain should be most cordial." He had made no impression on the Canadians, however, and, when asked by Fish whether they intended to stick to the course adopted, was forced to say they did. To Granville[51] he had to admit that he had had little success in Canada "whether from the soreness which the Canadian Government feel just now with regard to the U. S., or from their determination to protect the fisheries at all risks and to render the pursuit as unprofitable as possible to American fishermen." The captures made of vessels within the three-mile limit seemed, he said, "to cause little irritation except to the owners and persons immediately interested," but "the restriction . . . of preventing vessels from entering the ports for the purpose of trading, landing & transshipping fish &c., is most severely felt; for it affects every American fisherman and considerably diminishes his gains." Mr. Fish, he remarked, was aware of the losses involved and perhaps it was on that account that he was so "earnest in denouncing it as a false interpretation of the Treaty and as a very unfriendly act."[52]

Despite the assurances of Tupper and Hincks that the Dominion Government were a unit on the new policy, it began to appear that there were some, in governmental circles as well as out, who doubted the wisdom of the course. Premier Macdonald began to be skeptical and speculate whether it was not possible to "meet the U. S. Gov^t on some fair terms or arrangement if any can be found as to the point in question."[53] On the other hand, more intimate inquiry seemed to cast a shadow of doubt over the universality of American privilege in ports

51. Confidential, Sept. 12, 1870; FO 115:508 (P.R.O.).
52. Scammon wrote from Charlottetown (Sept. 19, 1870; Consular Letters, Vol. II [D.S.]), that never in the past twenty-five years was it supposed that the act of the Prince Edward Island Legislature of 1843 had any purpose except to prevent smuggling. He repeated that it was all a device to coerce the island and Newfoundland into the Dominion.
53. According to Sir John Young in Young to Kimberley, Sept. 23, 1870; G [unnumbered], pp. 270–271 (P.A.C.).

before the Reciprocity Treaty went into effect;[54] it seemed to have depended on local custom. Neither Canada nor the United States was too sure of its position, but both realized that an impossible situation was in the making. Great Britain occupied, as usual, the middle ground: it would not coerce Canada, yet it was reluctant to let that Dominion handle the situation in a way that would preclude the settlement of any of the issues which it so anxiously desired to get rid of.

As a way of getting out of the *impasse* Lord Kimberley approached the Canadian Government[55] with a proposition, which he said had been sent to Thornton to bring before the American Government, suggesting the appointment of a commission on which Great Britain, Canada, and the United States would be represented to inquire "what ought to be the Geographical limits of the exclusive Fisheries of the British North American Colonies." The British and American Governments should come to a clear understanding in the case of each bay, harbor, and creek and "define those limits in such a way as to be incapable of dispute, either by reference to the bearings of certain headlands or other objects on shore, or by laying the lines down on a Map or Chart." If an agreement were reached it might be in the "form of an understanding between the two Govts. as to the practical interpretation which [should] be given to the Convention of 1818." To ease in such an undertaking the Colonial Office disavowed the course the Dominion had taken respecting ports,[56] sincerely regretting "that the Canadian Govt: should have taken so serious a step without previously consulting [the Imperial Government], as they are most desirous that in dealing with a question of so much difficulty there should be no divergence in the action of the Imperial & Colonial Govts: & they also regret it because such a step is evidently not calculated to further the success of the proposal for the appointment of a Commission wh: with the assent of the Canadian Govt: they are about to make to the U. S." Orders to Admiral Wellesley put a point to this rebuke when the British Navy was directed no longer to enforce the regulation about enter-

54. Malmros (Pictou) to Davis, Sept. 26, 1870; *For. Rel., 1870*, pp. 427–428. Jackson (Halifax) to Davis, Oct. 3, 1870; Consular Letters: Halifax, Vol. XII (D.S.).

55. Kimberley to Young, Sept., 1870, with a Colonial Office Memorandum elaborating the proposal; FO 115:504 (P.R.O.).

56. Kimberley to Young, Oct., 1870; FO 115:504 (P.R.O.).

ing ports, without, however, admitting "Mr. Fish's interpretation of the Treaty of 1818 as regards the exclusion. . . ."[57]

The appointment of a commission, with the possibility of a protracted negotiation, however, did not appeal to Fish. He wanted immediate action. The political situation in the United States was such that a semblance of toleration of the existing situation would make the Administration's position too difficult; it was necessary to have affairs so in hand that a majority in Congress was assured for major issues, and apparent yielding to England would weaken the President's hand. Mr. Fish, reported Thornton,[58]

does not seem disposed to admit of any delay or even discussion upon the subject, but states in pretty plain terms that American Citizens have already during the fishing season now ending suffered such serious losses from the proceedings of the Canadian Authorities that the United States will be under the necessity of retaliating upon Canada by withdrawing the privilege now enjoyed of transporting goods in bond from Portland thro' the U. S. to the Canadian frontier.

Whether M^r: Fish really means what he says, or is merely parading a Menace for the purpose of influencing the decision of the Canadian Gov^t: with regard to the question at issue, it is difficult to discover. There is no doubt however that the American fishermen are returning from their labours, having had but scanty success, and in a very bad humour.

However unjust their complaints, Thornton wrote, the New England fishermen exercised a powerful political influence, especially at a time just before elections, and no doubt the next session of Congress would be filled with violent speeches and retaliation would be proposed. The speeches did not wait until Congress was in session, for within a week Thornton was reporting "the substance of a speech recently made by General Benjamin F. Butler at Salem in Massachusetts, in which he comments in pretty severe terms upon the action of the Canadian Gov^t: with reference to the U. S. fishermen who pursue their calling in the seas adjacent to the Canadian coast."[59]

The warning and rebuke from London had its effect in the Do-

57. Hammond to Thornton, Oct. 24, 1870; FO 115:505 (P.R.O.).
58. Thornton to Granville, Oct. 17, 1870; FO 115:509 (P.R.O.).
59. Thornton to Granville, Oct. 24, 1870; FO 115:509 (P.R.O.). "Made on the eve of the elections in Massachusetts, General Butler's speech is of course principally for electioneering purposes; but I presume that it will be

minion, for the Premier notified the Governor-General that the Council "have come to the conclusion that we will not for the present enforce any such exclusion" of American fishing vessels from Canadian ports.[60] The Government had directed Mitchell to prepare a report presenting his view and then Macdonald would make one "viewing the subject in all its phases for the Consideration of the Council." Meantime, it was Macdonald's opinion that Thornton had better postpone "any application to the United States Government for the appointment of a mixed Commission."[61] He need have had no fears about the American Government's desire for immediate recourse to a commission, for nothing was farther from the thoughts of the President and his advisers. This, however, did not mean that Secretary Fish was indifferent to the matter or wished to prolong the controversy; on the contrary, he was only too anxious to find some way to settle the differences as soon as possible, since friction over fisheries complicated adjustment of other issues, especially that of the *Alabama* Claims, but policy dictated allowing nothing to strengthen the anti-administration forces in Congress by adopting too conciliatory an attitude.[62]

The fishing season was ended and for the next two months nothing

followed by similar declamations during the approaching Session of Congress." See Halifax *Recorder* of October 3, 1870, quoted in *Cape Ann Advertiser,* October 14, which pointed out the buncombe of Butler's speech, yet called the measures provoking it "insane," and "adopted apparently for the deliberate purpose of irritating and annoying our neighbors, who have shown so much forbearance and such a peaceable disposition toward us."

60. Oct. 31, 1870; Macdonald Papers: Letterbooks, XIV, 403–405 (P.A.C.).

61. The rebuke evidently got under the skin of the Canadian Government, since Macdonald referred to it as "a very unpleasant Despatch respecting Fisheries [which had] come from England in consequence of the too energetic action of the irrepressible Minister of Marine." Macdonald to Alex. Campbell, Nov. 1, 1870; Macdonald Papers: Letterbooks, XIV, 414 (P.A.C.). Thornton to Granville, Confidential, Nov. 7; FO 115:509 (P.R.O.).

62. Davis noted in his Diary (Nov. 6, 1870 [L.C.]), that in a conversation with Fish the latter agreed with him that if the question of the ports were not soon settled it was bound to make trouble. Fish told the Assistant Secretary, in confidence, what he no doubt had privately from Thornton, that the British Government had "soundly rated" the Dominion officials for their course, and, without accepting the American interpretation of the convention, had reversed the policy.

occurred except oratory and sparring for position.[63] Correspondence accumulated upon issues which had been raised and the public speculated on the probable outcome, even raising the question of possible war. Canadians wanted reciprocity in exchange for fisheries, while Americans were bent on maintaining their protective walls. In England the most profound feeling was one of wishing to clear up all the controversies, together with some exasperation at Canada for complicating the situation. Adam Badeau, who had been sent to the Legation in London as secretary, wrote Davis:[64]

. . . As to the fishery question, they neither know nor care anything about it. I was staying at Lord Halifax's last week, and he told me that he had been talking up the matter with Lord Kimberley (who you recollect is the Secretary of State for the Colonies) and Kimberley told Halifax that he had recently read up all that was written on the subject. He came to the conclusion that the British had international law on their side, but that it would be impolitic to press the matter. Lord Halifax assured me that he had no doubt that all difficulties on that account would be avoided.

Thornton busied himself trying to find out from American precedent what stand had been taken by the United States respecting its own waters and came to the conclusion, often pointed out before, that "exclusive right [is] generally claimed by the respective States of this Country to the Fisheries adjacent to their coasts and in the bays, even though the mouths of the bays be of great width, as is the case with Chesapeake and Delaware Bays, in which the States of Virginia, Maryland, and Delaware exercise exclusive State authority over the whole of those Bays."[65] Massachusetts alone seemed to assert jurisdiction only over the three-mile area, even in the case of Cape Cod Bay. In the latter case, he said, since many of the fishermen came from that State "they might have a claim to a liberal interpretation of the Treaty of 1818 with regard to Canadian Bays."

63. "Things are going very quietly here, the Colonial Office being a little nervous about Fishery matters." Macdonald to Rose, Nov. 17, 1870; Macdonald Papers: Letterbooks, XIV, 536 (P.A.C.).

64. Nov. 26, 1870; Davis Papers, Vol. VIII (L.C.).

65. Thornton to Lisgar, Dec. 2, 1870; G '69–'71 (P.A.C.). Sir John Young had been recently raised to the peerage as Baron Lisgar.

When Congress met, Grant's Annual Message had an extended reference to the fisheries.[66] "The course pursued by the Canadian authorities toward the fishermen of the United States during the past season has not been marked by a friendly feeling." The Imperial Government, he said, had delegated "the whole or a share of its jurisdiction" to the Dominion Government and "this semi-independent but irresponsible agent has exercised its delegated powers in an unfriendly way"; vessels were seized without notice, officers were authorized to bring in vessels hovering within three miles of the coasts, and heavy penalties could be imposed upon the masters if truthful answers were not given. American vessels, the Canadians claimed, could enter ports only for wood, water, shelter, and repair, although it was not known that any vessel had been seized under this claim. Since Canada might "repeat their unneighborly acts" in the coming season he recommended that Congress give him power to suspend the bonding privilege, and possibly to refuse permission to Canadian vessels to enter American ports. "A like unfriendly disposition," asserted the President, had been manifested in claiming a right to exclude American citizens from the navigation of the St. Lawrence. This, he maintained, was contrary to the spirit of the times as well as a potential hardship to Americans who were interested in cheap transportation of western goods to the seaboard and abroad.

Commenting on the Message, Thornton wrote[67] that the two points of interest to Her Majesty's Government were the questions of the *Alabama* Claims and the fisheries. He contented himself with summarizing what the President had stated, but, as to the charge that vessels had been seized without warning, he noted that "they could not have been ignorant that during this year's season no such notice would be given to them; for an announcement to that effect had been made by the Secretary of the Treasury of the U.S." As to the St. Lawrence he believed that "practically . . . the American flag enjoys at present equal freedom upon the St. Lawrence with the British flag. But the very treaties which the President quotes, appear to prove the inherence of the right in the nation possessing the river, and of her power to grant it to other nations."

Canadian comments on the Message were less temperate than those

66. Richardson, *Messages and Papers,* VII, 102 ff.
67. Thornton to Granville, Dec. 6, 1870; FO 115:509 (P.R.O.).

of the British Minister. "The President falsifies the language of the Treaty of 1818," wrote a correspondent to the editor of the *Gazette*. "He grossly misrepresents the action of our Government, and ignores the very existence of his own proclamation." Canadians, however, had long since ceased to be surprised at such treachery; three-fourths of existing American territory had been wrested from Great Britain "under the same pretensions as are now set up as to the fisheries." Sooner or later Canadians must take a stand, and the fisheries afforded an opportunity for doing so.[68] Officially there was a disposition to read politics into the President's statements. "You need be afraid of no storms from the West," wrote Macdonald to a London correspondent,[69]

although President Grant chooses to be a little saucy in his message about the Canadian Fisheries. We know what that means. The Republican Party which elected him is split in two, the better half of them being for the present opposed to him. He hopes, however, by an appearance of vigor to succeed in getting the nomination of the Republican party as their Candidate for President next year, believing that if he succeeds in getting the nomination party discipline will whip in the recalcitrants. . . . We have, however, completely broken up the stealing of our fish by American fishermen, hence General Butler's howl, & General Grant's grumble.

On American soil, particularly in the maritime regions of the Northeast, the President's Message was none too strong. The Canadians, said the editor of one "Down East" paper,[70] had profited by the Rebellion, and now when Congress was trying to reduce taxation the Canadians asked to be admitted into American markets, a request the Government properly refused. Since service in "Confederate pirates" was no longer available they were doing a little business on their own hook by seizing American vessels, refusing admission to their ports and the like. President Grant had exactly met the case and the remedies he proposed were the only ones likely to be efficient. General Butler's "howl" took the form of a resolution introduced in the House on December 13.[71] It stated that "to obtain satisfaction for the Fenian

68. Montreal *Gazette,* Dec. 9, 1870.
69. To D. G. Bruce Gardyne[?], Dec. 30, 1870; Macdonald Papers: Letterbooks, XIV, 731–732 (P.A.C.).
70. *Cape Ann Advertiser,* Dec. 9, 1870.
71. *Cong. Globe,* 41st Cong., 3d Sess., p. 88.

raids; to force the United States to renew the reciprocity treaty; to drive American fishermen from their waters, thereby reducing the number of fishing vessels, weakening the marine power of the United States, and making a monopoly of the fishing business in the hands of the Canadians to supply our markets," they had seized vessels, refused the use of ports and generally "harassed the fishermen in a manner peculiar to British authority." Consequently there should be passed a non-intercourse act,

similar in its effects to that of Canada, whereby the same treatment may be applied to all vessels hailing from the British Provinces as that suffered by American fishermen; also an act prohibiting the importation of English or Canadian fish or mackerel so long as American vessels are prohibited from taking fish and mackerel in so-called British waters; also that transportation in bond of merchandise through American territory be prohibited until Canadian ports are opened for transportation in bond of American fish, mackerel, or other merchandise to and from the United States [and also that full indemnity be demanded for] all detentions and outrages [committed on American vessels by British armed vessels].

On a call from the House for correspondence covering the issue the President, on December 21, sent a special message announcing that all papers had been transmitted with the Annual Message,[72] a statement which came fairly near the literal truth. Meantime, Butler had presented a petition, said to be signed by two thousand persons, relative to the capture of vessels during the late season. "The petitioners," remarked Thornton, "refrain from acknowledging that the principal seizures were made on account of violations of the Treaty of 1818 with regard to the inshore fisheries, which they had been previously warned to respect by Circulars from the Treasury Department of the United States."[73]

Butler's fulminations, irate editorials, and petitions did not, however, stir up the expected storm of recrimination, for it was being quietly circulated around that the Department of State had in train action which would, or might, result in some sort of solution of all the issues between Great Britain and the United States, including the Canadian problems. On both sides of the Atlantic businessmen were

72. *Cong. Globe,* 41st Cong., 3d Sess., p. 276.
73. Thornton to Granville, Dec. 19, 1870; FO 115:1195 (P.R.O.).

tired of the protracted squabble, and the more sober portion of the two countries yearned to settle down and forget old scores. Even Canada thought that something might come out of an amicable discussion and so, with reservations, was willing to try her luck with the others.[74]

74. The Toronto *Globe,* February 2, 1871, in an editorial, quoted in full the queries put by the Nova Scotia House of Assembly in 1841, prefaced by the comment that they were "worth giving in full now when this same business is being brought prominently forward, and a good many quasi Englishmen, with one or two of those trifling bores among Canadians who are always speaking about their 'broad views,' are quite sure that in order to have peace, Canadians ought to surrender the whole point at issue *simpliciter.*"

General R. C. Schenck, who was about to leave the United States as Minister to England, could not have created a very favorable impression when he was quoted as saying at an interview on the fisheries (Montreal *Gazette,* Jan. 5, 1871) "that England feels annoyed at the conduct of the Canadians, and will probably send out a delegate to the Government of the Dominion, with instructions to put a curb on their arrogance, and bring them to a sense of the duty they owe to the people of the United States!! Without regard to the merits of the case, I must say that their behavior has been churlish and offensive in the highest degree."

CHAPTER XIII

YEARNING FOR RECIPROCITY AGAIN

GRUMBLINGS against the Reciprocity Treaty in the United States and the growing sentiment for its abrogation during the Civil War had been noted with apprehension in the British Provinces. While this treaty was not all that was desired and had, indeed, been looked upon by some as unnecessarily yielding,[1] it had been, after all, of great benefit to Canada, at least, and not without some value in the other Provinces. Aware that a portion of American resentment came from dissatisfaction with rising Canadian duties, nevertheless pique against anything British was charged with causing the principal animus. Hence, when the North had overwhelmed the secessionists and the Union had been vindicated, there was a not illogical feeling that different counsels would prevail and temporary irritation give way to sound business judgment. Nor was it unreasonable for the Canadian Government to undertake such steps as might conceivably lead to a renewal, perhaps on a modified basis, of the arrangement which Congress, on March 17, 1865, said was to become inoperative a year hence. In London, in the summer of 1865, the delegates sent by order of the Canadian Council to take up the question of confederation also discussed reciprocity with Imperial authorities. In the words of their report:[2]

We explained how advantageously the Treaty had worked for Canada, and the desire of our people for its renewal; but we showed at the same time how much more advantageously it had operated for American interests, and we expressed our inability to believe that the United States Government seriously contemplated the abolition of an arrangement by

1. Joseph Howe had not concealed his belief that the exigencies of Canada had caused the interests of the Maritime Provinces to be overlooked; the fisheries, he was convinced, had been too lightly tossed into the balance in order to open a market for Canadian grain. "Paper on the Reciprocity Treaty," Howe Papers (P.A.C.).

2. Macdonald, Cartier, Brown, and Galt were the delegates. Their report was dated August 14, 1865. Macdonald Papers: Reciprocity, pp. 50–51 (P.A.C.).

which they had so greatly increased their foreign Commerce, secured a vast and lucrative carrying trade, and obtained free access to the St. Lawrence and to the invaluable fishing grounds of British America, and that on the sole ground that the Provinces had also profited by the Treaty. We explained the immediate injury that would result to Canadian interests from the abrogation of the Treaty, but we pointed out at the same time the new and ultimately profitable channels into which our foreign trade must, in that event, be turned and the necessity of preparing for the change if indeed it was to come. . . .

The British Government made good its promise to have the matter taken up in Washington, but Sir Frederick Bruce pointed out that the assassination of Lincoln and the illness of Secretary Seward prevented an immediate consideration.[3] "I do not think," he added, "this delay is to be regretted. I am in hopes that the bitterness engendered by the proceedings of the [Confederate] raiders will have greatly subsided, and that the question will be approached in a more dispassionate spirit, than would have been the case before the termination of the Civil War." He called attention to the convention to be held at Detroit for a consideration of Canadian-American commercial relations, and proposed to ask Joseph Howe, then in the United States, to attend and communicate "confidentially what he can gather of the feelings & motives which sway the parties which will compose it." This suggestion was not too favorably received in London, for, as Russell stated to Bruce,[4] Edward Cardwell, Secretary of State for the Colonies, believed that Howe, as a member of the Nova Scotia Government, might by attending give rise to dissatisfaction in that as well as in the other Provinces; moreover, the employment of a person thought to be actively opposed to both Great Britain and Canada on the subject of confederation could hardly be presumed to be politic. Howe did, however, attend the Detroit Convention in August and did take a part somewhat more active than Bruce had anticipated.

To the convention[5] came some five hundred delegates from the

3. Bruce to Russell (draft), Confidential, June 7, 1865; FO 115:438 (P.R.O.).
4. July 1, 1865; FO 115:434 (P.R.O.).
5. The newspapers of Canada and those of the western cities of the United States, especially Detroit and Chicago, gave extensive accounts of the meetings, including *verbatim* reports of many of the speeches.

United States and about seventy from the British Provinces, chosen by Boards of Trade and like organizations in the principal cities; Howe was designated as a delegate from the Chamber of Commerce of Halifax. According to his son's preface to Howe's speech made there,[6] "the British Americans, to a man, were in favor of maintaining the Treaty, but the great body of the Americans were apparently hostile or were disposed to insist upon such modifications as might, if conceded, make it of little value to us." Delegates from the western grain-growing regions were not unfriendly but insisted on enlargement of the canals; but, on the other hand

powerful and very able delegations had come to the Convention, representing the Lumbering interests of Maine and Michigan, the Iron and forwarding interests of New York, the great Coal interests of Pennsylvania, and generally such other interests, manufacturing and agricultural as were favorable to protection. These men were led by the Hon. [Hannibal] Hamlin, late Vice President of the United States, and others of great experience and ability, and a gentleman who was said to represent the State Department came westward and harangued a large number of the Members a day or two before the vote was taken in a spirit of hostility to the Treaty. The only person who actively interfered to save it was the venerable Lorenzo Sabine. . . .

After general discussion the last day was given over to a consideration of the treaty, and the Provincial delegates were informed that they might have their day in court. At a caucus of the Provincials, Howe was selected to present their side, a task which he somewhat reluctantly undertook, since he had some compunctions with respect to his position as observer for Bruce. "I have conversed," wrote his son, "with many gentlemen who were present, and who have assured me that the night before my Father spoke bets to any amount would have been taken that the Treaty would be condemned by an overwhelming majority," but

the effect of the speech was magical. From the start he commanded the ear of the audience, carried them with him to the close, won a unanimous verdict in favor of the Treaty, and, vindicated the oratorical power and mental elevation of his country before such a body of men as for commer-

6. Howe Papers (P.A.C.). The speech itself is in J. A. Chisholm, *The Speeches and Public Letters of Joseph Howe* (Halifax, 1909), II, 438–455.

cial influence, sagacity and experience, will rarely again be assembled on the Continent.

Votes taken immediately after a stirring address and action which followed second thought were different things. Already A. T. Galt and W. P. Howland had been in Washington on reciprocity business. In their interview on July 22 with Seward he "made repeated references to the irritation still existing against Canada in the public mind from events arising during the war, and said that if official application were now made to the American Government for the renewal of negotiations respecting the Reciprocity Treaty, it would be met with a refusal."[7] A later interview with Hugh McCulloch, Secretary of the Treasury, produced a similar response: the Government, he said, must positively await some expression from Congress before it could or would move in the matter. The whole subject of taxation was undergoing examination and its relation to trade arrangements must be seriously considered. Sir Frederick agreed with Galt and Howland that there was no use trying to go forward with the matter at the moment, although he admitted that, as a precaution, the Governor-General ought to send a dispatch to him stating the willingness of the Canadian Government to open discussion of a new treaty.

Here the matter appeared to rest until Congress assembled in the winter, in that session when President Johnson and the Radicals locked horns over Reconstruction.[8] Under the surface, however, there was a stirring. Galt entered into correspondence with the chairman of the Financial Commission, then conducting hearings in New York preliminary to the meeting of Congress, and gave him a written statement of what Canada wished to propose. They met in New York; Galt was introduced to E. H. Derby, who had been appointed by the Treasury

7. Galt and Howland, Aug. 3, 1865; Macdonald Papers: Reciprocity (P.A.C.). On August 8, 1865, Seward wrote to Chandler asking him to call if he were in the city, for he would like his views on the matter of Canadian trade before taking into consideration the overtures made to him for the revival of the Reciprocity Treaty. Chandler Papers (L.C.).

8. Bruce dropped the matter too for the time. He did inform both Lord Monck and the Foreign Office that in his opinion a union of British North America afforded "the best, if not the only hope, of obtaining a fair Reciprocity Treaty from the United States." Bruce to Russell, Aug. 28, 1865; FO 115:438 (P.R.O.).

Department to report on the working of the Reciprocity Treaty; then Galt went to Washington where he again saw Seward and Mc-Culloch, and it was decided to make an attempt to secure from the House Committee on Ways and Means resolutions recommending extension of the period beyond March 17, 1866, for such resolutions could be carried by a majority vote, while a treaty would demand the support of two-thirds of the Senators.[9] Bruce and Galt agreed to the procedure. W. P. Fessenden of Maine and E. D. Morgan of New York agreed to help this plan and Derby was understood to favor it. Until the result of the attempt should be known, no official overture for a treaty would be made. One of the principal stumbling blocks, as Bruce reported, appeared to be McCulloch's desire for revenue which, he thought, was seriously reduced by admission of duty-free goods from Canada; another was presented by Morrill, who said to Galt that the House of Representatives "regarded a commercial treaty as an infringement of their Constitutional rights, and would not . . . entertain it." Mutual legislation was the proper procedure. This, Galt said, was difficult to accomplish when action had to be obtained from so many different legislative bodies; if confederation had carried the previous year it would have made the situation more hopeful. To forward the scheme it was advised that Canada have a mission in Washington when Congress met, not to make proposals but, as Galt put it, to find out what were objections to continuing the existing treaty and ascertain whether the two governments were sufficiently in accord to make it worth while to inaugurate negotiations for a new one.

Back in Canada, Galt outlined to the Council the whole situation. That body authorized him and Howland to proceed once more to Washington to find out on what basis action could be had, although it was pointed out that the fisheries privileges then enjoyed by citizens of the United States could not be continued and made permanent while Americans insisted on maintaining control over all the subjects which the Canadians had looked upon as equivalents of the concession. Since, in the short time that remained before the expiration of the treaty, it would be impossible to secure action from all the Provinces, and in view of probable early confederation of these colonies, it was

9. Bruce to Clarendon, Confidential, Dec. 4, 1865; FO 115:434 (P.R.O.). The Macdonald Papers: Reciprocity (pp. 26 ff. [P.A.C.]) contain two long reports by Galt and Howland dated December 19 and 20, 1865.

urged that the British Minister in Washington be asked to suggest the propriety of continuing the treaty until a permanent arrangement could be perfected. Meantime the other Provinces should be invited to send delegates to Washington to coöperate with the Canadians in considering any propositions made by the United States.

By this time it had become generally known that attempts were being made to extend or replace the Reciprocity Treaty. In Canada opinion was almost unanimously favorable to the proposition, although there was difference of opinion as to how far to go to promote it. Not a few agreed with Brown in the *Globe* when he asserted[10] that there was evidence coming in from every part of the United States that the real purpose of the "howl raised . . . against the Reciprocity Treaty" was to "frighten us into annexation," and quoted with approval from an editorial in the New York *World* which said:

We are weary of refuting arguments and statements brought forward with a preconceived and prevailing belief that the Provinces can in this way be forced into annexation. The silly and pernicious notion that whatever has been or can be profitable to Canadians, has been, and must be injurious to us, steams up through the arguments of all who are opposed to a fair system of reciprocity. . . . Not one influential representative of public opinion among the Canadian journals—nor, we believe, one newspaper of an inferior class—now advocates annexation to the United States.

Papers like the New York *Herald* and the Chicago *Tribune* continued their diatribes on inevitable annexation and their denunciation of the inequities of the Reciprocity Treaty, but other voices were heard too. The New York *Evening Post*[11] hoped that the Canadian delegates would get a respectful hearing and wished that "their arguments might be reinforced by the representations of the multitudes of Eastern and Western producers and consumers, whose interests are threatened by the protectionists, who are laboring to repeal the Reciprocity Treaty." The New York *Times*[12] remarked that consumers were ranged against coal and lumber interests, who would gouge with increased prices, and that Congress should be as anxious to protect

10. Toronto *Globe,* Jan. 30, 1866.
11. Quoted in Detroit *Free Press,* Jan. 25, 1866.
12. *Ibid.*

farmers, mechanics, and the great mass of consumers as to listen to the plea of vested interests who feared competition. The Board of Trade of Boston, in its annual report, came out with this statement:[13]

Upon this important question the views of the Board have been stated at length in former annual reports. The delegates to the Commercial Convention at Detroit were active in the committee room, and on the floor of the Convention, in support of the resolution which passed that body; while the Special Committee here has endeavored during the whole year, by personal conference and by correspondence, to induce the Federal Government to continue in force the treaty of June, 1854, until Commissioners shall have agreed upon, or fail to agree upon, a new Convention.

Evidence there is in plenty that reciprocity, its maintenance or its elimination, aroused more than a passing interest in the United States, but to few did the issue seem so vital as it appeared to Canadians.

Galt and Howland for Canada, W. A. Henry for Nova Scotia, and A. J. Smith for New Brunswick met with members of the House Committee on Ways and Means January 25 and 26, and February 2, 5, and 6. Morrill, Samuel Hooper, James Brooks, J. A. Garfield, John Wentworth, Roscoe Conkling, J. K. Moorhead, W. B. Allison, and John Hogan were present at all or part of the meetings.[14] On the first days the discussion was rather general, with Morrill doing most of the talking. He stated and restated his belief that establishment of reciprocity by treaty was unconstitutional and the House would never agree to it. Twice he referred to the probability of annexation, once when making inquiries about the country beyond the Rockies and once in speaking of neutralizing the canals: "That," he said, "will have to be postponed until you, gentlemen, assume your seats here." On February 2 Galt submitted a memorandum of what Canada would be willing to do: trade in natural products under normal circumstances should be free between the two countries, but as American internal taxes existed at the time, the Provinces would agree to put

13. Toronto *Globe*, Jan. 17, 1866.

14. *Report of the Conference between the Colonial Delegation and the Committee of Ways and Means of the House of Representatives* (a thirty-two page, confidential, printed report found in Macdonald Papers: Reciprocity [P.A.C.]). See D. C. Masters, "Reciprocity and the Genesis of Canadian Commercial Policy," *Can. Hist. Rev.*, XIII, 418–428.

duties upon such goods equivalent to the American excise, but both parties might add certain articles to the existing list; as to the fisheries, the Provinces were willing to allow present arrangements to continue; Canada was willing to improve water access to the sea providing the United States did not by legislation divert western trade from its natural channels; if the United States should not be prepared to consider a general opening of their coasting trade, it was desirable that in the internal waters no distinction should be made between vessels of the two countries. If these points could be satisfactorily arranged, then Canada would adjust her excise duties on beer, spirits, and tobacco on "the best revenue standard" to be mutually agreed upon, and if there should be a desire to treat any other articles in a similar manner, Canada stood ready to meet any overtures of the United States in a friendly spirit with a view to stopping illicit trade across the border. The transit trade, it was suggested, should be under the same regulations in both countries, and Canada would make her patent laws conform to those of the United States.

Three days later Morrill presented a counter-memorandum. The Committee of Ways and Means, with the approval of the Secretary of the Treasury, were prepared to submit to the House a law proposing to continue some of the provisions of the Reciprocity Treaty: Canadians should be allowed to use the waters of Lake Michigan in return for American use of the St. Lawrence and the canals, subject to the same conditions imposed on British subjects; transit of goods in bond across territory of the United States from Portland to Canada and back by railroad should be balanced by similar privileges from Windsor, Sarnia, or other western ports to Buffalo, Ogdensburg, and points east, and free ports in the Provinces should be abolished; bounties given to American fishermen should be abolished and duties on Canadian fish in American ports should be no higher than those of the attached schedule,[15] providing all the rights of inshore fisheries allowed in the treaty should be continued for American citizens in Provincial waters and for British subjects in American waters; and the following articles should be mutually free from duty: unwrought burr millstones, cotton and linen rags, firewood, rough and unfinished grindstones, and unground gypsum or plaster. To these proposals was ap-

15. Black mackerel, $1.50; herring, $1; salmon, $2.50; shad, $2; all other pickled fish, $1.50.

pended a list of articles, which had been free under the treaty, with duties of varying amounts, which the Provincial delegates insisted were on the average far above 20 per cent and suggested more with the idea of protection than revenue.

In the opinion of the Colonials this was a proposition for them to surrender the fisheries for what amounted to nothing in return, and on the next day Galt presented a memorandum rejecting the proposals. Bruce concurred with the Provincials in considering that there was little here which offered a basis for negotiation, and the conferences came to an end. Reviewing the work, Sir Frederick expressed his regret that, after the hopeful indications given by officials like McCulloch, Seward, and others, the results should be so disappointing.[16]

I am inclined [he wrote] to think that independently of the strong party in Congress which adopts the Protectionist theory, the desire to impose exorbitant duties may be attributed in part to a feeling that the extent of the operation of the Internal Revenue Law on the industry of the country is very imperfectly understood; the Report of the Revenue Commission shows that even the present high tariff does not place the American producer on a level with the foreign manufacturer. . . .

The exclusion of the Southern Representatives however throws an exceptional power in such matters into the hands of the protectionists of the North and centre of the country, and their ranks are swelled by the agriculturalists of the N. Western States who dread the competition of the wheat & barley-growers of Canada.[17]

When information of what had taken place in Washington began to be spread about, opinions were varied. In the United States some of those who had been scoffing at the Reciprocity Treaty as of benefit to the Provinces alone appeared to weaken a little and wonder if, after

16. Bruce to Clarendon, Feb. 11, 1866; FO 115:453 (P.R.O.).

17. In an exhaustive editorial in the Toronto *Globe* (reprinted in the Montreal *Gazette,* Feb. 8, 1866) there was a detailed analysis of the Derby Report showing that American-Canadian trade had increased under reciprocity from eighteen millions in 1851 to sixty-eight millions in 1865; that the fisheries had increased by nearly 50 per cent; that there were but seven articles—wheat, oats, barley, coal, lumber, fish, and possibly horses—largely exported to the United States upon which duties could be levied, and if such duties were levied it would merely mean change of form of the commodities or inconvenience and expense for the Americans.

all, it had been such a one-sided bargain, and whether the Committee on Ways and Means had not, by its intransigent attitude, used a sword that cut both ways. Those who had been friendly to the arrangement were outspoken in their denunciation of the American proposal; in commenting upon it the New York *Times*, not usually overly sympathetic with the northern neighbors, did not spare its scorn.[18]

. . . The list of articles which the Committee liberally place upon the free list is a curiosity, considering the circumstances in which it originates, and the parties for whose acceptance it is designed. Let there be no mistake about it. The Committee are prepared to agree that five articles— positively five!—"shall be mutually free." And these five are—what think you? Burr mill-stones, unwrought; rags; firewood; rough grindstones; gypsum! Of which but one is imported from Canada, and that in small quantities—we mean firewood. His excellency the Asiatic Tycoon, may profit by this lesson in exclusiveness. On this continent, we fear, it will be laughed at irreverently. . . .

But the protectionists in Congress did not lack support from their constituents. Coal[19] and lumber interests, sometimes wheat and others, united in rejoicing that the Reciprocity Treaty was passing off the scene, and did not fail to let their representatives know that they wished no relaxation in duties upon these competitive articles.

In Canada and the other Provinces the consensus of opinion was that no self-respecting government could entertain the American counter-proposals and, moreover, there was a disposition to condemn the delegates for having made the suggestions which called them forth.[20] The Toronto *Globe*,[21] an opposition paper with politics coloring its comments, raised the question of responsibility for the fiasco and came to the conclusion that the Government's delegates had laid themselves open by their too generous offer: "*Has not the whole trouble in this matter been created by the senselessness of our own people, in teaching the Americans erroneously to fancy that our prosperity was in their hands, and that the repeal of the Treaty was sudden ruin to us?*" For weeks the battle went on between government and

18. Quoted in Montreal *Gazette,* Feb. 19, 1866.
19. See *House Misc. Docs.,* No. 46, 39th Cong., 1st Sess.
20. Montreal *Gazette,* Feb. 20, 1866. Letter signed "Merchant."
21. Quoted in *ibid.,* Feb. 20, 1866.

opposition papers as to whether the former were culpable in going as far as they had, but there was practical unanimity of sentiment in one point—that the American proposals were inadmissible, verging on the insulting and absolutely not to be considered. How much of this was bravado it is impossible to say, but there can be no doubt that at the bottom there was a feeling that commercial prosperity could be bought at too great a price. When March 17, 1866, came around it was signalized as something more than St. Patrick's Day; it was to be a "date long remembered in British American annals. Today the reciprocal trade which, under treaty stipulations, has subsisted between our neighbours and ourselves for the past eleven years, is at an end, and a new commercial policy becomes essential to our very existence."[22] It was also a day when mutterings of "an armed invasion *from*, though not *by* the United States" were heard on every hand.

Throughout the remainder of the year 1866, until the time approached for the meeting of Congress, echoes of reciprocity were occasionally heard, but discussion of Canadian-American relations had to do mostly with Fenian threats, the working of the fishing license system, and reminiscent references to the war. Diplomatically the issue was at stalemate. As early as February 21 Seward had definitely informed the British Minister[23] that proposals for the temporary extension of the treaty provisions were declined: the matter had been referred to the appropriate committees of Congress. Bruce, however, was not without hope that a more tolerant attitude might come to prevail. As he wrote the Lieutenant-Governor of Nova Scotia,[24] if collision over Fenians and fisheries could be avoided, "even in this Congress something may be done in favour of commercial intercourse with the provinces"; David A. Wells of the Revenue Commission was for it; "the Secretary of the Treasury and the Gov^t generally wish it"; and even Morrill saw the necessity of an arrangement more strongly than he did when the delegation was in Washington. To the Foreign Office he sent a dispatch[25] enclosing a copy of Raymond's resolution and the debate on the fisheries and an article from the New York *Times*

22. Montreal *Gazette,* Mar. 17, 1866.
23. Bruce to Monck, Feb. 21, 1866; G 237 (P.A.C.).
24. Bruce to Sir Fenwick Williams, Apr. 8, 1866; FO 5:1064 (P.R.O.).
25. Bruce to Clarendon, Apr. 12, 1866; FO 5:1064 (P.R.O.). For Raymond's resolution, see above, p. 264.

wherein confederation in Canada was advocated as "tending to facilitate the settlement of relations between the United States and the British Provinces, by the constitution of a united legislature which would secure uniformity of tariff," and obviate risk of endangering a good understanding on outstanding questions. In June he had a conversation with Morrill about a reduction of the duty on fish and found that gentleman "contented with a ten per cent duty which he considers necessary to compensate for the heavy taxes imposed on articles used by the U. S. fishermen"; the fifty cent per ton license fee he thought was not excessive, although he trusted that each province would not insist upon its own license.[26] A little later he forwarded a copy of James W. Taylor's report to London.[27] Taylor, he said, had talked with him frequently, urging confederation as "a necessary preliminary to a renewal of the Reciprocity." Taylor looked "upon the question of British N. America, mainly as it affect[ed] the interests of Minnesota, and the farthest N. Western States"; resources for Provincial development were demanded far beyond their means and he proposed "a union with the States as the only means of executing" the necessary works. Bruce felt that Taylor was in error, for competition between railway and canal interests in the American Northeast and the Canadian route to the east created great jealousy, and the "same feeling" would be "created against a Pacific Railway through the North West." Taylor's observations, thought Bruce, were important, for they showed the "intimate connection that exists between the interests of the N. Western States & the water communications through the British Provinces." The West felt the hampering restrictions of limited means of transportation and so swelled "the cry for the annexation of Canada by fair means or foul." If the "material wants of the West" united with "the prejudices and monopolists of New England & the Central States, we shall have against us in this question the influences which would otherwise become the best guarantees for peace & harmony on the Canadian frontier."[28]

26. Bruce to Monck, June 4, 1866; G 237 (P.A.C.).
27. Bruce to Clarendon, June 28, 1866; FO 115:453 (P.R.O.). See T. C. Blegen, "A Plan of Union . . . ," *Miss. Val. Hist. Rev.*, IV, 470. For Taylor's Report, see above, p. 192, n. 27.
28. This question of transportation occupied much of the attention of Congress in both sessions of the Thirty-ninth Congress. For the most part it cen-

The second session of the Thirty-ninth Congress had the subject of reciprocity before it in many indirect ways, although there was no specific proposition for the renewal of the treaty.[29] Two reports, as well as the Annual Report of the Secretary of the Treasury, afforded texts for discussion. The report of Israel D. Hatch[30] presented a consideration of the "revenue, trade and commerce with the British Provinces," while the Derby Report,[31] brought into the Senate on February 16, 1867, was an elaborate analysis of conditions in the British Provinces, based upon conferences with leading men and a personal tour over much of the region. A detailed discussion of the nature of the trade which had been promoted by the treaty was followed by a statement of the results of abrogation. Since March, American duties on articles formerly on the free list had been restored; the Maritime Provinces, where duties had been low and "satisfactory to us," now retaliated by advances,[32] while Canada, on the other hand, "in a more liberal and magnanimous spirit," had reduced duties on manufactures, raised them on spirits, proposed to discontinue its free ports,

tered on a proposition to construct a canal on the American side of Niagara Falls. *Cong. Globe,* 39th Cong., 1st Sess., Parts II and IV, *passim; ibid.,* 2d Sess., Part II.

29. Bruce made it a point to talk with most of the leading Senators and Representatives when they assembled in Washington. He found that abrogation had worked badly for woolen manufacturers, the lumber trade, the gas companies of northern cities which wanted Nova Scotia coal, and railroad and shipping interests of New England, but these were "balanced by a powerful protectionist party in the North Western and central States, and I fear that the latter are too strong to give much hope of carrying a Treaty through the Senate so long as the Southern States are unrepresented in Congress, particularly as political passions can be appealed to, to ensure the defeat of any measure to which Great Britain is a party." I. D. Andrews had a long conversation with Bruce, spoke of the discontent in New England over abrogation, and frankly offered to perform a service similar to what he had done in the Fifties, utilizing something of the same methods. Bruce to Stanley, Secret, Dec. 24, 1866; FO 5:1068 (P.R.O.).

30. Transmitted Feb. 6, 1867; *House Ex. Docs.,* No. 78, 39th Cong., 2d Sess.

31. *Senate Ex. Docs.,* No. 30, 39th Cong., 2d Sess.

32. New Brunswick on tobacco, horses, oxen, sheep, swine, beef, and salt meats; Nova Scotia on flour, horses, cattle, swine, beef and pork, hams, tongue, bacon, and lard; Prince Edward Island on flour and meats; Newfoundland on oat and corn meal, flour, pork, beef, and lard.

and, said Derby, was really ready to make a new treaty "on equitable terms." In general, the Provinces were making efforts to rival the United States in foreign trade, especially in the West Indies and South America. Deprecating rivalry between the Provinces and the United States, Derby said of course the "most effective mode to remove all difficulties would be the union of all parts of our continent in one harmonious whole," something which required the sanction of England. Most Americans would like to see the "continent occupied by one republic . . . [rather] than to have it hemmed in by a French empire at one end and a monarchy or vice-royalty of the British Empire at the other." Under existing conditions France gracefully withdraws, but England

bids us be silent while she consolidates the provinces into a military power; expends millions on military roads; plants, or proposes to plant, heavy cannon at Halifax and Victoria; or at Esquimault Harbor, adjacent to Victoria; establishes free ports to undermine our revenue, and sends out cruisers to watch our coasts and fisheries. . . . Can she wonder that we, under the circumstances seek alliances with France and Russia, and forget the home of our fathers?

Failing an amicable union between the United States and the British Provinces, the next best thing would be a Zollverein after the plan presented by the Secretary of the Treasury. If such a tariff union could not be secured by negotiation, there was reason to believe a treaty, eliminating the defects of the former agreement, could be obtained. Derby suggested the application of a "new principle" for such a treaty: instead of putting everything together he would make three classifications of commodities, each to be handled differently. Schedule A would contain a few staple articles taxed in both countries to a limited extent; Schedule B would comprise most of the products of the sea, mine, field, and forest—articles largely entering the United States from the Provinces—and these would be on the free list; while Schedule C would comprise articles entering Canada free from the United States, such as fruits, butter, cars, carriages, clocks, flour, engines, furniture, corn and meal, petroleum, instruments, and various other manufactured articles.

Neither the Hatch nor the Derby Report came up for specific discussion in the short session of Congress, but, incidentally, trade with the Provinces received considerable attention in discussion of a general tariff measure. Proposals to lower duties upon salt and lumber[33] inferentially brought in Canadian reciprocity. Proposals both to raise and to lower duties upon coal[34] provoked discussion of Nova Scotia competition. In the Senate, G. F. Edmunds of Vermont, answering G. H. Williams of Oregon, who had pleaded for no increase in duties upon flour, meal, middlings, etc., contended that no legislation beneficial to foreigners and harmful to Americans should be indulged in; while T. O. Howe of Wisconsin chimed in to say that if the Senate refused to raise the duty on flour after raising that on wheat it would merely mean that the farmer would export the grain in the shape of flour: "It will cheat our bill, and still the Canadians will have all the benefit."[35] B. F. Wade of Ohio put in an eloquent plea to protect from Nova Scotia competition the makers of grindstones in Michigan, Pennsylvania, Ohio, and other states. Without multiplying illustrations it is sufficient to state that the dominant majority in Congress showed no disposition to entertain either general reciprocal concessions or specific reductions on items which were prominent in Canadian-American trade relations.

For over two years reciprocity as an issue remained outwardly rather quiescent. Incidental and sporadic references showed that the idea was not dead, especially since it was connected with the cognate questions of transportation facilities, the fisheries, shipments in bond, and the like. General Butler's visit to Prince Edward Island in the summer of 1868 stirred a momentary flurry by calling attention to both annexationist agitation and certain undoubted inconveniences created by loss of privileges under the treaty.[36] Nova Scotia coal operators had felt the pinch of restricted markets in New England, and they complained the more bitterly since Pennsylvania coal continued to enter Canada free of duty.[37] Nevertheless, few of the ills

33. *Cong. Globe,* 39th Cong., 2d Sess., pp. 680–682.

34. *Ibid.,* pp. 731 ff., 765, 832 ff.

35. *Ibid.,* p. 871. The proposed amendment raising the duty from 15 per cent to 30 per cent was carried by a vote of 29 to 8.

36. Lt.-Gov. George Dundas to Buckingham and Chandos, Aug. 27, 1868, with Report of the Executive Council of Prince Edward Island of Aug. 20; FO 115:474 (P.R.O.). Report on the Butler mission of Aug. 29; FO 115:485 (P.R.O.). Numerous newspaper references.

37. Stanley to Thornton, Apr. 29, 1868; FO 115:473 (P.R.O.).

prophesied for Provincials with abrogation of reciprocity had been experienced. In general, trade dropped off very little, and in some cases increased, a factor which was pleasing to those in charge of administering American finances, for it meant that goods hitherto free were paying duties and helping a little to ease the burdens on the Treasury.[38] Agitation in the American Northwest for better communication facilities led Bruce to believe that "if the Provinces, aided by Great Britain are unable to meet [the demand] when it becomes necessary, and show themselves incapable of providing greater facilities for the transit of produce from the Lake region through the St Lawrence to the Atlantic, the desire of the United States to drive their British rivals off this continent will be powerfully reinforced by the material interests of the North West which will be enlisted in favor of conquest or annexation." Every effort, therefore, should be made to organize and populate this region north of the border, for, with people pushing up from the States especially into the mining regions which were understood to extend across the boundary,

it is evidently of vital importance to the security and well-being of British North America, and to her political future, that this intermediate space, lying between the Canadas and Columbia should be at once secured, and that an authority emanating from the British Crown should be found in possession, empowered to grant titles to land, to administer justice, and to assert British proprietary rights.[39]

Interspersed among acrimonious debates on Reconstruction, Johnson's impeachment, and other matters arising from the Civil War there could not fail to be some references to the British Provinces and to reciprocity during the three sessions of the Fortieth Congress. They were, however, much the same old story, which showed that opponents of renewed reciprocal relations were still in the ascendant, intermingling their comments on Canada with expressions of their animosity against England. The few feeble voices lifted in behalf of friendlier commercial relations with the northern neighbor were lost

38. McCulloch's reply of Mar. 30, 1868, to House Resolution of Mar. 7; *House Ex. Docs.,* No. 240, 40th Cong., 2d Sess. Montreal *Gazette,* Mar. 22, 1867, Apr. 4, 1867. Hatch Report (second), Jan. 12, 1869; *House Ex. Docs.,* No. 36, 40th Cong., 3d Sess.

39. Bruce to Stanley, Jan. 12, 1867; FO 5:1104 (P.R.O.).

in the dominant chorus of opposition, or made the theme of annexationist arguments.[40]

But in the summer of 1868 there began to be a little evidence that perhaps a change might come in American opinion on reciprocity.[41] Macdonald feared that impeachment proceedings would prevent any action during that session of Congress; nevertheless he thought he saw signs of American opinion "steadily though slowly veering round to a return to our old condition of Commercial relations."[42] There was, however, a disposition to proceed cautiously and let the first move come from the United States; Canada should not appear too anxious.[43] This advice appeared sound, especially if the resolutions adopted by the legislature of Vermont were indicative of a general attitude in the United States. When the Fortieth Congress opened its third session in December of 1868 the Vermont legislature had ready for presentation two sets of resolutions; one urged their senators and representatives

40. It was on December 7, 1867, that Senator Ramsey brought in his resolutions containing a comprehensive program covering readjusted tariffs, fisheries, use of the boundary waters, common laws for patents, copyrights, and the like, and the proposition for the acquisition of the Hudson's Bay Company's land and British Columbia. *Cong. Globe,* 40th Cong., 2d Sess., p. 79; *Senate Misc. Docs.,* Nos. 4 and 22, 40th Cong., 2d Sess.

41. In April the Dominion Government had been approached by G. W. Brega, who had "managed to get a Resolution carried in the House of Representatives asking for a report on the Reciprocity question," and by D. A. Wells, who would like to be "employed as Canadian representative in Reciprocity matters." Macdonald thought nothing must be done before the impeachment was over and in any case it must not be known that Wells or anyone else had any connection with the Canadian Government. Macdonald to Galt, Apr. 13, 1868; Macdonald Papers: Letterbooks, XI, 656–657 (P.A.C.). *House Ex. Docs.,* No. 295, 40th Cong., 2d Sess., shows Brega's interest, this time in the fishery aspect of the situation. *House Ex. Docs.,* No. 240, 40th Cong., 2d Sess., contains a supplementary report of Brega's dated May 14, 1868. Thornton said Brega had little influence with members of Congress; to Monck, Confidential, June 11, 1868; G 239 (P.A.C.).

42. Macdonald to Swinyard, June 4, 1868; Macdonald Papers: Letterbooks, XI, 833.

43. This was the advice of Lord Monck both to Macdonald (Oct. 5, 1868; Macdonald Papers: Governor General Correspondence, II, 376 [P.A.C.]) and to the Colonial Office, whence had come an inquiry whether the time was ripe to instruct the British Minister to sound the American Government (Oct. 10, 1868; FO 115:474 [P.R.O.]).

to exert their best efforts to prevent the consummation of any reciprocity treaty with Canada and to insist that the subject of trade and commercial intercourse was not a "proper matter of treaty stipulation." The other suggested that free navigation of Canadian waters, and free transit of American merchandise might be exchanged for similar privileges in the United States, with the proposition that, if New York would consent, there should be constructed a canal from Lake Champlain to the River St. Lawrence which Canadians could use on the same terms as Americans.[44] Presentation of these resolutions afforded Senator Morrill an opportunity to launch one of his customary invectives against reciprocity and against Canada.[45] The Americans of the North "lifted off their feet by the will-o'-the-wisp of annexation" and the South by sectional advantage had accepted the Reciprocity Treaty, but "the arguments used to that end, without regard to the merits or demerits of the question itself, have been buried too deeply by our eleven years of cruel experience under the treaty ever to be resuscitated." Americans had expected an era of good feeling but Canadians assumed their true shape during the Rebellion. The Convention of 1818 had been a weak surrender; by "any rule of facts or principle in the partition of territory and rights" the Americans were entitled to *all* the fisheries and should have insisted on excluding Great Britain entirely. After waving the bloody shirt of the Rebellion, Morrill proceeded to flaunt the banner of American nationalism. For the present the United States had enough undeveloped territory to occupy its man-power and its capital, and if the neighboring provinces were so shortsighted as to cling to an outmoded form of government and lag behind for half a century, the United States could afford to wait, but

when these provinces seek that aggrandizement which naturally flows over all the parts of a free, independent, and prosperous nation by union of interests and honors, by a fraternal welding together of all their material forces and political aspirations, by an unreserved and uncalculating

44. *House Ex. Docs.,* Nos. 15 and 18, 40th Cong., 3d Sess. Thornton sent copies to the Foreign Office with merely a comment that Vermont objected to reciprocity. Jan. 11, 1869; FO 5:1158 (P.R.O.).

45. Jan. 14, 1869; *Cong. Globe,* 40th Cong., 3d Sess., p. 349. Justin S. Morrill entered the United States Senate on March 4, 1867, when the Fortieth Congress first convened.

assumption of privileges and duties, it will be time enough to consider what measures will best advance their general welfare. Until then it is a study exclusively their own about which it will be unbecoming for us to waste diplomacy.

A second Hatch Report[46] brought before Congress details of trade, transportation, and other aspects of Canadian relations; it emphasized the "anomalous spectacle" of two nations with customhouses facing each other, of expenses to the American Government of collecting taxes exceeding the sum taken in, while Canada collected "large revenues from taxing American commodities," the result of ever-mounting duties across the border, although the United States was her most profitable market.[47] Had the Canadians, said Hatch, been willing to accept the "liberal privileges extended to them in the fraternal spirit they were granted, yielding to the destiny unalterably fixed by geography, climate, and the boundaries established under the Ashburton treaty, and not vainly attempted to exercise a commercial dominion . . . over our western trade, and its transit lines to the Atlantic" they would still be enjoying commercial freedom and access to American markets. In short, the old treaty had been a mistake. Butler's report on his Prince Edward Island mission,[48] Spaulding's resolution denouncing reciprocity treaties in general as contrary to public policy,[49] Garfield's report for the Committee on Military Affairs recommending defense of the Northeastern frontier,[50] renewed agitation for an American canal around Niagara Falls,[51] and other incidents not only made it appear that no vital change had taken place in the temper of Congress, but drowned any puny attempts to secure a favorable hearing of those who still believed there was something in reciprocity.[52]

46. Jan. 12, 1869; *House Ex. Docs.*, No. 36, 40th Cong., 3d Sess.

47. He rather contradicted himself later in the report when he said that during reciprocity an average of $75,000 in duties was collected annually on Canadian goods, while in the two years after the abrogation of reciprocity about $14,000,000 had been received. He stated that duties received on Canadian imports for the fiscal years 1867 and 1868 had been $5,144,166.25 and $5,400,000 respectively.

48. *Cong. Globe,* 40th Cong., 3d Sess., p. 1809.

49. *Ibid.,* p. 937.   50. *Ibid.,* p. 1446.

51. *Ibid.,* pp. 367 ff.; App., p. 54.

52. Such as the petition by citizens of Massachusetts asking renewal of reci-

Caution, indeed, seemed the better course for Canadians to follow, as Macdonald stated to an American correspondent[53] when he wrote:

We are quite ready to enter into a renewed Reciprocity Treaty, but we are satisfied that the initiative must come from your Government. Until Congress thinks the American interests will be advanced by such a Treaty, there is no use in our moving in it. I am satisfied that a fair interchange, on equal terms, of the products of the two countries will be greatly to the advantage of both.

In spite of all unpropitious indications, however, there was a stirring which gathered momentum, especially after the Johnson administration gave place to Grant's. Even in Congress there had been one episode which seemed to open a small door to hope. The Committee on Ways and Means brought before the House a resolution which, while denying to the Executive the right to make a treaty involving the alteration of import duties without the assent of Congress, nevertheless recommended that the President inaugurate negotiations with England regarding commercial intercourse as well as with respect to the fisheries and the navigation of the St. Lawrence. "The language of the proposed resolution," observed the British Minister,[54]

is obscure and even contradictory; but General Schenck, the chairman of the Committee, has informed me that it is the decided opinion of the Committee, and as he believes of the House, that no treaty engagements should be entered into as to a Reciprocal reduction of duties, between the United States and Canada, but that such measures should be adopted by the Legislature of each country, as it may suit its own convenience.
    It is believed by a great many American Statesmen that had it not been for the reciprocity Treaty which lately existed, their favourite dream of the annexation of Canada might before now have become a reality. . . .

When Schenck brought up the resolution later it was adopted with no opposition,[55] a fact which appeared to belie the stand Schenck had assumed and to indicate that more people than had been suspected

procity, introduced by Wilson in the special session in March. *Cong. Globe,* 41st Cong., 1st Sess., p. 47.
    53. To Gen. W. W. H. Davis, Jan. 15, 1869; Macdonald Papers: Letterbooks, XII, 429 (P.A.C.).
    54. Thornton to Clarendon, Feb. 22, 1869; FO 115:490 (P.R.O.).
    55. *Cong. Globe,* 40th Cong., 3d Sess., p. 1869.

approved the idea of reciprocity, even by treaty. Thornton, however, was going to play a waiting game and let the new Secretary of State introduce the subject; if he did this, then Thornton would write immediately to Sir John Young requesting him to send a Canadian representative to Washington. But, pessimistically added the Minister, he did not place entire confidence in the information he had received about the disposition of the Administration, nor did he have any positive expectation that the President would direct the Secretary to act in the spirit of the resolution.[56] The pessimism was well founded, for weeks passed and no intimation came from Fish to signify his desire to open the subject.

Meantime, signs both encouraging and discouraging were observed. Sumner's intransigent speech on the Johnson-Clarendon Convention was hardly to be taken as a promising symptom of a changing attitude.[57] On the other hand, there were not wanting indications that Sumner failed to represent universal feeling in the United States on British and Canadian questions. The Michigan legislature, stimulated by difficulties in moving western crops, inquired by resolution why negotiations were not inaugurated looking to opening to Americans the navigation of the Canadian waterways.[58] The Board of Trade of Boston adopted a resolution calling attention to the Congressional resolution and "urging the importance of liberalizing trade with the British Provinces."[59] The New York Chamber of Commerce[60] took a similar step. Across the ocean, in France the Foreign Minister took occasion to warn General Dix, the retiring American Envoy, and his successor, Elihu B. Washburne, that France would view as a *crime de lèse-civilisation* any development which was provocative of hostilities

56. Thornton to Clarendon, Mar. 22, 1869; FO 115:490 (P.R.O.).

57. Benjamin Moran's Journal contains an interesting comment: "Mr. Wilkins, the Rebel stockholder, came up to know if the Stock Exchange rumor was true that the U. S. as an aid to enforce the Alabama Claims had decided to achieve the independence of Canada, and also if General Grant were ill-disposed to England. It seems the Stock Exchange is much excited by such a rumor." (Apr. 4, 1869, Vol. XXII [L.C.].)

58. *Cong. Globe,* 41st Cong., 1st Sess., p. 439. Thornton to Clarendon, May 5, 1869; FO 5:1160 (P.R.O.).

59. Thornton to Clarendon, May 31, 1869; FO 115:491 (P.R.O.).

60. Macdonald to Gwinn, June 5, 1869; Macdonald Papers: Letterbooks, XII, 886 (P.A.C.). Thornton to Clarendon, June 7; FO 115:491 (P.R.O.).

between the United States and Great Britain: "There was hardly any event which could give more pain to the Emperor and his Gov^t."[61]

Finally, in June, Fish requested the British Minister to call upon him to consult as to a time agreeable for considering "the question of commercial intercourse between this country & Canada, and the Fisheries &c. &c."[62] On the thirteenth Thornton saw Fish, who informed him that

> although he considered it difficult, in consequence of the Resolutions of the House of Representatives . . . to conclude a Convention which would be acceptable to Congress, he was willing, in consequence of the representations made to him by his countrymen interested in the trade with Canada, to use his best efforts to arrive at so desirable an end, and, if any arrangement could be come to between the two countries, to use all his influence to bring about its acceptance by Congress.

Informing the Secretary that he would not take the "responsibility of discussing the subject with him" without the assistance of a Canadian representative, Thornton said he would ask the Governor-General to have someone sent, and Fish agreed to the proposition.[63] Only one gentleman, Thornton told Young, ought to be sent then, for he had "observed in recent conversations with the Secretary of State that there is not much inclination on his part to agree to reciprocal free trade betw: the two countries, and as the negotiation" might be futile it would be better not to send a delegation.[64] It was the Honorable John Rose who was selected for the mission; since he was going to Washington primarily on affairs connected with the Hudson's Bay Company[65] he could meet in an unofficial capacity the Secretary of State and others to sound out the prospects of a treaty.

61. Lyons to Clarendon, June 3, 10, 1869; FO 115:487 (P.R.O.). Lord Lyons was then Ambassador to France.

62. Thornton to Clarendon, June 14, 1869; FO 115:491 (P.R.O.).

63. A few days earlier Clarendon had had a long conversation with Motley, just arrived in London, in which on both sides there was expressed a desire to adjust amicably the differences between the two governments. No special mention was made of Canadian issues but those were obviously included among the "existing differences." Clarendon to Thornton, June 10, 1869; FO 115:487 (P.R.O.).

64. Thornton to Clarendon, June 28, 1869; FO 115:491 (P.R.O.).

65. Macdonald to J. M. Machar, July 12, 1869; Macdonald Papers: Letterbooks, XII, 977 (P.A.C.).

Rose reached Washington on July 8 and had an interview with Fish the same day, not a very satisfactory one, for Fish "was more than usually silent and difficult to draw out upon the subject we had in hand, and [Thornton] was obliged to remind him that it was he who had requested Sir J. Young to send a gentleman from Canada."[66] Fish could not be persuaded that the resolution of the House of Representatives which "authorized the Executive to negotiate for Commercial intercourse with Canada, empowered it to come to an arrangement for a reduction or abolition of certain import duties." George S. Boutwell, Secretary of the Treasury, who dined with Fish, along with Rose, Thornton, and others, was of the same opinion as his host. But, undeterred by this cool reception, Rose and Thornton called upon Fish on the tenth, when, after an informal discussion, it was agreed to meet again the next day. At that time the Secretary, regretting that Congress was not in session so that he could confer with its members, asked if the Britishers had thought of any method of proceeding which might hold out a prospect of success. Rose thereupon produced "a paper somewhat in the nature of a protocol" which contained a "general indication of the articles to be embraced in the Schedule which it was proposed each country should exchange freely, embracing those enumerated in the former Treaty. Mr. Fish replied that he thought that under existing circumstances it would probably be necessary to have two schedules—one a free list, and the other embracing articles which might have to be subject to certain rates of duty." After some discussion the proposition was reduced to writing under six heads. The first stated that, if satisfactory trade relations could be established between the United States and the Dominion and other British Provinces, to be embodied in a treaty, then Americans should enjoy the same rights in the fisheries as under the Reciprocity Treaty, with necessary extensions demanded "under the altered circumstances of

66. The account of these informal negotiations is contained in a dispatch from Thornton to Clarendon and in three memoranda drawn up by Rose. These documents are printed in A. H. U. Colquhoun, "The Reciprocity Negotiations with the United States in 1869," *Can. Hist. Rev.,* VIII, 233–242. Colquhoun points out that there was long a controversy over the question whether any definite proposals were made by the Macdonald Government in 1869, and especially whether it was proposed that there should be reciprocal free trade in certain manufactured products.

the present time." Secondly, under the same proviso, Canadian inland waters would be opened to Americans if American waterways were similarly opened to British subjects of the Dominion and Provinces, and Canada would take steps to enlarge and deepen the canals "on proper assurance of the permanency of the reciprocal commercial intercourse . . . , and that the Trade of the Western States will be left free to seek its natural channels, and not be diverted elsewhere by legislation." Thirdly, under like proviso, Canada would be prepared to consider: (1) laws regulating the coasting trade, with a view to opening it to citizens of both countries "when corresponding concessions [were] made by the U.S."; (2) patent and copyright laws, with a view to "placing them on a liberal and reciprocal footing"; (3) making over present extradition treaties to include all but political crimes. Fourthly, transit trade should be rendered mutually free and unrestricted. In the fifth place, both countries would agree to allow for a term of years reciprocal exchange "as nearly free of duty as possible" of "natural productions of the Sea, Forest, Mines, and of Agriculture" and animals and their products; articles enumerated in the Treaty of 1854 were to be the basis of the arrangement, but "the list may be added to by both parties, and may embrace certain articles of manufacture." The duty, if any, should be levied after taking into consideration internal taxation in the United States. Finally, if Canada accepted these arrangements, she would adjust her excise on spirits, beer, tobacco, and cognate articles "on the best Revenue standard which after due and mature consideration . . . may be mutually agreed upon," and would use every legitimate device to secure cooperation between Canadian and American revenue officers to prevent smuggling.

Mr. Thornton explained to Secretary Fish that any arrangement would have to have the sanction of the British Government and perhaps action by Parliament. This apparently was as far as things could go at the moment, and Rose returned to Canada. When Fish had received from Thornton a copy of the "paper somewhat in the nature of a protocol," he requested that it be "considered as an informal and confidential communication," and at the same time said that

he did not expect to be able to do much in the matter until Congress [should] meet in Dec^r: next, because he wished to consult upon the sub-

ject with the Senate Committee for F.A. and the House Committee of
Ways & Means, the members of wh. [were] now spread over the world,
M^r: Schenck, the Chairman of the latter, being at this moment in Europe
& perhaps in England.

Thornton and Rose had not expected to make much more progress
than this and considered "M^r: Fish's tone upon the subject as in general satisfactory."

In London there immediately rose the question whether the mention
of manufactures meant that it was proposed to make with the United
States an agreement discriminating against British products. Both
the British Minister in Washington and the Dominion Government
were definitely told that no such scheme would be approved; any reductions in duties must be on the most-favored-nation basis and apply
not only to British goods but also to all foreign manufactures. This,
came the answer from Washington and Ottawa, was exactly the intention of the proposition: the only exception would be articles imported
wholly or almost exclusively from the United States, where there was
no question of competition with the Mother Country.[67]

It was obvious that there was nothing to be done to further negotiations until the American Secretary gave the signal, and that would
not be earlier than November, when Congressmen began to straggle
into the capital for the long session. The signal was slow in coming, at
least in the opinion of interested persons in Canada. Macdonald suggested to Sir John Young that Thornton be asked to make an appointment for some Canadian delegates, and, since Fish had intimated to
Rose that sometime in November would be convenient, it would be
well to get the conversations started before Congress met in December.
But Thornton put a damper on any premature move by the Cana-

67. Clarendon to Thornton, July 17, 1869, FO 115:487; Thornton to Clarendon, July 31, 1869, FO 115:491; Otway to Thornton, Aug. 27, 1869, FO
115:488 (P.R.O.). Young to Macdonald, Sept.[?] 7, 1869; Macdonald
Papers: Governor General Correspondence, III, 176–183 (P.A.C.). Nevins,
Hamilton Fish, pp. 212–214. Rose's suggestion that, as he was about to go to
London, he might sound the British Government on the possibility of reopening
discussions on the *Alabama* Claims, was approved by Fish and there was even
some talk of a special British envoy's coming to Washington in the winter.
There should, however, be made a distinction between the claims and an ordi-
nary commercial understanding, perhaps separate treaties.

dians; let the Americans speak first.[68] The first American official statement, however, was the paragraph contained in Grant's Annual
Message:

The question of renewing a treaty for reciprocal trade between the United
States and the British Provinces on this continent has not been favorably
considered by the Administration. The advantages of such a treaty would
be wholly in favor of the British producer. Except, possibly, a few engaged in trade between the two sections no citizen of the United States
would be benefited by reciprocity. Our internal taxation would prove a
protection to the British producer almost equal to the protection which
our manufacturers now receive from the tariff. Some arrangement, however, for the regulation of commercial intercourse between the United
States and the Dominion of Canada may be desirable.[69]

"I am sorry, though not surprised," commented Thornton,[70]

to see the declaration that the United States Government are opposed to
renewing reciprocal trade with Canada. I presume therefore that the commercial intercourse to which Mr Fish formerly, and the President now,
have alluded, merely signifies the free navigation of the St. Lawrence for
the American Flag and the right of Americans to fish in Canadian waters,
without any return for such important advantages.

Fish, two days later, recorded in his Diary:[71]

68. Macdonald to Young, Nov. 18, 1869; Macdonald Papers: Letterbooks,
XIII, 467–468 (P.A.C.). Young to Macdonald, Nov. 18, 1869; Macdonald
Papers: Governor General Correspondence, III, 214 (P.A.C.). To an Ameri-
can correspondent Macdonald wrote (Nov. 23; Letterbooks, XIII, 526), "I
believe that it is the intention of your Secretary of State to invite the British
Ambassador shortly to enter upon the discussion of the whole subject [of reci-
procity]; in which case probably Sir Francis Hincks, our present Finance
Minister and myself, will take a run to Washington to watch events. . . ."

69. This was sandwiched in between a statement about the *Alabama* and the
recently rejected Johnson-Clarendon Convention, and an announcement that
the commission for adjusting the claims of the Hudson's Bay Company and
Puget Sound Agricultural Company had settled upon an award of $650,000
as compensation for all the rights of those companies in the territory awarded
to the United States in the Treaty of 1846. Richardson, *Messages and Papers*,
VII, 34–35.

70. To Clarendon, Dec. 7, 1869; FO 5:1163 (P.R.O.).

71. Nevins, *op. cit.*, p. 298.

Mr. Thornton has nothing particular to say but wishes to express his satisfaction with what the President has said in his message. "Of course he has his views, which are not entirely ours, but the manner and tone in which they are presented is entirely satisfactory, and in the spirit in which alone we can hope to reach a solution. . . ."

The Secretary, who had by this time become pretty well acquainted with the British Minister, probably knew that Thornton made the remark with his tongue in his cheek and was aware that Thornton knew he knew it.[72]

Privately, official Canadians were more outspoken. "Grant's remarks on Reciprocity are quite unintelligible," wrote Macdonald.[73]

He evidently thinks that Reciprocity means Trade free of all duties, and not Trade on equal terms. The truth of the matter is that the first part of the passage was put in to please Kelly of Pennsylvania, the Coal owners & the Maine Lumbermen; while the latter part was inserted to please Sumner, Butler and the Bostonians generally. Before Parliament meets we shall know finally and decidedly what course Congress will take on the matter, and then we will be guided altogether by the consideration of what is most for the interest of Canada. I quite agree with you that we have been playing the waiting game long enough. I may state to you, entre nous, that Mr. Fish has expressed his intention, since the message, of inviting Mr. Thornton to enter upon the subject immediately after Christmas. . . .

Wishful thinking must have colored the Canadian Premier's statement, for a few days later Fish confided to his Diary that Thornton had called upon him and asked "if there be any idea of a negotiation with Canada." Fish had replied that he could not see much: an exchange of natural products free from duty appeared wholly impracticable, but there was a desire that some arrangement would continue to promote free interchange of commodities. "The difficulty is in concentrating different views and interests."[74]

72. On December 8 the Senate passed a resolution asking for information relative to negotiations on the subject of trade and commerce with the Dominion, to which Fish had replied that there were no negotiations, and the conversations on the matter were too informal to be made the subject of an official report. *Senate Ex. Docs.,* No. 19, 41st Cong., 2d Sess.

73. To T. N. Gibbs, Dec. 11, 1869; Macdonald Papers: Letterbooks, XIII, 709–710 (P.A.C.).

74. Nevins, *op. cit.,* p. 298.

The strongest intimation that something might take place was when, on December 21, Fish was visited by a delegation of Western Congressmen,[75] who inquired about the condition of negotiations, and were told what had happened the previous summer: how through Caleb Cushing it had been suggested that a Canadian delegation come to Washington; how Rose had come on other business and incidentally talked about reciprocity and had submitted a proposition; and how Fish had declined to take any steps without having first consulted with at least members of the Committee on Ways and Means. Fish went on to say that he understood that recent elections in New Brunswick had returned a majority of "21 to 28 opposed to the Confederation," that an annexationist movement was gaining force. When asked what the Administration proposed to do, Fish replied "that while we wish not to retard the advancing feeling in favor of annexation, the Administration desires to be guided in arranging the commercial relations by the wishes of Congress." This Western impetus did not die with this interview, for, in February, Thornton was informed[76] by the Secretary that some Western Congressmen "whose constituents are interested in obtaining an additional outlet for the agricultural produce of those regions so as to defeat the combination which is now formed against their interests by those who are able to control the present means of communication between the Western States and the Sea," had a proposition they wished to have submitted to the Canadian Government. Would the Dominion be willing to enter a negotiation on some such basis as this: free navigation of the Welland Canal and the St. Lawrence, with some improvements thereon, and opening of the fisheries to Americans in return for a "very considerable" reduction of duties upon lumber, fish, salt, and coal, possibly an entire removal of duties upon all but coal? It is almost unnecessary to state that this proposal met with no cordial response in Canada. A memorandum of a Committee of the Council concluded that Mr. Fish had not "made any proposition on the part of the American Government. Had he done so, the Committee would have been prepared to give it prompt

75. *Ibid.*, p. 299. The men were James A. Garfield, Ebon C. Ingersoll, Job E. Stevenson, J. V. Smith, William Lawrence, James J. Winans, and Donn Piatt.

76. Thornton to Young, Private and Confidential, Feb. 10, 1870; G '69–'71 (P.A.C.).

and respectful consideration."[77] Shortly after, in a confidential Minute of the Privy Council,[78] a counter-proposition was put forward,
accompanied by a statement that, in view of repeated rejection by the
United States of Canadian overtures, there was increasing pressure in
the Dominion for adoption of a retaliatory policy; the Government
would, therefore, be obliged to announce its course in the Parliament
then sitting. Out of courtesy to Mr. Fish, however, they would propose two schedules, one of articles free of duties and one on which
moderate duties might be levied; if the United States would adopt
these, then Canada was prepared to "concede the free navigation of
the St. Lawrence and the use of her canals" and maintain the latter in
"a state of the greatest efficiency."[79]

By the end of March, 1870, it was seen that this latest attempt to
secure renewal of reciprocity had failed. On several occasions Thornton recorded his impressions of Fish's sympathy and expressed his

77. Thornton to Clarendon, Feb. 28, 1870; FO 115:506 (P.R.O.). A little
earlier a Minute of the Council had passed some rather severe strictures upon
Thornton, being of the opinion that he had been negligent of Canadian interests. The Governor-General refused to sign the Minute until the references to
the British Minister were deleted. Young to Macdonald, Jan. 20, 1870; Macdonald Papers: Governor General Correspondence, III, 244–251 (P.A.C.).

78. Mar. 9, 1870; G '69–'71 (P.A.C.).

79. On March 28 Thornton wrote Clarendon (FO 115:506 [P.R.O.]) he
had seen Fish on the twenty-fourth to ask if he had reached any conclusion on
the counter-proposal of the Canadians relative to navigation of the St. Lawrence and canals and reduction of certain duties, and Fish replied that "he had
communicated with most of the Western Members who had originally asked
him to make inquiries upon the subject, as well as with other persons interested
in the matter, and that they had expressed the strongest opinion that it would
be impossible in the first place to obtain the assent of Congress to a reduction
of duties on so extensive a scale. . . . And that further no arrangement could
be entertained unless the freedom of the fisheries in Canadian waters for citizens of the U. S. sh[d]: form a part of it. . . ." Commenting on the proposition
of the Westerners, Macdonald (to Brega, Apr. 4, 1870, Macdonald Papers:
Letterbooks, XIV, 111–112 [P.A.C.]) said: ". . . Canada will not entertain
for a moment the proposition to give the freedom of the St. Lawrence and the
right of fishing in our waters to Americans for the sake of a reduction or abolition of the import duties on coal, lumber and salt." On May 23 Lawrence of
Ohio introduced a bill framed on the lines of the proposition. *Cong. Globe,* 41st
Cong., 2d Sess., App., p. 367. Thornton to Clarendon, May 30; FO 115:507
(P.R.O.).

belief that were it not for the implacable attitude of Congress the Administration would be willing to go ahead with some sort of negotiation. Fish "mildly favored reciprocity,"[80] but Grant was either indifferent, probably through ignorance, or hostile. The attitude of Congress was fairly well indicated in a vote on a resolution introduced in the House by Peters of Maine expressing assent to Grant's statement on reciprocity in his Message; on the vote to lay the resolution on the table there were 129 against and 42 in favor. As in the previous Congresses, alignment was to some extent sectional: New England wanted cheap Nova Scotia coal, while Pennsylvania, Maryland, and West Virginia opposed reduction of duties thereon; Maine, Wisconsin, and Michigan were inalterably set against reducing duties on lumber, while those who bought this commodity were for lowered rates or their entire abolition; New England fishermen yearned for free salt, and salt producers of New York and Michigan clamored for greater protection; the grain-producing states sought cheap use of the waterways to the Atlantic to protect themselves from the extortions of the railroads, but they were indifferent to Canadian demands for some compensatory concessions. In short, the whole affair ended in a deadlock by the time Congress brought its protracted session to an end, and shot through all was the thread of persistent annexation agitation, intertwined with demands for settlement of the *Alabama* Claims, more or less sympathy for the Fenians in their expiring efforts, while Canada's putting the screws on American fishermen in the season of 1870 produced howls of anguish and consternation.

All this had been watched closely in Canada. The Dominion Parliament convened in February, late enough in the congressional session to have become convinced that whatever their hopes, there was no chance then of securing a renewal of reciprocity. American relations tinged almost every question that came up for discussion: the fisheries; the late unfortunate experiences at Red River; British Columbia; transportation; and, above all, commercial intercourse. This came up in many ways, but perhaps the most fervent discussion arose over L. S. Huntington's resolutions on a customs union.[81] Summarized, they demanded a continental system of commercial intercourse "bringing un-

---

80. According to his biographer, Nevins, *op. cit.*, p. 213.
81. Mar. 16, 1870; *Dom. Parl. Deb.*, I, 449.

der one general customs union with this Dominion the countries chiefly interested in its trade," which would place in a position of commercial equality all the countries which were parties to it; it would allow Canada to have direct communication with the states willing to enter the arrangement without interposition of England, although in all cases where the proposed commercial arrangements were made, the approval of Her Majesty would be necessary to the treaties. In support of his resolutions Huntington maintained that the policy of Canada and of the Dominion Government since 1864 had been utterly inefficient and public confidence had been lost. One of the things expected from confederation had been expansion of trade, but the Government's course in its first tariff had prevented this, as in the case of the report of a commission on trade with Brazil. As to the United States, the Government had made no proper effort to get reciprocity; postponing abrogation of the Treaty of 1854 for one year had been the result of a promise to enlarge the canals, thereby gaining the support of the Western States, but the promise had not been carried out. With canals, fisheries, and the St. Lawrence, Canada had bargaining factors which had not been effectively used. It was well known that a large portion of the people of the United States desired free trade with Canada, as was shown by the recent vote in the House of Representatives, and this was no time to adopt the suicidal policy of retaliation, nor was it a time to be hampered by American resentment against Great Britain over the *Alabama* Claims—the "chief difficulty in securing new trade relations," as an American "in high official position" had told a friend of Huntington's. Canada should be placed in a position where she could make her own bargains "free from the embarrassment of British diplomacy."[82]

The resolutions and the speech precipitated a protracted debate, in which charges of disloyalty, of neglect of Canada's interests, of leaning toward annexation flew back and forth. Huntington was accused of being willing to let the Dominion become subservient to the Americans, who, as Cartier remarked,[83] individually were kindly neighbors, "but as a nation they were the most illiberal in the world

82. *Dom. Parl. Deb.*, I, 464. The speech, interspersed with questions and comments, is found in *ibid.*, pp. 449–466.

83. *Ibid.*, p. 487.

except the Chinese." Most of the heavy guns of the Government, including the Premier and Finance Minister, were brought to bear upon the proposition, which, however, received support equally able, notably from Galt, who introduced an amendment to the resolutions almost identical with the original except that it contained no reference to a Zollverein with the United States and concentrated upon the theme of Canadian independence in managing her commercial affairs.[84] There were, he declared, two courses before the Government: restriction and retaliation or developing trade with foreign countries on the basis of free trade as far as that was consistent with revenue purposes. Canada had two principal markets, Great Britain and the United States, the latter taking "our white wheat, our coarse grains, our sawn lumber, our cattle, horses, our minerals and a variety of minor produce." Now, since Americans were unwilling to renew reciprocity, the thing to do was to develop markets elsewhere and compete with them until they should be willing to change their attitude; retaliation would do no good, for it would arouse animosity and put off the day when the American Government would change their policy.

In the course of the debate frequent reference was made to the informal negotiations Rose had been engaged in, and futile attempts were made to smoke out the Government; just what had taken place would not be divulged, although spokesmen of the Government did not hesitate to say that very erroneous ideas were current. The specific policy Macdonald's Government intended to propose was foreshadowed in his speech in answer to Huntington and Galt,[85] a policy made clear when Hincks brought in the Government's budget with a pro-

84. *Ibid.,* pp. 558–575.

85. *Ibid.,* pp. 575–583. The response of the House as a whole was made clear by the vote on an amendment introduced by Macdonald, which read: "That this House, while desirous of obtaining for the Dominion the freest access to the markets of the world, and thus augmenting and extending its prosperity, is satisfied that this object can be best obtained by the concurrent action of the Imperial and Canadian Governments, and that any attempt to enter into a treaty with a foreign power, without the strong and direct support of the Mother Country, as the principal party, must fail, and that a Customs Union with the United States, now so heavily taxed, would be unfair to the Empire and injurious to the Dominion, and weaken the ties now so happily existing between them." This amendment was carried by a vote of 100 to 58. *Ibid.,* pp. 653–654.

posal to raise duties on a number of articles[86] and to place on the dutiable list certain commodities which were then free. He did this, as he said, because it was time that Canada should adopt a national policy and frame its fiscal laws in accordance with Canada's interests. It was not a protective tariff he proposed, said he, but one based on the revenue policy. Macdonald, defending the commercial and fiscal policy proposed by the Government, asserted that patience had ceased to be a virtue:[87]

Since 1865 to the present moment the Government had pursued the same course. They had waited from year to year, and from session to session, to see if there was any desire, on the part of the American Government or Legislature, to return to the old state of affairs. They found there was no prospect now of such a return, and that it had been settled that no Reciprocity Treaty should be made with Canada. Still the Canadian Government did not propose to adopt a retaliatory policy. Before these resolutions [on the budget] had been introduced honorable members had brought down petitions from all parts of the country, for the adoption of a national policy (no, no). He would ask—judging from the petitions presented to this House since the beginning of the session—if there had not been a general *pronunciamento* from all parts of Canada in favour of a national policy (hear). . . .

Since 1865 Canada had waited long and patiently, and had not resented, the policy that had been observed and carried out on the other side of the line—a policy by which Canadian interests had been snubbed wherever they could, and United States interests as against Canadian interests furthered as much as possible. Canada could not make one single remark, nor was there any attempt to carry out a revengeful or retaliatory policy. Canada took a straightforward course—a much better policy than was taken by the American Republic. We took our own ground; we were not to be seduced, either by the strong course taken against us, or by the threats that were held out against us; we took a higher course.

While the Dominion Government may have taken the ground that its policy was not one of retaliation, nevertheless it might easily become one, for there was more than a grain of truth in the strictures of

86. *Dom. Parl. Deb.*, I, 939–940. Flour, meal, wheat, coal, salt, hops, animals, fruits, roots, steam engines.
87. Apr. 26, 1870; *ibid.*, p. 1201.

the opposition. If it was not a preliminary step in the direction of a tariff war, it was at least a shift toward a national economic policy.[88] Reciprocity was still desirable but apparently unattainable under existing conditions. Perhaps a combination of pressure through the fisheries, the waterways, and now a little added weight through tariff changes might eventually effect some change of attitude.

88. It was at this time that William Alexander Foster and his friends were formulating their "Canada first" ideas, the first public pronouncement of which was in the Toronto *Globe* of July 17, 1871. See the article on Foster by J. B. Brebner in the *Encyclopaedia of the Social Sciences*, VI, 400.

CHAPTER XIV

BREAKING THE DEADLOCK

OUTWARDLY during the summer of 1870, especially after Congress had adjourned, public attention in the United States was but very little drawn to Canadian issues, nor was there any particular concern expressed even over the *Alabama* Claims. Those more intimately connected with the solution of all these problems, however, were none too easy over the situation; no one of the issues had been met. The recent abortive Fenian attempt had stirred again in Canada the anger and fear which had flared up in 1866, while talk of pardoning those arrested did nothing to calm such feelings. American fishermen were complaining bitterly that their season had been ruined and demanded that something be done. Annexation talk, while it had died down temporarily, seemed bound to break out again at any moment, perhaps in a more virulent form than before. Americans might be complacent over the trade situation, but the temper of the Dominion Parliament and the beginning of a national policy contained germs of future quarrels. The San Juan boundary controversy was hanging fire, but the uneasy status there could not be indefinitely maintained. There was plenty of dynamite which could be detonated by a very small cap, and while such unsolved problems as that of the *Alabama* Claims, tied up as they were with agitation for annexation, lay about, no one knew when the initial explosion would take place.

Potential dangers in the situation were, perhaps, more clearly realized by the American Secretary of State and the British Minister, both of whom were anxious to clear the board and start anew. Fish, as has been seen, had been playing around with the idea of Canadian independence, obviously with the notion that this would involve annexation sooner or later. More than once he had not only hinted but broadly suggested to Thornton that Great Britain had it in her power to resolve the whole situation by cutting at once the bonds which held the Dominion and the separate colonies to the Mother Country, or at least by seeking in them some expression of opinion on the subject. Just as often Thornton had replied that his Government could not do this: if the North American possessions of their own volition expressed a desire for separation, Great Britain would place no obstacle in the way; but every indication showed that the Imperial bond was growing stronger and not weaker—British North American subjects were not drawn either to independence or to inclusion within the American Union.[1] If Fish evinced a tepid sort of expansionism at the expense of British possessions, President Grant was more than a little interested in the matter, while the, as yet, powerful Chairman of the Senate Committee on Foreign Relations, Charles Sumner, was in the front rank of those who maintained that no solution of British-American differences was possible without it.

It is evident that when September found the Secretary of State back at his office in Washington, he had come to the conclusion that some other method of handling Canadian problems must be found than in withdrawal of England from the North American continent.[2] For the last time he brought up the subject while he and Thornton one Sunday afternoon talked over various aspects of the Canadian

1. This was apparently true even in Nova Scotia, for, as Consul Malmros wrote Davis (Sept. 30, 1870; Consular Letters: Pictou, Nova Scotia, Vol. VIII [D.S.]): "No portion of the people of Nova Scotia, with a few individual exceptions, bear any love for republican institutions in general or American in particular nor have they any faith in manhood suffrage, but prefer their own laws and system of government. Nova Scotians do not by any means think, as they sometimes express it, that 'Jack is as good as his master,' nor that it is desirable that he should be. All parties anticipate and none with pleasure that the incorporation of the Provinces into the American Union will have an inevitable tendency to assimilate many of their local laws [e.g., elective officials, divorce laws, etc.] to those prevailing in the States. . . ." Renewal of reciprocal trade relations, thought Malmros, would, by enhancing the material well-being of Nova Scotians, "decree the annihilation of the present annexation movement." See Chapter IX, pp. 204 ff., for the views of Fish and Grant on annexation.

2. Information from the American Consul at Halifax (Aug. 25, 1870; *For. Rel., 1870,* pp. 423–424) that recent action by both Dominion and Imperial authorities had resulted in withdrawal of shipping-in-bond privileges no doubt strengthened his conviction that it was getting dangerous to dally with the situation. "This sudden prohibition of the Bonding system which has existed for years without interruption," wrote Jackson, "and which has been mutually beneficial to the fisheries and traders of both countries, evinces a determination on the part of the Dominion and Imperial authorities to throw every obstacle in the way of American fishing vessels visiting for any purpose a Canadian or Colonial port."

issues.[3] A week later a determination to try new tactics was made clear when, again at Fish's house and after fruitless bickering over Canadian sins against American fishermen and England's stubborn backing of Canadian sinners, the Secretary broke out with a proposal, astounding in the light of American attitude for the past five years:[4]

Disclaiming any official character or purport in the suggestion, I asked whether Great Britain would settle all the questions pending between the countries at once. That the United States had refused the arbitration of the *Alabama* Claims, and Great Britain would not settle except upon arbitration. The United States declined a partition of San Juan or arbitration. That if the United States abandoned their opposition to arbitrating the *Alabama* Claims, Great Britain might agree to the American claim of the San Juan boundary line. All commercial claims may be referred to arbitration. The inshore fisheries be opened to American vessels, and in return a more free trade be allowed in certain articles between the United States and its colonies.

He [Thornton] thought there was not enough given in return for what Great Britain would thus concede, and excepted particularly to the cession of their claim to San Juan without arbitration, as involving a "point of honor." I reminded him of what he had told me, that Great Britain attached no importance to the possession and was quite willing to have the question decided against her claim, and to the fact that now it was a joint possession and an acknowledged disputed boundary. On parting he promised to think of it.

Having thus thrown overboard with one gesture the American uncompromising stand of half a decade, Fish invited a consideration *de novo* of the vexing problems which had come to threaten more seriously than ever good understanding between Great Britain and the United States and good neighborhood between Canada and America. It was but the first step, although a significant one. There remained tasks of no inconsiderable proportions: Grant, and especially Sumner, must be won over to this point of view or at least brought to acquiesce in it; England likewise must swallow its pride and reach out to grasp the hand extended by Fish. Both Thornton and Fish had their work cut out. For the former, the path was smoothed by the death of Clarendon

3. Nevins, *Hamilton Fish*, p. 424.
4. Fish's Diary, Sept. 26, 1870, in *ibid.*, pp. 425–426.

and the passing of immediate control of British foreign affairs into the no more able but certainly more conciliatory handling of Earl Granville, who, in the Colonial Office, had especially come to realize the potential danger of the fisheries question which now loomed up in English view as the most serious stumbling block of them all. Moreover, England's position in Europe was none too secure. The Franco-Prussian War had brought home a realization of her relative isolation; Russia's flouting of the restrictions imposed in 1856 upon the activities of her Black Sea fleet was ominous, and there was no other European power in a position to aid England in maintaining those limitations; besides which there was the traditional though fundamentally inexplicable rapport between the Muscovite and Uncle Sam. It would have been flying in the face of Providence to court trouble with the American Republic under these circumstances. Beyond all this, there was a real desire to avoid hostilities with the United States on general grounds, apart from the fact that they would mean invasion and probably conquest of Canada.

Fish's task was the more difficult one. Sumner, from his commanding position in the Senate, was a force to be reckoned with, while his jingoistic pronouncements had fanned American expansionist aspirations in a people that sincerely believed itself impregnable and at the same time equipped to impose its will upon the North American continent if so minded. Fortunately for Anglo-American peace, Sumner had already aroused the animosity of the President through his opposition to the latter's cherished Santo Domingo annexation plans. Anything to thwart Sumner would find a response with Grant, even if it meant abandonment of half-formed Canadian ambitions. Shrewdly through the autumn Fish worked upon the susceptibilities of his chief, so that by the time the Annual Message was in course of preparation Grant was ready to follow, reluctantly it may be, the skilful leading of his Secretary of State. At the same time, Fish did not let the seed he had sown in Thornton's mind wither and die. Not that it was likely to, for Granville encouraged the Minister to nurture the growth of any sprout that might appear: "I am glad to see that Fish is constantly recurring to the questions which are in dispute between us," he wrote Thornton.[5]

5. Oct. 13, 1870, Private. In Nevins, *op. cit.*, p. 431.

I have always thought a dilatory despatch would have been better than the hurrying a Convention with Reverdy Johnson, but the firmness with which Clarendon lately adhered to his reticent policy has worked admirably. One proof of it is in the recent conversations you have had, and which you have conducted on your part with great skill and tact. I do not, however, pretend in this state of things on the continent of Europe, that I should not like to make all things snug on your side of the water, and I should be disposed to grease the wheels for the United States to slide back upon if I knew where such an ointment was to be found. . . .

Even more incentive to "making things snug" came from various little annoying things which continued to exasperate on both sides of the Canadian border. Earlier in October, for example, Thornton was instructed to take up with the Department of State a recent complaint based on the operation of an act of the recent Congress whereby cattle for breeding purposes, imported from Canada into the United States, were taxed 20 per cent *ad valorem* while "such animals [were] admitted duty free when imported 'from beyond the seas.' "[6] Arthur Otway, at the Foreign Office, told Secretary Moran of the American Legation that he thought "the Fishery question likely to lead to bad blood and I told him that there really was danger of it."[7] Some of Minister Motley's remarks were, to say the least, tactless in their implication that he, too, considered the possibility of a collision on the fishing grounds.[8]

Between Granville's assuming the portfolio of the Foreign Office and the time Grant sent his Annual Message to Congress, unostentatious progress toward a settlement of Anglo-Canadian-American problems was being made. Fish's private and confidential intimation to Thornton had opened the way and the British Government were not slow to proceed upon it, for Gladstone's Cabinet included several influential members who believed cordial relations with the United

6. Minute of Canadian Privy Council, Aug. 27; Young to Kimberley, Sept. 8; Hammond to Thornton, Oct. 7, 1870; FO 115:504 (P.R.O.).

7. Nov. 10, 1870; Moran Journal, XXVII, 116–117 (L.C.).

8. "What is the meaning of Mr. Motley's speech? It is ridiculous to apply it to anything about the Fisheries—and the small squadron the U. States are preparing would seem to betoken operations in China, Cuba or some point of S. America." Lisgar to Macdonald, Nov. 14, 1870; Macdonald Papers: Governor General Correspondence, III, 431 (P.A.C.).

States should be a corner stone of their policy. Lord Tenterden, Assistant Under-Secretary of Foreign Affairs, in the middle of November suggested in a memorandum to Granville that while a special mission, new negotiations, or another convention would be ineffectual, it was possible to make the new questions which had arisen the occasion of suggesting to the United States a Joint International Commission empowered to take up all the questions. Rose, now permanently in business in England, urged the feasibility of such a course, and the Prime Minister gave his approbation to the proposal. Thornton reported a conversation with Fish late in November which indicated that the door was still being held open; that Fish, at least, was animated by "a little good will," which Tenterden thought was the one thing needful "on the part of the American Government and Congress" to set things in motion.[9]

When the Annual Message was read in Congress, however, the casual hearer might well have doubted whether any advance had been made toward an amicable adjustment.[10] After a reference to the boundary line near Pembina, where it was found that surveys had been erroneous and that the Hudson's Bay Company's fort was actually on American territory, the President regretted that "no conclusion [had] been reached for the adjustment of the claims against Great Britain growing out of the course adopted by that Government during the rebellion," recommended appointment of a commission to "take proof of the amount and ownership of these several claims" and advised their taking over by the United States. Then came the sentence which showed the results of Fish's activities during the past months:

It cannot be necessary to add that whenever Her Majesty's Government shall entertain a desire for a full and friendly adjustment of the claims the United States will enter upon their consideration with an earnest desire for a conclusion consistent with the honor and dignity of both nations.

The very next paragraph, however, started out by saying that "the course pursued by the Canadian authorities toward the fishermen of the United States during the past season has not been marked by a

9. See, in general, Nevins, *op. cit.*, pp. 432–435; Paul Knaplund, *Gladstone and Britain's Imperial Policy* (London, 1927), pp. 121–123; Lord Edmund Fitzmaurice, *Life of Granville* (London and New York, 1905), II, 29, 83 ff.

10. Dec. 5, 1870. Richardson, *Messages and Papers,* VII, 102 ff.

friendly feeling." On the interpretation of "three marine miles of any of the coasts, bays, creeks, or harbors" of Canada, the United States and Great Britain were far apart; British assertion that American fishing vessels could not enter British ports in North America for anything except wood, water, and shelter and must, even in such cases, depart within twenty-four hours, could not be assented to by the United States, "so far as the claim [was] founded on an alleged construction of the convention of 1818." Nor could the American Government agree to the British proposition that fishing vessels could have on board no merchandise of any variety. Whether the claims were founded on "provincial or colonial statutes, and not upon the convention, this Government can not but regard them as unfriendly" and opposed to the spirit if not the letter of the treaty, for the execution of which "the Imperial Government [was] alone responsible." So,

anticipating that an attempt may possibly be made by the Canadian authorities in the coming season to repeat their unneighborly acts toward our fishermen, I recommend you to confer upon the Executive the power to suspend by proclamation the operation of the laws authorizing the transit of goods, wares, and merchandise in bond across the territory of the United States to Canada, and, further, should such an extreme measure become necessary, to suspend the operation of any laws whereby the vessels of the Dominion of Canada are permitted to enter the waters of the United States.[11]

Passing to another point, Grant stated, "a like unfriendly disposition [had] been manifested on the part of Canada in the maintenance of a claim of right to exclude the citizens of the United States from the navigation of the St. Lawrence." Such a claim would exclude American citizens from access to lake ports: "to state such a proposition is to refute its justice." The right of a nation through whose territory a river flowed into the sea to regulate commerce from hinterland country "should be framed in a liberal spirit of comity, and should not impose needless burdens upon the commerce which has the right of

11. It was not many days after Congress heard the Message that Chandler, on December 12, introduced a bill in line with this suggestion, and on December 15 it was reported out of committee with no material changes. Thornton to Granville, Dec. 19, 1870; FO 5:1195 (P.R.O.). Chandler tried to bring it up February 6, but on objection that it touched foreign relations it was allowed to lie over. *Cong. Globe,* 41st Cong., 3d Sess., p. 980.

transit." He pointed out that the whole trend of international policy was in the direction of liberalizing the rules governing such waterways as well as emphasizing the need of the West to such an outlet.

This mixture of truculence and conciliation was calculated to kill a whole flock of birds: its language was sufficiently jingoistic to make Congress believe that the Administration was neglecting no point of American interest; it rebuked Canada; it made it possible for England to consider taking up negotiations again openly with no loss of national honor, since the United States thus practically invited some proposition looking toward adjustment. It did not call attention to Canada's offer of the previous winter, an offer which was generous and statesmanlike, the rejection of which had not unnaturally aroused much resentment in the Dominion. It was not the sort of a Message that could be counted on to remove exasperation; indeed, one wonders how Secretary Fish could reconcile this combination of threats and insinuations with his evident purpose of attempting to reach a settlement of differences, and yet such a consummation he had obviously been working toward for the past months. Only four days after the Message went to Congress, Fish "triumphantly announced"[12] he had just had word that the British Government, according to a letter he had received from Rose, was apparently ready to enter upon negotiations to bring about that result.

Dominion and Provincial newspapers were unsparing in their comments on Grant's message, ranging from sarcastic paragraphs to long and ponderous expositions of the untenability of his position. "The system of giving warnings," observed the Montreal *Gazette*,[13] was only in operation after 1866, and

it is rather too bad for the President, instead of acknowledging the great liberality exhibited by Canada in giving warnings and issuing licenses while negotiations were pending, to charge her with unfriendliness because, when all her efforts to negotiate had failed, she determined to maintain her rights.

The St. Lawrence navigation question may fairly be passed over without serious consideration. Even the American newspapers have admitted that the President has made himself ridiculous by his reference to the navigation of the St. Lawrence, which has suddenly been revived after the lapse of 46 years. The absurdity of the claim must be manifest to all ac-

12. Nevins, *op. cit.*, p. 435.   13. Dec. 28, 1870.

quainted with facts. Practically, the Americans are not, and have never been, excluded from the use of the St. Lawrence or the Canadian canals. Without the privilege of using the canals, to which they cannot pretend to set up any claim of right, the use of the river would be of no value whatever. . . .

But, in spite of official intransigence publicly exposed in the United States, the one small olive branch in the Message was welcomed in England. Sir John Rose was sent to America to sound out the situation. As Granville wrote Bright:[14]

We are taking several bites at that big cherry—reconciliation with the States.

I have sent Sir John Rose to New York and Washington to do that which is difficult for Thornton to do without committing us. He is to go on his own commercial business. He is to have no authority, but a boast that he was intimate with me when I was in the Colonial Office. He is to ascertain from the Government and from the Opposition what chance there is of our simultaneously agreeing to some beginning of a negotiation, if it were only to assent to a Joint Commission, who, without being commissioned to settle anything, might arrange in what manner each question in discussion might be best considered.

A becoming reticence about what Rose was doing was maintained in London without specifically putting a quietus on rumors which were circulating. Moran, who was acting as Chargé after the recall of Motley, assured Secretary Fish that there was nothing in the rumor that Rose was going to Washington on an official mission connected with the fisheries; he was going merely on private business.[15] The next day he sent a dispatch acknowledging receipt of a telegraphic inquiry as to whether Rose was coming to America and stating that while that gentleman sailed on December 24 he had no official mission about the fisheries, and his recent visit in Canada had no relation either to that or any other question pending between the United States and Great

14. Dec. 18, 1870. Fitzmaurice, *Granville*, II, 29. Knighthood had recently been conferred on Rose.

15. Dec. 28; Despatches, Vol. CVII (D.S.). In his Journal (L.C.) the same day Moran recorded: "For some days there has been a rumor in town that Sir John Rose has gone to Canada in Govt. interests about the Fisheries, but Mr. Hammond says the story is not true.

Britain. The American Secretary probably indulged in a smile when he received these communications, for he, certainly, was not surprised to have Rose turn up in Washington on January 9.

That evening the unofficial British envoy accompanied Assistant Secretary of State Bancroft Davis to Fish's residence where they dined and afterwards were closeted until the small hours of the next morning; when the guests withdrew an understanding had been reached on many points—a proposal from Great Britain for a Joint Commission to take up Canadian questions would be answered by the United States with a suggestion of a simultaneous consideration of the *Alabama* Claims which would be agreed to by the British. Fish's insistence on Great Britain's acknowledgment of liability together with an expression of regret respecting the Confederate cruisers was met with equally firm refusal, although eventually Rose and Thornton succeeded in getting their Government to yield the latter point, while Fish, with the reluctant approval of Grant and the Cabinet, who had been kept informed of the progress of the conversations, gave up the demand for previous admission of liability. The claims were to be subjected outright to an arbitration with no strings attached. Meantime, Fish had been seeing various senators to find out how the Senate would probably receive a treaty based upon the informal proposals. One by one they gave assurance that such a treaty would probably receive the approbation of the ratifying body, except for Sumner, who grew more and more unyielding, finally delivering an ultimatum that Great Britain must withdraw entirely from the American continents and the adjacent islands, and Carl Schurz, who was loath to commit himself to anything although he admitted the desirability of settling the issues. On January 24 Fish could inform Rose that the British Commissioners would be cordially received and that no effort would be spared to reach a satisfactory result, "even if it involves a conflict with the chairman of the Foreign Relations Committee."[16]

16. Nevins, *op. cit.*, p. 442. On January 24, 1871, Hammond telegraphed for Granville to Thornton: "Request Sir John Rose to remain. We adhere to arbitration as to the point of international law in the Alabama question, but we should express regret at the fact of escape and depredations." FO 115:518 (P.R.O.). On the same day Granville wrote Thornton (Confidential, *ibid.*) that H. M. Government were ready to appoint a commission to deal with all questions between the governments, but they adhered to arbitration "as to the

The British Government promptly gave its assent to the under-standing. Grant was shown how important it was that General Schenck, who had been appointed Minister to England[17] to replace Motley, should remain in the United States as a member of the Joint Commission rather than proceed immediately to his post. On Feb-ruary 1 came from the Foreign Office a cipher telegram to Thornton authorizing him to propose formally a Joint High Commission.[18] The next day the British Minister, through Rose, announced to Secretary Fish the acceptance by his Government. On February 3, having early in the morning seen Thornton and smoothed over final details includ-ing an arrangement to antedate several notes "so as to allow an inter-val sufficient for them to have been transmitted and considered,"[19] Fish related to the Cabinet the latest developments and urged immedi-

point of international law in the Alabama question," and they would not cede outright San Juan as Fish had suggested. For a more detailed account of the steps by which the goal was reached see Nevins, *op. cit.*, pp. 435–442.

17. Benjamin Moran wrote Bancroft Davis, January 11, 1871 (Davis Papers, Vol. VIII [L.C.]), that Schenck would be received and that he would probably be able to settle the *Alabama* Claims: "You will have no trouble in arranging the Fishery question at Washington and in bringing those imperti-nent Canadians to reason. People don't care much about retaining them and if they were to ask their independence I believe it would be granted with but little regret. An attempt on our part however to acquire the Colony by pressure would be resisted. Ours the province must be sooner or later, and this idea is generally accepted here. Indeed the whole of the North American possessions of Great Britain are an encumbrance to her and an annoyance to us. This at-tempt of a lot of Colonies to construe an Imperial Treaty is flat insolence. As you say make these portions of the British Empire independent and Gr. Britain and the U.S. will not be subject to the disturbances that no[w] arise between them."

18. FO 115:518 (P.R.O.). The next day Granville sent an instruction stat-ing that if the *Alabama* Claims were referred to the Commission, the British Government also expected that "all other claims of British subjects and Ameri-can citizens should be similarly referred."

19. Fish Diary in Nevins, *op. cit.*, p. 443. Thornton to Granville, Feb. 4, 1871; FO 115:524 (P.R.O.). In a dispatch of February 6 (*ibid.*) Thornton said: "The four Notes enclosed were communicated by M^r: Fish and myself to each other before any one of them was sent in, and I can only express my earnest hope that they will be satisfactory to H. M. Gov^t:, and beg Y.L. to be assured that in taking upon myself the responsibility of addressing M^r: Fish the two notes of which copies are enclosed, I have been guided by what I believed to be the wishes of H. M. Gov^t: as expressed in Y.L. telegram of the 2nd Inst."

ate consideration of the American personnel of the commission. He wanted a fairly large group, representative of all parts of the country, and he believed the commission should begin its task as soon as possible in order to have the work well advanced before the adjournment of Congress. There was also another reason for taking action quickly, as Fish explained to Thornton:[20]

I understand [wrote Thornton] that the President considers that he is empowered by the Constitution to name Commissioners on the part of the U. S. without any appeal to the Senate; he prefers however and thinks it expedient, when he shall have decided upon the persons who shall be appointed, to send their names to the Senate for confirmation, so that no opposition may hereafter be made to any conclusions which they may arrive at, on the ground that the Senate was not consulted as to the fitness of the negotiators for the U. S. But the President has no doubt that the Senate will sanction the appointments. . . .

Every precaution was being taken to assure the successful outcome of the proceedings.

In like manner Fish urged upon Thornton a similar speed in naming the British Commissioners, but the recommendation was unnecessary, for on February 6 there was received from London a cable naming three of the Commissioners and on the ninth another announcing the other two.[21] Heading the list, which Thornton confidentially disclosed to Fish, were the names of the Earl de Grey and Ripon, President of the Council, and Sir Stafford Northcote, representing the Opposition in Parliament. To these were added Thornton himself, Professor Mountague Bernard of All Souls' College, Oxford, and Sir John A. Macdonald, Premier of the Dominion of Canada. As soon as it had been decided that a commission was to meet, Thornton had suggested that Rose be permitted to announce the agreement to the Governor-General of Canada and that his Government be invited "to send a delegation to Washington for the purpose of communicating with the Commission on permanent settlement of Fishery question & a temporary arrangement in view of next season being so near, and to urge upon the Canadian Gov't conciliatory spirit."[22] The British Govern-

20. Thornton to Granville, Feb. 6, 1871; FO 115:524 (P.R.O.).
21. FO 115:518 (P.R.O.).
22. Thornton to Granville, Feb. 4, 1871; FO 115:524 (P.R.O.).

ment, however, had decided to go even farther than this, and make a
Canadian a member of the commission. Naturally the name of Rose
presented itself at once in view of what he had done to promote the
arrangement, and Rose would have been most acceptable to the American Administration, but Macdonald obviously would be the person to
be first considered. Indeed, both Rose and Macdonald would have been
named but for the fact that the former had now definitely taken up his
residence in England and on that account would not be considered a
real Canadian representative.[23]

Sir John A. Macdonald had some compunctions about accepting
the appointment. He was "embarrassed by the injunction of secrecy,"
as Lisgar reported to the Colonial Office, and it was not until after he
had been given permission to consult his colleagues in the Dominion
Government that he consented to become a commissioner. "I was under the apprehension," wrote the Governor-General,[24] "that the Privy
Council would advise Sir J. A. Macdonald not to serve, and would
refuse to take part in a Commission constituted as it is announced the
proposed Commission will be constituted. This course would have been
more in accordance with the previous declarations of a majority of
the Members of that Council. Fortunately more acceptable Counsels
have prevailed."[25] Later on, according to his own testimony, Sir John
many times regretted that he had accepted the, to him, doubtful honor
of being a commissioner. Certainly his was no bed of roses while in
Washington, with a critical and sometimes querulous Council sitting
in Ottawa to check his every move.

Grant's Cabinet was no less prompt in making a selection of the
American Commissioners. On February 3 four of them were decided

23. Lisgar to Kimberley, Secret, Feb. 6, G [unnumbered] (P.A.C.); Granville to Thornton, Feb. 6, 8; Thornton to Granville, Feb. 13, FO 115:518
(P.R.O.). Rose himself believed there were "serious objections to his being a
Commissioner; that his being married to an American, his banking relations
with the U. S., his bank having been named one of the Agents in London for the
conversion of the U. S. debt might be used against H. M. Gov^t: with regard to
the result of the negotiations." Thornton to Granville, Feb. 12, 1871; FO 115:
524 (P.R.O.).

24. Lisgar to Kimberley, Feb. 9, 1871; G [unnumbered] (P.A.C.).

25. Lisgar believed that rumors of what was going on had leaked out from
members of the Canadian Privy Council; this had happened before when information had been submitted to them in confidence.

upon: Senator Rockwood Hoar; General Robert C. Schenck, the newly appointed Minister to England; George H. Williams of Oregon, whose term as Senator was just expiring; and the Secretary of State himself. The fifth chosen was Justice Samuel Nelson of the United States Supreme Court, after two or three others had been considered and rejected for one reason or another. Accordingly, the day after Thornton had announced confidentially to Fish a part of the British personnel, the latter could tell him who would make up the American group.

News that something was in the wind had got about, but, considering the number of persons Fish had consulted, as Thornton commented in one of his dispatches[26] to the Foreign Office, "it [was] remarkable in a country like this that it should not have become public until it was officially communicated by the President to the Senate on the 9th Inst."

It is true that a variety of surmises were made by the various newspapers but these contained nothing approaching the truth till the 8th Inst. when a Telegram appeared in the New York World containing what was said to be a skeleton of H. M. Speech to Parliament which contained an allusion to the prospect of a settlement of the questions between the two countries. Mr: Fish had intended to give the substance of the arrangement as to the Commission to the Public thro' the press on the 7th Inst.; but on Sir J. Rose's suggestion that H. M. Govt: might wish to announce it simultaneously to Parliament in the Queen's Speech, I begged Mr: Fish to defer any publication until the 9th Inst. To this he readily consented, and he subsequently determined to make no announcement thro' the press, but to let the matter become known thro' the Message which the President would send to the Senate on the 9th Inst. . . .

The Senate promptly confirmed the appointments with apparently little opposition or comment, although rumors were running about that Senator Sumner had tried to block the action.[27]

26. Thornton to Granville, Feb. 14, 1871; FO 115:524 (P.R.O.).

27. The Boston *Journal* on February 10 carried a special dispatch from Washington to the effect that "some of the correspondents have represented Mr. Sumner as having opposed the confirmation of the Commissioners in the executive session yesterday. This is an error, and it is understood that Mr. Sumner merely advised caution—that the United States might not again invite Great Britain to enter into the negotiations which would not be ratified."

Immediately expressions of general approbation were numerous, and a sigh of relief went up to show that Americans at least felt there was now an opportunity to eliminate the issues which had been causing so much friction. The Boston *Journal*,[28] for example, spoke with commendation of the whole project and of the choice of commissioners and then went on to say: "It will be seen that the initiative in this auspicious work was taken by the British Government in its proposal to submit the difficulties arising out of the Canadian fisheries to the adjudication of a Joint High Commission." The belief that Great Britain actually invited the negotiation was widely held, and since that was pleasing to American self-esteem the British Government was surely not going to upset that complacency by revealing how things actually got started.

Canadian approval was somewhat more guarded. Administration papers, of course, had to support the move heartily, but the opposition press tempered its jubilation. Its leading paper in Ontario, the *Globe* of Toronto,[29] was of the opinion that

Much will now depend upon the character of the British Commissioners. In general John Bull has been apt to allow himself to be gulled when it came to negotiation. He has been so afraid of being thought guilty of a shabby proceeding, or of standing upon trifles, that he has yielded a great deal of the matter in dispute, though he would have fought for it to the death. In American matters this has been specially noticeable, as the Ashburton and other treaties made manifest. British politicians have been generally so triumphantly ignorant of almost everything connected with this continent, and so ready to believe that a few millions of acres here or there did not matter much, that they have generally had the worst of the bargain. It is so fine to assume a grand air and to look as if above paltry haggling, that Yankees have known how to make use of the vanity and ignorance thereby manifested. In Sir Edward Thornton we have little confidence. His silly desire to get credit for "broad views" and superiority to colonial prejudice would lead him a very long way in undue concession. If Sir John Macdonald manages to keep straight, we don't suppose that he is likely to sacrifice the interests of Canada. If he does he will hear of it. . . .

In the meantime it is a matter for congratulation that there is a prospect of these unpleasantnesses being peacefully settled. . . .

28. Feb. 10, 1871.   29. Feb. 11, 1871.

In Congress, as in the country at large, news of the appointment of the Joint High Commission was bound to start speculations about annexation, and professional agitators of that issue did not fail to seize the opportunity to insinuate that now was the time to strike. But the peak of that movement had already been passed, so that speeches and editorials were received with amusement or scorn in most quarters. Already the House of Representatives had received the report of J. N. Larned, made in conformity with the joint resolution of June 23, 1870, on trade with the British North American Provinces.[30] It ran along much the same lines as earlier reports. It had been referred to the Committee on Ways and Means and had not been brought back before the President's Message, transmitting the correspondence regarding proposed negotiations, had gone to the Senate; consequently attention concentrated not upon the report, with its rehashing of old topics, but upon possibilities opened up by the imminent meeting of the commission. That this commission might not miss an opportunity, Senator Howard of Michigan introduced on February 18 a resolution recommending the advisability of their considering the surrender to the United States of at least the territory west of Hudson's Bay.[31] Upon objection of Simon Cameron the resolutions went over under the rule, to be brought up on February 21 and referred to the Committee on Foreign Relations. "Some opposition to its being passed was made on various grounds," reported Thornton,[32] "one of which was an insinuation that it was not worth while considering the question at present, inasmuch as it was not improbable that the whole of the territory north of the Boundary not yet laid down would be ceded to the U. S. by the High Commission." This argument, said Thornton, was so absurd that it had little influence on votes, and the resolution was carried 120 to 73.

It was on the same day, February 18, that the Washington *Republi-*

30. *House Ex. Docs.*, No. 94, 41st Cong., 3d Sess. Transmitted by Secretary of the Treasury Boutwell, February 3.

31. *Cong. Globe,* 41st Cong., 3d Sess., p. 1382; *Senate Misc. Docs.*, No. 68. Thornton, sending copies to London, remarked that he could "hardly suppose however that M^r: Howard [would] be able to gain many supporters to a proposal which, if adopted by the U. S. Commissioners, would probably put an end to all hopes of agreement." Feb. 20, 1871; FO 115:524 (P.R.O.).

32. Thornton to Granville, Feb. 21, 1871; FO 115:524 (P.R.O.).

can carried an item, under the caption "Canard Extraordinary,"[33] saying that "we are authorized to state that the dispatch from Washington in the *Evening Post* and other papers of February 15, to the effect that the subject of purchasing the British territory in North America would be embraced in a proposition before the Joint Commission and that President Grant has given his entire approval of the scheme, is utterly without foundation. The dispatch comes from the same source to which many previous dispatches have been traced, as the work of pure invention." The Administration, and this meant Secretary Fish, was not going to have the negotiation jeopardized at the outset by a proposition that would make impossible any coöperation from Canada.

And in Canada that coöperation was needed if success was to crown the efforts of the commission. Canadian issues must be settled as well as the *Alabama* Claims. From shortly after the announcement of plans for the Washington conferences until the middle of April the Dominion Parliament was sitting; consequently there was ample opportunity to air suspicions and voice grievances. Lord Lisgar's Speech from the Throne reviewed most of the points at which friction or differences had arisen. The latest Fenian outrages were adverted to and the prompt, energetic action of the militia complimented, while the expense to which the Government had been put was not forgotten. British Columbia, knocking at the door of the Dominion, and Manitoba were remembered, together with the necessity of establishing rail connection with these distant parts of the Empire. As to the fisheries, Canada, recited his Lordship, would be represented on the Commission where there would be urged no demand "beyond those to which she is entitled by Treaty and the law of nations. She has pushed no claim to an extreme assertion, and only sought to maintain the rights of her own people fairly and firmly, but in a friendly and considerate spirit and with all due respect to foreign powers and international obligations."[34] No specific reference to reciprocal trade was made but this topic was implicit in the whole speech.

If the Government's position was stated in the Speech from the Throne, the opposition was no less positive, for, speaking through its leader, Alexander Mackenzie, it showed that it intended to compel the

33. Quoted in Boston *Journal,* Feb. 20, 1871.
34. *Dom. Parl. Deb.,* II, 3–4.

Government to assert and maintain without wavering a nationalist point of view *vis-à-vis* the southern neighbor:[35]

. . . Coming to the position of Canada, it was but right her relations towards the United States should receive attention. President Grant had spoken of it as in a semi-independent position, and there was truth in this view of it. Doubtless it was on this account that we had been continually and systematically subjected to offensive remarks and ill-judged acts of administration from the people of the United States. The inhabitants of this country had reason for complaint on this head, but were not willing to submit to ill will or aversion with the object of forcing them from their present constitutional position. That policy he for one repudiated in the strongest possible terms and he announced his strongest opposition to yielding any of our rights to an arrogant demand from them (hear, hear). If we were to maintain an independent position on this continent we must cultivate that natural love of liberty which prevailed in our midst and maintain our internal rights intact. . . .

The Government of the United States, thought Mackenzie, had been negligent in the Fenian matter; they had easily put down Mormon organizations in Utah and could easily have done as much with the Fenians if so minded, although, when representations had been made by the Canadian Government they had "acted in the most prompt and friendly manner." In the Senate, Letellier de St. Just questioned whether Canadian interests had been sufficiently guarded in the fisheries in the forthcoming negotiations.[36]

. . . Was the High Commission to mature an arrangement which would be a mere repetition of the Ashburton Treaty, in which the rights of the British Provinces had been notoriously sacrificed? England was very desirous of coming to some amicable adjustment of the difficulties between herself and the United States, and was it not just possible that her interests might not always coincide with those of Canada when the questions in dispute were discussed and arranged?

This was a note frequently sounded throughout the session: would Canadian interests be sacrificed to British needs? Robert B. Dickey of Amherst, Nova Scotia, expressed in the Senate the doubts of the Maritimes, although professing to believe that Great Britain was not willing to barter away the invaluable resources of the seas without safe-

35. *Ibid.,* pp. 18–21.   36. Feb. 17, 1871; *ibid.,* pp. 34–35.

guarding her Provinces in some way.[37] In the discussion of the address in the House examples were numerous of similar apprehensions, and on February 20 Macdonald brought down at least a portion of the correspondence on this subject.[38] He outlined[39] the course pursued by the Government since the abrogation of the Elgin Treaty and showed how ineffective the licensing system had become and what significance the headland question had attained. It was on account of this that Postmaster General Alexander Campbell had been sent to England to see what could be done and in due time this Minister had received approval of a plan to submit the whole matter to a commission;[40] this, in turn, had opened up the whole series of issues and led to the proposition of a Joint High Commission. No rights of Canada, he assured the House, would be surrendered without Canadian consent. As to the Fenian claims, he admitted that he had not seen the exact wording of the understanding between the British and American Governments: all that he knew was that a dispatch had been received conceding Canadian demands and giving Canada representation on the commission.

In a sense, Sir Alexander Galt precipitated a discussion and eventually a division on the whole subject of the fisheries and the commission by introducing on February 24 a series of resolutions, the purport of which was that "the control and disposal of the inshore fisheries and the navigation of the inland waters of the Dominion" were "within the powers conveyed to the Parliament of Canada under the British North America Act," and any proposal to alter or diminish these powers without the consent of the Dominion would be viewed with "the utmost concern and apprehension." But the House was always disposed to grant the fisheries and the use of the waters in return for a "modification of the United States commercial system, directed to the more free and liberal interchange of the products of labour in the two countries." The House would willingly make any sacrifices in the interests of the Empire "so far as they do not compromise the national interests and security of this country, and directly tend to their

37. *Dom. Parl. Deb.*, II, 38–39.
38. Canadian *Sessional Papers*, No. 12 (1871).
39. *Dom. Parl. Deb.*, II, 56–61.
40. The primary purpose was to confer on the proposed removal of British troops.

undue subordination to the United States in the future."[41] Defending his resolutions, Galt did not impute dishonorable motives to the Imperial Government but, in trying to establish cordial relations with the United States, "they might look at our Canadian interests in these questions as of comparatively minor importance. It was a favorite idea with the Americans, that Canada should become a part of the Republic. The States would prefer, that the concessions to be made should be such as to place us in a position of subordination and inferiority. This, rather than English concessions or money payments would be particularly welcome to our neighbours." The correspondence which had been placed before the House was incomplete and unsatisfactory instead of being plain and distinct. So, too, with the Fenian claims; there should have been a bill for damages presented by the British Government to the United States. Then again, the withdrawal of British military forces from the Provinces showed little consideration for Canadians in its haste and precipitancy. Up to February 10 the Imperial officials had communicated freely with the Canadians, but after that date "the British Ministers entirely ignored our Government." While he would not accuse them of intentional sacrifice of Canadian interests, he believed "mixing up of Canadian with Imperial questions in this Commission would be disadvantageous. . . . Both sets of questions should have been kept separate. The fisheries were of paramount importance" to Canadians.[42]

The Premier himself felt called upon to answer Sir Alexander, and he did so not because of anything that was in the resolutions but because they "would be quoted and republished in every journal in the United States, and turned to our disadvantage." "Why show," said he, "the fissure through which the entering wedge could be put?" Most of what Galt had said he agreed with, although he maintained that there was nothing on which to base an opinion that Great Britain would not defend Canada and her rights with all the power of the Empire; at all events he, as Commissioner, must have a free hand not tied by hampering resolutions no matter how unexceptionable they might be in themselves. Following Macdonald several other members of the House expressed themselves, Government supporters to assert that the course

41. *Dom. Parl. Deb.*, II, 99–100.
42. The speech is in *ibid.*, pp. 100–104. Macdonald's reply followed immediately, *ibid.*, pp. 104–111.

taken was a justifiable one and that fears of being left in the lurch by England were groundless, the opposition to voice doubts whether Canadian rights had been sufficiently emphasized. Macdonald stated in categorical terms that the headland issue would not be abandoned although he considered it unimportant in comparison with the whole fishery question. Upon that note the matter was dropped with permission to withdraw the resolutions.[43]

Woven into the warp of practically every specific proposal of legislation at this session was some reference to American relations and the commission, now, after February 27, actually sitting in Washington. When Hincks presented his budget, among other things proposing to take 5 per cent off the duties imposed at the last session, and suggesting that the next thing to be considered would be removal of duties on coal and flour, he remarked that, since negotiations were then proceeding, it would be inadvisable to act at the moment.[44] This did not meet with universal approval. Galt, for one, thought that the excuse made for the retention of the duties "was unworthy of anyone in the position of Minister of Finance," especially when he admitted that no revenue was derived from them; if the duties were not in the interest of Canada they should be removed, negotiations or no negotiations.[45] Luther M. Holton, when the bill came from the Committee of the Whole for its third reading, moved recommitting to amend to remove duties on coal, coke, flour, and wheat, thus giving Tupper an opportunity to explain how beneficial these duties had been and how the duty on coal had broken the stranglehold of Pennsylvania producers despite Thomas Workman's dictum that coal in Canada was dearer than ever before. Tupper also took the opportunity to defend the Government's course with the fisheries, whose importance the highest authorities in the United States admitted.[46]

Holton's motion carried by a vote of 83 to 55, fairly indicative of

43. In the Senate (*Dom. Parl. Deb.*, II, 130 ff.) there was a short debate along similar lines.

44. Mar. 10, 1871; *ibid.*, p. 385.

45. *Ibid.*, p. 399. Tupper defended the Government; Parliament at the last session had provided for the removal of these duties whenever the United States reduced or removed the duty on one or all of these articles, but nothing had been done. *Ibid.*, p. 409.

46. Mar. 22; *ibid.*, pp. 587–588.

the division of sentiment and presaging carrying of the amendment which would place these articles on the free list, even though C. C. Cameron of Huron maintained that the removal of the duty on salt could not fail to injure the salt-boilers of Western Canada.[47] How much influence negotiations at Washington had on this reversal of the Government's policy and how much it was a mere question of pure economic demand in Canada is impossible to determine, although it is probable that the latter factor was the stronger of the two. Canada was not yet prepared to enter upon a full-fledged protectionist program.

The bill for accepting the conditions under which British Columbia was ready to enter the Confederation met with a little rough sledding, especially since it contemplated Dominion assistance in putting a railroad through to the Pacific. There were some who believed that this was too heavy a price to pay and deprecated using threats of annexation to the United States as a means of bludgeoning both British Columbia and the Dominion into line. Supporters of the Government, however, were firm in their conviction that not only was it imperative that the Dominion should be rounded out by the inclusion of the western province but that this was impracticable, if not impossible, without a railroad. Advocates of economy who saw no danger to British Columbia from the United States were unable to stem the tide, and Parliament supported the Government by passing the measure.[48]

On the fisheries, Parliament supported the policy pursued during the past year. Here, too, the question was asked whether it was politic to continue such stringent control while negotiations were going on; "needlessly aggressive" they might be considered by the United States, thought Holton.[49] But the fisheries touched very closely the whole Canadian case, and it may well be thought that Canadians of all political hues believed there must be an object lesson not only to the United States but to the British Commissioners, a warning that

47. Apr. 4, 1871; *ibid.*, p. 881. Cameron predicted that if the salt duty were removed, "the whole trade would revert to the Americans in two months, and Canada salt boilers would see their business ruined." On March 30 Hincks had announced in reply to a question from Holton that customs officials had been informed that the repeal of duties on coal, coke, flour, wheat, etc., would take effect on April 1. *Ibid.*, p. 710.

48. *Ibid.*, pp. 671, 700, 712, 761, 842, 916, 935–941.

49. *Ibid.*, p. 743.

this ace was going to be held in reserve. There had, indeed, been little opportunity for the Dominion Government to forget the significance of this issue in Canadian and particularly in Maritime opinion. All through the winter, news items and editorials had played up the matter and one and all had let it be understood that no yielding on this point would be tolerated. "Certainly Canadians would be the meekest of people if they were to allow American fishermen, under the pressure of the Presidential *brutum fulmen* of non-intercourse, to fish freely and without molestation in Canadian waters, while Canadian fishermen are excluded from American waters and the fish caught by Canadian fishermen are subject to a heavy duty on importation to the United States. It is the old story over again, however; self-seeking, grasping, exacting, the Americans would fain have the handle all on one side of the jug."[50]

After quoting a dispatch in the Rochester *Democrat and Chronicle* which asserted that Great Britain had peremptorily called upon Canada to "submit to the demands of the United States in relation to the fishery question," the Toronto *Globe*[51] delivered itself of this outburst:

We thought the *Democrat* was far too sensible to believe anything telegraphed from Washington by the Associated Press. How could it have fallen into such an error? Great Britain never thought of paying the Alabama's damages with our fisheries; she is prepared to pay in cash. She is incapable of such an act of meanness. No Englishman ever thought of such a thing. Only an American Associated Press reporter could have conceived the idea. . . . Our representatives go to England with confident expectation of a cordial reception and the most kindly consideration of what they have to urge. On the other hand, from the States we meet nothing but rebuffs. The ingenuity of Washington officials is strained to the utmost to keep out our products, and the assertion of our just rights in the matter of the fisheries is met with threats of even more perverse regulations. . . .

Examples like these from two of the leading dailies in Canada, papers on opposite sides of the political fence, could be matched by scores of

50. The Montreal *Gazette,* Jan. 5, 1871.
51. Feb. 10, 1871.

others from all over the country. No government could be in doubt about public opinion on this issue.[52]

An issue of minor significance in itself came before this same session of Parliament, as it did before the Joint Commission. This grew out of the construction by the United States of a canal through the St. Clair Flats[53] some time before the Civil War. In August, 1870, one Hiram Little was arrested at Detroit and two of his boats seized on the ground that he discharged at the Flats a cargo of wood for the use of a concern engaged in deepening the channel. The alleged grounds for the arrest and seizure were that Little was smuggling the wood into the territory of the United States, while the defense was that the canal actually ran through Canadian territory. There was a discrepancy in the maps made of this area, and strong reason to believe that the canal had really been constructed within Canadian jurisdiction. The Dominion Government, on the advice of the Governor-General, made no formal application through the British Minister at Washington to the Government of the United States until the point of jurisdiction could be definitely ascertained, although, as Sir John Young observed, while "several newspapers in the United States have commented upon these proceedings not one of them suggests a doubt as to

52. From the other side of the boundary, from a place where the Canadian regulations bore most oppressively, came outbursts like this from the *Cape Ann Register* (January 6, 1871) in commenting on a statement that Canada's acts were in a friendly spirit:

"Thank you, gentlemen, but we don't propose to turn the other cheek. The words and spirit which characterized the debate on the equipment of your cutters, the consequent appointment of men to their command, peculiarly fitted to be your instruments, their action and your applause, are better testimony than any excuses of convicted culprits. The first duty you owe to American fishermen is to right the wrong done to them by returning their vessels and paying for the damage done. . . . Then and not till then will the question of reciprocity be considered. . . ."

53. See *Senate Ex. Docs.*, No. 78, 34th Cong., 1st Sess. (1856); *Senate Ex. Docs.*, No. 71, 34th Cong., 1st Sess.; *Senate Ex. Docs.*, No. 46, 34th Cong., 3d Sess. (1857); *Senate Ex. Docs.*, No. 6, 36th Cong., 1st Sess. (1860). For the issue which arose in 1870 see *Dom. Parl. Deb., 1870*, II, 62, 227, 644; Cartier to Young, Aug. 25, 1870, FO 5:1194; Thornton to Granville, Oct. 24, 1870, FO 5:1195 (P.R.O.); Young to Kimberley, Sept. 23, 1870, G [unnumbered] (P.A.C.).

the Canal's being within the limits of Canada." This, however, did not prevent a call for papers and questions in the Dominion House of Commons. A minor point itself, it did not present any serious problem to the Commission, nor was it difficult to adjust the complication.

While all this comment, friendly and otherwise, was being made about the probable action of the Joint High Commission, that body proceeded to take up its work in Washington. On the morning of February 24, Sir Edward Thornton ushered into Fish's office at the Department of State the members of the British delegation, except Northcote and Sir John Macdonald, who had not yet reached Washington. On the twenty-fifth Thornton took De Grey, Bernard, and Tenterden, Secretary of the British group, to the White House, where Fish presented them to the President, who, according to Thornton,[54] "was most friendly and cordial in his manner to Lord de Grey, and conversed with him for nearly an hour, and I have reason to believe that H. L. made a very good impression upon the President. Indeed I am glad to observe that the High Commissioners have been received with kindness by the principal personages on all sides, and that the public Press has generally expressed itself in favour of the objects of their mission." After Macdonald and Northcote had arrived, the whole delegation visited the Capitol and were introduced on the floor of both houses. The Senators, reported Macdonald,[55] all professed hopes that the negotiations would result in a permanent treaty. "The joke was that before going into the Senate General Schenck said he would send for a Senator to conduct us, and he sent for Chandler of Michigan, telling him that the British Lion was waiting for him and he must come out and confront him." But, remarked Macdonald, Chandler was very civil.

The greatest obstacle to the conclusion of a satisfactory outcome of their deliberations was, apparently unknown to himself, about to be removed from the position where he could block all efforts. The differences between Grant and Sumner had become so pronounced and the latter's opposition to any sane agreement with England so implacable that his retention in the strategic position of Chairman of the Senate Committee on Foreign Relations was recognized as politi-

54. Thornton to Granville, Feb. 27, 1871; FO 115:524 (P.R.O.).
55. Macdonald to Tupper, Mar. 5[?], 1871; Macdonald Papers: Letter-books, XV, 390 ff. (P.A.C.).

cally impossible, and the ground for his removal was being carefully prepared. When the Senate met in the special session of the Forty-second Congress, at a time when the commission had barely started its work, Sumner's name was left off the list of that most important committee, and, despite the protests of some of his friends, he was relegated to a position of innocuity.[56]

56. Writing to Elihu Washburne (February 20) Fish said: "Sumner is bitterly vindictive and hostile; he is determined to oppose and if possible defeat everything that the President proposes or wishes or does. He is at work in advance, endeavoring to prevent any settlement of the English questions. I am convinced that he is crazy; vanity, conceit, ambition have disturbed the equilibrium of his mind; he is irrational and illogical, and raves and rants. No mad bull ever dashed more violently at a red rag than he does at anything that he thinks the President is interested in. He exhibits what I believe is a very common incident to insanity, and an equally unfailing sign of it, a constant apprehension of designs to inflict personal violence on him." Nevins, *op. cit.*, p. 461.

CHAPTER XV

THE JOINT HIGH COMMISSION

IT was a distinguished group which met in the library of the Department of State, an able one as well. Not the least able and distinguished was the Canadian delegate, Sir John A. Macdonald. He had accepted the appointment with misgivings, fearing that Britain would be disposed to sacrifice her colony's interests to forward the Empire's well-being, and he knew that, whatever he did, his course would be scrutinized closely by his countrymen, who would not hesitate to criticize. It might even involve his political future. His colleagues in the Dominion Government were equally solicitous and they had not failed to impress upon him the importance of his undertaking, as well as to load him with advice. Sir Francis Hincks, the Finance Minister, perhaps looked at the situation as realistically as any.

I wish [he wrote the Premier] your colleagues understood as well as you do that the coming negotiation is really a game of brag, and that by bragging high you must win. We have no object to gain of vital importance and even if the whole negotiation broke off England must be the gainer. The U. S. have already refused to ratify one treaty, and if they again refuse whatever terms your colleagues are now prepared to offer for settling the Alabama Claims, and this no doubt will be reasonable, *they* will be in a very awkward position. *They will not declare war against England* on any pending issue of that you may be assured.[1]

The Americans would wish to settle first of all the Claims, and if this question should be adjusted then they would be anxious to hurry the remainder of the issues to a conclusion. Macdonald should use the fisheries, navigation, the San Juan question, and all the rest as bargaining points. Since Great Britain would wish Canada to yield something and since they would be likely to get very little from the United States in return, it would give an opportunity to require of England as a makeweight a guaranty of a bond issue for a Pacific Railroad, for im-

1. Feb. 15, 1871; Macdonald Papers: Washington Treaty, I, 308–316 (P.A.C.). In Pope, *Memoirs of Macdonald*, II, chaps. xx and xxi, are printed parts of Macdonald's letters written from Washington.

proving the canals and for other important works. Hincks placed no high value upon the bonding privileges; mutual registration of vessels and the coasting trade he did not believe the United States would admit unless persuaded it was to their distinct advantage; these, as well as the use of Lake Michigan, should not be pressed but merely put forward as trading points. The really great points the Americans had to gain were the fisheries and the use of the St. Lawrence, and "really we have no object in refusing them on the contrary the fisheries are a mere expense. Our equivalents that should be pressed are full reciprocal trade—If we yield on this England *must compensate us*. But we cant yield the fisheries without *at least* free importation of our fish & free or low duty coal lumber & salt particularly the first." The Americans, thought Hincks, knew as well as the Canadians that "the mere question of headland or permission to trade in certain ports are of no real importance & I therefore hope that they will press for the entire fisheries."

When Macdonald arrived in Washington he found the other British members of the Commission established in a house taken by Earl de Grey, who had brought along his own cook, for they intended to make themselves comfortable, if not "gay," as the Canadian put it. The British had been met in the same spirit in which they came, although Fish had had some misgivings about Tenterden and Bernard,[2] despite the assurances which had come from London, whence Benjamin Moran wrote his impressions of the personnel of the British contingent.[3]

The strongest man in the party is Tenterden. You will find him a good fellow, but he has heretofore entertained the Foreign Office tradition that the U.S. always wants to bully England. . . . But he has been cured in a measure of his old views about us. Manage him and you manage the commission. He will be the soul of it, and he knows our history very well. I have always found him frank and honest, but he dreads the Senate. . . .

Moran's opinion was to some extent borne out in the subsequent weeks; if Tenterden was not the "soul" of the Commission and De Grey was found to be the guiding spirit, at least the former was very useful in

2. Nevins, *Hamilton Fish,* p. 471.
3. To Davis, Feb. 20; Davis Papers, Vol. VIII (L.C.).

rounding difficult corners, while he as Secretary of the British group and Bancroft Davis in a similar capacity for the Americans were able to smooth many a rough passage.

With a round of entertainments which accompanied serious business, the negotiations threatened to rival those which Lord Elgin had conducted in the Fifties; parties, dinners, receptions followed each other in rapid succession, and the British delegation could not go home underestimating the hospitality of their diplomatic opponents.[4] This spirit carried over into the informal conferences, for between Lord de Grey and Secretary Fish were frequent and long conferences in which knotty points which had baffled the Commission as a whole were calmly threshed out to some sort of a compromise.[5] Tact and patience were needed. Although the British Government sent its representatives charged with the duty of bringing back a treaty which would contain some solution of all the difficulties between the two countries and put at rest forever the animosity attending the *Alabama* Claims; although they were prepared to submit that issue to arbitration with the expectation the award would go against them and require them to pay the direct losses—there must also be a solution of Canadian and Provincial issues which would call for some sacrifice. One can understand that British America felt that it was likely to be the sacrificial goat. This meant that its representative had to be a thorn in the flesh not only of the American negotiators but of his own colleagues as well; perhaps this feeling made him unduly suspicious and prone to impute motives which did not exist. But his rôle obligated him frequently to appear obstinate, unyielding, even ungracious.

Hincks's idea that the *Alabama* Claims would be disposed of first and thus ease the way for Canadian issues was not realized. The Americans contended that the fisheries and other points of difference with Canada were first on the agenda and must be taken up in that order. In the "Confidential Memoir for Use of the Commissioners on the Part of the United States in the American-British Joint High

4. "Dinner parties, dances, receptions, and a queer kind of fox-hunt, with picnics and expeditions in the beautiful Virginia country, alternated with serious business and grave discussions." Andrew Lang, *Life, Letters and Diaries of Sir Stafford Northcote, First Earl of Iddesleigh* (Edinburgh, 1891), p. 238.
5. See Nevins, *op. cit.*, pp. 474 ff.

Commission"[6] the fisheries took precedence over everything else; then followed the St. Lawrence question, and finally reciprocity.

After a meeting of the British Commissioners at De Grey's on Friday, March 3, the whole High Commission assembled on Saturday and spent some three hours "marshalling the subjects" and settling the order of discussion.[7] The Americans expressed a wish that this order should not be revealed, since they would be "overwhelmed with interviews with those interested." Indeed, through the weeks of negotiation this idea of secrecy was constantly impressed on the Commissioners, and Macdonald urged in nearly every communication he sent to Ottawa the same reticence. At this preliminary meeting it was intimated that the fisheries would be the first topic for consideration. On Sunday after church De Grey sought out Macdonald to tell him of an unofficial but significant conversation with a "leading statesman."[8]

This man said that there would doubtless be a good deal of gas talked about the fisheries. That without any question as to the right, the United States must have the inshore fisheries, but were ready to pay for them. Lord de Grey very properly said that he had no instructions on that matter, but would, of course, submit any proposition for the con-

6. Treaty of Washington Papers (D.S.). This Memoir outlined the history of the fisheries dispute, considered the meaning of the Convention of 1818, and stated that questions arising under the issue could be adjusted by (1) agreeing on terms on which all reserved fishing grounds could be opened to Americans, together with repeal of obnoxious laws respecting ports; or (2) agreeing on the construction of the disputed renunciation in the Convention of 1818, on principles by which a line could be run between the area open to Americans and that which should be closed, repeal of obnoxious laws, and agreement on measures to be taken to enforce colonial rights.

7. A detailed account of the meetings of the Commission was written out by Bancroft Davis. A copy of this, entitled Papers and Proceedings relating to the British and American Joint High Commission, in three manuscript volumes, is in the archives of the Department of State. A copy was also found by Nevins in the Fish Papers. The printed Protocols, giving a bare outline of essential facts, are found in Foreign Relations, 1871, pp. 495–531.

8. Macdonald to Tupper, Private and Confidential, Mar. 5; Macdonald Papers: Letterbooks, XV, 400 (P.A.C.). Macdonald said the Postoffice was not to be trusted and so did not name the "statesman," who was probably Fish. See also Pope, Memoirs of Macdonald, II, 90–91. Charles Tupper, Minister of Public Works, received most of Macdonald's communications on the conference.

sideration of his Government. He asked if the United States were ready for a renewal of the Reciprocity Treaty on the same terms as before. The man replied that he did not think Congress could be brought to sanction anything of the kind just now, but what he alluded to was a pecuniary equivalent.

Macdonald told De Grey that his Government had not taken into consideration any other equivalent "but that of enlarged commercial intercourse" as much like the old treaty as "the exigencies of the U. S. revenue would permit." He did not know how the proposal for a money payment would be received, but certainly Canada would not consider a perpetual surrender "for any compensation, however great." He did, however, promise to write in general terms to his colleagues to get their impressions, while De Grey would write to Granville on the same subject.[9]

To fortify himself when this suggestion of purchasing the fishing rights came up in a formal manner, Macdonald telegraphed Tupper to have the Council telegraph him and the Colonial Office that "Canada considers inshore fisheries her property and that they cannot be sold without her consent."[10] On Tuesday, March 7, the American Commissioners came forward with a tentative suggestion of a pecuniary equivalent.

We retired [wrote Macdonald][11] to consult and replied that Canada would be satisfied with a return of the Reciprocity Treaty. I was the spokesman and stated that we thought that under the Treaty the United States had the best of the bargain. That the interchange of agricultural products was equally advantageous to the two Countries and that therefore we got nothing in exchange for the use of our canals, the navigation of the St. Lawrence or the Fisheries. That I always thought that the

9. De Grey said that he would ask Granville to destroy or return to him all private letters, and Macdonald suggested that Tupper pursue the same course "so that by no possibility can [the letters] at any future time become public property." Macdonald Papers: Letterbooks, XV, 408 (P.A.C.). Tupper returned the letters, and today the correspondence is among the Macdonald Papers in the archives at Ottawa.

10. Mar. 8, 10, 1871; Macdonald Papers: Washington Treaty, II, 1, 30 (P.A.C.).

11. To Lisgar, Mar. 11; Macdonald Papers: Letterbooks, XV, 418–419 (P.A.C.). Compare Fish's account, Nevins, op. cit., pp. 475–476.

coasting trade should have been added. That we would ere long have a large addition to the Atlantic Coasting Trade by the construction of the Bay Verte Canal. The U. S. Commissioners withdrew and after some time returned to inform us that they did not see their way at all clear to a renewal of the Reciprocity Treaty, that it would involve an alteration of the Tariff and that therefore a Bill must be passed through both Houses of Congress, the Senate alone not having the power by Treaty to interfere with the Tariff. This they said was now a fixed principle of the Constitution. I may say en passant that I do not believe that there is any such fixed principle and that they would sweep it away like a cobweb if it suited their purpose to do so.

The American Commissioners averred that if such a bill were introduced it would not be passed; that the original Reciprocity Treaty had been concluded in the expectation that it would lead to the annexation of Canada to the United States, and since that had not come about they feared Congress would refuse to extend commercial advantages "as if we were a portion of the United States without bearing the burdens." They did, however, say that if anything could be done in the way of purchasing the fisheries by a money payment "they thought there might be a reduction or repeal of the duties on coal, salt, fish and firewood." Being asked for how long, they replied "in perpetuity." "I am myself," Macdonald wrote, "strongly opposed to the surrender in perpetuity of our fisheries. They are now merely in their infancy, and their present value is no indication of what their annually increasing development may make them in the future. I think it would be a crime against posterity for us to deprive Canada for all time to come of the control of these sources of wealth." The British Commissioners said they would seek instructions from their respective Governments on the point and take it up again if allowed to do so.[12]

For over a week the fisheries were pushed into the background but

12. In a reply to this letter dated March 11, Lord Lisgar (Macdonald Papers: Washington Treaty, I, 364–371 [P.A.C.]) said he had concluded that the American Government "had not the power, if it had the will, to induce or coerce the powerful cliques banded together in Congress, to forego any of the advantages or supposed advantages which they desire from protection. . . ." Canada might, he thought, make some fair arrangement about the fisheries for a limited time, say ten to fifteen or twenty-five years, in order to give time "for the subsidence of the dregs and muddiness—the Protectionist theories—which the Civil War threw up to confuse and blind men's minds."

during that time telegrams and letters in profusion passed between Washington and Ottawa and London. The British Government agreed to consider a money equivalent, and the Canadian Council struggled first to reconcile themselves to the idea at all and then to the form in which it might be acceptable. On March 19 Macdonald telegraphed three alternatives on which he wished instructions in order to be prepared when the question came up again before the Commission.[13] How much money would Canada take for the fisheries in addition to the coasting trade, and free admission of fish, coal, lumber, and salt; how much without the coasting trade but with these articles free; how much without coasting trade and only fish, coal, and salt free? The next day Tupper telegraphed him that the second and third propositions were inadmissible, but the first would be accepted if $200,000 were paid annually.[14]

The Canadian member of the commission had meantime been subjected to considerable pressure from his English colleagues to agree to this idea of a money equivalent and already he was beginning to feel keenly the awkwardness of his position; the Americans, he thought, would be glad to get the British Commissioners to quarreling among themselves and thus "strengthen that party in England who desire to get rid of the colonies as a burden."[15] He was between two fires; if he continued to act on the commission he would be "attacked for making an unworthy sacrifice of Canada's rights"; if he withdrew it would show the split in the delegation. On Monday, March 21, the subject

13. Macdonald to Tupper, Mar. 19; Macdonald Papers: Washington Treaty, II, 79 (P.A.C.). Copies of telegrams and letters are in *ibid.*, and in the Macdonald Papers: Letterbooks, especially Vol. XV (P.A.C.).

14. Hincks privately wrote the Premier (Mar. 21; Macdonald Papers: Washington Treaty, I, 388–389 [P.A.C.]) that while it was to the interest of Canada to get the question settled they could hardly do so leaving certain interests unsatisfied. He hoped that it was true there was some expectation of securing free coal, salt, and lumber; if live animals could be added it would be better than a money payment; once, however, the principle was settled that something *more* than a money payment must be had, the details ought to be easy to arrange. Hincks approved a suggestion Macdonald had thrown out of submitting to arbitration the question of headlands and himself added that the port issue might also be adjusted in this manner.

15. Macdonald to Tupper, Mar. 21; Macdonald Papers: Letterbooks, XV, 455–466 (P.A.C.). The letter was written after the discussion outlined below.

of the fisheries was formally before the commission again by Lord de Grey's announcing that they had received permission to discuss the whole question without any restriction of any kind as to the nature of equivalents and, therefore, he was ready to receive a proposition. The American Commissioners withdrew and, after a long delay, returned and Fish stated for them that

since the subject was last mentioned they had received sundry communications from very intelligent persons concerned with the Fisheries who had represented that they are of small value, and that they (the Fishermen) would prefer things to remain as they are than that the American market should be opened to our fish.

But there was a political consideration of importance, so, though they did not think them worth the money, they were willing to offer $1,000,000 for perpetual rights. Naturally, De Grey said that this sum was so utterly inadequate that he could not think Mr. Fish serious. Then, after a long discussion of the value of the fisheries,

Mr. Fish thought it was a proper occasion to try on the statements of the unfriendly conduct of the Dominion Government—that we had altered our laws, and had prohibited trading, purchase of bait &c., &c., &c. That in fact we had entered into a course that if persisted in might lead to serious complications between the two Nations.

Much talk, more or less at cross-purposes, followed, and in the course of it Fish "alluded in strong terms" to the *White Fawn* case,[16] a recent seizure under the fishing laws. Macdonald made the best defense he could of what he did not consider a strong case, saying that he as Attorney-General had ordered no appeal from the decision of the local court and no prosecution for breach of the customs law. Altogether this day's conference left the Canadian, at least, much discouraged. He thought there was no chance of obtaining coasting privileges, even of the inland waters; in fact,

16. Before leaving Canada, Macdonald had expressed the opinion (to Tuck, St. Johns, Feb. 14; Macdonald Papers: Letterbooks, XV, 302 [P.A.C.]) that the vessel should not have been detained and should be released with compensation to the owners. "The Americans are in an amicable humour at present, and we must endeavor to keep them so."

having nearly made up my mind that the Americans want everything, and will give us nothing in exchange, one of my chief aims now is to convince the British Commissioners of the unreasonableness of the Yankees. This they are beginning to find out, and are a good deal disappointed.

In a private letter to Tupper of the same day[17] Macdonald was even more pessimistic. Senator Hoar, he said, told him plainly that the United States would agree neither to a reciprocity treaty nor to the coasting trade, although he admitted that duties on coal and salt would probably be removed in December.

On the next day, March 22, the fisheries were still the main topic of discussion. At the outset the American Commissioners refused to consider a return to reciprocity, just as the British refused the offer of $1,000,000. A British suggestion of free fish, coal, salt, and lumber, plus the coasting trade, was met by an offer for a term of years of free coal and salt, together with free mackerel, herring, and cod, also free lumber after the first of July, 1876, without any money payment; they also desired free fishing in the Lakes and in the St. Lawrence above St. Regis. This, Macdonald considered, was probably the best offer to be got and asked for the Council's opinion.[18] On the twenty-fourth came the opinion to the effect that no government could carry through Parliament a proposal so obnoxious to the people; anxious as they were to settle the matter this solution would only make matters worse.[19] To De Grey, Macdonald unbosomed himself[20] both orally and in writing. The Canadian right to everything within three miles of the shore was incontestable, and the Secretary of State for the Colonies had assured the Governor-General on February 16 that this "right" should be conceded to Americans only for an adequate consideration; free coal, fish, salt, and lumber were not adequate, for duties on coal and salt were to be repealed in December anyhow and so should not be looked upon as a part of the equivalent. Besides, the Americans were

17. Mar. 21; Macdonald Papers: Letterbooks, XV, 469–471 (P.A.C.).
18. Cipher telegram to Tupper, Mar. 22; Macdonald Papers: Washington Treaty, II, 91–92 (P.A.C.). Privately, Tupper was informed that Macdonald's British colleagues looked at matters only from an English point of view.
19. Tupper to Macdonald, cipher telegram; Macdonald Papers: Washington Treaty, II, 103–104 (P.A.C.).
20. Mar. 25; Macdonald Papers: Letterbooks, XV, 472–476 (P.A.C.).

suggesting that the thirty-ninth rather than the thirty-sixth parallel should be the limit of Canadian reciprocal rights in American waters.

More and more, Macdonald came to be looked upon by his British associates as unnecessarily stubborn, a stumbling block in the path of an amicable adjustment: in separate caucuses, he said, his colleagues were always pressing him to yield and he was obliged to stand out and make himself very disagreeable.[21] On the twenty-third of March there was a long discussion of the fisheries by the whole Commission, with questions of the canals, the St. Lawrence, Lakes Michigan and Champlain raised in connection with the principal topic. Macdonald remarked that while Canada had no present intention of laying discriminating tolls, nevertheless she would do as her interests dictated unless adequate compensation was afforded. After the formal meeting was over, again the other British Commissioners urged acceptance of free coal, fish, salt, and lumber in return for a ten-year surrender of the fisheries with a requirement of two years' notice of abrogation. But Sir John had in hand letters and telegrams from Ottawa showing that not only were the Council behind him but they were inclined to be even more stiff-necked than himself. Two days later he proposed that De Grey take to the conference the letters and telegrams which demonstrated the Canadian attitude, but the latter was not prepared to take that step; it would, he thought, show the Americans that there was a rift in the British delegation and would make them more difficult than ever to deal with. At the conference that day he did inform them that the British Government thought that the offers which had been made were insufficient both as to the fisheries and the navigation, whereupon the Americans offered to make July 1, 1875, the date at which lumber might be made free, and said that if the fisheries of the Lakes could not be common property, then there must be a specification of the kinds of fish which might enter American ports free.

De Grey consented to Macdonald's putting his views in writing, but, when he read the letter at the next meeting of the British Commissioners on Monday, March 27, he objected to several things therein, especially to the statement that the Canadian Parliament

21. Macdonald to Tupper, Mar. 29; Macdonald Papers: Letterbooks, XV, 478 ff. (P.A.C.). This letter contains an account of the negotiation from March 23 through March 27.

would reject the treaty and that Macdonald himself would be unable to defend it before that body. The other British members of the Commission that day also "made speeches *at*" the Canadian Prime Minister, all of which made him feel that they were going to hold him and the Canadians responsible if the negotiations failed. At the conference of the whole Commission on Monday, Macdonald explained why the lake-fishing issue had better remain as it was. When De Grey pressed for retaining the thirty-sixth parallel, Fish explained that no Canadians had fished or would fish south of the thirty-ninth and to change would mean heavy cost in determining the mouths of rivers. Secretary Fish then stated the American concessions: for American participation in the fisheries as under the Reciprocity Treaty the United States would grant free fish and fish oil (except fish in oil, and the fish of the lakes and their tributaries), and free lumber after July 1, 1874. This would never satisfy the Canadians, was Macdonald's opinion, and if this was the best that could be obtained then he considered that he had merely a watching brief, but would stay to see that the treaty provided an article stipulating that provisions affecting Canada should not take effect without submission to and ratification by the Dominion Parliament.[22]

In Ottawa, where the Ministry were up to their necks in Parliamentary maneuvers, news from Washington was eagerly awaited. The realists in the group, like Hincks, recognized the necessity of capitulating on some points but they were one in desiring Canada's problems affecting the United States to be included in the general settlement, even if they did not gain all they had hoped for. They did not want to be "left out in the cold," as Cartier put it.[23] On April 5 Tupper informed Macdonald[24] that the Council "reluctantly" consented to accept $150,000 per annum plus free fish, coal, salt, and lumber, with $50,000 additional for each year that lumber was not free. But qualms of uneasiness attended the dispatch of this telegram, for it was fol-

22. *Ibid.* In a postscript Macdonald remarked rather sarcastically on Fish's statement that no change could be effected by treaty to alter tariff schedules; "he forgot this statement and now finds that a Treaty may be ratified affecting coal, salt and fish, to come into effect on its ratification, by the Senate in Executive Session. I may have occasion to remind him of it hereafter."

23. Mar. 29; Macdonald Papers: General Letters, 1871, p. 94 (P.A.C.).

24. Macdonald Papers: Washington Treaty, II, 178 (P.A.C.).

lowed closely by another asking whether they could afford to accept a smaller sum; in this case, however, they "confidently expected" that England would in some way make up for Canada's sacrifices. Hincks would even go to the point of taking $100,000, with $25,000 additional for the years lumber remained dutiable. The backing the British Government gave Macdonald's stand was a distinct encouragement and gave him "rather a victory over" his colleagues when the Home Government informed Lord de Grey that they considered "Sir John Macdonald's propositions were quite reasonable, and that there should be a substantial money payment and an immediate repeal of the duty on lumber."[25] De Grey admitted that he had never thought the equivalent adequate but political considerations weighed with him.

My uniform reply to an observation of that kind [said Macdonald] has been that while I admitted the importance to Canada as well as to England, of friendly relations with the United States, I could not suppose that these relations were endangered by the maintenance of an undisputed right. That no civilized nation could take umbrage at the assertion of such a right, and that the only complaint that really had any force in it was that our officers had carried out the law too strictly. I denied that there was good ground for such a charge, but said that in the future we would take still more pains to prevent even the semblance of harshness, or overeagerness to capture.

In spite of his frequent differences with his colleagues and his apparently unyielding stand toward the Americans, the Dominion Prime Minister began to feel that the situation was fairly well in hand. He was content now to keep back the settlement of the fisheries until other questions had been adjusted, and then, if agreement on the fisheries and navigation proved impossible, he thought he would propose that the Joint Commission should recommend a minor commission to meet the following winter to settle Canadian questions: "This arrangement as it will hold out hopes of a satisfactory settlement to the Western members, will carry the treaty through the Senate and at the same time give Canada a far better chance than she has just now where her pecuniary interests are considered as altogether secondary to

25. Macdonald to Tupper, Apr. 5, 1871; Macdonald Papers: Letterbooks, XV, 542 (P.A.C.). A part of the letter, including the quotations here, is in Pope, *Memoirs of Macdonald,* II, 106–107.

present Imperial necessities."[26] To Lord Lisgar he summed up the negotiations in a private and confidential letter of April 7.[27]

With respect to the Fisheries we came rather to a standstill. After a good deal of discussion my colleagues offered to accept free coal, salt, fish and lumber. I dissented on the ground that the coal and salt duties were to be taken off by the Americans whether or not, and that such was the unpopularity of the tax that there was no chance of its being reimposed. That with respect to free fish and lumber, while these concessions as make weights, in addition to a substantial money payment, would be of importance I felt that they could not be considered as an adequate equivalent. . . . The chief value of free lumber to Canada would be the finding of a market for inferior qualities of lumber for fencing, outhouses, &c, which is of such little value as scarcely to more than pay the cost of transportation with a small profit, and on which the present 20 per cent duty operated as a prohibition. . . .

I am not in a very enviable position at present as I stand alone. The Americans are constantly depreciating the value of our property and making absurdly low offers, which my colleagues, in their anxiety for a settlement, are constantly pressing me to yield to. . . .

If Macdonald thought he stood in a tactically safe position and could, by hanging on, wear down the opposition of the Americans and the temporizing of his colleagues, he was soon to be disabused of the idea. On April 12 De Grey, in a conversation with Fish, told the latter that it was useless to expect an agreement unless provision was made for submitting Canadian issues to the Canadian Parliament and it was found to be impossible to secure the approval by that body of the propositions which the American Commissioners had made. Fish thereupon said he was glad to hear this because in conversation with several Senators he had discovered they believed too generous an offer had been made and since it had proved unacceptable, the offer was withdrawn.[28] De Grey then asked if it would be possible to unite Cana-

26. Macdonald to Tupper, Apr. 5; Macdonald Papers: Letterbooks, XV, 548 (P.A.C.).

27. Macdonald Papers: Letterbooks, XV, 570 ff. (P.A.C.).

28. Papers and Proceedings relating to the American and British Joint High Commission, III, 143 ff., 181 ff. (D.S.); Fish Diary in Nevins, *op. cit.*, pp. 477–478; Macdonald to Tupper, Private and Confidential, Apr. 16, Macdonald Papers: Letterbooks, XV, 597 ff. (P.A.C.). Chandler promised to "fight

dian trade and fisheries issues with a monetary consideration. To this Fish replied that it was too late: Congress was nearing the end of its special session and was unwilling to take up any new matters; earlier an appropriation could probably have been obtained but it was out of the question now. To Fish's suggestion that the commission attempt to deal with the *Alabama* Claims alone and leave the Canadian issues to future disposition, De Grey replied that this was impossible; he did not see how an accommodation could be reached unless some disposition of those issues were made, and that the San Juan boundary affair, being British and not Canadian, was one on which the former could not make a concession and renewed an earlier proposition to submit this to an arbitration.

Nearly a month earlier the San Juan issue had come before the Commission only to find the two groups wide apart: the Americans were firm in their determination not to yield on their contention, particularly Williams, who felt that the people in his part of the country would never forgive any surrender of their claims; the British were equally obstinate in maintaining that at least the question should be submitted to arbitration, although Macdonald thought of this issue more as a bargaining point than as one on which Great Britain had any substantial basis of claim.[29] Yet San Juan was proving a problem which presented "more difficulties than all the other cases put together."[30] It seemed almost "to be a point of honor with both nations not to give way." Macdonald privately suggested to his colleagues that, if no other mode of accommodation could be reached, the disputed islands be jointly occupied for a period of twenty-five years, with a guard of ten instead of one hundred men kept there by each party. "I shall tell the American Commissioners jocularly," he wrote,

to the last ditch any treaty" admitting lumber and salt free. Nevins, *op. cit.,* p. 479.

29. Macdonald to Tupper, Mar. 17; Macdonald Papers: Letterbooks, XV, 436 (P.A.C.). "We have had two or three days discussion of the San Juan business. This matter offers great difficulties and between ourselves, I think the United States have a very strong case; stronger in equity than ours which can only be maintained by the most technical construction of the actual words of the Treaty. However we are fighting the battle stoutly and do not intend to give up San Juan. . . ."

30. Macdonald to Tupper, Apr. 5; Macdonald Papers: Letterbooks, XV, 547 (P.A.C.). See also Macdonald to Lisgar, Apr. 7; *ibid.,* pp. 575–576.

"that that is the best mode of settlement as long before the quarter century is out the infallible destiny of absorption which they all believe awaits us, will have settled the difficulty."

Navigation of the rivers, lakes, and canals and the question of transit in bond had likewise cropped up in the discussions from time to time. At an early date, before the subject came before the commission as a whole, Macdonald in a private conversation with Fish[31] had stated that the present canals were sufficient for Canadian use, but it had been "nearly resolved" to extend them considerably, although, as this would entail a great expense, tolls might have to be raised to meet the increased cost. "I further said that even if Canada intended to continue the policy of charging against her own shipping a toll simply sufficient for maintenance, the United States and other foreign shipping had no right to expect that the same principle would be extended to them, but that they ought to be prepared to contribute to the cost of enlargement by a higher rate of tolls than might be imposed on our own vessels." Secretary Fish appeared to attach no especial value to the St. Lawrence and the canals; the situation as it stood was satisfactory, but "the west attached an exaggerated importance to an arrangement for free navigation," and the Western Senators would have to be placated in order to get their votes for the treaty.[32] At the same time he was willing to admit a system of give and take: he would

allow the St. Lawrence to stand against Lake Michigan and Lake Champlain, and Sault Ste. Marie & St. Clair Flats Canals against the Welland and the St. Lawrence. . . . He desired the bonding system to be made a permanent arrangement instead of being at the discretion of both Governments, and . . . he would give the right to our [Canadian] vessels to carry from American Port to American Port on the Lakes, in bond, where land transportation intervened, and in that respect make a breach in their Coasting Laws under our granting the same privileges to them. . . .

As a part of the arrangement Fish asked that the export duty on lumber at St. John, New Brunswick, be taken off, and that no export

31. Macdonald to Tupper, Mar. 17; Macdonald Papers: Letterbooks, XV, 440 (P.A.C.).

32. Macdonald to Tupper, Private, Apr. 1; Macdonald Papers: Letterbooks, XV, 530 ff. (P.A.C.). Macdonald was sure that Fish took this ground in order to scare De Grey into thinking that no treaty might be obtained otherwise.

duty should be charged on the products of either country when shipped from the other.

The St. Clair Flats Canal case was presented by Macdonald on March 17, when he took the line that it was a minor question and principally involved customs; he suggested that "two sensible men," one Canadian and one American, be sent to see what could be done.[33] But four days later, when discussing the issue with his colleagues, who were strongly opposed to fighting the question on alleged discrepancies in plans, Macdonald referred to the Ashburton Treaty, with its provision for joint and equal use of the channels; if either built an artificial channel it must be for the use of both parties, although the Canadians were prepared to pay a proportionate share of the expenses of such construction. When put to the whole commission in this form the Americans gave no "express assent" to the proposition, but the Canadian Premier gathered they saw the reasonableness of his position, and the matter dropped for the time.[34] The Fenian claims had not arisen, although the Canadian representative had been informed by his colleagues in Ottawa that a dispatch had been received from England saying that their minute on the subject had been referred to the Joint High Commission; they trusted that he would "willingly press them," for they might help the fishery negotiations.[35]

But, with the blunt announcement of Secretary Fish that the offer of free coal, fish, salt, and lumber after a period of years, together with a possible monetary payment, was withdrawn, the fisheries tangle appeared to be back where it was when the negotiations started.[36] This was driven home the more firmly since the Canadian Council, at Macdonald's behest, had rejected Fish's comprehensive proposal which lumped navigation, bonding, and New Brunswick lumber duties, along with a modification of the coasting laws with respect to

33. Macdonald to Tupper, Mar. 17, 1871; Macdonald Papers: Letterbooks, XV, 437–439 (P.A.C.).

34. Macdonald to Tupper, Mar. 21; Macdonald Papers: Letterbooks, XV, 467 ff. (P.A.C.).

35. Tupper to Macdonald, cipher telegram, Mar. 25; Macdonald Papers: Washington Treaty, II, 115 (P.A.C.).

36. On the same day this announcement was made by Fish, Lord Lisgar wrote Macdonald (Macdonald Papers: Washington Treaty, II, 114 ff. [P.A.C.]) that Tupper had moderated the money demand to $50,000 per annum in addition to free fish, coal, lumber, and salt.

the lakes. Outwardly there seemed to be an unbreakable deadlock. Nevertheless, nine of the commissioners were reluctant to allow the negotiations to break off without some treaty, especially since agreement, except as to some details, had been reached on the *Alabama* Claims. The Canadian member stood alone, subjected to pressure from his British colleagues and argument from the Americans; he was, as he put it in one of his letters, the "nigger on the fence." But something more than argument had to be used. A step was taken that very day when the American Commissioners stated that, while reluctant to submit the San Juan boundary to arbitration, they were willing to yield the point as a last resort if everything else was settled.[37] That evening De Grey called at Davis' house, where they threshed over the questions again. De Grey had grasped at a hint from Fish about a reference of the question of the value of the fisheries to arbitrators; it would have the advantage of hanging up the question for a couple of years. On the other hand, if they could only get San Juan arbitrated they did not care who was the arbitrator, even the Emperor of Russia if the Americans wished. Davis' saying that if an arbitration came they would insist upon bringing in all the correspondence since 1827 did not disturb De Grey; they might bring in anything they wanted so long as the British had the same privilege.

On the following morning Fish saw the President:[38]

. . . I ask his opinion as to the purchase of the right of the inshore fisheries, at a price to be named by arbitrators without any trade privileges; he thinks favorably of it, provided the St. Lawrence navigation be settled satisfactorily, and as a last resort will consent to arbitration of San Juan in a separate treaty. I tell him the English Commissioners have insisted that all the questions be united in one treaty; he then advises me to consult with my associate Commissioners, and with some leading Senators. . . .

Later in the morning Fish saw Chandler, the Senator who stood in a position to make as much trouble as anyone; showed him the "British expression of regret" about the Rebel cruisers, with which he was

37. Papers . . . relating to the . . . Joint High Commission, III, 143 ff. (D.S.).

38. Diary, Apr. 13, in Nevins, *op. cit.,* pp. 477–478. The gist of the interview is also noted in Papers . . . relating to the . . . Joint High Commission, III, 161 (D.S.).

satisfied; obtained from him a promise to support a treaty providing for purchase of the inshore fisheries and submission of San Juan to arbitration of the German Emperor. The next day Fish had a conversation with De Grey and a long talk with Macdonald to try to find some formula which would handle Canadian issues. Sir John, still clinging—at least in appearance—to the idea that tariff concessions were to be obtained, stated that if live animals were added to the proposed free list, Canada would be satisfied with the concessions, only to be told that the offer was withdrawn and that the Americans preferred to make a money payment, and, since they could not agree on the value, to let this question be arbitrated. This, said Macdonald, would be very distasteful to the Canadians, whereupon Fish urged the necessity of some settlement, emphasizing the danger which might at any minute arise from the rash act of some fisherman. At the meeting of the commission that afternoon Fish announced how far his Government would go: arbitrate the value of the fisheries and, as a last resort, arbitrate San Juan.[39] In the course of the session Tenterden sent for Davis and told him that if the Americans were willing to arbitrate the value of the fisheries it would be necessary to allow entrance of Canadian fish free from duty, and the arrangement must be for a term of years. When Davis reported this to the American delegation they immediately said no; nor would they take to the idea of a limited period only—they still clung to a settlement in perpetuity.

Cables between London and Washington and telegrams from Washington to Ottawa and back were the order of the day on April 15 —no new thing, for cable and telegraph bills of the British Commission were mounting to a prodigious sum. Macdonald informed his Council of the withdrawal of the previous American offer and put to them for their consideration two propositions: free fish and a sum of money to be determined by an arbitration, or a sum to be settled by arbitration without free fish. Promptly the same day came back the answer that neither proposal was satisfactory; "either . . . would be promptly rejected by Parliament and cause incalculable mischief by creating the impression that the right of Canada has been sacrificed

39. Williams was still reluctant; he did not wish as yet to agree to this course, for the people in his part of the country opposed any settlement which did not leave the island to the United States. Papers . . . relating to the . . . Joint High Commission, III, 189 (D.S.).

to Imperial interest."[40] Rightly supposing that the stiff-necked attitude of the Canadian Cabinet was inspired, at least in part, by the Premier, Northcote undertook to labor with that gentleman and make him see reason.[41] "We are now coming close to the end of our work," he wrote, "and there seems every possibility of our bringing it to a satisfactory conclusion." *Alabama* Claims and San Juan appeared on the verge of settlement and "none of us would like to take the responsibility of breaking off the whole negotiation at this stage." The time had come, then, for Macdonald to come forward and propose, at least to his colleagues, a practicable arrangement even though it might not be one completely acceptable to Canada. "The importance of the arrangement being made in that manner is in my judgment hardly inferior to the importance of the arrangement being a good one in itself." He begged him, therefore, not to let the opportunity escape. The Premier might fear unfortunate political results for himself if he came back with an unsatisfactory treaty, but "forgive me for saying that they would be equally ready to attack you if the arrangement were made, as it were, in spite of you, and if they had it in their power to say that you had been forced to sacrifice the interests of Canada to the exigencies of England; and that while you would fail to please England you would likewise fail to please Canada." By standing out Macdonald would encourage the "small anti-British party" and put the administration in a very embarrassing position, unless he was "prepared, which you certainly would not be, to make a quarrel with the Home Government." Northcote maintained that he would not take the position he did if he thought he was asking Canada to make any real sacrifice; free fish with a money payment would be as advantageous to Canada as it would be to the United States. After all, it was only a question of bargaining and, in Northcote's opinion, the British had "overstayed their market." He hinted pretty strongly that Macdonald had made a mistake in not closing with the offer which the Americans had now withdrawn.

At a caucus of the British delegation the same day all the members worked upon Macdonald as Northcote had done privately, expressing

40. Macdonald to Tupper and Tupper to Macdonald; Macdonald Papers: Washington Treaty, II, 208, 213 (P.A.C.).

41. Northcote to Macdonald, Apr. 15; Macdonald Papers: Washington Treaty, I, 422 ff. (P.A.C.).

very much the same opinions, and letting the Canadian understand that they felt he was blocking the way to a treaty which, if not perfect, at least offered to put an end to the constant bickering which had been going on for years. Naturally, Macdonald did not find his position comfortable and cast about to find someone to share the burden. He apparently took some rather cold comfort in the thought that the act of the Canadian Parliament in repealing coal and salt duties had put a weapon in the hands of the Americans, who thought that if Canadians wished to open this market to them without reciprocal legislation, then so much was gained without payment.[42] But on the latest American proposition he was adamant. His stand was viewed by De Grey "with deepest regret," although the Home Government was put in possession of the telegrams which had been received from Ottawa and their advice would be awaited.[43]

It was about this time that the Fenian claims were mentioned, and the American Commissioners stated that these could not be taken up under the terms of the correspondence which had passed between Thornton and Fish to lay the foundation of the conference.[44]

With regard to the Fenian claims Lord de Grey and I had a talk on our way home after the Conference & after the Americans had taken the objection. He evidently felt that the English Government and Thornton had made a mistake in the language of the correspondence. He said that he would sound his Government as to their willingness to pay Canada a sum of money to get rid of the question. I availed myself of the opportunity of speaking about a Guarantee for Railways as being a preferable mode of aiding Canada in any money arrangement for any purpose that might be

42. Macdonald to Tupper, Private and Confidential, Apr. 16; Macdonald Papers: Letterbooks, XV, 597 ff. (P.A.C.). In this letter Macdonald told at length of the position he was in and how his colleagues were bringing pressure to bear upon him. He, however, stood upon his original proposal: Canada would only be satisfied with free fish, salt, coal, and lumber, with a money payment. "We would fix our own price and that if the buyer would not pay the price, then we would keep our property." To Cartier he sent another letter for the use of the Council. Macdonald Papers: Washington Treaty, I, 126–143 (P.A.C.).

43. De Grey to Macdonald, Apr. 16; Macdonald Papers: Washington Treaty, I, 423 (P.A.C.).

44. Macdonald to Tupper, Apr. 16, Macdonald Papers: Letterbooks, XV, 607 ff. (P.A.C.); Pope, *Memoirs of Macdonald*, II, 108–113.

made with England. That it did not involve an advance of money but was a mere pledge of credit. . . .

De Grey, a little later, told Macdonald and permitted him to state in strictest confidence to his Council, that "if all other matters were settled & if it were not to be drawn into a precedent," Her Majesty's Government "would agree to pay a sum of money to Canada for the Fenian claims, if the United States did not." He thought there was no chance to get a guaranty from the Gladstone Government and so did not raise the question. The guaranty, of course, was what the Canadian Government wanted; the seed had been planted and time might cause it to sprout.

Until April 22 the sparring went on, principally over the fisheries.[45] The Canadian Premier himself admitted that he had been the cause of this prolonging of the discussions: "I had managed to keep things standing for a week but at last the U. S. Government became restive, and there was danger of breaking up all the arrangements." The informal withdrawal of the earlier American offer was made formal by announcement in a meeting of the Joint Commission. The British insisted, however, that there must be at least free fish, with a money equivalent, which they agreed might be determined by an arbitration; the British Government gave permission to their representatives to make this a basis of an understanding, and finally, on April 22, this was accepted as the way out. All the way along, however, Macdonald fought bitterly at each step, backed by his Council in Ottawa, which, through Cartier, in a communication written the same day the agreement was reached, emphasized again its opposition to this kind of adjustment.[46] With or without the backing of the Canadian Cabinet, Macdonald was waging a losing fight. On April 21 had come a cable

45. The details are given at length in Papers . . . relating to the . . . Joint High Commission, III, 217 ff. (D.S.); Macdonald to Tupper, Apr. 18, 21, Macdonald Papers: Letterbooks, XV, 650–652, 664–669 (P.A.C.); Hincks to Macdonald, Apr. 21, Macdonald Papers: Washington Treaty, I, 428 (P.A.C.). The letter to Tupper is in Pope, *Memoirs of Macdonald,* II, 120–125.

46. Cartier to Macdonald, Apr. 22; Macdonald Papers: Washington Treaty, II, 234 ff. (P.A.C.). Macdonald, writing to Hincks April 24 (Macdonald Papers: Letterbooks, XV, 685–686 [P.A.C.]), said that it was unfortunate that this answer did not reach him in time to make use of it: "Before its receipt matters had gone so far that it was of no value."

from London instructing the commission to negotiate on the basis of free fish and arbitration of the money value, and the die was cast. For ten years, then, and "further until the expiration of two years after either of the high contracting parties shall have given notice of its wish to terminate" the agreement, the fisheries were to be open to Americans, providing the necessary legislation should be enacted.

San Juan, which had also been lingering in the background, emerged and, with American yielding to arbitration, that too was put among the *faits accomplis*. Macdonald made a last-minute stand by urging that

it should be made a portion of the agreement that whether the decision be in favor of the Rosario Channel as we contend, or the Haro Channel as the Americans claim, it should be agreed that all the Channels should be free to both Nations, and that none of the Archipelago of Islands lying between Vancouver and the main land should be fortified. . . . If San Juan be awarded to the United States and they are not allowed to fortify during peace, England, so long as she is mistress of the seas, can, on the first breaking out of war seize upon the Island and hold it against all comers.[47]

But the Americans would have none of this; they "refused to split the difference," saying that such a provision would cause the rejection of the treaty.

The other questions affecting Canada were dealt with in short order, either to make some provision regarding them or to omit them altogether. Free navigation of the St. Lawrence to Americans, and to Canadians that of three Alaskan rivers, the Yukon, Porcupine, and Stikine, was accorded, but, except in a limited way, the navigation of the St. Lawrence meant little to Americans if they did not also have the right to use Canadian canals. All that was done in this regard was that the British Government agreed to urge upon Canada to open her canals to Americans on a footing of equality with her own citizens, while the Government of the United States stipulated to open the St. Clair Flats Canal to Canadians, and to urge upon the various States the opening of canals under their respective jurisdictions where these connected with the border lakes and rivers. Transit in bond was made mutual for twelve years, with only the ports of New York, Boston, and

47. Macdonald to Tupper, Apr. 21; Macdonald Papers: Letterbooks, XV, 667–668 (P.A.C.).

Portland opened on the American side, although the President might declare from time to time other ports where a similar privilege could be enjoyed. The limited breach of the American coasting laws, suggested earlier by Fish, was incorporated in the treaty by allowing carriage in Canadian bottoms of goods from one American port on the lakes to another where land carriage in Canada intervened, while the same privilege was extended to American vessels under similar circumstances.

As early as April 26 De Grey could say that only the matter of the Fenian raids remained. Thereupon ensued a discussion as to whether the correspondence with Thornton had specifically included this issue. The Americans were unanimous in saying it did not, while De Grey for the British maintained, not very strongly in view of what he had confided to Macdonald earlier, that they and their Government took the contrary view, and, when Fish took the ground that these claims were distinctly outside the agenda, referred the question to London. There the Cabinet concluded that there was enough doubt as to the meaning of the language to make it inexpedient to press the matter.

Sir Edward [wrote Macdonald to Lisgar][48] said he certainly intended by his language to include such claims. However, they were ruled out, and, I think, correctly. But this is another instance of diplomatic blundering, the fault to be divided between Thornton & Rose, who settled the correspondence, and Lord Granville who approved of it. It is rather fortunate for Canada that this mistake has happened, as I fancy we would have got but a small award if any, and I have secured the promise of Her Majesty's Government to pay Canada a sum of money in settlement of our claims, leaving England to deal with the question with the United States, as she may deem proper. In other words we will get the money from England, and she will never demand it from the United States.

Canada could well, as Macdonald did not hesitate to point out to everybody, complain that she had got very little from the treaty except for one thing: all the parts which affected the Dominion must be referred to her Parliament for ratification before they went into effect. The articles themselves were "a precious lot" in the view of Sir John.[49]

48. May 7; Macdonald Papers: Letterbooks, XV, 772–773 (P.A.C.).
49. In a letter to Tupper, Apr. 27; Macdonald Papers: Letterbooks, XV, 644–649 (P.A.C.).

His colleagues, on the other hand, were not so sure that Canada had come off badly. As Sir Stafford put it[50] in a letter to Disraeli:

. . . I think that the general effect of Acts xviii. to xxxiii. is decidedly favourable to Canada, and that the only thing she loses (and that for a short term of years) is a whip which she liked to crack for the purpose of driving Americans into bargains, but which she would have been very foolish if she had attempted to use,—I mean the power of excluding American vessels from her canals. But beyond this, I am convinced that if it could truly be said that any local interests had been sacrificed for the sake of a general settlement of imperial questions, it could not be said that the interests sacrificed were those of Canada, and that the party for whose benefit the sacrifice was made was England; for I believe that no part of the empire has so direct and immediate an interest in the maintenance of friendly relations between us and the Americans as Canada herself.

When the treaty was completed except for its final wording, and that was effected by May 3, some of the questions raised therein were not settled, for the Americans strongly wished to have the fishery provisions go into operation at once so that there would be no friction during the season of 1871. Macdonald did not prove at all helpful on this point.[51] When the question was up in the latter days of April, all that he would say to the Commission was that he had no suggestion to make as to how the difficulty could be solved; he admitted it was probable that there would be greater danger than ever of conflict on the fishing grounds, especially after "Butler's infamous advice to use armed resistance." But if there was trouble it would not be Canada's fault; if the United States Commissioners had agreed to a treaty with any semblance of fairness, then the Canadian Government might have "assumed the power of making a provisional arrangement for the present season in the belief that their conduct would be confirmed by Parliament at its next session." As it was, his Government had no right to make any temporary measures which would assume that Parliament would ratify the treaty. Nevertheless, he confided to Tupper:

It has at last been arranged that Sir Edward Thornton as British Ambassador, is to write a humbugging note to Mr. Fish stating that if the Treaty is ratified by the Senate Her Majesty's Government will under-

50. Lang, *Life . . . of Northcote*, pp. 244–245.
51. Apr. 29; Macdonald Papers: Letterbooks, XV, 719 ff. (P.A.C.).

take for itself and urge upon the Governments of Canada, Newfoundland and Prince Edward Island the making of such regulations for the opening of the inshore fisheries during the present season as may not be inconsistent with the present state of the law, such regulations to take effect as soon as the U. S. Government shall have opened the American Market to our fish in accordance with the proposed Treaty.

When Thornton, De Grey, and Northcote showed him a letter in line with this idea, Macdonald objected to its stating that Her Majesty's Government "would take such steps as the law would allow to open the inshore fisheries," for that would be taken by the United States as meaning that if the Colonial Governments did not give their consent the British Government would withdraw their moral support; it would encourage Americans to encroach on forbidden fishing grounds in the expectation that the trespass would be condoned.

As if his attitude of non-coöperation, to say the least, in the matter of immediate arrangement of the fisheries had not shown sufficiently his general attitude, Macdonald raised further difficulties about signing the completed treaty. Just how much of his hesitation was due to genuine dissatisfaction with the terms obtained for Canada, and how much was simulated in order to impress his colleagues on the one hand and to safeguard his political position at home on the other, it is very hard to say. In the light of his subsequent defense of the treaty before Parliament, one is inclined to believe that at least a part of his reluctance was feigned, possibly to induce on the part of the British Government a more tolerant attitude toward the guaranty of a railway loan. At any rate, Sir John consulted his Ottawa associates on the subject and to Lord de Grey expressed grave doubts as to whether he could with a good conscience put his signature to such a document. "My easiest course and the one most conducive to my own advantage would be, I think, to withhold my signature, but I doubt whether it is not my duty to obey my instructions regardless of consequence to myself."[52] To De Grey he suggested the possibility of either declining to sign, having an entry in one of the protocols expressing his opposi-

52. To Hincks, Apr. 29; Macdonald Papers: Letterbooks, XV, 736 (P.A.C.). Hincks told him he had to sign, but could save himself by protesting to the Imperial Government. May 2; Macdonald Papers: Washington Treaty, II, 281 (P.A.C.).

tion to the fisheries article, or writing to Granville a letter with the same sentiment. De Grey saw no objection to a letter, but, to save the political situation in Canada, it must be published at once, although that would cause "great irritation" in the United States and perhaps "thwart or impede the arrangements" regarding the *Alabama* Claims and the San Juan boundary.

Monday, May 8, was the day on which the treaty was to be signed. On Saturday, Sir John was still undetermined, or so he let his colleagues understand. Oral arguments had been used with him at length and De Grey made a final attempt to win him over by an earnest letter.[53] As a whole, he wrote, the treaty was all that could be expected, "fair and honourable to all parties and calculated to confer very important advantages upon our respective countries." Every treaty, unless negotiated under "the shadow of a triumphant army," had to be a compromise, and the one now before them, he was convinced, was the very best that could be secured. Over Sunday, Sir John decided to hold back no longer. Whether this was because he felt that he had stood out long enough to impress his colleagues and the British Government or whether he became convinced that no other course was possible his correspondence does not reveal.[54]

The next problem was whether the Senate of the United States would ratify the treaty. All those who had been concerned in making the pact recognized that the outcome would depend in some degree on Sumner's attitude. Sir Stafford Northcote, who had become intimate with the aging Senator, was hopeful.[55]

. . . I had a long talk with Sumner yesterday, and De Grey is to see him today. He is very cautious, but I do not think him unfriendly. He is very anxious to stand well with England; but, on the other hand, he would dearly like to have a slap at Grant. We have paid him a good deal of attention since he has been deposed, and I think he is much pleased at

53. May 6; Macdonald Papers: Washington Treaty, I, 442 (P.A.C.).
54. In his Diary, Fish wrote: "When Sir John Macdonald was about to sign, while having the pen in his hand, he said to me (in a half-whisper), 'Well, here go the fisheries.' To my reply, 'You get a good equivalent for them,' he said, 'No, we give them away—here goes the signature'; and thereupon signed his name, and rising from the table, said, 'They are gone.' " Nevins, *op. cit.*, p. 490.
55. Northcote to Disraeli, May 9. Lang, *Life . . . of Northcote*, p. 245.

being still recognised as a power. He certainly is one, for though I think the Government could beat him in the Senate, he could stir up a great deal of bad feeling in the country, if he were so minded. . . .

Macdonald, too, was inclined to think that Sumner would not prove an insuperable obstacle,[56] although he admitted that much would depend on his course. "It is said by some that from his hatred of the President and his Cabinet, he will continue his opposition to the Alabama settlement. If he does so, and causes a split in the Republican ranks, the temptation to join may be too great for the virtue of the Democratic Senators." On the whole, Sir John was inclined to think that while Sumner might speak against certain provisions of the treaty, he would not finally oppose it. The American Commissioners and the Cabinet, noted Macdonald, all along showed keen desire to have the thing carried through, but he observed that

as the time for completing the Treaty approaches Mr. Fish & Bancroft Davis, the asst. Secretary—who is the power behind the throne and a very able man,—are becoming more nervous.

Davis told me at dinner the day before yesterday, that the Administration had staked everything on the Treaty, and that they and especially Mr. Fish and himself, were lost men if it were defeated. The President intends to make it a great card in his presidential programme for the next election. He will take the ground that he has removed every cause for war with England; that the United States can now pursue a course of economical reforms and reduction of taxation without fear, and, that they will now be able to carry out the Treasury scheme of funding the debt by the aid of European capital, at a low rate of interest.[57]

Most of the many Senators to whom Fish showed and explained the treaty prior to its submission for ratification had expressed their satisfaction with it. The Foreign Relations Committee could be counted on to make a favorable report. A small group of Senators was either noncommittal or wavering. How much Sumner's anger at Fish and

56. To Cartier, May 6; Macdonald Papers: Letterbooks, XV, 750–770 (P.A.C.).

57. Writing to Lisgar on May 7 (Macdonald Papers: Letterbooks, XV, 582–583 [P.A.C.]), Macdonald said of Sumner and the treaty: "Its fate will depend a good deal on Sumner's course. He hates the President and his Cabinet with a deadly hatred."

Grant would color his views remained to be seen. Throughout the negotiations Commissioner Hoar had kept him in contact with the proceedings step by step, and now, when the instrument was ready to go to the Senate, Hoar had a long talk with him and was able to report that "all was well." When the treaty came up in executive session on May 24, Sumner suggested modifications he would like to see, but did not press them, and, with forty-nine other Senators, voted for ratification, with only twelve opposed.[58] Reporting the result of the Senate deliberations Thornton said that, owing to investigations started to discover how a copy of the treaty became public,[59]

Senators have been more than usually reticent as to their proceedings in secret Session during the discussion of the Treaty. It is however well understood that its approval was carried by a vote of 50 to 12, much more than the necessary two thirds. It is further said that all the Republican Senators present voted in favour of the Treaty, with the exception of three, Mess.[rs]: Sprague, Hamilton of Texas and West, who voted against it, and Mess.[rs]: Ferry of Connecticut and Howe, who are stated to have paired in favour with Mr: Blair against it. Two Democratic Senators, Mess.[rs]: Bayard and Hamilton of Maryland voted in favour of the Treaty, whilst it is supposed that nine Democratic and the three above mentioned Republican Senators voted against. Some days before the 24th Inst. several of the Democratic Senators who subsequently voted with the minority, had expressed high approval of the Treaty and were supposed to intend to vote in its favour. It would seem however that on the 23d: Inst. a private meeting of all the Democratic Senators was held, at which it was decided that as it appeared certain that the Treaty would be confirmed, it would be in the interest of the party to oppose it. Mess.[rs]: Bayard and Hamilton of Maryland, alone refused to be guided by the dictates of their party, altho' great efforts were used to induce them to do so.

58. Nevins, op. cit., pp. 492–493; E. L. Pierce, Memoir and Letters of Charles Sumner (Boston, 1877–93), IV, 489–491. All the suggestions had to do with the articles bearing on the Alabama Claims; none had any reference to Canadian issues.

59. Thornton to Granville, May 29, 1871; FO 115:525 (P.R.O.). The Committee appointed to investigate the matter found that Z. L. White of the New York Tribune had secured a copy of the treaty but he would not reveal the donor. Senator Wilson accused Chandler of passing out information about the executive session; he said they had all talked too much. May 16, 18, 1871; Cong. Globe, 42d Cong., 1st Sess., pp. 846, 849–886.

Now all that remained for the treaty was to run the gantlet of the British Parliament, the Dominion Parliament, the legislative bodies of Newfoundland and Prince Edward Island, public opinion in the United States, already committed by the action of the Senate, and public opinion in England and in the British North American Provinces. In England and in the United States attention would be largely centered on the *Alabama* adjustment; in Canada and the Provinces this would be taken as settled, while specific articles dealing with Canadian issues, particularly the fisheries, would be under fire, and Canada's Premier took his departure from Washington anticipating a strenuous fight before the electorate and in Parliament—a fight in which not only the treaty as a national factor would be involved but perhaps his own political future.

CHAPTER XVI

RECEPTION OF THE TREATY OF WASHINGTON

PRECAUTIONS taken by the Joint High Commission to keep the progress of their negotiations secret met with a considerable degree of success. Only once or twice did newspapers come out with dispatches which showed that there had been a slight leak. It was a matter of much chagrin to the Administration, then, when, after the treaty had been submitted, some Senator divulged the essential provisions, which became public even before the Senate had had time to get a report from the Committee on Foreign Relations. Immediately editorial comment was rife.

In general in the United States there was a feeling of satisfaction that the American Commissioners had done their job well; there was a British apology of sorts, the *Alabama* Claims were to be submitted to arbitration and the rules which were to guide the tribunal stacked the deck in favor of the complainants. On the issues which affected British North America there was a well-grounded belief that considerable had been gained and little had been given in return. Only here and there, where special interest was involved or where political expediency dictated opposition, was sounded a note of dissatisfaction or complaint. Incidentally, publication of the document proved that some of the pessimistic prognostications indulged in by some persons and papers were without foundation; the Boston *Journal*,[1] for example, had said that it would prove to be a "log-rolling" treaty embodying five main issues each of which had its own partisans in the Senate: the only things definitely to be established were the neutrality question and the navigation of the canals and the St. Lawrence. But a few days later, with the treaty before him, the editor of this paper maintained that the essential requirements of the United States had been met; while critics were found on both sides of the Atlantic, they were driven to desperate straits to find items about which to quibble.[2]

The New York *Tribune* regarded the treaty as a "triumph of

1. May 3, 1871.   2. May 15, 1871.

American principles and American diplomacy"; what trouble was to be anticipated would come from Canada rather than from Great Britain, but even here opposition would not be so great as to prevent ratification. The New York *Herald* could not "conceal its jubilant feelings over England humiliated." True to his inveterate Anglophobism, Bennett could not fail to find a great triumph over the ancient foe.

Above all, in this Great Treaty of Washington we have the virtual recognition from England of our "manifest destiny." So far as human foresight can fathom the events of the future it is the "manifest destiny" of these United States to occupy and govern the North American continent and the islands thereof, and England, in the reciprocities of this treaty, if she does not accept this idea, ceases to resist it. She abandons the idea of war, and consents to a settlement of the great question through the moral agencies of peace.

The Boston *Advertiser* compared the Washington Treaty with that of 1842. "Each treaty may be regarded as successful, but the second is much the greater success of the two." England granted a substantial concession on every "point and principle" ever officially demanded by the United States. The Chicago *Tribune* admitted that the fisheries provisions were a great concession and not a yielding of rights.

We have no such rights. We can catch fish three miles from land, but have no right to enter bays and inlets, or to land, without which right fishing is unprofitable. We should also bear in mind that, if we were the exclusive owners of these fisheries, it is doubtful, extremely so, whether "protection to home industry" would permit any foreign vessel under any circumstances, to take fish from our waters. . . . We cannot expect to use the British fisheries, with the privilege of landing and curing the fish, without making some compensation either in money or reciprocal privilege.

The Detroit *Post* remarked, "This treaty proposes to clear the docket, clean the slate, of all the questions pending between the two nations. It is comprehensive, moderate, well executed. It is equally just and unambiguous. It is a new and noble starting point for both parties concerned in it." According to the Chicago *Republican* the treaty was conceived in "a spirit of unusual liberality and sound policy," while the St. Louis *Democrat* opined that it was a "great moral victory" for the Americans, and the Philadelphia *Telegraph* thought its ratification would be a most beneficent and important triumph for American diplomacy. According to the Detroit *Press*, American newspaperdom was all but unanimous in favor of the agreement.[3]

The New York *Tribune*, pausing in its pæan of satisfaction over the *Alabama* clauses, hoped that "the sober second thought of our Northern neighbours will induce them to accept the accomplished fact, and pass the requisite legislation to carry the treaty into effect." And the Cleveland *Herald* said that no one had

for a moment harboured a doubt of our having irrefragable proof of the justice of our demands in every particular. America stands before the world in a position to command respect, whilst Great Britain has, by its successive blunders—to use a mild term—provoked unfriendliness or contempt from nearly every important nation. . . . Our part is done. Here we rest waiting for the others to perform their part of the agreement. If this adjustment of difficulties should fail through the hesitancy of England, *or the stupidity of the Provincial marplots*, there can be no other settlement short of the sword, and war, under the circumstances, would be as popular with our people as is the desire for peace general now.[4]

It was impossible, of course, that in this chorus of jubilation there should not be here and there a sour note. No doubt there were headshakings and expressions of doubt such as E. J. Penniman wrote to Senator Chandler:[5]

That was a smart game that exhibited the Treaty to the public and it may get some support that it would not otherwise have. For myself I can only say that no umpire should ever be allowed to measure the infinite damage done us by Great Britain. Her regrets (real regrets) are that her infamous conduct failed of success—and her only grief today, is that until this Treaty is ratified she is under highly respectable Bond to keep at Peace with all the world. She is fully the exponent of that old song which begins

> When the Devil was sick the Devil a Saint would be,
> When the Devil was well the Devil a Saint was he.

I would never give her a quit claim short of 500 millions of Dollars, and no arbitration at that.

3. All the above excerpts are found in the Toronto *Globe,* May 24, 1871.
4. These excerpts are in the Toronto *Globe,* May 29, 1871.
5. May 17, 1871; Zachariah Chandler Papers (L.C.).

Outspoken attack on the treaty, however, came almost exclusively from the fishermen and those who represented them. Ben Butler appeared before the Committee on Federal Relations at the Massachusetts State House two days before the United States ratified the treaty and read them a letter which he had written to General Ames.[6] In it he expressed his objection to the provision for American use of British-American shores until they were privately owned; almost all these shores were already so owned, he said, and the concession was virtually nothing. The treaty as it stood would absolutely ruin American fisheries: there would be competition with American fishermen in American ports; the low wages paid in Canada would fill American fishing boats with Canadians instead of Americans; the yearly value of the right to import fish free of duty was worth more than the supposed money value of the *Alabama* Claims; no immunity from seizure of American vessels before the ratification by Canada was provided. Moreover, the concessions granted to Canadians in American waters were very valuable; they could get menhaden there for bait. Whale- and seal-oil fishermen all over the world would have the competition of Canadians. In fact, no part of the treaty pleased Butler and he assured the Committee that it would never be ratified, especially by the House of Representatives, where the members would not be hoodwinked as the American Commissioners had been.

A real wail came from the fishing precincts when the *Cape Ann Advertiser*, on the twelfth of May, exploded with:

It does not take a great quantity of brains to interpret such a treaty as this, as its ratification would conclusively prove the system of spoliation adopted by the Dominion Government toward the American fishermen a complete success. By providing a free market for the Provincial fishermen, we simply transfer the fishing business to the hands of foreigners, and punish our own fishermen for complaining when they have been maltreated by Canadian officials.

Whatever the interest of the speculators might be, the producers would be ruined. It was to be hoped that the Massachusetts Senators had not lost sight of the interests of their constituents, the fishermen, who had asked: "First, protection from British insolence, insult and

6. Boston *Journal*, May 23, 1871. Two members of the committee spoke in support of what Butler had to say.

spoliation (this is an old complaint, commencing with the settlement of the country and continuing ever since). Second, American markets for American fish. Anything less than the first is base cowardice. Less than the second is suicide!" A week later the *Advertiser* returned to the fray with a long editorial to prove that Massachusetts fishermen could not tolerate the treaty. With a duty of two dollars per barrel on mackerel and fifty-six cents per quintal on fish, American fishermen were barely holding their own. Figures showed that under reciprocity Nova Scotia exports to the United States rose by leaps and bounds, and now it was proposed to reëstablish this same iniquitous system. The following week, after receipt of news that the Senate had ratified the treaty, the *Advertiser* sadly commented that all that could be said was that the British Commissioners had hoodwinked the United States. One strongly suspects that the Gloucestermen wished to eat their cake and have it.

Opposition to the treaty on grounds of purely domestic politics existed but was surprisingly little. The Detroit *Free Press*, bitterly anti-Radical and anti-Grant, observed that there was little doubt about ratification, but, "in expressing this opinion we are not led to it by considering the treaty particularly favorable to this country—for we really think that under its own concessions it is shown that the British Government gets off cheap." The fisheries provisions were satisfactory and "if, as the abstract assures us, 'all privileges of fishing, navigation and transit accorded to the United States by the treaty of 1854' are again conceded 'without the burdensome conditions of that treaty in matters of reciprocity,' we have gained everything without conceding much that is valuable to the Dominion in return."[7] There was room for criticism in the cumbersome machinery, but perhaps this was not as bad as it appeared in the abstract. The New York *World*, a Democratic paper, asserted that it would not "withhold from Mr. Secretary Fish because he is a political opponent the credit which is justly his due"; he had "yielded little or nothing, while the Commissioners on the British side sent home again and again for new instructions, and made repeated concessions."[8]

Where there was so nearly unanimous approbation of this treaty on the American side, it can scarcely be surprising that in Canada suspicion should grow that they had received the little end of the bargain;

7. May 10, 1871.   8. In the Toronto *Globe,* May 29.

if the Americans were so well satisfied it must mean that British North America was expected to foot the bill. Sir John Macdonald himself, before the treaty was ratified and even before it had been signed,[9] summed up the manner in which he hoped it would appear to his countrymen:

[Canada] has been refused a renewal of the Reciprocity Treaty. Her demand (which has been declared reasonable by H. M. Government) that in addition to free fish, coal, salt and lumber she should get a sum of money in exchange for her inshore fisheries, has also been rejected. That by direct instructions from H. M. Government those inshore fisheries have been ceded in exchange for free fish & a sum of money to be settled by arbitration:—That this provision however is of no effect until Canada gives it force by Statute: That therefore the whole question remains at her absolute disposal according to her will, and in the meantime she will continue to enjoy the exclusive possession of her own Fisheries.—The Alabama and San Juan questions being both settled there is no danger of Canada being made the battle ground between the two Nations. The right of transit in bond is continued for twelve years absolutely, so that the United States cannot, as she threatened to last season, shut us out if we protect our inshore fisheries & close our ports to American fishermen, the provision being abolished & not continuing upon the ratification of the Treaty by Canada. And in exchang[e] for the navigation of the St. Lawrence between Montreal and Cornwall, where it is not navigable, we get the navigation of three fine rivers in the North West, which is absolutely necessary for the development of that country.

With an eye to political repercussions Sir John, some time before the treaty had been completed but when its general outlines were clear, wrote to Alexander Morris, saying:[10]

I want you to make arrangements with the friendly newspapers, such as the Leader, Montreal Gazette, Ottawa Times & Citizen, and the Maritime Provinces papers friendly to the Government, to hold back, if possible, any expression of opinion on the Treaty when it is promulgated, until the Globe commits itself on the Treaty. I want to endeavor so to manage it as to let the Globe write under the impression that I have assented to the Treaty. Brown will then pitch into the Treaty and into me for sacri-

9. To Cartier, May 6, 1871; Macdonald Papers: Letterbooks, XV, 750–770 (P.A.C.).

10. Apr. 21, 1871; Macdonald Papers: Letterbooks, XV, 680–683 (P.A.C.).

ficing the interests of Canada. He will afterwards find out when it is too late that he is on the same side as myself and will not be able to retreat. My chief object in doing this is, that if Brown finds that I was opposed to the Treaty he will try to find reasons for supporting it. He may take up the loyalty cry and state that it is the bounden duty of Canada to sacrifice something for the sake of insuring peace to the Empire.

While there were some speculations here and there, on the whole the strategy outlined by Macdonald had been employed; the papers which supported the Government did abstain very largely from embarrassing comments during the course of the negotiations. Neither did the opposition papers have much to say that would be in the way of committing them. But, when the work was practically done although not yet announced, the barrage began. On May 1, commenting on an article in the London *Spectator*, the *Globe* of Toronto came out with a warning that neither the British Commissioners nor the British Government would be well advised to sell out Canada's interests, especially in the fisheries. Mischievous news items, such as that in the *Spectator*, received undue prominence in American eyes and led to the belief that England was ready to shuffle off her colonies. "If the Spectator really believes it will purchase a settlement of all vexed questions between the two nations, now and in time to come, by giving up a single just claim, it will one day find out its mistake. In the meantime it should be careful either to inform its mind before speaking or be judiciously silent." Then, when the terms of the arrangement did become known, Brown and his *Globe* came out with a note of "I told you so," even though they were careful not to commit themselves too deeply:[11]

As was to have been expected, the threatened surrender of the Canadian fisheries to the United States for a money consideration has excited strong indignation in all sections of the Dominion yet heard from. It could not be otherwise.

Sir John A. Macdonald, it appears, is anxious to be heard on the subject before the people of Canada pronounce against the measure. The gravity of the matter will, we doubt not, secure what he desires; the whole subject in all its bearings must be calmly and fully discussed; but the more deliberately the question is considered, the firmer must be the decision arrived at and the action upon it.

11. May 11, 1871.

As the weeks passed until well into the summer, evidence piled up that a general burst of wrath was exploding not alone among the opposition but to some extent all over the country, although, more or less, Conservative opinion was willing to wait for Sir John's explanations before going too far. From Toronto the American Consul wrote:[12]

In Canada, with the Reform Party, the Treaty is a bitter dose. Sir Jno. A. Macdonald is blamed and berated for being "jolly green" in agreeing to the basis of the fishery settlement.

I am not certain what the effect will be hereafter. The feeling against the Treaty is pretty general now—and yet the "Reformers" do not desire to offend England—and I think will finally "come down."

This treaty, thought Shaw, ought to bring home to Canadians that it was not possible to browbeat the United States into another reciprocity treaty as well as convince them of the "poor condition they now occupy as a hanger-on to England"; it would stir up discussion and hasten annexation.

"There will be a great fever in the Lower Provinces about the Fisheries and I am not surprised at it," wrote Macdonald[13] on May 12, shortly after he returned to Canada. There was a fever indeed. The New Brunswick legislature was in session when the news of the treaty came through, and this body, without waiting for an official copy, "proceeded to condemn certain points and place their opinion on record without loss of time. . . ."[14] One of the members exclaimed, "If we were to be sold as so many sheep, either by the British Government or Sir J. A. Macdonald, away went our boast that we were British subjects and could receive British justice."[15] In Nova Scotia, where Provincial elections were in progress, there was reason to fear that both Unionists and anti-Unionists would

take the same line as that taken in New Brunswick as soon as the opportunity is offered by the meeting of the Provincial Parliament, for the Coal owners and miners looked for the taking off of the duties on their Coals imported into the United States and the lumberers of both the one

12. A. D. Shaw to Davis, May 17, 1871; Davis Papers, Vol. IX (L.C.).

13. To Lisgar, Macdonald Papers: Letterbooks, XV, 811 (P.A.C.).

14. Lisgar to Kimberley, May 25, 1871; G [unnumbered], pp. 321 ff. (P.A.C.).

15. Montreal *Gazette*, May 16, 1871.

and the other Province export mostly of the quality on which the high duties of the United States weigh very heavily.[16]

The Halifax *Chronicle*,[17] representing anti-Confederation sentiment, called the loss of the fisheries "a blow from which [Nova Scotia] will never recover." "The treaty," it maintained, "is a monstrous and derisive proposition to make to Nova Scotia; and the Commissioners have been dreaming in false security if they believe that we shall submit to the loss of our valuable in-shore fisheries without violence. . . ."

The *Globe*, as the leading paper of the opposition, set itself to gather from the papers of British North America expressions about the treaty and produced a formidable array of condemnatory evidence.[18] The Carleton (N.B.) *Sentinel* opined that it was always the Provincial fortune when North American interests were subjected to Imperial Commissioners for the Provinces to come off the losers; the Webster-Ashburton Treaty and the loss of "a million acres" was dragged out to be compared with the Washington Treaty. "Brother Jonathan thirsted for an opportunity to 'take it out' of John Bull, and his chance came with the Joint High Commission," said the Montreal *Sun*. Canada was a fair field for American rapacity, and the blows aimed at her were meant for England; the surrender of the fisheries would whet appetite for territorial acquisitions and would probably bring on a bloody war. "If, to maintain the Imperial tie, it is necessary to surrender so great a possession [as the fisheries], we say the sooner that tie is severed the better, and we believe we echo the opinion of all true Canadians." Could any sane man believe that Canada would submit to this imposition? was the question put by the Woodstock *Review;* the present Parliament would probably do almost anything on order from Cartier, but surely shame would prevent adding to the infamies by ratifying treaty conditions "which on the face of them

16. Lisgar to Kimberley, May 25; G [unnumbered], pp. 321 ff. (P.A.C.).

17. Quoted in the Montreal *Gazette,* May 16, 1871. Writing to De Grey on May 17, Macdonald remarked: "In order to give you some idea of the storm I shall have to encounter on my return home, I send you certain excerpts from the Canadian Press both French and English. I have not seen the New Brunswick and Nova Scotia papers, but I understand that they are quite rabid." (Macdonald Papers: Letterbooks, XV, 821–822 [P.A.C.]). One can see, of course, the building up of the case for the loan guaranty.

18. Quoted in the issue of May 25, 1871.

mean the ultimate absorption of the Dominion into the Republic," and, while Canadians had always been strongly attached to Britain, if the "overreached and baffled" diplomatists had been victims of a "Yankee sell," it would not follow that they would always submit tamely to humiliation. The Waterloo *Chronicle* found it difficult to contemplate without indignation such "wanton sacrifice of honour, position and future opportunities as made by this disgraceful capitulation. . . . We regret to add that the Treaty of Washington appears to be another step in the direction of what designing American and supine British statesmen have conjoined to make The Inevitable." The Cobourg *Star*, a Government paper, called upon the Canadian people to hold public meetings to voice resentment at having their rights parceled out among enemies; local politics should be forgotten until the question of the existence of Canada was settled. The *Gleaner* of Cannington said that the treaty had scarcely a friend in that community; it was a joke to exchange the navigation of the St. Lawrence for that of the "Yucan"; the Americans had got all they wanted in return for a trifling sum of money and the privilege of selling to the Yankees such fish as they left to be caught by British subjects.

According to the Peterboro *Examiner* the Americans had got the better of the British, and the latter had lost a fine opportunity to get arrangements which would benefit both sides equally; whether Macdonald sat and allowed their rights to be taken away or whether he protested remained to be seen, but one thing was certain: all hopes of reciprocity for at least twelve years must be abandoned, and whatever happened then, a valuable consideration was lost forever. If any doubt remained after reading the treaty that all the advantage was on the American side, that doubt disappeared after reading the protocols, was the view of the Belleville *Intelligencer;* a more humiliating position than that occupied by the British Commissioners could scarcely be conceived. The Napanee *Standard* warned all members of the Dominion Parliament that they would be held strictly accountable for words and votes relating to the treaty; it was rightly designated the "Treaty of Washington," and it would have to be amended in many respects before it could also be considered a "Treaty of Ottawa." The Prince Albert *Observer* said: "We should judge that the States have got their share of the good things, and have therefore no reason to demur at the arrangement. Britain too will most likely get off on pretty easy terms; and as for the Dominion, she will have to grin and bear it till she can help herself, unless she has sufficient courage through her representatives to say No to the conditions of the treaty."

These are but samples of the comment which found expression in newspapers of various political stripes in the Canadas and the Maritimes. Macdonald was on firm ground when he had said that the terms of the treaty would create a furor when they were known. Day after day new evidence appeared to confirm the *Globe's* assertion[19] that "so far as the country possesses information on the case before it, its judgment is one of unqualified condemnation." In private conversation and in letters, not a few of which went to Macdonald himself, the same attitude was demonstrated. The only saving feature in the situation was the fact that articles affecting British North America needed confirmation there, and the only hope lay in Parliament's rejection of those articles.[20] All, however, awaited an explanation from Canada's representative: what was he going to say for himself and for the treaty? Brown in the *Globe* voiced the sentiments of many Government supporters as well as those of the opposition when he called upon the Premier to render an account.[21]

The British "High Joints" have sailed by the *Cuba* for home, and before leaving the United States were entertained with all the liberality for which he is famous by Mr. Cyrus W. Field, at a banquet at Delmonico's. . . . The Commissioners were there, but not all. Sir John A. Macdonald was significantly absent. Perhaps he felt it would be a little too bold a challenge to accept the congratulations of the well-satisfied New Yorkers as a preliminary to facing the stern demand to give an account of his doings which awaited him in Canada. . . .

The veteran politician was not to be smoked out. The strategy he had outlined before the treaty was signed was working out the way he had expected it to work. He intended to let "disappointment and chagrin"[22] have full expression before saying anything. Early in June he wrote to De Grey to explain what his further procedure would

19. May 26, 1871.
20. Fredericton (New Brunswick) *Reporter,* in the *Globe,* May 29, 1871.
21. May 26, 1871.
22. This was how Consul Dart at Montreal, May 25, characterized the feeling in Canada. Consular Letters: Montreal, Vol. XI (D.S.).

be.[23] "I have been pressed very much to make some explanations respecting my course, but have declined to do it until the Treaty is ratified by Her Majesty and the debate in Parliament ended." If he made a statement at the time, he said, it would probably be commented on and misrepresented by the press of the United States, and those comments might create embarrassment in Parliament; for the same reason he had refrained from writing Lord Granville, but when the ratification was completed in England he would write Granville and make his explanatory speech in Toronto.

The line I intend to take at Toronto is that I think the Treaty in every respect beneficial to Canada except as to the Fishery Articles. That viewing them from a commercial point of view it is evidently a bad bargain for Canada.—That I so expressed my opinion as did the Canadian Government and that Her Majesty's Government were fully informed to that effect. That notwithstanding this H. M. Government instructed the Commissioners to assent to the Fishery Articles, subject to the approval of our Legislature.—That I still continue of the same opinion, as do my Colleagues; but that H. M. Government having taken the responsibility of ordering the execution of the Treaty, notwithstanding the Canadian protest, it is for them when they invite the Canadian Legislature to a consideration of the Treaty, to state the ground on which they deemed it necessary to take that course:—

That the Canadian Government as well as Parliament will, as in duty bound, give the most respectful consideration of the views of H. M. Government, with a sincere desire to act as much in accord with them as possible, consistently with the just protection and assertion of the rights and interests of Canada.

This course, Sir John hoped, would keep things quiet in Canada until the next February, and he trusted that the delay, together with "liberal action of Congress next December," would bring people to "a calm state of mind."

While he did not as yet say it in so many words, the intimation is clear that Macdonald intended to support the treaty; but, at the same time, he intended to let the situation work to the political advantage of his party and himself and make sure that England came through with a guaranty of a bond issue. One is forced to conclude that a great many of the things Sir John said to his fellow Commissioners and

23. June 6, 1871; Macdonald Papers: Letterbooks, XV, 771–776 (P.A.C.).

wrote to his friends in Canada were for effect, but if he played a part to gain an end he was successful. Even his friend Rose appeared to think that Sir John had meant most of what he said, for he wrote at length[24] to persuade him that Canada would be making a tremendous mistake if she rejected the treaty. Would rejection bring better terms? Did Canada wish to hold on to her fisheries regardless of the irritation that policy aroused in the United States? Retaliation hardly ever paid, especially when used by a smaller toward a larger country.

The American people are guided perhaps more by feeling than any other nation. They want Canada. Are they not rather resentful that Canada will not be wooed, and will they not be specially averse to letting people situated as we Canadians are, and who daily tell them we will not be of them coerce them into Commercial arrangements?

Canada and the United States were near neighbors with daily political and social irritants to keep things agitated. The fisheries were at the American doors and, rights or no rights, could it be expected that Americans would refrain from using them? Could it be expected that after what had taken place in Congress the United States would withdraw from its protective policy just to please Canada? "The great bulk of the American people who live in the middle Southern and Western States care nothing about the Fishery interests and would not modify their fiscal policy to suit them,—however ready they might be to make common cause in a national assertion to secure the use of them by force." After all, when viewed dispassionately, did abrogation of reciprocity make much change in Canada's economic life? "Though for the purpose of the present argument it might be better that the facts were otherwise it is difficult to gainsay the conclusions they involve viz:—that Canada is really independent of the commercial policy of the United States."

The first breaking of silence in Government ranks occurred when Hector Louis Langevin, speaking to his constituency, revealed the fact that Macdonald and the Conservative Government had protested the terms accorded to Canada. This assertion aroused "almost frantic exultation" in the Government Press.[25] Sir John, said the Belleville

24. June 8; Macdonald Papers: Washington Treaty, I, 481–498 (P.A.C.).

25. The characterization is from the Toronto *Globe*, June 21, which quoted the comments, in "gushing style," of the Belleville *Intelligencer*.

Intelligencer, signed the treaty as Imperial Commissioner but not until he protested and not *"until a clause had been inserted in the treaty providing for its ratification or rejection by the Parliament of Canada,"* leaving him and the Government unfettered with respect to the future. Langevin, according to Macdonald, "completely cut away the ground of the Opposition" which now began to maintain that he should not have signed the treaty at all.[26] While "the storm here against the Fishery Articles continues to be intense, and were our Parliament assembled now, they would be summarily rejected,"[27] the first hot indignation against the treaty was subsiding and the instrument was beginning to be "studied and considered on its own merits."[28]

Two classes of objectors to the course pursued by the Canadian Government now began to be differentiated.[29] First, there were those who maintained that Sir John should not have signed the treaty at all; the second group, the "ultra-loyalists," claimed that Canada was not free to reject the articles affecting her, no matter what the treaty said. In reply to the latter assertion parts of the debate in the House of Lords were cited to show that the treaty did mean what it said; that Canada was free to accept or reject. The Earl of Derby, leader of the opposition, acknowledged that the Government had acted fairly in giving Canada the veto power, but he hoped that no pressure would be put upon her to influence her decision. The Marquis of Ripon[30] agreed that the option for Canada was included in good faith, but he thought that arrangements made in her behalf and which were dependent on the will of the Canadian Parliament were "perfectly fair as far as the interests of the Canadian people" were concerned and it

26. Macdonald to Gowan, June 27, 1871; Macdonald Papers: Letterbooks, XV, 973 (P.A.C.). See also comment of the *Globe,* June 21, which doubted whether in the end the Government would stand up to its protest.

27. Macdonald to Thornton, June 29; Macdonald Papers: Letterbooks, XV, 985 (P.A.C.).

28. Macdonald to John Elliott, July 7; Macdonald Papers: Letterbooks, XVI, 1 (P.A.C.). This subsidence of feeling made Sir John feel that he could choose his own time for making a public pronouncement.

29. Montreal *Gazette,* July 1. Here are found excerpts from the discussion in the House of Lords.

30. Earl de Grey and Ripon had been created a marquis in recognition of his work at Washington.

would be a serious matter to reject them. Lord Granville made no bones of stating that it would be the duty of the Secretary of State for the Colonies "to urge on the Canadian Government the propriety of adopting an arrangement which we believe will be honourable and advantageous to them," while the Earl of Carnarvon, formerly Colonial Secretary, considered that "it would be wrong for us to say anything to prejudge the decision of the Canadian Parliament, but, at the same time, we ought not to flinch from the expression of any opinion which may be justly called for."[31] Furthermore, on the merits of the issue itself, it was questioned whether the fisheries articles left Canada in any worse position than she had been.[32]

But it was on the fisheries provisions that practically all criticism was centered. Passing references, usually of a sarcastic nature, were made to the exchange of navigation of the St. Lawrence for that of rivers in far-off Alaska, and there was some adverse comment based on the mistaken idea that the treaty gave Americans the right to use Canadian canals.[33] There was some comment on the failure to make any arrangement about the Fenian claims, but on the whole, despite deep feeling, surprisingly little. It is understandable why Government organs should refrain from raising this issue, but that opposition papers paid so little attention is less comprehensible. It almost seemed as though there was more indignation in England than in Canada over shoving these aside. In the House of Commons, Sir

31. Montreal *Gazette,* July 1. Lord Lisgar wrote Macdonald, July 7 (Macdonald Papers: Governor General Correspondence, IV, 492–495 [P.A.C.]), that Lord Kimberley, the Colonial Secretary, wrote him that every speaker in the debate had expressed a "hearty good will" toward Canada, but at the same time considered that the treaty on the whole demanded no greater concessions from Canada than from England. Ripon wrote Macdonald July 7 to state how favorable was the opinion in England toward the treaty and telling why both he and Canada should be satisfied. (Macdonald Papers: Washington Treaty, I, 500–510 [P.A.C.].)

32. Montreal *Gazette,* July 6. An editorial in reply to the position of John Young, who advocated independence.

33. Lisgar wrote Macdonald, July 4 (Macdonald Papers: Governer General Correspondence, IV, 489 [P.A.C.]), that the Bishop of Ontario had been under the impression that the use of the canals had been surrendered; he said that if people were reassured on that point and England would show some sympathy, excitement and aversion to the treaty would subside.

Charles Adderley maintained[34] that there "was no possibility of defending the course which Government had instructed the Commissioners to take" in this matter. "Whatever gave weight to the Alabama claims gave tenfold weight to the Fenian claims," where it was not the amount involved but the principle, for the American Government had been aware that "fifty regiments of Fenians were drilling from day to day," and if the principle of "due diligence" could be applied in the *Alabama* case, how much more was it implicated here. Whatever was said in England that supported these claims strengthened Macdonald's hand. "I have read the debate in the Commons on the Treaty, with great interest," he wrote Ripon.[35] ". . . Mr. Gladstone's remarks quoad the Fenian claims have been read in Canada with great satisfaction. I am looking anxiously for the communication from the Colonial office, in the sense of our conversations at Washington. It would strengthen my hands immensely."

Nothing was to be left undone to impress the British Government that that guaranty of a bond issue was imperative. Indeed, that had come to be the trump card if Macdonald and his Government were to get the support of the Canadian Parliament in upholding the treaty. "I have no doubt," Lord Lisgar wrote,[36] "that Sir J. A. Macdonald finds himself in a most embarrassing position, caused mainly by the lofty language and pledges of never yielding either on the Fishery question or in regard to the Navigation of the St. Lawrence in which the rival parties in Parliament have indulged, and vie with each other in repeating and enforcing for years past." The Governor-General was not allowed to forget the issue, and he in turn impressed its importance on the Colonial Office. "My Council fear increased difficulty in carrying Fishery article through Parliament from present misunderstanding with United States, as there is no certainty of friendly relations being permanently established," he telegraphed to London.[37]

34. *Hansard*, 3d Ser., CCVII, 861–873. Extracts from the speech are found in *Foreign Relations, 1871*, pp. 454–455.

35. Sept. 18, 1871; Macdonald Papers: Letterbooks, XVI, 210–211 (P.A.C.). Aug. 4, 1871; *Hansard*, 3d Ser., CCVII, 914.

36. To Kimberley, Secret, July 26, 1871; G [unnumbered], pp. 333–336 (P.A.C.).

37. Lisgar to Kimberley, no date [but in December, 1871]; Macdonald Papers: Governor General Correspondence, IV, 673 (P.A.C.). "The present misunderstanding" grew out of the American Case, prepared chiefly by Ban-

But, he added, they would endeavor to pass the necessary legislation if the Imperial Government would offer a guaranty of bonds to the amount of £4,000,000 to be expended on railroads and canals instead of spending over a million on fortifications.

"The present misunderstanding" proved to be a very real stumbling block, not only in the path of the *Alabama* Claims settlement but in that of the adjustment of the Canadian situation with its manifold angles. It prevented the British Government from giving attention to the demand for a guaranty;[38] it held up action by Congress on legislation calculated to put the treaty into effect so far as the United States was concerned;[39] it threatened, in short, loss of the whole treaty at a time when opinion north of the boundary was slowly swinging around from its original hostility at least to one of temperate consideration. In November, Sir John had sized up the situation in this way:[40]

Quoad the Treaty & its prospects, the case I think, stands thus:—The Commercial Classes on the whole in favor of it—the Fishermen in Nova Scotia ditto, except those in the Bay of Fundy—the Legislature and the majority of New Brunswick strongly against it—the agriculturalists in Ontario ditto, and, I understand, the French rather against than for. The whole Opposition (excepting Holton) will unite against it in Parliament & will agitate the Country at the next Election against it. . . .

croft Davis, where he revived the indirect claims. See Nevins, *Hamilton Fish,* chap. xxii, where there is an account of the course taken by Davis and backed by Fish in pressing these claims which the British Commissioners had thought tacitly dropped; i.e., the claims based on the charge that by allowing the Rebel cruisers to leave British ports the war had been prolonged and therefore Great Britain should pay such a sum as would compensate the United States for the additional cost. These indirect or "consequential" claims were finally ruled out by the Arbitral Tribunal itself.

38. Kimberley to Lisgar, Feb. 17, 1872; Macdonald Papers: Governor General Correspondence, IV, 674 (P.A.C.).

39. *Cong. Globe,* 42d Cong., 2d Sess., p. 1811. On March 19, 1872, in the House of Representatives, Banks carried a motion to postpone for four weeks consideration of the report of the Committee on Foreign Affairs. Macdonald wrote Rose, March 5, that it was stated in several American newspapers that the Committee on Foreign Affairs was not going to report out the bills until further progress had been made with the Geneva arbitration of the *Alabama* Claims. (Macdonald Papers: Letterbooks, XVII, 321 [P.A.C.].)

40. To Rose, Nov. 30, 1871; Macdonald Papers: Letterbooks, XVI, 519 (P.A.C.).

Much, he said, would depend on the action of Congress; if a liberal disposition with the tariff were exhibited it would ease things in Canada, but that country felt "very sore about the Fenian claims, which were withdrawn to suit Imperial interests." This testimony was corroborated by Consul Dart, who visited Ottawa and incidentally conversed with most of the members of the Government. The Governor-General told him that it would be difficult for the Government to carry the treaty through Parliament unless Congress did something to allow the Ministers to say that the situation had been changed so they could now support it.[41] Elections in Ontario had an ominous portent.[42] And from England came a pessimistic note. "I may say," wrote Rose,[43] "I think the chances are, that the Treaty is at an end. I learn that the people about the U. S. legation say that if one part is repudiated, the *whole* must go. So *you* may be remitted to the status quo."

In the United States the Administration evinced a desire, even a determination, to see that the treaty was carried into effect so far as legislation could do it, notwithstanding the fact that Secretary Fish's approval of the American Case as presented by Bancroft Davis raised a barrier which was going to be difficult to surmount.[44] In his Annual Message President Grant recommended "legislation on the part of the United States to bring into operation the articles of the treaty relating to the fisheries, and to other matters touching the relations of the United States toward the British North American possessions."[45] He also stated that he had addressed to the Governors of New York, Pennsylvania, Ohio, Indiana, Michigan, Illinois, and Wisconsin letters urging them to press action necessary "to carry into effect the object of the article of the treaty which contemplates the use of the

41. Dart to Davis, Dec. 7, 1871; Consular Letters: Montreal, Vol. XII (D.S.).

42. Macdonald to Rose, Dec. 28, 1871; Macdonald Papers: Letterbooks, XVI, 693 (P.A.C.).

43. To Macdonald, Jan. 8, 1872; Macdonald Papers: Rose, '64–'74, pp. 593–594 (P.A.C.).

44. Macdonald was inclined to lay the blame for the deadlock over the indirect claims to Fish and to Gladstone, who, he considered, had by his first speech made it impossible for the American Government to back down. Macdonald to Rose, Mar. 7, 1872; Macdonald Papers: Letterbooks, XVII, 341 (P.A.C.).

45. Dec. 4, 1871; *Cong. Globe*, 42d Cong., 2d Sess., p. 4.

canals on either side." Within a week Nathaniel Banks of the Committee on Foreign Affairs had introduced a House resolution in the spirit of the Message, although on the same day Campbell came out with another resolution asking that the President be instructed to open negotiations with both Great Britain and Mexico to ascertain on what terms and conditions they would consent to annexation to the United States of their possessions on the North American continent.[46] The customary legislative resolutions from Massachusetts and Maine urging Congress to protect their fishermen were not wanting.[47] When Banks's bill for carrying the fisheries provisions into effect came up on the calendar, it was reported and, on motion of Banks, made a special order of the day for March 5, but when that day arrived it was again postponed and no action was taken in either House during the session: the controversy over the indirect claims halted all consideration.

Tariff schedules came in for attention, not particularly by way of easing the situation for the treaty but because 1872 was a year in which American political exigencies demanded at least a gesture toward lowered duties, for no one knew yet how strong the anti-Grant Liberal Republican movement was going to be. The regulars could afford to take few chances, so strongly was the tide of disfavor setting in against the Grant administration. Indeed, from what debate there was on the various schedules, Canada figured very slightly, and it is doubtful whether many legislators turned more than a passing thought to her. This was not, however, from want of attempt by Canadians to impress their wishes upon Congressmen where it could be done not too obtrusively. Sir John A. Macdonald took advantage of having met various Senators the previous spring to write F. T. Frelinghuysen[48] that the Canadians were more than usually interested in American legislation. The Senator would agree with him that the treaty should be ratified "in all respects," for with that done it hardly seemed possible that another cloud could again arise between England and

46. Dec. 11; *ibid.*, pp. 55, 62. Butler introduced a bill to promote and sustain American fisheries under the Washington Treaty (Jan. 22, 1872; *ibid.*, p. 497) while Banks, on January 29, brought in his bill for further protection of the fisheries. (*Ibid.*, p. 624.)

47. Feb. 5, 28, 1872; *ibid.*, pp. 829, 1254.

48. Jan. 8, 1872; Macdonald Papers: Letterbooks, XVII, 61–63 (P.A.C.).

the United States. The general feeling in Canada, however, was that unless something approaching the conditions set up by the Treaty of 1854 were reëstablished, the fisheries ought not to be surrendered, and strongest opposition to ratifying the articles affecting this subject was to be anticipated in the coming session of Parliament. If, however, Congress lowered or repealed duties on coal, salt, lumber, etc., he, Sir John, could see his way to meet this opposition. If no chance of speedy action existed, he feared Parliament would approach consideration of the matter in no favorable frame of mind. The Honorable John Young of Montreal took upon himself to visit Washington to see what he could do in a quiet way, although his going was no special pleasure to Government circles in view of the gentleman's notorious predilection for an independent Canada. Sir Edward Thornton watched the situation and dropped a word here and there where he felt it might do some good.

Canada or no Canada, pent-up resentment against war-time import duties and the threatened split of the Republican party necessitated some kind of conciliatory action. This took the form of a more or less general tariff revision by the House Committee on Ways and Means, including some reduction of duties on the commodities which figured so largely in the discussions of the Joint High Commission. Over the hot protests of Representatives and Senators from such States as Maryland, Pennsylvania, Michigan, and Wisconsin, the bill when signed[49] had reduced duties on bituminous coal, salt, lumber of the cheaper varieties, laths, shingles, pickets, clapboards, and a few agricultural products, although none of the latter, except potatoes, figured largely among the imports to the United States. Stark ruin was pictured by Representatives of Maryland and West Virginia as facing their constituents if the duty on bituminous coal and slack went below a dollar per ton; as it was, they contended, with a duty of $1.25 the operators of the United States barely withstood Nova Scotia competition.[50] Chandler maintained that Goderich, Ontario, stood ready to supply the entire American market with salt the minute

49. June 6, 1872; *Statutes at Large,* XVII, 230–231.
50. May 8, 1872; *Cong. Globe,* 42d Cong., 2d Sess., p. 3207. The duty as finally written into the act was 40 cents per ton on slack and 75 cents on bituminous. The Committee had recommended 50 cents.

duties were lowered,[51] and Duell of New York was sure that Canadians, with lower wages than prevailed in the United States, could put it on the market at half the price Americans had to charge.[52] Nevertheless, the duty went from a flat eighteen cents per hundredweight to eight cents for bulk and twelve cents for packed salt. When a bill was introduced to admit free of duty lumber for use in rebuilding Chicago after its disastrous fire, Chandler objected[53] because it would be a breach in the protective system; he would vote any reasonable sum for the relief of the stricken city but he could not countenance this attack on "ruined lumbermen throughout the States of Wisconsin and Michigan."

Long before Congress had completed its tinkering with the tariff the Dominion Parliament had assembled to have as its principal subject of discussion the question whether the articles of the Treaty of Washington affecting British North America should be ratified or not. All through the autumn and winter the Premier had been at work to arrange matters so that he could get a favorable vote and at the same time preserve intact his own political future. Congressional action was slow and none too promising as an aid. The British Government, hampered by the controversy over indirect claims, was almost equally slow in making the promise of a guaranty which Sir John could use in triumphant demonstration of his subtle strategy. His own colleagues who had followed him, sometimes reluctantly, when in Washington and had backed him up in every stand he took, had apparently learned their lesson too well: they were unconvinced that the treaty should be ratified, for they had taken too seriously their leader's words and could not keep up with his tactical moves. Hincks felt that about all that could have been gained had been secured and he would be satisfied if the British Government would make the guaranty of bonds. Most of the rest of the Cabinet were still seething.

It was Hincks, Finance Minister of the Dominion, who took a step which incurred the wrath of Macdonald. On his own responsibility he had made the proposition, forwarded to London by Lord Lisgar, that Canada would forego assistance in building fortifications, to which the British Government was committed, if a guaranty of £4,000,000 in

51. *Ibid.*, p. 2001. 52. *Ibid.*, p. 3214.
53. *Ibid.*, pp. 582–583.

bonds for railroads, especially the Pacific road, and canals could be
assured. It was a most unhappy suggestion, Macdonald informed
Rose:[54] while there was no idea of erecting the fortifications at an early
date, to renounce the assistance would make it appear that Canada
would not defend the country if England got into difficulties with the
United States. Hincks was as fertile as ever in matters of finance, but
"his rashness, always a defect of his character, seems to increase with
years & strange to say he is quite a stranger to public opinion of
Canada as it is. His Canada is that of 1850."[55] As a matter of fact the
Premier's ideas were not far from those of Hincks; it was only that his
method of approach was different. He would forego a money payment
for the Fenian claims, either from the United States or England, in
return for a guaranty which would allow Canada to borrow at a much
lower rate than could be obtained if acting alone; he would also forego
the specific guaranty of £1,100,000 for fortifications which had been
proposed at the instigation of the Imperial Government; but to come
out openly and renounce the fortifications guaranty would encourage
the annexationists and the large party in the United States which believed in "the manifest destiny by which all North America is to be
absorbed in the great Republic."[56] Opinion in Government circles in
England was friendly to Macdonald's idea, but there was some doubt
still whether the whole strength of the Canadian Government would
back ratification of the treaty.[57] Moreover, in the existing dubious condition of the Geneva arbitration, it was impossible to give the matter
the attention it required; could not the session of the Dominion Parliament be postponed as long as possible?[58] Parliament had been summoned for April 4, but at the suggestion of the Governor-General it
was postponed a week to meet Kimberley's views: "a week is a week,
and it may be that the farther delay for that period would obviate the

54. Jan. 19, 1872; Macdonald Papers: Letterbooks, XVII, 98 (P.A.C.).

55. Hincks had been absent from Canada for ten years as governor of some
British Islands in the West Indies.

56. Macdonald to Lisgar, Jan. 22, 1872; Macdonald Papers: Letterbooks,
XVII, 112–118 (P.A.C.).

57. Rose to Macdonald, Feb. 7–8, 1872; Macdonald Papers: Washington
Treaty, I, 559 (P.A.C.).

58. Kimberley to Lisgar, Feb. 17; Macdonald Papers: Governor General
Correspondence, IV, 624 (P.A.C.).

awkwardness of silence or a dubious paragraph in the opening speech or the recurrence to so inconvenient a course as an adjournment."[59]

Cables and letters between the Governor-General and the Colonial Office accompanied by unofficial communications between Macdonald and Rose eventually straightened out the tangle so far as Canada was concerned, and on March 18 came a message with a definite proposition which would enable the Government to go ahead.[60]

Cable from England says: "Secret. We think Canadian Legislation to bring Treaty into executive operation should provide that the Acts should come into force by Orders in Council issued by the Governor General. He will engage that when Treaty shall take effect by such Orders we will propose to Parliament to guarantee two million five hundred thousand to be expended on Canals and Railroads through British territory from Canada to Pacific on understanding Canada abandons all claims on this country on account Fenian claims. . . ."

This was not the £4,000,000 Macdonald had been talking about, but, if the £1,100,000 guaranty for fortifications, which Canada did not intend to construct, were added, it was not too far from the original sum. The path was open for the Canadian Cabinet to proceed, but that did not necessarily mean they would follow it. Stragglers still had to be whipped into line. One of them was Joseph Howe, veteran Nova Scotian, whose presence in the Government was part of the price of keeping his Province lined up with the Confederation. In a speech made before the Y.M.C.A. in Ottawa the old man delivered himself of a tirade which might make it appear that the Dominion was not at all inclined to go out of the way to help England. According to the Premier, who was much incensed, he "made a mess of it."[61]

He did not at all mean to preach Independence or Annexation; his tone was that of a despairing & unwilling belief that English Statesmen were regardless of the existence of the Colonial tie. His remarks about England

59. Lisgar to Macdonald, Feb. 19, 1872; Macdonald Papers: Governor General Correspondence, IV, 625–626 (P.A.C.).

60. Macdonald to Langevin, Macdonald Papers: Letterbooks, XVII, 421 (P.A.C.).

61. Macdonald to Sidney Bellingham, Mar. 6, 1872; Macdonald Papers: Letterbooks, XVII, 332 (P.A.C.). See also Macdonald to Rose, Mar. 5, *ibid.,* p. 323.

buying her peace by the sacrifice of our interests & the Comedy of Errors were much more untimely than untrue. They are the last words however that should be spoken by a Cabinet Minister. . . .

But it was not alone Howe who held back. At a meeting of a portion of the Cabinet the Governor-General was requested to put before the Colonial Office the difficulties of the Canadian situation.[62] Congress had postponed legislation on the treaty and was not likely to complete any that session; no bill had been introduced in the British Parliament. Nevertheless, Canada was asked to carry out an unpopular measure before action was taken anywhere else, and strong opposition was to be expected. Would the British Government, if Ministers did undertake to carry appropriate legislation, agree that the guaranty would mature within a reasonable time, since it really was only an equivalent for abandoning the Fenian claims? Ministers would not, at the present crisis, assume the responsibility for the transference of the Fortification Loan guaranty.

Another stumbling block was San Juan. The Dominion Government feared that, whatever happened about the *Alabama* Claims, arbitration of the territorial dispute would go ahead, and they were pretty sure that the Americans would win the award, especially since information had been received which seemed to strengthen the American claim. From Rose, who acted as unofficial *liaison* agent between the two governments, came the assurance that the San Juan and the *Alabama* arbitrations would proceed *pari passu*. Furthermore, they could be assured that England would send to the fishing grounds at least as strong a force as had been there the previous season. In short, no effort would be spared to show the world that England was not abandoning the Dominion to its fate.

By the time Parliament assembled in Ottawa, what with assurances about the guaranty and the fisheries, and an understanding that no legislation which might be enacted would take effect until corresponding acts had been passed by Congress and the British Parliament, Macdonald had won his victory. A few days after the opening of Parliament, when news about Geneva had become much more encouraging, Macdonald could sigh with relief and feel convinced that "after

62. Lisgar to Kimberley [probably Mar. 27, 1872]; Macdonald Papers: Governor General Correspondence, IV, 671 (P.A.C.).

many months of labor and anxiety" he had finally "screwed up his colleagues to the sticking point." They had agreed to go to Parliament with an act to carry the fishery provisions into effect, even though faced with the fact that George Brown and his paper were prepared to go to the electorate in the summer and use the Government's course as a basis for campaigning against it.[63]

63. Macdonald to Rose, Apr. 17, 1872; Macdonald Papers: Letterbooks, XVII, 564–566 (P.A.C.).

CHAPTER XVII

THE PARLIAMENTARY HURDLE

THE delayed session of Parliament convened at Ottawa on April 11, 1872. Lord Lisgar's speech[1] necessarily dealt at considerable length with issues touching the United States. The "young Province of Manitoba," which had been threatened with a Fenian invasion from the United States, was now once more allowed to proceed without apparent further molestation from below the border, although the Government had been put to a large expenditure of money to afford protection and prevent recurrence of similar troubles. But it was the Treaty of Washington that occupied the center of the stage. Immediately, discussion centered upon it both on account of the measure introduced by the Government to carry into effect its provisions and incidentally upon many other topics which came up. In seconding the address a fledgling member, Carter, announced:[2]

The importance of the Treaty of Washington cannot be overrated. We must look back to the time anterior to the events which took place, and which resulted in the appointment of the High Commission. There was a great feeling of anxiety in the country owing to the unsettled state of the relations between England and the United States. Fortunately the clouds of war which threatened us have been dispersed, and the effect has been a quietening of the public mind and a restoration of the trade of the country. . . .

While it would be premature at this point to discuss details of the arrangement, Carter went on, it could be said from the manner in which the treaty was framed that England had every desire to extend protection to Canada and to sustain undoubted Canadian rights, and the Dominion had every reason to be congratulated that the Premier had been made one of the commissioners.

The opposition made no delay in coming to grips on the treaty. Mackenzie said that the member from British Columbia had spoken of the great credit which the treaty reflected on the distinguished

1. *Dom. Parl. Deb.*, III, 3.
2. Apr. 12; *ibid.*, p. 18.

statesman who had represented Canada, but that gentleman would find great difference of opinion and probably a majority of the House would take an opposite view. There was, he heard, talk of appointing a new commission; if so, there certainly would not be the same commissioners; allowances might be made for some of the British members, who could not have been expected to know Canadian conditions, but no such excuse could be made for the Commissioner who did represent Canada. He understood that the Secretary of State (Howe) had termed the treaty a Comedy of Errors, and another member of the Cabinet (Langevin) had asserted that the Government had protested vigorously when it was understood that the fisheries were to be given up, nevertheless the Government of Britain had instructed its representatives to sign the treaty; such instructions never contemplated that all the Commissioners should sign, and he did not comprehend how the "distinguished statesman" could have signed a document he did not approve.[3] Then, too, there was the delay in calling Parliament: that needed explanation.

Hincks took up the challenge.[4] He defended both the Government and the First Minister. There were, he said, two distinct subjects to be considered: the merits of the treaty, which would have to be dealt with by the House, and the responsibility of the Government because the Premier had signed it. According to Mackenzie, apparently the First Minister should have announced that he would not be bound to sign a treaty unless he agreed with all its terms, whereas everybody knew that if he had taken this stand he would not have been appointed at all. As it was, the Premier had stated Canadian views with fidelity and frankness; leading statesmen in England placed responsibility of signing the treaty not on the commissioners but upon the British Government which directed them to do so—Disraeli had charged and Gladstone had accepted that responsibility, consequently it was unfair to single out the one Canadian representative because he too had followed instructions. Members, he felt sure, would see when papers were brought before the House that the Minister had faithfully performed his duties.

Following Hincks, L. H. Holton, another of the opposition, representing the constituency of Chateauguay, Quebec, asked[5] why, if Macdonald had been sent to Washington to present Canadian interests,

3. Apr. 12; *ibid.*, p. 21.   4. *Ibid.*, pp. 23–25.   5. *Ibid.*, p. 25.

he was responsible to any body except the Canadian Parliament; none could control his actions except Parliament and to that House he should be responsible for his acts. He hoped that the Treasury Bench would explain this apparent discrepancy. J. L. Macdougal of Renfrew, Ontario, asserted that he was prepared to support the treaty. He was surprised that members of the Government were, as he understood the Minister of Finance, ready to throw obstacles in the way of ratification; if that was the case he stood ready to oppose them. Thereupon, Hincks quickly rose to say that he had been misunderstood if members thought he was opposed to the treaty; he had intended to say that the Government had been dissatisfied but, after correspondence with the Imperial Government, they were now in accord. Holton again expressed his opinion that the House ought to hear from the head of the Government respecting his action in subscribing to the treaty when he went to the United States as a Minister for Canada and in that capacity responsible to the House. But Macdonald was not yet to be drawn into a statement: he said it was highly inexpedient and not to the public interest that he speak to the subject then; a question of such grave importance should not be discussed before papers were brought down. As to the Government, every member was responsible to the House and to the country, but as to his personal responsibility as a member of that Government and as a commissioner he declined to discuss the matter until the whole course of Government in its relation to the treaty was before the House.

Such papers as were deemed advisable by the Cabinet were laid before the House on April 18,[6] but meantime there had been more or less sniping from the side lines, all calculated to draw from the Premier some statement. Mackenzie moved an address for papers covering the correspondence with Lieutenant-Governor Archibald relative to the Fenian invasion of Manitoba, as well as for those incorporating the report of engineers appointed to investigate the location of the canal across the St. Clair Flats.[7] He also demanded other papers bearing on the canal and "alluded to certain events that took place in Washington in connection with the Treaty, which showed that the Canadian Government tacitly acknowledged that the United States held dominion

6. *Dom. Parl. Deb.,* III, 62–63. Canadian *Sessional Papers,* No. 18 (1872).
7. Apr. 16; *Dom. Parl. Deb.,* III, 33–34.

over that portion of the Lake [St. Clair]." If such an admission had been made, it was well known that if the canal were recognized as being under American jurisdiction there would be no way for a Canadian vessel to find its way from Lake Huron to Lake Erie if the Americans chose to close the canal.[8]

When Charles McGill of Hamilton, Ontario, moved for a select committee to inquire into the state of manufacturing interests of the country, Francis Jones, representing Leeds and the West Riding of Grenville, would amend to add agricultural interests, pointing out that while manufacturers were protected by a 15 per cent duty there was none for farmers, who, especially in Ontario, were suffering for want of protection; they were practically shut out of the American market, where a duty of 20 per cent was levied upon agricultural imports.[9] The brief discussion of McGill's motion led to a passage involving Howe, Mackenzie, and Edward Blake of West Durham, Ontario, wherein charges of disloyalty were bandied about and Howe was accused of maintaining that England desired to break the connection with the Dominion. Macdonald came to the rescue of his colleague by saying that while he regretted the language Howe had used, the provocation was great. Moreover, if Blake used the words reported in the *Globe,* that in the relations of Canada and England they must look to a reorganization of the Empire, there was not much difference between what the two had said, yet Blake had not been accused of disloyalty. "The organization of the Empire was to be changed because for a few years the Americans were to have the right to catch fish in Canadian waters (cheers)." Furthermore, Macdonald could agree with Howe as to the unwisdom of withdrawing British troops from the Dominion.

The papers relating to the treaty were naturally examined with great care and interest by members of the House. They were, however, not complete enough according to Holton, and Blake said that only those which strengthened the Government's case had been presented.[10] Three days later Mackenzie wanted to know when they might expect more papers relating to the treaty and to the fisheries, whereupon Macdonald announced that with respect to those asked by Blake they

8. *Ibid.,* p. 39.   9. Apr. 17; *ibid.,* pp. 45–59, *passim.*
10. Apr. 19; *ibid.,* pp. 78–80.

had been carefully read and it had been decided that they could not be submitted to the House without injury to the public interest and injustice to the Imperial Government; their omission would in no way affect an intelligent discussion of the treaty.[11] He then announced that as soon as the budget speech had been made the Government would submit its bill to carry the treaty into effect.

Hincks, in bringing his budget before the House,[12] regretted that it was necessary to refer to the Treaty of Washington before it had been discussed in Parliament but it could not be helped. He had always objected to mixing fisheries with Imperial issues, and he had felt deep regret that the First Minister had been asked to be a member of the Joint High Commission, for he was bound to be criticized no matter what the outcome; he had been charged with selling Canadian rights for a mess of pottage while generally opponents of the Government and the treaty had overlooked the very real concessions which Canada had gained. After all, members should remember that England had been very considerate in settling the fishery question, and should also recall that without England's protection the fisheries were worth nothing. Before Americans had raised the issue of consequential or indirect damages, England had been disposed to accept the treaty; now if Canada refused to ratify the clauses affecting her, which she had a legal right to do, she would be placed in a position of antagonism not only to the existing Government but to leading statesmen of all parties. Under those circumstances was it at all certain that British public opinion would sanction further expense for protecting those fisheries? Could it be that opponents of the treaty were blind to the results of failing to carry it into effect, especially when the most prominent opponents were loudest in their protestations of devotion to the British connection? It had been said that there could be no question of money compensation in return for the injuries Canada had endured, but how otherwise were the Fenian claims to be recompensed without a direct or indirect pecuniary compensation? There could be no idea of asking money as a bribe, but there should be some compensation for Fenian losses which England admitted, and the best mode of securing it had seemed to be a guaranty of a loan for aid of public works, especially a railroad to the Pacific. The Government had, indeed, hoped to

11. Apr. 22; *Dom. Parl. Deb.*, III, 107.
12. The speech, on Apr. 30, is in *ibid.*, pp. 223–229.

secure a guaranty of a bond issue of £4,000,000; they had been promised one for £2,500,000. This would mean much more for Canada than a direct money payment, for it would mean that securities could be marketed at a low rate of interest.

Hincks also paid his respects to those who apparently desired to have Canada pursue an independent course within the Empire by erecting a tariff barrier. Some of these would go as far as to urge complete independence of Canada, so that some sort of customs union could be formed with the United States. But they forgot that England had a most-favored-nation clause in a commercial treaty with the United States, and Canada would also have to make a treaty with the Mother Country containing a similar clause. "The object then of the advocates of independence is unattainable by the means which they contemplate, and few of them, I hope, are inclined to recommend annexation, any agitation for which would, in my humble judgment, be neither more nor less than civil war." Nevertheless, the economic life of Canada was intimately bound up with that of the United States in many ways; hence, if duties on tea were removed in that country—and action had already been taken in each house of Congress in that direction—then they must be removed in Canada, otherwise there would be an encouragement to smuggling, with nearly as great loss to revenue as if the duty were removed. As things were, the Government felt that at the time it was unwise to meddle with the tariff schedules in general.

It would be unfair to say that the debate following Hincks's budget speech was a discussion of the Treaty of Washington; nevertheless, so much of it was devoted to this topic that one might almost have thought the House had forgotten the real question before them. Mackenzie, Galt, Blake, and R. J. Cartwright of Lennox, Ontario, among others, did not spare the Government or the Finance Minister as they scoffed at the little return Canada was expected to have for the great sacrifices made. Galt believed that the last part of Hincks's speech was "pointing the finger of scorn" at those who did not share his political opinions; while he did not wish to terminate the connection with England recklessly or suddenly he was not prepared to say that they were dependent on the Imperial Government, but so long as the connection lasted he would do his duty in all matters concerning the Empire.[18]

13. *Ibid.,* p. 241. One must believe that practical politics were pretty well mixed with this apparent genuine objection to the treaty. A year before, Hincks

Galt's reference to his well-known predilection for an independent Canada calls attention to an undercurrent which ran through much of the debate on the treaty and on other subjects which involved that instrument directly or indirectly: how would its ratification or rejection by Canada affect the relations of the Dominion with England on the one hand and with the United States on the other? What came out in Parliament was only an echo of what had been cropping up throughout the preceding months. One version is well summed up in a letter written by Macdonald to Thomas Marshall, editor of the *Evening Post* of Chicago, in February.[14] Marshall, he began, had asked him if he wished to make any statement for publication "respecting the allegation made as to the signing of a Secret Treaty by myself on the part of Canada, & by Lord de Grey on the part of England, providing for the declaration of independence of Canada should Great Britain find it necessary to sever the connection between the two countries in consequence of war or for other reasons."

I have hitherto taken no notice of this statement which originated, I believe, with the Halifax Morning Chronicle. Nobody in Canada believes the story, and I have left it to the ridicule of the Canadian Press. As I gather, however, from your note, that some credence has been given it in the United States, I readily comply with your invitation.

I assure you that the story is altogether untrue, that it has no semblance or shadow of truth and that the subject of the severance of Canada from the Mother Country has never even been a matter of discussion between the Government of Great Britain and the Dominion, or between Lord de Grey and myself.

Nevertheless, Macdonald, as well as others, was not altogether easy on the persistent talk of independence and annexation. Writing to W. H. Gibbs on March 23, 1872,[15] to congratulate him on his election to Par-

had written Macdonald (May 10, 1871; Macdonald Papers:Washington Treaty, I, 469 [P.A.C.]) that at Montreal he had talked with Galt, Holton, and others and was surprised that they showed satisfaction with the fishery provisions; they could not understand why the Americans had not pressed a claim for the St. Albans raid.

14. Macdonald Papers:Letterbooks, XVII, 281–282 (P.A.C.).

15. *Ibid.*, pp. 444–445. By "Grits," as used here, Macdonald means the whole Liberal party, not merely the radical wing.

liament he said it was of the utmost importance to carry the next general election.

I fully believe that the future existence of Canada as a British Confederation depends upon the defeat of the Grits. Should the Grits, from the supineness or neglect of our friends, get possession of the reins, they would be obliged to yield to the Independence, or Annexation, movement. The words are almost synonymous.

It has been said that a party, like a snake, is moved by its tail. The tail of the Grit party is the Annexation section, hence my great anxiety that the Canadian Constitutional party should triumph next summer.

With five years more over our heads I think that the Confederation will have hardened from gristle into bone, and that no attempt, external or internal, to destroy it would be successful.

Subsequent events have shown not only that the annexation party in Canada was small, even if articulate, but that the peak of blatant annexationism in the United States had been passed. In Canada, however, even among responsible leaders this was not grasped. Nevertheless, the same leaders were convinced that, whatever the future might hold, the rejection of the parts of the Treaty of Washington affecting Canada was likely to increase friction not only between Canada and the United States but between England and America, and that above all things Canada must have a period of repose, freed from threat and menace, in order to establish the Confederation upon a lasting foundation; hence leading Government organs were intent on reconciling public opinion and paving the way for acceptance of the treaty.

However much newspaper comment may have prepared the public mind, what everybody wanted to hear, in Parliament and out, was Macdonald's explanation of his course in Washington and his attitude on the treaty. It was, then, a full house which crowded the chamber on the third of May to listen to the Premier's defense and plea. For four and a quarter hours he developed his subject, holding his audience to the end.[16] Moving the bill to carry into effect the clauses of the Treaty

16. *Dom. Parl. Deb.,* III, 293–345. On May 1, R. J. Cartwright of Lennox had moved the House to go into Committee of the Whole to consider a series of resolutions which, at Macdonald's instance, were postponed until after he brought in the Government's bill. The resolutions expressed regret that the

of Washington, Macdonald made a brief exposition of its terms. Then he took up *seriatim* the parts which were submitted to the Canadian Parliament for ratification, emphasizing that

no matter what may be the consequences of the action of this Parliament, no matter what may be the consequences with respect to future relations between Canada and England, or between Canada and the United States, no matter what may be the consequences as to the existence of the present Government of Canada, it must not be forgotten that this House has full power to reject the clauses of the Treaty if they please, and maintain the right of Canada to exclude Americans from inshore fisheries, as if the Treaty had never been made (hear, hear).

Reviewing the situation before the Marcy-Elgin Reciprocity Treaty, the abrogation of that treaty, and the efforts of Canada to secure its renewal, Macdonald said it had come to be thought that it would be humiliating for Canada to press the matter further. At the request of the British Government, Canada, at the expiration of the treaty, had not exercised at once her undoubted rights over the fisheries, but had inaugurated the license system, which had proved a failure. Then, assured by England of moral and material support, a policy of closing entirely exclusive Canadian waters to American fishermen had followed, and this policy, although accompanied by some complaints of unnecessary harshness, had accomplished its purpose. The introduction of this exclusion policy had brought to the fore not only the headland question but also rights of American fishermen in Dominion ports where they claimed the privilege of trading, though it was alleged that this claim frequently cloaked a design to fish in the forbidden waters. As a result of this situation the British Government, after Canada had sent the Postmaster-General to London to present both the fisheries issue and the Fenian claims, had agreed to take up with the United States and attempt to settle all questions.

Already England was engaged in the *Alabama* controversy, which was a standing obstacle to a return to the old friendly footing between the two countries. Not only was the prestige of England seriously affected by lack of an *entente cordiale*, but there was danger that the

Fenian claims had been withdrawn, since such a course would encourage more outrages and make the United States careless in maintaining international obligations. *Ibid.*, p. 261.

United States might take advantage of some European complication to force the issue. But Canada was even more vitally implicated than England, for, in case of war between Great Britain and the United States, "Canada would, as a matter of course . . . be the battle ground." Hence it was quite as much Canada's interest that the *Alabama* question should be settled as it was England's, consequently, he continued, "I am pleased and I was pleased, that the fact of Canada having asked England to make these demands upon the United States, gave an opportunity for reopening the negotiations with respect to the Alabama and other matters," for England herself could not with self-respect reopen them. How fortunate this was had been impressed on him by remarks of British statesmen who had said that unfriendly European powers had learned with dismay that the *entente cordiale* between the nations was to be resumed; it was common knowledge, although officially denied by Russia, that Minister Catacazy in Washington had made "active exertions for the purpose of preventing the Treaty of Washington from receiving the sanction of the Senate of the United States," and he, Macdonald, could vouch for the truth of this fact.[17] Not only in England but also in the United States, where the animosities arising from the Civil War were subsiding, there was desire for renewal of cordial relations, hence the opening presented by Canada's demands was welcomed on both sides. Then, as the correspondence before the House showed, steps were taken for the work of the Joint High Commission. He personally had felt considerable reluctance and embarrassment when asked to be a member. Nevertheless, even though he knew he would be criticized and would not get "fair play," a sense of duty and the urging of his colleagues persuaded him to accept the mission.

In Washington he found a general desire in both branches of the commission to settle all questions, but, as was well known, while it was easy for the American and British Commissioners to make a treaty, "in the United States there is a power above and beyond the Government, the Senate of the United States which had to be considered." A second rejection of a treaty would be disastrous: "An American statesman said to me, 'the rejection of the Treaty now means war.' Not war

17. Thornton wrote the same to Granville, Dec. 18, 1871. FO 5:1218 (P.R.O.).

tomorrow or at any given period, but war whenever England happened to be engaged in other troubles, and attacked from other sources (hear, hear)." The position, then, of the Canadian member could easily be seen; while Canadian interests were constantly before him, Imperial interests also had to be considered. He could refer members to Kimberley's message of February 16, 1871,[18] on the fisheries to demonstrate how much he had Canada's interests at heart. The result of communications between Washington, Ottawa, and London was a cable stating that it was never the intention of the British Government to part with the fisheries without Canada's consent, a substantial concession, for England could have given them away without that consent and the treaty would have been valid; as it was, Canada's rights were established beyond dispute.

Specifically, while the protocols did not show the day-by-day procedure of the commissioners, they did demonstrate that there was a desire on both sides to settle all questions permanently. They showed, moreover, that renewal of reciprocity was out of the question, for there was not the slightest chance that Congress would pass the necessary legislation. He [Macdonald] thereupon had urged upon his colleagues retention of the inshore fisheries while satisfying the United States in some other way, but the other British Commissioners, backed by Her Majesty's Government, felt that this would leave the door open to further collisions and greatly prejudice the outcome of the negotiations. Again, the protocols showed that at first the Americans had made an offer of limited reciprocity and then had withdrawn it. The reason for this, he felt sure, was Canada's action in taking off her coal and salt duties at the last session; under the circumstances he was powerless, so, when the Americans made the offer that was in the treaty, he accepted it. As things had developed since the treaty became known he had become more convinced that the action was correct, for the provisions which he had thought would be most unpopular in the Maritimes were acceptable there, while American fishermen almost to a man denounced them. Beyond all this, all fishing privileges had not been given away; those of the Pacific Coast and of Hudson Bay were reserved, and with their development during the next twelve years

18. Canadian *Sessional Papers,* No. 18 (1872), p. 6. Kimberley stated that the "right of Canada to exclude Americans from fishing in the waters within the limits of three marine miles of the coast, is beyond dispute."

there would be something to bargain with when the present treaty provisions expired. There were reserved the lake fisheries which, if Americans were allowed to share, would cause no end of trouble and would remove all hopes of real reciprocity. Another long-standing difference of opinion had been abolished by the treaty; namely, whether the War of 1812 did or did not put an end to the concessions of the Treaty of 1783, or whether the Treaty of 1854 "obliterated" the Convention of 1818. The Treaty of 1871 set this controversy at rest by recognizing Canadian property in the inshore fisheries; the offer to buy an entry into Canadian waters was the strongest proof of Canadian claim.

The other affirmative concessions of the treaty were, according to the Premier, minor matters. There was nothing but sentiment to exclude Americans from the St. Lawrence, which was usable only if they had access to the canals; the cities on Lake Michigan would see to it that Canadian vessels could enter their ports; there was a real gain to Canada from the opening of the Yukon and other Alaskan rivers, although the Opposition might scoff at the concession. Real gain, too, there was in the continuation of the bonding system for twelve years, a privilege which American newspapers had attacked from time to time and Congress had threatened to cancel. "They have said at times when they thought an unfriendly feeling existed towards them in Canada, that if the Canadians *would* be so bumptious, they should be deprived of this system, and allowed to remain cooped up in their frozen country." Now this was safe for twelve years, and after that the completion of the Canadian Pacific Railway would obviate the necessity of its continuance if the United States chose to withdraw the concession. One article represented a slight relaxation of the "extreme, almost harsh exclusive coasting trade system of the United States," which could be taken advantage of if Canada chose to open the canals to Americans on equal terms with Canadians and New Brunswick would withdraw its export duties on American lumber.

As to the omission of the Fenian claims, it could not be denied that Canada had been deeply wronged, and England admitted it. Canada, however, could only press its claims through England, and had, indeed, been invited to send a statement of them to London. But what a spectacle it would be to have Canada pressing claims and England questioning them! It was not seemly that such a contest should arise between the Mother Country and a colony, hence the suggestion of a guaranty which would not encroach on the dignity of either country; both would retain their self-respect. Such a guaranty would be an open avowal of the great interest England took in the great public enterprises of the Dominion. This gesture would end the hopes of "all dreamers or speculators" who might desire alienation or separation of the Dominion from the Empire. If it had not been for the cloud unhappily arising over the relations between England and the United States, there would have been the guaranty of £4,000,000 instead of £2,500,000; the guaranty made several years ago for fortifications, not yet built and which probably never would be built, would be a standing menace to the United States; it would undoubtedly in time be added to the £2,500,000 guaranty for public works.

If, as Howe said in his Y.M.C.A. speech, Canada had made sacrifices for England, what sacrifices had not England made for Canada? The whole treaty was primarily in the interests of the Dominion, for England had made herself liable to pay out millions, exclusive of the indirect claims, so that there could be peace between the Empire and the United States.

Let Canada be severed from England—let England not be responsible to us, and for us, and what could the United States do to England? Let England withdraw herself into her shell, and what can the United States do? England has got the supremacy on the sea—she is impregnable in every point but one, and that point is Canada; and if England does call upon us to make a financial sacrifice; does find it for the good of the Empire that we, England's first colony, should sacrifice something, I say that we would be unworthy of our proud position if we were not prepared to do so. (Cheers.) I hope to live to see the day, and if I do not that my son may be spared to see Canada the right arm of England, (cheers) to see Canada a powerful auxiliary to the Empire, and not a cause of anxiety and a source of danger.

Believing that the treaty called upon Canada to make no unusual sacrifices, for it contained more of benefit than disadvantage; believing that the saving clause for Canada's right to ratify or reject the portions affecting her interests had been inserted at his instance, he did not hesitate to think that the sober second thought of the country was with him and the Government in considering that the agreement should be ratified, despite what the Opposition, at the dictates of a power outside Parliament,[19] said against it and against him personally.

At last, then, after a year of silence, the Premier had come into the open and definitely pronounced for the treaty. A shrewd mixture of telling argument, demagogic appeal, and patriotic fervor, the speech produced a tremendous effect. "It leaves your opposition without a peg on which to hang an argument," wrote M. Taffray. "Coming as it did upon D'Isralli's [*sic*] exposition of Conservative Principles and Policy at Manchester [it] will infuse new life into the Conservative party of Canada, and teach them that they have but manfully to do their duty by their cherished principles of connexion with Great Britain, as you have done, to secure the same re-action of opinion in Ontario as is taking place in Great Britain upon the policies of the two political parties."[20] After this exposition, wrote William Anglin of Kingston, Macdonald's friends need have no fear of the "treaty bill."[21] The argument, said the Montreal *Gazette*,[22] fell into two parts: "the question as it affects the interests of the Empire, and the question as it affects the Dominion alone," and the first part would receive equal consideration with the second.

The new doctrine which has recently been promulgated, that on Imperial questions, or on questions in which the Empire and the Dominion have a joint interest, the people of this country may ignore the wishes of the British Government, and act simply upon their own narrow and selfish conceptions of duty, is utterly inconsistent with the continuance of the connection between the two countries. . . .

No doubt those urging such a course were honest and loyal, but they encouraged the comparatively small but influential "anti-colonial party in England" whose hands could in no way "be better strengthened than by following the advice of the new doctrinaires, who are advising the rejection by the Canadian Parliament of the Washington

19. George Brown of the *Globe* was not in Parliament, but he was charged by the Premier with being the real power behind the Liberal party there.

20. May 6, 1872; Macdonald Papers: General Letters, 1872, pp. 188–189 (P.A.C.).

21. May 8, 1872; Macdonald Papers: General Letters, p. 198 (P.A.C.).

22. May 7, 1872.

treaty." According to these "doctrinaires" Canadian interests were paramount, not to be relinquished "even in international disputes, disputes which might involve, not Canada alone, but the whole Empire in a bloody and relentless war."

It was, in fact, this Imperial argument that Macdonald largely relied upon to rally around him his party as he had already used it to win over his colleagues in the Government. While he might argue that the treaty was not nearly as bad as it could have been, he could scarcely expect that its concessions to Canada would be hailed as a great victory. If, however, he could swing enough wavering Conservative votes, the trick would be turned. He could scarcely expect to move many of the Opposition.

While Mackenzie protested that he had not expected to discuss the treaty critically at that time, preferring to wait until the second reading, nevertheless he did consume some time in running over the principal points Sir John had made.[23] His line of attack was not markedly dissimilar from that taken earlier; it amounted to contending that the danger pictured by the Premier was far less than he seemed to fear, even if it existed at all. Whenever the United States had wanted anything, England and Canada had yielded. Concessions granted to Canada by the treaty were so small as to be ridiculous because the British Commissioners had given in at the slightest show of opposition on the part of the Americans; Canada's great weapons—the fisheries and the navigation of the St. Lawrence—had been handed over in a cowardly manner. Furthermore, the repeal of coal and salt duties could have no influence because the Americans had known about them before they made their original offer.

The real discussion of the bill started when Macdonald moved its second reading on May 8; this lasted until May 16, and was participated in by many members. Blake opened the case for the opposition in a four-hour speech[24] in which he emphasized the surrender of the fisheries for a money payment, the giving up of the navigation of the St. Lawrence without reference to Canada, and abandonment of the Fenian claims for an Imperial guaranty. The original stand of the Government had been correct; its reversal had resulted in loss of prestige and of sovereignty. Following his speech he introduced an

23. *Dom. Parl. Deb.*, III, 345–354.
24. *Ibid.*, III, 431–447. The speech is summarized in the *Debates*.

amendment, seconded by Dorion, which was greeted with "loud cheers":

That before proceeding further with the said bill, this House feels bound to declare that, while Her Majesty's loyal subjects, the people of Canada, would at all times make any reasonable sacrifice in the interests of the Empire, there is [sic] just grounds for the dissatisfaction pervading the whole country as to the mode in which our rights have been dealt with in the negotiations at Washington, and the subsequent proposal of our Government that England should adopt a Canadian loan as the price of the adoption of the treaty, and the abandonment of the claims in respect to the Fenian raids, which affect not merely our peace but also our honour and our peace.[25]

William McDougall of Lanark, Ontario, felt that in view of his "peculiar position" toward both parties he should give his opinions on the course of the Premier. It struck him as interesting that it was in Ontario, where there was no direct interest in the fisheries, that the strongest opposition to the treaty was manifested; the people of Prince Edward Island, Nova Scotia, and Newfoundland were all in favor, for they considered they would once more enjoy the prosperity which had come under the Treaty of 1854. Canadian honor, he believed, was not involved, since England had assumed the responsibility. As to the Fenian raids, while in his opinion the United States had not properly exerted its powers to prevent them and the three rules laid down in the treaty to guide the arbitrators at Geneva might equally apply here, nevertheless, under the Act of 1867 treaty-making powers remained with England, and England did not choose to make an issue, because of Canada's vulnerable position.[26] L. S. Huntington of Shefford,

25. *Ibid.*, p. 447. In the Montreal *Gazette,* May 10, was this comment: "The speech of Mr. Blake, who, if not the leader, is at least the cleverest man in the Opposition ranks . . . was undoubtedly a very able effort. . . . It was clear and logical, and as a piece of special pleading deserves a high place in the records of Canadian Parliamentary discussions. . . . He had the advantage of having his bill and answer both before him, and he pleaded the case of his clients, the dissatisfied factionists of Ontario, with wonderful skill. The eminent chancery barrister was apparent in every argument, almost in every sentence. And the only regret which could be felt, as he sat down amid the well earned cheers of his friends, was simply that he was the eminent chancery barrister, nothing more."

26. *Dom. Parl. Deb.,* III, 459–460. The whole speech is on pages 447–

Quebec, thought the debate was to no purpose, for the whole treaty was likely to fall; if, then, the Canadian Parliament ratified the clauses affecting her interests it would be a matter of great embarrassment.[27] Privately the Premier shared at least a part of this opinion, for, as he wrote Sir Edward Thornton,[28] the unfortunate complications between Great Britain and the United States put Canada in a false position, since her Government were told that the legislation might be so much waste paper. "However, as I commenced I am resolved to carry it through."

David Mills of Bothwell, Ontario, was one of the most outspoken opponents of the treaty.[29] It was, he maintained, "the hole through which America would get possession of this country." Sir John's argument about England's sacrifice for Canada was all bosh; the danger of war was removed when the United States gave up Seward's claim of damages on account of premature recognition of belligerency. Canada had made sacrifices "which certainly point to a severance of relations between Canada and the Mother Country. (Hear, hear.)" Ratification of this treaty as a removal of all difficulties with the United States was an old story; they had been told that about every other treaty. "The difficulty between Great Britain and America did not grow out of the *Alabama* case, but had existed years before. We might trace it to elementary education in the United States, where the people were educated from their youth up to a cordial dislike of Great Britain and her institutions. A great change for a better end, however, had taken

462. Joseph Rymal remarked on McDougall's references to Brown and said he thought McDougall was one of his "most subservient followers," going into the Liberal party on his account. It looked as though he were ready to take another somersault and go over to the Treasury benches: "Oh whistle and I'll come to thee lad." *Ibid.*, p. 462. At Hamilton, McDougall had made a public address in April. His remarks were interpreted as aligning him with those "demanding the severance of the Imperial tie." Montreal *Gazette,* Apr. 9, 1872.

27. *Dom. Parl. Deb.,* III, 465.

28. May 10, 1872; Macdonald Papers: Letterbooks, XVII, 588 (P.A.C.).

29. *Dom. Parl. Deb.,* III, 470–474. Mills had written Thornton asking information as to interpretation of the fisheries clause and the Minister had informed Macdonald of the fact. The latter said Mills had acted in a "very disingenuous" manner by writing at all; nothing could reconcile him to the treaty and he was only trying to get more ammunition to use against it. Macdonald to Thornton, May 10; Macdonald Papers: Letterbooks, XVII, 587 (P.A.C.).

place now; but much of the ill-feeling had been traceable to this." Another source of annoyance was the American idea that the United States should embrace the whole North American continent, and a third grew out of the former misgovernment of Ireland. Ratification of the treaty would never efface these fundamental notions.

The views of a considerable number of members, especially on the Government side, were expressed by Galt,[30] who aligned himself definitely with neither party. He proposed to vote for the treaty although he was not satisfied with it. He believed that the licensing system, if it had been rigorously enforced, would have avoided all the troubles which arose from the subsequent policy, since an insistence on Canada's extreme rights had caused them to be mixed up with a general discussion of Imperial affairs. It was necessary to support the treaty because neither side was willing to take the steps and accept the consequences which would follow its rejection; besides, in ten years, aside from the navigation of the St. Lawrence, the whole matter would again be submitted to the people of Canada. It was wiser to accept the terms which England offered and remain under her protection because it had been proved that the Canadian people were unable to protect themselves. Galt's speech, especially since it was followed by one from Howe, turned the course of the debate into a discussion of separation or remaining in the Empire. Each side accused the other of shifting position; each avowed its fidelity to the Imperial connection and charged its opponents with wavering. Insinuations that there was something behind the documents and spoken arguments—that England had practically threatened to leave Canada to her fate if she did not ratify the treaty—were emphatically denied by Macdonald, who asserted that in no way, officially or privately, had the British Government tried to influence the Canadian Government except by fair arguments; each Member of Parliament should vote on the merits of the question and not be moved by supposed motives of Great Britain. Surely the relations between Sir Alexander and the Government were such as to give no reason to think that he spoke for it; his supposition that the Canadian Government had changed its stand as a result of some Imperial communication was purely imaginary.[31]

30. May 10; *Dom. Parl. Deb.,* III, 474–483.
31. *Ibid.,* p. 491.

The word "separation" inevitably brought up annexation, and E. V. Bothwell, prominent in the opposition,[32] did not hesitate to say that, having given up the potent weapons of fisheries and navigation, "the Treaty was a step in the direction of annexation, and as such highly unacceptable to the people of this country." He reinforced his remarks by offering an amendment to strike out of the proposed bill all except the enacting clause and substitute the words: "Having regard to the existing differences between the United States and Great Britain, concerning the proceedings necessary to give effect to the Treaty of Washington, it is inexpedient to proceed further at this time with the said bill." Thereupon the First Minister replied that, as Bothwell was a member of the opposition, he supposed that the amendment had the backing of that party; Blake had already moved what amounted to a vote of want of confidence, but apparently he was now afraid of it and so got the member from South Oxford to bring forward a substitute. It was not in accord with parliamentary rules, it was not fair play, to get another member to move another amendment. Was he to suppose that the opposition would not press Blake's amendment, being now afraid of it and trying to get rid of it? Or did not Blake's meet the case and so Bothwell was trying to make a better one? In any case the House ought to have an explanation. Whether or not it was an explanation, Mackenzie announced that Blake's amendment would be pressed; from the Premier himself the House had learned that the situation had changed since it was introduced and so did not meet existing conditions.[33] The opposition did not look upon it as simply one of want of confidence; they merely desired to express an opinion on a subject which affected all parties.

The debate jogged on. Hincks made an elaborate argument following much the same lines as Macdonald's;[34] Hillyard Cameron of Inverness, Nova Scotia, came to the defense of the Premier and maintained that objections to the treaty were ill-founded;[35] P. Power of Halifax regretted that the reciprocity provisions were not more

32. May 13; *Dom. Parl. Deb.*, III, 493. The name seems to have been spelled indifferently "Bothwell" and "Bodwell."

33. This has reference to the latest information received regarding the controversy over the American *Case* and the indirect claims. The remarks are in *ibid.*, pp. 495–497.

34. *Ibid.*, pp. 498–505.   35. *Ibid.*, pp. 505–518.

liberal, but asserted that those obtained were far from negligible—he was not a supporter of the Government but he favored the treaty because it would promote peaceful relations with the United States. Members from Nova Scotia, British Columbia, Ontario, and a few from Quebec, including Holton and Cartier, and New Brunswick, of whom the most prominent was S. L. Tilley, avowed with varying enthusiasm their intention to vote for the treaty. R. W. Harrison of Toronto West, who denied that "the people of Canada had ever shown an unfavorable feeling to the people of the United States, and regretted that he could not say as much for the people of the United States," maintained that the treaty was neither so good nor so bad as it had been represented. While it had been a mistake to go on with negotiations when the Americans ruled out Fenian claims, for if the British had insisted they would have settled all issues, nevertheless much had been obtained of mutual advantage. Canada had not made any sacrifices, and if she had, it was her duty to. "There was no reason why nations like men, should not settle disputes by the rule of reason, and he trusted that the Treaty would be a precedent for the future, not only to the two nations concerned, but also to the nations of the world."[36] Charles Tupper,[37] from the constituency of Cumberland, Nova Scotia, was in favor of the treaty "because it was the only means left to obtain reciprocal trade, by allaying all enmities between the two countries. This was already found to be the result, and every one who had visited the United States since the ratification of the Treaty came back in favour of it, for the reason that there was a wonderful difference in the state of feeling towards Canada. All the acrimonious feeling that had formerly existed had been allayed. Let Honourable gentlemen study the proceedings of Congress, and they would find the same change evidenced there." L. H. Holton declared that he had been almost alone on his side of the House as an original friend of the treaty; it was not such a treaty as would have been obtained if Canada had been independent, and not such as England would have made had she no colonies in America, but the existing situation made it necessary to take the action best for the Empire. While he did not believe that the fisheries had been surrendered without an equivalent, he was "more reticent than the Honourable President of the Council, [and] he did

36. May 14; *ibid.*, pp. 533–546.   37. *Ibid.*, pp. 548–566.

not propose to put arguments into the mouths of General Butler and others to show the advantages the people of Canada would gain." He proposed to vote for Blake's amendment to express reprobation of the course of the Government, but against Bothwell's as tending to defeat the treaty.[38]

The veteran S. Campbell of Guysborough said that he had been a member of the Nova Scotia legislature when the Treaty of 1854 had been passed upon and heard the same arguments now being advanced against the Treaty of Washington: "The prejudices and hostilities of a particular class of the population, supposed to be affected by that measure, were invoked and sought to be arrayed against it." In spite of opposition, the earlier treaty had worked beneficially and he expected the one before them to do the same.[39]

It was A. A. Dorion, astute leader of the French wing of the Liberals, who came out flatly to voice suspicions of the course which had been taken by the Premier.[40] Proponents of the treaty had said that the *Globe* was the first to cry out against the treaty. They forgot that as early as May 13, 1871, the *Gazette* had really raised the first cry, presumably at the direction of the Government, and on May 20 had come out against the treaty and the British Commissioners. Then all the ministerial press had followed in condemnation, and on July 28 the Government themselves had said the treaty was not acceptable. If they had believed that it was not satisfactory but nevertheless ought to be accepted by Canada, they should have said so, and Canada would have supported it. He, personally, was willing to make any sacrifice which England demanded, but it was not on this ground that the case had been put. He was convinced that from the first the Government had determined to support the treaty in order to get the guaranty; Ministers held the treaty in one hand and the purse in the other. "He would have desired to condemn the action of the Government and then support the Treaty; but, after mature consideration, he could only come to the conclusion to condemn the Government and the Treaty, considering the circumstances under which it was presented." Canada would not always be a colony, but when the time came to separate there could be no greater evil than separation accompanied by coldness and

38. May 15; *Dom. Parl. Deb.*, III, 569–573.
39. *Ibid.*, pp. 581–582.   40. *Ibid.*, pp. 585–589.

ill-feeling of the Mother Country. The action of the Ministry, he feared, would make England feel that Canada was only selfish. P. Fortin of Gaspé voiced the sentiments of that part of Quebec which had a direct interest in the fisheries when he said he could not agree with those who maintained that the Dominion fishing interests were benefited; Canadians would be at a disadvantage on account of American bounties, superior equipment, and the like. All in all, he could not see why ratification or rejection would affect in any way the settlement of the *Alabama* or other questions between Great Britain and the United States.[41] To much the same effect but at greater length T. Anglin of Gloucester, New Brunswick, spoke for his constituents, of whom he knew of only two who had a good word to say for the treaty. All the provisions of the treaty, good as well as bad, were likely to be terminated at the expiration of twelve years "and if we had not at that time lapsed into independence, as one honourable gentleman had expressed it, or become annexed as others apprehended, we should find ourselves face to face with a new difficulty," for the United States would make more demands or put an end to the concessions. It had been his intention at first merely to oppose the treaty in silence, but after he saw the correspondence and found they were asked to dishonor the country, degrade Parliament, and disgrace the Government he felt bound to declare that he for one would be no party to the measure.[42]

Little was added to the arguments for or against ratification by the numerous speeches of the last days. Even Mackenzie's summing up was not much more than a repetition of what had gone before, although he stated that the principal reason adduced for ratification seemed to be that by doing so England and the United States would be kept out of war. Such talk he believed to be nonsense, for "while he believed that the diplomatic policy of the United States was almost always aggressive, . . . also he believed there was a sufficient number of public men in that country who were sufficiently devoted to the cause of maintaining public law, and who scorn to make such a petty pretense a cause for hostilities." Really the only cause of trouble was the headland question. If Canada was going to get justice she must insist upon every atom of right; whenever there came a controversy

41. *Ibid.*, p. 599.   42. *Ibid.*, pp. 606–620.

between Great Britain and the United States, the former got the worst of it and he did not believe in blindly rushing to place the latter in a position to demand more.[43]

The vote on the second reading of the bill took place on the evening of May 16, preceded by roll calls on the Bothwell and Blake amendments. In general, voting followed party lines, although a few Liberals voted against both amendments and for the treaty and an occasional Conservative refused to support the Government. Sir John, however, had a more than two-to-one majority on each test.[44] Nor was there marked sectionalism in the voting. As might have been expected both from discussion before Parliament convened and from the debate in that body, the most concentrated resistance came from Ontario, with about a four-to-three victory for the Government. Quebec, with no special interest particularly affected by the treaty, strongly conservative, influenced to some extent by the Montreal merchants who expected great things from opening the river and from enhanced trade, gave a three-to-one support, while the two Maritimes were equally favorable. It is, of course, impossible to estimate which factor weighed most: the idea that England wanted the treaty ratified; belief that there was a possibility of hostilities if it was not; satisfaction that something had been gained in the exchange with the United States, even though it was not much; a notion that the treaty was an entering wedge which might eventually pry open the door of reciprocity. All no doubt played their parts. But, whatever may have been modifying factors in each individual vote it is apparent that party ties were potent; the Dominion was on the eve of a general election and no trick must be lost. For Sir John A. Macdonald it was a personal triumph. It was the more gratifying because light was just beginning to appear in the clouds which hung over the whole *Alabama* affair, so that it could be assumed that eventually the whole treaty would go into effect.

On May 21 Macdonald moved the House into Committee of the Whole on the bill; it was carried without discussion and without divi-

43. *Dom. Parl. Deb.*, III, 625–638.

44. *Ibid.*, pp. 646–648. Bothwell's amendment was defeated by a vote of 124 to 50; Blake's was defeated by 123 to 52. The bill was carried by a vote of 119 to 55. The summaries given by the Parliamentary reporter and the actual count of names as given for the division do not quite coincide. The above figures represent the votes as indicated by the names of the voters on each side.

sion, reported to the House, read the third time and passed.[45] In the
Senate, where Campbell introduced the bill and explained its terms,[46]
the debate was perfunctory; what discussion there was followed much
the same lines as that of the House and nothing new was brought out.
The second reading passed with no division and the measure passed
through its final stages without hitch, to become law with the provision that it should come into force "upon, from, and after a day to be
appointed for that purpose, by a proclamation based upon an order
of the governor in council, and shall remain in force during the term
of years mentioned in article thirty-three" of the Treaty of Washington.[47]

Replying to Sir John Rose to thank him for congratulatory letters
respecting the outcome of the struggle, Macdonald wrote:[48]

You may tell Lord Granville for me confidentially, that if he wants his
business done up correctly at Washington at any time he must send me
alone. But seriously, the whole thing was badly managed [i.e., the *Alabama* Case], first in Washington and still more in England. I suppose
that the Treaty will come to something in the end, but instead of removing
heart burning it has laid the foundation of new suspicions, and all without the slightest necessity.

45. *Ibid.,* pp. 718–719.
46. May 28; *ibid.,* pp. 833–839, 897.
47. *Statutes of Canada Passed in the Session Held in the Thirty-fifth Year
of the Reign of Her Majesty Queen Victoria* (1872), pp. 4–6.
48. June 18, 1872; Macdonald Papers: Letterbooks, XVII, 701–702
(P.A.C.). On August 6, 1872, royal approval was given to an act passed by the
British Parliament to put into effect, so far as this action was necessary, the
provisions of the Treaty of Washington as they affected Canada and, prospectively, Newfoundland. *The Public General Statutes, Passed in the Thirty-fifth
and Thirty-sixth Years of the Reign of Her Majesty Queen Victoria,* pp. 279–
280.

CHAPTER XVIII

THE EVERLASTING FISHERIES QUESTION

THE passage of the Dominion bill to carry into effect the provisions of the Treaty of Washington which touched Canadian interests by no means closed the chapter or ensured immediate compliance with stipulations contained in that instrument. Canada had acted, but the United States had as yet taken no legislative action. The *Alabama* Claims imbroglio, while emerging from the clouds which had enshrouded it, was not cleared up, and Congress adjourned leaving the whole situation legislatively *in statu quo ante*. The most pressing issue, so far as Canada and certain interests in the United States were concerned, was whether the fisheries would be open during that season and whether fish and fish products would be admitted into each country from the other free of duty.

On the day following the crucial vote in the Dominion House of Commons, T. Robitaille, representing Bonaventure, Quebec, asked the Government whether they were prepared to pledge, in case the pending legislation were passed, that it should not go into operation while the *Alabama* Claims remained unsettled; whether the Government would afford the same protection as before to the fisheries until those claims should be settled; and whether they would bind themselves to expend such money as might be awarded under the fishery clauses for the direct benefit and improvement of those fisheries.[1] Macdonald explained that the bill itself provided that no change would take place until after an Order in Council, but he would give no pledge: the Government would provide efficient protection until the fisheries were opened to the Americans, and whatever money might be awarded would be subject to Parliamentary vote, so no pledge about it could be given. He did explain, in answer to a question, that the money was wholly at the disposal of the Canadian Parliament and not subject to any arrangement with the British Government.

This matter of protecting the fisheries pending full operation of the treaty was not up for the first time; in fact it had been on the boards

1. *Dom. Parl. Deb.*, III, 653–654.

from the very time the Treaty of Washington was drafted. On May 4, 1871, four days before the signing, Lord Lisgar, in response to Kimberley's dispatch of April 13, had informed the Colonial Secretary that, in compliance with a request, the Privy Council of Canada had assented to a suspension of the order prohibiting entrance of "U. S. Fishing Vessels from entering Bays or Harbours for the purpose of trade," and commanders of the policing squadron had been so instructed.[2] But this relaxation had been insufficient, according to the American Government. On the day of the signing Secretary Fish addressed a note to Sir Edward Thornton[3] to say that "in furtherance of the objects and spirit of the treaty" American citizens ought to enjoy fishing privileges during that season, hence "I am directed by the President to express to you his hope that Her Majesty's government will be prepared, in the event of the ratification of the treaty, to make on their own behalf, and to urge the governments of the Dominion of Canada, of Prince Edward Island, and of Newfoundland, to make . . . such relaxations and regulations as it may respectively be in their power to adopt, with a view to the admission of American fishermen to the liberty which it is proposed to secure to them by the treaty." In return, the United States Government would admit British fishermen to American waters. But, since the President could not suspend operation of the customs laws, it would not be possible to remit duties in American ports on fish brought in by British fishermen; if, however, the concessions were granted on the part of Great Britain and her colonies, the President would "recommend and urge upon Congress at their next session that any duties which may have been collected on and after the 1st day of July next on fish-oil and fish, (. . . except fish preserved in oil) . . . be returned and refunded to the parties paying the same" if a like arrangement would be made in the Provinces for American-caught fish. The terms of the note, which had been "discussed with M^r: Fish by Lord de Grey, who also gave his valuable assistance in inducing Sir John Macdonald to acquiesce in them,"[4]

2. Lisgar to Kimberley; Kimberley to Lisgar, May [?], 1871; FO 115:520 (P.R.O.).

3. *For. Rel., 1871,* pp. 485–486.

4. Thornton to Granville, May 8, 1871; FO 115:524 (P.R.O.). "Mr Fish," wrote Thornton, "is extremely anxious that copies of a note couched in such terms and of the answer which he hopes I may be instructed to give him, should

were immediately cabled to London, whence came the next day to De Grey a telegram[5] saying that Her Majesty's Government were willing to recommend to the Colonial Governments acceptance of the provisional arrangement, but, since the concession asked by the United States was immediate and positive and the promise merely prospective and contingent, Her Majesty's Government must not be understood to remove the decision from Canada.

Evidently Sir John Macdonald had not given his assent to this step too easily and his reluctance was not feigned. When sending to Cartier copies of the notes[6] and warning him that the Canadian Government might expect a communication from Lord Kimberley soon, he voiced his pessimism:

Even if the Treaty is ratified by the Senate it does not follow that Congress will, next session, pass the acts necessary to bring the Fishery Articles into operation. Strange as it may appear from our point of view, there is more opposition to these articles than any other part of the Treaty, as the Gloucester Fishermen have somehow or other contrived to impress the Senatorial mind with the idea that in giving us a free market for our fish they have given us much more than they will get, in the use of our inshore fisheries.

Events were to prove that his pessimism was only too well founded. It was, moreover, shared by Macdonald's associates in Ottawa, for they exhibited no undue haste in complying with the request of the Colonial Office; they shared the common feeling in the Dominion that too little had been got for Canada by the treaty, and gratuitously to hand over the disputed privilege in advance was going too far. As the Premier put it in a letter to Lord de Grey,[7] the rescinding of the orders to the British squadron was not only unwise but unwarranted; it was simply a notice to Gloucestermen to go ahead and do as they pleased,

accompany the Treaty in its submission to the Senate on the 10th Inst: he thinks that they will contribute to its obtaining the sanction of the Senate, and without them, it will be considered that there still remains a difficulty for the removal of which no provision has been made."

5. A copy of the telegram is in Thornton to Granville, May 9, 1871; FO 115:524 (P.R.O.). Thornton to Fish, May 9, 1871; *For. Rel., 1871*, p. 486. Fish acknowledged receipt of the information the same day.

6. May 18, 1871; Macdonald Papers: Letterbooks, XV, 824–825 (P.A.C.).

7. June 6, 1871; Macdonald Papers: Letterbooks, XV, 875–876 (P.A.C.).

and if the fishery articles were to be carried into effect by the necessary legislation,

we *must* enforce the laws as they exist. The consequences will probably be collision and bloodshed, and all by this hasty order which I see originated with the Admiralty.

Even if such dire results should not happen, the order will have a most unfortunate effect in Canada. It is in effect saying that although nominally the option of accepting the Fishery Articles was reserved to Canada, there is no reality in it. The withdrawal of the Fleet will be considered the first step to coerce the Canadian Parliament to accept the Treaty whether they like it or not.[8]

After the Senate had ratified the treaty on May 24, 1871, Fish returned to the issue. "Much anxiety is expressed and made known to this Department," he informed Thornton,[9] "on the part of those concerned in the mackerel fishery near the coasts of the British provinces." He was aware that these waters could not technically be claimed on behalf of Americans, but he had hoped through the forbearance of the British and Colonial Governments these fishermen "might no longer be subjected to the annoyances to which they have hitherto been liable." Much irritation, he was sure, would be aroused, and legislation by Congress would be retarded if the privileges were withheld during the season then opening. While privately, in view of their close personal relations, the British Minister may have hinted to Fish that the difficulties were raised by the Dominion Government, officially he could only call attention to the fact that the strict provisions of the Convention of 1818 respecting use of Provincial harbors were relaxed and express the hope that American citizens would do their part in preventing "untimely collisions, by refraining from encroaching, for the purpose of fishing, upon those waters from which . . . they are ex-

8. To Captain Harding of H.M.S. *Valorous,* Macdonald wrote on June 21: "The fisheries must still be protected, notwithstanding the Treaty, until the Articles connected with the Fisheries are brought into effect by the Canadian Parliament next February. Very great opposition is shown to these articles and it is quite uncertain whether they will be adopted or not." *Ibid.,* p. 947. To Gowan (Private and Confidential, June 24), he stated that the treaty was satisfactory to the Government in everything except the fishery articles. *Ibid.,* p. 968.

9. June 24; *For. Rel., 1871,* p. 489.

cluded, until the legislation for insuring to them the privileges and immunities agreed upon by the treaty of the 8th ultimo shall have been carried out."[10] To Granville, Sir Edward noted the use of the word "annoyances" and said that when he expressed verbally his regret that Fish had sent him the note, in view of the liberal instructions given Her Majesty's commanders, the latter told him "he had received a multitude of letters upon the subject from persons interested in the fisheries who had suffered great losses during the last fishing season, and who now expressed their fears that they would not be allowed to enter Canadian ports nor to fish in the Bays."[11]

It was not for want of prodding from the Colonial Office that the Dominion Government remained obdurate. After receipt of a Report of a Committee of the Privy Council to Lord Lisgar wherein complaint against the orders to the British squadron was strongly put, Kimberley went to great lengths to explain how it had been at the instance of Canadians that negotiations had been started and how the British commission had attempted to secure as good a bargain as possible for them, but that the Americans had insisted on tying the fisheries question with other issues. In vain did the commissioners attempt to find some other equivalent for American concessions. Canada, he wrote,[12]

cd not reasonably expect that this Country should for an indefinite period incur the constant risk of serious misunderstanding with the U. S. imperilling perhaps the peace of the whole empire, in order to endeavor to force the American Gt to change its commercial policy, and H. M. G. are confident that when the Treaty is considered as a whole the Canadian people will see that their interests have been carefully borne in mind, and that the advantages which they will derive from its provisions are commensurate with the concessions which they are called upon to make.

Subsequent elucidations seemed to indicate that the policy of the Imperial Government in patrolling the disputed waters was not as exceptionable as it had first appeared. As Lisgar told Macdonald,[13]

As I understand it H. M. Ships are to remain on the station and cruise as heretofore. They are to abstain from active measures against the

10. June 26; *For. Rel., 1871,* p. 490.   11. June 26; FO 115:525 (P.R.O.).
12. To Lisgar, June 17, 1871; FO 115:521 (P.R.O.).
13. July 4, 1871; Macdonald Papers: Governor General Correspondence, IV, 483–485 (P.A.C.).

U. States Fishermen, but they are to preserve order and to protect the Canadian Police schooners against violence or armed molestation by encroaching foreigners.

In other words, British vessels were to act as a sort of super-police to prevent those very collisions which the Canadian Government appeared to fear so much. Macdonald himself admitted[14] that the instructions were, on the whole, satisfactory. "If the squadron is not allowed to make captures, so much the worse for the officers, and our people will get more prize money." Nevertheless, he continued to maintain that "the Treaty is greatly beneficial to Canada in every respect except as to the Fisheries, and with regard to them the Canadian Parliament has full power to do as it pleases,"[15] and he was at one with his colleagues in insisting that no further relaxation of regulations, that is, opening the inshore waters, should come until Congress acted. It was not long before a case arose to demonstrate that the Canadians meant what they said, for one of the police schooners seized a vessel within the three-mile limit and took it to Quebec for adjudication.[16] The master pleaded that he committed the offense in ignorance, for he thought that the terms of the treaty applied immediately, and threw himself on the mercy of the Government and sought release. "This," said Macdonald, "we cannot afford to do, lest it might verify McDougall's statement that Mitchell's fleet is an expensive farce. We shall condemn the vessel but probably after condemnation act with great liberality to the owner. I am curious to see the effect of the seizure on the American newspapers."

If Canada was skeptical and preferred deeds to words, little Prince Edward Island had more faith in the assurances of the American Government. On July 26 the British Chargé in Washington announced

14. To Lisgar, July 11; Macdonald Papers: Letterbooks, XVI, 11–13 (P.A.C.).

15. To George Jackson, July 17; Macdonald Papers: Letterbooks, XVI, 30 (P.A.C.).

16. Macdonald to Alexander Morris, July 31; Macdonald Papers: Letterbooks, XVI, 119 (P.A.C.). F. J. Pakenham to Granville, Aug. 1; FO 115:525 (P.R.O.). Chargé Pakenham said Fish told him that a violent attack would be made on the articles at the next session of Congress and he "thought that seizures similar to the present one would probably serve to revive the ill feelings so happily allayed."

that he had been informed by the Lieutenant-Governor of that Province that his Government, the day before, had decided not to enforce the fishing laws during the current season, pending consideration of appropriate articles by the Legislature.[17] This action was not taken on account of any great advantages the Island would derive from the treaty, for it was considered that those would accrue more to Canada than to the Maritime Provinces; nor was it on account of prospective free admission of fish and fish oil into American markets, for "this w^{ld} not be generally felt by the people, inasmuch as this trade is now principally in the hands of a few American Citizens"; nor, furthermore, was the concession of inshore fisheries on the American coast as far as the thirty-ninth parallel of any particular value; in addition to all this, there was nothing in the treaty which specifically guaranteed that the Island would receive a money consideration. The action was taken solely

in deference to the strongly expressed wish of the Brit: G^t in the matter—and for the same reason the Committee now recommend that the application made by the U. S. G^t be acceded to so that American fishermen may be at once allowed during the present season the provisional use of the privileges granted to them by the Treaty without any pledge, however, on the part of the Gov^t that the Legislature will pass the Acts to give effect to the Treaty, in which they feel that the interests of P. E.'s Island have not been fairly considered.

Newfoundland, too,[18] readily yielded to the request of the Colonial Office. The Executive Council, however, desired to know whether seal oil was to be understood as coming within the definition of the term "fish-oil." It was pointed out that it would be exceedingly difficult to

17. Pakenham to Davis, July 26; *For. Rel., 1871*, p. 492. O. D. Russell to Pakenham, Aug. 25; FO 115:522 (P.R.O.). Fish to Thornton, July 28; Great Britain: Notes to, XV, 312 (D.S.). William Robinson to Kimberley, July 25, enclosing minute of Committee of the Executive Council of Prince Edward Island of same date; FO 115:522 (P.R.O.).

18. When the initial correspondence over this matter passed between Fish and Thornton, Newfoundland was inadvertently omitted. When, however, this was called to the attention of the American Secretary, the deficiency was rectified. Hill to Kimberley, July 14, 1871; FO 115:522 (P.R.O.). Fish to Davis, Sept. 20; Davis Papers, Vol. X (L.C.). Davis to Thornton, Sept. 30; Great Britain: Notes to, Vol. XV (D.S.).

prevent American poachers' trespassing on the floes which bordered the island in the parts where seal were accustomed to whelp, and all trouble could be avoided if mutual concessions were made; Americans might share the right with British subjects in taking seal, while Newfoundlanders could take their products free of duty to American markets. After considerable correspondence the Administration decided that seal oil was not specifically comprehended in the general term, hence they would be unable to make this concession in advance of an act of Congress.[19]

So passed the fishing season of 1871. In waters of the Dominion, Americans were debarred from entering upon inshore fisheries, although fishing craft could visit ports for bait and other supplies in addition to the wood and water mentioned in the Convention of 1818. In the waters of Prince Edward Island, American fishermen stood on an equality with the Islanders themselves, and in Newfoundland waters the situation was practically the same, although technically the inclusion of this island in the list prepared by the Secretary came so late in the season as to be of no significance. In spite, however, of continued restrictions in portions of British American waters there was little friction; that is, there were only two or three cases which elicited complaints grave enough to cause any diplomatic consideration. Early in the season, on June 7, the *Lizzie A. Tarr* was ordered from Lambley Harbor, Grand Jarvis, Newfoundland, by a British naval officer who, when the master of the fishing vessel was attempting to secure bait, tripped "the seine then in the hands of English fishermen, and let out the herring, so that no bait could be sold, saying to the fishermen, 'What are you doing? If I catch you selling bait to the Yankees I will cut up your seine. Where are you to get bread next winter?' "[20] Another case was that of the schooner *Samuel Gilbert*. This craft had been seized for infringement of the Dominion fishing laws and "some little anxiety" was expressed to Chargé Pakenham by both Fish and Davis about the stringency of the regulations.[21]

19. See especially minute of the Executive Council of Newfoundland, July 14, 1871, FO 115:522 (P.R.O.); Davis to Pakenham, Sept. 23; *For. Rel., 1871*, pp. 494–495.

20. Davis to Pakenham, Aug. 9, 1871; *For. Rel., 1871*, p. 493.

21. Pakenham to Granville, Sept. 5, 1871; FO 115:525 (P.R.O.). As late as the following April, Lisgar was being petitioned by Richard Hanan, one of

Mr Bancroft Davis told me confidentially that the particulars connected with the seizure of this vessel had been got together & forwarded to the State Dep^t by Genl Butler, of Mass: who would probably use them to the best of his power, & naturally in an unfriendly sense, during the approaching session of Congress. Mr Fish, however, a few days ago informed me he would not lay the matter officially before me, as he had grave doubts whether the action of the Capt of the schooner had been bona fide, & he, Mr Fish, even hinted that the vessel might have been despatched for the express purpose of being captured.

It was Pakenham's opinion that "these incidents would be largely diminished in number, if not prevented altogether, by the authorities of the United States issuing such instructions as they may think necessary for guidance of Masters of American fishing vessels, warning them of the impropriety of illegal fishing in Canadian waters, and pointing out the embarrassments that might arise from a persistence in such a course of action."[22] Fish replied that while the Secretary of the Treasury had issued such instructions in 1870, he had not done so in 1871 because it had been supposed that the Dominion authorities would have desired to anticipate as far as possible the execution of the provisions of the treaty. Before another season, Fish hoped, both the Dominion Parliament and Congress would have taken proper legislative action;[23] now, since the 1871 season was over there was no need of such instructions, as it was not thought necessary to take any such step in advance of legislative action.

Meantime, the people and Government of Prince Edward Island were beginning to be anxious as to whether throwing open their inshore fisheries would be recompensed by a return of duties paid on fish imported into the United States after July 1. At first there had been no doubt in their minds that this would be the case, but there began to be rumors that "the refusal of the Dominion of Canada to give

the owners of the *Gilbert,* who asserted he would be ruined if the vessel were confiscated. Lisgar to Macdonald, Apr. 6, 1872; Macdonald Papers: Governor General Correspondence, IV, 687 (P.A.C.).

22. Pakenham to Fish, Oct. 5, 1871; Great Britain: Notes to Department, Vol. XCI (D.S.).

23. Fish to Thornton, Oct. 7; Great Britain: Notes to, XV, 365–367 (D.S.). Pakenham to Granville, Oct. 10; FO 115:525 (P.R.O.).

effect to the Treaty of Washington [might] work adversely to the interests of this Island and prejudice her claim to such return of duties."[24] Unfortunately, it appeared that there was a basis for the rumors, for when the matter was taken up in Washington at the instance of the Colonial Office, it was found that the Administration did, indeed, take just that view: since Canada had not relaxed her restrictions, the Government of the United States did not feel under obligation to return the duties paid by the citizens of the Province which had. "From the somewhat querulous tone of Mr Fish's ans^r it would seem that the prompt & liberal conduct of the Legislature of P. E. I. in this matter has but small chance of being reciprocated by the Gov^t of the U. S.," was the view Pakenham imparted to Lord Granville.[25] The intimation that the Administration was not prepared to recommend to Congress legislation to refund the duties drew from Granville a scathing commentary in which the circumstances attending the proposition were recited. Each colony, said His Lordship, was considered competent to act independently of the others and this had been recognized by the Treaty of Washington; Prince Edward Island had complied with the request of Her Majesty's Government in the expectation that the American Government would fulfil its part of the bargain.

No intimation was given by the United States Government that they did not intend to fulfil their part of the arrangement unless united action was taken by all the Colonies and the Government of the Island could not therefore have anticipated that such a course would be pursued, nor did Mr Fish's original proposal make the refunding of the duties contingent on such united action.

He hoped, therefore, that the Administration would reconsider the decision and "not persist in refusing to carry out their part of an arrangement which they themselves originated and which was proposed to the Government of Prince Edward Island . . . in the full confidence

24. I. C. Hall to Lt.-Gov. Robinson, Sept. 26, 1871; FO 115:523 (P.R.O.). Hall was an American merchant at Charlottetown.
25. Nov. 28, 1871; FO 115:525 (P.R.O.). See correspondence between Charlottetown and London, and London and Washington; FO 115:523 (P.R.O.). Pakenham to Fish, Nov. 14, 1871; Great Britain:Notes to Department, Vol. XCI (D.S.).

that that Colony would receive an equivalent for the concessions which it was recommended to make."[26]

No comfort had been obtained when Grant sent his Annual Message to Congress on December 4, 1871. Not a word was said about return of duties, although the President did recommend "the legislation necessary on the part of the United States to bring into operation the articles of the treaty relating to the fisheries, and to the other matters touching the relations of the United States toward the British North American possessions, to become operative as soon as the proper legislation shall be had on the part of Great Britain and its possessions."[27] He added that it was desirable that such legislation become operative before "the fishermen of the United States begin to make their arrangements for the coming season." A week later Nathaniel Banks introduced House Resolution No. 489 to give effect to provisions of the treaty relating to the fisheries, but it failed to progress on account of the friction engendered by the quarrel over indirect claims. If, however, there was no discussion of moment on the subject of the required legislation, it did not mean that the topic was tabu. It brought out another annexation proposal;[28] it stimulated to activity the groups who felt themselves likely to be affected adversely by the operation of the treaty; it brought memorials urging Congress to offset remission of duties by some system of bounties.[29]

Quietly—that is, outside regular proceedings in the House, for it is

26. Granville to Thornton, Mar. 26, 1872; FO 115:534 (P.R.O.). The essential parts of this instruction, in part *verbatim*, are in Thornton to Fish, Apr. 12, 1872; *For. Rel., 1872,* Part I, pp. 219–220.

27. *Cong. Globe,* 42d Cong., 2d Sess., p. 4.

28. *Ibid.,* p. 62. A. D. Shaw, Consul at Toronto, wrote at length on the attitude toward annexation in Ontario, ending his communication with this sentiment: "I am sincerely glad you have taken an interest in the matter, for the people in Canada are possessed of a vast amount of *developing power* at present, and unless we act wisely they will grow alongside of us into a strong alien people." To Bancroft Davis, Jan. 16, 1872; Davis Papers, Vol. XI (L.C.).

29. Resolutions of the Massachusetts Legislature (*House Misc. Docs.,* No. 64); a Memorial of an *ad hoc* Committee on Fisheries of Boston (*House Misc. Docs.,* No. 69); Resolutions of the Maine Legislature (*House Misc. Docs.,* No. 101). A message of Johnson's, with a report of the Secretary of State relative to the resources and extent of the fisheries, was printed (*Senate Ex. Docs.,* No. 34). On the other hand, resolutions such as those of the National Board of Trade at St. Louis, December, 1871, urged Congress to enact the necessary

doubtful whether it can be truthfully said that he ordinarily did anything quietly—Ben Butler was doing "his utmost" to prevent fisheries legislation, but he was meeting with some opposition in his own district, for one Loring hoped to get Butler's seat by proposing an alternative and, according to him, more attractive plan.[30]

Dr Loring has been endeavouring to persuade the Gloucester fishermen that Genl: Butler is injuring their interests in attempting to prevent legislation to carry out the fishing stipulations of the Treaty and that their object should rather be to make no opposition to them but to urge Congress to allow to the New England fishermen a bounty upon their vessels employed in the fisheries.

Fish, when Thornton spoke to him about this proposition, said that he understood that Canadian fishermen received bounties, but, if they did not,[31] "could always fit out, equip and navigate their vessels at a much cheaper rate than citizens of the U. S." But Fish added that he was not sorry to learn of Loring's suggestion, "because it would create a division amongst the enemies of the Treaty, and would render General Butler's opposition much weaker than it otherwise might be." Neither the friends nor the enemies of the treaty, however, could get any affirmative action in this session of Congress, and the whole issue had to be postponed another year.

But, legislation or no legislation, fishing would go on and exasperation was likely to increase. It was to minimize this that, on March 6, 1872, the Treasury Department issued a circular[32] addressed to collectors of customs who were directed to bring it to the attention of all parties concerned with its contents, which consisted principally of a copy of the circular which had been issued in June, 1870. Fishermen were instructed as to just what privileges they had under the Convention of 1818 and were particularly warned that the Canadian law of May 22, 1868, authorized naval officers of Great Britain and duly commissioned officials of the Dominion to

legislation (*Senate Misc. Docs.*, No. 99). (All documents of 42d Cong., 2d Sess.)

30. Thornton to Granville, Jan. 15, 1872; FO 115:539 (P.R.O.).

31. Thornton got from the Foreign Office assurance that no bounties were paid. Hammond to Thornton, Mar. 30, 1872; FO 115:534 (P.R.O.).

32. *For. Rel., 1872*, Part I, pp. 217–219.

go on board of any ship, vessel, or boat, within any harbor in Canada, or hovering (in British waters) within three marine miles of any of the coasts, bays, creeks, or harbors in Canada, and stay on board so long as she may remain within such place or distance; and that any one of such officers or persons . . . may bring any ship . . . into port, and search her cargo, and may also examine the master upon oath touching the cargo and voyage; and if the master or person in command shall not truly answer the questions put to him . . . he shall forfeit four hundred dollars; and if such ship . . . be foreign, or not navigated according to the laws of the United Kingdom or of Canada, and has been found fishing, or preparing to fish, or to have been fishing (in British waters) within three marine miles of any of the coasts, bays, creeks, or harbors of Canada not included within the [excepted] limits, without a license, or after the expiration of the period named in the last license granted to such ship . . . , [it] shall be forfeited.

Fishermen were likewise notified *"that the warning formerly given is not required under the amended act, but that vessels trespassing are liable to seizure"* forthwith. The Department circular furthermore called attention to the fact that the Dominion Government had, in January, 1870, provided for a naval police force to see that the law was carried into effect. Such a warning as contained in this circular was needed. As Macdonald had assured Robitaille in the House of Commons, there was to be no relaxation in the vigilance of officials in preventing foreign fishing in territorial waters.[33]

Despite the warning and despite the intention of the Dominion Government not to complicate matters further by bringing in the headland issue, the season of 1872 opened rather inauspiciously. On June 20 the schooner *James Bliss* owned by William Parsons, 2d, and Company and commanded by Allan MacIsaacs, a Nova Scotian-born Gloucesterman, was seized for violation of the regulations and taken into Gaspé Basin by the Dominion marine police cutter *Stella Maris*. But this was far from the worst of it. Some little time after the vessel had been brought into port under orders of Commander Lachance, Consul George H. Holt was horrified to see that the American flag, union down, was hoisted *beneath* the Dominion flag and, notwithstanding the protest he immediately lodged with Lachance, the next morn-

33. Macdonald to Peter Mitchell (Minister of Fisheries and Marine), Apr. 2, 1872; Macdonald Papers: Letterbooks, XVII, 489 (P.A.C.).

ing when the flags were run up they occupied the same relative position. This episode, originating, as Holt himself believed, in the perversity and obstinacy of Lachance, encouraged by the natives of Gaspé, was immediately the subject of prolonged telegraphing and correspondence involving Gaspé, Washington, Ottawa, and London, and lasting until well toward the end of September.[34] Fish quite properly was inclined to think that the whole affair grew out of the self-assertiveness of a minor official;[35] nevertheless, when newspapers took it up and bellicose editorials were printed, the matter had to be pursued to the bitter end.[36] The Colonial Office, which did not wish any unfortunate though trivial happening of this kind to stir anew belligerent feelings on both sides of the line, was much relieved on receiving a report of the Canadian Privy Council, which had caused an exhaustive investigation to be made.[37] This inquiry showed

that . . . when bringing into the harbor of Gaspé the captured vessel in question, the seizing-officer, in disregard of . . . instruction, and probably misapprehending his duty, did intentionally cause the Dominion flag to be hoisted above the American flag, but that the fact of the latter being so hoisted with the union downward was entirely unintentional, and occurred through inadvertence on the part of a subordinate.

That the government have already officially disavowed any intention to show disrespect toward the flag of the United States, and taken precautions to prevent recurrence of any such objectionable acts, and the minister recommends that the facts established by this inquiry be communicated to the United States authorities.

He also recommends that the seizing-officer, through whose inattention to his official instructions this difficulty has occurred, should be severely reprimanded.

34. All the pertinent notes are found in *For. Rel., 1872,* Part I, pp. 200 ff. There is considerably more correspondence in FO 5:1365 and 115:537 (P.R.O.).

35. The New York *Herald,* June 24, 1872, stated that Fish remarked when it was called to his attention: "It amounts to nothing. Some hairbrained Dominion official thinks he can make trouble by insulting our flag. We have become accustomed to such insolence."

36. See, for example, the Montreal *Gazette,* June 26, which paid its respects particularly to the New York *Herald.*

37. Sept. 30, 1872; *For. Rel., 1872,* Part I, p. 207.

Secretary Fish acknowledged Thornton's note of October 15 relating the course of the Dominion authorities and expressed his satisfaction at its disposition, and so the case of the *James Bliss* was relegated to the realm of things past and forgiven.

If this case stands out as the only one in which there was even momentary friction, it was probably due to the fact that few American fishermen attempted to indulge in the mackerel fishery in Canadian or other British American waters during the season. This fishery was, as the *Gazette* of Montreal noted at the season's end,[38] an almost "total failure," although the "bankers" had had a fairly profitable time. One reason, probably the most significant, was that the Government of Prince Edward Island refused to become a second time the victim of, let us say, a misunderstanding. The Committee of the Executive Council, on June 13, addressed to His Honor the Lieutenant-Governor a minute wherein they considered it was inexpedient to withdraw all privileges conceded on July 24, 1871, still allowing American fishermen "the right of entry at the Customs, the purchase of supplies, and transshipment of cargoes," yet they could not "recommend that the privilege of fishing within the 3 mile line be conceded during the present season, unless satisfaction be given relative to the refund of duties paid last year."[39] In this determination the British Government upheld them and, since they had no force with which to protect their interests, directed Her Majesty's naval establishment to see that there were no violations of the regulations.[40] Upon Thornton's informing the Department of State of this stand, Fish somewhat disingenuously maintained that the proposition of May, 1871, contemplated "the united action of all the British colonies." As to the Island's decision he hoped "that in carrying that measure into effect, a spirit of justice and forbearance will be made apparent, so that unnecessary and unprofitable irritation upon the subject may be avoided."[41] Thornton

38. Oct. 28, 1872.

39. FO 115:537 (P.R.O.). The minute and correspondence relating to it were transmitted by Granville to Thornton on June 26; FO 115:536 (P.R.O.).

40. Colonial Office to Secretary of the Admiralty, June, 1872; FO 115:536 (P.R.O.).

41. Thornton to Fish, July 10; Fish to Thornton, July 18; Thornton to Fish, July 19, 1872; *For. Rel., 1872*, Part I, pp. 220–222.

agreed that "due justice and forbearance" should be exercised, but he
did not hesitate to retort by saying:

I am at the same time confident that the Government of the United States
will, on its part, contribute toward preventing all grounds of dispute by
doing its utmost to induce its citizens to abstain from fishing in those
waters, for their admission to which the necessary legislation has not yet
been carried out by the Congress of the United States.

Yet it would appear that the Islanders yearned for the fleshpots.
The small number of American fishing vessels, which appeared in their
harbors to buy bait, ice, supplies, and various other commodities and
which had ordinarily brought in an appreciable amount of money,
affected adversely the economic life of the little community, so much
so that in July the way was cleared for a *rapprochement* if the United
States saw fit to take advantage of it. A minute of July 10 contained
this statement:[42]

Read a letter from the Lt. Governor to the Pres: of the Council, whereupon the Com[tee] recommended that His Honor the Lt. Governor do, if
applied by the Impl. Govt. sanction the renewal of the provisional arrangement by which American fishermen were admitted to the Inshore
fisheries of this Island during last summer, provided a sufficient guarantee
is given for the refund of duties paid last year, & which will under such
arrangement become payable this year.

The British Government, however, would have none of it. They were
not going to approach the American Administration, and the latter
showed no signs of reversing the position already taken. The attitude
of the Dominion and of Prince Edward Island produced no effect upon
Newfoundland, the colony which was always prone to go its own way,
for the Colonial Office received from the Lieutenant-Governor a telegram saying that "the Americans are fishing on the S. Coast of that
Colony, the Colonial Govt. having given them leave to do so, although
the Treaty of Washington has not yet come into operation."[43]

Thus the season of 1872 drew to a close and the time approached

42. FO 115:537 (P.R.O.).
43. Colonial Office to Secretary of the Admiralty, June, 1872; FO 115:536
(P.R.O.).

when the Forty-second Congress would meet for its third and final session. The election of that year was over, and Grant had been triumphantly returned to office in spite of the Liberal Republican revolt. There was little doubt that the Administration very much desired Congress to act to bring the treaty into effect, the more so because by this time not only had the Geneva Tribunal settled the *Alabama* Claims, by making an award to the United States and leaving only actual payment to be completed, but the German Emperor had handed down his decision in the San Juan case, vindicating the contentions Americans had persistently maintained as to the channel designated by the Treaty of 1846. This determination of the Administration to complete the job was indicated in Grant's Annual Message where he said:[44]

In my last annual message I recommended the legislation necessary on the part of the United States to bring into operation the articles of the Treaty of Washington . . . relating to the fisheries, and to other matters touching the relations of the United States toward the British North American possessions, to become operative as soon as the proper legislation should be had on the part of Great Britain and its possessions.

The legislation on the part of Great Britain and its possessions had not then been had, and during the session of Congress a question was raised which for the time raised a doubt whether any action by Congress in the direction indicated would become important. This question has since been disposed of, and I have received notice that the imperial parliament and the legislatures of the provincial governments have passed laws to carry the provisions of the treaty on the matters referred to into operation. I therefore recommend your early adoption of the legislation in the same direction necessary on the part of this Government.

Four days after the message was read Banks called to the attention of the House the resolution which had been made a special order during the previous session but which had been passed over and still remained to be acted upon. In view, he said, of information communicated by the President which should be considered by the Committee, he asked that the subject be postponed until the second Tuesday in January provided it did not conflict with any special arrangement al-

44. *Cong. Globe*, 42d Cong., 3d Sess., p. 4. Certified copies of the Dominion and Prince Edward Island acts were transmitted to Fish on December 4, 1872, and January 11, 1873.

ready made.[45] All these moves were, of course, watched with keen interest by Sir Edward Thornton. He did not understand the reason for the delay and said so to Secretary Fish, who told him that he had understood at the close of the last session there was an agreement that the bill would not be taken up until after the holidays, "but he stated his conviction that as soon as the Bill did come up, it would be passed without any difficulty."[46]

Your Lordship [he confided to Granville] may be aware that General Banks during the late Presidential election, sided with the party which supported M[r] Greeley in opposition to General Grant. As a consequence of his having thus abandoned the Republican party, General Banks lost his re-election to Congress from his District in Massachusetts. On the meeting of Congress, he offered to resign his position of Chairman of the Committee of Foreign Relations; his resignation however was not accepted by the House though the majority against accepting it was small, and he therefore retains the position. But as he no longer sympathises with the Administration, neither has it much confidence in him.

Privately Thornton wrote to the Earl of Dufferin, the new Governor-General of Canada, that he was "half inclined to think that this move has been taken with a view to divert General Butler in his opposition to the treaty."[47]

As the date set for bringing up the bill approached, Thornton became uneasy.[48] There were rumors that there was to be great opposition in Congress, but the reasons for this he could not ascertain unless they were "the general desire of the New England fishermen that they should enjoy the privilege of fishing in our waters without giving the Canadians the right of importing their fish duty free into the U. S.; but this idea is too extravagant to gain much support even from Americans." Senator Morrill of Vermont, he said, had called upon him the day before to say he was going to oppose the treaty because when Canadian vessels passed through the canals to Canadian ports they

45. Dec. 8; *ibid.*, p. 22.

46. Thornton to Granville, Dec. 16, 1872; FO 5: 1366 (P.R.O.).

47. Dufferin to Macdonald, Dec. 18, 1872; Macdonald Papers: Governor General Correspondence, V, 123–125 (P.A.C.).

48. Thornton to Macdonald, Jan. 12, 1873; Macdonald Papers: Washington Treaty, I, 588–594 (P.A.C.).

received back 90 per cent of their tolls, though he did not deny that American vessels would have the same concession under similar circumstances. But, he maintained, most of the trade was in Canadian bottoms for Canadian ports and in American bottoms for American ports, so that it was actually a discriminatory charge against Americans. To Granville[49] Thornton voiced some of the doubts he expressed to Macdonald and told of Morrill's visit and complaints, and said that although Fish still insisted that the legislation would go through he admitted that opposition from an unexpected quarter had arisen, while insisting he did not know the grounds on which it was based. "I have learnt from other quarters," Sir Edward wrote, "that Senators have found great fault with the American negotiators and particularly with Mr: Fish, because no precautions were taken by them during the Negotiation of the Treaty to remedy the evil complained of."[50]

The first of February came and nothing had been done about the bill. Sir Edward was beginning to lay the blame at the door of Banks, who, he said,[51] with the worst taste in the world was taking pleasure in annoying the Administration and paying no attention to business. The Minister had been constantly at Fish, who professed that he was doing everything he could to get action and still believed the bill would be passed before the end of the session. It was on that very day, however, that Banks gave notice that the next Thursday he would ask the House to consider the resolution and make it a special order, but not to the exclusion of everything else.[52] True to his word Banks did call the bill up but it was laid over in favor of the Post Office Appropriation Bill; on Friday, Banks again tried but had to give way to the Military Academy Bill. On the eighteenth once more Banks made an attempt, but Butler succeeded in having the measure sidetracked for the Civil

49. Jan. 13, 1873; FO 115:555 (P.R.O.).

50. Macdonald wrote Dufferin, Jan. 22, 1873 (Macdonald Papers: Letterbooks, XIX, 632–633 [P.A.C.]) that there was "a screw loose at Washington about the Bill" and that "Beast Butler is the 'nigger in the fence,'" using Morrill, who was a "loco style of Yankee and . . . always opposed to the extension of trade relations with Canada," as a tool.

51. To Macdonald, Feb. 1, 1873; Macdonald Papers: Washington Treaty, I, 594a–c (P.A.C.).

52. *Cong. Globe,* 42d Cong., 3d Sess., p. 1037. *House Reports,* No. 52, 42d Cong., 3d Sess. This would be February 6.

Appropriation Bill. The next day Grant and Fish went to the Capitol, where

they summoned into their presence General Banks. . . . In reply to the President's inquiries why the Bill had not been advanced, General Banks is said to have stated that several members of Congress belonging to the party wh. supports the Administration were opposed to the progress of the Bill, and amongst others he cited Genl: Butler. It is supposed however that Genl: Banks greatly exaggerates the opposition to the Bill. The President insisted upon its being pressed, and is said to have stated that unless the Bill were passed during this Session, H. M. Govt might refuse to pay the amount awarded by the Tribunal of Arbitration at Geneva.[53]

On the next day Banks did call up the measure again and in the course of some desultory discussion, principally between Banks and Sargent, the former charged that all the Administration wanted had been the money from Great Britain and now that that seemed to be assured they did not care what happened to other parts of the treaty; if Congress adjourned without action there would be feelings more bitter than ever. If the House persisted in the present course the "money wrung from England by false pretenses and fraud would prove a curse and a dishonor to us."[54] It was on this same day that Simon Cameron for the Senate Committee on Foreign Relations introduced a bill similar to that in the House except that it provided that fish imported prior to the President's proclamation or which should be held in bond in the United States on that date should not be exempt from duties. "This," remarked Thornton, "is no doubt intended to prevent the refunding of the duties paid upon fish imported from Prince Edward's Island during the summer of 1871, when American fishermen were allowed to fish in the inshore waters of that Island."

By now the Administration was really in earnest. On February 24 Grant sent a special message to Congress[55] reciting what had been done

53. Thornton to Granville, Feb. 24, 1873; FO 115:555 (P.R.O.).

54. Washington *Morning Chronicle,* Feb. 22, 1873, enclosed in Thornton's dispatch of Feb. 24. Thornton thought these remarks, which had not appeared elsewhere, would be suppressed entirely, for the Washington *Daily Globe* stated that Banks's remarks were reserved for revision; at any rate the speech did not appear in the *Congressional Globe.*

55. *Cong. Globe,* 42d Cong., 3d Sess., p. 1646; *House Ex. Docs.,* No. 216, 42d Cong., 3d Sess.

in the way of legislation by Great Britain and her colonies and how the *Alabama* and San Juan issues had been settled. He could not, he wrote, too strongly urge an early consideration of the pending measure by Congress. The good faith of the United States was in question. Directly after the reading of this message in the House, Banks called for consideration of the bill. For a short time he was blocked by the regular order, but as soon as he could get the floor he called it up again, and, after a little parliamentary sparring, in which Butler proposed an amendment that October 1 instead of July 1 be the day fixed for the President's proclamation in order that the money for the *Alabama* Claims might have been paid, and after Banks accepted an amendment to make the measure correspond with the Senate bill, he secured a vote and the bill was on its third reading. At this stage occurred more debate and considerable bickering. One representative particularly objected to allowing lake fish caught by Canadians to enter free of duty; another maintained that fixing of tariffs by treaty was unconstitutional, while Eugene Hale joined in the chorus with the statement that the ten years of reciprocity had ruined the American fishermen. S. S. Cox said he never thought much of the Washington Treaty where the United States had gone in for two or three hundred million and come out with fifteen, but the fisheries provisions were an advance: "Now when we are doing something to bring Canada to order . . . and get something like real reciprocity in the carrying trade, when we are making a large advance in the interest of commercial liberality, gentlemen representing local interest come here and place impediments in the way of carrying out a solemn treaty which we are bound to carry out." Banks, summing up for his committee, maintained that he had never been enthusiastic about the treaty but, after all, the United States did get the use of the Canadian canals; they got five thousand miles of navigation for which they had been struggling since the government was formed with no obligation except to pay for its use. "Does my colleague [Butler] mean to say that those 'Bluenoses' can circumvent us and destroy the people of this country by their superior capacity or their greater enterprise or bravery?" Could they overreach the people of the West, as Omar D. Conger had argued? He, for one, did not think that was possible. When he moved the question Conger tried to table the bill and Butler wished to extend the debate. Both lost, and the vote stood 145 in favor to 30 opposed with 65 not voting. The negative vote was fairly well scattered but such concentration as there was, was accounted for by New England's representatives.[56]

When the President's message was read in the Senate, Hannibal Hamlin thought it had better lie on the table, since, while the Committee on Foreign Relations had reported a bill, this was a matter involving revenue and so could not originate there; furthermore, in a few minutes the House bill would be before them. Two days later, on February 26, 1873, the House measure was taken up, the calendar laid aside, and, after Hamlin briefly explained its provisions, it was passed without a record vote. The act recited that as soon as the President was satisfied that the British Parliament, the Dominion Parliament, and the legislature of Prince Edward Island had passed laws to give effect to the treaty, he should issue his proclamation declaring Articles XVIII to XXV and Article XXX in effect, and should likewise proclaim that all fish and fish oil, except fish preserved in oil, and except fish of the lakes and of the rivers flowing into them, should be admitted to the ports of the United States free of duty. Whenever Newfoundland should give its assent and the British Parliament had enacted necessary laws, that island also should be given the same privileges. From the date of the proclamation, July 1, 1873, the ports of New York, Boston, Portland, and such others as the President might designate should receive goods destined for the British possessions without the payment of duty, but this exemption should not apply to merchandise held in bond on that day. British subjects, moreover, could then transport goods in British bottoms from place to place on the lakes and rivers of the United States without paying duty, provided a part of the transportation was through Canada by land carriage and in bond.[57]

After the bill had passed the House and before it was taken up in the Senate, Thornton had expressed his regret that its operation was to be postponed until July 1. Fish had said that he, too, regretted this condition and could not understand why it was interpolated; possibly the Senate might eliminate it, but then the measure would have to go back to the House and that might mean the defeat of the whole busi-

56. *Cong. Globe,* 42d Cong., 3d Sess., pp. 1647, 1661, 1663–1665.
57. *Ibid.,* pp. 1738, 1778, 1779; App., p. 257.

ness. On the whole, he believed it was better to accept it as it was rather than run this risk.[58] The Dominion Government, now that Congress had finally acted, did not stand on ceremony but moved at once. A Report of a Committee of the Privy Council noted that while the Act of Congress did not take effect until July 1, and that until then American fishermen would have no legal right to the inshore fisheries, nevertheless they were of the "opinion that no steps should be taken by the government to prevent American vessels from fishing within the three-mile limit, and they should have full permission to fish so far as the government [could] grant it." Seizures might, however, be made at the instance of private parties, but in that case the committee were prepared to advise the Governor-General to order the release of vessels and remission of any penalties.[59] Now there remained only the steps to bring into operation the commission to assess the difference in money value between American and Canadian fishery concessions.

58. Thornton to Granville, Mar. 3, 1873; FO 115:555 (P.R.O.).
59. Dated Mar. 3, 1873. *For. Rel., 1873*, Part I, I, 418.

CHAPTER XIX

AWARD vs. RECIPROCITY

THE necessary legislation had been passed to put the Treaty of Washington into operation, nevertheless there still remained some minor obstacles to be cleared away. To make the law effective it must be proclaimed to the world, but over this apparently simple matter there were still to be weeks of haggling and yards of red tape unrolled. It was not, indeed, until April 26, 1873, that Minister Schenck, now for some time established in the London Legation, was able to inform Secretary Fish that Lord Granville had told him that instructions had been issued to draft directions to Sir Edward Thornton.[1] Then there was a delay over whether it was understood that the protocol should be signed in Washington and not in London.[2] At last, on May 31, Thornton handed to Fish "a copy of the Draft of a Protocol . . . fixing the 1st: of July next as the day on wh. Articles 18 to 25 . . . should come into operation and told him that if he concurred in it, I was authorized by Y.L. to sign it."[3] Fish took the copy, made a few verbal corrections in which the British Minister concurred, and both signed it on June 7. Copies were transmitted to the Governor-General of Canada and the Lieutenant-Governor of Prince Edward Island so that, on July 1, proclamation issued simultaneously from the executives of these units and from the President of the United States.

The delay had been caused in part by the desire of Newfoundland to be included in the President's proclamation. Through the Colonial Office, Lieutenant-Governor Stephen J. Hill had brought to Thornton's attention the act his legislature passed during the session just ended in the expectation that there would be no trouble in having the island comprehended in the scope of the American proclamation.[4] But

1. *For. Rel., 1873,* Part I, I, 355–356.
2. Thornton to Granville, May 19, 1873; FO 115:555 (P.R.O.). Davis to Schenck, May 20; *For. Rel., 1873,* Part I, I, 366. Schenck to Fish, June 9; *ibid.,* pp. 377–378.
3. Thornton to Granville, June 9, 1873; FO 115:555 (P.R.O.).
4. Hill to Kimberley, enclosing copy of Newfoundland act, May 6, 1873; FO 115:552 (P.R.O.).

one clause caused unexpected difficulty. After stating that "all laws of this Colony which operate to prevent the said Articles from taking full effect" should be suspended during the operation of the treaty, there was added the proviso "that such laws, rules & regulations relating to the time & manner of prosecuting the Fisheries on the coasts of this Island, shall not be in any way affected by such suspension." The act had been submitted to the Law Officers of the Crown by Lord Kimberley,[5] and those gentlemen had ruled that it "sufficiently" complied with the provisions of the treaty and that Her Majesty's assent should be given it, although they were of the opinion "that the clause should be so framed as expressly to cover the close time for the herring fishery & the observation by American fishermen of the Rules & Regulations imposed upon the fishermen of Newfoundland in that particular."[6] This statement raised a question in both the Colonial and Foreign Offices whether the Law Officers thought the act ought to be amended before the treaty could be brought into operation because objections could be raised by the Government of the United States, or merely desirable for the purpose of more clearly expressing the object intended by the "proviso . . . namely to put American fishermen on the same footing as Newfoundland fishermen."[7] In either case, Lord Kimberley suggested that copies of the correspondence be sent to Thornton, together with the act, and that he be instructed to ask Fish whether he was prepared to sign a protocol affecting Newfoundland as well as the Dominion and Prince Edward Island.

Mr. Fish should be distinctly informed by Sir E. Thornton, in order to prevent misunderstanding hereafter, that the laws rules and regulations . . . include the close time for the herring Fishery, and the observation by American fishermen of the rules and regulations imposed upon the Newfoundland fishermen in that particular.

The Newfoundland House of Assembly, it was pointed out, had been prorogued and would not meet again that year; moreover, it would be hard to demonstrate to them the necessity of a change unless it were

5. H. G. Holland to Under-Secretary of State, May 23; FO 115:552 (P.R.O.).

6. J. D. Coleridge, G. Jessel, and I. P. Deane to Granville, May 29, 1873; FO 115:552 (P.R.O.).

7. R. G. W. Herbert to Hammond, June 3, 1873; FO 115:552 (P.R.O.).

shown that the act did not sufficiently comply with the terms of the treaty. If the Government of the United States raised no objection, then there would appear to be no reason why the act should not be proclaimed along with those of the other colonies.

In accord with this suggestion Lord Granville instructed Thornton[8] that, since the protocol relating to Canada and Prince Edward Island would probably already have been signed, he should "propose to Mr. Fish to sign a similar protocol respecting Newfoundland, with the addition of a clause following as nearly as possible the proviso. . . ." This Thornton did as soon as he received his instructions. Fish's reaction was what had been feared: he doubted "whether he could agree to sign a Protocol with the Proviso," for no restrictions had been inserted in the treaty and,

whilst he would certainly be disinclined to sign another Protocol for Newfoundland with the Proviso of the Act without knowing the exact restrictions to which it referred, he should even hesitate to accept the Act in question as a law of the form required by the Treaty to carry into operation Articles XVIII to XXV, inasmuch as it spoke of restrictions to wh. the Treaty made no allusion.[9]

Thornton in vain pointed out that the restrictions applied only to a certain kind of fishing and were enforced against all alike, and he presumed that there were local laws in the United States which would have the same effect. While Fish admitted that fishermen on both sides would have to observe local regulations, "such restrictions had not formed a part of the Treaty or of the laws of the different countries interested in the matter with the exception of Newfoundland, and . . . he thought that there was no ground for this exception." To this position the American Secretary stuck tenaciously through a correspondence which lasted until the following spring: admitting that American fishermen would have to abide by reasonable and fair local restrictions, he was determined not to admit any *formal* exception. July first came and passed, and Newfoundland was still outside the pale, for it was not until the House of Assembly, meeting in 1874, modified the Act of 1873 that Fish was willing to advise the President

8. June 7, 1873; FO 115:552 (P.R.O.).

9. Thornton to Granville, June 23, 1873; FO 115:556 (P.R.O.). Fish's formal answer to Thornton is in *For. Rel., 1873,* Part I, I, 429–430.

to issue the requisite proclamation. No kind of assurance that the original law really made no difference produced the slightest impression upon him; he stuck to his guns to the end, having, no doubt, an eye to the correspondence he would have to publish and avoiding any risk of a backfire from Gloucester fishermen and their advocates in Congress. Eventually, on May 18, 1874, he could write to Thornton that Newfoundland's amended act satisfied the Government of the United States, and, as soon as the Lieutenant-Governor of that island issued his proclamation, the President's would follow.[10] Meantime American fishermen were enjoying the inshore fisheries along Newfoundland's shores, but Newfoundlanders were not exempt from paying duties upon the fish they shipped into American ports until June 1, 1874.

Intermingled with the question of associating Newfoundland with the Dominion and Prince Edward Island in applying the provisions of the Treaty of Washington, there had arisen again the question of the seal fisheries and the admission of seal products duty free to American ports. No progress had been made when the subject had been broached in 1871, nor had Congress taken up the matter. Lieutenant-Governor S. J. Hill therefore reopened the issue on May 3, 1873, by addressing to Lord Kimberley a communication requesting that the British Minister in Washington be instructed to "ascertain if the Gov^t of the United States has obtained the approval of Congress to admit into their ports [these products] duty free in exchange for the right of taking Seals in Newfoundland Waters and of making outfits in the ports of the Island."[11] On June 19 Sir Edward recalled to Fish the correspondence which had taken place in the latter part of 1871 and inquired "whether any steps have been taken by your Department with a view to carry out the proposal of the Government of Newfoundland."[12] The Secretary's reply, Thornton was obliged to report to Lord Granville,[13] was no more satisfactory than the earlier one, for it indicated "that the measure involved in the proposal is one which must receive the sanction of Congress, and that it is not considered probable that the assent of that Body would be given to it."

Much closer to the American Secretary's heart than either of these

10. *For. Rel., 1874,* pp. 557–558.   11. FO 115:552 (P.R.O.).
12. Thornton to Fish, *For. Rel., 1873,* Part I, I, 426.
13. June 30; FO 115:556 (P.R.O.).

suggestions was the question of appointing the commission to assess the money value of the difference between British and American fishery concessions. Back in December Fish had brought up the matter.[14] The President, he had told Thornton, would be ready to appoint the American Commissioner as soon as the bill putting the treaty into operation should have been passed; as to the third member he agreed that it should be someone familiar with the English language, but he doubted whether it would be possible to find anyone not an American or Britisher who would be willing to go to Halifax to serve. British and Canadian officials were likewise casting over the field, and Minister of Marine and Fisheries Mitchell was the person most favorably considered in Canada and approved by the Colonial Office.[15] He was, Lord Dufferin thought, inclined to too much "bounce and bluster," qualities, however, which might be useful in "diplomatizing with the Yankees." The Premier thought he would "make a good Comn^r. Like all New Brunswickers he [is] half Yankee in style—has a rough and ready."

When the implementing bill was finally signed by the President, Thornton, pursuant to a telegraphic instruction from Granville, said to Fish that he understood that the three months mentioned in Article XXIII during which the third commissioner should be agreed upon would begin with the date of approval of the act. Fish, on the other hand, felt pretty sure that the three months should be reckoned from the day on which the act went into effect, namely, July 1, but he would not have any time to consider the matter in detail until Congress should have adjourned.[16] He did not see, however, why in the meantime the two governments might not try to agree upon some individual. A week later, still sticking to his notion that any time before October 1 would be within the spirit of the treaty, Fish was willing to canvass the possibilities; the only person "who had passed thro' his mind was Mr. Justice Nelson," one of the American members of the Joint High Commission whose long judicial career would make

14. Thornton to Granville, Dec. 16, 1872; FO 5:1366 (P.R.O.).
15. Macdonald to Cartier, Dec. 20, 1872; to Dufferin, Jan. 22; Macdonald Papers:Letterbooks, XIX, 422, 632–633 (P.A.C.); Dufferin to Macdonald, Jan. 15; Macdonald Papers:Governor General Correspondence, V, 37–40 (P.A.C.).
16. Thornton to Granville, Mar. 3, 1873; FO 115:555 (P.R.O.).

him thoroughly impartial and whose age "placed him beyond all political ambition." Thornton did not venture any opinion to Granville on this suggestion "because Y. L. will be able without difficulty to consult the remaining four of H. M. High Commissioners who negotiated the Treaty."[17] Nelson, naturally, did not make any great appeal to either the Colonial or Foreign Secretary, but, while the former had been trying to think of someone to propose, he had not found it an easy matter.[18] It appears, however, that Fish was serious in suggesting Nelson, for, after prodding Thornton once or twice, he definitely stated that "as he had already confidentially proposed Judge Nelson who had not been considered acceptable, it was but fair that H. M. Govt: should mention some other person whom it might consider more suitable."[19] Fish's linking the naming of a commissioner with the signing of the protocol, as he did at this time, rather irritated Sir Edward, who was led to suspect that Fish "wished to force the installation of the commission by delaying the signature of the Protocol and perhaps even the President's Proclamation."

On June 25 Thornton received from the Foreign Office a telegram which admitted they were finding some difficulty in "naming a third fishery commissioner whose nomination would be acceptable to the Canadians and to whom some objection might not be made by the American Government." They therefore suggested that the British and American ministers at The Hague be authorized to see if they could agree "upon some Dutchman who would be acceptable to both Governments."[20] This idea did not strike Fish at all favorably, although he would neither decline nor accept the proposition until he had consulted with the President; it would put the United States at great disadvantage and to great expense for cable tolls, and frankly he considered it a device to delay matters and to throw the appointment to the Austro-Hungarian Ambassador in London. Moreover, it would probably postpone the meeting of the commission until the next year, for it could hardly be expected that this third commissioner could be induced to stay at Halifax during the cold season. Besides all

17. To Granville, Mar. 10, 1873; FO 115:555 (P.R.O.).
18. Extract of Kimberley to Dufferin, Mar. 27; Macdonald Papers: Governor General Correspondence, V, 261–263 (P.A.C.).
19. Thornton to Granville, Confidential, June 9; FO 115:555 (P.R.O.).
20. FO 115:556 (P.R.O.).

that, Fish confided to Thornton, "Mr: Gorman, the U. S. Minister at the Hague, was not a man of high order and that as he spoke nothing but his own language, he would not probably be well acquainted with the principal people of the country."[21] Nothing had been done when Secretary Fish went back to New York to escape the heat of Washington; he had, however, left with Davis instructions to keep after the British Minister and made up a list of persons who would be satisfactory to the President. These were Ignacio Mariscal, Henri d'Offenberg, A. P. de Carvallo Borges, José Polo de Bernabé, the Marquis de Noailles, and Bernhard de Westenberg, ministers respectively from Mexico, Russia, Brazil, Spain, France, and the Netherlands.[22]

Thornton's comments on the individuals proposed, which he wrote in a confidential dispatch to Lord Granville from Catskill, where he had gone to cool off from the heat of Washington,[23] were interesting if somewhat frank and not altogether flattering. Mariscal, who had an American wife, was not likely "either personally or as the Mexican Representative to resist the influence which would certainly be brought to bear upon him by a people whom the Mexican Nation may not love but certainly dreads." The Russian Minister was "a very intelligent and well informed man, tho' rather slow and heavy"; he knew English well, was not prejudiced against England and could hardly be "induced to decide unjustly against us either for the sake of diminishing the prestige of England or of conciliating the United States." The Brazilian did not know English well enough to handle the situation, and he was, moreover, an "indolent man and not likely to make himself acquainted with the subject, which . . . would require a good deal of reading and research." Admiral Polo spoke English fairly well and read and wrote it better.

I consider him a completely honest and straightforward man whom nothing could induce to decide in a way wh. he did not consider in accordance with justice. He is not perhaps brilliant nor deeply read; but his common

21. Thornton to Granville, Confidential, June 30; FO 115:556 (P.R.O.). Fish to Schenck, June 28; Great Britain:Instructions, XXIII, 377–379 (D.S.).

22. Davis to Thornton, July 7, 1873; Great Britain:Notes to, XVI, 150–153 (D.S.).

23. July 14; FO 115:556 (P.R.O.). Thornton had been in Washington when he received Davis' note on July 11.

sense would make up for such defects. He has certainly no prejudice against England but on the contrary has a great admiration for her political institutions.

The Marquis de Noailles who had not been in the United States long, was not much accustomed to business "particularly of the sort for which he would now be required"; besides, he would probably be too much influenced by "the view which his Government might wish him to take." The Netherlands Minister Thornton could not recommend very highly, "tho' in some points of view his nomination might be very desirable."

M. de Westenberg is well acquainted with the English language, is extremely intelligent, and possesses a great fund of general knowledge; he is also very studious and laborious, and would take great pains to make himself thoroughly acquainted with the subject. But unfortunately his manner is disagreeable and he on that account generally disliked; he is occasionally so eccentric as almost to lead one to believe that his mind is slightly affected; but this may be due to, or have been brought about by, the impossibility under wh. he seems to labour, of abstaining from the excessive use of intoxicating liquors.

Of all the suggestions Thornton inclined to Admiral Polo and Baron Offenberg, with some slight leaning in favor of the former "because he inspires me with greater confidence in his honesty and with a conviction that he would be determined to be just to the best of his judgment."

From the Governor-General of Canada, Thornton received a telegram saying that his Government would prefer the Belgian Minister at Washington for the third commissioner.[24] Because he feared that this suggestion, especially from that source, would not be acceptable to the American Administration, he did not intimate to Fish that the idea had come from Ottawa, but merely asked him why the Belgian's name had not been included in the suggested list. "He understood English extremely well," commented Thornton, "having been in London for several years, was a very intelligent man, and having but little official business at Washington connected with his Legation, could more easily absent himself for a time than almost any of his Col-

24. Thornton to Granville, Aug. 11, 1873; FO 115:556 (P.R.O.).

leagues." But, true to Thornton's expectations, Fish would have none of him.

Belgium was so completely under the control and protection of Gr: Britain that the American people would never be persuaded that her Representative could be anything but partial towards England; indeed, Belgium was looked upon in the U.S. almost as a Province of Gr: Britain.

Besides, Grant did not like him; he was too outspoken about the United States. Since Fish would not consider M. Delfosse, Lord Granville once more[25] suggested that, as the two governments did not seem to be able to agree, the only thing to do was to leave the selection to the Ambassador of Austria-Hungary at London. But Thornton, not having "asked Mr: Fish in the name of H. M. Govt: to consent to the appointment of the Belgian Minister," had one more try, and in a private letter definitely stated that the British Government hoped this gentleman would be acceptable. Fish received this communication while at his summer home in Garrison, New York. Immediately he dictated an answer couched in more peevish tone than was his wont. He resented the suggestion of a man who was known to be unacceptable and expressed his surprise that no response had come to his own list of suggestions, adding that if Lord Granville objected to all of them he hoped he would name one or more "known in advance not to be incapable of acceptance." Before this note reached Thornton the latter had received another telegram from the Foreign Office stating that the Dominion Government objected to the appointment of any of the ministers at Washington.[26]

In explanation of the British Government's disinclination to accept one of the persons named by the Secretary of State, Davis, with whom Thornton continued to carry on correspondence and oral conversations, ascertained that it was really the attitude of the Dominion that blocked progress. This aroused the ire of Fish, who maintained[27] that the President still retained his confidence in the gentlemen suggested

25. Telegram to Thornton, Aug. 18, 1873; FO 115:556 (P.R.O.).

26. Fish to Thornton, Aug. 21, 1873; Great Britain: Notes to, XVI, 187–188 (D.S.). Thornton to Granville, Confidential, Aug. 25, 26; FO 115:556 (P.R.O).

27. Fish to Thornton, Sept. 6, 1873; Great Britain: Notes to, XVI, 200–204 (D.S.).

and went on to say that "the reference in your [Thornton's] note to the people and Dominion of Canada seems to imply a practical transfer to that Province of the right of nomination which the Treaty gives to her Majesty." The President was of the opinion that *his* refusal on account of some local interest to accept someone might be considered by the British Government as a departure from the spirit of the treaty which might justify their remonstrance and possibly hesitation as to their future relations to such a commission. This, thought Thornton, was a detractory and ridiculous comparison of Gloucester fishermen with the Government of Canada, and he was "at the same time convinced that the fishing interests of New England have been consulted in every step that has been taken since the beginning of the discussion upon the fisheries question."[28]

The last day of September arrived and no progress had been made toward naming the third commissioner, unless Granville's renewed proposal to let the British and American ministers at The Hague do it might be so considered. Fish chose to view this as the first *official* suggestion of such a course and quoted from his Diary to show that when Thornton had broached it to him, he had said it did not strike him favorably and he would neither accept nor decline until he had consulted the President. He adverted to Granville's bringing up the name of the Belgian Minister, "so overlooking Canadian objection to the ministers at Washington," and hoped that he might, "disregarding as we do local interests," still be willing to name the third man.[29] The proposal to try to find "some Dutchman" Fish was pleased to regard as a departure from the Treaty of Washington which would require a new convention, while Granville was equally sure that Fish's idea of still trying to come to some agreement, despite the fact that the three months had elapsed, was "wholly inconsistent with the letter of the Treaty,"[30] which specifically demanded that if in this period no

28. Thornton to Granville, Sept. 12, 1873; FO 115:556 (P.R.O.).

29. Fish to Thornton, Oct. 3, 1873; Great Britain: Notes to, XVI, 222-228 (D.S.). In a note of September 30 Fish had deeply regretted that H. M. Government had made no effort to comply with the provisions of Article XXIII. (*Ibid.*, pp. 218–219. Thornton to Granville, Oct. 6; FO 115:556 [P.R.O.].) This insinuation Thornton opposed, and insisted that his Government had tried to carry out the stipulations.

30. Granville to Thornton, Oct. 7; FO 115:553 (P.R.O.).

agreement had been reached "the nomination should then rest with the Representative of the Emperor of Austria and King of Hungary in London." Accordingly, Thornton was instructed to propose "to Mr Fish that it is desirable that he should agree with you upon an identic note to be addressed to the Austrian Government . . . requesting that Government to be good enough to authorize their Ambassador at this court to take the necessary steps for selecting a commissioner."[31] It was obvious that the American Administration still had hopes that the two governments could come to an agreement without having recourse to the alternative plan, and it was as nearly apparent that the British Government despaired of naming a person who would be acceptable to both Canadians and Americans, and consequently would be glad to put the task to a third party. Fish was in no hurry to respond to Granville's suggestion of applying to the Austro-Hungarian Government, even after it had been brought a second time to his attention,[32] for a new factor had now appeared. Canada was making another attempt to secure a reciprocity treaty.

On November 5, 1873, Sir John A. Macdonald announced in the House of Commons that his Excellency the Governor-General had accepted the Government's resignation and had sent for Alexander Mackenzie, leader of the Opposition, to form a new one. This not unexpected occurrence was the direct result of the so-called Pacific Railway Scandal, which brought about a shift in Parliament so that the veteran Conservative leader lost his majority.[33] Wedded to free trade

31. Granville to Thornton, Oct. 11, 1873; FO 115:553 (P.R.O.).

32. On Dec. 2, 1873. Thornton to Granville, Dec. 8; FO 115:556 (P.R.O.).

33. One of the principal inducements to get British Columbia into the Dominion had been an agreement that the Government would bring in a bill to construct within ten years a railroad to the Pacific Coast. After various efforts at forming a company had failed, there was organized the Canadian Pacific Railway Company, with Sir Hugh Allan as the guiding spirit. The act had provided that there should be no American interest in this undertaking and also that for six years there should be no transfer of stock.

During the hotly contested parliamentary election of 1872, Allan, who was alleged not to have completely severed his connection with American capital, advanced considerable sums to aid the Conservatives, some of which had been solicited by Sir John himself. Toward the close of the session of 1873 Lucius S. Huntington, a Liberal, had brought charges of corruption against the Government and especially against the Premier. The Governor-General appointed a

as a principle, in contrast to the growing mildly protectionist policy of the Conservatives, Mackenzie and the Liberals believed that they could bring about limited reciprocal arrangements and secure other advantages from the United States although Macdonald had failed. The impending organization and meeting of the commission to assess the money value of the fisheries appeared to offer an opportunity to bargain: the Government of the United States might be willing to grant concessions in return for escaping a payment which the Canadians were sure would be awarded to them. Political gain for the Liberal party as well as economic advantages for Canada would doubtless result if Mackenzie could win where Macdonald had failed, hence there was a double motive for striking at a time when the Conservative party was very much under a cloud.

For some reason Mackenzie's government and particularly George Brown, who, though not in office, was the patron saint of the Liberals, were of the opinion that this was an opportune time to approach the American administration. Just why there should have been this confidence is hard to comprehend. Surely nothing had taken place in Congress to warrant it, and while there had been some sporadic manifestations of a desire for closer commercial relations the dominant sentiment was still protectionist. The slight reductions in duties made in 1872 catered to a political necessity, but the presidential and congressional elections of that year did not indicate that the Republican

Royal Commission to investigate. When Parliament met after prorogation an attack centered upon the Government and particularly upon Macdonald. Perceiving from the trend of the debate that he would no longer command a majority, Sir John tendered the resignation of his Government.

Except for the fact that one of the American capitalists with whom Allan had been previously associated, George W. McMullen, appeared to be still connected with the Canadian Pacific enterprise, although this was denied by Allan, there does not seem to be any relation of the whole matter to Canadian-American affairs in general. Perhaps as satisfactory an account of the matter as appeared is found in the dispatch of the Earl of Dufferin to Kimberley on August 15, 1873, printed in William Leggo, *History of the Administration of the Right Honorable Frederick Temple, Earl of Dufferin, etc.* (Montreal and Toronto, 1878), pp. 140–173. The newspaper accounts of the affair were for the most part highly exaggerated and frequently abusive. See H. A. Innis, *A History of the Canadian Pacific Railway* (London and Toronto, 1923), pp. 82 ff.

party, beginning to be so closely identified with protectionism, was in any immediate danger of collapse. Nor was there any evidence of weakening in the reluctant and hardly gracious passage of legislation necessary to put into operation the parts of the Treaty of Washington affecting Canada. If one cannot go wholly with the opinion expressed by a Canadian politically opposed to Brown, Mackenzie, and their group, that it was "sufficiently obvious that the movement was taken to gratify Mr. Brown's ambition to figure as a treaty maker, without duly considering the inopportuneness of the attempt, or the inefficiency of the chief plenipotentiary [Brown],"[34] one can hardly fail to think that the new Canadian Government was motivated more by ill-founded hope and rather heedless enthusiasm than by solid reason.

No obstacle was placed in the path of Canadian aspirations by the British Government, although it was made clear that no other course than that specified by the treaty, i.e., carrying on with the Halifax Commission, should be followed unless the Canadian Government expressed a "spontaneous and unmistakable desire" to do otherwise.[35] Sir Edward reported that Fish himself had introduced the subject, probably as a result of talks which H. C. Rothery had had with him and Davis; the Minister had not encouraged enlargement upon the topic, nor did he place much confidence in Fish's saying that he personally favored reciprocity, for he had found that

he, like most statesmen in this country, endeavors to find out the opinion of influential Members of Congress before he commits himself upon any question, and however desirable it may be that I should obtain M[r] Fish's private feelings and opinions upon any subject, he supposes that I understand that his letting me know them does not in any way commit him.[36]

But even Thornton's skepticism began to waver a little, for, on February 9, he telegraphed that recent occurrences had made him "tolerably certain" that both the President and the Secretary favored the

34. Leggo, *op. cit.*, p. 211.
35. Granville to Thornton, cipher telegram, Jan. 24, 1874; FO 115:573 (P.R.O.).
36. To Granville, Confidential, Jan. 26, 1874; FO 115:573 (P.R.O.). Henry Cardogan Rothery, registrar of the High Court of Admiralty in England, had come to America to prepare the Canadian case for the arbitration of the award.

idea of renewing the reciprocal arrangement. That same day Brown and Rothery arrived in Washington with assurances that the Canadian Government much preferred renewal of reciprocity to a money payment. Thornton agreed that this was probably true but he could take no steps until he had specific instructions to proceed, and advised their having the matter taken up with Lord Kimberley; he would, however, suggest that the Canadians merely propose to renew Article III of the old treaty, which provided mutual free trade in natural products, and let the United States offer modifications. Then followed a series of telegrams between Ottawa and London which resulted in permission to the Canadian Government to go ahead, with the distinct understanding that the initiative was Canada's.[37]

A mere renewal of Article III, however, Fish "with an air of disappointment" told Thornton when the matter was opened, was hardly enough to warrant delaying the fishery provisions of the Treaty of Washington. The United States wanted admission of manufactured articles and wished the Canadian canals enlarged, something which Macdonald in 1871 had led them to think would be done; New York had already admitted Canadians to their canals. If free admission of manufactures was *sine qua non*, Thornton replied, then it was useless to go on with the discussion for the United States could hardly expect Her Majesty's Government to adopt "so suicidal a policy." Moreover, he was under the impression that Canada had already begun to enlarge her canals.[38] But Canada was willing to advance somewhat in the direction indicated by the Secretary of State, for on February 23 Lord Dufferin approved and forwarded to the Colonial Office a minute of the Privy Council, based upon a memorandum of Mr. Mackenzie, which stated that it was considered "a most favorable opportunity for the renewal of negotiations for a Reciprocity Treaty between Canada and the United States . . . , by which the claim for compensation as regards the Fisheries might be settled without the reference provided for by Article XXII" of the Treaty of Washington, and recommended that the British Minister in Washington be instructed to enter

37. The correspondence is in FO 115:566 and 115:573, especially Carnarvon to Dufferin, Secret, Mar. [?], 1874, enclosed in Holland to Under-Secretary, Foreign Office, Mar. 3, 1874; FO 115:566 (P.R.O.). The Earl of Carnarvon was now back in the Colonial Office.

38. Thornton to Derby, Mar. 2, 1874; FO 115:573 (P.R.O.).

upon such negotiation. With great promptness the Colonial Secretary, the Earl of Carnarvon, answered that Her Majesty's Government acceded to the desire of the Dominion Cabinet, "though they had been fully prepared to abide by, and were in no way apprehensive of the results of, the reference contemplated by the provisions of the Treaty," and instructions had been transmitted to Sir Edward Thornton to this effect. It was made clear, however, that the step was taken "at the express instance and solicitation of the Canadian Government." At the further request of this Government, George Brown was named "Joint Plenipotentiary with Her Majesty's Minister at Washington, for the purpose of negotiating and concluding a Treaty with the United States, relating to Fisheries, Commerce and Navigation."[39]

What Brown and the Government behind him hoped to obtain were: (1) renewal of the Treaty of 1854 for twenty-one years, "including the Fisheries, with addition of free admission of salt, manufactures of wood, iron or steel, or of those jointly, agricultural implements, and a few other trifling articles";[40] (2) opening of the coasting trade mutually on the lakes and the St. Lawrence; (3) opening of Canadian and American canals on equal terms to both countries; (4) right of navigating Lake Michigan in perpetuity without restrictions imposed by the United States for the ten-year period of the Treaty of Washington; (5) ownership and navigation of vessels of both countries by citizens of Canada or of the United States; (6) joint reciprocal admission to patent rights; (7) a joint commission to improve the navigation of the St. Clair River at joint expense; and (8) a joint commission to secure propagation and protection of fish in the lakes and to coöperate in establishing lighthouses. Canada was willing to forego any money payment for the inshore fisheries and to engage to enlarge the canals of the St. Lawrence to take vessels up to fourteen-foot draft.[41]

39. Canadian *Sessional Paper* No. 51, Second Session of Third Parliament, 1875, pp. 2, 7–8. Thornton to Derby, Mar. 9, 1874; FO 115:573 (P.R.O.).

The British Government yielded reluctantly to the appointment of Brown to full rank. Holland to Foreign Office, Mar. 10, 1874; FO 115:567 (P.R.O.).

40. Not, however, to include articles manufactured in England and exported to Canada. Telegram from Dufferin, Mar. 3, 1874; FO 115:566 (P.R.O.).

41. Report of Committee of the Privy Council, Mar. 26, 1874; Carnarvon to

While in Washington, Brown had been hard at work trying to get in touch with leading men in Congress as well as with the Department of State. "So far everything looks well," he wrote home on February 12.[42] He saw Butler at the latter's request and understood that he would support the arrangement. "Charles Sumner is heart and hand with us, and is most kind to me personally." Two days later he could write:

Everything has gone on as well as we could have hoped for. It is always difficult to say beforehand what any legislative body will do, . . . but without overestimating the favourable symptoms, I feel confident that were a bill for the renewal of the reciprocity treaty (with some amendments) submitted to both Houses next week, it would be carried. Whether such a bill will get before congress, or what new influences may arise to affect its chances when it does, is a different thing.[43]

Toward the end of March, Thornton and Brown, now definitely instructed to negotiate for a treaty, called upon Fish. "Mr. Brown," Fish recorded in his Diary, "does most of the talking and wishes the Treaty, not for any material advantages, but to promote amicable relations and close intercourse between the two peoples." When Brown inquired what were the wishes of the United States, Fish replied that "we have nothing to propose at all, the suggestion comes from them, and I doubt if any proposition could be made which would be accepted by the Senate and House, but am willing to see and consider any proposal which they have to make."[44] Intimation that the old Reciprocity

Dufferin, Apr. 23, Canadian *Sessional Paper* No. 51 (1875). While agreeing to allow Thornton and Brown to negotiate on these points, the Colonial Secretary asked Lord Derby to instruct the former that "the proposals should not be made as being the result of the matured decision of Her Majesty's Government, but as preliminary only—and Sir E. Thornton was desired to explain this to Mr. Fish." Edward Henry Stanley, fifteenth Earl of Derby, was back as Foreign Secretary in Disraeli's Ministry.

42. Mackenzie, *Life . . . of . . . Brown*, p. 212.

43. The only reference to reciprocity in the *Congressional Record* for the first session of the Forty-third Congress was a speech printed in the Appendix (Part VI, p. 357) as of May 19, 1874, purporting to be the remarks of E. Crossland of Kentucky, who was favorably disposed toward the renewal of the 1854 agreement.

44. Nevins, *Hamilton Fish*, p. 919. When Brown told how favorably his suggestions had been received by many gentlemen, Fish dryly insinuated they

Treaty might be reinstated brought from Fish a refusal to consider the idea; it had already been rejected many times. Nor would he make any move or offer any suggestions; all initiative must be left to the British. Many consultations between Brown and Thornton, aided somewhat by the new Canadian Minister of Marine and Fishery, Albert J. Smith, resulted late in April in a determination to smoke out the wily American Secretary.[45] The smudge was provided by a report of the Canadian Privy Council of April 18 containing a long and detailed account of the advantage of the Elgin Reciprocity Treaty as well as a statement of what Ottawa was prepared to concede.[46]

On April 27 Brown and Thornton laid all their cards on the table, reading from a memorandum based on the report and the Mackenzie memorandum, and asked Fish if he would have this printed "for limited distribution."[47] Again came a noncommittal answer, for Fish, as he noted in his Diary,[48] could not see that they had brought forward any suggestion which would be likely to produce an effect on Congress. But Brown was either blinded by his own hopefulness, or read into Fish's words more than was meant, or received from others encouragement which he might think the Secretary too cautious to express.

We have made a good deal of progress since I got back here. I had a long talk with Bancroft Davis, and he assures me they mean business, but do not feel they can deal with it without advice. . . .

I have visited several prominent men whose views were doubtful, among others Senator Conkling, who goes heartily for a treaty, and will urge Mr. Fish to go ahead; I also saw General Garfield and Secretary Schurz, both of whom are favourable.

I shall go to New York for a day to obtain, if possible, the *Herald*, the *Times*, and the *Sun*. We have already had articles in the *World* and *Evening Post*. I have sent off our first despatch to the London *Times*.[49]

had used such language "out of courtesy to strangers," but had talked very differently to him. Unlike Brown, Thornton believed Fish's tone was "most discouraging." Thornton to Derby, Mar. 30, 1874; FO 115:573 (P.R.O.).

45. Thornton to Derby, Apr. 7, 1874, FO 115:573; Apr. 13, FO 115:574 (P.R.O.).

46. FO 115:568 (P.R.O.).

47. Thornton to Derby, Apr. 28, 1874; FO 115:574 (P.R.O.).

48. Nevins, *op. cit.*, p. 919.

49. May 10. Mackenzie, *op. cit.*, pp. 212–213.

A few days later he reported that he had promise of support from the *Herald* and the *Times*, that the Chicago *Tribune* had had a "grand article," and that he had heard of but had not seen many other papers equally favorable; but, he reminded his correspondent,

Don't, I pray you, come to the conclusion that all is safe for the treaty. We know of not one thing more against us than we did when you were here, and we know of much that is favourable which has turned up since. But political matters are in such a mess here that it seems hopeless to get anything satisfactory done this session, unless Mr. Fish signs a treaty, and to do that he seems more and more unwilling. He is frightened at his shadow, and seems to have neither knowledge enough of the subject, nor breadth of grasp sufficient to cast his fears aside. If he had, the treaty would be carried without much trouble.[50]

On May 27 Brown thought that Fish was now "thoroughly in earnest" and believed he would send the treaty to the Senate for advice and that the Senate would assent to it, "but that is not certain." Two days earlier Fish had written in his Diary that he told Brown and Thornton he "would not submit in any form to the Senate the proposition which they had made," and informed them that he doubted whether it would "be possible at this session to obtain any action from either branch of Congress, partly on account of the lateness of the session, but mainly on account of the revenue question. . . . They then stated that they had prepared a modified proposition omitting the coasting trade and had reduced it to the form of a Convention. They read this Convention and I cautioned them that my silence was not to be construed one way or the other."[51] From Ottawa a halt was called on the concessions that Brown appeared to be willing to make: the free list was growing to such an extent that it threatened the Dominion revenue; but, when this protest was brought to the attention of the

50. May 15; *ibid.*, p. 213. A week later he reported that the newspapers were "coming out famously," and that "excellent resolutions" had been adopted or soon were to be by the Boards of Trade of Chicago, New York, Boston, and Detroit. To Thornton, who had called on other matters, Fish, in a "somewhat peevish tone," said there was no use in submitting the paper to the Senate, that the proposals were not at all reasonable. Thornton to Derby, May 23, 1874; FO 115:574 (P.R.O.).

51. Nevins, *op. cit.*, p. 919. Thornton to Derby, May 25, 1874; FO 115:574 (P.R.O.).

Secretary, "he fought hard against any amendment," although finally conceding the demands "subject to three concessions by us: 1st, That we surrender for ever to the United States the right of passage through the Gut of Canso; 2nd, That we make our canals 14 feet deep; and 3rd, That the tolls on the Welland and St. Lawrence canals shall not discriminate by lighter charges on through vessels than on vessels going only part of the way down." As a counter demand Brown put in a bid for opening in perpetuity to British vessels both the Rosario and Douglas channels on the Pacific coast.[52] Then came a delay of a few days while Thornton was trying to get Derby's consent to the changes, and Brown was becoming more and more impatient, for Congress was on the point of adjourning. On June 11 came the British Government's assent, but now there was trouble again with Fish.

Would you believe it? he was showing his timidity nearly as much as ever. "The difficulties were immense;" "the senate would certainly throw the draft treaty out." In short, there was no hope unless we made concessions now proposed for the first time. All this within ten days of the adjournment. We kept cool, made a memo. of his proposals, and retired to consider the situation. Sir Edward was downcast and angry; my bump of hope, as usual, kept me up, and determined me to make one more attempt to bring Mr. Fish back to reason.[53]

The new propositions advanced at this eleventh hour by Secretary Fish included denial of perpetual free navigation of Lake Michigan, refusal of fishery rights on the Pacific coast, postponing free entry of lumber for three and a half years, elimination of ochres, seal oil, and salt from the free list, insistence on fourteen-foot channels in the canals, and the demand for perpetual right of navigation of the Gut of Canso without corresponding concession in the Rosario channel. Furthermore, the Canadians should construct the Caughnawaga canal to Lake Champlain without any offset by the United States. "After a long tussle" Fish gave up most of these new demands, while Brown compromised on a twenty-one-year concession of Lake Michi-

52. June 7, 1874. Mackenzie, *op. cit.,* p. 214. Farrar to Colonial Office, June 10; Herbert to Foreign Office, June 11; Derby to Thornton, June 11; FO 115: 569 (P.R.O.).

53. June 12. Mackenzie, *op. cit.,* p. 215. Thornton to Fish, June 15, 1874; FO 115:574 (P.R.O.).

gan navigation and agreed to the Caughnawaga canal. Then salt proved a stumbling block; if that were left in, the treaty had no chance. On June 13 the three men worked over the draft with no new demands from either side: Mr. Fish "made several sensible suggestions for the improvement of the paper, and was most courteous throughout. He hoped to get it completed and ready for the senate on Monday."[54] But it did not go to the Senate on that day; it was not until June 17 that the President sent it in.

Brown's incorrigible optimism received an added fillip when he dined at the White House on the evening of June 17 and remained to talk with Grant about the whole matter. The President spoke "most enthusiastically for it, and congratulated me on the great success that had been accomplished. He assured me he would take every means to have the senate endorse it."[55] Nevertheless the draft had gone unsigned by the Secretary of State and was transmitted to the Senate by the President with at most a tepid recommendation. "I am of the opinion," he wrote, "that a proper treaty for such purposes would result beneficially for the United States." While the draft had many features to commend it to "favorable consideration" it was a question whether it made all the concessions "which could justly be required of Great Britain, or whether it calls for more concessions from the United States than we should yield, I am not prepared to say."[56] Brown thought the message "very good," but it had "the defect of not speaking definitely of this particular measure as his own and his government's, and calling on the senate to sustain him. Had he done this the treaty would have been through now."[57] Evidently the Senate, too, was struck with the fact that the Administration was not pushing the affair, for no report from the committee came in that session and adjournment took place with the Brown-Thornton Convention dangling in the air.

Even granted that George Brown was deluded by his own hopes, it is a strain upon the imagination to believe that he did not receive some encouragement when in Washington. Of course, it is possible

54. June 13. Mackenzie, *op. cit.*, p. 215. Thornton to Derby, June 17; FO 115:574 (P.R.O.).

55. Mackenzie, *op. cit.*, p. 216.

56. June 18. Richardson, *Messages and Papers,* VII, 266–267.

57. June 20. Mackenzie, *op. cit.*, p. 216.

that his personal appeal to a wide range of acquaintances, and his popularity from the stand taken by his paper during the Civil War made it difficult for any of them to damp his enthusiasm when he talked about the proposed treaty. On the other hand, Secretary Fish might well have been too pessimistic about the whole situation. A mild believer in reciprocity, neither he nor the Administration had anything to lose in giving real support to the proposition, especially if, as Brown was told, Zach Chandler failed in his attempt to have the draft treaty sent to his committee and it was sent instead to the Committee on Foreign Relations where the members were seven to two in favor of it, although at least two of the seven thought the sense of the country should be tested before action was taken.[58]

When the Forty-third Congress assembled for its last session, in December of 1874, the Democratic party could look back on a congressional election in which for the first time in eighteen years they had secured a majority in the lower house and could look forward to two years of successful opposition even though a Republican Senate could block all partisan legislation. Even if the "democrats [were] stronger than ever with us," as Brown thought when he returned to Washington to watch proceedings,[59] they did not control the Senate and could not force action. Yet, in spite of this and of Thornton's gloomy but well-founded opinion that the treaty was dead and would not have ten supporters, Brown refused to be utterly despondent. Again he interviewed Senators, talked with the President, and had a long conversation with Secretary Fish, who was convinced that the treaty had no chance that session, although he said he believed it might be agreed to in a year or so. "The money question," Fish told the Canadian, "occupied everyone's thoughts to the exclusion of every other subject. . . . There was no great hostility to the treaty, but utter apathy. To get a two-third majority was hopeless; to get a majority vote in the senate

58. The British Chargé reported later that he found the press and conversations with people "who may be supposed to form a correct opinion" indicated that the feeling of the country was favorable to the treaty. Watson to Derby, July 7, 9, Confidential, 13, 1874; FO 115:575 (P.R.O.).

59. In a letter to a relative, Dec. 15. Mackenzie, *op. cit.*, p. 216. Thornton was very much surprised to see Brown appear, for he shared none of the Canadian's optimism. Thornton to Derby, Dec. 21, 1874; FO 115:574 (P.R.O.).

he did not believe possible. This was sure, that nothing would be done until Congress met after the holidays."[60] Fish's fears were only too well founded: "apathy" described the situation.[61] Brown himself was forced to admit that now there was no hope, even before the Senate, toward the end of January, accepted the report of the Committee on Foreign Relations to the effect that the draft treaty should not be considered. Two rebuffs coming so close together convinced even the Mackenzie government that it would be unwise as well as undignified to pursue the subject, and reciprocity sank into the background.

Now Articles XXII and XXIII of the Treaty of Washington with the troublesome question of the third commissioner must be revived.[62] A report of the Dominion Privy Council went through the usual channels of Governor-General, Colonial Secretary, Foreign Office, to the British Legation in Washington, thence to Secretary Fish, announcing that

Inasmuch as the Arbitration proceedings under the 22nd Art. of the Treaty of Washington were delayed, pending the result of the negotiations for [a] Reciprocal Treaty, it is now deemed desirable that no time should be lost in proceeding, under the Treaty of Washington, to ascertain the compensation due to Canada for the concession of the Fishery rights to citizens of the United States.[63]

60. Dec. 16. Mackenzie, *op. cit.*, pp. 216–217. The "money question" was over resumption of specie payments.

61. The Vermont legislature did send resolutions, adopted January 1, 1875, stating that it was the duty of their Senators and Representatives "to use their influence against the consummation of any treaty relating to reciprocity in trade with the Dominion of Canada." *House Misc. Docs.*, No. 50, 43d Cong., 2d Sess.

62. Thornton to Derby, May 10, 1875; FO 115:589 (P.R.O.). In July, 1874, both sides had agreed to postpone further effort to pick the third man on the understanding that "no rights under the Treaty of Washington, which may have existed in behalf of either party thereto at the date when the negotiations with respect to the proposed reciprocity treaty were begun, are to be prejudiced by the delay which has occurred, or that may occur, in consequence of such negotiations up to the action of the Senate upon the proposed treaty." Watson to Fish, July 17; Fish to Watson, July 18; *For. Rel., 1874*, pp. 563–564.

63. Canadian *Sessional Paper* No. 51 (1875). FO 115:584, 115:585 (P.R.O.).

Unable still to agree upon the third commissioner, Fish had to fall back on the alternative provided by the treaty of submitting the choice to the Austrian Ambassador in London, who proceeded to name M. Delfosse, the Belgian Minister in Washington. Then, between May and November, 1877, the commission sat at Halifax and decided the United States would owe Canada $5,500,000 for the privileges during the life of the treaty, thus paving the way for another period of bickering and then abrogation of the mutual privileges by the United States in 1885.[64]

64. The details of these proceedings fall outside the scope of this study, but the official account may be found in *Record of the Proceedings of the Halifax Fisheries Commission* (London, 1877), and *For. Rel., 1878*.

CHAPTER XX

THE END OF AN ERA

WHILE the Treaty of Washington, when finally put into operation with respect to British North America, did not remove all causes of difference between the Dominion and the United States; while there were many details of administration still to be worked out; and while hopes of reciprocity on something like the old scale were definitely dashed by the rejection of the Brown-Thornton Convention of 1874, nevertheless there was a breathing spell for both countries. The fisheries issue passed into a quiescent stage, for Gloucestermen were now enjoying legally what they had seemed determined to take, law or no law—the inshore privileges and rights of trade, repair, recruitment, and transshipment in British North American ports. They grumbled, it is true, over free admission of British-caught fish in American ports, and, after the Halifax award, their mutterings swelled in volume until Congress provided for ending the arrangement on July 1, 1885.[1] But for the country at large there was a welcome respite from what was, after all, a tempest in a teapot stirring up waves all out of proportion to the originating cause.

Trade across the border was, after some preliminary friction, adjusted so that only minor issues were raised. If there were occasional differences of opinion about whether the American States were carry-

1. Permanent articles of the treaty were not affected; Article XXVI, relating to free navigation of the St. Lawrence, Yukon, Porcupine, and Stikine rivers, and Article XXVII, wherein Great Britain engaged to urge upon Canada opening of canals along the border to American citizens, and the United States agreed to open the St. Clair Flats Canal to British subjects and to urge upon the border states the opening of their canals, remained in force. Articles XVIII to XXV and Article XXX were abrogated, pursuant to an Act of Congress signed March 3, 1883; by separate acts of July 2 and October 16, 1883, the President was directed to give notice of abrogation of Article XXIX, relating to transit in bond, and Article XXXII, dealing with Newfoundland fisheries. No mention was made of Article XXVIII, which dealt with the navigation of Lake Michigan. For a discussion of Article XXIX, see John Bassett Moore, *A Digest of International Law, etc.* (Washington, 1906), V, 330–335.

ing out in good faith the spirit of the treaty with respect to its canals,[2] while Canadians allowed American boats to enjoy to the full the privileges of their canals, there seemed to be a desire not to make invidious distinctions. Governor J. T. Hoffman of New York, for example, had explained, when the matter was called to his attention,[3] that so far as he knew no State law discriminated against Canadian vessels in the use of the canals of that Commonwealth; if there were such regulations he would call the matter to the attention of the legislature in order to have the situation remedied. Complaints, nevertheless, continued to come in to such an extent that, in 1874, Governor Dix caused special inquiry to be made of tenders of the locks at Whitehall and was able to say, on the basis of their replies, that there had been no complaints there, for British registered craft were allowed to use the canal on exactly the same terms as American, and that the Canadian authorities must have been misinformed. Governor Hoffman, he stated, had recommended to the New York legislature in 1872 the passage of any necessary laws, but none had been passed because they were not needed.[4] Even this positive assertion was not accepted as sufficient by the Canadian Privy Council. In a minute of February 18, 1875,[5] they came to the conclusion that after the trouble in 1871 the principal Canadian forwarders and canal-boat owners agreed that

the probable reason why no case can be cited of Canadian vessels having been refused permission since 1871 to navigate these canals is that the persons engaged in this trade on both sides of the line were so convinced that no change had taken place in the policies of the authorities of the State of New York . . . that they made no attempt to test the question since 1871 as the boats usually employed by Canadian forwarders are too

2. Report of a Committee of the Privy Council, Nov. 12, 1874; FO 5:1485 (P.R.O.). The Committee maintained that, with the exception of the Sault Ste Marie Canal, restrictions, particularly in New York, still applied to Canadian craft.

3. Hoffman to President, Dec. 12, 1871, in Fish to Thornton, Apr. 4, 1874; FO 5:1482 (P.R.O.).

4. See correspondence in FO 5:1485 and 115:572 (P.R.O.), especially Dix to Fish, Dec. 4, 1874, with enclosures; also Thornton to Fish and Fish to Thornton, Nov. 23, 1874 in *For. Rel., 1875,* Part I, pp. 642–644.

5. FO 115:585 (P.R.O.).

large to navigate the New York Canals & they c^d not afford to build canal boats specially adapted for such canals until they were assured that they w^d be allowed to navigate them.

But, as the Governor of New York now definitely asserted that these Canadian vessels were not prohibited from using the canals "on terms of equality with American vessels," this "important information" should be officially promulgated so that Canadians might take advantage of the privilege.

Details of operation in the transit of goods in bond, of utilization of Lake Michigan, of transport of goods from one Canadian port to another with intervening land carriage through the United States, all had to be ironed out, with the usual complaints of discrimination and hampering regulations.[6] Nevertheless, a working basis more or less acceptable was finally reached, although the Treasury Department was adamant in refusing to allow Canadian barges to carry foreign merchandise beyond the first point of entry; in particular these barges could not pass from Rouses Point to New York with merchandise in bond.[7]

A little friction arose over the position of British subjects residing on the Island of San Juan after formal title of the United States had been established by the German Emperor's award. Squatters found that as aliens they had no status and were in danger of being ousted, no matter what their length of residence had been or what improvements they had made,[8] and the British Minister was instructed to urge upon the Government of the United States the practice of "fairness and liberality." Little comfort was obtained, since the attitude of the Administration and Congress was that the island had been American from the beginning of the controversy, hence the law of 1841 giving preëmption rights only to citizens of the United States applied; British subjects who had not declared their intention of taking out naturalization papers and who had made settlements after June 1,

6. Considerable correspondence on these points is found in *For. Rel., 1875,* Part I, pp. 546 ff., and in FO 5:1513 and 115:550 (P.R.O.).

7. Parmenter, Collector of Customs, to Captain Jones, Montreal, June 28, 1875; FO 5:1513 (P.R.O.).

8. Granville to Thornton, Oct. 9, 1873; FO 115:553 (P.R.O.). Morris and Wylly to Granville, Dec. 20, 1873, in Granville to Thornton, Jan. 29, 1874; FO 115:566 (P.R.O.).

1840, did not come under the protection of the statute. Congress did, however, in the session of 1873–74, take care of those who had settled before the Treaty of 1846, but made no provision for those who had taken up residence on the island between 1846 and 1871. Thornton did press the equitable claims of the latter class, only to have Fish ask him "what rights the same settlers would have had, supposing it had been decided that the island was British or in short what rights would have been acquired by the mere act of settling or squatting on public lands in British Columbia?"[9] The Minister could not answer this question and put the problem to the Governor-General of Canada.

Preliminary rumblings of future disputes of the Alaska boundary sprang up in connection with granting free navigation of the Stikine River to both British and Americans. Gold was discovered near Deane's Lake, not far from the river, and the usual rush began. As this area was in British Columbia, immediately the question whether American river boats carrying supplies to the gold fields would have to detour to Victoria or Esquimalt to make declarations was put before the Department of State and the Foreign Office. Since river boats were not built to navigate the high seas it was obvious that inconvenience, to say the least, would result from such a regulation. A spirit of accommodation, however, was demonstrated when arrangements were made for declarations at some point within British territory without the establishment of a formal port of entry.[10] A proposal from Thornton that a survey of the boundary between Alaska and British Columbia be undertaken brought from Fish the reply that there was such an economical streak in Congress that it would be impossible to get appropriated the amount necessary for the first year's work and that it would be inadvisable to try.[11] The successors of Secretary Fish may well have wished that Congress had not been so parsimonious and that the Secretary had at least urged the matter.

In short, setting aside the fisheries-reciprocity issue which was passing through one of its numerous expiring spasms in 1874, a calm unknown for a quarter of a century descended upon Canadian-American

9. Thornton to Derby, July 18, 1874, copy; FO 115:570 (P.R.O.).

10. Thornton to Fish, July 31, 1873; Great Britain: Notes to Department, Vol. XCV (D.S.). Memorandum of Minister of Customs, Ottawa, June 4, 1874; FO 5:1484 (P.R.O.).

11. Thornton to Derby, Feb. 23, 1874; FO 115:573 (P.R.O.).

relations. None of the old issues was in an acute stage and the Halifax award had not yet been made to re-arouse acrimonious bickerings. Americans had troubles enough at home, with political scandals and hard times following the crisis of 1873, to prevent their giving more than an occasional passing glance at what went on north of the border. Protectionism, while not yet formally adopted as a basic tenet of Republicanism, was so firmly entrenched that it became almost sacrilegious to question its supposedly beneficent workings. Confederation and the gradual expansion of the Dominion of Canada no longer disturbed the average American; indeed, he generally ignored the fact that a colony was disappearing and a nation was rising in its place. Even annexationism was quiescent, although now and then some reverberation of the storm that had raged through the Sixties received momentary attention. It is improbable that many Americans gave a thought to an article which appeared on April 20, 1875, in the Washington *Morning Chronicle* and which seemed of enough significance to the British Minister to comment on and send home.[12] It is, nevertheless, worth quoting as an illustration of the eternal hopefulness on the part of those who could not see the signs of the times.

A Convention, to take into consideration the best means for the speedy union of the United States and the Canadian Dominion, will assemble at Buffalo, New York, on July 4, 1875. Three delegates from each congressional district in the United States and three delegates from each parliamentary district in the British Provinces will compose the Convention. As the union of adjacent States, with kindred peoples, the same language, identical interests, and a common destiny, has, in all ages and countries, and especially in America and Europe, been attended with the happiest results, therefore it is natural that a very large number, if not even a large majority of the people in both the United States and the British Provinces, believe that the union of these kindred States would forever prevent war, that dire calamity of mankind, secure complete fraternity, obliterate all restrictions upon trade and commerce, increase immigration, and finally result in an immense and lasting advantage to all. To encourage, increase, and consolidate the friends of this union into active co-opera-

12. Thornton to Derby, with copy of article enclosed, Apr. 20, 1875; FO 5: 1510 (P.R.O.). Thornton doubted "whether the assertion is true that a large number of people in the British Provinces believe in the expediency of such a measure."

tion, will be the purpose of the convention. It is believed that the time for such a union is exceedingly opportune, and that through this convention arrangements may be inaugurated by which it may be effected on the 4th of July, 1876, the Great American Centennial.

Little did the ever-hopeful sponsors of this grand gesture realize that what had been taking place in the past fifteen years had made impossible any such consummation, whether desirable or not. Those few Americans who took the trouble to learn what was being thought and done in the Dominion could easily perceive that the United States had been the most potent factor in creating a nation which had no desire to link its political future with theirs. Neither threats nor cajolery had produced results other than cementing colonial bonds, which had been none too tight when the American Civil War began. Resolved to maintain its identity and its connection with the British Empire, the Dominion of Canada was becoming more and more conscious that its future was bound up in peaceful relations with, but not political assimilation to, its southern neighbor.

Twenty-five years is a short time in the lives of nations, even of such relatively young nations as the United States of America and the Dominion of Canada, but in that quarter century could be packed more delicate situations, more critical issues, than can be found in many a period extending over a far greater span of years. Such a period was the one between 1849 and 1874. No similar concentration of so many serious problems arising between British North America and the United States can be found in the time between the separation of the thirteen colonies from the Mother Country and the present day. Surely no other quarter-century saw such an aggregation of momentous episodes affecting their internal evolution. A sectional division in one reacted upon separatism in the other and hastened a movement which might otherwise have been long delayed. This was not merely an outward physical amalgamation; it was accompanied by a change of outlook, by a different inner spirit. The Civil War completed the work of making a nation of the United States even though the brutal method left wounds slow to heal; the Civil War was one of the most potent forces in making Canada a nation, although there, too, the process left heartburnings.

In 1849 the spirit of "manifest destiny" was pushing a people flushed with territorial acquisitions yet farther afield. Yearning eyes cast over the northern border saw enough to encourage the belief that Provincial dissatisfaction with the Imperial course foretold early separation which could mean only annexation. But a combination of forces stood in the way: sectionalism in the United States urged the South to throw its influence and votes for any course which would prevent expansion in a direction that could only mean more states in which the "peculiar institution" would never exist; predominant opinion in the Provinces, backed by the British Government, sought a detour around a danger that seemed real. The result was the Reciprocity Treaty of 1854. The War between the States not only scrapped reciprocity but raised old specters and created new ones. Annexationism again was rampant south of the border. Then common sense came to the rescue with a resulting adjustment which, if it did not leave all parties completely satisfied, did at least remove the greater obstacles and allowed time to emphasize again the desirability, the necessity, of kindred people's living in amity. Friction there was to be subsequently, but it is not too much to say that the Treaty of Washington and its immediate aftermath marked the end of one period in Canadian-American relations and inaugurated a new day.

APPENDIX I

MANUSCRIPT MATERIALS

THE manuscript materials principally used in the preparation of this work were found in the Public Archives of Canada at Ottawa, and in the archives of the Department of State and the Library of Congress in Washington.

In the Public Archives of Canada the "G" series contains dispatches which passed between the Colonial Office and the Governors-General in Canada, correspondence between the latter and the British Ministers in Washington, interprovincial correspondence, and correspondence between the Colonial Office and the Lieutenant-Governors of certain Provinces. Some of the portfolios of the "G" series are numbered, while others, particularly those containing correspondence after about 1870, are unnumbered.[1] The extensive manuscript collection of the John A. Macdonald Papers, also found in the Public Archives of Canada, was especially useful; this collection contains, in addition to the Letterbooks, volumes of correspondence grouped as Governor General Correspondence, Visits to England, Rose, Reciprocity, Washington Treaty, and General Letters. The Joseph Howe Papers in the same depository added some material.

At the Department of State in Washington the following were utilized: Consular Letters from various cities of British North America; Index to Despatches; Great Britain: Despatches, Instructions, Notes to Department, Notes to (British Legation); Special Agents (especially Volume XVI); Reciprocity Treaty (miscellaneous material bearing on the Treaty of 1854); Treaty of Washington Papers, 1871; and Papers and Proceedings relating to the British and American Joint High Commission (three volumes prepared by J. C. Bancroft Davis, Assistant Secretary of State and the American secretary of the commission).

In the Library of Congress at Washington were found several manuscript collections of personal papers of which, for this study, most extensively used were those of Franklin B. Pierce, William L. Marcy, Zachariah Chandler, and J. C. Bancroft Davis, whose Diary is also in this depository. The Journal of Benjamin Moran, long-time secretary of the American Legation in London, was not without value.

The Library of Congress also possesses copies, part of which were ob-

1. See *A Guide to the Documents in the Manuscript Room at the Public Archives of Canada*, prepared by David W. Parker (Ottawa, 1914), Vol. I.

tained through the efforts of the Carnegie Endowment for International Peace, of manuscripts in the British Public Record Office. Of these, Foreign Office Correspondence (FO 5 and 115) was especially valuable, while some use could be made of Colonial Office Correspondence (CO 188). The Library of Congress also has in photostatic copy parts of the "G" series, noted above as located in the Public Archives of Canada, especially the Correspondence between the Governors-General and the British Ministers in Washington, which, in these photostatic folios, is arranged chronologically and so designated, as, for example, "G '44–'58." These copies, both of documents in the Public Record Office in London and of those in the Public Archives at Ottawa, were used at the Library of Congress.

The Diary of Hamilton Fish, now in the possession of Representative Hamilton Fish, Jr., is a source which no student of the subject can neglect. Its most essential information has been made available in the recent biography of Fish by Allan Nevins, and large parts of it are to be published verbatim within a few years.

APPENDIX II

ARTICLES IN THE TREATY OF WASHINGTON AFFECTING BRITISH NORTH AMERICA AND THE UNITED STATES[1]

Article XVIII

IT is agreed by the high contracting parties that, in addition to the liberty secured to the United States fishermen by the convention between the United States and Great Britain, signed at London on the 20th day of October, 1818, of taking, curing, and drying fish on certain coasts of the British North American colonies therein defined, the inhabitants of the United States shall have, in common with the subjects of Her Britannic Majesty, the liberty, for the term of years mentioned in Article XXXIII of this treaty, to take fish of every kind, except shell-fish, on the sea-coasts and shores, and in the bays, harbors, and creeks, of the provinces of Quebec, Nova Scotia, and New Brunswick, and the colony of Prince Edward's Island, and of the several islands thereunto adjacent, without being restricted to any distance from the shore, with permission to land upon the said coasts and shores and islands, and also upon the Magdalen Islands, for the purpose of drying their nets and curing their fish; provided that, in so doing, they do not interfere with the rights of private property, or with British fishermen, in the peaceable use of any part of the said coasts in their occupancy for the same purpose.

It is understood that the above-mentioned liberty applies solely to the sea fishery, and that the salmon and shad fisheries, and all other fisheries in rivers and the mouths of rivers, are hereby reserved exclusively for British fishermen.

Article XIX

IT is agreed by the high contracting parties that British subjects shall have, in common with the citizens of the United States, the liberty, for the term of years mentioned in Article XXXIII of this treaty, to take fish of every kind, except shell-fish, on the eastern sea-coasts and shores of the United States north of the thirty-ninth parallel of north latitude, and on the shores of the several islands thereunto adjacent, and in the bays, harbors, and creeks of the said sea-coasts and shores of the United States

---

1. For the complete text of the treaty, see *Foreign Relations, 1871,* pp. 517–531.

and of the said islands, without being restricted to any distance from the shore, with permission to land upon the said coasts of the United States and of the islands aforesaid, for the purpose of drying their nets and curing their fish, provided that, in so doing, they do not interfere with the rights of private property, or with the fishermen of the United States in the peaceable use of any part of the said coasts in their occupancy for the same purpose.

It is understood that the above-mentioned liberty applies solely to the sea fishery, and that salmon and shad fisheries, and all other fisheries in rivers and mouths of rivers, are hereby reserved exclusively for fishermen of the United States.

ARTICLE XX

IT is agreed that the places designated by the commissioners appointed under the first article of the treaty between the United States and Great Britain, concluded at Washington on the 5th of June, 1854, upon the coasts of Her Britannic Majesty's dominions and the United States, as places reserved from the common right of fishing under that treaty, shall be regarded as in like manner reserved from the common right of fishing under the preceding articles. In case any question should arise between the governments of the United States and of Her Britannic Majesty as to the common right of fishing in places not thus designated as reserved, it is agreed that a commission shall be appointed to designate such places, and shall be constituted in the same manner, and have the same powers, duties, and authority as the commission appointed under the said first article of the treaty of the 5th of June, 1854.

ARTICLE XXI

IT is agreed that, for the term of years mentioned in Article XXXIII of this treaty, fish oil and fish of all kinds, (except fish of the inland lakes, and of the rivers falling into them, and except fish preserved in oil,) being the produce of the fisheries of the United States, or of the Dominion of Canada, or of Prince Edward's Island, shall be admitted into each country, respectively, free of duty.

ARTICLE XXII

INASMUCH as it is asserted by the government of Her Britannic Majesty that the privileges accorded to the citizens of the United States under Article XVIII of this treaty are of greater value than those accorded by Articles XIX and XXI of this treaty to the subjects of Her Britannic

Majesty, and this assertion is not admitted by the Government of the United States, it is further agreed that commissioners shall be appointed to determine, having regard to the privileges accorded by the United States to the subjects of Her Britannic Majesty, as stated in Articles XIX and XXI of this treaty, the amount of any compensation which, in their opinion, ought to be paid by the Government of the United States to the government of Her Britannic Majesty in return for the privileges accorded to the citizens of the United States under Article XVIII of this treaty; and that any sum of money which the said commissioners may so award shall be paid by the United States Government, in a gross sum, within twelve months after such award shall have been given.

ARTICLE XXIII

THE commissioners referred to in the preceding article shall be appointed in the following manner, that is to say: One commissioner shall be named by the President of the United States, one by Her Britannic Majesty, and a third by the President of the United States and Her Britannic Majesty conjointly; and in case the third commissioner shall not have been so named within a period of three months from the date when this article shall take effect, then the third commissioner shall be named by the representative at London of His Majesty the Emperor of Austria and King of Hungary. In case of the death, absence, or incapacity of any commissioner, or in the event of any commissioner omitting or ceasing to act, the vacancy shall be filled in the manner hereinbefore provided for making the original appointment, the period of three months in case of such substitution being calculated from the date of the happening of the vacancy.

The commissioners so named shall meet in the city of Halifax, in the province of Nova Scotia, at the earliest convenient period after they have been respectively named, and shall, before proceeding to any business, make and subscribe a solemn declaration that they will impartially and carefully examine and decide the matters referred to them to the best of their judgment, and according to justice and equity; and such declaration shall be entered on the record of their proceedings.

Each of the high contracting parties shall also name one person to attend the commission as its agent, to represent it generally in all matters connected with the commission.

ARTICLE XXIV

THE proceedings shall be conducted in such order as the commissioners appointed under Articles XXII and XXIII of this treaty shall determine. They shall be bound to receive such oral or written testimony as either government may present. If either party shall offer oral testimony, the other party shall have the right of cross-examination, under such rules as the commissioners shall prescribe.

If in the case submitted to the commissioners either party shall have specified or alluded to any report or document in its own exclusive possession, without annexing a copy, such party shall be bound, if the other party thinks proper to apply for it, to furnish that party with a copy thereof; and either party may call upon the other, through the commissioners, to produce the originals or certified copies of any papers adduced as evidence, giving in each instance such reasonable notice as the commissioners may require.

The case on either side shall be closed within a period of six months from the date of the organization of the commission, and the commissioners shall be requested to give their award as soon as possible thereafter. The aforesaid period of six months may be extended for three months in case of a vacancy occurring among the commissioners under the circumstances contemplated in Article XXIII of this treaty.

Article XXV

THE commissioners shall keep an accurate record and correct minutes or notes of all their proceedings, with the dates thereof, and may appoint and employ a secretary and any other necessary officer or officers to assist them in the transaction of the business which may come before them.

Each of the high contracting parties shall pay its own commissioner and agent or counsel; all other expenses shall be defrayed by the two governments in equal moieties.

Article XXVI

THE navigation of the river St. Lawrence, ascending and descending, from the forty-fifth parallel of north latitude, where it ceases to form the boundary between the two countries, from, to, and into the sea, shall forever remain free and open for the purposes of commerce to the citizens of the United States, subject to any laws and regulations of Great Britain, or of the Dominion of Canada, not inconsistent with such privilege of free navigation.

The navigation of the rivers Yukon, Porcupine, and Stikine, ascending and descending, from, to, and into the sea, shall forever remain free and open for the purposes of commerce to the subjects of her Britannic Majesty and to the citizens of the United States, subject to any laws and regulations of either country within its own territory, not inconsistent with such privilege of free navigation.

Article XXVII

The government of Her Britannic Majesty engages to urge upon the government of the Dominion of Canada to secure to the citizens of the United States the use of the Welland, St. Lawrence, and other canals in the Dominion on terms of equality with the inhabitants of the Dominion; and the Government of the United States engages that the subjects of Her Britannic Majesty shall enjoy the use of the St. Clair Flats Canal on terms of equality with the inhabitants of the United States, and further engages to urge upon the State governments to secure to the subjects of Her Britannic Majesty the use of the several State canals connected with the navigation of the lakes or rivers traversed by or contiguous to the boundary line between the possessions of the high contracting parties, on terms of equality with the inhabitants of the United States.

Article XXVIII

The navigation of Lake Michigan shall also, for the term of years mentioned in Article XXXIII of this treaty, be free and open for the purposes of commerce to the subjects of Her Britannic Majesty, subject to any laws and regulations of the United States or of the States bordering thereon, not inconsistent with such privilege of free navigation.

Article XXIX

It is agreed that, for the term of years mentioned in Article XXXIII of this treaty, goods, wares, or merchandise arriving at the ports of New York, Boston, and Portland, and any other ports in the United States which have been or may, from time to time, be specially designated by the President of the United States, and destined for Her Britannic Majesty's possessions in North America, may be entered at the proper custom-house and conveyed in transit, without the payment of duties, through the territory of the United States, under such rules, regulations, and conditions for the protection of the revenue as the Government of the United States may from time to time prescribe; and under like rules, regulations, and conditions, goods, wares, or merchandise may be conveyed in transit, without the payment of duties, from such possessions through the territory of the United States for export from the said ports of the United States.

It is further agreed that, for the like period, goods, wares, or merchandise arriving at any of the ports of her Britannic Majesty's possessions in North America, and destined for the United States, may be entered at the proper custom-house and conveyed in transit, without the payment of duties, through the said possessions, under such rules and regulations and conditions for the protection of the revenue as the governments of the said possessions may from time to time prescribe; and, under like rules, regulations, and conditions, goods, wares, or merchandise may be conveyed in transit, without payment of duties, from the United States through the said possessions to other places in the United States, or for export from ports in the said possessions.

ARTICLE XXX

IT is agreed that, for the term of years mentioned in Article XXXIII of this treaty, subjects of her Britannic Majesty may carry in British vessels, without payment of duty, goods, wares, or merchandise from one port or place within the territory of the United States upon the St. Lawrence, the great lakes, and the rivers connecting the same, to another port or place within the territory of the United States as aforesaid: Provided, That a portion of such transportation is made through the Dominion of Canada by land carriage and in bond, under such rules and regulations as may be agreed upon between the government of Her Britannic Majesty and the Government of the United States.

Citizens of the United States may for the like period carry in United States vessels, without payment of duty, goods, wares, or merchandise from one port or place within the possessions of Her Britannic Majesty in North America to another port or place within the said possessions: Provided, That a portion of such transportation is made through the territory of the United States by land carriage and in bond, under such rules and regulations as may be agreed upon between the Government of the United States and the government of Her Britannic Majesty.

The Government of the United States further engages not to impose any export duties on goods, wares, or merchandise carried under this article through the territory of the United States; and Her Majesty's government engages to urge the Parliament of the Dominion of Canada and the legislatures of the other colonies not to impose any export duties on goods, wares, or merchandise carried under this article; and the Government of the United States may, in case such export duties are imposed by the Dominion of Canada, suspend, during the period that such duties are imposed, the right of carrying granted under this article in favor of the subjects of Her Britannic Majesty.

The Government of the United States may suspend the right of carrying granted in favor of the subjects of her Britannic Majesty under this article, in case the Dominion of Canada should at any time deprive the citizens of the United States of the use of the canals in the said Dominion on terms of equality with the inhabitants of the Dominion, as provided in Article XXVII.

Article XXXI

The government of Her Britannic Majesty further engages to urge upon the Parliament of the Dominion of Canada and the legislature of New Brunswick, that no export duty, or other duty, shall be levied on lumber or timber of any kind cut on that portion of the American territory in the State of Maine watered by the river St. John and its tributaries, and floated down that river to the sea, when the same is shipped to the United States from the province of New Brunswick. And, in case any such export or other duty continues to be levied after the expiration of one year from the date of the exchange of the ratifications of this treaty, it is agreed that the Government of the United States may suspend the right of carrying hereinbefore granted under Article XXX of this treaty for such period as such export or other duty may be levied.

Article XXXII

It is further agreed that the provisions and stipulations of Articles XVIII to XXV of this treaty, inclusive, shall extend to the colony of Newfoundland, so far as they are applicable. But if the imperial Parliament, the legislature of Newfoundland, or the Congress of the United States, shall not embrace the colony of Newfoundland in their laws enacted for carrying the foregoing articles into effect, then this article shall be of no effect; but the omission to make provision by law to give it effect, by either of the legislative bodies aforesaid, shall not in any way impair any other articles of this treaty.

Article XXXIII

The foregoing Articles XVIII to XXV, inclusive, and Article XXX of this treaty, shall take effect as soon as the laws required to carry them into operation shall have been passed by the imperial Parliament of Great Britain, by the Parliament of Canada, and by the legislature of Prince Edward's Island on the one hand, and by the Congress of the United States on the other. Such assent having been given, the said articles shall remain in force for the period of ten years from the date at which they may come into operation; and further until the expiration of two years after either of the high contracting parties shall have given notice to the other of its wish to terminate the same; each of the high contracting parties being at liberty to give such notice to the other at the end of the said period of ten years or at any time afterward.

[Articles XXXIV to XLII contain provision for submitting the disputed San Juan water boundary to the arbitration of the German Emperor, and regulations governing the arbitration.]

INDEX

Abbott, Sir John, 3

Aberdeen, Earl of, 45; correspondence with Everett, *1845,* regarding fishing rights of Americans, 51, 54; Northwest boundary, 254

Adams, Charles Francis: instructions regarding Confederate activity in Canada and United States naval armament on Great Lakes, 133, 134, 138, 147, 156, 168, 169; Fenian agitation, 219, 223, 231; succeeded by Reverdy Johnson, 204, 253; instruction regarding protocol to create fisheries commission, 264

Adams, John Quincy, 30

Adderley, Sir Charles, 392

Alabama episode, and subsequent claims, 129, 130, 138, 204, 210, 253, 258, 260, 282, 284, 308, 312, 313, 317, 318, 322, 327, 332, 338, 344, 350, 373, 376, 380, 382, 392, 393, 410, 411, 418, 423–426, 446; suggested cession of Canadian Northwest in settlement of claims, 200; annexation of the Dominion in settlement, 205; Joint High Commission, 331, 361, 364, 366, 400; attitude of Sumner, 374, 375; editorial comment, 379; Geneva Tribunal and award, 377, 393, 398, 400, 417, 426, 442, 445, 446

Alaska: purchase by the United States, 199; relative to annexation of Canada, 201–202, 203; river navigation, 369, 386, 391, 413, 472, 475; Treaty of Washington, 413; survey proposed of Alaska-British Columbia boundary, 475

Alexandria, case of the, 139

Allan, Sir Hugh, 459

Allison, W. B., 294

Ames, General, 380

Ancona, S. E., 230–231

Anderson, Deputy Inspector-General of Canada, 76

Anderson, negro, extradition from Canada, 184

Andrew, John Albion, 136

Andrews, Israel DeWolf: special agent to British North America, 17, 26, 122; reports: regarding Canadian independence and annexation, 18, Canada's attitude to slavery, 19, reciprocal free trade, 21; items of suggested reports, 25–26; completed report filed with

United States State Department, 50–51, 52, 58; efforts to modify hostile Canadian opinion regarding fisheries, 72–75, 77, 82; expenditures and reimbursement, 76, 77; opinion of the Reciprocity Treaty and proposed abrogation, 99, 110, 160, 300

Anglin, T., 423

Anglin, William, 415

Annette, brigantine: examination by United States officers, 122

Annexation: Montreal Manifesto, 1–3, 7, 8, 10, 12, 14, 18, 25, 26; overthrow of the "Family Compact," and resulting bitter feeling, 3–4; Rebellion Losses Bill, 4, 8; removal of Colonial preference, 5, 9, 20, 182; Canadian efforts to offset losses by English free trade, 6; immigration problem, 7; relaxation of Navigation Laws, 7, 14; election of *1848,* 8, 10; British-American League, 8; sentiment centered in Montreal and Eastern Townships, 10; among the French, 11, 16; eventual separation of the Colonies, 12; Lord John Russell's speech on attitude of the Crown, 13, 14; movement the result of political disappointment, 14; Maritime Provinces, 14, 15; Nova Scotia, 15; hard times of *1848–1849,* 15; interest in annexation in the United States, 16, 172, 180, 182–183; the Northwest, 16; "Manifest Destiny," 17; reports of Israel D. Andrews, 17, 72; annexation or confederation, 18, 180–213, 232; attitude of Southern States, 19, 82, 176, 478; British reaction, 26; effect of reciprocity on desire for annexation, 88, 94, 175, 180, 186, 283; suggestion in the Northern States as a counterbalance for the South, 98, 182, 183; attitude of Seward on annexation, 115; the probable result of a war, 128; campaign of James Gordon Bennett, New York *Herald,* 159–160, 183, 184, 269; proposal of annexation as compensation for secession of Southern States, 184; annexationist Press in the States, 185, 191, 194, 198; need for capital, 187; attitude of United States annexationists to confederation, 188, 197; sub-

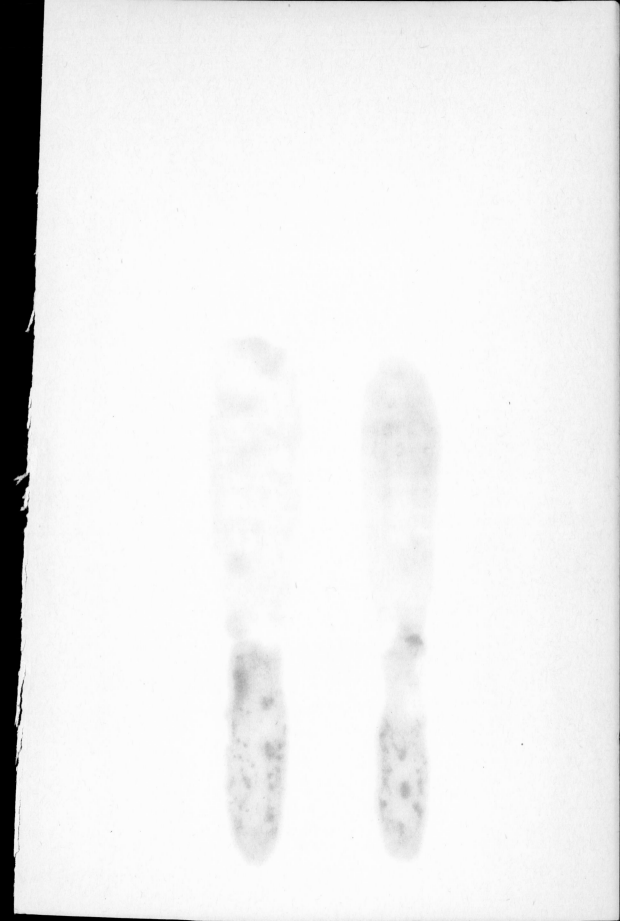

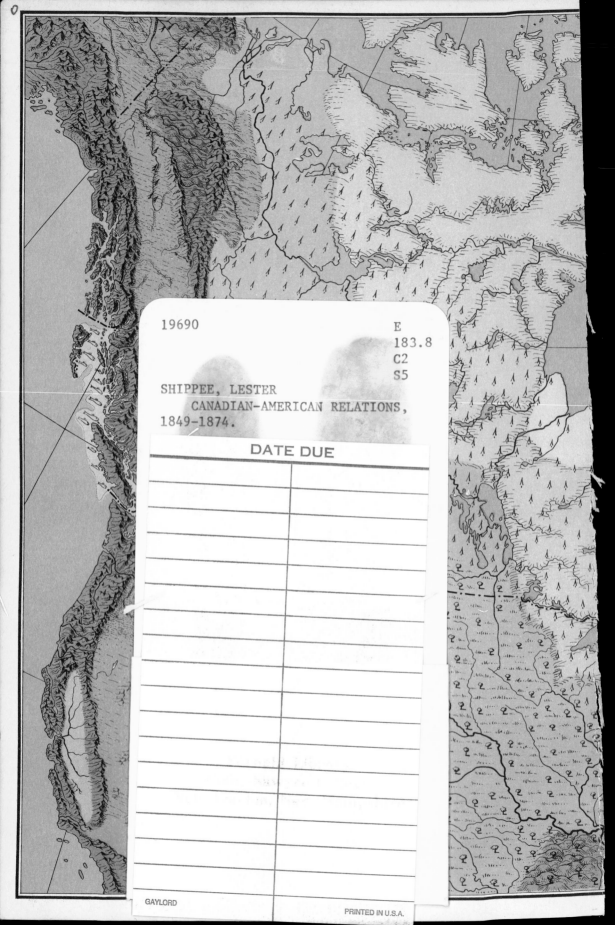

DATE DUE